Book of Days

The Wordsworth
Book of Days

—

Gerald Masters

Wordsworth Reference

First published 1990 as *The Pan Book of Dates* by Pan Books Ltd,
Cavaye Place, London SW10.

This edition published 1995 by Wordsworth Editions Ltd,
Cumberland House, Crib Street, Ware, Hertfordshire SG12 9ET.

ISBN 1-85326-358-3

Printed and bound in Denmark by Nørhaven

The paper in this book is produced from pure wood pulp, without the use of chlorine or any other substance harmful to the environment. The energy used in its production consists almost entire of hydroelectricity and heat generated from waste materials, thereby converting fossil fuels and contributing little to the greenhouse effect.

To Nora for 10 October 1933
To Brenda for 4 July 1984
– otherwise there would be no dates for me

To the many people who provided information for this book and the thousands of sources I tapped, from reference books to newspapers, my sincere thanks, but because of space, have to remain uncredited. I owe my editors at Pan a debt not only for their skills in licking this book into shape and saving my blushes by spotting inevitable errors, but also for their patience in dealing with my frequent calls for guidance and help.

Gerald Masters
London, 1990

THE PAN BOOK OF DATES

JANUARY

The past is but the beginning of a beginning
(H. G. Wells)

1 JANUARY

New Year's Day.

BORN THIS DAY

HISTORY

1449 Lorenzo de' Medici, 'Lorenzo the Magnificent', Florentine statesman, poet and patron of the arts during a period when the power and influence of the city was at its height.

1735 Paul Revere, American patriot, famous for his ride from Charlestown to Lexington (18.4.1775) to warn of the advance of the British during the American War of Independence.

ARTS

1879 E(dward) M(organ) Forster, British novelist who was briefly the literary editor of the *Daily Herald*. His novels include *A Room with a View* (1908) and *A Passage to India* (1926).

1920 J(erome) D(avid) Salinger, reclusive US author of *Catcher in the Rye* (1951), a cult novel of adolescence.

ENTERTAINMENT

1879 William Fox, born in Hungary as Wilhelm Fried. He bought an ailing penny arcade in the US and turned it into a successful cinema chain before starting Fox Films (later 20th Century-Fox) to bring in his audience.

1901 Xavier Cugat, Spanish-born bandleader who arrived in Hollywood via Cuba, where he played at the Coconut Grove and was known as 'The Rumba King'.

1909 (Carver) Dana Andrews, US film actor, brother of the actor Steve Forrest. His films include *Laura* (1944) and *A Walk in the Sun* (1946).

1933 Joe Orton, British playwright of black comedies, including *Entertaining Mr Sloane* (1964) and *Loot* (1966). In 1967, he was murdered by flatmate and lover, Kenneth Halliwell.

SCIENCE

1854 Sir James George Frazer, Scottish anthropologist, author of *The Golden Bough* (1892), which traced the development of thinking from a belief in magic to an understanding of science.

SPORT

1863 Baron Pierre de Coubertin, French founder of the modern Olympics.

RELIGION

1892 Pastor Martin Niemoller, German priest and First World War U-boat commander who was persecuted for his stand against the Nazification of the German church.

CRIME

1895 J(ohn) Edgar Hoover, US lawyer, founder and head of the Federal Bureau of Investigation (FBI), 1924 to 1972. He established the world's largest fingerprint file and crime-detection laboratory.

1912 Harold 'Kim' Philby, British traitor who became a Soviet agent in 1933 and then joined British intelligence. Together with Burgess, Maclean, and Blunt, he passed top secrets to the Russians. (*See* 23.1.1963)

DIED THIS DAY

1716 William Wycherley, English playwright of *The Country Wife* (1675).

1766 James Stuart, 'the Old Pretender',

father of Bonnie Prince Charlie, in Rome.

1894 Heinrich Rudolph Hertz, German physicist who discovered radio waves.

1944 Sir Edwin Landseer Lutyens, English architect of the Whitehall Cenotaph.

1972 Maurice Chevalier, French stage and film entertainer.

1989 Hans Schlumf, Swiss vintage-car collector. With his brother Fritz, he built up a collection of over 500 vintage cars in France, fleeing to Switzerland in 1976 to avoid prosecution over their alleged misuse of company money.

ON THIS DAY

1583 German and Swiss states introduced the Gregorian calendar. Now used throughout the world, it was only adopted by England in 1752 and by Russia in 1918, while Greece adopted it as late as 1923.

1660 Samuel Pepys began his *Diary*, which he wrote in an early form of shorthand for just over nine years.

1772 The first traveller's cheques were introduced by the London Credit Exchange Company. They were guaranteed against theft and could be used in 90 cities.

1781 Iron Bridge, Shropshire, England, opened to traffic, the first all-iron bridge in the world.

1785 The *Daily Universal Register* was first published by John Walter. It was renamed *The Times* in 1788.

1808 The importing of slaves into the US was halted.

1841 Voigtlander of Vienna marketed the first all-metal camera.

1858 The island off Australia's south coast, Van Dieman's Land, was renamed Tasmania after its European discoverer, Abel Tasman, who had originally named it after the expedition's Dutch admiral.

1876 The first British trademark was registered, for Bass Pale Ale.

1881 The first British postal orders were issued.

1887 British Prime Minister, Disraeli, had Queen Victoria proclaimed Empress of India.

1890 Football nets were used in the goalmouth for the first time, for a match in Bolton, England.

1891 Old age pensions were introduced in Germany. 18 years later, in 1909, pensions for people over 70 were introduced in Britain.

1894 The Manchester Ship Canal was opened, linking the city to the River Mersey, Liverpool.

1901 The Commonwealth of Australia was established. Edmund Barton became Prime Minister.

1905 The Trans-Siberian Railway officially opened, offering the chance to travel from Paris to Vladivostok in 21 days.

1914 The first scheduled airline began operating from Florida.

1947 Britain nationalized the coal industry, followed by the railways in 1948 and the steel industry in 1951.

1955 Luncheon Vouchers, the office-worker's perk, were introduced into Britain.

1958 The EEC came into being, the Treaty of Rome having been signed on 25.11.1957 by the Six – France, Italy, West Germany, Belgium, Holland and Luxembourg. 16 years later, in 1973, Britain also joined, together with Ireland and Denmark, followed in 1986 by Spain and Portugal.

1959 Fidel Castro overthrew the Batista regime in Cuba.

FLOPS AND TOPS In 1962, the Beatles auditioned for Decca Records, but were rejected in favour of Brian Poole and the Tremeloes. In 1964, the first *Top of the Pops* was aired, with Jimmy Savile as its presenter.

1965 Stanley Matthews, legendary footballer who played on the right wing for Blackpool, became the first professional footballer to be knighted.

1975 John Erlichman, H. R. Haldeman and John Mitchell were found guilty of obstructing the course of justice for their part in the Watergate affair.

LAST KNIGHTS In 1975, two controversial and elderly ex-pats, Charles Chaplin and author P.G. Wodehouse, received knighthoods. Wodehouse, at last forgiven for broadcasting from occupied France when trapped there by the invasion, enjoyed his knighthood for just one month.

2 JANUARY

The Feast Day of St Marcarius, patron saint of confectioners.

BORN THIS DAY

HISTORY

1727 James Wolfe, British general who captured Quebec (1759) from the French at the cost of his life.

ARTS

1866 Professor Gilbert Murray, English classical scholar, in Sydney, Australia. At the age of 11 he was sent to England to be educated, where he remained. He translated Greek drama into English, resulting in many new productions.

1905 Sir Michael Tippett, English composer, who was imprisioned during the war for failing to get exemption as a conscientious objector. His involvement with serious social concerns is demonstrated in his oratorio *A Child of Our Time* (1939).

1920 Professor Isaac Asimov, Russian-born US biochemist and science fiction writer of some 200 books, including the 'Foundation' trilogy.

PHOTOGRAPHY

1938 David (Royston) Bailey, English photographer.

DIED THIS DAY

MINUS TWO 17AD saw the deaths in Rome of Ovid (Publius Ovidius Naso), the celebrated poet, and the historian Livy, who wrote a 142-book history of the city.

1883 General Tom Thumb (Charles Sherwood Stratton), US 31-inch (90cm) midget, who was publicly exhibited by circus impresario P. T. Barnum.

1974 Tex Ritter, US stage and screen singing cowboy.

ON THIS DAY

1635 Cardinal Richelieu established the Académie française to maintain the purity of the French language.

1757 Clive of India captured Calcutta after it had been seized by the Nawab of Bengal. The latter imprisoned 146 British prisoners in the 'black hole'. Only 23 survived.

1769 English painter Sir Joshua Reynolds became the first president of the Royal

Academy, which opened on this day.

1788 Georgia became the fourth state of the Union.

1839 French photographic pioneer Louis Daguerre took the first photograph of the moon.

1900 The first electric omnibus ran in New York City.

1903 President Roosevelt closed a Missouri post office for refusing to employ a black postmistress.

1905 The Russians surrendered Port Arthur, Manchuria, to the Japanese.

1935 The trial of Bruno Hauptmann for the kidnapping and murder of the 19-month old son of US aviator Charles Lindberg and his wife Anne began in New Jersey. Hauptmann was found guilty and electrocuted on 3 April 1936 at Trenton State Prison.

1944 Three US Sikorsky helicopters began patrol duty with an Atlantic convoy, the first time helicopters had been used in warfare.

1959 The USSR launched the unmanned *Luna I* to pass close to the moon.

1971 A barrier collapsed at the Ibrox Park football ground, Glasgow, Scotland, crushing 66 spectators to death.

1979 The murder trial of Sex Pistol's singer, Sid Vicious, began in New York. Accused of murdering his girlfriend Nancy Spungen in her apartment in Greenwich Village, he died of a heroin overdose exactly one month later while out on bail. He was 21 years old.

1987 The publishers of Enid Blyton's Noddy books bowed to pressure groups and agreed to expunge all 'racism' from them. Golliwogs would now become neutral gnomes.

1988 A New York accountant waited 45 days before claiming a $3m New York state lottery jackpot on this day. He said it had saved him about $15,000 in taxes by waiting until the New Year.

3 JANUARY

BORN THIS DAY

HISTORY

106BC Marcus Tullius Cicero, Roman orator and statesman. After Caesar's assassination, he spoke in favour of a republican Rome, which led to his eventual death.

TWO OF A KIND In 1883, Clement (Richard) Attlee, British Labour Prime Minister (1945-51), who made sweeping social reforms. Five years later, in 1888, Herbert (Stanley) Morrison, the Labour MP who would lead the House of Commons during his premiership.

ARTS

1888 J(ohn) R(onald) R(euel) Tolkien, British author of *Lord of the Rings* (1954-5), in Bloemfontein, South Africa.

ENTERTAINMENT

1908 Ray Milland (Reginald Truscott-Jones), US actor who won an Oscar in 1945 for his role as an alcoholic in *The Lost Weekend*.

1909 Victor Borge (Borge Rosenbaum), pianist and musical comedian, in Denmark.

1942 John Thaw, British stage, film and television actor, best known for his part in the television series *The Sweeney*.

1945 Victoria Principal, US film and television actress, best known for her part in the long-running television series, *Dallas*.

POP

1926 George Martin, British record producer, at his own Polydor Records, of the Beatles and other leading pop groups.

INVENTION

1823 Robert Whitehead, British inventor of the self-propelled torpedo, which he developed in Austria.

RELIGION

1840 Father Damien (Joseph de Veuster), legendary Belgium missionary who worked with lepers on the Hawaiian island of Molokai. He later died of the disease.

DIED THIS DAY

1795 Josiah Wedgwood, English founder of the famous pottery that still bears his name.

1875 Pierre Larousse, French editor and encyclopaedist.

1923 Jaroslav Hašek, Czech author of *The Good Soldier Schweik*. He planned six volumes, but only lived to complete the first four of this monumental satire.

1946 William Joyce (Lord Haw-Haw), the Irishman who broadcast propaganda from Nazi Germany during the Second World War, was hanged in London for treason.

1967 Jack Ruby, the man who shot Lee Harvey Oswald before he could be tried for the alleged assassination of President John F. Kennedy. He was sentenced to death, but died in hospital from a blood clot in the lungs.

1979 Conrad Hilton, US hotel magnate.

ON THIS DAY

1521 Martin Luther, founder of Protestantism, was excommunicated following his refusal to retract any of his views about the wrongs of the Catholic Church.

1777 George Washington defeated the British, led by Cornwallis, at the Battle of Princeton during the American War of Independence.

1888 Paper drinking straws were patented in the US.

1911 The Siege of Sidney Street began when two members of a group of foreign anarchists were trapped by police in a house in London's East End. Three weeks earlier, the group had committed a robbery, killing three policemen. In Sidney Street, the fugitives fired at police. The Scots Guards from the Tower of London were sent in and Winston Churchill, then Home Secretary, arrived to see the house in flames. Firemen were not sent in to stop the blaze and the house eventually collapsed. The anarchists were burnt to death.

1924 English explorer Howard Carter discovered the sarcophagus of Tutankhamun in the Valley of the Kings, near Luxor, Egypt. When it was opened on 12.2.1924, they found the golden effigy of the young king.

1940 Unity Mitford, one of the famous 'Mitford girls', returned to England having failed to commit suicide in the Englischer Garten in Munich. She had flirted with both Fascism and Hitler, but when Britain went to war with her idol, Hitler, she tried to shoot herself.

1947 The US House of Representatives was televised for the first time.

1958 Sir Edmund Hillary, British conqueror of Everest in 1953, reached the South Pole.

1959 Alaska became the 59th and largest US state.

1961 The US severed diplomatic relations with Fidel Castro's Cuba.

1961 The millionth Morris Minor, the highly successful British car designed by Sir Alec Issigonis, came off the assembly line at Oxford.

1988 The first advertisements in a Soviet newspaper appeared in *Izvestia*. One was a full-page advertisement by a French industrial company, the other was shared by Soviet, West German and Belgian industrial companies.

4 JANUARY

BORN THIS DAY

ARTS

1785 Jakob Grimm, the elder brother of the famous German folklorist duo who published the first volume of their *Fairy Tales* in 1812.

1878 Augustus (Edwin) John, Welsh portrait painter and Royal Academician, who was also passionately interested in gypsy lore.

1937 Grace Bumbry, US opera singer who studied with Lotte Lehmann and was the first black singer to perform at Bayreuth (1961).

ENTERTAINMENT

1914 Jane Wyman (Sarah Jane Faulks), US film actress who won an Oscar for her performance as a deaf mute who was raped in *Johnny Belinda* (1948), the year her marriage to Ronald Reagan ended in divorce.

INVENTION

TWO OF A KIND Two people who devised new ways of transcribing language were born this day: in 1809, Louis Braille, French inventor of the alphabetic system for the blind that bears his name and, in 1813, Sir Isaac Pitman, English publisher and inventor of shorthand.

SPORT

1935 Floyd Patterson, US heavyweight boxing champion, and youngest world title holder.

DIED THIS DAY

1958 Ralph Vaughan Williams, English composer.

CRASH! In 1960 Albert Camus, Algerian-born French novelist and winner of the Nobel prize for Literature (1957), was killed in a car crash. On the same day in the English Lake District, Donald Campbell, son of Sir Malcolm Campbell, attempted to break the world water speed record in his ageing *Bluebird*. After a good first run on Coniston Water, he inexplicably failed to stop to refuel and began the second run, eventually hitting the wake which had not yet calmed. *Bluebird* somersaulted at high speed, killing Campbell instantly.

1965 T(homas) S(tearns) Eliot, US poet and critic, who wrote *The Waste Land*.

1980 Joy Adamson, German-born naturalist who wrote about Elsa the lioness in her book, *Born Free*, found murdered at her home in Kenya.

1986 Christopher Isherwood, English novelist and playwright, whose novel,

Goodbye To Berlin, was adapted as the musical *Cabaret*.

1985 Lt-Gen Sir Brian Horrocks, British military strategist and commander in North Africa during the Second World War.

ON THIS DAY

1835 The first chess column appeared in a newspaper, *Bell's Life in London*.

1884 The Fabian Society was founded. This British socialist organization took its name from the Roman, Fabius Maximus, who wanted to introduce gradual reforms. Its members included Bernard Shaw and Beatrice and Sydney Webb.

1885 The first successful appendix operation was performed by Dr Williams West Grant, in Iowa. His patient was a 22-year-old farm girl, Mary Gartside.

1895 Captain Alfred Dreyfus, the French army officer falsely accused of treason, was ritually degraded on the parade ground of the Military Academy. Found guilty at his trial, he was sent to Devil's Island before eventually being exonerated (1906).

1896 Utah became the 45th state of the Union.

1932 Gandhi's National Congress of India was declared illegal by the British administration, and he was arrested.

1936 The US magazine *Billboard* published the first pop music chart based on national sales.

1944 The attack on Monte Casino was launched by the British Fifth Army in Italy.

1948 Burma became fully independent outside the British Commonwealth.

1951 Seoul, the South Korean capital, was captured by the Communists during the Korean War.

A SHORT NOSE AND A LONG STRIKE In 1957, a man who thought his nose was too short as a result of plastic surgery, threatened the surgeon with a gun and was sentenced this day in London to ten years imprisonment. In 1961, a strike in Copenhagen by apprentice barbers that began in 1938 finally ended.

1972 Rose Heilbron became Britain's first woman judge at the Old Bailey.

1982 The buxom Erika Rowe became famous when she streaked across the pitch during the England v. Australia rugby match at Twickenham.

1988 Indian moustache-growing champion, Karni Bheel, who boasted a growth of 7ft 10in from tip to tip, was decapitated and his head removed; the remainder of his corpse was found in a cart in west Rajasthan city, an area where there is fierce competition to grow the most luxuriant moustache.

5 JANUARY

BORN THIS DAY

HISTORY

1779 Stephen Decatur, US naval commander who coined the phrase 'Our country, right or wrong'.

1787 John Burke, British genealogist, founder of *Burke's Peerage*, first published in 1826.

1876 Konrad Adenauer, German statesman known as the 'Old Fox'. Imprisoned by the Nazis, he became Chancellor of the Federal Republic in 1949.

1906 Kathleen Kenyon, British archaeologist who dated the remains of Jericho using the radio-carbon method.
1938 King Juan Carlos I of Spain.

ARTS

1902 Stella (Dorothea) Gibbons, English novelist and journalist. *Cold Comfort Farm*, published 1932, is a satire on the melodramatic rural novel.
1931 Alfred Brendel, Austrian concert pianist who, in 1962, played all Beethoven's sonatas in a single season in London.

ENTERTAINMENT

1887 Clifford Grey, English lyricist, best known for his songs 'If You Were the Only Girl in the World' and 'Spread a Little Happiness'.
1909 Jean-Pierre Aumont (J.-P. Salomons), French actor who appeared in Hollywood films as a handsome continental.
1931 Robert Duvall, US film actor, son of an admiral, who made his debut with Gregory Peck in *To Kill a Mockingbird* (1963) and later proved himself a leading character actor in *Apocalypse Now* (1979).
1946 Diane Keaton (Diane Hall), US film actress. A former understudy for the musical *Hair* (1968), she starred in several Woody Allen films after playing opposite him on Broadway in *Play it Again Sam* (1969). *Annie Hall* (1977) won her an Oscar for best actress.

INVENTION

1855 King Camp Gillette, US inventor of the safety razor which went on sale in 1903. Within a year, he was producing 90,000 razors and over 12.4m blades.

SPORT

1943 Eusébio (Ferreira da Silva Eusébio), Brazilian footballer.

DIED THIS DAY

1066 Edward the Confessor, English king, known for his piety, whose death led to the Norman Conquest.
1477 Charles the Bold, Duke of Burgundy, killed at the Battle of Nancy, his invasion of France halted by the combined French and Swiss forces.
1589 Catherine de Medici, wife of Henry II of France.
1933 John Calvin Coolidge, 30th US President.

ADVENTURERS In 1922 Sir Ernest Shackleton, British Antarctic explorer, died on the island of South Georgia in the South Atlantic during his expedition to Enderby Land. In 1941 Amy Johnson (Mollison), record-breaking English aviator who flew solo from Britain to Australia, died while ferrying an aircraft on a flight across a foggy Thames estuary. The plane was found in the muddy water, but not Amy's body.

ON THIS DAY

1896 Rontgen gave the first demonstration of X-rays. The German physicist had made the discovery the previous year when investigating the passage of electricity through gases.
1919 Anton Drexler, a Munich plumber, formed the German Workers Party which was later transformed by Hitler into the Nazi Party.

1925 Mrs Nellie Taylor Ross in Wyoming became the first US woman governor.

SMILING In 1938, 'When You're Smiling (The Whole World Smiles with You)' was recorded by Billie Holiday in New York. In London, the BBC began its first radio comedy series, *Bandwagon*, starring Arthur Askey and Richard 'Stinker' Murdoch.

1940 FM Radio was demonstrated for the first time in the US by Major Edward H. Armstrong. A year later, the first FM transmitter was broadcasting.

1960 The oldest railway in the world made its final journey. The Mumbles Railway, which ran from Swansea to Mumbles Head, Wales, was set up in 1804 as a goods railway and carried passengers from 1807. On 28 October 1988, Swansea Council announced it would carry out a feasibility study to see if it could bring back the railway to run around the bay.

1964 During his tour of the Holy Land, Pope Paul VI met the Ecumenical Patriarch of Constantinople in Jerusalem. It was the first time in 500 years that leaders of both the Roman Catholic and Orthodox churches had met.

1968 Alexander Dubček succeeded Antonin Novotny as party leader in Poland. 16 months later he was ousted in favour of Gustáv Husák, after five Warsaw Pact countries sent in tanks to halt his reforms.

1971 The body of former world heavyweight boxing champion Sonny Liston was found at his US home. He had been dead at least a week.

1971 One-day cricket was born when 46,000 turned up to watch England play Australia at Melbourne. The test match had been aborted by the previous days' rain.

1976 No more real or fractured anglais for French advertisements. French premier Giscard d'Estaing promulgated a law making French the only language permitted in advertising.

1981 The hunt for the Yorkshire Ripper, who killed 13 women over four years, ended when long distance lorry-driver Peter Sutcliffe was charged with murder.

6 JANUARY

Twelfth Night (after Christmas). In the mid-19th century, it was the custom in London for groups of boys to assemble around pastry shops and nail coat-tails of unsuspecting pedestrians to the wooden window frame as they lingered to peer into the shop. A boy would deftly – with just one hammer blow – strike a nail through the coat-tail, much to the amusement of other passers-by until they, in turn, also found themselves nailed.

BORN THIS DAY

HISTORY

1367 King Richard II of England, son of Edward the Black Prince, in Bordeaux.

1412 St Joan of Arc, known as the Maid of Orleans, French heroine who believed she had a divine mission to expel the British from France. It ended with her capture by the Burgundians, who sold her to the British.

1745 Jacques Etienne Montgolfier, French balloonist and paper manufacturer. With his brother Joseph (1740–1810), he made the first successful flight in a hot-air balloon.

1822 Heinrich Schliemann, German archaeologist who discovered and excavated the legendary cities of Troy and Mycenae, where he thought he found the grave of Agamemnon.

ARTS

1832 Gustave Doré, French artist and illustrator of over 90 books.

1838 Max Bruch, German composer mainly of choral works. He also taught; one of his pupils was Vaughan Williams.

1878 Carl Sandburg, US poet and biographer of Abraham Lincoln. He was also a journalist and folk-singer.

1931 P(atrick) J(oseph Gregory) Kavanagh, Irish poet, novelist, critic and actor. He won the Guardian Fiction Prize for *Song & Dance* (1968).

ENTERTAINMENT

1880 Tom Mix, US film actor who made his name in early Westerns and became one of the silent screen's most popular cowboy stars, appearing in over 100 one- and two-reelers before retiring in 1934.

1913 Loretta (Gretchen Michaela) Young, US film actress who began as a child extra. Later she won an Oscar for *The Farmer's Daughter* (1947) and several awards for appearances on television.

1934 Sylvia Sims, British film actress who was allowed to play sensual women in a period when French actresses were usually hired for that type of part. Her films include *Ice Cold in Alex* (1958).

1955 Rowan Atkinson, English comedian and stage and screen actor, best known for his successful television comedy series *Blackadder* and the multi award-winning *Mr Bean*.

SPORT

1943 Terry Venables, British footballer and later manager.

1945 Barry John, schoolmaster who became a Welsh and Lions rugby international.

1957 Nancy Lopez-Melton, US professional golfer since 1977. She was voted US Sportswoman of the Year in 1978 and has attracted big prize money to women's golf tournaments.

1959 Kapil Dev, Indian cricket captain who led the underdogs to a World Cup victory against the West Indies in 1982.

DIED THIS DAY

1840 Fanny Burney (Madame d'Arblay), British novelist and diarist, at the age of 87.

1852 Louis Braille, inventor of the reading system for the blind.

1918 Georg Cantor, German mathematician who worked on the theory of infinity.

1919 Theodore Roosevelt, 26th US President.

1981 A(rchibald) J(oseph) Cronin, Scottish novelist, author of *The Citadel*, in Switzerland.

ON THIS DAY

871 King Alfred defeated the Danes at the Battle of Ashdown.

1066 Harold II was crowned King of England in succession to Edward the Confessor. Ten months later he died in the Battle of Hastings (14.10.1066).

1540 King Henry VIII married 'the Flanders Mare', Anne of Cleves, his fourth wife.

1838 US inventor Samuel Morse gave the first demonstration of his electric telegraphic system.

1912 New Mexico became the 47th state of the Union.

1926 Lufthansa, the German national airline, was founded.

1928 The River Thames flooded causing four people to drown. It filled the moat of the Tower of London and the basement of the Tate Gallery, where many paintings were severely damaged.

1930 Australian batsman Don Bradman, batting for New South Wales, scored 452 not out against Queensland in his first innings, which included 49 boundaries.

1938 Sigmund Freud, the Austrian pioneer of psychoanalysis who was by now a frail 82-year-old, arrived in London with several of his students having fled the persecution of Jews in Vienna.

1977 EMI sacked the Sex Pistols after they took part in a television interview with Bill Grundy and behaved, according to Grundy, 'like foul mouthed yobs'. Grundy was suspended by Thames Television.

1988 La Coupole, the famous Parisian brasserie, was sold for £6m, destined to become an office block. Frequented by Vlaminck, Derain, James Joyce and later by Hemingway, Henry Miller, Gertrude Stein and other notable Americans, its most famous dish was Welsh rarebit.

7 JANUARY

BORN THIS DAY

HISTORY

1768 Joseph Bonaparte, eldest brother of Napoleon, who became King of Naples in 1806 and then of Spain, 1808.

1844 Marie-Bernard Soubirous, Saint Bernardette of Lourdes, an asthmatic French girl who claimed to see visions of the Virgin Mary at a spring near her home. This became the shrine at Lourdes.

ARTS

1873 Charles Péguy, French poet and socialist who experienced poverty before publishing an influential fortnightly journal, *Cahiers de la quinzaine*, expounding socialism.

1899 François Poulenc, French composer and pianist encouraged by Satie and Cocteau. He had a great success with his music for the ballet, *Les Biches* (1924), commissioned by Diaghilev.

1912 Charles Addams, *New Yorker* cartoonist and author of *Addams Family of Ghouls*. He is said to have been fascinated by graveyards at an early age.

TWO-REELERS Born 1867, Carl Laemmle, German immigrant who fulfilled the American dream by becoming a film producer and founder of Universal Pictures. He was the first to realize the full potential of publicity and the star system. Also born this day, in 1873, Adolf Zukor, Hungarian immigrant who worked in the penny-arcade business before becoming a film magnate. Under his chairmanship, Paramount Studios rose to prominence.

SCIENCE

1794 Eilhard Mitscherlich, German chemist involved in the examination of benzene and methyl while Professor of Chemistry at Berlin.

NATURAL HISTORY

1925 Gerald (Malcolm) Durrell, English author and naturalist, brother of Lawrence, and director of the Jersey Zoological Park. His most famous book, *My Family and Other Animals*, was published in 1956.

DIED THIS DAY

1536 Catherine of Aragon, first wife of Henry VIII.

1932 André Maginot, French politician who was responsible for the Maginot Line, a border fortification which was expected to, but failed to hold back the Germans in the Second World War.

1989 Michinomiya Hirohito, Emperor of Japan, aged 87, after a long illness.

ON THIS DAY

1450 Glasgow University, Scotland, was founded.

1558 The French recaptured Calais from the English.

1610 Galileo discovered the four satellites of Jupiter and named them Io, Europa, Ganymede and Callisto.

1618 Francis Bacon became Lord Chancellor of England. Later this year he would be accused of taking a bribe and be fined £40,000.

1785 Dr John Jeffries, an American who put up the money, and Jean-Pierre Blanchard, a Frenchman who piloted it, crossed the Channel from Dover to Calais in a hot-air balloon.

1789 The first national US elections were held. George Washington would become the first president.

1857 The London Central Omnibus Company started its first services.

1904 The CQD distress signal was introduced. CQ – seek you, and the D – danger. It lasted just two years before being replaced with SOS.

1927 The Harlem Globetrotters basketball team was founded by Abraham Sapperstein of Chicago.

1927 The transatlantic telephone service between New York and London opened.

1937 Princess Juliana of the Netherlands married Prince Bernhard.

1975 OPEC agreed to raise crude oil prices by ten per cent, which began a tidal wave of world economic inflation and near-bankruptcy for developing nations.

1988 A team of West German scientists at Bayreuth University, led by Professor Frank Pobell, announced that they had cooled a block of metal to 12 millionths of a degree above absolute zero, the lowest temperature ever achieved in a laboratory.

1990 For safety reasons, the famous leaning tower of Pisa was closed to the public for the first time since it opened around 1275.

8 JANUARY

BORN THIS DAY

HISTORY

1885 John Curtin, Australian Labour politician and Prime Minister in 1941.

1899 Solomon Bandaranaike, Prime Minister of Sri Lanka, husband of Sirimavo, who succeeded him after his assassination to become the world's first woman Prime Minister.

1902 Georgi (Maximilianovich) Malenkov, Soviet Prime Minister 1953–5, replaced by Kruschev.

ARTS

THRILLERS In 1824, (William) Wilkie Collins, English pioneer of the detective and suspense story, who wrote *The Woman in White* (1860) and *The Moonstone* (1868). Also born this day, in 1897, Dennis (Yates) Wheatley, English writer of thrillers and adventure stories featuring black magic and the occult. His books include *The Devil Rides Out* (1935).

ENTERTAINMENT

1912 José Ferrer (José Vincente Ferrer de Otero y Cintron), Puerto Rican-born US actor and director whose theatrical roles ranged from appearing in *Charlie's Aunt*, to playing Iago to Paul Robeson's *Othello*. He made his screen debut as the Dauphin in *Joan of Arc* (1948) and won an Oscar for *Cyrano de Bergerac* (1950).

1928 Ron Moody (Ronald Moodnick), English actor, Fagin in the musical *Oliver!* on both stage (1960) and screen (1968).

1935 Elvis (Aaron) Presley, US singer, guitarist, songwriter, film actor and world rock 'n' roll idol with record sales of over 500 million.

1937 Shirley Bassey, 'the girl from Tiger Bay', Welsh-born international singer with expressive hands and a strong emotional voice. Her hits include the theme from the Bond film, *Goldfinger*.

1947 David Bowie (David Robert Jones), British pop singer and actor who starred in the film *The Man who Fell to Earth* (1976) and the play *The Elephant Man* (1980) on Broadway.

SCIENCE

1942 Professor Stephen Hawking, English mathematician and author of *A Brief History of Time* (1988), who suffers from a wasting disease and is confined to a wheelchair.

DIED THIS DAY

1642 Galileo Galilei, Italian mathematician and astronomer.

1713 Arcangelo Corelli, composer and violinist. His major work, 12 *Concerti grossi*, was published posthumously.

1825 Eli Whitney, US inventor of the cotton gin.

1895 Paul Verlaine, French poet who took some 20 years to sell 500 copies of his *Poèmes Saturnias*. He briefly taught in a school in Bournemouth, on England's south coast, but returned to France where he drank heavily and died in poverty.

1941 Robert Baden-Powell, Boer War hero and founder of the Boy Scouts.

1948 Richard Tauber (Seiffert), Austrian-born tenor, in Australia.

1948 Kurt Schwitters, German painter and writer associated with the Dada movement.

1976 Chou En-Lai, Chinese Communist statesman and Prime Minister.

1988 Elizabeth Bather, Scotland Yard's first woman chief inspector.

1990 Terry-Thomas (Thomas Terry Hoar Stevens), English actor with the famous gap in his front teeth, who specialized in upper-class cads in films including *Carlton-Browne of the F.O.* (1959) and *Those Magnificent Men in Their Flying*

Machines (1965). He suffered from Parkinson's disease in his last years.

ON THIS DAY

1800 The first soup kitchens for the poor of London began.

1806 The Cape of Good Hope (Cape Town, South Africa), formerly in the hands of the Dutch, was occupied by Britain.

1815 The British, led by General Sir Edward Pakenham, were defeated at New Orleans in the last battle Britain ever fought against the US, in the War of 1812.

1889 Dr Herman Hollerith of New York patented an electrically operated computer to process data. The company he formed to market his invention would evolve into the giant IBM.

1921 David Lloyd George became the first British Prime Minister to occupy Chequers, a country mansion in Buckinghamshire, presented to the nation as a gift by Lord Lee of Fareham.

1926 Ibn Saud became King of the Hejaz, which he renamed Saudi Arabia.

1959 General Charles de Gaulle became the President of the French Fifth Republic.

1961 Canadian Gordon Lonsdale and four others were arrested for spying at the British Navy's Underwater Establishment in Portland, Dorset.

1963 A serious fire in the Empire State Building, New York, damaged seven floors.

1967 The first of 26 episodes of the television adaptation of John Galsworthy's *The Forsyte Saga* with Eric Porter, Kenneth More, Susan Hampshire and Nyree Dawn Porter was screened. It would keep half of Britain glued to their black-and-white television sets each Sunday evening for the next six months resulting in many of clergy having to change the times of church services!

1971 Sir Geoffrey Jackson, the British ambassador in Uruguay, was kidnapped by left-wing urban guerrillas of the Tupamaros movement. He remained a hostage until his safe release. (*See* 9.9.1971)

1982 Spain ended its siege of Gibraltar and reopened the frontier. In return Britain agreed to talks on the colony's future and ended its opposition to Spain joining the EEC.

1989 A British Midland 737-400 jet with 117 passengers and eight crew on board crashed on the M1 motorway less than half a mile from East Midlands Airport, where it was trying to make an emergency landing after one engine had had to be switched off, and the remaining engine had suddenly lost power. 47 were killed, over 80 were injured.

9 JANUARY

BORN THIS DAY

HISTORY

1735 John Jervis (Earl of St Vincent), British admiral who defeated the Spanish fleet off Cape St Vincent in 1797. Nelson, then a captain, shared in the victory and became a national hero. He was coincidentally buried this day, eight years later. (*See* ON THIS DAY)

1854 Jenny, Lady Randolph Churchill, wife of Lord Randolph and mother of Winston.

1913 Richard Nixon, the first US

president to resign (as a result of the Watergate scandal), and also the first US president to visit China.

ARTS

1890 Karel Čapek, Czech playwright whose play *R.U.R* (Rossum's Universal Robots) coined the term 'robot'.

1902 Sir Rudolf Bing, Austrian-born conductor and founder of the Edinburgh Festival. He became a British citizen in 1946.

1904 George Balanchine (Blanchivade), influential Russian-born dancer who was Diaghilev's last choreographer. In the US, he created the first ballet sequence in a musical with 'Slaughter on 10th Avenue' in *On Your Toes* (1936), and was co-founder of the New York City Ballet.

1908 Simone de Beauvoir, French novelist and critic who wrote *The Second Sex* (1949). She also wrote a biography of Jean-Paul Sartre, her long-time companion.

STRIPPERS Born 1901, Chic Young (Murat Bernard Young), US cartoonist who created the famous 'Blondie' strip in 1930 that was later syndicated to more than 1,500 newspapers throughout the world. Born 1914, Gypsy Rose Lee (Rose Louise Hovick), actress, strip-tease artist and author, who made her stage debut with her sister 'Baby' June (film actress June Havoc) aged four, and became the Queen of Burlesque in the 30s, starring in the Ziegfeld Follies and other Broadway shows. Her autobiography, *Gypsy*, became a Broadway hit musical.

ENTERTAINMENT

1898 Gracie Fields (Grace Stansfield), English singer, actress and comedienne, born in Rochdale, Lancashire, who became one of the most popular entertainers of the 30s with songs such as 'Sally' and 'The Biggest Aspidistra in the World'. She was made a Dame of the British Empire in 1979.

1917 Herbert Lom, (Herbert Kuchacevich ze Schluderpacheru), in Prague. He came to England in 1939, where he worked at the Old Vic, later appearing in *The Seventh Veil*, and three Pink Panther films.

1922 Clive Dunn, British actor, best remembered for his portrayal of Corporal Jones in the *Dad's Army* comedy series on BBC television.

1941 Susannah York (Susannah Yolande Fletcher), English actress whose films include *Tom Jones* (1963) and *The Killing of Sister George* (1968). She was nominated for an Oscar for *They Shoot Horses, Don't They?* (1969).

1941 Joan Baez, US singer. Known for her protest songs, she played an active part in the US civil rights movement.

DIED THIS DAY

1848 Caroline Lucretia Herschel, English astronomer who discovered nine comets. She was the sister of William Herschel, for whom she worked as an assistant.

1873 Napoleon III, Emperor of France and Bonaparte's nephew, in exile, at Chislehurst, Kent.

1878 Victor Emmanuel, the first King of Italy.

1923 Katherine Mansfield (Kathleen Beauchamp Murry), New Zealand-born author, in France, aged 34, of a pulmonary haemorrhage.

1949 Tommy Handley, English radio comedian of *I.T.M.A* (It's That Man Again) fame.

1985 Sir Robert Mayer, German-born musical philanthropist.

ON THIS DAY

1799 The Napoleonic Wars forced the British Prime Minister, William Pitt the Younger, to introduce income tax: two shillings (10p) in the pound.
1806 Nelson, Viscount Horatio, British naval hero, was buried at St Paul's Cathedral, London.
1811 The first women's golf tournament took place in Scotland between locals in the fishing town of Musselburgh.
1902 New York State introduced a bill to outlaw flirting in public.
1909 Ernest Shackleton's polar expedition got within 11 miles of the South Pole before being forced to turn back.
1920 The Bolsheviks defeated the last of the White Russian troops under Admiral Koltchak.
1923 Spanish aviator, Juan de la Cierva, inventor of the autogyro, made the first successful flight in Spain.
1929 Alexander Fleming used a penicillin broth to successfully treat his assistant Stuart Craddick's infection, at St Mary's Hospital, Paddington.
1951 The first British X Certificate was awarded to the film *La Vie Commence Demain* (Life Begins Tomorrow).
1957 Anthony Eden resigned as British Prime Minister due to ill-health following the Suez fiasco. Harold Macmillan took over the following day.

ONE UP, ONE DOWN In 1969, the first trial of Concorde, Britain's supersonic airliner, took place at Bristol. In 1972, the liner *Queen Elizabeth*, fitted out as a sailing university, caught fire and sank in Hong Kong harbour.

1972 The British miners strike for improved pay and conditions began, their first since 1926. Power cuts and candles were the order of the day.
1987 Ernest Saunders, chief executive of the brewing giant Guinness, resigned as the Department of Industry began investigating the company's take-over of the huge Distiller's Group.
1988 It was reported this day that Edgar Dakin from Yorkshire was now the owner of Patent No. 8721872, the Dakin Plastic Tombstone which would cost one tenth the price of a conventional marble stone.
1989 In Tiberias, Israel, a rabbi revoked the kosher food licence of a local hotel for allowing a couple to have sex in a helicopter hovering above its pool during a party.

10 JANUARY

BORN THIS DAY

HISTORY

1769 Michel Ney, the most famous of Napoleon's marshals, who commanded the Old Guard at Waterloo.
1913 Gustáv Husák, President of Czechoslovakia 1975–87, who took control after the 'Prague Spring' which led to the suppression of democratic aspirations.

ARTS

1903 Dame Barbara Hepworth, English abstract sculptor.

1910 Galina Ulanova, Russian prima ballerina.

ENTERTAINMENT

1880 Grock (Karl Adrien Wettach), the great clown, son of a Swiss watchmaker. He worked both in the circus and theatre, and played 17 different musical instruments during his performance.

1904 Ray Bolger, US actor and dancer, famous on Broadway before he reached a larger audience as the Scarecrow in the film *The Wizard of Oz* (1939).

1908 Paul Henreid, Viennese actor discovered by film director Otto Preminger when he worked with Max Reinhardt's theatre as a business manager. His films include *Now Voyager* (1942) and *Casablanca* (1942).

POP

1927 Johnny Ray, US singer, all the rage in the 50s with his hit song 'Cry'. He also appeared in films, including *There's No Business Like Show Business* (1954).

1945 Rod Stewart, Scottish pop star discovered by blues singer Long John Baldry playing a harmonica on a station platform. Stewart's hits include 'Maggie May', 'Sailing' and 'Do You Think I'm Sexy?'.

SPORT

1949 George Foreman, US world heavyweight boxing champion.

DIED THIS DAY

1645 Archbishop of Canterbury, William Laud, beheaded on Tower Hill for treason. He introduced press censorship, persecuted Puritans, provoked the Civil War with Scotland by trying to impose the Prayer Book, and seems to have alienated just about every group in English society.

1778 Carl Linnaeus, Swedish botanist.

1862 Samuel Colt, US gunsmith.

1917 Colonel William Cody, one-time US army scout, Indian fighter and showman known as 'Buffalo Bill'.

1951 Sinclair Lewis, the first US novelist to win the Nobel prize.

1961 Dashiel Hammett, former detective with the Pinkerton Agency, who wrote *The Maltese Falcon* and influenced a generation of crime writers, including Raymond Chandler.

1985 Anton Karas, composer and zither player, whose playing was featured on the soundtrack of *The Third Man*, sparking a revival of interest in the instrument.

1988 August T. Baden, the US drugstore owner who gave the world cinnamon-flavoured Baden's Hot Toothpicks.

ON THIS DAY

1839 Indian tea was auctioned for the first time in Britain. Until now, only expensive China tea was available. Tea prices were to fall to make it affordable as the national drink.

1840 In Britain, Sir Rowland Hill introduced the Penny Post. 112,000 letters were posted in London on the first day. To coincide with this event, Sir Isaac Pitman started the first correspondence course for his shorthand system.

1863 The London Underground railway was opened by Prime Minister Gladstone. The first route of the Metropolitan Railway went from Paddington to Farringdon Street stopping at seven stations.

1888 Frenchman Louis Aimé Augustine le Prince was granted a US patent for the first single-lens film camera. The true father of cinematography, he settled in Leeds, Yorkshire, and disappeared while on a rail trip between Dijon and Paris. Both equipment and inventor were never seen again. When le Prince's son tried to prove his father was the originator of the motion picture, he too was found dead, in a wood in Long Island, New York.

1918 The US House of Representatives voted in favour of women's suffrage. The vote would go to married women over 30.

1919 The new Rt Hon Minister of State for India, was Sir S. P. Sinha, the first coloured man to hold the position. On the 22nd of this month he became the first non-white to be elevated to the British peerage by Lloyd George.

1920 The League of Nations was inaugurated in 1920. On this same day, 1946, the UN Assembly held its first meeting in London.

1920 The official end of the First World War with Germany and the ratifying of the Treaty of Versailles.

1928 English pioneer aviators, Hood and Moncrieff, were lost over the Tasman Sea attempting to fly from Australia to New Zealand.

1929 Tintin and his dog Snowy, the cartoon creation of Belgium artist Hergé (Georges Remi), made their first appearance in *Vingtième Siècle*.

1934 Dutchman Marinus van der Lubbe, a Communist, was guillotined for allegedly burning down the German Reichstag, but many believed it was the work of the Nazis who then blamed van der Lubbe. (*See* 27.2.1933)

1935 'The King and Queen of Hollywood', Douglas Fairbanks and Mary Pickford were divorced.

1949 Seven-and-a-half-inch 'microgroove' records from RCA went on sale in the US. They played at 45 r.p.m., while rivals Columbia produced 12-inch 'long player' (LP) records to be played at 33.3 r.p.m.

1985 Sir Clive Sinclair demonstrated his C5 electric car. The £399 battery-driven car flopped.

11 JANUARY

BORN THIS DAY

HISTORY

1716 Daniel Dancer, who came from a long line of celebrated English misers and lived in seclusion, taking one meal a day of a little baked meat and a hard-boiled dumpling. Lady Tempest was the only person who visited him in his later years. When he died, on 9.9.1794, he left her his estate but she died soon after, having contracted a severe cold through looking after the old man in his damp, unheated house.

1807 Ezra Cornell, founder of Cornell University, New York.

1815 Sir John Alexander, Canada's first Prime Minister.

1859 George Nathaniel Curzon (Lord Curzon of Kedleston), Viceroy of India who was passed over as Prime Minister in favour of Baldwin. Romantic novelist, Elinor Glyn, was the love of his life.

1896 Sir William Stephenson, Canadian-born head of British intelligence in the US who was codenamed 'Intrepid'.

1922 Neville Duke, English test pilot and

one-time holder of the world air speed record.

ARTS

1903 Alan Paton, South African writer whose novel *Cry the Beloved Country* brought him international acclaim and made the world more aware of the racial inequalities of his country. He was one of the founders of the South African Institute of Race Relations.

ENTERTAINMENT

1929 Rod Taylor, Australian actor who achieved success in Hollywood in films such as *The Birds*.

SPORT

1857 Fred Archer, English champion jockey who had 2,748 wins including five Derbys, in just over 8,000 races, with 246 winners in one season.

BUSINESS

1857 Henry Gordon Selfridge, US founder of Britain's first large department store.

DIED THIS DAY

1753 Sir Hans Sloane, British physician and naturalist whose collection of books formed the basis of the British Museum.

1762 Louis François Roubillac, French-born sculptor, in London.

1843 Francis Scott Key, US lawyer and poet who wrote the words of 'The Star-spangled Banner'.

1891 Georges Eugène Haussmann, architect responsible for re-planning Paris, in poverty.

1928 Thomas Hardy, English novelist and poet, in Dorset, aged 87. His books include *Tess of the D'Urbervilles*. (*See* 16.1.1928)

1966 Alberto Giacometti, Italian sculptor and painter.

1966 Lal Bahadour Shastri, Indian Prime Minister.

1969 Richmal Crompton (Lamburn), English children's author of the popular 'William' books.

1972 Padraic Colum, poet and founder of the Irish National Theatre.

ON THIS DAY

1569 The first state lottery was held in England. 40,000 lots at 10s (50p) each, which could be further subdivided, were available from the West Door of St Paul's Cathedral, London. Prizes were £20,000 and £30,000. Critics claimed it encouraged crime.

1813 Joachim Murat, King of Naples, deserted Napoleon and joined the Allies. He later tried to make himself King of Italy, but was captured and shot.

1864 London's Charing Cross station was opened.

1867 Benito Juarez, Mexican President, returned to Mexico City following the defeat of foreign forces, and the death by firing squad of the hated Maximilian.

1898 Major Esterhàzy was acquitted in Paris of forging documents which were exhibited at the trial of Captain Alfred Dreyfus. Years later, when further evidence against Esterhàzy was available, he fled the country, and the following year Dreyfus was brought back from Devil's Island.

1922 At Toronto General Hospital, Canada, 14-year-old Leonard Thompson, who was suffering from diabetes, became the first person to be successfully treated with insulin.

1946 King Zog, who smoked well over 100 cigarettes a day, was deposed *in absentia* and Albania became a republic.

1954 All Comet airliners were grounded following a mystery crash off the island of Elba the day before, which killed 35 people. The cause of a previous Comet crash near Calcutta in 1953, when the aircraft 'fell out of the sky for no apparent reason', was finally diagnosed as a structural fault and set British aviation back many years.

1970 General Ojukwe, the Biafran leader, fled the country as Nigerian troops occupied Owerri, centre for the Ibo people in southern Nigeria.

1974 The first sextuplets were born to Mrs Sue Rosenkowitz of Cape Town, South Africa.

CAR TROUBLE In 1977, a London court tried Rolling Stone Keith Richards for possession of cocaine which was discovered in his car following an accident. He was fined £750. In 1987, 25 motorists who staged an unofficial race in the Saudi capital, Jeddah, were lashed in public.

12 JANUARY

The Feast Day of Benedict, patron saint of speleologists (cavers and potholers).

BORN THIS DAY

HISTORY

1729 Edmund Burke, British statesman and writer, in Dublin. An eloquent Member of Parliament, he was the author of *Reflections on the French Revolution*.

1746 Johann Heinrich Pestalozzi, Swiss teacher and educational reformer who highlighted the importance of a close mother-and-child relationship in early teaching.

1852 Joseph Joffre, French army marshal and Commander-in-Chief on the Western Front during the First World War.

1893 Hermann Wilhelm Goering, German field marshal and Nazi leader. A former First World War fighter ace, he enlarged the Luftwaffe.

1926 P(ieter) W(illem) Botha, first executive state president of South Africa (1984). He hinted at reforms, but a right-wing backlash trapped him in the Boer laager.

ARTS

1628 Charles Perrault, French writer and collector of fairy tales. *Tales of Mother Goose* (1729) included 'Little Red Riding Hood', 'Sleeping Beauty' and 'Puss in Boots'.

1856 John Singer Sargent, US painter of stylish high society portraits, in Florence. Educated in the US, he 'deserted its provincial life' for Europe. He was elected to both the British Royal Academy and the National Academy in New York, while the French gave him the Légion d'honneur.

1876 Jack (John Griffith) London, US adventure novelist whose books include *Call of the Wild* (1903) and *White Fang* (1906).

ENTERTAINMENT

1905 Tex Ritter (Woodward Maurice Ritter), US singing cowboy who recorded the title song for the film *High Noon*. While studying political science, he became interested in cowboy ballads which he sang on stage and radio. In the

30s and 40s he appeared in many films, including *The Old Chisolm Trail* (1942).

1910 Luise Rainer, Viennese born actress who was hailed by Hollywood as a second Garbo. She won Oscars for *The Great Ziegfeld* (1936) and *The Good Earth* (1937) before her career fizzled out.

1948 Anthony Andrews, English actor who starred in the television adaptation of *Brideshead Revisited*.

1932 Des O'Connor, British comedian and singer, host of the long-running *The Des O'Connor Show* on television.

SCIENCE

1580 Jean Baptiste van Helmont, Belgium chemist and scientist, who coined the word 'gas' from the Greek *chaos*. He is regarded as having been the bridge from alchemy to chemistry by identifying carbon dioxide and other gases.

1899 Paul Hermann Muller, Swiss chemist who formulated the insecticide DDT (dichlorodiphenyltrichloroethane), for which he was awarded the Nobel prize in 1948.

POP

1941 Long John Baldry, British blues singer, songwriter and guitarist who discovered and influenced Rod Stewart and Elton John.

SPORT

1947 Joe Frazier, US world heavyweight boxing champion in 1970, when he knocked out Jimmy Ellis in New York, but in the 'thriller in Manila', in 1975, Muhammed Ali took back the crown.

DIED THIS DAY

1519 Maximilian I, King of Germany, Holy Roman Emperor from 1493.

1665 Pierre de Fermat, French mathematician.

1897 Sir Isaac Pitman, shorthand inventor.

1960 Nevil Shute (Norway), English novelist. His books include *A Town Like Alice* (1949).

1976 Dame Agatha Christie, the world's most successful detective story writer, and author of the world's longest-running play, *The Mousetrap*. Her last book, *Curtains*, was also Hercule Poirot's last case.

1990 Laurence Johnston Peter, Canadian-born educationist and author of *The Peter Principle* published in 1969, ('In a Hierarchy Every Employee Tends to Rise to His Level of Incompetence').

ON THIS DAY

1866 The Aeronautical Society of Great Britain was formed in London.

1948 The London Co-op opened the first supermarket in Britain, at Manor Park.

1950 The *Truculent*, a British submarine, collided in the Thames with a Swedish ship and sank with the loss of 65 lives.

1954 The Queen opened the New Zealand parliament; the first time a reigning monarch had done so in the country's history.

1959 Henry Cooper became British and European heavyweight boxing champion when he defeated Brian London on points over 15 rounds.

1964 The Sultan of Zanzibar was banished and the country declared itself a republic.

1970 The Boeing 747 jet touched down at London's Heathrow Airport at the end of its first transatlantic flight from New York.

TERROR SQUADS In 1971, the Angry Brigade planted two bombs at the home of Robert Carr on the outskirts of London. They exploded, but the British Secretary of State for Employment escaped unscathed. In 1977, France released PLO terrorist Abu Davoud, leader of the Black September group responsible for the Munich Olympic killings of 11 Israeli athletes. Israel withdrew its ambassador from France in protest.

1978 Lady Churchill's executors admitted she had burnt the controversial Graham Sutherland portrait of Sir Winston 18 months after it had been presented to him by the House of Commons in 1954. Sir Winston called it, with bitter irony, 'a remarkable example of modern art'.

1982 Mark Thatcher, son of the British Prime Minister, went missing in the Sahara on the Paris-Dakar Rally. Rescued two days later having lost his way, he became the subject of hundreds of jokes and cartoons about his sense of direction.

SPERM BANKS In 1985, a British high court allowed the surrogate baby born to Kim Cotton, a 28-year-old mother of two, to travel to the US with the couple who had paid £14,000 to an agency to have Kim artificially inseminated with the man's sperm. In 1988, Chinese scientists announced it was now possible to breed test-tube pandas having completed research into the use of frozen panda sperm the previous October.

13 JANUARY

BORN THIS DAY

HISTORY

1921 Sir Johannes Bjelke-Petersen, New Zealand-born former Prime Minister of Queensland, Australia. After Taabinga Village Primary School, most of his education was by correspondence courses and private tuition.

ARTS

1926 Michael Bond, English creator of Paddington Bear.

ENTERTAINMENT

1884 Sophie Tucker, Russian-born US singer and vaudeville star known as 'the last of the red hot mamas'. She immortalized songs including 'Some of these Days'.

1918 Lord Ted Willis, British playwright and screenwriter. His films include *The Blue Lamp* (1949), which led to the television series *Dixon of Dock Green*.

1919 Robert Stack, US film actor, nominated for an Oscar for his supporting role in *Written in the Wind*, but best known for his portrayal of Eliot Ness in the TV series, *The Untouchables*.

1920 Harry Worth, British comedian who created a gentle, dithery character on both stage and television in such shows as *How's Your Father*.

DIED THIS DAY

1599 Edmund Spenser, English poet who wrote the allegorical poem, *The Faerie*

Queene (1590–96), and was buried in Westminster Abbey.

1691 George Fox, English founder of the religious group the Society of Friends, or the Quakers as they are usually called.

1832 Thomas Lord, founder of Lord's Cricket Ground in 1787.

1864 Stephen Foster, US composer and songwriter of such classics as 'Swanee River' and 'Beautiful Dreamer', in poverty and obscurity, of alcoholism, aged 37, in a charity ward of the Belle Vue Hospital, New York.

1929 Wyatt Earp, US lawman who, with his brothers (Virgil and Morgan) and Doc Holiday, fought the Clanton Gang at O.K. Corral, of old age, aged 81, in Los Angeles.

1941 James (Augustine Aloysius) Joyce, Irish author of *Ulysses* (1922).

ON THIS DAY

1838 William Lyon Mackenzie, the Scottish-born Canadian radical, fled to the US after he had led an abortive uprising against the establishment families that virtually ruled Toronto.

1893 The Independent British Labour Party was formed by Keir Hardie.

J'ACCUSE! In 1898, following the acquittal of Major Esterhàzy, French author, Émile Zola's letter headlined 'J'accuse!' was published on the front page of *L'Aurore*, addressed to the French President. He accused senior government and military figures of a cover-up in their involvement in the Dreyfus Affair. Zola, in turn, was accused and found guilty of criminal libel. He fled to England to continue his fight to free Dreyfus from Devil's Island. In 1976, another French newspaper, *La Libération*, published a list of 32 CIA agents operating undercover in Paris.

1910 Lee De Forest carried out a broadcast demonstration of opera for the first time from the stage of the New York Metropolitan. Enrico Caruso sang *Pagliacci* followed by music from the opera *Cavelleria Rusticana*.

1915 South African troops under Louis Botha occupied Swakopmund in German South West Africa, the most southerly stronghold of the crumbling German Empire. After the war, the area was mandated to South Africa. It became independent as Namibia in 1989.

1964 A reluctant Capitol Records released the first Beatles record in the US 'to see how it goes'. 'I Wanna Hold Your Hand' became their fastest selling single ever. One million copies were sold in the first three weeks.

1974 The world's largest airport was opened at Dallas, Texas.

1978 NASA selected its first women astronauts 15 years after the USSR had a female astronaut orbit the earth. The US chose six women to join as mission specialists.

1982 A Boeing 737 crashed into a bridge hitting five ships and killing 78 people on the Potamac River in Washington DC.

1989 Anxious computer users switched on to see if their discs had been infiltrated by a special virus known as the Friday the 13th Virus. Devised by an unknown operator to destroy data, it had already filled screens with random numbers at a staff training centre near Brussels.

14 JANUARY

BORN THIS DAY

HISTORY

1741 Benedict Arnold, American general and spy who provided British forces with information during the American War of Independence.

1875 Dr Albert Schweitzer, French missionary surgeon, organist, and Nobel Peace prize winner (1952), who also wrote *On the Edge of the Primeval Forest*. His hospital at Lambaréné in Gabon was founded in 1913, financed by Schweitzer's organ recitals in Europe.

1911 J. Skelly Wright, US judge and hard-line racist who was instrumental in enforcing the desegregation of New Orleans schools. His change of heart began when he saw blind black and white people segregated at a party.

ARTS

1836 Henri Fantin-Latour, French painter, who showed his portraits and still lifes in the Salon de Refuses, set up for talented painters rejected by the established art galleries. Many of his paintings now hang in the Tate and Louvre.

1850 Jean de Reszke, Polish tenor who sang Faust at its 500th performance in Paris while his younger brother Édouard sang Mephistopheles. Their sister, Joséphine, was also an opera singer.

1886 Hugh Lofting, British-born author and illustrator who lived in the US. There he wrote his 'Dr Doolittle' books, about a man who talked to animals.

1925 Yukio Mishima, Japanese novelist, who wrote *Confessions of a Mask*. A great traditionalist, he believed Japan had become corrupted by westernization and, on 11.12.75, committed *hari kiri*: ritualistic suicide in the tradition of the Samurai.

ENTERTAINMENT

1892 Hal Roach, US film producer, director and screenwriter who started as a bit player in silent films before making his own two-reelers with Harold Lloyd, Laurel and Hardy, Will Rodgers and others.

1904 Sir Cecil Beaton, English photographer and stage designer. He snapped the rich and famous and was involved in both theatre and film design, winning Oscars for his work on *Gigi* (1958) and *My Fair Lady* (1964).

1909 Joseph Losey, US film director who, during the communist witch hunt in the US in the 50s, was forced to work in Britain, where some of his finest films were made: *The Servant* (1963), *Accident* (1967) and *The Go-Between* (1971).

1926 Warren Mitchell, English actor who immortalized the bigoted, foul-mouthed Alf Garnett in BBC television's *Till Death Us Do Part*.

1940 Trevor Nunn, artistic director of the Royal Shakespeare Company from 1968. His productions of *Nicholas Nickleby* (1981) and *Les Misérables* (1987) won him awards on both sides of the Atlantic.

1941 Faye Dunaway, award-winning US film actress. She won an Oscar for her performance in *Network* (1976), as well a nominations for *Bonnie and Clyde* (1967) and *Chinatown* (1974).

1934 Richard Briers, English stage and television actor, best known for his roles in the comedy series *The Good Life*, and *Ever Decreasing Circles*.

POP

1938 Jack Jones, US nightclub, recording and TV singer.

DIED THIS DAY

1742 Edmond Halley, English Astronomer Royal who discovered the cycle of the famous comet that bears his name.

1867 Jean Ingres, French painter.

1898 Lewis Carroll (Charles Lutwidge Dodgson), English author of *Alice's Adventures in Wonderland* (1865).

1957 Humphrey Bogart, US film actor, best remembered for his roles in *The Maltese Falcon* (1941) and *Casablanca* (1942).

1965 Jeannette MacDonald, US singer and actress who was teamed with Nelson Eddy in Hollywood movies.

1977 Anthony Eden, Earl of Avon, British Prime Minister.

1977 Peter Finch (William Mitchell), English actor who was discovered in Australia, and who won a posthumous Oscar for his performance in *Network* (1976). Faye Dunaway, who also won an Oscar for her role in the film, had her 36th birthday this day, while he died of a massive heart attack.

1990 Gordon (Cameron) Jackson, Scottish actor best remembered for his role as Hudson in the television series *Upstairs, Downstairs*.

ON THIS DAY

1814 The King of Denmark ceded Norway to the King of Sweden, sparking off a rebellion in Norway.

1814 The last London Frost Fair was held. Crowds flocked on to the frozen river Thames to enjoy all manner of entertainments, such as Punch and Judy shows, piemen, oyster-wenches and spit roasts.

1878 Alexander Graham Bell's telephone was demonstrated by W. H. Preece to Queen Victoria at Osborne House on the Isle of Wight.

1900 The first performance of Puccini's *Tosca* was staged in Rome.

1907 An earthquake killed over 1,000 in Kingston, Jamaica and virtually destroyed the capital.

1918 Joseph Caillaux, former French Prime Minister, was arrested for treason after advocating a peace settlement with Germany.

1938 *Snow White and the Seven Dwarfs*, Walt Disney's first full-length Technicolor cartoon had its screening in the US. When it opened in London, on 7 February 1939, the Board of Film Censors gave it an 'A' certificate instead of the expected 'U'.

1947 The newly formed Covent Garden Opera Company opened with *Carmen* directed by Karl Rankl in the renovated theatre which had been a dance hall during the Second World War.

1983 In central London, Stephen Waldorf narrowly escaped death when police opened fire on his Mini believing him to be escaped convict, David Martin. He was later awarded £120,000 as compensation.

1988 A legal dispute over a frozen head caused problems for the Alcor Life Extension Foundation. They had frozen Dora Kent's head, on her instruction, as she wished to come back to life at a future date, but the coroner's office in Los Angeles wanted to examine the head on the grounds that Mrs Kent was not dead when the head was removed. Both the Foundation and Saul Kent, the woman's son, contested the demand saying it would damage the skull and brain so that Mrs Kent could never be brought back from the dead.

1989 Muslims in Bradford ritually burned a copy of Salman Rushdie's *The Satanic Verses*. This was the first serious protest in Britain, although the book had been banned in some Muslim countries.

15 JANUARY

The Feast Day of Isidore, patron saint of labourers.

BORN THIS DAY

HISTORY

1809 Pierre Joseph Proudhon, French social reformer and anarchist who said 'All property is theft'.

1906 Aristotle Onassis, millionaire Greek shipowner who will probably be best remembered as a collector of famous women, first opera diva, Maria Callas and then the widowed Jackie Kennedy, whom he married.

1918 General Gamal Nasser, Egypt's first president. He overthrew the playboy King Farouk and made his ailing country a republic.

1929 Martin Luther King, charismatic US clergyman, leader of the Negro civil rights movement, and Nobel Peace prize winner (1964).

ARTS

1622 Molière (Jean Baptiste Poquelin), French playwright and actor. *Tartuffe*, written in 1664, was a biting satire of Parisian society and hypocrisy and was banned for five years. His other plays include *Le Misanthrope* (1666), and *Le Malade imaginaire* (1673).

1885 Mazo de la Roche, Canadian novelist, author of the 'Whiteoaks of Jalna' books.

ENTERTAINMENT

1893 Ivor Novello (David Ivor Davies), Welsh-born composer, actor, director and playwright. With Christopher Hassall, he created lush, romantic London shows, including *King's Rhapsody* (1949) and the now-classic song, 'We'll Gather Lilacs'. During the First World War, he wrote the imperishable 'Keep the Home Fires Burning'.

1913 Lloyd Bridges, US actor who appeared in *High Noon* (1952) and *The Rainmaker* (1956). Two of his sons, Beau and Jeff, became actors.

1937 Margaret O'Brien, US child film actress of the 40s who starred in *Thousand's Cheer* (1943), and *Little Women* (1949).

SCIENCE

1877 Lewis Terman, US psychologist who devised intelligence tests.

1908 Edward Teller, Hungarian-born physicist who played a major role in Dr Robert Oppenheimer's team developing the atomic bomb at Los Alamos.

JAZZ

1909 Gene Krupa, US drummer whose innovative technique allowed him to raise drumming to near-solo status.

DIED THIS DAY

1815 Emma, Lady Hamilton, mistress to Lord Nelson, a pauper in Calais.

1896 Matthew B. Brady, the man who photographed the American Civil War, destitute in New York.

1919 Rosa Luxembourg, socialist and founder of the Spartacus League, murdered shortly after her arrest by the Nazis in Berlin. Her body was thrown into a canal.

1964 Jack Teagarden, US jazz trombonist and band leader. One of the giants of jazz, he died of bronchial pneumonia alone in a hotel room.

ON THIS DAY

1559 Queen Elizabeth I was crowned.

1759 The British Museum was opened at Montague House, London.

1779 A London haberdasher, John Hetherington, wore the first top hat.

1790 Fletcher Christian and eight fellow mutineers from the *Bounty* landed on the remote Pitcairn Island, accompanied by six Tahitian men and 12 women.

1867 A severe frost caused London's Regents Park lake to freeze, attracting crowds on to the ice. When it gave way, 40 people died.

1878 Women received degrees for the first time at the London University.

TELEPHONE LINES In 1878, the telephone was used for the first time in a public emergency when 21 doctors were summoned to a railway disaster at Tariffville on the Connecticut Western Railway. In 1880, the first telephone directory was published by the London Telephone Company. It listed 255 subscribers.

1881 'My Bonnie Lies Over the Ocean' was published, without the songwriter being identified.

1890 The first performance of Tchaikovsky's *Sleeping Beauty*, choreographed by Petipa, based on the tale of Charles Perrault, was given by the Russian Imperial Ballet at St Petersburg.

1912 Italian aircraft dropped the first ever propaganda leaflets during the Italo-Turkish War of 1911–12. The leaflets offered a coin (a golden napoleon), and a sack of wheat or barley to every Arab in Tripolitania (Libya) who surrendered.

1916 The Irish Free State, as southern Ireland was formally called, came into being, and on this day in 1922, Arthur Griffith was elected president following the resignation of Eamon de Valera.

1927 The first live rugby commentary on BBC radio of the match at Twickenham between Wales and England was given by Captain Teddy Wakelam. A blind man was hired to sit by his side to give him 'some sort of feel of what the new-fangled thing was about'. The following Saturday Wakelam gave the first football commentary from Highbury, when Arsenal played Sheffield United.

1963 Moishe Tshombe surrendered Katanga, the breakaway Congo state, after asking for an amnesty for himself, his government, and 200 white mercenaries.

1970 General Gowon accepted the unconditional surrender of the Biafran commanders in Nigeria.

1971 The Aswan High Dam was officially opened by President Sadat of Egypt and President Podgorny of the USSR, whose country had been responsible for both financing and building the Dam.

1972 Queen Margrethe II acceded to the throne of Denmark.

1973 Golda Meir became the first Israeli head of state to be received by the Pope.

1973 President Nixon called a halt to the US's Vietnam offensive.

16 JANUARY

BORN THIS DAY

ENTERTAINMENT

1853 Sir Johnston Forbes-Robertson, actor-manager who, in 1895, took over the Lyceum in London with Mrs Patrick Campbell.

1906 Diana Wynyard, British actress who was a leading lady during the 20s and 30s before going to Hollywood to make *Cavalcade* (1933), for which she received an Oscar nomination.

1907 Alexander Knox, Canadian actor with a long, distinguished career on both sides of the Atlantic. *Wilson* (1944) brought him an Oscar nomination. Other films include *Reach for the Sky* (1956) and *The Longest Day* (1962).

1909 Ethel Merman (Zimmerman), US singer and actress whose belting voice enhanced both Broadway and Hollywood musicals, including *Annie Get Your Gun*, *Call Me Madam* and *There's No Business Like Show Business*.

BUSINESS

1853 André Michelin, French tyre manufacturer; the first to mass-produce tyres.

1921 Lord Thomson of Monifieth, Canadian media magnate and one-time owner of *The Times*.

DIED THIS DAY

1794 Edward Gibbon, English historian, author of the monumental *Decline and Fall of the Roman Empire* (1776–1788).

1891 Leo Delibes, French composer.

1906 Marshall Field, US retail magnate who gave us the modern department store.

1942 Carole Lombard (Jane Alice Peters), US actress, killed with her mother in an air crash at the peak of her career. Her death deeply affected her second husband, Clark Gable.

1957 Arturo Toscanini, Italian conductor.

1967 Robert Van de Graaf, US physicist and inventor of the particle accelerator.

1979 Shah Mohammed Reza Pahlavi, Shah of Persia (Iran), in Egypt, having fled with his family after reigning for 37 years.

1990 Sam Chippendale, English property developer who gave British towns Arndale shopping centres. The name is a combination of that of his partner, Arnold Hargenbach, and his own surname.

ON THIS DAY

1547 Ivan the Terrible was crowned first Tsar of Russia.

1769 A conjuror who claimed he would get into a quart tavern bottle 'and there sing several songs' failed to turn up at the packed Haymarket Theatre, London, causing one of worst riots in theatre history.

1780 Admiral Rodney defeated the Spanish at Cape St Vincent and relieved Gibraltar.

1909 Ernest Shackleton's British expedition reached the area of the South Magnetic Pole, but could go no further.

1920 The US introduced prohibition, making the sale of alcoholic beverages illegal. Bootleg spirits produced and run by leading gangsters enabled Americans to drink more alcohol during the years of prohibition than ever before. It wasn't repealed until 5.12.1933.

1924 The BBC broadcast the first play specially written for radio, *Danger* by Richard Hughes.

1925 Leon Trotsky was dismissed as Chairman of the Russian Revolutionary Council.

1928 The funeral took place of the British author Thomas Hardy, who died on 11.1.1928. His heart was buried in the village cemetery in Stinsford, Dorset, and his ashes in Westminster Abbey.

1932 'It Don't Mean a Thing' was recorded by Duke Ellington and his Orchestra in New York.

1944 General Eisenhower was appointed Supreme Commander of Allied Forces in Europe.

1957 The Sadler's Wells Ballet was granted a royal charter and became the Royal Ballet.

1957 The Cavern Club, which would become a major showcase for young rock 'n' roll talent including the Beatles, opened in Liverpool.

1963 Yvonne Pope of England became the first woman to fly an international airline route when she took off from Gatwick to Dusseldorf.

1970 Colonel Gaddafi became Prime Minister of Libya.

1973 A guest at a Walt Disney promotion party in Harrogate helped himself to ice from the wrong bucket. The cubes contained a prize – a concealed diamond. The guest was put under observation until the diamond could be retrieved in nature's own good time.

IT TAKES TWO In 1979, just nine days after her marriage to musician Greg Allman, the singer and actress, Cher filed for divorce. In 1988, an 85-year-old merchant, Khafan Askour, from Abu Dhabi married two teenage girls simultaneously and consummated both marriages the same night. He said he married them both so they could keep each other company.

17 JANUARY

The Feast Day of Antony of Egypt, the patron saint of pigs. His name gives us the word 'tantony', a diminutive applied to pigs, meaning the smallest of the litter.

BORN THIS DAY

HISTORY

1706 Benjamin Franklin, American statesman and scientist who demonstrated that lightning was a form of electricity (*see* 15.6.1752). He also helped draft the Declaration of Independence and still found time to invent the rocking chair.

1863 David Lloyd George, Welsh politician born in Manchester who introduced old age pensions (1909), health and unemployment insurance (1911), and became Prime Minister of a coalition government in 1916. He was re-elected with a huge majority at the end of the First World War and remained in office until 1922.

ARTS

1820 Anne Brontë, youngest of the three English novelist sisters, author of *The Tenant of Wildfell Hall* (1838) and *Agnes Grey* (1845) as well as poetry.

1863 Konstantin Stanislavsky, Russian actor, director, teacher and co-founder in 1898 of the the Moscow Art Theatre. His naturalistic style of acting and production (the basis of 'The Method' in the US) greatly influenced Western theatre and was ideal for Chekhov's plays, which were first produced at his theatre.

1883 Sir Compton Mackenzie, (Edward Montague Compton), English novelist who is best remembered for *Whisky Galore* (1947).

1899 Nevil Shute (Norway), English novelist who settled in Australia, where he wrote the very popular *A Town Like Alice* (1949) and *On the Beach* (1957).

1926 Moira Shearer, Scottish ballerina with the Royal Ballet and star of the first major ballet film, *The Red Shoes* (1948).

ENTERTAINMENT

1880 Mack Sennett (Mikall Sinnott), Canadian who went to the US, where he worked as a chorus boy before becoming both an actor and director with Biograph films in 1908. He later formed Keystone to make slapstick comedies. The advent of sound put an end to Sennett's reign as 'The King of Comedy', but he received a special Academy Award in 1937.

SCIENCE

1501 Leonhard Fuchs, German botanist and physician. The fuchsia is named after him.

1761 Sir James Hall, Scottish scientist who was the founder of experimental geology.

POP

1956 Paul Young, English singer, with several hits, including 'Wherever I Lay My Head', No. 1 in the UK in 1983.

CRIME

1899 Al(phonse) Capone, America's most notorious gangster, nicknamed 'Scarface' because of a scar he got through a street brawl in his youth. In 1927 Capone took over the syndicate set up by Johnny Torrio, who had fled to Italy. 227 rivals or challengers were murdered in the 1920s, while Capone made millions from bootlegging, protection and other rackets. He was eventually indicted for tax evasion and sent to Atlanta's Federal Jail and later to Alcatraz. Released in 1939, an elderly, sick syphilitic man, he died in 1947.

SPORT

1926 Clyde (Leopold) Walcott, in Barbados, one of the great West Indian cricketers who, with schoolmate Frank Worrell, hit an unbroken 544 for Barbados against Trinidad. He was awarded an OBE for services to the game.

1942 Muhammad Ali (Cassius Clay), US Olympic and world heavyweight boxing champion from 1964–7. He changed his name on becoming a member of the Black Muslim Movement. Stripped of his title for refusing military service, he later won it back on two more occasions, the first boxer ever to achieve this.

FASHION

1928 Vidal Sassoon, English hair stylist with an international reputation.

DIED THIS DAY

1893 Rutherford Birchard Hayes, 19th US President.

1903 Quintin Hogg, English philanthropist and founder of the London Polytechnic.

1964 T(erence) H(anbury) White, English author of *The Sword in the Stone*.

1990 (Augustus John) Ruskin Spear, English painter and founder-member of the Bonzo Dog Doo Dah Band.

ON THIS DAY

1827 The Duke of Wellington was appointed commander in chief of the British Army.

1912 One month too late, Captain Robert Falcon Scott reached the South Pole, beaten by the Norwegian Amundsen.

1933 A telegram was received by the MCC at Lords Cricket Ground from the Australian Cricket Board: 'Body-line bowling has assumed such proportions as to menace the best interests of the game, making protection of his body by a batsman his main consideration. It is causing intensely bitter feeling between players as well as injury to them. In our opinion it is unsportsmanlike. Unless it is stopped at once it is likely to upset the friendly relations existing between Australia and England.' The third test was being played at Adelaide. Jardine captained England. The body-line bowler was Larwood. In the Australian team was Bradman; two of his team mates had been injured by head-high bowling.

1934 A 500-carat diamond discovered near Pretoria, South Africa, by a 'poor white' named Pohl was rumoured to be the stolen half of the famous Cullinan diamond found in 1905.

1966 A B-52 carrying four nuclear weapons collided with a refuelling tanker killing eight of the 11 crew members. Both planes crashed. One of the four hydrogen bombs fell to earth intact, one fell into the ocean (it took three months to locate), the other two landed over the fields of Polomares, Spain, releasing plutonium.

1977 Gary Gilmore, a double murderer, became the first man to be executed in the US since the reintroduction of the death penalty in 1976. He elected to die by firing squad.

1983 Breakfast television came to Britain with the BBC beating TV-am to it. Frank Bough and Selina Scott were the presenters.

1989 The trial of those responsible for Britain's biggest armed robbery at a Knightsbridge deposit centre, which involved £40m in cash and illegal drugs, began at the Old Bailey. The manager admitted being associated with the gang, and the robbery was described as being like 'a clip from a *Carry On* film'.

18 JANUARY

BORN THIS DAY

HISTORY

1779 Peter Mark Roget, English doctor and lexicographer, whose *Thesaurus* took 47 years to compile and was first published in 1852.

1782 Daniel Webster, American statesman who negotiated the Ashburton treaty (1842) setting the US – Canada boundary.

1818 George Palmer, British biscuit manufacturer, other half of Huntley and Palmer, who introduced the first biscuit tins for their Napoleon and Leopold biscuits.

1888 Sir Thomas Sopwith, British air pioneer and the first pilot to land in the grounds of Windsor Castle. On his 100th birthday, a Sopwith Pup built after the First World War led a fly-past over his Hampshire home. Now blind, he could only hear the engines. It was a Sopwith Camel which shot down the Red Baron (Von Richthofen).

ARTS

1841 Emmanuel Chabrier, French composer who influenced Satie.

1867 Ruben Dario, Nicaraguan poet who wrote *Songs of Life and Hope*.

1882 A(lan) A(lexander) Milne, English author of *Winnie-the-Pooh* (1926) and *The House at Pooh Corner* (1928).

1884 Arthur Ransome, English author, best remembered for his children's adventure story, *Swallows and Amazons*, written in 1930.

1935 Raymond Briggs, English author and illustrator of *Fungus the Bogeyman*.

ENTERTAINMENT

1892 Oliver Hardy, US film comedian. In 1926, he teamed up with Stan Laurel to form probably the most successful comedy duo in film history. Their films include *Another Fine Mess* (1930).

VERY SPECIAL Two stars born on this day both won special Academy Awards. Cary Grant (Archibald Alexander Leach), born in Bristol in 1904, left a life of poverty to try his luck in the US and found success in Hollywood, where he played a string of romantic male roles in films such as *Bringing Up Baby* (1938) and *Charade* (1963). Danny Kaye (David Daniel Kaminsky), born in 1913, found success on Broadway where he stopped the show, *Lady in the Dark*, with his song 'Tchaikovsky', in which he named 54 Russian composers in 38 seconds. His films include *Up in Arms* (1954) and *Hans Christian Andersen* (1952). Special Oscars went to Kaye in 1954 and to Grant in 1970.

INVENTION

1813 Joseph Farwell Glidden, US farmer who devised a machine to make barbed wire, patented in 1874.

SCIENCE

1933 David Bellamy, English botanist who encouraged public interest in ecology through his many television programmes.

DIED THIS DAY

1677 Jan van Riebeck, in what is now Indonesia. He was the founder of Cape Town.

1835 Diving Mouse, aged 26, squaw to Red Indian chief Muk Coonce, the Little Bear of the Michigan tribe, in London on a visit to negotiate the sale of land. Forced because of financial difficulties to perform in an Indian spectacle at the Victoria Theatre, she died from pneumonia at a lodging house in the Waterloo Road and was buried in nearby St John's churchyard.

1936 Rudyard Kipling, English author of the *Jungle Books* (1894–5).

1954 Sydney Greenstreet, English actor remembered for his role in *Casablanca* (1942).

1963 Hugh (Todd Naylor) Gaitskell, British Labour Party leader.

1980 Sir Cecil (Walter Hardy) Beaton, English theatrical designer and photographer of the famous.

1987 George Markstein, British author who created the cult television series *The Prisoner*.

ON THIS DAY

1485 The Houses of Lancaster and York were united by the marriage of Henry VII to Elizabeth, eldest daughter of Edward IV.

1778 Captain Cook discovered the Sandwich Islands, now known as Hawaii.

1871 Wilhelm of Prussia was proclaimed the first German Emperor in the Hall of Mirrors, Versailles.

1879 England beat Wales 2–1 in their first international football match, played at the Oval, Kennington, London.

1879 The first edition of *Boy's Own Paper* was published, edited by S. O. Beeton, husband of Mrs Beeton of cookery book fame. The paper closed 88 years later on 16 January 1967, during which time it published stories by Conan Doyle, G. A. Henty and R.M. Ballantyne.

1911 Eugene Ely became the first pilot to land his aircraft on a ship. His Curtis pusher-bi-plane landed on a special 120ft platform on the US cruiser, *Pennsylvania*, in San Francisco Bay.

1919 The Versailles Peace Conference opened. Georges Clemenceau of France was chairman.

1934 The first arrest was made in Britain as a result of issuing 'pocket' radios to policemen. A thief in Brighton was arrested just 15 minutes after stealing three overcoats from a shop.

1943 After a 16-month siege by the Germans, Leningrad was relieved when the Soviet army broke through.

1972 Former Prime Minister Garfield Todd and his daughter Judith were placed under house arrest by the Ian Smith government in Rhodesia for campaigning against the granting of legal independence to the country.

1982 Colonel 'Mad' Mike Hoare and four mercenaries were charged in South Africa with hijacking an aircraft after an abortive coup bid in the Seychelles which had had South African backing.

1988 A Hindu used his own skin to make a pair of sandals and travelled across India to offer them to his family deity.

19 JANUARY

BORN THIS DAY

HISTORY

1544 Francis II, King of France, son of Catherine de' Medici and husband of Mary, Queen of Scots.

1807 Robert E(dward) Lee, American general, Commander-in-Chief of the Confederate Army in the Civil War.

1920 Javier Pérez de Cuéllar, Peruvian-born secretary-general of the UN from 1982.

ARTS

1809 Edgar Allan Poe, US short story writer and poet, author of the first true detective story, *Murders in the Rue Morgue* (1841), and undisputed master of the macabre with *The Tell-Tale Heart* and *The Pit and the Pendulum*, both 1843.

1839 Paul Cézanne, French Post-Impressionist painter. A friend of Zola, he was persuaded by the writer to give up his law studies and take up painting instead. He produced some 900 paintings and 400 watercolours; his bold style directly influenced Cubism.

1921 Patricia Highsmith, US-born mystery novelist. Her first book, *Strangers on a Train* (1950), became a classic Hitchcock film.

1925 Nina (Mary) Bawden, English novelist of *Afternoon of a Good Woman* (1976) and several children's books.

1955 Simon Rattle, English conductor with the Birmingham Symphony Orchestra and BBC Scottish Symphony Orchestra. He conducted the Liverpool Sinfonia aged 15, and won a conducting award at 19.

ENTERTAINMENT

1931 Richard Lester, US film director who settled in Britain. He made the first films with the Goons, (Sellers, Milligan, et al.) and the Beatles' *A Hard Day's Night* (1964).

1942 Michael Crawford, actor and singer, who appeared in the long-running *No Sex Please, We're British*, but who made his name in the television comedy series *Some Mothers Do 'Ave 'Em* before starring in the musicals *Barnum* and *Phantom of the Opera* (in London and on Broadway).

INVENTION

1736 James Watt, the Scottish engineer who developed the steam engine, which he built in association with Matthew Boulton.

1798 Auguste Comte, French philosopher and social reformer who founded modern sociology.

1813 Sir Henry Bessemer, British metallurgist, pioneer of mass produced, low-priced steel using the blast furnace method he invented in 1856.

POP

1939 Phil Everly, who, with his brother Don, formed the Everly Brothers in 1957. They had several hits including 'Bye Bye Love' before they parted on stage.

1943 Janis Joplin, rock singer from Texas who rose to fame before dying of a heroin overdose, aged 27 (4.10.1970). Her No. 1 in the US was with ex-boyfriend Kris Kristofferson's 'Me and Bobby McGee', which went to the top six months after her death.

1946 Dolly Parton, big bosomed US country singer who was born in a cabin on the banks of the Little Pigeon River. She released her first single 'Puppy Love' aged 13, which was followed by 'Jolene' and 'Islands in the Stream'.

DIED THIS DAY

1547 Henry Howard, Earl of Surrey, courtier, poet and soldier, beheaded at the Tower accused of high treason.

1729 William Congreve, English Restoration playwright, after a carriage accident in London.

1881 Auguste Mariette, French egyptologist who excavated the Sphinx.

1990 The Bhagwam Shree Rajneesh, the

richest of the gurus who had a huge Western following in the 60s and 70s.

ON THIS DAY

1793 King Louis XVI, King of France, was found guilty of treason and guillotined. His wife, Marie Antoinette, would meet the same fate on 16.10.1793.

1853 The first performance of Verdi's *Il Travatore* in Rome.

1870 Two New York sisters became the world's first stockbrokers. Victoria Caffin Woodhall and Tenessee Caffin attracted mainly female customers, but the business collapsed because of their outspoken views on Marxism, racial equality and free love.

1884 Massenet's *Manon* was first performed in Paris.

1903 It was announced in Paris that a new bicycle race would be held. It would be called 'Tour de France'.

1915 The first raid on England by German Zeppelins caused casualties when they bombed Great Yarmouth and King's Lynn.

1937 The first play written for British television, *The Underground Murder Mystery* by J. Bissell Thomas, was broadcast by the BBC. The 30-minute play was set in Tottenham Court tube station.

1942 The Japanese invaded Burma.

IN AND OUT In 1966, Indira Gandhi became Prime Minister of India, following her father Jawaharlal Nehru, while Sir Robert Menzies resigned as Australian Premier after 16 years in office.

1969 Jan Pallach, a Czech student, set himself alight in Wenceslas Square as a protest against the Russian invasion, and was buried as a martyr on the 25th.

1988 Christopher Nolan, an Irish writer, aged 22, completely paralysed and only able to write at a frustratingly slow speed with a 'unicorn' attachment on his forehead, won the £20,000 Whitbread Book of the Year Award for his autobiography, *Under the Eye of the Clock*.

20 JANUARY

The Feast Day of Sebastian, patron saint of athletes.

St Agnes Eve. On this day, legend has it that a woman can divine her future husband. 'They told her how, upon St Agnes Eve/Young virgins might have vision of delight' (Keats).

BORN THIS DAY

HISTORY

1763 Theobald Wolfe Tone, Irish nationalist. He enlisted French support to fight against the British in Ireland.

1907 Sir Roy Welensky, former Prime Minister of the Federation of Rhodesia (Zimbabwe) and Nyasaland, from 1956–63.

1910 Joy (Friederike Victoria Gessner) Adamson, German-born author and conservationist, whose books about Elsa the lioness, including *Born Free* (1960), became world best sellers and films.

SPACEMEN In 1930, Dr Edwin 'Buzz' Aldrin, US astronaut who followed Neil Armstrong on to the Moon, and in 1939, Professor Nalin Chandra Wickransinghe, astronomer and co-author, with Sir Fred Hoyle, of *Space Travellers* (1982).

ARTS

1873 Johannes Jensen, Danish poet and author of 'The Long Journey' (1904). He won the Nobel prize for Literature in 1944.

1891 Mischa Elman, Russian-born violinist. A child prodigy, he became a US citizen in 1923, playing concerts in the US and Europe.

ENTERTAINMENT

1896 George Burns, (Nathan Birnbaum), US comedian who, with his wife Gracie Allen, had a successful career on radio and television and in films. Aged 79, he won an Oscar for *The Sunshine Boys* (1975).

1920 Frederico Fellini, Italian film director. He won an Oscar for best foreign film, *Le Notte di Cabiria* (1957), and a second Oscar for *La Dolce Vita* (1960).

1926 Patricia Neal, US actress whose films include *Hud*, for which she won an Oscar in 1963. She married author Roald Dahl, but her traumatic life included a series of severe strokes; one of their children had eight brain operations after being hit by a cab, and a daughter died of measles. Finally her marriage ended in divorce.

1934 Tom Baker, British stage and television actor best known for his role as Dr Who.

POP

1924 Slim Whitman, US country singer. His recording of 'Rose Marie' (1955) was in the UK charts for 11 consecutive weeks.

1947 Malcolm McLaren, US-born pop manager who created the Sex Pistols.

DIED THIS DAY

1779 David Garrick, English actor. He was buried in Westminster Abbey.

1837 Sir John Soane, English architect.

1875 Jean François Millet, French painter.

1900 John Ruskin, English art and social critic.

1907 Dmitri Mendeleyev, Russian chemist who formulated the periodic table of chemical elements.

1936 King George V of England.

1965 Alan Freed, US DJ who coined the term 'rock 'n' roll'.

1974 Edmund Blunden, British poet and literary critic.

1984 Johnny Weismuller, US Olympic swimming champion who played Tarzan in Hollywood films.

1988 Baron Philippe de Rothschild, French wine producer, poet, translator and sportsman.

1990 Barbara Stanwyck (Ruby Stevens), US actress who won a Special Oscar in 1981, and was six times nominated for Best Actress.

ON THIS DAY

POLITICS In 1265, the first English parliament met at Wesminster Hall. This same day, in 1649, parliament tried King Charles I.

1841 Hong Kong was occupied by the British.

1882 The first shop in the world was lit by incandescent electric light, a draper's, Coxon & Company, in Newcastle-upon-Tyne. It used Swan lamps.

1892 In Springfield, Massachusetts, the first game of basketball, devised by Dr James Naismith, a Canadian, was played at the YMCA.

1936 Edward VIII became the first British monarch to fly in an aeroplane when he flew as a passenger from Sandringham to London on the death of George V, to succeed to the throne.

1942 In a 30-roomed villa in Berlin, Reinhard Heydrich and Adolf Eichmann met to prepare plans for the Final Solution of the 'Jewish problem'. The meeting lasted 90 minutes.

1944 The RAF dropped 2,300 tons of bombs on Berlin.

WHITE HOUSE US Presidents inaugurated this day: 1945 Franklin Delano Roosevelt (his record fourth term); 1953 General Dwight D. Eisenhower; 1961 John F. Kennedy; 1965 Lyndon B. Johnson; 1969 Richard M. Nixon; 1977 Jimmy Carter; 1981 Ronald Reagan (at 69, the oldest of the 40 presidents to take office); 1989 George Bush.

1971 The famous Red Arrows aerial display team was involved in a mid air collision resulting in four deaths.

1981 The 52 Americans taken hostage when student followers of Ayatollah Khomeini stormed the US Embassy in Tehran were released after being held for 444 days, following an agreement to unfreeze Iranian assets held in the US.

1986 A mother's three-year fight for justice ended this day at St Alban's Crown Court when the man who injected her drug-addict son with a fatal painkiller was jailed for 15 months for manslaughter. Mrs Pauline Williams of Luton had become the first person to bring a private prosecution for manslaughter to a Crown Court trial.

1986 In 1975 France and Britain once again abandoned the Channel Tunnel proposal. 11 years later to the day, France and Britain finally decided to go ahead with the project promising that trains would run under the Channel by 1993.

1987 Terry Waite, special envoy to the Archbishop of Canterbury, was last seen just before 7 p.m. in Beirut prior to being kidnapped.

1988 It was announced that Russian goldminers had found the remains of a prehistoric mammoth with flesh so well preserved that it looked edible.

21 JANUARY

The Feast Day of Agnes, virgin and martyr, patron saint of girls.

BORN THIS DAY

HISTORY

1813 John Charles Fremont, US explorer and later senator who showed it was possible to cross the Rockies.

1824 Thomas Jonathan 'Stonewall' Jackson, Confederate general in the American Civil War who acquired his nickname because of his stubbornness at the Battle of Bull Run when his troops resisted an attack by the northern forces.

1829 Oscar II, King of Sweden and Norway. During his reign, the two countries were separated.

ARTS

1941 Placido Domingo, Spanish-born opera singer who has lived in Mexico since 1950.

ENTERTAINMENT

1922 Paul Scofield, English actor who played Hamlet on the first English company tour to Russia in 1955. He also played Sir Thomas More in the film *A Man for All Seasons* (1966).

1925 Telly (Aristotle) Savalas, US film actor who won an Oscar for best supporting actor in *The Birdman of Alcatraz* (1962). He also starred as Kojak in the popular television detective series of the same name.

1925 Benny Hill, English comedian known mainly for his internationally successful television show.

1945 Martin Shaw, English actor, best known for his role in the television series *The Professionals*.

SPORT

1940 Jack (William) Nicklaus, US champion golfer, nicknamed 'The Golden Bear'. He has won many major titles, including the US Masters (1986), the oldest contestant to achieve this.

FASHION

1905 Christian Dior, French fashion designer who created the 'New Look' in 1947, whereby long, full skirts came back after wartime austerity.

DIED THIS DAY

1793 Louis XVI, King of France. Found guilty of treason, he was guillotined in the Place de la Révolution.

1901 Elisha Gray, US inventor of the telephone.

1924 Lenin (Vladimir Ilyich Ulyanov), revolutionary Russian leader.

1932 Lytton Strachey, member of the celebrated Bloomsbury Group.

1950 George Orwell (Eric Arthur Blair), English novelist and essayist, aged 46, of a lung haemorrhage as a result of tuberculosis. His books include *Animal Farm* (1945) and *Nineteen Eighty-Four* (1949).

1959 Cecil B(lount) de Mille, US film director, producer, and screenwriter of biblical epics.

ON THIS DAY

1846 The first edition of the *Daily News*, edited by Charles Dickens, was published.

1907 Taxi cabs were officially recognized in Britain.

1911 The first Monte Carlo Rally began. The winner on 28 January 1911 was Henri Rougier.

1935 Snowdonia in Wales became a national forest park.

1937 Marcel Boulestin became the first television cook when he presented the first of BBC televisions's *Cook's Night Out* programmes.

1941 The *Daily Worker*, the British communist newspaper, was suppressed in wartime London.

1954 The US launched the first nuclear submarine, *Nautilus*.

1976 A British Airways (then BOAC) Concorde made its inaugural flight to Bahrain, and an Air France Concorde also took off at 11.40 a.m. from Paris *en route* to Rio de Janeiro.

22 JANUARY

The Feast Day of Anastasius, patron saint of goldsmiths.

BORN THIS DAY

HISTORY

1440 Ivan (III) the Great, Grand Duke of Muscovy, who rebelled against the Tartars in 1480 and made himself the first Tsar.

1561 Francis Bacon, Viscount St Albans, English statesman, lawyer, philospher, essayist, Lord Chancellor of England and, some say, the true writer of Shakespeare's works.

1858 Beatrice Potter Webb, English social reformer who with husband Sydney Webb, founded the Fabian Society and the *New Statesman*.

ARTS

1788 Lord (George Gordon) Byron, English liberal and romantic poet who wrote *Childe Harold* (1812–17) and *Don Juan* (1819–24). His divorce caused a scandal, forcing him into exile, where he became involved in revolutionary struggles in both Italy and Greece.

1849 August Strindberg, Swedish playwright, novelist and poet. His three marriages were the source of his dramas. In *The Father* (1887) a captain is driven insane by his wife's strong will, and *Miss Julie* (1889) deals with sexual conflict.

ENTERTAINMENT

1875 D(avid) W(ark) Griffith, influential US film director who helped raise the medium to an art form, both as a writer and director. His use of camera angles and movement, skilful editing and more naturalistic acting were demonstrated in *Birth of a Nation* (1915) and *Intolerance* (1916). He was awarded a special Oscar for services to the film industry, but he died in 1948, mostly forgotten, alone in a hotel bedroom, of a brain haemorrhage.

1936 Nyree Dawn Porter, New Zealand-born actress who made her name in the television series *The Forsyte Saga*.

1940 John Hurt, English actor who has played leading roles on television in *The Naked Civil Servant* (1975) and *I, Claudius* (1976), as well as in films such as *Elephant Man* (1980) and *Midnight Express* (1978), for which he won an Oscar.

1959 Linda Blair, US actress who won an Oscar nomination for her role as the possessed child in *The Exorcist*.

SCIENCE

1775 André Ampère, French physicist who experimented with electromagnetics and gave us the term 'amp', a measurement of electrical power.

SPORT

BALL BOYS 1907, Dixie (William Ralph) Dean, English footballer who played for Everton in the late 1920s, scoring a record 60 goals in 39 League games. 1920, Sir Alf Ramsey, former England footballer and Ipswich manager who was England's manager from 1963-74. Under Ramsey England, captained by Bobby Moore, won the World Cup, beating West Germany in 1966.

DIED THIS DAY

1719 William Paterson, Scottish financier and founder of the Bank of England.

1887 Sir Joseph Whitworth, English

mechanical engineer who standardized screw threads.

1900 David Edward Hughes, the English inventor of the carbon microphone, who settled in the US but left his fortune to London hospitals.

1901 Queen Victoria, at Osborne House on the Isle of Wight, aged 81, after a reign of over 63 years.

1959 Mike Hawthorn, 29-year-old British and world motor racing champion. He was killed not on the race track, but on the Guildford bypass, when he lost control of his Jaguar on a bend.

1973 Lyndon B(aines) Johnson, who became President after the assassination of John F. Kennedy.

ON THIS DAY

1879 The Zulus massacred British troops at Isandlwana.

1902 Marconi's first radio transmission experiments proved successful when he transmitted from the Lizard, Cornwall, across water to St Catherine's on the Isle of Wight, on the first anniversary of Queen Victoria's death on the island.

1905 'Red Sunday' in St Petersburg when Russian troops fired on workers protesting against repressive conditions.

1924 Stanley Baldwin resigned as British Prime Minister at the end of an unsuccessful election, and the new Labour Party had their first Prime Minister, Ramsay MacDonald.

1944 The Allied landings in Anzio, Italy, began.

1962 The 'A6 Murder' trial, in which James Hanratty was accused of murdering Michael Gregston at a lay-by near Bedford, began. The longest murder trial in British legal history, it ended on 17 February 1962 with Hanratty sentenced to hang, despite his claims of innocence and disquiet amongst some observers of the trial.

1964 Kenneth Kaunda was sworn in as the first Prime Minister of Northern Rhodesia, later renamed Zambia.

1972 The United Kingdom, the Irish Republic and Denmark joined the Common Market.

1983 Anne Winter became British Rail's first woman engine driver.

1988 Amsterdam's Schipol airport opened a special departure lounge for cows, serving pre-flight food and drink to travelling cattle.

23 JANUARY

BORN THIS DAY

ARTS

1783 Stendhal, the French novelist Marie Henri Beyle, author of *The Red and the Black* (1831).

1832 Édouard Manet, French Impressionist painter and printmaker, famous for his *Déjeuner sur l'herbe*, which scandalized many who came to see it.

ENTERTAINMENT

1898 Sergi Mikhailovich Eisenstein, influential Russian film director who, despite harassment from both his own government and suspicious western officialdom, put the Soviet film industry on the world map. His films include *The Battleship Potemkin* (1925) and *Alexander Nevski* (1938), which had a musical score by Prokofiev.

1928 Jeanne Moreau, French stage and screen actress. Her films include *Les*

Liaisons Dangereuses (1959) and *Jules et Jim* (1961).

SPORT

1919 Bob Paisley, a former Tyne and Wear apprentice bricklayer who went to Liverpool FC, first as a player in 1939, then became a trainer in 1959, and finally the manager in 1974, and made Liverpool one of the finest teams in Europe.

FASHION

1943 Bill (William Elphinstone) Gibb, Scottish fashion designer who played an influential role during the 'Swinging Sixties' in London.

DIED THIS DAY

1622 William Baffin, English explorer. Baffin Island is named after him.

1806 William Pitt, 'the Younger', twice British Prime Minister, first when he was just 25 years old.

1883 Charles Kingsley, English clergyman who wrote *The Water Babies* (1863).

1883 Gustave Doré, French artist and illustrator.

1931 Anna Pavlova, Russian prima ballerina, died in Holland.

1936 Dame Clara Butt, English contralto.

1944 Edvard Munch, Norwegian painter and lithographer, whose predominant theme was death.

1947 Pierre Bonnard, French painter.

1956 Sir Alexander Korda (Sandor Laszlo Korda), Hungarian-born British film producer and director.

1973 Edward 'Kid' Ory, jazz musician.

1976 Paul Robeson, US actor, singer who symbolized black consciousness, neglected and almost alone in Harlem, aged 77.

1981 Samuel Barber, US composer.

1989 (Félipe Jacinto) Salvador Dali y Pubol, eccentric Spanish surrealist painter and sculptor. He was buried in a crypt under a glass dome in the Dali Museum in Segerras, north-east Spain.

ON THIS DAY

1556 An earthquake in Shensi Province, China, is thought to have killed some 830,000 people.

1571 Queen Elizabeth I opened the Royal Exchange, London, founded by the financier Sir Thomas Gresham as a bankers' meeting house.

1938 16 oil companies were convicted in the US under the Anti-Trust laws for price fixing. They included Standard Oil, Shell and Continental Oil.

1943 The British captured Tripoli. The Eighth Army crossed into Tunisia in pursuit of the retreating Germans.

1960 In the Pacific Ocean, Professor Piccard descended a record 35,800 feet in the bathyscaphe *Trieste*.

1963 At 7.30 p.m. in Beirut, Kim Philby, Middle East correspondent for two London journals, was expected to collect his US wife Eleanor. He never arrived. 'The most damaging double agent in British history' had begun his journey to Moscow.

1968 North Korean patrol boats boarded the US 'spyship' *Pueblo*, which was claimed to be within territorial waters. Several crew were killed and wounded.

1985 PC George Hammond was viciously stabbed while on the beat in London, needing 120 pints of blood to save his life. He never fully recovered from the attack and committed suicide two years later.

1989 The gallon sign began to disappear from Britain's 20,000 petrol stations as legislation came into force which allowed them the option to offer fuel prices by litre measurements only.

24 JANUARY

The Feast Day of Francis of Sales, who wrote several popular books on theology and so was adopted as patron saint of authors and journalists.

BORN THIS DAY

HISTORY

76AD Hadrian (Publius Aelius Hadrianus), Roman Emperor born in Spain whose defensive policies led to the building of Hadrian's Wall on the border of Scotland and England.

1712 Frederick the Great, King of Prussia, who earned his name by his courage both in victory and defeat, and by his administrative skills, which made his country prosper. Yet he was a reluctant ruler and was nearly executed as a young man for trying to flee from his future responsibilities and settle in England.

1749 Charles James Fox, British Whig statesman and brilliant orator who supported the French revolutionaries and later, as Foreign Minister, persuaded the Prime Minister, Pitt, to abolish slavery.

ARTS

1670 William Congreve, English playwright who wrote five plays before he was 30, including *Love for Love* (1695) and *The Way of the World* (1700).

1732 Pierre Beaumarchais (Pierre Augustin Caron), French playwright of the politically provocative *The Marriage of Figaro*, and *The Barber of Seville*. Both were the basis of operas by Mozart and Rossini respectively.

ENTERTAINMENT

1909 Ann Todd, English stage and screen actress, best known for her role in *The Seventh Veil* (1945). Her third husband was film director, David Lean.

1917 Ernest (Ermes Effron) Borgnine, US actor who won an Oscar as the stout butcher looking for love in *Marty* (1955).

1961 Nastassja Kinski, daughter of German actor, Klaus Kinski, who was in *Tess* (1979) and *Paris, Texas* (1984).

SCIENCE

1928 Dr Desmond Morris, English zoologist, author of *The Human Ape* and *Body Language*.

POP

1945 Neil Diamond, US singer and songwriter, who wrote hits such as 'I'm a Believer' and 'Kentucky Woman'.

DIED THIS DAY

AD41 Caligula, notorious Roman emperor, murdered by a tribune of the guard.

FATHER AND SON 1895, Lord Randolph Churchill, leader of the Conservative party, and, 70 years later in 1965, his son, Sir

Winston Leonard Spencer Churchill, in London, aged 90.

1920 Amadeo Modigliani, Italian sculptor and painter, from drink and drug abuse. On the 26th his pregnant mistress threw herself from a fifth-floor window.

1983 George Cukor, US film director of *A Star is Born.*

ON THIS DAY

1236 Henry III of England married Eleanor of Provence.

1848 Just a week before the peace treaty with Mexico, James Marshall discovered gold in California at Sutter's sawmill. The gold rush would follow.

1900 British troops under General Sir Charles Warren captured Spion Kop, South Africa, after outnumbering the Boers 20,000 to 500. The British lost 1,200 men, the Boers 300.

1915 The British defeated the Germans at the Battle of Dogger Bank, a First World War sea battle which resulted in the superior speed and gunnery of the British fleet sinking the German armoured cruiser *Blucher*. To hit her, British shells had to travel 15 miles on a trajectory reaching an apex at 22,500ft (Mont Blanc is only 15,755ft) before descending. *Blucher*'s design had been based on a stolen forecast of the *Invincible.* German Intelligence was unaware that these plans were false, planted by the British.

1916 Conscription was introduced in Britain to provide more fodder for the trenches on the Western front.

1941 Josslyn Hay, 22nd Earl of Erroll and Kenyan socialite, was found shot dead in his car. The Earl had fallen in love with Diana, the young wife of the very much older Sir Henry Delves 'Jock' Broughton. Sir Henry was tried for murder, but was acquitted, although he later killed himself in Liverpool's Adelphi Hotel in 1942. Some believe a jilted Diana was the murderer. The story inspired a book and film called *White Mischief*.

1961 Elsa, the lioness of Joy Adamson's books, was reported found dead in Kenya.

1961 A US B-52 bomber broke up in mid air. Three of the eight crew were killed and two 24-megaton nuclear bombs were released. One parachuted safely to earth, but five of its six safety devices had failed. The other bomb landed in a waterlogged field near Goldsboro, North Carolina, US, and was never found.

1976 The *Olympic Bravery*, a 270,000-ton oil tanker, ran aground off France. The largest shipwreck recorded, she broke in two on 13 March 1976.

1978 An orbiting Russian satellite crashed near Yellow Knife in Canada's Northwest Territory.

1986 Staff of the newspapers the *Sun* and the *News of the World* were told they were moving to Wapping in London's new Dockland's development area. This was the start of an exodus of major newspapers from Fleet Street.

25 JANUARY

Burns Night in Scotland.

BORN THIS DAY

HISTORY

1540 St Edmund Campion, English scholar and Jesuit martyr, who went to Rome and later returned as a missionary. Accused of spying, he ended up being hanged, drawn and quartered on Tower Hill. He was canonized in 1970.

1928 Edvard Shevardnadze, Soviet foreign minister who brought a more pragmatic and co-operative style to the Soviet Union's dealings with the West during the introduction of *perestroika*.

ARTS

1759 Robert Burns, Scotland's national poet who used the Scottish dialect in his poems and many songs, including 'Tam o'Shanter' and 'To a Mouse'. He married Jean Armour and became an excise officer when his farm failed.

1874 William Somerset Maugham, English novelist and playwright born in Paris, who is best remembered for his novels *Of Human Bondage* (1915) and *The Moon and Sixpence* (1919).

1882 Virginia Woolf (Adeline Virginia Steven), English novelist and critic. A key figure of the influential Bloomsbury Group, her books include *To the Lighthouse* and *The Waves*.

1886 Wilhelm Furtwängler, German conductor and composer identified with the Berlin Philharmonic and the Bayreuth Festival. After he was cleared of pro-Nazi activities, he was able to conduct in the West.

SCIENCE

1627 Robert Boyle, Irish physicist and chemist and one of the founder's of the Royal Society. Boyle's Law relates to the pressure and temperature of gases.

1736 Joseph Louis Lagrange, French mathematician and physicist. He chaired the commission in 1793 that introduced the metric system.

SPORT

1857 Lord Lonsdale (Henry Cecil Lowther), fifth Earl, English sportsman and president of the National Sporting Club, who gave boxing its official rules and 'Lonsdale Belts' to its champions.

DIED THIS DAY

1855 Dorothy Wordsworth, sister of William Wordsworth, whose journals describe their life together in the Lake District.

1947 Al Capone, Chicago gang boss in the Prohibition era, nicknamed 'Scarface', of a brain haemorrhage.

1969 Irene Castle, US actress and dancer who created 'The Turkey Trot' and 'The Cake Walk' with her husband and partner, Vernon.

1990 Ava Gardner, US actress (*The Snows of Kilimanjaro* (1952)), in London.

ON THIS DAY

1327 Edward III acceded to the English throne.

1533 King Henry VIII and Anne Boleyn (wife number two of six), were married secretly by the Bishop of Lichfield.

1878 A Turkish steamer was sunk by the first torpedo fired in war from a Russian torpedo boat.

1882 The London Chamber of Commerce met for the first time.

1895 The first hockey international was held at Rhyl, Wales. Wales lost 3–0 to the Irish.

1899 Manufacture of the first radio sets began at the Wireless Telegraph & Signal Company, Chelmsford, England.

1917 It cost the US $25 million to buy the Virgin Islands (formerly the Danish West Indies).

1919 The League of Nations, forerunner of the UN, was founded.

1924 The first Winter Olympics began at Chamonix, France, and ended on 4 February.

1938 The aurora borealis ('northern lights') were seen as far south as London's West End and throughout western Europe. This was due to intense sunspot activity.

1944 The Reverend Florence Tim-Oi Lee of Macao became the first Anglican woman priest due to the shortage of ordained priests in that part of the world as the Second World War neared its end.

1950 American Alger Hiss was found guilty of perjury, having concealed his membership of the Communist Party, and was sentenced to five years, despite there being no evidence of him spying against the US.

1955 Approximately ten years after the end of the Second World War, the USSR proclaimed the end of belligerency with Germany

BARBARISM In 1971 Idi Amin deposed Milton Obote and became President of Uganda, ushering in a period of unprecedented barbarism. On the same day, in California, 'Mad' Charlie Manson was found guilty along with three members of his 'family' of the brutal murder of actress Sharon Tate, then several months pregnant, and others in her luxury Hollywood home.

1981 'The Gang of Four' (Roy Jenkins, Dr David Owen, Shirley Williams and Bill Rodgers) broke away from the British Labour Party to set up the Social Democrats.

1981 Chiang Ch'ing, Mao's 67-year-old widow, was dragged shouting from a Peking court having been found guilty of 'counter-revolutionary' crimes during China's Cultural Revolution.

1985 Bernard Goetz, who shot four black youths trying to mug him in a New York subway, was told he would only face a charge of possessing an illegal weapon. The public were divided: he was a hero to some, criminal to others.

1989 Actor John Cleese won libel damages at the High Court over an article in the *Daily Mirror* which claimed he had become like Basil Fawlty.

26 JANUARY

The Feast Day of Paula, patron saint of widows.

Australia Day, marking the founding of Sydney in 1788 by Governor Arthur Philip as a penal colony comprising 1,030 people, of which 736 were convicts. Transportation of convicts, often for petty crimes, was only ended in 1865.

Republic Day, India, celebrating the day in 1950 when it became a democratic republic within the Commonwealth.

BORN THIS DAY

HISTORY

1880 Douglas MacArthur, US general and Supreme Commander of the Allied

Forces in the Pacific in the Second World War.

ARTS

1908 Stephane Grappelli, virtuoso French jazz violinist who formed the Quintet of France with guitarist Django Reinhardt in 1934.

1946 Christopher Hampton, English playwright. His plays include *Savages* (1973).

ENTERTAINMENT

1913 Jimmy Van Heusen (Edward Chester Babcock), US songwriter who wrote many Sinatra and Crosby hits. He won Oscars for 'Swinging on a Star' (1944), 'All The Way' (1957) and 'Call Me Irresponsible' (1963).

1922 Michael Bentine, Peruvian-born British actor, comedian and writer who was one of the originators, with Peter Sellers, Spike Milligan and Harry Secombe, of the classic radio comedy, the Goon Show.

1925 Paul Newman, US film actor, director and producer. He received an Oscar nomination for his performances in *Cat on a Hot Tin Roof* (1958), *The Hustler* (1961), *Hud* (1963) and *Cool Hand Luke* (1967). He directed his second wife, Joanna Woodward, in *Rachel, Rachel* (1968).

1928 Roger Vadim (Roger Vadim Plemiannikov), French film director who made his name with the erotic *And God Created Women*, starring Brigitte Bardot (1956), then his wife.

1928 Eartha Kitt, sexy US singer, actress in revues, musicals and films who came to attention in *New Faces of 1952* with 'An Old-fashioned Millionaire'.

SPORT

1907 Henry Cotton, English golf champion; three times winner of the British Open in the 30s and again in 1948.

1954 Kim(berly James) Hughes, Australian cricketer who became only one of five batsmen ever to bat every day of a five-day Test match. In the 1980 Centenary Test at Lords he scored 117 in the first innings and 84 in the second.

DIED THIS DAY

1823 Edward Jenner, English physician who introduced vaccinations.

1885 General Charles George Gordon, British soldier and Governor of the Sudan who defended a besieged Khartoum, two days before his 52nd birthday, from a spear wound inflicted by a Muslim soldier as the city fell to the Mahdi.

1891 Nikolaus August Otto, German inventor of the first four-stroke internal combustion engine.

1947 Prince Gustav Adolf of Sweden, killed in an aircrash near Copenhagen. Travelling with the Prince was US singer and actress, Grace Moore (Mary Willie Grace Moore), who was also killed.

1973 Edward G. Robinson (Emmanuel Goldenberg), US actor who made his name playing gangster roles in Hollywood films.

1983 Nelson Aldrich Rockefeller, US Republican Vice-President to Gerald Ford, and one-time Governor of New York.

1988 Edmond Sébeille, the French detective who tracked down 75-year-old Gaston Dominici for the murder of Sir Jack and Lady Drummond and their daughter Anne, who were murdered on a camping holiday in France, 1952. Condemned to death, Dominic retracted his confession and was set free, leaving Sébeille a bitter man.

ON THIS DAY

1500 Vicente Yáñez Pinzón discovered Brazil and claimed it for Portugal.

1802 Napoleon was made President of the Italian Republic.

1828 The Duke of Wellington became British Prime Minister.

1837 Michigan became the 26th US state.

1841 Hong Kong was proclaimed British sovereign territory.

1871 The Rugby Football Union was formed in London by an initial 20 clubs.

1875 The first battery-powered dentist drill was patented by George F. Green of Kalamazoo, Michigan. A truly electrical drill would not be developed until 1908.

1886 Karl Benz patented his three-wheel drive motor car and internal combustion motor which he had put on test early in 1885.

1905 Captain Wells discovered the largest diamond in the world, at the Premier Mines, Pretoria, South Africa. Called the Cullinan diamond, it weighed over 1¼lbs.

1907 'Foul language' caused a riot in the Abbey Theatre, Dublin on the first night of J.M. Synge's *Playboy of the Western World*. The riots continued through the following week, but the play continued to be performed with a heavy police presence.

1908 The first Boy Scout group (the 1st Glasgow) was registered.

1931 Mahatma Gandhi was released from prison to have discussions with the British government in India.

1939 Franco's rebel forces, with Italian aid, took Barcelona in the Spanish Civil War.

1965 Hindi became the official language of India.

27 JANUARY

BORN THIS DAY

HISTORY

1859 Kaiser Wilhelm II, third German emperor, eldest son of Prince Frederick (Frederick III) and Victoria, daughter of the British Queen Victoria. He was forced to abdicate after the First World War and fled to Holland.

1901 Art(hur Joseph) Rooney, Snr, a spectacularly successful gambler who bought an American Football club on the winnings from a single bet and whose subsequent winnings enabled the Pittsburg-Steelers to win the Super Bowl in 1972 for the fourth time.

1945 Mairead Corrigan-Maguire, co-founder of the Northern Ireland 'Women for Peace' movement, which sought to unite both factions, and joint Nobel Peace prize winner.

ARTS

1756 Wolfgang Amadeus Mozart, Austrian composer and infant prodigy, who produced 20 operas including *The Marriage of Figaro*, *Don Giovanni* and *The Magic Flute*, 17 masses, 41 symphonies, 27 string quartets and other chamber music, 21 piano concertos, as well as many concertos for other instruments. Despite all this, he would die a pauper, aged 35, in 1781.

1832 Lewis Carroll (Charles Lutwidge

Dodgson), mathematician, author of *Alice in Wonderland* (1865), *Through the Looking Glass* (1872) and *The Hunting of the Snark* (1876).

1937 John (Howard Andrew) Ogdon, English concert pianist who, in 1962, won the Moscow Tchaikovsky competition jointly with Ashkenazy. He later suffered from a severe bout of schizophrenia, which temporarily ended his career, but successful treatment enabled him to return to the concert hall shortly before his untimely death in 1989.

ENTERTAINMENT

1885 Jerome Kern, US composer, 'father of the modern musical'. His major works are *Show Boat* (1927) and *Roberta* (1933). His songs include 'Look for the Silver Lining', 'Smoke Gets in Your Eyes', 'Ol' Man River', 'They Didn't Believe Me' and 'All the Things You Are'.

1924 Sir Brian Rix, English actor who appeared mainly in farces. He left the theatre to become secretary-general of Mencap. One of his own children was mentally handicapped.

DIED THIS DAY

1731 Bartolemmeo Cristofori, Italian harpsicord and piano maker.

1901 Giuseppe Verdi, Italian composer, whose famous operas include *Rigoletto* (1851), *La Traviata* (1853) and *Aida* (1871), aged 87.

1972 Mahalia Jackson, US gospel and jazz singer.

1989 Thomas Octave Murdoch Sopwith, pioneer English aircraft manufacturer.

ON THIS DAY

1822 Following war against Turkey, Greece won her independence.

1868 E. D. Young reported to the Royal Geographical Society that Dr Livingstone, the British explorer and missionary in 'darkest Africa', was still alive.

1913 US athlete Jim Thorpe was stripped of his Olympic decathlon and pentathlon gold medals when it was ruled that he was a professional having been paid £25 a week to play baseball.

1926 John Logie Baird gave a special public demonstration of television to members of the Royal Institution in London.

1943 The US made their first bombing raid on Germany.

1952 The famous Shepheard Hotel in Cairo was burnt down during an anti-British riot. 17 people died in the fire.

1967 Three US astronauts died just 218 feet above the ground on Launch Pad 34 at Cape Kennedy. Virgil 'Gus' Grissom, Ed White and Roger Chafee were burnt to death in the *Apollo 1* during a ground test when an electrical fault ignited pure oxygen in the capsule.

1967 Round-the-world yachtsman Francis Chichester was knighted by Queen Elizabeth II on the quay at Greenwich. The sword that lightly touched his shoulders was that of another Francis and seaman, Sir Francis Drake, and the ceremony took place the day before the 371st anniversary of his death.

1969 Serious flooding in California led to many deaths and several thousand people were left homeless.

1973 US action in Vietnam ended.

28 JANUARY

BORN THIS DAY

HISTORY

1457 Henry VII, the English king who founded the Tudor dynasty. He brought order after the Wars of the Roses.

1833 General Charles George Hamilton Gordon, British defender of Khartoum.

1841 Sir Henry Morton Stanley (John Rowlands), explorer-journalist born in Wales, who was sent by the *New York Herald* to find the missing Dr Livingstone in Africa.

1853 José Marti, Cuban poet and revolutionary leader who fought against Spanish rule.

1928 (Leonard) James Callaghan, former leader of the Labour Party and British Prime Minister.

ARTS

1873 (Gabrielle Sidonie) Colette, French author who wrote *Chéri* (1920) and *Gigi* (1945).

1874 Vsevold Meyerhold, Russian actor and director who, at his own theatre, trained actors to dance and perform acrobatics. Stalin closed the theatre as it did not conform with his ideas of social realism and Meyerhold disappeared mysteriously in 1939, never to be seen again.

1887 Artur Rubinstein, US concert pianist born in Poland, who gave his first recital aged five. Fluent in eight languages, he worked as an intepreter during the war. Afterwards, he settled in Hollywood and continued to perform throughout the world. In 1977, the Queen made him an honorary knight.

1912 Jackson Pollock, US abstract expressionist painter, who also experimented with action painting in the 40s.

1929 Claes Oldenburg, Swedish pop artist who did most of his work in the US.

1948 Mikhail Baryshnikov, Russian ballet dancer who defected to the US and became the artistic director of the American Ballet Theater.

ENTERTAINMENT

1892 Ernst Lubitsch, US film director, born in Germany. 'The Lubitsch Touch' brought style to many comedies, including *Ninotchka* (1939), starring Garbo.

1936 Alan Alda, US actor, best known for his role in the long-running, award-winning television series *M*A*S*H*.

INVENTION

1855 William Seaward Burroughs, US inventor of the first commercially successful recording adding machine in 1885. He did not perfect it until 1892, when he finally patented it, but he died before he could make much money from his invention.

SCIENCE

1884 Auguste Piccard, Swiss deep-sea explorer and balloonist who researched cosmic rays.

TWO BEATS IN A BAR 1927, Ronnie Scott, English saxophonist, band leader and owner of Britain's major jazz club. 1929, Acker Bilk, English jazz clarinettist and band leader, who helped popularize traditional jazz.

DIED THIS DAY

814 Charlemagne, Holy Roman emperor.

1547 Henry VIII, King of England, in London.

1596 Sir Francis Drake, Elizabethan seaman and adventurer, of dysentry; buried at sea off Porto Bello.

1696 Sir John Fenwick, executed for the attempted assassination of King William III.

1613 Sir Thomas Bodley, scholar and founder of the Bodleian Library in Oxford.

1829 William Burke, Irish body-snatcher who later moved to Scotland where he joined with William Hare in selling bodies to Dr Knox, who dissected them for research at medical classes. When the natural supply dried up, they jollied it along by committing a string of murders before being caught. Burke was hanged this day in front of a huge crowd, many prepared to pay a premium for a good view. Hare escaped the gallows by turning king's evidence. Later blinded in an attack when his identity was discovered, Hare was last seen alive begging outside the London Museum.

1928 Vicente Blasco Ibàñez, Spanish writer and politician, author of *The Four Horsemen of the Apocalypse* (1916). He died the day before his 61st birthday.

1939 William Butler Yeats, Irish poet and playwright, in France.

1988 Klaus Fuchs, German communist who spied in Britain and the US while working with the atom bomb team, in East Germany. Fuch's confession in 1949 and subsequent trial in Britain led to the suspension by the US of all co-operation in developing nuclear weapons. Fuchs served nine years of a 14-year sentence (1950–59) before being released for good behaviour.

ON THIS DAY

1807 London's Pall Mall was the first street in any city to be illuminated by gaslight.

1896 The first speeding fine was handed out to a British motorist, Walter Arnold of Kent, for exceeding 2 m.p.h. in a built-up area. He was doing 8 m.p.h.

1896 Mrs Rose Lee was given the first radiation treatment for carcinoma of the breast by Émile Grubbe of Chicago.

1930 Miguel Primo de Rivera's dictatorship in Spain came to an end.

1932 The Japanese occupied Shanghai; the start of a full-scale invasion of China.

1935 Iceland became the first country to introduce legalized abortion.

1953 19-year-old Derek Bentley was hanged at Wandsworth Prison. Along with 16-year-old Christopher Craig he had been apprehended by police on 2 November 1952, trying to rob a confectioner's warehouse in Croydon. Bentley was soon caught, and while held by the police is said to have egged on Craig to use the firearm he carried, injuring one policeman and killing another. Both boys were found guilty of murder, but, because of his age, Craig was to be detained while Bentley, despite considerable public protest, was sentenced to death.

1965 Crown Princess Beatrix of the Netherlands announced she planned to marry a German, sparking off protests that would mar her wedding day (10.3.1966).

1985 The Clive Ponting case opened in London. The civil servant would be found – 'much to my surprise' – not guilty of leaking secret information on the sinking of the *Belgrano* during the Falklands war.

1986 Nine years and a day after the first American space deaths (*see* 27.1.1967) the US space shuttle *Challenger* blew up shortly after lift-off from Cape Canaveral, killing five men and two women. The next shuttle would not fly until 29.9.1988.

29 JANUARY

BORN THIS DAY

HISTORY

1737 Thomas Paine, English social and political philosopher, author of *The Rights of Man* (1791).

1843 William McKinley, 25th US President who served two terms during the Spanish-American War and the annexation of the Phillipines.

ARTS

1862 Frederick Delius, English composer who first managed a Florida orange plantation and studied music with a Jacksonville organist, which inspired his *Florida Suite*. Other works include the opera *A Village Romeo and Juliet* (1901).

1867 Vicente Blasco Ibáñez, Spanish writer and politician, author of *The Four Horsemen of the Apocalypse* (1916).

1939 Germaine Greer, Australian feminist writer, author of *The Female Eunuch* (1970).

ENTERTAINMENT

1879 W. C. Fields (William Claude Dukinfield), US comedian who claimed he wouldn't act with children or animals.

1915 Victor Mature, US film actor who never took his own acting ability too seriously, having to use his beefcake appearance to enhance films such as *Samson and Delilah* (1949).

1923 Paddy (Sidney) Chayefsky, US playwright who brought a naturalistic style to both his television and film scripts. *Marty* (1955), *The Hospital* (1971) and *Network* (1976) all won awards.

1931 Leslie Bricuse, English musical composer who settled in the US after successes in Britain with Anthony Newley in *Stop the World I Want to Get Off*.

1933 Sacha Distel, French singer and songwriter who has sung more than 200 songs in French, English, Italian and German.

1941 Tom Selleck, US actor best known for his role in *Magnum*.

1943 Katherine Ross, US actress who moved from television to films, winning an Oscar for her role in *The Graduate* (1967).

SCIENCE

1700 Daniel Bernoulli, Swiss mathematician who studied the motion of liquids.

SPORT

1950 Jody Schecter, South African motor racing champion who won the World Driver's Championship in 1979.

DIED THIS DAY

1820 George III, King of England, at Windsor. At 81, he had both lived longer and reigned longer (over 59 years) than any previous monarch.

1899 Alfred Sisley, English Impressionist painter born in Paris.

1928 Douglas, first Earl Haig, British commander during the First World War and founder of the British Legion.

1962 Fritz Kreisler, Austrian-born virtuoso violinist.

1964 Alan Ladd, US film actor who found being short (5ft 5in) no handicap when playing tough guys, aged 50, from an overdose of sedatives and alcohol.

1980 Jimmy 'Schnozzola' Durante, US comedian, songwriter and vaudeville performer who was working almost until his death at the age of 87.

ON THIS DAY

1728 The first performance of John Gay's *The Beggar's Opera*, with a musical score derived from popular ballads of the time.

1853 Napoleon III married Eugénie de Montijo at the Tuilleries, Paris.

1856 Queen Victoria instituted Britain's highest military decoration, the Victoria Cross (VC).

1861 Kansas became the 34th US state.

1916 While German Zeppelins bombed Paris for the first time, British military tanks were having their first trials in Hertfordshire.

1942 The first broadcast of the BBC radio programme, *Desert Island Discs*, devised and presented by Roy Plomley.

1947 Buckingham Palace was lit by candles as the temperature dropped to an all-time low of −16°F producing nationwide power cuts.

1988 Failed opera singer Bantcho Bantchevsky leapt to his death from the balcony of the New York Metropolitan Opera House during an intermission of a matinée performance of Verdi's *Macbeth*.

1989 The artificial leg which once belonged to Sir Douglas Bader was catalogued for a sale later in the year. His widow was selling this and other war memorabilia to raise money to purchase a home of her own instead of the rented farmhouse she then lived in.

30 JANUARY

BORN THIS DAY

HISTORY

1882 Franklin Delano Roosevelt, lawyer, US Democrat statesman and 32nd President, who took the US out of the Depression with his 'New Deal'. He helped Britain with aid in the dark years before the US joined the conflict of the Second World War, but never lived to see out his record fourth term.

1913 Percy Thrower, English gardener and broadcaster who did much to popularize gardening in Britain in the post-war years.

1915 John Profumo, British Conservative War Minister who, as a leading figure in the political scandal known as 'The Profumo Affair', resigned after admitting having lied to the House of Commons on 22 March 1963 that there had never been any impropriety between him and Christine Keeler. As she had also slept with the Russian naval attaché, this gave rise to fears of security leaks. After the scandal, Profumo devoted himself to charitable work. His wife actress Valerie Hobson stood by him.

1927 Olaf Sven Joachim Palme, Prime Minister of Sweden, who was later assassinated.

ARTS

1860 Anton (Pavlovich) Chekhov, Russian playwright and short story writer. His works include *The Seagull* (1896), *Uncle Vanya* (1897), *The Three Sisters* (1900) and *The Cherry Orchard* (1903).

ENTERTAINMENT

1928 Harold Prince, US stage producer and director with a long list of credits including *West Side Story* (1957), *Fiddler on the Roof* (1964) and *Cabaret* (1966), as well as the Lloyd-Webber musicals *Evita* and *The Phantom of the Opera*.

1931 Gene Hackman, US actor who won an Oscar for his portrayal of the cop, Popeye Doyle, in *The French Connection* (1971).

1937 Vanessa Redgrave, English actress and eldest child of the Redgrave dynasty. Her left-wing views led her to stand unsuccessfully for Parliament.

JAZZ

1911 Roy (David) Eldridge, US jazz trumpeter and composer, a child prodigy who became one of the great creative musicians of his generation.

SPORT

1938 Boris Spassky, Russian chess champion who lost the world championship to Bobby Fischer in 1972 at Reykjavik.

DIED THIS DAY

DAY OF EXECUTIONS In 1606, Sir Everard Digby, Thomas Winter, John Grant and Thomas Bates were hanged, drawn and quartered in London for their part in the Gunpowder Plot of Guy Fawkes. In 1649, on a scaffold outside the Banqueting House in Whitehall, King Charles I, convicted of treason, was beheaded. The man believed to have wielded the axe was Richard Brandon, an experienced executioner who got £30 for his trouble.

1888 Edward Lear, English artist and writer, author of *The Book of Nonsense* (1846), in Italy.

1948 Mahatma Gandhi, Indian political and religious leader, assassinated by a fanatical Hindu on his way to prayers.

1948 Orville Wright, who, with his older brother Wilbur, made the first powered and controlled flights (17.12.1903).

1963 Francis Poulenc, French composer and pianist.

1982 Stanley Holloway, English actor, comedian and singer, who graduated from music hall to legitimate theatre.

ON THIS DAY

1790 *The Original*, the first purpose-built lifeboat was launched on the River Tyne at South Shields.

1858 The celebrated Hallé Orchestra was founded by Charles Hallé in Manchester. He remained its principal conductor, proprietor and performer until his death in 1895.

1889 At the royal hunting lodge of Mayerling, near Vienna, the beautiful 17-year-old Baroness Marie Vetsera and her lover, Austrian Crown Prince Rudolf, were found dead in his bedroom. No one is certain if it was a double suicide or murder.

1933 Adolf Hitler was appointed Chancellor by the President of Germany, von Hindenburg.

1945 The Duke of Gloucester became the first British royal to be appointed Governor General of Australia.

1958 Yves St Laurent held his first major Paris show, aged 23, and was hailed as Dior's successor.

1961 The contraceptive pill went on sale in Britain. It was not available through the National Health Service until December.

1965 The state funeral of Sir Winston Churchill, former Prime Minister of England, took place in London, the biggest of its kind since the Duke of Wellington's funeral 18.11.1852.

1972 In Londonderry, Northern Ireland, British paratroopers, believing they were under fire from Catholic protesters on a banned march which had turned into a violent riot, opened fire killing 13 people in what became known as 'Bloody Sunday'.

1973 Gordon Liddy and James McCord were convicted of spying on the Democratic headquarters at the Watergate building. McCord later wrote to Judge Sirica revealing that top White House officials were also involved.

1976 Muriel Naughton rode her own horse in an amateur riders chase at Ayr to become the first woman jockey to compete under National Hunt rules.

1989 Egyptian archaeologists discovered five life-sized black granite figures, Pharaonic statues dating back to 1470BC, close to the foundations of the Temple of Luxor in upper Egypt.

31 JANUARY

The Feast Day of John Bosco, the popular preacher who became patron saint of editors.

BORN THIS DAY

HISTORY

1938 Queen Beatrix of the Netherlands.

ARTS

1797 Franz (Peter) Schubert, Austrian composer who wrote his first symphony at 16. He went on to compose 600 songs, eight in one day. His famous *Unfinished Symphony* was actually written six years before his death.

1872 Zane Grey, US writer of westerns, in Zanesville, Ohio, which explains his first name.

1885 Anna Pavlova, Russian prima ballerina of the Imperial Ballet from 1906, who settled in London in 1913. She formed her own company and travelled the world performing many ballets, including *The Dying Swan*, which she made her own.

1893 Dame Freya Stark, English traveller and writer whose books include *A Winter in Arabia* (1940).

1923 Norman Mailer, US writer, author of one of the finest war books ever, *The Naked and the Dead* (1948).

ENTERTAINMENT

1892 Eddie Cantor (Edward Israel Iskowitz), US comedian and singer whose big rolling eyes, distinctive speech and singing style led to many song hits, including 'If You Knew Suzie'.

1903 Tallulah Bankhead, flamboyant US actress, daughter of a former Speaker of the House of Representatives.

1921 Mario Lanza (Alfredo Arnold Cocozza), US tenor and film actor whose promising career was ended by drink, barbiturate and obesity problems.

1921 (Elaine) Carol Channing, gravel-voiced, wide-eyed US actress, comedian and singer who made her mark on Broadway in *Gentlemen Prefer Blondes* (1949).

1929 Jean Simmons, English stage and

screen actress who appeared in *Great Expectations* (1946) aged 17.

SCIENCE

1881 Irving Langmuir, US chemist and physicist who developed an inert gas to displace the vacuum in electric lamps, giving them much longer life.

POP

1951 Phil Collins, English musician and actor, who was originally a member of Genesis.

RELIGION

1903 The Reverend Lord (Donald) Soper, British Methodist minister and brilliant orator with strong socialist and pacifist views.

SPORT

1931 Christopher Chataway, British athlete who became a government minister. In 1953, the Oxford blue ran a world-record breaking 5,000m at London's White City.

DIED THIS DAY

1788 'Bonnie Prince Charlie' (Charles Edward Stuart), the Young Pretender, in Rome.

1933 John Galsworthy, English author of *The Forsyte Saga*.

1956 A(lan) A(lexander) Milne, English author and poet, creator of *Winnie-the-Pooh*.

1974 Sam Goldwyn (Samuel Goldfish), Polish-born US film producer.

ON THIS DAY

1606 Guy Fawkes, the chief conspirator in the Gunpowder Plot, was hanged, drawn and quartered.

1747 The first VD clinic opened at London Lock Hospital.

1858 The five-funnelled steamship, *The Great Eastern*, designed by Isambard Kingdom Brunel and John Scott Russell, was launched at Millwall.

1876 All US Indians had to move into reservations or be deemed hostile. Many could not make it in time, others never even knew of the proclamation.

1901 Chekhov's *The Seagull* was performed at the Moscow Arts Theatre for the first time.

1910 The Crippens had the Martinettis to dinner. They were the last to see 'Belle' Crippin alive. After they left, Dr Crippen first poisoned 'Belle', then cut her up into small pieces, which he buried in the cellar. When the police finally unearthed the remains, the head, skeleton and limbs were never found.

1928 3M began marketing their clear Scotch tape.

1929 Leon Trotsky (Lev Davidovich Bronstein) was exiled by Stalin and found asylum in Mexico.

1943 In defiance of Hitler, Field Marshall Paulus surrendered the German 6th Army to the Russians at Stalingrad.

1953 The Thames estuary broke its banks and large areas of Kent and Essex were flooded, killing 307. There was also flooding in Holland and other parts of the Continent, which raised the death toll to over 2,000.

1955 RCA demonstrated the first musical synthesizer.

1957 The Trans-Iranian oil pipeline was completed.

1958 *Explorer I* was launched at Cape Canavarel, the first US earth satellite.

1983 Wearing car seat belts became compulsory in Britain.

1989 A man who had served 30 years on death row in Japan was finally found innocent of kidnapping and murdering a six-year-old girl. Masao Akabori, now 59, was hoping for £526,000 as compensation for his 12,660 days behind bars.

THE PAN BOOK OF DATES

FEBRUARY

I invent nothing. I rediscover
(Auguste Rodin)

I FEBRUARY

The Feast Day of Brigid, or Bride, patron saint of scholars.

BORN THIS DAY

ENTERTAINMENT

1895 John Ford, (Sean Aloysius O'Fearna), US film director who was a set builder, propman and stuntman before he began directing westerns. His films include *Stage Coach* (1939), *The Grapes of Wrath* (1940) and *How Green was My Valley* (1941).

1901 (William) Clark Gable, US film actor. Turned down by all the major film studios as having 'big ears and the looks of an ape' he eventually became the 'King of Hollywood'. He won an Oscar for *It Happened One Night* (1934) and played Rhett Butler in *Gone with the Wind* (1939).

1908 George Pal, Hungarian-born US film director who made special effects his forte, first with his *Puppetoons* which won a special Oscar in 1943, and later with *When Worlds Collide* (1953), which also won him an Oscar.

ARTS

TWO OF A KIND In 1873, in England, the contralto Dame Clara Butt, who was the first to perform the song version of 'Land of Hope and Glory'; and in 1922, Renata Tebaldi, the Italian soprano who was chosen by Toscanini to sing at the reopening of La Scala, Milan, in 1946.

1874 Hugo von Hofmannsthal, Austrian playwright and poet, who wrote *Everyman* (1912), based on the morality play, and *The Tower* (1925).

1895 Stephen (Meredith) Potter, English author, best known for his humorous books *Lifemanship* (1950) and *One-Upmanship* (1952).

1904 S(idney) J(oseph) Perelman, US writer and humorist who scripted the Marx Brothers' film *Monkey Business* (1931).

1918 Muriel Spark, Scottish novelist, author of *The Prime of Miss Jean Brodie* (1961).

POP

1937 Don Everly, of the internationally successful US pop duo, the Everly Brothers, who had three No. 1s, including 'Cathy's Clown' (1960).

SPORT

1915 Sir Stanley Matthews, former Blackpool and England footballer, the first to be knighted. He won an FA Cup Winner's medal in 1953, when he was 38.

DIED THIS DAY

1650 Rene Descartes, French philosopher, known as 'the father of modern philosophy'. He was visited in his bedroom at 5 a.m. by his patron, Queen Christiana of Sweden, who wished to pursue her studies, and he died shortly after.

1851 Mary Wollstonecraft Shelley, English author of *Frankenstein, or the Modern Prometheus* (1818).

1878 George Cruikshank, English caricaturist and illustrator.

1908 Carlos I of Portugal, shot at point blank range, together with his son, Crown Prince Luiz, in his carriage.

1922 Prince Aritomo Yamagata, military commander and Prime Minister of Japan.

1940 John Buchan, Lord Tweedsmuir, Scottish author of *The Thirty-nine Steps* (1915).

1944 Piet Mondrian, Dutch abstract painter, in New York.

1966 (Joseph Francis) 'Buster' Keaton, film comedian.

ON THIS DAY

1787 The first edition of the *Botanical Magazine*, edited by a former English apothecary, William Curtis, was published in London.

1790 The first meeting of the US Supreme Court took place.

1840 The first dental college opened in Baltimore, Maryland, US.

1880 The *Stage* newspaper (*Stage Directory)* was published in London.

1884 The first edition of the *Oxford English Dictionary* was published.

1893 Thomas Alva Edison opened the first film studio. It was set up in New Jersey, US, to make films for peepshow machines.

1896 Mimi's tiny hand was frozen for the first time as Puccini's opera, *La Bohème* opened in Turin.

1910 The first 80 Labour Exchanges opened in Britain to try and find jobs for the unemployed.

1920 The North West Mounted Police ('The Mounties', who always get their man), became the Royal Canadian Mounted Police.

1924 The first British Labour Government recognized the Soviet government.

1934 Austrian Chancellor Dollfus dissolved all political parties except his own 'Fatherland Front'.

1939 A British White Paper proposing the formation of the Home Guard (which became better known as 'Dad's Army' because of the average age of the volunteers) was published.

1941 The British Air Training Corps was founded.

1942 Vidkun Quisling was made Norwegian Premier.

1958 The United Arab Republic was formed by a union with Egypt and Syria.

1965 P. J. Proby, the US rock singer, was banned by ABC Theatres and the BBC after he had deliberately split his trousers during his act. It had happened accidentally while playing south London the previous week. The mainly female audience and the tabloids, who claimed Proby's act was obscene, went wild. It was the beginning of the end for this flamboyant performer who years later ended up as a shepherd on the Yorkshire Dales.

1974 Great Train Robber Ronald Biggs, who escaped from a British jail, was arrested by Brazilian police in Rio de Janeiro. He escaped extradition because he was the father of a child by his Brazilian girlfriend.

1977 The ultra-modern Pompidou Centre for arts in Paris, designed by English architect Richard Rodgers and the Italian, Renzo Piano, was opened.

1979 Ayatollah Khomeini returned from 14 years of exile in France to become the Iranian leader following the forced departure of the Shah.

1979 Liverpool gravediggers called off their strike which resulted in a long queue of coffins awaiting burial.

1979 Trevor Francis, 24, became the first £1m footballer in England, signing for Brian Clough's Nottingham Forest.

1981 Gro Harlem Brundland became Norway's first woman Prime Minister.

1983 British Independent Television's breakfast time station, TV-am began broadcasting.

1989 Omiuri, the 16ft python believed by millions of Luo tribesman to have magical powers, died in Kenya. The subject of heated debates in the Kenyan parliament over her welfare, she was always shown to important visitors.

2 FEBRUARY

Candlemas Day, the Feast of the Purification of the Blessed Virgin Mary, when after the birth of Christ she was ritually cleansed in the Temple.

BORN THIS DAY

HISTORY

1650 Nell (Eleanor) Gwynne, former orange seller at Drury Lane Theatre, who became a comedy actress and later mistress of Charles II, by whom she had two sons.

1754 Charles Maurice de Talleyrand-Périgord, French statesman and politician who was Napoleon's foreign minister and later ambassador to Britain.

1850 Jesse Boot, first Lord Trent, English chemist and philanthropist, founder of the Boots the Chemist chain.

1926 Valéry Giscard d'Estaing, former French President, in Koblenz, Germany, although he was educated in France. He was elected President in 1974 and was defeated by Mitterand in 1981.

ARTS

TWO OF A KIND Two of the finest violinists of the past century were born this day. In 1875, Fritz Kreisler was born in Austria. He became a US citizen in 1943. At one point in his career he abandoned music for medicine, but he returned to the violin in 1899. He performed in most of the major concert halls and gave the first performance of Elgar's concerto, which was dedicated to him. He also composed several popular violin pieces. In 1901 Jascha Heifitz, who made his debut aged five years, was born in Russia. He became a US citizen in 1925.

1882 James Joyce, Irish novelist renowned for his innovative use of language. *Ulysses* (1922), his most famous work, is a stream-of-consciousness epic describing a single day in the lives of several Dubliners (*see* 16.6.1904). Originally banned in both the US and Britain, it was first published in serial form in a US magazine.

1911 Jussi Bjorling, Swedish tenor who made his debut at the Stockholm Opera in 1930, and later performed in both London and New York.

ENTERTAINMENT

1920 Hughie Green, Canadian-born quiz showhost, and originator on British television of the talent show, *Opportunity Knocks*.

1927 Elaine Stritch, US actress, singer who starred in Noel Coward's London production of *Sail Away* and stayed on to appear on television.

1933 Les Dawson, English stage and television comedian, host of *Blankety Blank*.

1940 David Jason, English actor, best known as Del Boy in the highly successful television series *Only Fools and Horses*.

1946 Farrah Fawcett, US actress who added her former husband's surname,

Majors, when she starred in the television series *Charlie's Angels*.

JAZZ

1927 Stan Getz, US tenor saxophonist who played with all the named bands from the age of 16.

SEX

1859 (Henry) Havelock Ellis, English sex psychologist, author of *Studies in the Psychology of Sex*.

DIED THIS DAY

1918 John L(awrence) Sullivan, US bare-knuckle boxing champion and known as 'The Boston Strong Boy'.

1970 Bertrand Russell, 3rd Earl, English philosopher and writer.

1979 Sid Vicious (John Beverly), lead singer with the notorious British punk group, the Sex Pistols, of a heroin overdose.

ON THIS DAY

1709 The real Robinson Crusoe, Alexander Selkirk, on whom Defoe based his famous novel, was rescued by Captain Thomas Dover, having spent five years on the uninhabited island of Mas à Tierra.

1801 The first parliament of Great Britain in which Ireland was represented, was assembled.

1848 The war between the US and Mexico ended after the signing of the Treaty of Guadalope Hidalgo.

1852 The first 'Gents' opened in Britain in Fleet Street, followed on the 11 February with the first 'Ladies' at Bedford Street, off the Strand.

1878 Greece declared war on Turkey.

1901 Kaiser Wilhelm II attended the state funeral of his grandmother, Queen Victoria.

1914 Cub Scouts were formed in England, the first pack being in Sussex.

1943 The German Army surrendered to the Soviets at Stalingrad.

1971 Major-General Idi Amin declared himself the absolute ruler of Uganda.

1972 A mob burned down the British Embassy in Dublin during riots over the deaths of 13 Catholics in Londonderry the previous Sunday.

1986 Women were allowed to vote for the first time in Lichtenstein.

3 FEBRUARY

The Feast Day of Margaret, the patron saint of pregnant women. According to legend, having been swallowed whole by a dragon, she was able to burst out of its belly.

BORN THIS DAY

HISTORY

1821 Elizabeth Blackwell, in Bristol, who became the first woman doctor in the US where her parents emigrated.

1830 Lord Robert Cecil, 3rd Marquis of Salisbury, statesman and British Prime Minister.

ARTS

1809 (Jakob Ludwig) Felix Mendelssohn-Bartholdy, German composer, grandson of Jewish philosopher Moses Mendelssohn, whose banker son Abraham changed his name to Bartholdy when he became a Protestant. Felix composed the popular *Hebrides* overture, *Fingal's*

Cave, in 1830 and *The Midsummer Night's Dream* in 1842.

1826 Walter Bagehot, English economist, author and journalist who edited the *Economist*.

1874 Gertrude Stein, US author and critic who went to Paris in 1904 and befriended many new artists including Picasso, as well as fellow Americans such as Hemingway and F. Scott Fitzgerald. Her novel *The Autobiography of Alice B. Toklas* (1933) is typical of her style with its repetition and lack of punctuation.

1883 Clarence E(dward) Mulford, US writer of westerns who created Hopalong Cassidy in a short story, 'Bar-20' in 1907. The first Cassidy novel was published in 1912, the last in 1950, during which time Mulford only set foot in the West once – and hated it.

1898 Alvar Aalto, Finnish architect, one of the early Modernists. He also invented bent laminated plywood furniture.

1907 James (Albert) Michener, US novelist whose experiences in the South Pacific during the Second World War served as a basis for his novel, *Tales of the South Pacific* (1947).

1909 Simone Weil, French author whose books, which include *Waiting For God*, were published after her death in a English sanatorium in 1943.

1926 Glen Tetley, US choreographer who has worked with many of the major international ballet companies creating ballets such as *The Anatomy Lesson* and *Rag Dances*.

ENTERTAINMENT

1889 Carl Theodore Dreyer, Danish film director, internationally admired for *The Passion of St Joan* made in France in 1928, and *The Day of Wrath* (1945).

1928 Frankie Vaughan (Frank Abelsohn), English singer and actor who went to Hollywood to be Marilyn Monroe's leading man in *Let's Make Love* (1960), and came back home.

1929 Val Doonican, Irish-born ballad singer and entertainer.

1935 Jeremy Kemp (Walker), English character actor whose films include *The Blue Max* (1966).

DIED THIS DAY

1399 John of Gaunt, Duke of Lancaster, father of King Henry IV. The name Gaunt was originally 'Ghent', where he was born.

1762 Richard 'Beau' Nash, English gambler and dandy.

1832 George Crabbe, English poet, who wrote *Peter Grimes*.

1857 Mikhail Glinka, Russian composer, whose works include *Russlan and Ludmilla* (1842).

1924 Woodrow Wilson, US Democrat statesman and 28th President who served two terms.

1959 Buddy Holly, US singer and guitarist, killed in an aircrash, aged 23. With him were performers Richie Valens and J.P. 'Big Bopper' Richardson.

1969 Boris Karloff (William Henry Pratt), English actor who went to Hollywood and became famous as Frankenstein's monster.

ON THIS DAY

1488 The first European to land on southern African soil, the Portuguese navigator Bartholomew Diaz came ashore at Mossel Bay on the Indian Ocean side of the Cape.

1730 The first stock exchange quotations were published in the *Daily Advertiser*, London.

1809 Illinois was organized as a Territory of the US. Almost nine years later, on 3.12.1818, it became a state.

1877 'The Celebrated Chop Waltz' – better known as 'Chopsticks' – was registered at the British Museum. Arranged as a duet and solo for pianoforte by Arthur de Lull (a pseudonym for Euphemia Alten, the music publisher's sister who wrote it when she was 16), it has since been played on millions of pianos throughout the world.

1881 Belle Starr, the bandit queen of the Wild West who was also a horse thief, a murderess and close friend of the outlaws Jesse James and Cole Younger, was buried in front of her log cabin two days before her 41st birthday after being ambushed by an unknown assailant.

1916 Ottawa's parliament building was destroyed by fire.

1919 The first meeting of the League of Nations was held in Paris, with President Woodrow Wilson as chairman.

1931 A severe earthquake hit Napier and Hastings in New Zealand causing 216 deaths.

1945 The Allies used over 1,000 planes on daylight bombing raids on Berlin.

1954 The Queen visited Australia, the first reigning monarch to do so.

1957 Severe floods and high winds caused extensive damage to England's east coast from Lincoln to Kent. Over 280 people were drowned and thousands were made homeless.

1958 The Benelux Economic Treaty was signed.

1960 Macmillan made his historic 'The wind of change is blowing through this continent' speech to the South African parliament in Capetown.

1966 The first controlled landing on the moon was made by the USSR unmanned spacecraft, *Luna IX*.

1969 Yasser Arafat was appointed leader of the PLO at the Palestinian National Congress in Cairo.

1977 Teferi Bante, the Ethiopian Prime Minister, was executed, together with six others.

1989 British Telecom banned all chatlines because of the number of people running up huge phone bills. One 12-year-old landed his mother with a bill for £6,000.

4 FEBRUARY

The Feast Day of St Joan of Arc, patron saint of soldiers.

BORN THIS DAY

HISTORY

1740 Tadeusz Andrzej Bonaventura Kosciusko, Polish patriot who has Australia's highest mountain named after him. It took both the Russians and Prussians to defeat and imprison him.

1897 Dr Ludwig Erhard, German statesman who directed his country's economic recovery after the Second World War, before succeeding to the Chancellorship of the Federal Republic following Konrad Adenauer.

1902 Captain Charles Lindberg, US pioneer aviator, the first to fly solo across the Atlantic. He became an international celebrity and was in the news again, first when his baby was kidnapped and murdered, and later when he advised the Nazis on aviation matters prior to the outbreak of the Second World War.

1906 Dietrich Bonhoeffer, German theologian and anti-Nazi who took part in the failed plot to assassinate Hitler. He was later executed in Flossenberg concentration camp. His *Letters and Papers from Prison* (1951) was published posthumously.

ARTS

1881 Fernand Léger, French Cubist painter who featured cylindrical and machine forms in his paintings and ballet sets. He worked both in Paris and New York.

ENTERTAINMENT

1918 Ida Lupino, English film actress who described herself as the 'poor man's Bette Davis'.

1920 Norman Wisdom, English comedy actor who specialized in slapstick on both stage and screen.

POP

1948 Alice Cooper (Vincent Furnier), US pop singer who deliberately set out to shock his audience; his act included performing with snakes. His hits include 'Welcome to my Nightmare'.

SCIENCE

1893 Professor Raymond Arthur Dart, born Toowong, Brisbane, Australia. Discoverer of 'the missing link' in the evolutionary chain. (*See* 28.11.1924)

SPORT

1912 Byron Nelson, US golf champion who won the first two US Masters titles (1937) and, two years later, the US Open.

DIED THIS DAY

AD211 Lucius Septimius Severus, Roman emperor, in England. Although he was cremated in York his ashes were taken to Rome.

1555 Giambattista della Porta, Italian inventor of the camera obscura.

1925 Robert Koldewey, German archaeologist who excavated Babylon.

1925 Oliver Heaviside, English physicist who advanced electrical communications.

1983 Karen Carpenter, US singer who with her brother formed the successful Carpenters duo, from anorexia nervosa.

1987 (Lee) Liberace, flamboyant US pianist and entertainer, officially from a brain tumour, although the real cause is believed to have been AIDS.

ON THIS DAY

1861 The Confederate States of America was formed; an alliance of secessionist states which met at Montgomery, Alabama.

1904 The Russo-Japanese War began over the former's occupation of Manchuria.

THE ECSTASY AND THE AGONY In 1911, Rolls-Royce commissioned their famous figurehead 'The Spirit of Ecstasy' by Charles Sykes who used as his model Lord Montague's mistress, Eleanor Thornton. 60 years later to the day, Rolls-Royce was declared bankrupt due to a disastrous contract to supply aero engines to Lockheed.

The British government would come to its rescue.

1920 Two South African aviators took off from Brooklands, Surrey, on the first flight to Cape Town from England. The journey would take Lt Col Pierre van Ryneveld and Flight Lt C. J. Quinton 28 days.

1927 Malcolm Campbell reached over 174m.p.h. in *Bluebird* on the Pendine Sands in Wales to set a new land speed record. A year later in 1928 at Daytona Beach, Florida, he reached 206.35m.p.h. Four years and one day later, in 1931, he reached a record-breaking 245m.p.h., again at Daytona Beach.

1928 In Munich, black US singer Josephine Baker brought protests from the Nazis, but she was only banned from further appearances a year later because of her 'indecent behaviour' on stage.

1938 Adolf Hitler assumed command of the German Army. Von Ribbentrop became Foreign Minister.

1948 Ceylon became independent. It would later change its name to Sri Lanka.

1962 The first colour supplement in Britain was published by *The Sunday Times*.

1968 The world's largest hovercraft was launched at Cowes, Isle of Wight.

1976 The Guatemalan earthquake killed 23,000 people.

1987 Dennis Connor's US crew won back the America's Cup from Australia.

5 FEBRUARY

The Feast Day of Agatha, the patron saint of nurses and of Malta.

BORN THIS DAY

HISTORY

1788 Sir Robert Peel, the first commoner to become British Prime Minister (Conservative), although hardly from humble beginnings – his father was a cotton millionaire. Peel was the founder of the Metropolitan Police, first nicknamed 'Peelers', then 'Bobbies', after his name.

1900 Adlai Ewing Stevenson, US statesman and UN ambassador. His strong liberal views were once labelled 'red' by Senator McCarthy during the anti-communist witch-hunts.

1919 Andreas Papandreou, Greek Prime Minister who, aged 69, took an airline hostess as a companion while both in office and married. This and financial scandals cost him the 1989 elections.

TWO OF A KIND **Two British inventors were born this day in 1840; Sir Hiram Stevens, who perfected the machine gun that bore his name, and Scottish veterinary surgeon, John Boyd Dunlop, inventor of the pneumatic bicycle tyre.**

ARTS

1848 Joris Karl Huysmans, French novelist who wrote *Against Nature* (1884).

1914 William Burroughs, US 'beat' novelist who wrote *The Naked Lunch* (1959).

1921 Sir John (Michael) Pritchard, English conductor of the BBC Symphony Orchestra, who also conducted the first performances of operas by Britten and Tippett.

1942 Susan Hill, English novelist and playwright, author of *The Magic Apple Tree* (1982).

ENTERTAINMENT

1906 John Carradine (Richmond Reed Caradine), US film character actor known as the 'Bard of the Boulevard' because he recited poetry and Shakespeare in a booming voice while walking along Hollywood streets. He made over 170 films including *The Invisible Man* (1933) and *The Last Tycoon* (1976).

1920 Frank Muir, English humorous writer and broadcaster who with Dennis Norden, wrote many classic radio scripts, including *Take It From Here* with the immortal Glums.

1947 Charlotte Rampling, English actress who appeared in *The Night Porter* (1974).

POP

1945 Bob Marley, Jamaican reggae writer and performer who with his Wailers brought reggae to an international audience. One of his hits, 'No Woman No Cry', was recorded live at the Lyceum, London, 1975.

DIED THIS DAY

1679 Joost van den Vondel, Dutch poet and playwright.

1798 Luigi Galvani, Italian physiologist.

1881 Thomas Carlyle, English author and historian.

1941 A. B. 'Banjo' Peterson, Australian folk poet and journalist.

1946 George Arliss, English stage and screen actor.

1972 Marianne Craig Moore, US poet.

1988 Robert Richl, US inventor in the 1950s of thermal knitwear which was originally designed for use by the US army.

ON THIS DAY

1781 Lord George Gordon was acquitted of treason. He had organised the 'Gordon Riots' over the Catholic Relief Act of 1780 which removed penalties from British Roman Catholics.

1782 Minorca was captured by the Spanish from British forces.

1811 The Prince of Wales was declared Prince Regent. He later became George IV.

1816 Rossini's *The Barber of Seville* was first performed, in Rome.

1920 The RAF College at Cranwell was founded.

1935 In New York, boxing authorities ruled that no championship bout should exceed 15 rounds.

1945 US troops under the command of General MacArthur entered Manila.

1957 Bill Haley and the Comets arrived in London at the start of their British tour and received a wildly enthusiastic welcome.

1974 Patty Hearst, 19-year-old US heiress, was kidnapped from her San Francisco apartment. On the 22nd, it was revealed she was in the hands of the Symbionese Liberation Army, an extreme left-wing group who wanted the ransom money to be used to buy food for the poor of San Francisco.

1982 The small, independent Laker Airlines, created by former British pilot Sir Freddy Laker to cut prices and make air travel more accessible, collapsed with debts of £270m.

1983 Klaus Barbie, the Nazi war criminal

nicknamed 'the Butcher of Lyons', was flown to France to face prosecution for war crimes.

1983 Amongst old papers in Odense, Denmark, an unknown symphony by a nine-year-old Mozart was discovered.

6 FEBRUARY

New Zealand Day, or Waitangi Day. On this day, 1840, the Treaty of Waitangi between Britain and the Maori chiefs proclaimed British sovereignty and protection of New Zealand.
The Feast Day of Dorothy, one of the patron saints of gardeners.

BORN THIS DAY

HISTORY

1665 Queen Anne of Britain and Ireland, the last Stuart ruler, second daughter of James II. She bore Prince George of Denmark 17 children; 16 died in infancy, the remaining child when aged 12. Her desire for national unity led to the union of the English and Scottish parliaments (1707).

1905 Wladyslaw Gomulka, Polish Communist leader who led Poland from 1956 until 1970 when he was forced out of office because of riots over escalating food prices.

1911 Ronald Reagan, 40th US President and former film actor in mainly B-features. A one-time Liberal, he evolved into a staunch Republican Conservative. He proved to be one of the most popular presidents of modern times, serving the full two terms from 1980–89, despite the Irangate scandal.

1912 Eva Braun, Bavarian salesgirl who first met Hitler in the early 30s when he came into the Munich photographer's shop in which she worked, and later became his mistress. They married the day before their suicide in the Berlin bunker (30.4.1945).

ARTS

1664 Christopher Marlowe, English poet and playwright who wrote *Tamburlaine the Great* (1587) and *Dr Faustus* (probably produced soon after, first published in 1604). He was also suspected of being a government spy.

1903 Claudio Arrau, Chilean concert pianist who made his debut in Berlin in 1914 where, in 1935–6, he played all of Bach's keyboard music in a series of 12 consecutive recitals.

1929 Keith Waterhouse, English writer of novels, including *Billy Liar* (1959), as well as plays, television scripts and newspaper articles.

ENTERTAINMENT

1838 Sir Henry Irving (John Henry Brodribb), English actor, the first to be knighted (1895). During his management of the Lyceum in London, Ellen Terry was often his leading lady.

1897 Alberto Cavalcanti, Brazilian-born documentary film maker. He joined John Grierson's GPO Film Unit in 1934 and played a major role in the development of the British documentary. Later, he directed features including *Nicholas Nickleby* (1948).

1912 François Truffaut, French film director who won an Oscar for best foreign film with *Day for Night* (1973). He also directed and co-scripted the highly successful *Jules et Jim* (1961) and played a French scientist in Spielberg's *Close Encounters of the Third Kind*.

1920 Zsa Zsa Gabor (Sari Gabor),

Hungarian-born actress, bejewelled sister of Eva Gabor. She had her best part in *Moulin Rouge* (1952), but her career has been marriage to wealthy men, including hotelier Conrad Hilton.

1922 Patrick McNee, Scottish actor who starred in the popular television series, *The Avengers*.

1922 Denis Norden, English humorist, writer and broadcaster, who with his partner, Frank Muir wrote some of the most successful BBC radio comedy series.

1933 Leslie Crowther, English television comedian and quizmaster.

1940 Jimmy Tarbuck, English comedian and golf enthusiast.

POP

1966 Rick Astley, English singer who had international hits with 'Never Gonna Give You Up' and 'Together Forever' (1988) both of which were written and produced by the Stock Aitken Waterman team.

INVENTION

1802 Charles Wheatstone, English physicist, one of the main pioneers of telegraphy, who also invented the concertina and harmonica.

SPORT

1895 (George Herman) 'Babe' Ruth, who despite being a fat, heavy drinking womanizer, was also one of the best baseball pitchers in the US sport. His great weight also made him one of the best batters, the first to score 40, 50 and 60 home runs in one major league season.

1924 Billy Wright, English footballer who was capped 105 times, captaining England in the World Cup Final in 1950 when they were beaten 1–0 by the US novices in the shock first round.

1931 Fred Trueman, 'Fiery Fred', the Yorkshire fast bowler who played a key role in the England side that won back the Ashes in 1953 after 20 years.

DIED THIS DAY

1515 Manutius Aldus, Italian editor and printer who produced the first paperbacks (of Greek and Latin classics) in 1495 and invented italics, which were used for the first time for his edition of Virgil in 1501.

1685 Charles II, King of Great Britain and Ireland, at the end of several days of revelry with his concubines and favourite mistresses. There were rumours that he was poisoned.

1783 Lancelot 'Capability' Brown, English landscape gardener.

1793 Carlo Goldoni, Italian comic playwright who wrote over 250 plays.

1804 Joseph Priestley, English clergyman who discovered oxygen, in Pennsylvania.

1952 George VI, King of the United Kingdom.

1988 Marghanita Laski, English novelist who wrote *The Victorian Chaise-Longue*.

ON THIS DAY

1508 Maximilian I assumed the title Holy Roman Emperor.

1788 Massachusetts became the 6th state of the Union, and ratified the Constitution of the United States.

1804 A locomotive converted from a steam-hammer power source, ran on a line near Merthyr Tydfil, Wales, developed by Cornish engineer, Richard Trevithick.

1865 General Robert E. Lee became Commander-in-Chief of the Confederate Armies.

1897 Crete proclaimed a union with Greece.

1911 Ramsay MacDonald was elected Chairman of the British Labour Party.

1918 The Representation of Peoples Act passed by the British Parliament received the Royal Assent, granting the vote to women over 30. Their first opportunity to use it would come at the General Election on 14.12.1918.

1919 The German airline Lufthansa was established, flying between Berlin and Weimar.

1928 A 35-year-old woman arrived in New York claiming that she was Anastasia, the youngest daughter of the Tsar, and that she had managed to survive her family massacre.

1952 Queen Elizabeth succeeded to the British throne. She and her husband, the Duke of Edinburgh, were on tour in Kenya when they heard the news of the death of her father, King George VI.

1958 Seven Manchester United footballers – 'Busby's Babes' – were amongst the 23 killed when their plane crashed in thick snow on the runway at Munich airport during take-off. Manager Matt Busby, seriously ill, survived. The team had just won the European Cup in Belgrade.

1961 Spurs football team captain, Danny Blanchflower became the first person to say 'no' to Eamonn Andrews live on television's *This is Your Life* when he refused to take part in the show.

1964 France and Britain again agreed to a Channel Tunnel.

1989 Sky Television's satellite service was launched by Rupert Murdoch.

7 FEBRUARY

BORN THIS DAY

HISTORY

1478 Sir Thomas More, English statesman, Lord Chancellor and author of *Utopia*, who was executed by Henry VIII for refusing to deny Papal authority. He was canonized by Pope Pius XI in 1935.

ARTS

1812 Charles (John Huffam) Dickens, English novelist who was sent to work aged 12 because his father had been imprisoned for debt and the family faced destitution. He eventually became a journalist and was soon producing a string of highly successful novels, including *Pickwick Papers* (1836), *Oliver Twist* (1838) and *Nicholas Nickleby* (1839), which were serialized in magazines. In 1849, the largely autobiographical *David Copperfield* was published.

1885 Sinclair Lewis, US novelist and Nobel prize winner who wrote *Main Street* (1920), *Babbitt* (1922) and *Elmer Gantry* (1927).

ENTERTAINMENT

1924 Dora Bryan (Dora Broadbent), English stage and screen comedy actress who started in pantomime aged 11. She went on to make over 50 films including *A Taste of Honey (1961)*.

1937 Peter Jay, former British ambassador to the US, a founder of TV-am.

SCIENCE

1700 Philippe Buache, French geographer and cartographer who devised contour lines for maps and charts.

1870 Alfred Adler, Austrian psychoanalyst who was an associate of Freud in Vienna, but went on to develop his own theories on what influences human behaviour.

DIED THIS DAY

1779 William Boyce, English organist and composer of the song 'Heart of Oak'.

1873 Joseph Sheridan Le Fanu, Irish novelist of *In a Glass Darkly* (1872).

1894 Adolphe Sax, Belgian musical instrument inventor and maker, in Paris.

1959 Daniel François Malan, South African Prime Minister.

1960 Igor Vasilevich Kuchatov, Soviet nuclear physicist.

1990 Jimmy van Heusen (Edward Chester Babcock), US composer of songs including the Sinatra hit 'Come Fly with Me'.

ON THIS DAY

301 Edward of Caernarvon (later King Edward II) became the first Prince of Wales.

1845 The Portland Vase, a cameo-glass Roman vase believed to date from 25BC and to have belonged to the Emperor Augustus, was broken by William Lloyd, a drunken visitor to the British Museum. It was soon 'rebuilt', and reassembled again in 1949. Following the discoloration of the glue, work began yet again in 1988 when the 200 fragments were 'dismantled' and put back together once more, including 34 pieces which had been omitted earlier.

1863 The HMS *Orpheus* was wrecked on the New Zealand coast with the loss of 185 lives.

1886 While building a cottage for a prospector in the Transvaal, South Africa, an Englishman, George Walker found a clear streak of gold. On 7.10.1853, Pieter Marais had discovered a few specks of gold in the river Crocodile on the slopes of the Witwatersrand, but until Walker's discovery no one realized that they were above the richest gold reef in the world.

1974 Grenada became independent. Eric Gairy became the first Prime Minister.

LADIES FIRST Two ladies made sporting history in 1976. Joan Bazely became the first woman football referee of an all-male match at Croydon, Surrey, and Diana Thorne became the first woman jockey to win under National Hunt Rules on 'Ben Ruler' at Stratford.

1986 The hated Haiti dictator, 'Baby Doc' Duvalier, fled to exile in France to avoid a national uprising which began the following day, taking over £100m with him. He and his father, 'Papa Doc' ruthlessly ruled Haiti for over 28 years.

1989 It rained sardines over the Australian town of Ipswich, 30 miles from the Australian coast. A violent storm probably caused updraughts which took the fish from the shallow Brisbane waters into the atmosphere, scientists suggested.

1990 After 70 years of guaranteed monopoly rule, the Communist Party's

Central Committee agreed to back the amendment of Article Six of the Soviet Union's constitution which claimed 'full authority in government'. It was the first step towards democracy.

8 FEBRUARY

BORN THIS DAY

HISTORY

1820 William (Tecumseh) Sherman, Union general and military commander during the US Civil War who made a famous march to the sea with 65,000 men. When Grant became President, he was made head of the army.

ARTS

1819 John Ruskin, English writer and art critic, author of *The Stones of Venice* and *Modern Painters*.

1828 Jules Verne, pioneer French science-fiction writer who wrote *Journey to the Centre of the Earth* (1864) *Twenty Thousand Leagues Under the Sea* (1870), as well as *Around the World in Eighty Days* (1873).

ENTERTAINMENT

1888 Dame Edith Evans, English actress who was the definitive Lady Bracknell in Wilde's *The Importance of Being Earnest*.

1894 King (Wallis) Vidor, US film director who won a Special Oscar for his 'incomparable achievements as a cinematic creator and innovator'. His silent film *The Crowd* (1928) is now recognized as a masterpiece. He met the challenge of sound by directing a string of successes including *Duel in the Sun* (1947).

1920 Lana Turner (Julia Jean Mildred Francis Turner), US film actress. Legend has it she was discovered sipping soda at a Hollywood drugstore wearing a tight sweater that highlighted her main assets. She became known as 'The Sweater Girl' and her glamour girl roles included *The Postman Always Rings Twice* (1946) and *Peyton Place* (1957) which won her an Oscar nomination.

1925 Jack Lemmon (John Uhler Lemmon III), US film actor noted mainly for his comedy roles that are often tinged with tragedy in films such as *The Apartment* (1960). He won Oscars for best supporting actor in *Mister Roberts* (1955) and best actor in *Save the Tiger* (1973).

1931 James (Byron) Dean, US film actor and cult hero who died after crashing his Porsche on the way to a racing event. His film career lasted just 15 months, during which time he made three films: *East of Eden* (1955), *Rebel Without A Cause* (1955) and *Giant* (1956).

1932 John Williams, US composer and conductor mainly of film scores, including *Jaws* (1975) and *Star Wars* (1977) for which he won Oscars.

SCIENCE

1834 Ivanovich Mendeleyev, Russian chemist who formulated the periodic table of elements.

INVENTION

1906 Chester Floyd Carlson, US inventor of the Xerox copying process.

DIED THIS DAY

1587 Mary Queen of Scots, beheaded at Fotheringay Castle, Northamptonshire, where she had been imprisoned for 19 years following her attempt to overthrow Elizabeth and restore Catholicism to England.

1894 R(obert) M(ichael) Ballantyne, author of boys' adventure stories.

1921 Prince Peter Alekseyevich Kropotkin, Russian anarchist and geographer.

1926 William Bateson, English biologist who helped found the science of genetics.

1990 Del Shannon (Charles Weedon Westover), US pop musician whose hits included 'Runaway' (1961), shot himself.

ON THIS DAY

1725 Catherine the Great became Empress of Russia in succession to Peter the Great.

1740 The Great Frost of London, which started on Christmas eve 1739, came to an end. In contrast, this day 1750 was unseasonally hot and London experienced an earthquake. People fled to Hyde Park until the quakes, which caused little damage, ended.

1886 A peaceful demonstration by unemployed people started in Trafalgar Square and turned into a riot with looting in Oxford Street and Pall Mall.

1910 The Boy Scouts of America movement was formally incorporated.

1924 Gee Jon, a member of a Chinese *tong* (gang), became the first man to be executed in a gas chamber at Nevada State Prison, Carson City.

1964 A hysterical welcome awaited the Beatles on their arrival at J. F. Kennedy airport in New York at the start of their first US tour.

1965 Cigarette advertisements were to be banned from British television, it was announced by Health Minister Kenneth Robinson.

1969 The world's biggest passenger plane, the Boeing 747, made its maiden flight.

1971 At the Nuremberg International Toy Fair, a British plastics firm making educational toys was shown a board game which had been rejected by established companies. Invented by an Israeli telecommunications expert, Mordecai Meirowitz, the game, renamed 'Mastermind' by Invicta Plastics, would sell over 55 million sets in some 80 countries, making it the most successful new game of the 70s.

1972 The Albert Hall management cancelled a Frank Zappa and the Mothers of Invention concert because of the 'obscene lyrics' of one of their songs. Fans demonstrated outside the hall.

1974 After 85 days in Skylab space station, the US astronauts Gerald Carr, Edward Gibson and William Pogue returned safely to earth.

1976 The Dutch government ordered an inquiry into allegations that Prince Bernhard, Queen Juliana's husband, had taken bribes of around £555,000 from the US aircraft giant, Lockheed.

1983 The Derby winner Shergar was kidnapped in Ireland and a £2m ransom was demanded. The horse was never seen again.

9 FEBRUARY

The Feast Day of Apollonia, patron saint of dentists and toothache sufferers.

BORN THIS DAY

HISTORY

1773 William (Henry) Harrison, ninth US president. He was elected in 1840 and at the inaugural ceremony on 4 March 1841 he addressed the assembly in a cold drizzle, without a hat or coat. He contracted pneumonia and died a month later.

1854 Edward Carson, Anglo-Irish politician and barrister born in Dublin, who made his reputation cross-examining Oscar Wilde in 1895. As an MP, he organised opposition to Home Rule for Ireland with some 80,000 Ulster Volunteers.

1926 Dr Garret Fitzgerald, Irish Prime Minister who sought to reduce tensions between the republic and Northern Ireland.

ARTS

1863 Anthony Hope (Sir Anthony Hope Hawkins), English novelist, best remembered for *The Prisoner of Zenda* (1894).

1885 Alban (Maria Johannes) Berg, influential Austrian composer of the operas *Wozzeck* (1922) and the even more provocative, *Lulu* (1935).

1923 Brendan Behan, Irish poet, novelist and playwright, author of *The Quare Fellow* (1954) and the autobiographical *Borstal Boy* (1958).

ENTERTAINMENT

1865 Mrs Patrick Campbell (Beatrice Stella Tanner), English actress with an abrasive wit who created several famous roles including Eliza Doolittle in *Pygmalion* (1914). She had a close, well-documented relationship with Bernard Shaw.

1891 Ronald Colman, English actor who became a romantic star in such Hollywood films as *Lost Horizons* (1937) and *Prisoner of Zenda* (1937) and shares his birthday with the author of the latter.

1939 Janet Suzman, South African-born actress who has played leading roles on the British stage, in films and on television. She returned to Johannesburg in 1988 to direct the first *Othello* in South Africa starring a black actor.

1945 Mia Farrow, US actress who made her name in the television series *Peyton Place* before graduating to more serious roles in films such as *Rosemary's Baby* (1968).

POP

1941 Carole King (Klein), US singer and prolific songwriter who wrote hits such as 'It Might as Well Rain Until September' before embarking on her own successful recording career.

SCIENCE

1700 Daniel Bernoulli, Swiss mathematician from a family of mathematicians, who made important contributions to fluid dynamics. The Academy of Science had a Bernoulli as a member for 90 years.

SPORT

1922 Jim (James Charles) Laker, England cricketer who in 1956 at Old Trafford, Manchester, took all ten Australian wickets for 53 runs – the only Test bowler to do so.

CLUBMEN Two of the new breed of British golfers were born this day. In 1949, Bernard Gallacher, Scottish golfer who became the youngest British Ryder Cup international in 1969, and in 1958, Sandy Lyle, who became British Open golf champion in

1985 and the first Briton to win the Masters at Augusta in 1988.

DIED THIS DAY

1811 Nevil Maskelyne, English astronomer royal.

1881 Fyodor Mikhailovich Dostoevsky, Russian novelist of *Crime and Punishment* (1866) and other classics.

1966 Sophie Tucker, US entertainer, 'the last of the red hot mamas'.

1977 Sergei Vladimorovich Ilyushin, Russian aircraft designer.

1981 Bill Haley (William John Clifton), musician who, with the Comets, spearheaded the rock revolution.

1984 Yuri Andropov, Russian leader.

ON THIS DAY

1540 The first recorded race meeting in England was held at Roodee Fields, Chester.

1649 The funeral of King Charles I took place. He was buried at Windsor.

1801 The Holy Roman Empire came to an end with the signing of the Peace of Luneville between France and Austria.

1830 Explorer Charles Sturt discovered the termination of the Murray, Australia's longest river.

1849 Rome was proclaimed a republic by Giuseppe Mazzini.

1865 General Robert Lee took command of the Confederate Armies in the US Civil War.

1893 The world's first strip-tease took place (excluding Salome's alleged Dance of the Seven Veils), performed by Mona, an artist's model at the Four Arts Ball at the Moulin Rouge. The first professional stripper began gyrating a year later on 13.3.1894.

1923 The Russian state airline, known as Aeroflot, was formed.

1933 The famous Oxford Union Society debate on the proposal 'That this House will in no way fight for King and Country' was held.

1942 Fire gutted the French liner, *Normandie*.

1949 Robert Mitchum was jailed in Los Angeles for two months for smoking marijuana.

1972 The British government, led by Prime Minister Heath, declared a state of emergency as a result of the miners' strike, then in its third month.

1972 Britain and East Germany established diplomatic relations.

1981 General Wojciech Jaruzelski took over as Poland's Prime Minister to try and squash the 'Solidarity' movement.

1986 Halley's Comet made its expected return but poor weather conditions reduced opportunities to see it with the naked eye.

1988 For three months, the walls of a house in southern France echoed to an average 100 bangs from 10 p.m. until midnight and became a major tourist attraction. Police, geologists and Professor Yves Lignon, head of France's only paranormal research team, were unable to trace the source, although Professor Lignon felt the noise was probably provoked by tension within the family.

1989 At the Old Bailey, a Canadian artist, Rick Gibson, and a London art gallery curator were fined £500 and £350 respectively for displaying a pair of freeze-dried human foetuses hung from the ears of a mannequin. They were found guilty of outraging public decency.

1989 Polish archaeologists claimed to

have unearthed the world's oldest boomerang thought to be 23,000 years old.

10 FEBRUARY

The Feast Day of Scholastica, patron saint of convulsive children.

BORN THIS DAY

HISTORY

1824 Samuel Plimsoll, English reformer of the mercantile navy. He devised the Plimsoll Line, which acted as a regulation for the weight ships may safely carry. Rope sandals for sailors were also named after him.

1894 (Maurice) Harold Macmillan, 1st Earl of Stockton, who, as British Prime Minister after Eden's resignation following the Suez crisis, claimed 'You've never had it so good' and warned South Africa that 'the wind of change' was blowing through the continent. He was nicknamed 'Supermac' by cartoonist Vicky.

ARTS

1670 William Congreve, English Restoration comedy playwright, was baptized. *The Way of the World*, probably his finest play, flopped in 1700.

1775 Charles Lamb, English writer and essayist. After his sister Mary stabbed their mother to death in 1796, she spent periods in an asylum; while in Charles' care, though, they wrote *Tales from Shakespeare* (1807) and he contributed essays to the *London Magazine*.

1857 William Pember Reeves, New Zealand politician, journalist and author of *The Little White Cloud*.

1890 Boris Pasternak, Russian author of *Dr Zhivago* (1958) which was banned in the USSR because it showed the Revolution in an unfavourable light. The Russians claimed the awarding of the Nobel prize for Literature to Pasternak, which he declined, was 'a hostile act'.

1898 Bertold Brecht (Eugen Berthold Friedrich), German poet and playwright who expressed Marxist ideas through his plays; they included *The Threepenny Opera* (1928) (his adaptation of Gay's *Beggar's Opera*, with music by Kurt Weill), *Mother Courage* (1941) and *The Caucasian Chalk Circle* (1949).

ENTERTAINMENT

1893 Jimmy 'Schnozzola' Durante, US comedian, songwriter and vaudeville performer with the large proboscis.

1898 Dame (Frances Margaret) Judith Anderson, Australian actress who starred on Broadway and London where she played Gertrude to Gielgud's Hamlet.

1910 Joyce Grenfell (Joyce Irene Phipps), English writer and comedy actress. Besides her one-woman show, which she also took to the US, Canada, Australia and New Zealand, she appeared on radio and in films, including *Blue Murder at St Trinians* (1957).

1914 Larry (Laurence Cecil) Adler, US-born harmonica virtuoso and writer who settled in Britain where he composed and performed the score for the film *Genevieve*.

1930 Robert Wagner, US film and television actor who twice married Natalie Wood. He started as juvenile lead in films before graduating to better parts.

1940 Roberta Flack, US singer who had

hits with 'The First Time Ever I Saw Your Face' and 'Killing Me Softly'.

SCIENCE

1897 John Franklin Enders, US microbiologist who, with Thomas Weller and Frederick Robins, perfected a vaccine against polio. In 1954, all three were awarded the Nobel prize for Medicine, and later Enders isolated the measles virus.

SPORT

1893 William Tatem Tilden, US tennis champion, the first US player to win the men's singles at Wimbledon, 1920.

1920 Dr Alex Comfort, English physician and author of *The Joy of Sex*.

1926 Danny Blanchflower, Northern-Irish-born footballer who led Tottenham Hotspur to the double (the League and the FA Cup) in 1961.

1950 Mark Spitz, US Olympic swimming champion who won a record-breaking seven gold medals at the 1972 Munich Olympics.

1958 Greg Norman, Australian champion golfer who won the British Open in 1986.

DIED THIS DAY

1482 Luca della Robbia, Italian sculptor.

1567 Lord Darnley, the second husband of Mary Queen of Scots and father of James I, murdered near Edinburgh. The killer or killers used gunpowder to blow up their victim.

1837 Alexandr Sergeyevich Pushkin, Russian author of *Eugene Onegin*.

1868 Sir David Brewster, Scottish physicist, inventor of the kaleidoscope.

1878 Claude Bernard, French physiologist.

1912 Joseph Lister, English surgeon who introduced the antiseptic system.

1923 Wilhelm Konrad von Röntgen, German physicist, discoverer of X-rays.

1932 Edgar (Richard Horatio) Wallace, English thriller writer, in Hollywood.

1966 Billy Rose (William Samuel Rosenberg) Broadway producer and lyricist, in Jamaica.

ON THIS DAY

1354 Oxford University students clashed with townspeople in a three-day street battle. There were several deaths and many injuries until the students were overpowered.

1763 Following the Seven Years War, the Treaty of Paris was signed, with France ceding Canada to Britain, and on this day in 1840, Upper and Lower Canada were united.

1774 Andrew Becker demonstrated his practical diving suit in the Thames.

1840 Queen Victoria married Albert of Saxe-Coburg-Gotha.

1889 The use of the revised version of the Bible in church services was authorized by the Church of England.

1931 New Delhi became the capital of India.

1942 US bandleader and composer, Glenn Miller, was presented with the first gold disc ever, for officially selling over one million copies of 'Chattanooga Choo Choo'. (The first unofficial million-seller, achieved over many decades, was probably Caruso singing 'On With the Motley' from *Pagliacci*).

1988 Sir John Gielgud made theatrical history when, after an absence of ten years from the stage, he played the longest role ever for an actor of his age. Just weeks away from his 84th birthday he played Sydney Cockerell in *The Best of Friends* by Hugh Whitmore at the Apollo.

1989 Jamaican-born Tony Robinson was elected the first black Sheriff of Nottingham.

11 FEBRUARY

National Founding Day; Japan commemorates the Imperial House Law of 1889 which regulates the descent from the throne.

BORN THIS DAY

HISTORY

1821 Auguste Édouard Mariette, French egyptologist who excavated the Sphinx.

1920 King Farouk of Egypt who, in 1952, was forced to abdicate.

1908 Sir Vivien Fuchs, English geologist and leader of the Commonwealth Antarctic Expedition (1956–8).

ENTERTAINMENT

1909 Joseph L(eo) Mankiewicz, US film producer and writer who won Oscars for both his direction and script for *Letter to Three Wives* (1949), a feat he repeated with *All About Eve* (1950).

1936 Burt Reynolds, US film actor who began as a footballer, turning to acting when injury ended his career. He made a name for himself as the first male nude centrespread in *Cosmopolitan* (1972).

PHOTOGRAPHY

1800 Henry Fox Talbot, English photographic pioneer. He published the first book with photographic illustrations, titled *The Pencil of Nature* (1846).

SCIENCE

1839 Josiah Willard Gibbs, US physicist who specialized in thermodynamics.

INVENTION

1847 Thomas Alva Edison, US inventor who registered over 1000 patents, for the electrographic vote recorder (when just 22 years old), the phonograph, the dictaphone, the mimeograph, the film camera, storage batteries and the incandescent electric light bulb, amongst others.

SPORT

1934 John Surtees, British motor-cycle and motor racing champion.

FASHION

1934 Mary Quant, English fashion designer who played a major role in making London the centre of fashion in the 60s.

DIED THIS DAY

1799 Lazaro Spallanzani, Italian physiologist and chemist.

1868 Jean Foucault, French physicist and inventor of the gyroscope.

1879 Honoré Daumier, French caricaturist.

1931 Sir Charles (Algernon) Parsons, English steam turbine engineer and inventor.

1940 John Buchan (Lord Tweedsmuir), Scottish novelist of *The Thirty-nine Steps* (1915) who was also the Governor-General of Canada.

1949 Axel Martin Fredrik Munthe, Swedish writer and physician, author of

The Story of San Michele (1929).

1958 Alfred Ernest Jones, Welsh psychoanalyst.

1960 Erno von Dohnanyi, Hungarian composer who settled in the US.

1976 Lee J. Cobb, US actor.

1988 Marion Kirk Crawford, 'Crawfie', the British royal governess, and author of a book about life in the palace nurseries.

ON THIS DAY

1765 English wig makers petitioned George III seeking financial relief as the male fashion of wearing wigs came to an end.

1810 Napoleon, having divorced Joséphine, married Marie-Louise of Austria.

1826 London University was granted a charter.

1858 Bernardette Soubirous, a young asthmatic French girl, saw a vision of the Virgin Mary at Lourdes.

1858 Benito Juàrez was declared Constitutional President of Mexico by an assembly at Vera Cruz.

1861 Troops suppressed a riot in Chatham, Kent, when convicts broke out of a prison.

1878 The first weekly weather report was published by the meteorological office.

1889 The Japanese constitution was granted allowing the Emperor to retain wide powers.

1899 The first motorcyclist was killed in Britain when George Morgan crashed in Exeter.

1922 Honduras was declared an independent republic.

1929 The 109 acres of the Vatican in Rome was made an independent sovereign state by the Lateran Treaty.

1945 The Yalta Conference in the Crimea ended. The world leaders, Roosevelt, Stalin and Churchill had agreed to the formation of the United Nations Organization, and the division of Europe and the East when Germany and Japan were defeated.

1975 Mrs Thatcher became the first woman leader of a British political party.

WINNERS At the 1976 Winter Olympics at Innsbruck, John Curry became the first Briton to win a gold medal for men's figure skating. At the 1988 Winter Olympics at Calgary, English ski-jumper and plasterer Eddie Edwards, who had stayed at a mental home in Finland while training, became the surprise sensation of the Games. This bespectacled yet fearless contestant came last, but won all the headlines and the nickname 'The Eagle'.

1983 Dennis Andrew Nilsen, a civil servant, was accused of murdering between 14 and 16 young men over a period of five years and dismembering their bodies, burying some in the back garden of his north London bedsitter. Two heads and a hand were found in a sewage pipe.

1988 In the US, a paroled child molester was jailed for ten years for failing to display a proper sign on his house stating he was a dangerous sex offender.

1990 After more than 27 years in prison, Nelson Mandela, the world's most famous political prisoner, walked to freedom from a prison near Cape Town, watched by millions on television throughout the world.

1990 James 'Buster' Douglas, after being floored in the eighth round, got up after a controversial late count by the referee, and two rounds later knocked out the world heavyweight champion, Mike Tyson. The shock win in Tokyo was temporarily overuled because of the late count, but a few days later Douglas was declared the official victor.

12 FEBRUARY

BORN THIS DAY

HISTORY

1588 John Winthrop, Puritan and lawyer, the first Governor of the Massachusetts Bay Company.

1663 Cotton Mather, American writer and Puritan. He was the Congregational minister associated with the Massachusetts witch trials.

1809 Abraham Lincoln, 16th President of the US, who tried to preserve the Union during the Civil War having proclaimed freedom for slaves in 1863. His Gettysburg Address declared that 'all men are created equal'.

1893 Omar (Nelson) Bradley, US general and commander who led the US First Army's invasion of France during the Second World War.

ARTS

1567 Thomas Campion, English composer, lawyer and physician.

1828 George Meredith, English novelist, poet and critic, author of *The Egoist* (1879).

1898 Roy Harris, US composer of 11 symphonies and other works. He became composer in residence at the University of California.

ENTERTAINMENT

1870 Marie Lloyd (Matilda Alice Victoria Wood), probably the finest English music hall star. She made her name with slightly risqué comedy and songs such as 'My Old Man's a Dustman', but because her private life scandalized society (she was twice divorced on the grounds of adultery), she was never invited to appear at a Royal Command Performance.

1923 Franco Zeffirelli, Italian director of films, opera and plays.

NATURAL HISTORY

1637 Jan Swammerdam, Dutch naturalist who was the first to observe and describe the red blood cells.

1809 Charles Darwin, naturalist and author of *The Origin of Species* (1859) which formulated his theory of evolution and natural selection. These were based on his period as a naturalist on the HMS *Beagle* exploring South America and the Galapagos Islands. It aroused passionate resentment well into the 20th century from those who thought it anti-God to propose that man evolved from the apes.

DIED THIS DAY

1553 Lady Jane Grey, the queen who reigned only nine days. She was executed at Tower Hill, London for high treason, by her rival claimant to the throne, Mary.

1804 Immanuel Kant, German philosopher.

1894 Hans Guido von Bülow, German conductor.

1929 Lillie Langtry (Emilie Charlotte Le Breton), English actress. A vicar's daughter from Jersey, she was nicknamed 'Jersey Lily' because of her complexion.

1976 Sal Mineo, US actor, murdered on a street near his Los Angeles home. One of the films he appeared in was *Crime on the Streets* (1956).

1985 Henry Hathaway, US film director of *True Grit* (1969).

1986 Frank Herbert, science-fiction writer.

1987 Lorne Green, Canadian-born film and television actor best remembered for his part in the long-running television western series, *Bonanza*.

ON THIS DAY

1688 The conclusion of the 'Glorious Revolution'. James II fled with his family to France, and the Prince of Orange and Princess Mary were declared King and Queen of England, France and Ireland.

1818 Chile's independence was proclaimed in Santiago.

1831 Rubber galoshes were first marketed by J. W. Goodrich, Boston.

1851 A discovery at Summerhill Creek in New South Wales, Australia, set off a gold rush.

1861 The first inter-club football match was held at Sheffield between Sheffield and Hallam. It was also the first time admission charges were made.

1887 Alexander Graham Bell's 'articulating' telephone was demonstrated between Boston and Salem.

1898 Henry Lindfield of Brighton, Sussex, became the first British motorist to be killed in a car crash as a result of a steering failure, near Croydon, Surrey. Lindfield died of shock following a leg amputation.

1912 China became a republic with the overthrow of the Manchu dynasty.

1924 Howard Carter, having discovered the tomb of Tutankhamun 12 months before, lifted the lid off the sarcophagus to reveal a golden effigy of the young king. There was also a small wreath of flowers which still retained their original colours.

1954 The British Standing Advisory Committee on cancer claimed that the illness had a definite link with cigarette smoking.

1990 Dr Carmen Lawrence became the first woman Premier of an Australian state, three years after taking her seat in the Western Australian Parliament.

13 FEBRUARY

BORN THIS DAY

HISTORY

1728 John Hunter, Scottish physiologist, surgeon and dentist who wrote a treatise on 'Blood and Gunshot Wounds' and made important discoveries concerning arteries.

1849 Lord Randolph Henry Spencer Churchill, British Conservative politician who became Chancellor of the Exchequer in 1886. He later resigned over policy disagreements, and a sudden illness caused serious mental disabilities, forcing him to resign his seat in 1894. He had only a year to live. He married American Jennie Jerome in 1874.

ARTS

1873 Fedor (Ivanovich) Chaliapin, Russian operatic bass, who was considered one of the greatest ever.

1903 Georges Simenon (Georges Sim) Belgium-born prolific crime novelist and creator of Maigret. Simenon, who could turn out a novel in under two weeks, claimed to have made love to over 10,000 women.

ENTERTAINMENT

1933 Kim Novak (Marilyn Pauline Novak), glamorous US film actress who appeared in *Picnic* (1956).

1934 George Segal, US film actor who was nominated for an Oscar for best supporting actor in *Who's Afraid of Virginia Woolf?* (1966), and starred in many comedies, including *A Touch of Class* (1973).

1938 Oliver Reed, English film actor, nephew of film director Sir Carol Reed. A former bouncer and boxer, he made his name as Bill Sykes in *Oliver* (1968) and also appeared in *Women in Love* (1969).

POP

1950 Peter Gabriel, English pop musician. Originally lead singer with Genesis, he went solo in 1975.

DIED THIS DAY

1542 Catherine Howard, Henry VIII's fifth wife. Accused of adultery, she was executed on Tower Green.

1571 Benvenuto Cellini, Italian sculptor and goldsmith.

1728 Cotton Mather, American writer and Puritan, the day after his 65th birthday.

1883 Richard Wagner, German composer, of a heart attack in Venice.

1958 Dame Christabel Pankhurst, English suffragette.

1958 Georges Rouault, French Expressionist painter.

1979 Jean Renoir, French film maker, son of the painter.

ON THIS DAY

1668 Portugal's independence was recognized by Spain.

1689 William III and Mary II ascended the throne and would reign as British King and Queen until 27 December 1694. (*See* 11.4.1689)

1692 The massacre of the Macdonalds at Glencoe in Scotland was carried out by English forces lead by John Campbell, Earl of Breadalbane.

1793 Britain, Prussia, Austria, Holland, Spain and Sardinia formed an alliance against France.

1832 The first cases of Asiatic influenza were reported at Limehouse and Rotherhithe in London.

1854 Britain's first public school for girls, the Cheltenham Ladies College, was opened.

1866 The James-Younger gang carried out their first bank robbery in Liberty, Missouri. Jesse James was just 19.

1917 Mata Hari was arrested by the French for spying.

1920 Switzerland was admitted to the League of Nations.

1943 The Nuffield Foundation was established by Lord Nuffield (William Morris, the English motor car manufacturer) and became Britain's biggest charitable trust.

1945 1400 RAF and 450 US Airforce planes bombed Dresden in three waves over a 14-hour period, devastating one of the world's most beautiful cities.

1948 The Science Museum in London announced that it would return the

Wright Brothers' biplane, Kitty Hawk, the first to fly, to the Smithsonian Institution. It had been sent to England in 1928 by Orville Wright when he found that the Smithsonian had labelled another plane as the first capable of sustained flight.

1954 'Why could not mother die?' wrote a 16-year-old New Zealand schoolgirl in her diary. Then on 23 July, Pauline Yvonne Parker, with her close friend, Juliet Hulme, used a brick wrapped in a stocking to club Mrs Parker to death. It seemed her mother had been concerned at the intimate relationship between the two girls. They were found guilty, but were too young to be hanged and were detained 'at her Majesty's pleasure' until 1958.

1969 An announcement stated that eggs removed from a woman volunteer had been fertilized in a test tube as a result of work done at Cambridge University in collaboration with Dr P. Steptoe at Oldham General Hospital.

1971 US Vice President Spiro Agnew hit three spectators with his first two shots in the Bob Hope Desert Classic golf match.

1974 Alexander Solzhenitsyn, author of *The Cancer Ward* (1968) and Nobel prize winner, was expelled from the Soviet Union following internment in labour camps.

1987 London's property boom resulted in a 5ft 6in x 11ft broom cupboard opposite Harrods being offered for sale at £36,500 – over £600 per square foot.

1989 Pakistan cricketer Shoaib Mohammed scored the second slowest 150 in cricket history, taking 11½ hours to reach 159 not out against New Zealand at Wellington.

14 FEBRUARY

The Feast Day of Valentine, patron saint of lovers, probably based on a pagan holiday to honour Pan and Juno that fell on this day.

BORN THIS DAY

HISTORY

1766 Thomas Robert Malthus, English economist and author of *An Essay on the Principles of Population* (1798), which saw famine, disease and disaster as a method of controlling the earth's fast-growing population.

1912 Juan Pujol Garcia, Spanish wartime double agent codenamed 'Garbo' by MI5 (who got him an MBE for his services) and 'Arabel' by the Germans (who gave him an Iron Cross). His activities saved thousands of Allied lives. He died sometime in October 1988 leaving behind one unsolved mystery. As a friend of the English traitor Blunt, was he also working for the Russians?

1944 Carl Bernstein, US journalist who with Bob Woodward exposed the Watergate scandal and co-authored the award-winning *All the President's Men* (1976).

ENTERTAINMENT

1894 Jack Benny (Benjamin Kubelsky), US comedian who failed as a violin player until he decided to incorporate his act in comedy. He became a major performer on radio, then television, aided and abetted by a black valet, Eddie 'Rochester' Anderson.

1944 Alan Parker, English film director of the gangster spoof *Bugsy Malone* played by youngsters dressed in 30s costumes. Parker's birthday falls on the same date as the famous Chicago gangster massacre (*see* ON THIS DAY).

INVENTION

1819 Christopher Latham Scholes, US inventor of the modern typewriter.

SPORT

1907 John Longden, US jockey, in Wakefield, Yorkshire.
1951 Kevin Keegan, Liverpool and England international footballer.

DIED THIS DAY

1400 Richard II, the deposed English king, starved himself to death on or about this day in Pontefract Castle, where he had been imprisoned.
1525 Fiorenzo di Lorenzo, Italian painter.
1779 Captain James Cook, British explorer, murdered by natives in Owyhee (Hawaii). When Cook first came ashore, the chiefs believed he was the incarnation of the great god of the elements. He set sail, but when he had to return due to a storm which broke his mast, doubts set in and he was clubbed, knifed and then held under water in a frenzied attack.
1891 William (Tecumseh) Sherman, Union general and US Civil War military commander.
1975 Sir P(elham) G(ranville) 'Plum' Wodehouse, English-born writer of humorous 'Jeeves' novels and musicals, in the US.
1975 Sir Julian Sorell Huxley, biologist and philosopher.
1990 Norman Parkinson (Smith), English fashion and portraiture photographer, in Singapore.

ON THIS DAY

1477 Margery Brews sent a letter to John Paston in Norfolk, addressed 'To my right welbelovyd Voluntyne', probably the world's first known Valentine.
1797 The Spanish fleet were defeated off Cape St Vincent by Admiral John Jervis and Captain Horatio Nelson who subsequently became a British national hero for his part in the action.
1852 London's famous children's hospital in Great Ormond Street accepted its first patient, three-and-a-half-year-old Eliza Armstrong.
1893 Hawaii was annexed by the US on the 114th anniversary of Captain Cook's death.
1894 The planet Venus became both a morning and evening star this day by rising 43 minutes before the Sun, and setting 43 minutes after it.
1895 The first night in London of *The Importance of Being Earnest* by Oscar Wilde.
1912 Yuan Shi-kai became the first president of the Chinese republic.
1922 Marconi began regular broadcasting transmissions from Essex, England.
1929 'The St Valentine's Day Massacre' took place, when seven members of George 'Bugs' Moran's gang were 'rubbed out' at 10.30 a.m. in a Chicago garage. The Al Capone gang was suspected of the killings.
1939 The German 35,000 ton battleship, *Bismarck* was launched.
1946 The Bank of England was nationalized.
1946 At the University of Pennsylvania, IBM began operating its computer

using 18,000 electronic valves.

1956 Nikita Kruschev denounced the policies of Joseph Stalin at the 20th Soviet Communist Party Conference.

1963 Harold Wilson became leader of the British Labour Party.

1984 Britain's Torvill and Dean skated their way to a Gold at the Winter Olympics in Sarajevo, getting maximum points for artistic expression.

1989 The spiritual leader of Iran, Ayotollah Khomeini, condemned Salman Rushdie's award-winning novel, *The Satanic Verses* as an insult to Islam and issued a *fatwa* (edict) calling on Muslims to kill the author for committing blasphemy. Rushdie and his family went into hiding.

1989 Skyphone, the world's first satellite telephone service, was launched on the British Airway's 14.00hrs flight from London to New York. The cost of a call was from $9.50 (£5.47).

15 FEBRUARY

BORN THIS DAY

HISTORY

1519 Pedro Menedez de Aviles, Spanish navigator and explorer who established Florida as a Spanish colony.

1710 Louis XV, King of France who concerned himself more with his mistresses, Madame Pompadour and Madame du Barry, losing both Canada and India to the British.

1748 Jeremy Bentham, English philosopher and founder of utilitarianism who believed that the object of legislation should be to bring 'the greatest happiness to the greatest number'. The French Republic made him a citizen in 1792.

1812 Charles Lewis Tiffany, US jeweller, founder of the famous New York shop.

1845 Elihu Root, US Secretary of State, and winner of the Nobel Peace prize in 1912 for advocating an international organization to avoid wars. The League of Nations, however, was a world war away.

1874 Sir Ernest Shackleton, British Antarctic explorer, in Ireland. He went on Scott's original expedition in 1901–4 before leading his own in 1907, which got within a short distance of the South Pole.

ENTERTAINMENT

1882 John Barrymore (Blythe), US actor, the younger brother of Ethel and Lionel. His great profile often resulted in him being cast in romantic roles in films such as *Don Juan* (1926).

1931 Claire Bloom (Blume), English stage and film actress who played Ophelia at Stratford-upon-Avon before also going into films such as *Limelight* (1952) and *The Spy who Came in From the Cold* (1972).

1951 Jane Seymour, English film actress who first made her name as a James Bond girl in *Live and Let Die* (1973).

SCIENCE

1564 Galileo Galilei, Italian astronomer and mathematician. The Inquisition made him recant his observation that the world revolved around the sun, considered as heresy by the Church.

INVENTION

1809 Cyrus Hall McCormick, US engineer and inventor of the first practical mechanical harvester.

SPORT

1929 Graham Hill, British world motor racing champion, who was also the first man to win the daunting Indianapolis 500 on his first attempt.

DIED THIS DAY

1744 John Hadley, English inventor of the sextant.

1918 Vernon Castle, US dancer who partnered his wife Irene, in a plane crash in Houston, Texas.

1928 Herbert Henry Asquith, Earl of Oxford and leader of the British Liberal Party and Prime Minister, 1908–16.

1965 Nat King Cole (Nathaniel Adams Cole), US singer and pianist, of cancer.

1970 Lord Dowding, British air chief marshal and Commander-in-Chief of Fighter Command during the Battle of Britain.

ON THIS DAY

1882 The first cargo of frozen meat left New Zealand bound for Britain on the SS *Dunedin*.

1898 The US sent their battleship *Maine* to Havana on a goodwill mission, but in the harbour she struck a mine and sank; it was enough to spark off the Spanish-American War.

1913 Sir Barry Jackson opened the first repertory theatre at Birmingham with *Twelfth Night*.

1922 The first session of the Permanent Court of International Justice in the Hague was held.

1933 An attempt by an Italian-born anarchist, Giuseppe Zangara to assassinate US President F. D. Roosevelt failed.

1942 The Japanese captured Singapore.

1944 Allied bombing of Monte Casino monastery began.

1945 British troops reached the Rhine.

1971 Britain went decimal. Out went old pennies and half crowns.

1974 The battle for the Golan Heights between Israeli and Syrian forces began.

1982 A violent storm off Newfoundland wrecked an oil rig killing 84 people.

16 FEBRUARY

BORN THIS DAY

ARTS

1884 Robert Flaherty, documentary film maker who made the classic *Nanook of the North* (1922).

1922 Sir Geraint Evans, Welsh operatic baritone, famous for his roles as Falstaff, Figaro and Papageno.

1943 Anthony Dowell, English dancer, now director of the Royal Ballet.

ENTERTAINMENT

1926 John Schlessinger, award-winning English film director who has a list of highly acclaimed features to his credit including *A Kind of Loving* (1962), *Midnight Cowboy* (1969) and *Sunday, Bloody Sunday* (1971).

POP

1920 Patty Andrews, member of one of the first female singing groups, the legendary Andrews Sisters.

1935 Sonny (Salvatore) Bono, one-time singing partner and former husband of Cher. One of their hits was 'I've Got You Babe'.

SPORT

1959 John McEnroe, US international tennis champion, a temperamental but highly talented player who won his first Wimbledon title from Bjorn Borg when he was just 22 years old.

DIED THIS DAY

1754 Richard Mead, English doctor, physician to George II, who promoted inoculation for smallpox.

1834 Lionel Lukin, English inventor of the modern lifeboat.

ON THIS DAY

1659 The first British cheque was written by Nicholas Vanacker and is now in the archives of the National Westminster Bank.

1801 Pitt (the Younger) resigned as British Prime Minister when George III rejected his plans for the emancipation of Irish Catholics.

1887 To celebrate Queen Victoria's Jubilee, 25,000 prisoners in India were set free.

1932 The *Fianna Fail* party led by Eamon de Valera, won the Irish General Election.

1937 Dr Corothers and his US research team patented nylon.

1940 In a daring night raid, a boarding party from HMS *Cossack* successfully rescued over 300 British prisoners from the *Altmark*, a 12,000-ton German tanker in Norwegian waters. The prisoners had all been taken from ships sunk by the *Graf Spee*.

1945 US forces captured Bataan in the Philippines.

1959 Fidel Castro, aged 30, became president of Cuba after the constitution had been amended to lower the age of qualification.

1960 The first nuclear submarine to travel around the world under the sea, the US *Triton* began its journey.

1983 Fires started in South Australia in temperatures over 110°F. Arson was suspected as they grew and spread, destroying homes and livestock. Over 8,500 were left homeless, 200,000 sheep were burnt to death and damage was estimated at around £500m.

1987 The trial of John Demanjanuk, a 66-year-old Ukrainian who had settled in Ohio after the Second World War, began in Israel. Allegedly 'Ivan the Terrible', once a guard at the Treblinka death camp, he had been extradited by the US. He claimed it was a case of mistaken identity.

1989 Dr Raymond Crockett, a Harley Street nephrologist resigned as the director of the National Kidney Centre after revelations that kidneys had been purchased from impoverished Turks to be used in transplants for wealthy patients.

17 FEBRUARY

BORN THIS DAY

HISTORY

1929 Yasser Arafat, co-founder of *al-Fatah* and President of the Palestine Liberation Organization from 1969.

ARTS

1864 Andrew Barton 'Banjo' Paterson, Australian folk poet and journalist. He was a war correspondent during the Boer War for Australian newspapers. His popular verses included 'Waltzing

Matilda', which he adapted from a traditional source.

1902 Marian Anderson, US contralto; the first black singer at the New York Metropolitan. She also sang at the inauguration of President John F. Kennedy.

1923 Dr John Allegro, English scholar and author of the controversial *The Sacred Mushroom* (1970) in which he suggested that all religions are based on anxiety about fertility, and that there was evidence that ancient religions used hallucinatory drugs derived from mushrooms in their rites.

ENTERTAINMENT

1934 Alan Bates, English actor who made his stage debut in 1955. His films include *Women in Love* (1970) and *The Go-Between* (1971).

1934 Barry Humphries, Australian actor, creator of Dame Edna Everidge, international celebrity and chat show hostess, and Les Patterson, Australian 'Minister of Culture'.

INVENTION

1781 René Laënnec, French army doctor and inventor of the stethoscope.

1856 Frederick Eugene Ives, US inventor of the half-tone printing process, enabling pictures and photographs to be printed.

SPORT

1740 Horace Benédict de Saussure, Swiss traveller who was the first to promote the idea of climbing Mont Blanc. He was eventually beaten by his rival Paccard, who had the help of a guide, Balmat, in August 1786.

DIED THIS DAY

1405 Tamerlane (Timur) the Great, Mongol leader.

1673 Molière (Jean Baptiste Poquelin), French playwright and actor. He collapsed on stage on the third night of his play, *Le Malade imaginaire* (The Imaginary Invalid) and died at his home the same night from a haemorrhage as a result of a burst blood vessel.

1856 Johann Heinrich Heine, German poet.

1890 Christopher Latham Scholes, US modern typewriter inventor.

1909 Geronimo, 'One Who Yawns', the last of the Apaches, in custody at Forest Still, Oklahoma.

1968 Sir Donald Wolfit, English actor-manager.

1980 Graham Sutherland, English painter.

1982 Lee Strasburg, US actor and founder of the Actor's Studio.

1982 Thelonius Monk, US jazz pianist.

ON THIS DAY

1818 Baron Karl von Drais de Sauerbrun patented the 'Draisine', the forerunner of the bicycle which he exhibited in Paris that April.

1864 The US corvette *Houstanic* was sunk in Charleston harbour by the Confederate submarine *Hunley* armed with a ram torpedo. The small hand-propelled submarine was the first to use a torpedo to sink a ship and was blown up by the force.

1880 A bomb exploded in an attempt to assassinate the Tsar of Russia, Alexander II, in his Winter Palace in St Petersburg.

1883 Mr A. Ashwell of Herne Hill, south

London, patented Vacant/Engaged signs for toilet doors.

1938 A surprise item at the Dominion Theatre, London; the first public experimental demonstration of Baird colour television on a big 12ft x 9ft screen. Transmitted from Crystal Palace, the short programme consisted of fashion plates and a cartoon.

1968 One of the greatest Alpine skiers ever, Austrian Jean-Claude Killy won three Gold medals at the Winter Olympics, Grenoble.

1972 The British parliament voted to join the European Common Market.

1972 Volkswagen motor cars broke the record held by the Model T. Ford by selling the 15,007,034th production model of the Beetle.

1987 A group of male Tamils stripped to their underwear at London's Heathrow Airport in an attempt to prevent their return to Sri Lanka.

18 FEBRUARY

BORN THIS DAY

HISTORY

1517 Mary I, Queen of England, 'Bloody Mary' or 'Mary Tudor', daughter of Henry VIII and Catharine of Aragon.

1892 Wendell Lewis Wilkie, US politician who stood against Roosevelt for President. He was against US isolationism and made many trips to Europe on behalf of the President who defeated him in 1940.

1922 Sir Eric Gairy, Prime Minister of Grenada whose autocratic rule was eventually ended by a bloodless coup.

1922 Helen Gurley Brown, US magazine editor who established *Cosmopolitan* as a leading international journal.

ARTS

1784 Nicolo Paganini, Italian violin virtuoso and composer. Considered the greatest violinist ever, he was a great showman demonstrating his skill with outrageously difficult compositions such as *The Witches' Dance*. He was also an innovator introducing new tuning and bowing techniques.

1894 Andres Segovia, virtuoso Spanish classical guitarist who was responsible for the revival of interest in the instrument. Special works were composed for him by Falla and others.

1896 André Breton, French founder of the Surrealist movement.

1929 Len Deighton, English novelist who was previously a member of the RAF Special Investigation Branch, an airline steward and an around-the-world navigator. His first book, *The Ipcress File* (1962) had difficulty in finding a publisher, but its success prompted further spy stories such as *Funeral in Berlin* (1964) and *The Million Dollar Brain* (1966).

ENTERTAINMENT

1915 Phyllis Calvert (Phyllis Bickle), English stage and screen actress best remembered for her role in *The Man in Grey* (1943).

1919 Jack Palance (Walter Palahnuik), US film actor. Plastic surgery following a bomber crash during the Second World War gave him his distinctive features which he put to good use in *Sudden Fear* (1952) and *Shane* (1953), both of which won him Oscar nominations for best supporting actor.

1931 Ned Sherrin, English writer, producer and presenter who was involved in the renaissance of the British satirical scene in the 60s with the innovative television programme *That Was The Week That Was*.

1932 Milos Forman, Czechoslovakian-born US film director. His major success was *One Flew Over the Cuckoo's Nest* (1975), which won five Oscars including best director.

1954 John Travolta, US actor who made his name in the film *Saturday Night Fever* (1977).

SCIENCE

EPONYMS Two scientists, both born this day, have scientific terms derived from their surnames. 1754, Count Alessandro Volta, Italian physicist who made the first battery and gave his name to the measure of the power of electricity (volt). 1838, Ernst Mach, Austrian physicist who researched airflow. Mach numbers, indicate air speed (Mach 1 is the speed at which an aircraft breaks the sound barrier).

POP

1933 Yoko Ono Lennon, Japanese avant-garde artist, writer, performer and peace campaigner who became John Lennon's second wife. She also recorded several songs with him and with the Plastic Ono Band.

SPORT

1898 Enzo Ferrari, legendary Italian sports car builder and motor racing pioneer, who began as a test driver for Alfa Romeo before starting his own company. His racing team scored over 4,000 wins, 93 of them in Grand Prix, as well as 13 world titles.

1933 Bobby Robson, England football manager.

DIED THIS DAY

1455 Fra Angelico (Giovanni da Fiesole), Italian painter.

1478 George, Duke of Clarence, murdered in the Tower of London on the orders of his older brother, Richard, Duke of Gloucester. He was drowned in a butt of Malmsey wine.

1535 Heinrich Cornelius Agrippa (von Nettesheim), German scholar and astrologer who wrote books on the occult.

1546 Martin Luther, German leader of the Protestant Reformation.

1564 Michelangelo Buonarroti, Italian painter, sculptor, architect and engineer.

1833 (Wilhelm) Richard Wagner, German composer.

1855 Nicholas I, Tsar of Russia.

1933 James 'Gentleman Jim' Corbett, US prize fighter and world heavyweight champion from 1892 to 1897.

1967 (Jacob) Robert Oppenheimer, US physicist, 'father of the atomic bomb'.

ON THIS DAY

1678 *Pilgrim's Progress* was published. Bunyan began it during his second term in prison for preaching on behalf of the Baptists.

1876 A direct telegraph line was established between Britain and New Zealand.

1911 Over 6,000 letters and postcards were flown five miles from Allahabad to Naini Junction in India by Henri Pecquet – the first official airmail.

1930 At Lowell Observatory in the US,

Clyde Tombaugh discovered the planet Pluto as a result of a series of pictures taken the previous month.

1948 After 16 years as Irish Premier, Eamon de Valera lost his office due to discontent at the economic decline of the Republic.

1949 Mrs Durand-Deacon was shot through the back of the head in a storeroom she was taken to in Crawley, Sussex, by John George Haigh. Her body was submerged in a vat of acid and the slurry was later poured out into the yard, but traces of human remains were discovered. Haigh admitted she was his eighth victim for financial gain. He was hanged on 6 August.

1988 A thoroughbred, unbeaten female racing camel was sold by a breeder in Muscat for the equivalent of £85,000.

19 FEBRUARY

BORN THIS DAY

HISTORY

1960 Prince Andrew, second son of Queen Elizabeth II.

ARTS

1843 Adelina Patti, Italian soprano, the highest paid of her day. She was born in Spain, made her debut in New York (1850), gave her farewell concert in London (1906), retired to Craig-y-nos, her castle in Wales, and was buried in Paris.

1917 Carson McCullers, US novelist of *The Heart is a Lonely Hunter* (1940).

ENTERTAINMENT

1717 David Garrick, English actor, manager and dramatist who introduced a naturalistic style to acting. He made his debut at Goodman's Fields Theatre, London (19.10.1741) and later took over the Drury Lane Theatre, where his many innovations advanced theatrical style and production.

1893 Sir Cedric Hardwicke, English actor who, after a distinguished career on the British stage, went to Hollywood.

1911 Merle Oberon (Estelle Merle O'Brien Thompson), Tasmanian-born film actress discovered by Korda, whom she married and later divorced. She played Cathy Linton in *Wuthering Heights* (1939).

1924 Lee Marvin, US film actor who, despite being invalided out of the US Marines, specialized in tough guy parts. He won an Oscar for his role in *Cat Ballou* (1963).

SCIENCE

1473 Nicolas Copernicus (Mikolaj Kopernik), Polish astronomer who propounded the heliocentric theory of the Solar system; the Sun did not go around the Earth, we and the other planets went around it. Galileo would attract the displeasure of the Inquisition for promoting this idea a century later.

JAZZ

1912 Stan Kenton (Stanley Newcombe), US bandleader, composer and pianist. As well as hits like 'Peanut Vendor' and 'Artistry in Rhythm', he wrote music for the ballet *Homage to a Princess* which was performed at the wedding of Prince Rainier and Grace Kelly in Monaco in 1966.

POP

1960 Holly Johnson, front man of the pop group, 'Frankie Goes to Hollywood', in Khartoum.

DIED THIS DAY

1837 George Buchner, German poet and playwright of *Danton's Death* (1835) who also left an incomplete work, *Woyzeck* which was not produced until 1913, 100 years after his birth.

1897 Charles Blondin (Jean François Gravelet), French tight rope walker. (*See* 28.2.1824)

1951 André Gide, French novelist.

1952 Knut Hamsun (Pedersen), Norwegian novelist and poet.

1972 John Grierson, Scottish film maker, 'father of the documentary'.

1990 Michael Powell, English film director, producer and scriptwriter whose films include *The Battle of the River Plate* (1956).

ON THIS DAY

1800 Napoleon established himself as first Consul after overthrowing the French government. It made him a dictator.

1855 Bread riots took place in Liverpool.

1878 Thomas Alva Edison patented the phonograph two months after he first demonstrated the model (7.12.1877).

1897 Considered essentially English, the Women's Institute was actually founded this day in Ontario, Canada by Mrs Hoodless. A Mrs Watt introduced the WI to Britain during the First World War.

1906 William S. Kellogg formed the Battle Creek Toasted Cornflake Company to make a breakfast cereal he had invented for patients suffering from mental disorders.

1909 President Theodore Roosevelt called for a world conference on conservation.

1914 'Colonel Bogey March' was registered at the British Museum by its composers Kenneth J. Alford and F. J. Ricketts.

1922 When Ed Wynn's *The Perfect Fool* was broadcast in New York, a new sound was heard for the first time on radio – the studio audience.

1942 Japanese aircraft bombed Darwin, Australia.

1959 Cyprus's independence was guaranteed by an agreement signed between Britain, Turkey and Greece in London.

1975 The Queen knighted cricketer Gary Sobers on her visit to Barbados, the island of his birth.

1976 Iceland broke off diplomatic relations with Britain after the two countries failed to agree on limits in the 'cod war' fishing dispute.

1985 The first episode of the BBC soap opera, *EastEnders* was screened.

20 FEBRUARY

BORN THIS DAY

HISTORY

1904 Alexei Nikolayevich Kosygin, Russian Prime Minister from 1964, succeeding Khruschev. He resigned two months before his death in 1980.

ARTS

1694 Voltaire (François Marie Arouet de), French poet, playwright, historian, philosopher and opponent of intolerance, which led him to be twice imprisoned in the Bastille, and exiled three times. His work includes the satirical comedy *Candide* (1759).

1808 Honoré Daumier, (or 26.2.1808), French painter who produced some

4,000 lithographs and also drew biting caricatures of French society; Louis-Philippe had him jailed for one that attacked him.

1888 Dame Marie Rambert, founder of the Ballet Rambert, Britain's oldest ballet company.

ENTERTAINMENT

1892 Carl Mayer, German film director, best remembered for the classic silent film, *The Cabinet of Dr Caligari* (1919).

1925 Robert Altman, US film director who made his name directing the film *M*A*S*H* (1969).

1927 Sydney Poitier, the first black US film actor to win an Oscar, for *Lilies of the Field* (1963). His other films include *In the Heat of the Night* (1967).

SPORT

1940 Jimmy Greaves, English footballer. After his playing career ended, he became a successful television commentator.

DIED THIS DAY

1437 James I, King of Scotland, assassinated by a group of dissident nobles led by Sir Robert Graham who had previously tampered with the bolt on the door of the bedroom of the king in a Dominican monastery where he was residing. The murderers were later tortured to death.

1677 Baruch Spinoza, Dutch philosopher.

1707 Aurangzeb, the last Mogul emperor of India.

1920 Robert Peary, US Arctic explorer.

1960 Sir Leonard Woolley, English archaeologist who excavated Ur.

1961 Percy Grainger, Australian-born composer.

1966 Chester Nimitz, US admiral and Pacific Fleet commander in the Second World War.

1972 Walter Winchell, influential US journalist on the *New York Mirror* from 1929–69.

ON THIS DAY

1653 Admiral Blake defeated the Dutch Fleet under Van Tromp off Portsmouth.

1811 Austria informed the world she was bankrupt.

1817 An event at the Drury Lane Theatre indirectly affected American history. A promising young actor, Junius Brutus Booth, played Othello to Edmund Kean's Iago to see which of the two was the nation's finest actor. Booth patently failed to impress and retreated to the US. Here, his sons became leading actors. The younger, John Wilkes Booth, also became Lincoln's assassin.

1861 Violent storms hit England. Crystal Palace was damaged and the steeple was blown off Chichester cathedral.

1938 Anthony Eden resigned as British Foreign Secretary, no longer able to support Prime Minister Baldwin's appeasement policies.

1947 Lord Louis Mountbatten was appointed the last Viceroy of India, the same day London announced that the British would leave India by June 1948.

1962 Colonel John Glenn in the Mercury capsule *Friendship 7*, became the first American to orbit the earth three times before making a safe splashdown in the sea.

1971 Major General Idi Amin promoted

himself to General and President of Uganda.

1982 US entrepreneur John de Lorean's luxury sports car project in Belfast set up with over £17m of British taxpayers money, went into receivership. On his return to the US he was asked bluntly, 'Are you a con man?'

1985 The Irish Republic made the sale of contraceptives legal for the first time.

1988 Torrential rain in Rio de Janeriro caused flooding and severe damage. Over 10,000 were reported homeless and around 500 dead.

21 FEBRUARY

BORN THIS DAY

HISTORY

1728 Peter III, Tsar of Russia, who married the future Catherine the Great. Feeble-minded, he was soon deposed in favour of Catherine and murdered by her lover.

1794 Antonio López de Santa Anna, Mexican revolutionary and President, who won his country's freedom from Spain and later led the attack on the Alamo.

1801 John Henry, Cardinal Newman, English Roman Catholic who also wrote the hymn 'Lead kindly light' and the poem 'The Dream of Gerontius', which Elgar set to music.

1924 Robert (Gabriel) Mugabe, ZANU leader and the first Prime Minister of Zimbabwe (Rhodesia) after waging guerrilla warfare against the former regime.

ARTS

1836 (Clement Philibert) Léo Delibes, French composer best remembered for his ballet music for *Coppélia* (1870).

1903 Anaïs Nin, French author of *A Spy in the House of Love* (1954). She settled in New York and was closely involved in the literary and artistic scene there.

1907 W(ystan) H(ugh) Auden, US poet who was educated at Oxford.

1937 Jilly Cooper, English novelist and journalist.

ENTERTAINMENT

1879 Gertie Millar, English musical comedy actress, star of *The Quaker Girl* (1910), composed by her first husband, Lionel Monkton.

1885 Sacha Guitry, French actor, playwright and film director who began acting and writing in his teens. He was arrested after the Second World War as an alleged collaborator, but was later vindicated.

1903 Madeleine Renaud, French actress, wife of Jean-Louis Barrault with whom she co-directed their internationally famous stage company.

JAZZ

1934 Nina Simone, US jazz and soul singer.

SCIENCE

1866 August von Wasserman, German bacteriologist who made important advances in the diagnosis of syphilis.

DIED THIS DAY

1595 Robert Southwell, English poet and Jesuit martyr, hanged, drawn and quartered at Tyburn.

1741 Jethro Tull, English agricultural pioneer.

1852 Nikolai Gogol, Russian short story

writer, novelist and playwright, author of *Dead Souls*.

1941 Sir Frederick Banting, Canadian physiologist and joint Nobel prize winner with Charles Best for the discovery of insulin, killed in an air crash.

1965 Malcolm X (Malcolm Little), the Black Muslim leader, who believed black power would have to be achieved by violent struggle, shot dead in New York as he was about to address a meeting of his followers.

ON THIS DAY

1764 John Wilkes MP was expelled from the House of Commons for reprinting and publishing *The Essay on Women*, an 'impious libel'.

1858 The first electric burglar alarm was installed by Edwin T. Holmes of Boston, Mass.

1885 The 555ft high George Washington Memorial obelisk was inaugurated in Washington, DC.

1916 The Battle of Verdun began. It would last until December 16th.

1943 General Dwight D. Eisenhower became Supreme Commander of the Allied forces in North Africa.

1947 *A Woman to Remember*, the first televison soap opera, began in the US.

1969 A device to monitor the function of the human heart was granted a patent. The inventor was 'Sa Majeste H, Roi du Maroc II', King Hussan of Morocco. This was the first patent granted by the US Patents Office to a king.

1973 Israel shot down a Libyan airliner, killing 74 people for failing to land after it overflew an Israeli military airfield in the Sinai.

1975 Former US Attorney-General John Mitchell, Chief-of-Staff H. R. Haldeman, and domestic advisor John Erlichman were given prison sentences for trying to obstruct the course of justice in the Watergate Affair.

1988 The grave of Boadicea, the warrior queen who fought the Romans in Britain nearly 2,000 years ago, was located by archaeologists under Platform 8 at King's Cross railway station, London. British Rail said they had just refurbished the platform and anyone wanting to dig it up would have to come up with a strong case.

1989 Two members of Winnie Mandela's bodyguard, the so-called Mandela Football Club, were charged with the abduction, assault and murder in Soweto of 14-year-old Stompie Mocketsi.

22 FEBRUARY

BORN THIS DAY

HISTORY

NEW WORLDS **The man who gave his name to the New World, and the man who became its first President, share the same anniversary. Italian navigator, Amerigo Vespucci died this day, 1512. On the same day in 1732 George Washington was born in Virginia. He became President in 1789.**

1857 Sir Robert (Stephenson Smyth) Baden-Powell, English hero of the siege of Mafeking during the Boer War. His innovative approach to the situation kept morale high and his experiences led to the founding of the Boy Scouts. His daughter, Lady Olave St Clair Baden-Powell, Chief Guide from

1930, was born on his 32nd birthday in 1889.

1932 Senator Edward Kennedy, US senator, John F.Kennedy's younger brother who lost the chance to be nominated for president first in 1972, and later in 1980 because of his involvement in the Chappaquidick island car accident in which Mary Jo Kopechne was drowned (18.7.1969).

1933 The Duchess of Kent (Katharine Worsley) wife of Edward, second Duke of Kent.

ARTS

1788 Artur Schopenhauer, German philosopher whose pessimistic view of life was reflected in his writings.

1872 Eric Gill, English artist and propagandist for the revival of craftsmanship.

1908 H(erbert) E(atton) Todd, English writer of children's books, creator of Bobby Brewster, and was also sales manager for a shoe manufacturer.

ENTERTAINMENT

1900 Luis Buñuel, surrealist Spanish film director whose first film *Le Chien Andalou* (1928), ran for 24 minutes. Co-scripted and directed by Salvador Dali, it included a scene of a young woman's eyeball being slashed.

1907 Robert Young, US actor, best known for his leading role in the television series *Marcus Welby, M.D.*

1908 Sir John Mills, English actor and former chorus boy, who made his film debut in 1932. His memorable films include *Great Expectations* (1946), *Hobson's Choice* (1954) and *Ryan's Daughter* (1970), for which he won an Oscar.

1926 Kenneth Williams, English comedy actor with a rich, nasal voice and camp style, who appeared in 22 'Carry On' films.

1928 Bruce Forsythe, British entertainer who made his name compering television's *Sunday Night at the London Palladium.*

1933 Sheila Hancock, English actress who established herself on TV in *The Rag Trade.*

1950 Julie Walters, English comedy actress who made her name in *Educating Rita* (1983).

SCIENCE

1857 Heinrich Rudolph Hertz, German physicist who discovered radio waves (electromagnetic waves), and has his name on just about every radio set, if only in an abbreviated form: 'MHz' (Megahertz), an FM waveband measurement.

SPORT

1949 Niki Lauda, Austrian motor racing driver who was world champion three times.

DIED THIS DAY

1903 Hugo Wolf, Austrian composer who was confined to a mental asylum when venereal disease affected his mind. Believed to be cured, he was released, but in October 1902 he tried to drown himself. He was returned to the asylum where he died.

1973 Elizabeth (Dorothea Cole) Bowen, Irish novelist whose books include *The Death of the Heart* (1938).

1989 Aldo Joseph Jaccuzzi, US whirlpool pump manufacturer.

ON THIS DAY

1797 The French landed in Britain at Fishguard, but were soon captured and no other foreign force has managed to invade Britain since.

1819 Spain ceded Florida to the US.

1847 The Mexicans were defeated at the Battle of Buena Vista by the American forces under General Taylor.

1862 Jefferson Davis was inaugurated as President of the Confederate States of America.

1879 Frank Winfield Woolworth opened his first 'five and ten cent' store in Utica, New York.

1886 *The Times* ran the first ever classified personal column.

1946 Dr Selman Abraham Waksman announced his discovery of streptomycin.

1956 The first football match to be played under floodlighting in Britain took place at Portsmouth. The home side lost 2–0 to Newcastle United.

1989 The Finnish Health Ministry proposed that people suffering from stress should be given 'sex holidays, when they would be able to forget their worries and concentrate on recuperating in an erotic atmosphere'.

23 FEBRUARY

BORN THIS DAY

ARTS

1633 Samuel Pepys, English civil servant attached to the Navy office whose famous diary was written in a form of shorthand.

1685 George Frederick Handel, German composer who came to England in 1711 to present his opera *Rinaldo*. He continued to work in England, where he wrote the *Water Music* for a river procession by George I.

1817 Sir George (Frederick) Watts, Victorian English painter whose sentimental compositions were immensely popular. His marriage to actress Ellen Terry lasted only a year.

1899 Erich Kästner, German author of the famous children's book, *Emil and the Detectives*.

ENTERTAINMENT

1883 Victor Fleming, US film director, best remembered for *The Wizard of Oz* (1939).

1929 Leslie Halliwell, English writer on films and television.

BUSINESS

1743 Meyer Amschel Rothschild, German founder of the banking dynasty.

DIED THIS DAY

1468 Johannes Gutenberg, German inventor of printing using movable type.

1792 Sir Joshua Reynolds, English painter and first President of the Royal Academy, where he lay in state in the Great Room before being buried in St Paul's.

1821 John Keats, English poet, aged 25, of consumption, in Rome.

TWO OF A KIND Two US presidents died this day. In 1848, John Quincy Adams, sixth US President, and, in 1924, Thomas Woodrow Wilson, 28th US president and a founder of the League of Nations.

1855 Karl Friedrich Gauss, German mathematician and astronomer.

1900 William Butterfield, English architect largely responsible for the Gothic revival in Britain.

1931 Dame Nellie Melba (Helen Porter Mitchell), Australian diva.

1934 Sir Edward Elgar, English composer.

1942 Austrian writer Stefan Zweig and his wife, exiled in Brazil, by suicide. It was said they feared the continuing world war would mean they would never return to their homeland.

1944 Leo Hendrik Baekland, Belgium-born US inventor of Bakelite.

1965 Stan Laurel (Arthur Stanley Jefferson), the thin partner of the famous film comedy duo, Laurel and Hardy.

1976 L(aurence) S(tephen) Lowry, English painter.

1983 Sir Adrian Boult, English conductor.

1987 Andy Warhol, American pop artist, film and myth maker.

ON THIS DAY

1732 Handel's *Oratorio* was performed for the first time at the Crown and Anchor Tavern, London on the composer's 47th birthday, and was the first oratorio ever performed in Britain.

1820 The Cato Street conspiracy to assassinate the British cabinet and Prime Minister Castlereagh was uncovered. It was planned by Arthur Thistlewood in a house in Cato Street, off Edgware Road, London, where he was arrested. Found guilty, he was imprisoned in the Tower, (the last prisoner ever held there) before being executed with other accomplices in May.

1836 The siege of the Alamo in San Antonio, Texas by the Mexican army under General Santa Anna began.

1863 Captains Speke and Grant announced the discovery of the source of the Nile.

1874 Major Walter Wingfield patented an outdoor game he called 'Sphairistike', later known as lawn tennis.

1898 Émile Zola was imprisoned following the publication of his *'J'accuse!'* letter, which accused the French government of anti-Semitism and wrongly imprisoning Captain Dreyfus.

1905 The Rotary Club was founded in Chicago.

1906 Johann Hoch was executed in Chicago for murdering six of his wives. He used to advertise for 'widows without children', and married 13 times. (*See* also 25.2.1922)

1915 French actress, Sarah Bernhardt, had her right leg amputated, but she was to be back on stage by November.

1917 The February Revolution began in Russia.

1919 Benito Mussolini founded the Fascist Party in Italy.

1920 The first regular broadcasting service in Britain started from Marconi's studio in Chelmsford; the 30-minute programme was transmitted twice daily.

1945 The US forces raised the 'Stars and Stripes' on the island of Iwo Jima, only 750 flying miles from Tokyo, and within reach of the US bombers.

1981 It was announced that the heir to the British throne, Charles, Prince of Wales, would marry 19-year-old Lady Diana Spencer.

1981 Lt Colonel Antonio Tejero led a group of Civil Guards into the Spanish Cortes and fired shots into the ceiling of the parliament building in an attempted right-wing coup that was witnessed on television. That evening, a tough speech on television by King Carlos helped maintain Spain's new, fragile democracy.

24 FEBRUARY

BORN THIS DAY

HISTORY

1885 Chester Nimitz, US admiral and commander of the Pacific Fleet during the Second World War.

ARTS

1786 Wilhelm Karl Grimm, German philologist and collector, with his brother Jacob, of fairytales.

1852 George Moore, Irish novelist, playwright and critic, who wrote *Confessions of a Young Man* (1888).

1858 Arnold Dolmetsch, Swiss musical instrument maker and restorer, born in Le Mans, who set up shop in Haslemere, Surrey, and established an annual festival to encourage the playing of old and authentic musical instruments.

1932 Michel Legrand, French composer and conductor, known mostly for his many film scores such as *The Summer of '42* (1971), which won him an Oscar.

ENTERTAINMENT

1948 Dennis Waterman, English actor who began his career as a child actor in musicals before playing the lead on television in *Just William*. As an adult, he established himself in the successful television series *The Sweeney* and *Minder*.

SPORT

1931 Brian Close, former England cricket captain.

1940 Dennis Law, Scottish international footballer.

1955 Alain Prost, French world motor racing champion in 1985 and 1986.

POP

1942 Paul Jones (Paul Pond), who began as the lead singer with Manfred Mann in the early 60s.

DIED THIS DAY

1563 Francis, Duc de Guise, French military commander, killed by a Huguenot whilst besieging Orleans.

1810 Henry Cavendish, English physicist, discoverer of hydrogen and other gases.

1815 Robert Fulton, US engineer, submarine designer and inventor of the steam boat.

1825 Thomas Bowdler, expurgator of the 'naughty bits' in the works of Shakespeare, who gave the English language the word 'bowdlerized'.

1927 Sir Edward Marshall Hall, English lawyer who handled some of the most sensational cases of his time.

1945 Ahmed Pasha, Egyptian Prime Minister, assassinated.

1975 Nikolai Bulganin, Soviet Prime Minister 1955–8.

1987 Memphis Slim (Peter Chatman), US blues singer and songwriter, in Paris.

1990 Malcolm Forbes, US tycoon and owner of Forbes magazine.

ON THIS DAY

AD303 The persecution of the Christians officially began in Rome with the issuing of an edict by Galerius Valerius Maximianus.

1582 Pope Gregory XIII announced the

introduction of the new Gregorian calendar (in use to this day) which replaced the Julian calendar. It took Britain almost 200 years to follow suit, and as a result the year of its adoption, 1752, consisted of only 354 days – 11 days had to be deducted!

TELEPHONE LINES In 1887 the first two cities to be linked by telephone were Paris and Brussels, while in 1902, the London Telephone Service invited subscribers to join their system.

1920 The National Socialist German Workers Party published its programme for the creation of the Third Reich. Their spokesman was a former Austrian postcard painter, Adolf Hitler.

1920 Lady Nancy Astor became the first woman to speak in the British Parliament. She opposed a motion for the abolition of the Liquor Control Board.

1923 The *Flying Scotsman* locomotive began hauling scheduled services between London and Scotland.

1932 Malcolm Campbell in *Bluebird* beat his own land speed record at Daytona Beach by reaching 253.96 m.p.h.

1938 A nylon toothbrush went on sale in New Jersey, the first nylon product ever. Exactly one year later, nylon stockings would make their first appearance in US shops.

1946 Juan Perón was elected President of Argentina.

1966 Dr Kwame Nkrumah, first President of Ghana, was exiled following an army coup.

1969 The unmanned *Mariner 6* was launched by the US to fly close to Mars.

HAPPY BIRTHDAY In 1988, the first baby born from an embryo frozen after the fertilization of a donated egg was delivered at Dulwich Hospital, south London, to Mrs Ann Forrester, 37, by Caesarian section. In 1989, an elephant calf was born to South Africa's last wild elephants, staving off extinction.

25 FEBRUARY

BORN THIS DAY

HISTORY

1778 José de San Martin, Argentinian revolutionary who played a major role in gaining independence not only for his own country, but also for Chile and Peru.

1888 John Foster Dulles, US diplomat and Secretary of State.

1922 Donald MacLean, Scottish potato expert who had the world's largest private collection of potatoes; 367 varieties from the remotest parts of the world.

ARTS

1707 Carlo Goldoni, Italian playwright who wrote over 200 plays, mostly comedies, although it was a tragedy, *Belisario* (1732), that was his first success.

1841 Pierre Auguste Renoir, French Impressionist painter of voluptuous female nudes who first painted porcelain and fans before turning to canvas.

1873 Enrico Caruso, Italian operatic tenor.

1890 Dame Myra Hess, English pianist who made her debut in 1907 under Sir Thomas Beecham.

1914 John Arlott, English cricket radio commentator, writer on the game and wine authority. His distinctive voice and masterly descriptions of cricket matches put him on a par with Cardus.

1917 Anthony Burgess (John Burgess Wilson), English novelist, screenwriter, composer, and critic who achieved his first major success with the novel *A Clockwork Orange* (1962), which was also made into a film.

ENTERTAINMENT

1901 Zeppo (Herbert) Marx, youngest of the famous Marx Brothers. He sang and played the bland juvenile role until he gave up performing to become their agent.

1913 (Karl-Gerhard) Gert Frobe, corpulent German actor, best remembered for his part as Goldfinger in the Bond movie of the same name.

1937 Tom Courtenay, English stage actor who has also appeared in films including *The Loneliness of the Long Distance Runner* (1962) and *The Dresser* (1987).

1941 David Puttnam, English film producer who was largely responsible for the artistic and commercial revival of the British film industry with such films as the award-winning *Chariots of Fire*.

POP

1943 George Harrison, former Beatle who became a film producer with Handmade Films.

DIED THIS DAY

1601 Robert Devereaux, Earl of Essex, English soldier executed for high treason after trying to raise the City of London against Queen Elizabeth's councillors.

1723 Sir Christopher Wren, English architect of many notable buildings, including St Paul's Cathedral where he was buried in the crypt.

1899 Paul Julius von Reuter, German-born founder of Reuters, the international news agency.

1914 Sir John Tenniel, English artist, illustrator of *Alice in Wonderland*.

1983 Tennessee (Thomas Lanier) Williams, US playwright who wrote several of the major plays of the last half of the century, including *A Streetcar Named Desire* (1947), in a New York hotel.

LAUGH AND CRY Larry Shay, the US songwriter who wrote the ever-popular 'When You're Smiling', in 1987, and in 1990, Johnny (John Alvin) Ray, US singer who made his name with songs like 'Cry' and 'The Little White Cloud That Cried'.

ON THIS DAY

1308 Edward II of England was crowned.

1570 Queen Elizabeth I was excommunicated by Pope Pius V who declared her a usurper.

1841 Edward John Eyre set off to explore the Great Australian Bight.

1862 'Greenbacks' (green paper dollars) were introduced by Abraham Lincoln during the US Civil War.

1868 President Andrew Johnson was impeached because of his policy of reconciliation with the defeated South. He was acquitted in May.

1879 After a very large breakfast, Charles Frederick Peace, English burglar and murderer, was led to the scaffold at Armley Gaol, Leeds. Salty bacon had made him thirsty, as the hood was placed over his head, he asked for a glass of water. He was hanged, thirst unquenched.

1913 Federal Income Tax was introduced in the US.

1918 Food rationing began in the southern English counties.

1922 French mass murderer, Henri Landru, was guillotined for the murder of at least ten women whose bodies were never found. He had advertised for 'a widow with a view to matrimony'. (*See also* 23.2.1906)

1935 Louis Lumière screened an experimental 3D film to the Académie des Sciences.

1939 The first Anderson bomb shelter was erected in Britain in a garden in Islington.

1946 The first bananas arrived in Britain following the war, but a Bridlington girl died after eating four.

1953 At an inquest, crew members admitted that a ferry which sank off Belfast, the *Princess Victoria*, had sailed with her giant bow doors open, drowning 128 people. The same tragedy would be repeated on 6.3.1987 outside Zeebrugge harbour when the Herald of Free Enterprise capsized.

1964 Cassius Clay (Muhammad Ali), the 7–1 underdog, knocked out Sonny Liston in the seventh round in Miami to become the world heavyweight boxing champion.

1978 Princess Margaret and her friend, Roddy Llewellyn, left for a holiday on the romantic island of Mustique. On 10 May an announcement was made that the Princess intended to divorce Lord Snowdon after two years separation. A few days later, Roddy said he had no plans to marry the Princess.

1988 US television evangelist Jimmy Swaggart, who confessed to visiting a prostitute in Baton Rouge for the past three years, was suspended by church elders for three months. A notice in the prostitute's window stated: 'Positively no refunds after 15 minutes'.

26 FEBRUARY

BORN THIS DAY

ARTS

1802 Victor (Marie) Hugo, French novelist and poet, author of *Les Misérables* (1862) which he wrote while in temporary exile in Guernsey.

1808 Honoré Daumier, French painter and caricaturist. (*See also* 20.2.1808)

1888 Lotte Lehmann, German soprano who was chosen by Richard Strauss to sing in *Der Rosenkavalier*. In 1938, she settled in the US.

ENTERTAINMENT

WILD MEN, WILD WOMEN Born 1846, 'Buffalo Bill' (Colonel William Frederick Cody), frontiersman and showman. His Wild West Show also featured the legendary Annie Oakley and Sitting Bull. Besides touring America, he brought the show to England for Queen Victoria's Golden Jubilee fostering a romantic image of the American west. Born 1921, Betty Hutton (Betty June Thornburg), US comedy actress and singer who played Annie Oakley in the film version of *Annie Get Your Gun* (1950). She squabbled with her studio, walking out of two films, and finally filed for bankruptcy in 1967. The one-time millionairess became a cook and housekeeper in a rectory.

POP

1928 'Fats' Domino, US singer and pianist who composed and performed 'Blueberry Hill' and 'Goin' Home'.

1932 Johnny Cash, US country singer,

guitarist and film actor. His big hit in 1956 was 'I Walk the Line'.

1947 Sandie Shaw, English singer who made her name in the 60s singing in bare feet. She won the Eurovision Song Contest for Britain in 1967 with 'Puppet on a String'.

DIED THIS DAY

1834 Aloys Senefelder, Bavarian author and inventor of lithography.

1857 Émile Coué, French psychologist who wrote *Suggestion and Autosuggestion*.

1903 Richard Jordan Gatling, US inventor of the Gatling gun.

1909 Caran d'Ache (Emmanuel Poire), French illustrator whose pseudonym is Russian for 'pencil'.

1950 Sir Harry Lauder (MacLennan), Scottish music hall comedian.

1969 Karl Jaspers, German existentialist philosopher.

1969 Levi Eshkol, former Israeli Prime Minister.

ON THIS DAY

1531 Severe earthquakes caused the death of 20,000 people in Lisbon, Portugal.

1797 The Bank of England issued the first £1 note.

1815 Napoleon Bonaparte escaped from the island of Elba.

1839 The first Grand National Steeplechase was run at Aintree near Liverpool. The winner was 'Lottery' ridden by Jem Mason.

1848 The Second French Republic was proclaimed.

SINKING FEELINGS In 1852 the British troopship, *Birkenhead*, sank off Simon's Bay, near Cape Town, South Africa, with the loss of 485 lives. In 1916 the French transport ship *Provence II* was sunk by the Germans with the loss of 930 lives.

1901 The leaders of the Boxer Rebellion in China, Chi-hsui and Cheng-yu, were beheaded in public. Japanese troops escorted the men to the place of execution while American, French and German troops guarded the streets.

1935 At Daventry, England, Robert Watson-Watt first demonstrated Radar (radio detection and ranging).

1936 Hitler launched the 'people's car', the Volkswagen, designed by Ferdinand Porsche.

1951 From this date, with the passing of the 22nd Amendment, US presidents could serve no more than two terms of four years.

1952 Churchill told the House of Commons that Britain now had an atomic bomb which it intended to test in Australia.

1959 A State of Emergency was declared in Southern Rhodesia by Sir Edgar Whitehead to allow forces to round up African nationalists.

1979 Accused of forging old masters, painter Tom Keating's trial at the Old Bailey was halted due to Keating's ill health. Keating, a brilliant technician, went on to present a television series on painters and became a celebrity in his remaining years.

1980 Israel and Egypt established diplomatic relations.

1983 Irishman Pat Jennings became the first footballer to take part in 1,000 first-class matches in the English league.

1986 After rigged elections, President Marcos was finally deposed and Mrs

Corazon Aquino became the new President of the Philippines. A mob ransacked the palace as Marcos and his extravagant wife Imelda fled the country.

1988 A Malaysian witch doctor, Pak Awang, 84, who specialized in love charms, married for the 80th time. Most of his marriages ended in divorce.

27 FEBRUARY

BORN THIS DAY

HISTORY

274 Constantine the Great, the Roman Emperor who became a Christian. At one time, there were six emperors each claiming a section of the empire. Constantine eventually became sole Emperor, granting civil rights to Christians, but being equally tolerant to paganism.

1861 Rudolf Steiner, Austrian social philosopher and educationalist who developed techniques for teaching maladjusted children.

1940 Paddy Ashdown, British politician and leader of the newly formed SDLP, a merger of the Social Democratic Party – excluding Dr David Owen's SDP die-hards – and the old-established Liberal Party, previously led by David Steel.

ARTS

1807 Henry Wadsworth Longfellow, US poet who wrote the epic 'Hiawatha' and 'The Wreck of the Hesperus'.

1847 Dame Ellen (Alicia) Terry, English actress who was Sir Henry Irving's leading lady at the Lyceum. While he was the first actor to be knighted, she was the first actress to be made a dame.

1848 Sir (Charles) Hubert (Hastings) Parry, English composer who wrote the processional music for the coronations of Edward VII and George V, as well as choral works including *Prometheus Unbound* and the hymn 'Jerusalem' to words by William Blake.

1902 John (Ernst) Steinbeck, US novelist and Nobel prize winner, author of *The Grapes of Wrath* (1939), *Of Mice and Men* (1937) and *East of Eden* (1952), amongst others.

1912 Lawrence (George) Durrell, English poet and novelist born in India. His Alexandria Quartet, which includes *Justine* (1957), was at first well received by only a small group of critics, but by 1960 had been recognized as a major work.

1939 Antoinette Sibley, English prima ballerina who joined the Royal Ballet in 1956, dancing her first solo in 1960.

ENTERTAINMENT

1908 Elizabeth Welch, US singer who starred on Broadway in *Running Wild* (1923) in which she introduced the charleston to the world. She settled in Britain in 1933 and appeared in two Novello musicals as well as many revues.

1910 Joan Bennett, US actress who played a wide range of roles. She was in *Father of the Bride* (1951) and *We're No Angels* (1955).

1930 Joanne Woodward, US actress who won an Oscar with her third film, *The Three Faces of Eve* (1957). She won an Oscar nomination for *Rachel, Rachel* (1968) directed by her husband, Paul Newman. They had first acted together in *The Long Hot Summer* (1958).

1932 Elizabeth Taylor, English-born US actress and winner of two Oscars for *Butterfield 8* (1960) and *Who's Afraid of Virginia Woolf?* (1966), who appeared in *National Velvet* (1944) while still a child star. Her private life was as dramatic as any movie, with seven marriages. Her seven husbands included Michael Todd, Eddie Fisher, and, most famous of all, Richard Burton.

SCIENCE

1899 Charles Herbert Best, Canadian physiologist and co-discoverer with Banting of insulin in the treatment of diabetes.

DIED THIS DAY

1706 John Evelyn, English writer who kept a diary for the last 65 years of his life.

1735 John Abuthnot, English satirist and creator of the character symbolizing the British nation, 'John Bull'.

1795 Francis Marion, known as 'the swamp fox', American revolutionary commander.

1887 Alexander (Porphyrevich) Borodin, Russian composer of *In the Steppes of Central Asia*.

1906 Samuel Pierpoint Langley, US astronomer and aeronautical pioneer.

1936 Ivan Pavlov, Russian physiologist and phychologist who specialized in behaviour.

1990 Greville Wynne, British electronic engineer and spy who was arrested by the Russians in 1962.

ON THIS DAY

1558 Exactly one year to the day after opening the first Russian embassy in London, a trade mission from Russia reached London, bringing with it many sable skins with the teeth, ears and claws of the animals preserved.

1776 Pitt the Younger resigned his commission in the army rather than fight America.

1879 Saccharin had been discovered by Constantin Fahlberg and Professor Ira Pemson at John Hopkins University, Baltimore, it was reported this day.

WIN SOME, LOSE SOME In 1881 the Battle of Majuba in South Africa ended with victory by the Boers over the British forces. On this same day in 1900, however, Kitchener's British forces won the Battle of Paardenberg after ten bloody days outnumbering General Cronje's civilian militia six to one.

1897 Paris saw the first couple to leave their wedding in a decorated motor car.

1900 The British Labour Party was founded. Ramsay MacDonald became secretary.

1933 The Reichstag building (the German parliament) burned down. While a Dutchman was accused of arson, it was actually a ploy by the Nazis to suspend all civil rights and freedom of the press. (*See* 10.1.1934)

1939 General Franco's rebel government in Spain was recognized by both Britain and France.

1939 Britain's most haunted house, Borley Rectory, was mysteriously destroyed by fire.

1947 Walter Graham Rowland became the first man to be twice held in the condemned cell at Strangeways Jail, Manchester, first for the murder of his daughter, for which he won a reprieve, and then, in 1947, for the murder of a prostitute. This time there was no reprieve and he was hanged this day.

1948 The Communists seized power in Czechoslovakia and forced President Beneš to resign.

1952 The United Nations held its first session in its new building in New York.

28 FEBRUARY

BORN THIS DAY

HISTORY

1712 Marquis de Montcalm Gezan de Saint Véran, Commander of the French forces in Canada. He was the unsuccessful defender of Quebec against Wolfe in 1759.

ARTS

1820 Sir John Tenniel, artist, Punch cartoonist and original illustrator of *Alice's Adventures in Wonderland* (1865).

1894 Ben Hecht, US journalist and screenplay writer. His work includes *Scarface* and *Front Page*.

1909 Sir Stephen (Harold) Spender, English poet and critic, one of a group of poets which included Auden, Day Lewis and Louis MacNeice, all of whom shared a political viewpoint. A romantic, Spender earned the nickname of 'the Rupert Brooke of the Depression'.

ENTERTAINMENT

1824 Charles Blondin (Jean François Gravelet), legendary French tightrope walker who made several crossings of the Niagara Falls, the first in 1859, and subsequently blindfolded, with a man on his back, on stilts and with a wheel barrow.

1913 Vincente Minnelli, US film director who first directed Broadway shows such as *Ziegfeld Follies*. In 1943, he went to Hollywood, where he directed a string of both artistically and commercially successful films including the musicals *Meet Me In St Louis* (1944), starring his wife, Judy Garland, *An American In Paris* (1951) and *Gigi* (1958).

1915 Zero Mostel (Samuel Joel), US comedy actor who starred on Broadway in *A Funny Thing Happened on the Way to the Forum* (1963), as well as in films such as *The Producers* (1967).

INVENTION

1683 Réné Reaumur, French naturalist, writer and inventor of the thermometer scale.

SCIENCE

1901 Professor Linus Pauling, US chemist and physicist, who won two Nobel prizes, the prize for Chemistry (1954), for his work with quantum mechanics, and the prize for Peace (1962), for his strong anti-nuclear stance.

1915 Sir Peter Medawar, Brazilian-born English immunologist, who won the Nobel prize for his work on immunological intolerance.

POP

1942 Brian Jones (Lewis Brian Hopkins Jones), Rolling Stones guitarist who quit the group in 1969.

SPORT

1931 Peter Alliss, English golfer, born in Germany, whose father, Percy, was twice British PGA Match Play champion. Peter won 20 major events before retiring to become a television commentator.

1951 Barry McGuigan, Irish-born World Boxing Association featherweight champion.

DIED THIS DAY

1789 Big Heart Eclipse, the most successful race horse of its day, who won a fortune for owner Dennis O'Kelly. When the horse was opened up afterwards, it was found to have a heart weighing 13lbs – the reason given for its success.

1916 Henry James, American-born novelist, in England.

1967 Henry (Robinson) Luce, the founder of *Time* and *Life* magazines.

1986 Olaf Palme, Swedish Prime Minister, assassinated in a Stockholm street by an unidentified killer. In 1989, Christer Pettersen was tried for the murder, but acquitted.

1988 (Kathleen) Kylie Tennant, Australian novelist who enjoyed an international reputation with 11 novels including *The Battlers* (1941).

ON THIS DAY

1784 John Wesley signed the 'deed of declaration' of the Wesleyan faith.

1874 Arthur Orton, who claimed to be the long lost heir to the wealthy Tichborne estate, was found guilty of perjury after 260 days, the longest trial in England, and was sentenced to 14 years hard labour. The real Sir Roger Tichborne perished at sea in 1853.

1900 In the Boer War, General Buller finally managed to relieve Ladysmith, which had been besieged by Boer forces for 118 days. There were extraordinary scenes of jubilation in Britain.

1912 Albert Berry made the first parachute jump from a plane over Missouri.

1922 Princess Mary, only daughter of King George V and Queen Mary, married Viscount Lascelles in London.

1931 Having left the Labour Party, Oswald Mosley formed the New Party in Britain.

1948 King George VI, the Queen, Princess Elizabeth, her husband, the Duke of Edinburgh and Princess Margaret went to see Danny Kaye at the London Palladium, the first 'non-command performance' attended by a reigning monarch.

1966 The Cavern Club, Liverpool, where the Beatles and other pop groups began, was forced into liquidation.

1972 The French police seized 937lbs of pure heroin at Marseilles. The operation was later immortalized in the film *The French Connection*.

1975 At 8.37 a.m. in the London rush-hour, a Northern Line underground train crashed through the buffers at Moorgate station and hit a solid dead-end wall, killing 41 people and seriously injuring 50. The rescue operation took three days to complete.

1976 Spain withdrew from the Spanish Sahara.

1988 A 90-year-old man was charged in Miami with the murder of his 76-year-old bride. He beat her to death with a hammer because of an argument over honeymoon plans.

1989 In London's Covent Garden, the world's biggest litter bin was unveiled; it was sponsored, appropriately, by fast-food operator Kentucky Fried Chicken.

29 FEBRUARY

Leap Year Day, which occurs every four years to make the calendar year 'catch up' with the solar year which actually takes only 365.242199 days.

BORN THIS DAY

HISTORY

1896 Ranchhodji Morarji Desai, former Indian Prime Minister who was twice imprisoned with Mahatma Gandhi during the civil disobedience campaign. As leader of the Janata Party, he opposed Indira Gandhi in the 1977 elections which he won, but internal unrest forced him out of office in 1979.

ARTS

1792 Gioacchino (Antonio) Rossini, Italian composer of *The Barber of Seville* (1816) which flopped when first staged in Rome.

ENTERTAINMENT

1928 Joss Ackland, English stage and film actor who played classical roles at the Old Vic as well as the role of Perón in the musical *Evita*. Frequently seen on television, he was in *Tinker, Tailor, Soldier, Spy*.

INVENTION

1840 John Philip Holland, Irish-born US developer of the modern submarine.

RELIGION

1736 Ann Lee, the illiterate daughter of a blacksmith, in Manchester, England. She emigrated to the US in 1774 and in 1776 founded the American Society of Shakers, so named because of the way they expressed their religious ecstasy.

DIED THIS DAY

642 St Oswald, slain in battle. He had been converted to Christianity at Iona, and established Christianity in Northumbria. He also has the rare distinction of being the only saint to die on Leap Year Day.

1528 Patrick Hamilton, Scottish Protestant martyr, burnt at the stake.

1984 Roland Culver, English actor who appeared in the films *French Without Tears* (1939) and *The Life and Death of Colonel Blimp* (1943).

ON THIS DAY

1880 The St Gotthard tunnel linking Switzerland and Italy was completed. The rail link ran just over nine miles.

1904 A White Paper was published which claimed that the British colonies preferred a metric system (decimalization) to the Imperial measurement system.

1908 Dutch scientists produced solid helium.

1916 The German Navy was ordered to sink any armed merchantmen on sight.

1948 The Jewish Stern Gang mined the Cairo to Haifa train killing 27 British soldiers and injuring 35.

1956 Pakistan became an Islamic republic.

1960 Hugh Heffner opened his first Playboy club in Chicago, introducing the Bunny girls, scantily clad waitresses dressed as bunnies, fur tails and all.

1968 The discovery of the first 'pulsar', (pulsating radio source) was announced by Dr Jocelyn Burnell of Cambridge.

1984 The flamboyant Canadian Premier, Pierre Trudeau, resigned as leader of the Liberal Party. He had succeeded Lester Pearson in 1968.

1984 John Francome rode his 1,000th National Hunt winner at Worcester. He ended his career the following year with a record 1,138 winners.

TWO MILLION TO ONE Lisa Dluchik of Swindon, England, celebrated her first birthday this day, 1988. She had been born in 1984. Her mother, Suzanne, was also born on this day, in 1956, so she officially celebrated her eighth birthday. The odds of a mother and daughter sharing a Leap Year birthday are two million to one.

THE PAN BOOK OF DATES

MARCH

Since we cannot know all there that there is to know about everything,
we ought to know a little about everything
(Blaise Pascal)

1 MARCH

The Feast Day of St David, patron saint of Wales.
The Old Roman New Year's Day.

BORN THIS DAY

ARTS

1810 Frédéric (François) Chopin, composer and pianist who was born in Poland to a French father and a Polish mother. His romantic music includes popular mazurkas and polonaises.

1880 Lytton (Giles) Strachey, English biographer, author of *Eminent Victorians* (1918), who was a member of the Bloomsbury Set.

1886 Oskar Kokoschka, Polish-born Expressionist painter who became a British citizen. His colourful, daring paintings caused a sensation when first exhibited.

1917 Robert (Trail Spence) Lowell, US poet who wrote 'The Dolphin' (1973). He was professor of Literature at Essex University, 1970–72.

ENTERTAINMENT

1910 (James) David (Graham) Niven, Scottish-born actor. Originally a professional soldier, he began in films as an extra before eventually playing leads, for example in *Around the World in Eighty Days* (1956). He won an Oscar for *Separate Tables* (1958). He also wrote two bestselling autobiographies, *The Moon's a Balloon* (1971) and *Bring on the Empty Horses* (1975).

1917 Dinah Shore (Fanny Rose Shaw), US singer who made her name during the golden age of radio, later appearing in films and on television.

1927 Harry Belafonte, US actor and singer who spent much of his youth in Jamaica. His films include *Carmen Jones* (1955) and *Island in the Sun* (1957). His career has been mainly as a concert and television performer.

POP

1904 Glenn Miller, US trombonist, bandleader, composer and arranger. His band and its distinctive 'Miller sound', best heard in 'Moonlight Serenade' and 'In the Mood', lived on after Miller's untimely death in 1944.

1945 Roger Daltrey, English pop singer with The Who. He later played the title roles in the rock musical *Tommy* (1975) and the film *McVicar* (1980).

SPORT

1940 David Broome, English show jumper who was the first Briton to become world champion (1970, in Paris).

DIED THIS DAY

1912 George Grossmith, English comedian, singer and author.

1938 Gabriele d'Annunzio, Italian poet, playwright and politician.

1980 Richard Ralph (Dixie) Dean, English record-breaking footballer, at his former club Everton, while watching a game.

1983 Jackie Coogan, US film actor who, as a child, played opposite Chaplin in *The Kid* (1921).

1988 Joe Besser, US film actor, one of the famous Three Stooges who made over 190 films between 1934 and 1959. He played Curly.

ON THIS DAY

STATE OF PLAY In 1880, Pennsylvania became the first US state to abolish slavery. Exactly one year later, all the states ratified the Articles of Confederation. In 1803, Ohio became the 17th state of the Union and, in 1845, the US annexed Texas. Also on this day, in 1867, Nebraska became the 37th state of the Union.

1932 The 20-month-old son of US aviator Colonel Charles Lindberg was kidnapped from his nursery. He was found dead on 12 May. Bruno Hauptmann, a carpenter, was later charged with the crime.

1936 Golden Miller won the Cheltenham Gold Cup for the fifth consecutive year.

1940 Vivien Leigh won the Oscar for Best Actress for her role as Scarlett O'Hara in *Gone with the Wind*.

1949 Joe Louis, US world heavyweight boxing champion known as the 'Brown Bomber', retired aged 35, after a record 25 successful defences of his title.

1950 Klaus Fuchs was found guilty of passing British atomic secrets to Soviet agents. He eventually served seven years in prison.

1954 The US carried out the first hydrogen bomb test at Bikini Atoll in the Pacific.

1959 Archbishop Makarios ended his exile and returned to Cyprus.

1961 President Kennedy formed the Peace Corps of Young Americans to work overseas as part of US aid to developing nations.

1966 The Soviet unmanned spacecraft, *Venus 3*, touched down on Venus.

1972 A London schoolboy, Timothy Davey, was jailed by a Turkish court for 'conspiring to sell cannabis' despite pleas from British Prime Minister, Edward Heath. Timothy was 14 years old.

1978 Charles Chaplin's coffin was stolen from a Swiss cemetery three months after burial. It was later found ten miles away (on 17.5.1978).

1988 The massacre of Armenians in the Soviet republic of Azerbaijan began as a result of conflict over disputed regions with Muslim Azerbaijanis.

1990 Daily rum tots for sailors aboard Royal New Zealand Navy ships were stopped. It was the last navy in the world to scrap rum rations.

2 MARCH

The Feast Day of Chad, British patron saint of medical springs.

BORN THIS DAY

HISTORY

1793 Sam Houston, American soldier who became the first President of the Republic of Texas after defeating the Mexicans.

1923 Cardinal Basil Hume, Archbishop of Westminster, the first monk to hold this position.

1931 Mikhail (Sergeyevitch) Gorbachev, Soviet leader and general secretary of the Communist Party who introduced *glasnost* and sought better relations with the West.

ARTS

1824 Bedřich Smetana, Czechoslovakian composer who eventually went deaf. He is best known for *The Bartered Bride* (1866).

1900 Kurt (Julian) Weill, German-born

composer who collaborated with Bertold Brecht. Their success with *Der Dreigroschenoper* (The Threepenny Opera) with Weill's wife, Lotte Lenya singing the main role, was the last of their productions in Berlin before they fled from the Nazis to the US.

ENTERTAINMENT

1919 Jennifer Jones (Phillis Isley), US actress who won an Oscar for *The Song of Bernadette* (1943).

1920 Martin Ritt, US film and stage director whose credits include *Hud* (1963) and *The Spy Who Came In From The Cold* (1965).

POP

1943 George Benson, US singer whose hits include 'On Broadway'.

1944 Lou Reed, US singer best known for his 1973 hit, 'A Walk on The Wild Side'.

1950 Karen Carpenter, US singer who, with her brother Richard, formed the highly successful singing duo the Carpenters and had hits including '(They Long To Be) Close to You' (1970), 'Top of the World' (1973) and 'Please Mr Postman' (1975).

SPORT

1949 Dame Naomi (Christine) James, yachtswoman and author, educated in New Zealand, who sailed single-handed around the world in 1977–8 when she also became the first woman to sail solo around Cape Horn.

1949 J(ohn) P(eter) R(hys) Williams, Welsh rugby player who is also a consultant in trauma and orthopaedic surgery.

1958 Ian Woosnam, Welsh golfing champion who represented his country in the World Cup from 1980–5, and won the European Open in 1988.

DIED THIS DAY

1791 John Wesley, founder of English Methodism.

1797 Horace Walpole, fourth Earl of Orford, novelist and historian.

1835 Francis II, the last Holy Roman Emperor.

1855 Nicholas I, Tsar of Russia.

1930 D(avid) H(erbert) Lawrence, English novelist of *Women in Love* (1921).

1939 Howard Carter, English Egyptologist.

1988 Clive Jermain, 23-year-old English playwright, of cancer. His acclaimed television play *The Best Years of Your Life*, was largely autobiographical.

ON THIS DAY

1717 The first ballet was performed in England by dancing master, John Weaver. *The Loves of Mars and Venus* was staged at Drury Lane.

1725 A night watchman found a human head by the Thames, where the Tate Gallery now stands. It was later displayed on a pole until it was recognized as belonging to the husband of Catherine Hayes. She and her two lodgers were arrested for murder. One accomplice was hanged, the other died in prison before the execution, while Catherine was sentenced to be strangled and burnt. The executioner failed to strangle her, so she was burnt alive.

1882 Robert Maclean tried unsuccessfully to assassinate Queen Victoria at Windsor.

1909 The novelist Katherine Mansfield married musician George Bowden in

London while pregnant by a previous lover. The following morning she regretted her action and deserted Bowden, fleeing to Bavaria where her child was stillborn.

1946 Ho Chi Minh was elected President of North Vietnam.

1949 The first round-the-world non-stop flight was completed by Captain James Gallagher and his 13-man US Airforce crew. The flight took 94 hours, during which the plane, *Lucky Lady II* was refuelled four times in flight by tanker aircraft.

1955 Severe floods in North and Western Australia killed 200 people, leaving 44,000 homeless. Hundreds of thousands of sheep were also drowned.

1958 Sir Vivian Fuchs and a British team completed the first crossing of the Antarctic. The journey took 99 days using Sno-cat caterpillar tractors and dog teams.

1958 Gary Sobers scored 365 not out against Pakistan at Kingston, Jamaica.

1960 An earthquake in Morocco destroyed the town of Agadir, killing 20,000 and injuring many thousands more.

1970 Rhodesia broke away from Britain and the Commonwealth and became a Republic under Ian Smith.

1974 The US Grand Jury said Nixon was involved in the Watergate cover-up.

1986 The Queen signed the Australia Bill in Canberra, formally severing any Australian constitutional ties with Britain.

1988 In Britain, a new political party was born when Liberals merged with the Social Democrats to form the Social and Liberal Democrats.

1988 A report from China claimed that a worker at a boiler factory in Xinjiang province emitted electric charges strong enough to knock down people when he touched them. If he married, would his wife have to be earthed?

3 MARCH

BORN THIS DAY

ARTS

1869 Sir Henry Wood, English conductor and founder, in 1895, of the annual promenade concerts.

1920 Ronald (William Fordham) Searle, English cartoonist whose creations include the fiendish girls of St Trinians.

ENTERTAINMENT

1911 Jean Harlow (Harlean Carpenter), the platinum blonde US actress whose films include *Dinner at Eight* (1934) and *China Seas* (1935). Her life as a Hollywood sex symbol foreshadowed that of Marilyn Monroe: Harlow's marriages all failed – one husband committed suicide – and she died aged only 26.

INVENTION

1831 George Mortimer Pullman, US industrialist and inventor who designed and manufactured the de luxe railway carriages that bear his name.

1847 Alexander Graham Bell, Scottish inventor who settled in the US, where he opened a school for the deaf in Boston. While a professor of vocal physiology, he patented his invention, the telephone, in 1876. He also invented a cylinder recording machine.

SCIENCE

1831 Georg Cantor, Russian-born German mathematician who formulated the theory of infinity.

SPORT

1961 Fatima Whitbread, English woman's javelin champion, gold medallist in the World Athletics Championships in Rome, 1987, and silver medallist in the 1988 Olympics.

DIED THIS DAY

1703 Robert Hooke, English physicist who amongst his many scientific contributions invented the spirit level.

1792 Robert Adam, Scottish architect and interior designer, one of three architect sons of William Adam, the leading architect of his day.

1804 Domenico Tiepolo, Italian painter and engraver.

1954 Noël Gay (Richard Moxon Armitage), English composer and pianist who wrote the hit musical *Me and My Girl*, which features the popular 'Lambeth Walk', in 1937.

1959 Lou Costello (Louis Francis Cristello), US comedian, the other half of Bud Abbott.

1983 Arthur Koestler, Hungarian-born writer who settled in Britain. As a passionate believer in euthanasia, he committed suicide with his wife, who was suffering from leukaemia and Parkinson's disease.

1987 Danny Kaye (Daniel Kaminsky), US comedian.

ON THIS DAY

1802 Beethoven's 'Moonlight Sonata', 'the most famous piano composition in the world', was published.

1845 Florida became the 27th state of the Union.

1875 The first performance of Bizet's *Carmen* was staged at the Opera Comique, Paris.

1895 In Munich, bicyclists had to pass a test and display licence plates.

1924 In Turkey, the Caliphate was abolished and the Islamic religion was disestablished as Kemal Atatürk began his drastic programme to transform Turkey into a modern state.

1928 Ronnie Dix of Bristol Rovers scored a goal against Norwich in Division 3 (South) of the English Football League. Aged 15, he was the youngest goal scorer in League history.

1931 The US Congress adopted 'The Star-spangled Banner' as the US national anthem.

1933 The world première of *King Kong* was held in New York.

1943 At an air raid shelter in Bethnal Green, 178 people died, not as a result of a bomb, but because a woman carrying a baby fell down a flight of steps and an elderly man fell over her. People continuing to enter fell over others, causing the carnage. The mother survived; her baby died.

1974 A Turkish Airlines DC 10 on a flight from Paris to London, crashed in a wood, a favourite picnic spot for Parisians. All 344 people on board, of which 200 were British, were killed.

1988 A motorist in California who failed to use his seat belt was killed when his car spun off the road and plunged 37 feet. He had strapped his teddy bear in the passenger seat. The bear survived undamaged.

4 MARCH

BORN THIS DAY

HISTORY

1394 Prince Henry the Navigator, Portuguese explorer.

ARTS

1678 Antonio Lucio Vivaldi, Italian composer and violinist, best known for *The Four Seasons* (1725). In 1737, the papal authorities prevented the production of one of his operas because Vivaldi, a former priest, was having an affair with a woman singer.

1928 Alan Sillitoe, English novelist and playwright, author of *Saturday Night and Sunday Morning* (1958) and *The Loneliness of the Long Distance Runner* (1959) which dealt with working-class life in post-war Britain. Both were also successful films.

1929 Bernard Haitink, Dutch conductor, now Musical Director of Covent Garden. He was awarded an honorary knighthood in 1977.

JAZZ

1931 Miriam Makeba, South African singer who has sung and recorded her mix of jazz, African and protest songs internationally.

SCIENCE

1928 Patrick Moore, English astronomer who popularized the subject with his books and long-running BBC TV series, *The Sky at Night*.

SPORT

1936 Jim Clark, Scottish motor racing driver who became World Champion when only 27, in 1963.

1951 Kenny Dalgleish, Scottish footballer who made a record number appearances for Scotland. He also played for Liverpool – their most expensive player – who gave them the winning goal against FC Bruges of Belgium in 1978, to become European Champions for the second consecutive year. Later, as their manager, he saw his team win the 'double' (the League and FA Cup) in 1986.

DIED THIS DAY

1193 Saladin, Sultan of Egypt and Syria.

1832 Jean François Champollion, French egyptologist.

1948 Antonin Artaud, French actor, playwright and director of the Theatre of Cruelty. He went insane in 1937 and died in an asylum.

ON THIS DAY

1789 The first Congress of the US was held in New York. On its 124th anniversary, in 1913, Woodrow Wilson was inaugurated as the 28th US President.

1791 Vermont became the 14th state of the Union.

1824 The Royal National Lifeboat Instution was founded.

PICTURE PAPERS In 1873, The *New York Daily Graphic* became the first illustrated daily newspaper, and in 1986, Eddie Shah's *Today* newspaper became the first national daily to carry colour pictures in Britain.

1877 The first performance of *Swan Lake* (Le Lac des Cygnes) was staged by the Russian Imperial Ballet in Moscow.

1882 The first electric trams in Britain ran from Leytonstone, east London.

1890 The Prince of Wales opened the longest bridge in Britain, the 1,710ft Forth railway bridge in Scotland.

1919 Lenin formed the Communist International, better known as the Comintern.

1924 'Happy Birthday to You' was published by Clayton F. Summy.

1927 A diamond rush in South Africa included many trained athletes hired by major companies to stake claims.

1941 British forces, assisted by local Norwegians, raided the German-occupied Lofoten Islands, destroying 11 German ships.

1958 The US nuclear submarine *Nautilus* became the first to travel under the North Pole ice cap.

1964 Malta became fully independent.

1967 The first North Sea gas to reach mainland Britain was piped ashore in Durham.

1967 The first Third Division football club to win a Wembley final was Queen's Park Rangers, when they beat West Bromwich Albion 3–2 in the League Cup.

1971 Canada's Prime Minister, Pierre Trudeau married 22-year-old Margaret Sinclair in secret.

1974 Following the election, British Prime Minister, Edward Heath, failed to persuade the Liberals to join a coalition and resigned. Harold Wilson would become Prime Minister for a third time, but with a narrow majority.

1975 Charles Chaplin was knighted at Buckingham Palace.

1976 England's John Curry won the men's figure skating world championship in Stockholm, following his gold at the Winter Olympics.

5 MARCH

BORN THIS DAY

HISTORY

1133 King Henry II, the first Plantagenet king of England, in France.

1751 James Madison, fourth US president.

1871 Rosa Luxemburg, one of the founders of the extreme-left Spartacus movement in Germany, which was crushed by the Nazis.

1879 William Henry, 1st Baron Beveridge, English economist and civil servant who produced the famous Beveridge report which laid the foundations of the British welfare state.

ARTS

1852 Lady Augusta Gregory, Irish playwright who was an associate of Yeats, with whom she founded the famous Abbey Theatre, Dublin.

1887 Heitor Villa-Lobos, Brazilian composer whose music is characterized by native folk-rhythms.

ENTERTAINMENT

SEXY REXY AND THE FAIR LADY In 1908, Rex Harrison (Reginald Carey), English actor who made his stage debut in his home town aged 16, with the Liverpool Repertory Theatre, was born. He is perhaps best known for his portrayal of Henry Higgins in *My Fair Lady*, which he played on both stage and screen and which won him an Oscar in 1964. 'Sexy Rexy' as the gossip columnists called him, married six times. In 1939 Samantha Eggar, the English actress who played opposite him in *Dr Doolittle* in 1967, was born. *The Collector* had won her Best Actress award at Cannes in 1965.

1952 Elaine Page, English actress and singer who made her name in the Lloyd Webber musicals *Evita* and *Cats*.

POP

1958 Andy Gibb, English-born pop musician who was raised in Australia with his elder brothers, who became the Bee Gees. He died five days after his 30th birthday, ruined by drugs and debt.

SCIENCE

EQUAL MEASURES In 1512, Gerhardus Mercator (Gerhard Kremer), Flemish cartographer who developed Mercator's projection, and in 1575, William Oughtred, English mathematician who, it is believed, invented the first slide rule.

DIED THIS DAY

1534 Antonio Allegri da Correggio, Italian Renaissance painter.

1778 Thomas (Augustine) Arne, English composer of 'Rule Britannia'.

1790 Flora Macdonald, Scottish heroine who helped Bonnie Prince Charles after the Battle of Culloden.

1815 Franz Anton Mesmer, French physician who developed the theory of animal magnetism or 'mesmerism'.

1827 Alessandro Volta, Italian physicist, inventor of the first electric battery.

COMPOSER AND HIS CRITIC This day in 1953 saw the deaths of both Sergei Prokofiev, Russian composer, and his critic, Joseph Stalin, who condemned his 'formalism' and compelled him to confess his shortcomings. Stalin died after a brain haemorrhage.

1967 Mohammed Mossadeq, Iranian Prime Minister who tried to overthrow the Shah.

1981 William Powell, US actor, star of 90 films including *The Thin Man* (1934), died aged 89.

1982 John Belushi, US star of *National Lampoon's Animal House* (1978), from a drugs overdose.

1984 Tito Gobbi, Italian baritone.

ON THIS DAY

1461 Henry VI of England was deposed, and succeeded by Edward IV. Henry was unpopular for having lost English territories in France.

1770 British troops opened fire on a crowd in Boston, Massachusetts, killing five in what was called 'The Boston Massacre'.

1856 Covent Garden Theatre was destroyed by fire.

1857 James Townsend Saward, alias 'Jim the Penman', the most notorious forger of his age, was convicted of forging cheques. Saward was a respected solicitor with chambers in the Temple. He and his accomplices were sentenced to transportation to a penal colony in Australia.

1933 The Nazis won almost half the seats in the German elections.

1936 The Spitfire made its first flight from Eastleigh aerodrome, Southampton.

1946 Churchill, on a US tour, at Fulton, Missouri, said in reference to the Russian threat to the West, 'An iron curtain has descended across Europe.'

1960 Elvis Presley was discharged from the army having completed his service with US forces in Germany.

1988 A baby with two heads was born in Naples. Doctors said they expected it to lead a normal, healthy life although it would not be possible to remove one of the heads surgically.

6 MARCH

The National Day of Ghana, commemorating the independence of the former British Gold Coast. Ghana was the first British colony in Africa to gain independence.

BORN THIS DAY

HISTORY

1937 Valentina Nikolakyeva-Tereshkova, Russian astronaut, who, aged 26, became the first woman in space when she circled the world in the *Vostok* spacecraft in June 1963.

ARTS

1619 Savinien Cyrano de Bergerac, French novelist and playwright who was the model for the play by Rostand. He was said to have fought more than 1,000 duels because of insults about his large nose.

1806 Elizabeth Barrett Browning, English poet. Confined to bed because of a riding accident which damaged her spine, her marriage to fellow poet Robert Browning freed her from her repressive father.

1834 George (Louis Palmella Busson) du Maurier, English caricaturist and novelist, author of *Trilby* (1894), in Paris.

1870 Oscar Straus, composer, in Vienna, although he later became a French citizen. His most popular operetta, *The Chocolate Soldier*, based on Bernard Shaw's *Arms and the Man*, had its first performance in Vienna in 1894.

1885 Ring(old Wilmer) Lardner, US humorist and writer, particularly of sporting stories.

1944 Dame Kiri Te Kanawa, New Zealand soprano who made her debut in Britain in 1969. She played to her biggest audience when invited to sing at the wedding of the Prince of Wales and Lady Diana Spencer in St Paul's Cathedral which was televised to many countries.

ENTERTAINMENT

1922 Frankie Howerd, English comedian who made his name in radio comedy shows before making films such as *The Lady Killers* (1955). He is probably best remembered for his television series *Up Pompeii*.

1926 Andrzej Wajda, Poland's leading film director who made *Ashes and Diamonds* (1958).

POP

1944 Mary Wilson, US singer, who was a founder member, with Diana Ross and Flo Ballard, of the Supremes.

DIED THIS DAY

1888 Louisa May Alcott, US novelist, author of *Little Women* (1868–9).

1900 Gottlieb Daimler, German motor engineer and motor cycle inventor.

1932 John Philip Sousa, US bandmaster and composer.

1951 Ivor Novello (David Ivor Davies), Welsh-born composer, playwright and actor who died in his flat above the Strand Theatre, London, a few hours after performing in his own *King's Rhapsody*, which was running at the Palace Theatre.

1961 George Formby (George Hoy Booth), English comedian, banjo player and singer.

1965 Herbert (Stanley) Morrison, British Labour statesman.

1967 Zoltan Kodaly, Hungarian composer.

1967 Nelson Eddy, US singer and actor who partnered Jeanette MacDonald in Hollywood operetta musicals.

1971 Pearl (Sydenstricker) Buck, US Nobel Literature prize winner, author of *The Good Earth*.

1984 Donald Maclean, English diplomat who, together with Burgess, spied for the Russians.

ON THIS DAY

1834 York in Upper Canada was incorporated as a city under the name Toronto; its first mayor was W. L. Mackenzie.

1836 The Battle of the Alamo ended. The fort, besieged by the Mexicans under Santa Anna, fought to the death. Only six Texans survived out of the original 155. The legendary frontiersmen, Davy Crockett and Jim Bowie were both killed in the 12-day battle.

1853 Verdi's opera *La Traviata* was performed for the first time, in Venice.

1899 Felix Hoffman discovered the pharmacological properties of acetylsalicylic acid and formulated the world's most famous drug, the aspirin, which he patented this day.

1926 The Shakespeare Memorial Theatre in Stratford-upon-Avon was completely destroyed by fire.

1930 Birds Eye frozen foods, developed by Clarence Birdseye, went on sale for the first time in a US store in Springfield, Massachussetts.

1944 Daylight raids on Berlin from US bases in Britain began.

1953 Georgi Maksimilianovic Malenkov succeeded Stalin as Chairman of the Council of Ministers of the USSR.

1964 Constantine II acceded to the throne as King of the Hellenes on the death of Paul I.

1987 The *Herald of Free Enterprise* ferry capsized just outside Zeebrugge harbour. She had set out with her bow doors open allowing water to pour in. Over 200 passengers were drowned.

1988 Three IRA terrorists were shot dead by SAS men in Gibraltar reviving the 'shoot-to-kill' controversy.

1988 Dr Kurt Waldheim, Austrian President and former director-general of the UN, admitted he knew that Allied commandos interrogated by his unit during the war would be executed contrary to the Geneva Convention, sparking off fresh demands from both Austria and other countries for his resignation.

7 MARCH

BORN THIS DAY

HISTORY

1850 Thomas Garrigue Masaryk, Czechoslovakian patriot, scholar and philosopher who led the revolutionary movement against the Austrian Empire. When the Republic was finally formed he was elected the first President.

1905 Jacques Chaban-Dalmas, former French Prime Minister who was responsible for the military planning of the Resistance during the Second World War.

ARTS

1802 Sir Edwin Henry Landseer, English painter of animals, and sculptor of the Trafalgar Square lions.

1872 Piet(er) (Cornelius) Mondrian, Dutch abstract painter whose geometrical compositions influenced modern architecture and design.

1875 Maurice (Joseph) Ravel, French composer, best known for the popular *Boléro* (1928).

1930 Lord Snowdon, (Anthony Armstrong-Jones), former husband of Princess Margaret, photographer and design consultant to *The Times* and the *Sunday Times*.

ENTERTAINMENT

1958 Rik Mayall, English alternative comic and writer who first impressed in the television series *The Young Ones*.

PHOTOGRAPHY

1765 Joseph Nicéphore Niepce, French doctor who, in 1826, produced the very first photograph from nature on pewter plates using a camera obscura. It required an eight hour exposure.

SPORT

1952 Viv Richards, West Indian cricketer, in Antigua. He scored 291 in 1976 against England, the highest score by a West Indies batsman in a Test match in England. In 1984 he made the highest one-day score for the West Indies against England, 189 not out.

1960 Ivan Lendl, Czech tennis player, twice beaten in the men's finals at Wimbledon.

DIED THIS DAY

1932 Aristide Briand, French Socialist Prime Minister, and promoter of a United Europe.

1971 (Florence Margaret) 'Stevie' Smith, English poet.

1988 Divine (Harris Glenn Milstead), bloated US transvestite who made his name in an outrageous film called *Pink Flamingos* in which he swallowed fresh poodle droppings on screen. In *Polyester*, Divine played an alcoholic housewife who drove her dog to attempt suicide.

ON THIS DAY

1804 The Royal Horticultural Society was founded by John Wedgwood, son of pottery manacturer, Josiah.

1838 Jenny Lind, the 'Swedish Nightingale' made her debut at the Stockholm Opera in *Der Freischutz*.

1876 Alexander Graham Bell patented the first telephone capable of sustained articulate speech. Three days later on 10 March, the first telephone message, 'Come here, Watson, I want you', was relayed by Bell to his assistant.

1912 Frenchman Henri Seimet became the first aviator to fly non-stop from Paris to London. The flight took three hours.

1917 'The Dixie Jazz Band One-step' was issued by the US Victor Company – the world's first jazz record. A previous recording, in January, by Columbia, of the Original Dixieland Jazz band, was not thought a success and was never released.

1918 The Bolsheviks changed their name to the Russian Communist Party.

1975 Lesley Whittle's body was found down a 60-foot drain shaft. She had been strangled by 'The Black Panther' after being kidnapped and held for 52 days. The £50,000 ransom was never collected by Donald Neilson who was sentenced to four life sentences (21.6.1976).

1989 A convicted murderer in Columbia, South Carolina who successfully appealed against being sent to the electric chair, was electrocuted accidentally while sitting on the toilet trying to mend a pair of earphones.

8 MARCH

Feast Day of John of God, patron saint of hospitals and the sick, as well as booksellers and printers, because he used to peddle sacred books and pictures, eventually opening a shop in Granada, in 1538.

BORN THIS DAY

HISTORY

1930 Douglas Hurd, British Home Secretary in Mrs Thatcher's government, and author.

ARTS

1859 Kenneth Grahame, Scottish author who wrote the children's classic *The Wind in the Willows* (1908).

1939 Lynn Seymour, Canadian-born ballerina who danced with the Royal Ballet, and created the principal role in Ashton's *A Month In The Country*.

ENTERTAINMENT

1921 Cyd Charisse (Tula Elice Finklea), US dancer and actress who joined the Ballets Russes. Her classical training made her a superb partner for Fred Astaire in *Silk Stockings* (1957).

1943 Lynn Redgrave, English actress, the youngest of the Redgrave family, whose films include *Georgy Girl* (1966).

SCIENCE

1787 Karl Ferdinand von Graefe, German pioneer plastic surgeon who was born in Warsaw. By employing skin grafts, he was able to carry out elementary plastic surgery at military hospitals during the Napoleonic Wars.

1879 Otto Hahn, German physicist and chemist, and Nobel prize winner for Chemistry in 1944. He discovered nuclear fission, which made the atomic bomb possible.

SPORT

1955 David Wilkie, English gold medalist at the 1976 Olympics for the 200m breaststroke. He also won a silver for the 100m.

POP

1958 Gary Numan (Webb), British singer and songwriter who had big hits with 'Are Friends Electric' (with Tubeway Army) and 'Cars', both in 1979.

DIED THIS DAY

1717 Abraham Darby, English ironmaster, the first to use coke for iron smelting.

1874 The 13th US President, Millard Fillmore, and in 1930 the 27th, William Howard Taft.

1869 Hector Berlioz, French composer.

1889 John Ericsson, Swedish-born US ship designer who invented the first successful screw propeller.

1917 Count Ferdinand von Zeppelin, German soldier and airship pioneer.

1961 Sir Thomas Beecham, English conductor, founder of the Royal Philharmonic orchestra.

1971 Harold Lloyd, US silent film comedian.

1983 Sir William Walton, English composer, on the island of Ischia.

ON THIS DAY

1702 Queen Anne acceded to the British throne following the death of William III, who fell from his horse when it stumbled on a molehill at Hampton Court. He left no children and the crown passed to the daughter of James II.

1910 The first pilot's licences were granted to a Briton and a Frenchwoman. The Royal Aero Club granted licence number one to J.T.C. Moore Brabazon (later Lord Brabazon of Tara), while in France, Mlle Élise Deroche, who assumed the title Baroness de Laroche, also qualified for a licence.

1944 In an English Football League match between Third Division North Crewe and Bradford Park, four penalties were awarded in one five-minute period.

1952 An artificial heart was used for the first time on a 41-year-old man which kept him alive for 80 minutes; his death was not related to the heart machine.

1966 At 8.30 p.m., Ronnie Kray, notorious East End gangster, flanked by two Glaswegian 'hard men', walked into the *Blind Beggar* pub in Whitechapel Road. Kray, brandishing a 9mm Mauser automatic, shot rival gangster, George Cornell, through the head. This crime was to lead to the eventual imprisonment of the Kray twins.

1973 Paul McCartney was charged with growing pot on his farm in Scotland.

SHOW STOPPERS In 1988, soap opera writers in the US went on strike for improved terms, threatening major shows such as *Dynasty* and *Dallas*, while in a small southern Indian village, 3,000 residents were kept indoors by police who put up road blocks to enforce a government ban on the nude worship of a Hindu god.

9 MARCH

BORN THIS DAY

HISTORY

1454 Amerigo Vespucci, Italian explorer who made numerous voyages to the New World, which he was inaccurately credited with discovering, and which now bears his name.

1763 William Cobbett, English political journalist who championed the working class and became its first leader.

1881 Ernest Bevin, British union leader and Minister of Labour during the Second World War who created the 'Bevin Boys'; young men chosen by ballot to work down the mines as part of their war service.

1890 (Vyacheslav) Mikhailovic Molotov (Skriabin), former Soviet Prime Minister and foreign secretary who negotiated a non-agression pact with Hitler. He has the dubious honour of having the home-made bomb, a Molotov cocktail – a bottle with a wick filled with petrol – named after him.

1934 Yuri Alekseyevich Gagarin, Soviet astronaut, the first man in space, 1961.

ARTS

1892 Victoria Mary 'Vita' Sackville-West, English poet and novelist of *All Passion Spent* (1931).

1910 Samuel Barber, US composer

whose works include *Adagio for Strings* (1936).

1928 Micky Spillane (Frank Morrison), US pulp-fiction writer of tough, violent crime thrillers.

FASHION

1913 André Courrèges, French couturier who invented the 'mini' skirt in 1964.

SPORT

1943 Bobby Fischer, US chess champion who won the world title when he beat Boris Spassky in 1972. But Fischer's temperament led him to give away the crown by default to Anatoly Karpov in 1975.

1952 (William) Bill Beaumont, British Lions and England international rugby captain.

POP

1945 Micky Dolenz, US actor, drummer and vocalist with the Monkees, who were specially created for a television series of the same name, but managed to exist outside it. The group was revived in 1989 to enjoy a nostalgia boom.

DIED THIS DAY

1888 Wilhelm I, Emperor of Germany.

1918 Frank Wedekind, German Expressionist playwright.

1988 Richard C. Adams, US inventor of the paint roller, which he produced in his basement workshop in 1940.

ON THIS DAY

1562 Kissing in public was banned in Naples, contravention being punishable by death.

1796 Napoleon married Joséphine de Beauharnais, widow of a former French officer guillotined during the Revolution.

1831 The French Foreign Legion was founded with headquarters in Algeria.

1864 General Ulysses Grant was appointed General-in-Chief of the Union Forces in the US Civil War.

1891 Four days of storms began off England's south coast, sinking 14 ships.

1932 Eamon de Valera was elected President of Ireland.

1932 Pu-Yi, the last Chinese emperor, was installed as head of the Japanese puppet state of Manchukuo.

1937 George Orwell's examination of unemployment and life during the Depression in the north of England, *The Road to Wigan Pier*, was published.

1956 Britain deported Archbishop Makarios from Cyprus to prevent further conflict between Greeks and Turks on the island, and for 'actively fostering terrorism'.

1967 Svetlana Alliluyeva, the 41-year-old daughter of the late Joseph Stalin, defected to the West.

10 MARCH

BORN THIS DAY

HISTORY

1964 Prince Edward, third son of Queen Elizabeth II of England, and the most famous tea boy with Lloyd Webber's Really Useful Company.

ARTS

1885 Tamara (Platonova) Karsavina, leading Russian ballerina with Diaghilev's Ballets Russes who partnered

Nijinsky until 1913 and was famous for her roles in *Firebird* and *The Three-Cornered Hat*. She married a British diplomat, settled in London and was one of the founders of the Royal Academy of Dancing in 1920.

1892 Arthur Honegger, Swiss composer, member of the famous 'Les Six' group under the influence of Satie and Cocteau.

JAZZ

1903 Bix (Leon Bismark) Beidebecke, US cornet player and composer who was profoundly influenced by black jazz musicians. His harmonic skills influenced jazz development attracting white middle-class American interest. He died, aged only 28, in 1931.

DIED THIS DAY

1872 Giuseppe Mazzini, Italian nationalist.

1948 Jan Garrigue Masaryk, Czechoslovakian statesman, son of Thomas, who was found lying dead in the courtyard beneath his flat two weeks after the Communist coup. Official statements said he committed suicide, but it was not accepted by many.

1981 Sir Maurice Oldfield, British intelligence chief, considered to be the model for Ian Fleming's 'M' in his Bond novels.

1985 Konstantin Ustinovich Chernenko, Russian leader.

1986 Ray Milland, Welsh-born actor who became a star in Hollywood.

1988 Andy Gibb, member of the Bee Gees pop group who lost his battle with cocaine addiction five days after his 30th birthday.

ON THIS DAY

512BC The rebuilding of the Temple at Jerusalem after the Jewish deportation by Nebuchadnezzar was allegedly completed this day with much celebrating.

1906 London Underground opened the Baker Street to Waterloo section and named it the 'Bakerloo' line.

1914 The *Rokeby Venus* in London's National Gallery, one of the nation's most important paintings, was slashed by a suffragette Mary Richardson, using a meat chopper, who wanted to 'destroy the most beautiful woman in mythological history' as a protest against the government's efforts to 'destroy' Mrs Pankhurst, the suffragette leader. Velasquez's masterpiece was severely damaged.

1965 Goldie, the London Zoo golden eagle which escaped, was captured nearby on this its 13th day of freedom. Large crowds had been attracted to the zoo in Regent's Park to watch Goldie fly from tree to tree, occasionally landing to accept titbits from spectators.

1968 A New Zealand car ferry capsized in a severe storm in Wellington Harbour and 200 were drowned.

1969 James Earl Ray pleaded guilty to the murder of Martin Luther King and was sentenced to 99 years in jail.

1974 A Japanese soldier was discovered on Lubang Island in the Philippines. He still believed the Second World War was being fought, and was waiting to be relieved by his own forces.

THE END OF THE AFFAIR In 1979, Lee Marvin's ex-girlfriend, Michelle Triola Marvin, sued for a 'palimony', demanding half the $3.6m he made during the time they lived together. The case was later dismissed. In

1980, Jean Harris, a US headmistress, shot the inventor of the Scarsdale diet, Dr Herman Tarnower, four times in the back after a passionate 44-year affair ended.

1988 An avalanche in the Swiss ski resort of Klosters killed one member of the Prince of Wales' party and injured another, but Charles narrowly escaped.

31 MARCH

BORN THIS DAY

HISTORY

1916 (James) Harold Wilson, Lord Wilson of Rievaulx, British Labour Prime Minister from 1964–70, and again from 1974–6 until he resigned. During his period in office, according to Peter Wright in *Spycatcher* (1987), he was suspected of being a likely Soviet agent by British intelligence who may have been involved in 'dirty tricks' to destroy his reputation.

1931 Rupert Murdoch, Australian media magnate, owner of *The Times*, the *Sun* and Sky Television as well as media in the US.

1932 Nigel Lawson, former editor of the *Spectator* turned politician who was Margaret Thatcher's Chancellor of the Exchequer 1983–9.

ARTS

1819 Marius Petipa, French choreographer who created ballets for the Ballets Russes, including *Sleeping Beauty* (1890) and *Swan Lake* (1895).

1819 Sir Henry Tate, English sugar refiner who endowed the Tate Gallery in London.

1930 David Gentleman, English designer and painter, especially of London scenes.

1952 Douglas Adams, English author of the enormously successful *The Hitch-Hiker's Guide to the Galaxy* which began life as a BBC radio serial.

ENTERTAINMENT

1892 Raoul Walsh, US film director who made *High Sierra* (1941) and *The Naked and the Dead* (1958).

1898 Dorothy Gish (le Guiche), US silent film actress, younger sister of the more famous Lillian. Originally the sisters appeared together in films before going their separate ways. Dorothy eventually came to Britain, where she made her last films.

1898 Jessie Matthews, English actress, singer and dancer who was Gertrude Lawrence's understudy before appearing in many successful London revues in the 20s and 30s. Her films include *Evergreen* (1934). Her career took a new turn in 1963 when she began to play Mrs Dale in the long-running radio serial.

SPORT

1885 Sir Malcolm Campbell, English world speed record holder on both land and sea. His son, Donald, followed in his footsteps.

1928 Althea Louise Brough, US tennis champion and Wimbledon singles champion for three consecutive years from 1948. In 1951 she lost to 'Little Mo', 17-year-old Maureen Connolly. In 1955 she won her fifth title.

SCIENCE

1811 Urbain Jean Joseph Leverrier, French astronomer who predicted the existence of Neptune. In 1846 a German astronomer discovered the planet working from the calculations of an Englishman inspired by Leverrier.

DIED THIS DAY

1820 Benjamin West, US painter who became President of the Royal Academy, London.

1820 Sir Alexander McKenzie, Scottish explorer of Canada.

1936 Admiral of the Fleet, David Beatty (Earl Beatty), who won the Battle of Jutland in the First World War.

1955 Sir Alexander Fleming, Scottish bacteriologist, discoverer of penicillin.

1957 Earle Stanley Gardner, US lawyer and crime writer, creator of Perry Mason.

1957 Admiral Richard Evelyn Byrd, US aviator and explorer.

1988 Arthur d'Arcy 'Bobby' Locke, South African golf champion and four times British open champion.

1988 Ken Colyer, Brtish traditional jazz trumpeter, in southern France in his beach hut home.

ON THIS DAY

1682 The famous Chelsea hospital for soldiers ('Chelsea Pensioners'), and venue for the famous Chelsea Flower show, was founded.

1702 The first successful English newspaper, a single broadsheet called the *Daily Courant* was published.

1794 The Theatre Royal, Drury Lane, opened.

1845 A Maori uprising against the British in New Zealand began.

1845 Henry Jones invented self-raising flour.

1864 A reservoir near Sheffield burst its banks, killing 250 people.

1926 Eamon de Valera resigned as leader of Sinn Fein in Ireland.

1941 The US Congress passed the Lend-Lease Bill enabling Britain to borrow millions of dollars to purchase additional food and arms needed for the Second World War. The loan was only to be paid back after the war.

1945 The huge Krupps factory in Germany was destroyed when 1,000 Allied bombers took part in the biggest ever daylight raid.

1985 Mikhail Gorbachev, at 54 the youngest member of the ruling Politburo, became leader of the USSR following the death of Konstantin Chernenko.

1985 The Al-Fayed brothers won control of the House of Fraser group to become owners of Harrods.

1988 The Bank of England pound note, first introduced on 12.3.1797, ceased to be legal tender in Britain at midnight. When the deadline for returning old notes was reached, it was estimated that some 70 million were still outstanding. 'We have no idea where they are – perhaps they are with collectors,' a Bank spokesman said.

1990 Jennifer Capriati became the youngest finalist in a professional tennis tournament, in Florida, just 18 days before her 14th birthday.

12 MARCH

BORN THIS DAY

HISTORY

1832 Charles Cunningham Boycott, English estate manager in Ireland. Following the crop failure and famine in the

1880s, the demand for lower rents grew, but was rejected by Boycott. The Irish statesman Parnell urged tenants not to resort to violence, but instead to refuse to communicate with Captain Boycott, who gave his name to a new form of protest.

1863 Gabriele d'Annunzio, Italian soldier, poet, journalist, novelist and playwright who wrote *La Gioconda*. His escapades in the First World War inspired a new nationalism which would ultimately lead to Fascism. He was made a prince in 1924.

1881 (Mustafa) Kemal Atatürk, Turkish statesman and general who became President in 1923. His reforms to modernise Turkey included the creation of a secular state, encouraging western dress and banning the fez.

ARTS

1626 John Aubrey, English antiquarian and folklorist, best remembered for his *Brief Lives*, published well over a 100 years after his death.

1710 Thomas Augustine Arne, English composer who wrote the masque *Alfred* (1740), which included the song, 'Rule Britannia'.

1890 Vaslav Nijinsky, leading Russian dancer in Diaghilev's Russian ballet company that took Paris by storm in 1909. He was insane for the last 33 years of his life.

1922 Jack (John) Kerouac, US author of *On the Road* (1957), the definitive 'beatnik' novel of the 50s.

1928 Edward Albee, US playwright who wrote *Who's Afraid of Virginia Woolf?* (1962).

ENTERTAINMENT

1894 Joseph Meyer, US songwriter who wrote 'California Here I Come', 'If You Knew Susie' and 'Crazy Rhythm'.

1908 Max Wall, English comedian and actor who has been both a zany act in music halls and an acclaimed actor in Beckett's *Waiting for Godot*.

1917 Googie (Georgette Lizzette) Withers, English actress, born in Karachi. She appeared on the British stage and in films, including *Miranda* (1948), before settling in Australia where she worked in theatre.

1946 Liza Minnelli, US actress, singer, daughter of Judy Garland and film director Vincente Minnelli, who made her own name on Broadway, the West End and in Hollywood. In 1972, she won an Oscar for her role in *Cabaret*.

1948 James Taylor, US songwriter who wrote 'Fire and Rain' and 'Carolina On My Mind'.

SCIENCE

1790 John Frederic Daniell, English chemist who invented the Daniell electric cell.

1824 Gustav Robert Kirchoff, German physicist who invented the spectroscope, which can study atoms and molecules in a gaseous or liquid phase.

1838 Sir Henry Perkin, English chemist who, in 1856, discovered the mauve dye which made possible the aniline dye industry.

DIED THIS DAY

604 St Gregory, the son of a Roman senator who became a pope. He initiated the conversion of the Anglo-Saxons and was also involved in church music; Gregorian chant bears his name.

1507 Cesare Borgia, soldier and politician.

1563 John Bull, English composer and organist who ironically composed 'God Save the King', and then had to flee England to escape persecution as a Catholic. He died in Antwerp.
1884 Bedřich Smetana, Czech composer.
1908 Reverend Benjamin Waugh, founder, in 1884, of the National Society for the Prevention of Cruelty to Children (NSPCC).
1914 George Westinghouse, US inventor of the Westinghouse brake system.
1924 Hilaire, Count de Chardonnet, French inventor of rayon.
1925 Sun Yat-sen, Chinese revolutionary leader. He was succeeded by General Chiang Kai-shek.
1932 Ivar Krugar, Swedish industrialist and forger.
1942 Sir William (Henry) Bragg, English Nobel prize-winning physicist who worked on the structure of crystals.
1945 Anne Frank, the Jewish Dutch girl who kept her famous diary recording the events in the lives of a family hidden in a house in German-occupied Holland, in the Bergen-Bergen concentration camp.
1955 (Charles Christopher) Charlie Parker, influential US saxophonist known as 'Bird'.

ON THIS DAY

1609 Bermuda became a British colony.
1912 The Girl Guides (later called Scouts) were founded in the US by Juliette Gordon Low.

CAPITAL IDEA In 1913, Canberra became the federal capital of Australia. Five years later, in 1918, Moscow was designated the capital of Russia.

1930 Mahatma Gandhi began his 300-mile march to the sea in protest against the British tax law securing a monopoly for salt. With hundreds of supporters he planned to produce a symbolic amount of salt from the sea and provoke arrest.
1944 Britain banned all travel to and from Ireland and Ulster in an effort to prevent German spies operating in neutral Eire from learning of the Allied invasion preparations taking place in Britain.
1969 Paul McCartney married Linda Eastman, US photographer, and on the same day, another Beatle, George Harrison and his wife Patti were arrested and charged with possession of 120 marijuana joints at their home.
1988 Diamond mine owners, De Beers, unveiled a 599-carat diamond second only in size to the one in the British royal sceptre. Worth tens of millions of pounds, the diamond's discovery had been kept secret so that De Beers could present it in their centenary year.

13 MARCH

BORN THIS DAY

ARTS

1884 Sir Hugh (Seymour) Walpole, English novelist, born Auckland, New Zealand, who wrote *The Secret City* (1919).

ENTERTAINMENT

1898 Henry Hathaway, US film director who worked his way up from low-budget westerns to direct films such as *The House on 92nd Street* (1945) and *True Grit* (1969).
1918 Tessie O'Shea, English actress and

entertainer, known as 'Two-Ton Tessie' because of her size.

SCIENCE

1733 Dr Joseph Priestley, English chemist and Unitarian minister who discovered oxygen in 1774. His support for the French Revolution led to his house and chapel being sacked by a mob. He emigrated to America in 1794.

1855 Percy (Percival) Lowell, US astronomer who predicted the discovery of the planet Pluto. He established Lowell Observatory in Flagstaff, Arizona.

WEIGHTY MATTERS

1770 Daniel Lambert, English fat man, who weighed 52 stone 11 pounds (739lb/335.20kg). Crowds would line the riverbank to watch his regular swims in the River Soar, Leicester, where he usually charged for exhibiting his enormous bulk. He died in a barber's chair, and it took 20 men to lower his coffin into the grave.

POP

1939 Neil Sedaka, US singer, pianist and songwriter who wrote 'Breaking Up is Hard to Do'.

SPORT

1950 Joe Bugner, Hungarian-born British heavyweight champion who later settled in Australia. He took the British, European and Commonwealth crown off Henry Cooper in 1971, and went on to a dramatic points defeat at the hands of Muhammad Ali.

DIED THIS DAY

1619 Richard Burbage, English actor who built the Globe Theatre. His partners included Shakespeare.

1881 Tsar Alexander II, assassinated by anti-monarchists who threw a bomb at him near his palace.

1901 Benjamin Harrison, 23rd US President.

1943 Stephen Vincent Benet, US poet who wrote 'John Brown's Body', a poem about the Civil War.

1947 Angela Brazil, English writer of girls' school stories.

1967 Sir Frank Worrell, West Indian cricket captain.

ON THIS DAY

STAR STRUCK In 1781, Sir William Herschel discovered the planet Uranus, originally named Georgius Sidus after George III. In 1930, Clyde Tombaugh of Lowell Observatory announced on the 75th anniversary of Percy Lowell's birth the discovery of Pluto as predicted by the Observatory's founder. Then, in 1986, the Russians launched a Soyuz T-15 from the Baikonur Cosmodrome to establish a permanent human presence in space when it docked at the Mir space station, launched three weeks before. On the same day, Halley's comet was seen again just four minutes before midnight. The European Space Agency's *Giotto*, surviving the impacts of the dust particles from the comet's tail, passed within 605 km of the nucleus, sending back sensational pictures.

1873 Eight clubs met to form the Scottish Football Association.

1894 The first professional strip-tease performance took place at the Divan Fayonau Music Hall, Paris. 'Le Coucher d'Yvette', as the act was billed, showed a girl stripping to go to bed.

1914 Henriette Caillaux, 36, the wife of the French Finance Minister, entered the offices of the newspaper *Le Figaro* and shot dead chief columnist Gaston Calmette, who had published a copy of a letter written by her husband to his first wife. Fearing the first Madame Caillaux had further letters revealing more indiscretions, Henriette was told by lawyers that there was no law in France to protect her husband against libels by newspapers, so she took the law into her owns hands. In court, she pleaded the gun had gone off accidentally and was found not guilty.

1926 Alan Cobham landed at Croydon Aerodrome, near London, after a 16,000-mile flight to Cape Town and back to establish a commercial air route across Africa.

1928 Flooding from a burst dam near Los Angeles drowned 450 people and caused extensive damage.

1938 Germany invaded Austria, which was made a province named 'Ostmark'. The following day, Hitler arrived in triumph to be greeted by a huge welcoming crowd.

1961 Pablo Picasso, 79, married his model, Jacqueline Rocque, 37, in Nice.

1970 Susan Wallace, an English schoolgirl, became the first 18-year-old eligible to vote. She cast her vote in a by-election at Bridgwater, Somerset.

1972 Clifford Irving admitted to a New York court that he had fabricated Howard Hughes' autobiography after receiving a $750,000 advance from his publishers. He had hoped the reclusive millionaire would not venture into the public limelight to denounce him.

1974 The Charles de Gaulle Airport in Paris was opened.

1979 Sir Edward Gairy, Prime Minister of Grenada, was ousted while away at the UN by Maurice Bishop, leader of the People's Revolutionary Party.

1987 Rajendra Sethia, the world's biggest bankrupt, who fled from England in 1986 owing £170m, was charged in New Delhi with criminal conspiracy and defrauding an Indian bank of another £5m.

14 MARCH

BORN THIS DAY

HISTORY

1820 Victor Emmanuel II, who was proclaimed King of Italy in 1861. He reigned for 17 years as the first king of a united Italy.

ENTERTAINMENT

1933 Michael Caine (Maurice Micklewhite), English film actor who caught the public's attention in his tenth film, *Zulu* (1964). The following year he played Harry Palmer in *The Ipcress File* and in 1966 he starred in *Alfie*. He went to Hollywood and the cockney son of a fishmarket porter and a cleaning lady was soon one of the most successful international stars.

1933 Quincy Jones, US composer and producer whose film scores include *In The Heat of the Night*. He also produced Michael Jackson's record-breaking *Thriller* album.

1940 Eleanor Bron, English actress who started in satirical revues and went on to play both comedy and dramatic roles on stage and screen.

1943 Rita Tushingham, English actress who first made her name in the film, *A Taste of Honey* (1961).

1946 Jasper Carrott, English comedian.

1947 Pam Ayres, English folk poet who

made her name on radio and television with her light, amusing, anecdotal poetry.

SCIENCE

1835 Giovanni Viginio Schiaparelli, Italian astronomer who first discovered the 'canals' on Mars (1877), later seen by Lowell.

1879 Albert Einstein, German-born Swiss physicist and mathematician. He worked originally as an examiner at the Swiss Patents Office. He studied for his Ph.D and wrote scientific papers in his spare time, which attracted considerable interest. He published his special theory of relativity, which described the relationship of the universe to time, in 1905 and his general theory in 1916, winning the Nobel prize for Science in 1921. He worked in Germany until Hitler's rise to power where, as a Jew, he faced persecution. He went to the US to continue his work through the war. Later he urged controls on atomic weaponry and took a strong stand against the Un-American Activities Senate subcommittee.

SPORT

1957 Tessa Sanderson, English and world champion javelin thrower, gold medal winner at the Los Angeles Olympics, 1984.

DIED THIS DAY

1757 John Byng, British admiral who bungled the relief of Minorca, blockaded by the French fleet; shot for neglecting his duty, on board the *Monarque* at Portsmouth.

1883 Karl Marx, German philospher, the father of Communism, in London. He was buried in Highgate Cemetery.

1932 George Eastman, US inventor who founded the Kodak photographic company, committed suicide.

1975 Susan Hayward (Edythe Marrener), Oscar-winning US film actress.

1976 Busby Berkley (William Berkley Enos), US film choreographer and director.

ON THIS DAY

1805 Master Betty (William Betty), played *Hamlet* on the London stage, aged just 14. He was such a success, the House of Commons was adjourned to enable members to watch his performance. His success was short-lived and, not long afterwards, he was hissed off the stage.

1885 The first performance of Gilbert and Sullivan's *The Mikado* at the Savoy Theatre, London.

1891 Telephone cable was laid along the English Channel bed by the submarine *Monarch*.

1953 Nikita Krushchev replaced Malenkov as First Secretary of the Communist Party.

1964 Jack Ruby was found guilty in Dallas, Texas, of killing Lee Harvey Oswald, the alleged assassin of President John F. Kennedy, and was sentenced to death. He died of a blood clot in the lung in 3.1.1967.

1985 Five lionesses at Singapore Zoo were put on the pill because the lion population had grown from two to 16.

1988 A scuffle broke out at a Warwickshire restaurant when one diner took food from another man's plate and then bit off his ear when he objected. Stephen Flint, 23, admitted wounding and was jailed for two years.

15 MARCH

'Beware the Ides of March!' In 44BC, Gaius Julius Caesar was assassinated by conspirators, including Brutus and Cassius in the Senate House in Rome.

BORN THIS DAY

HISTORY

1767 Andrew Jackson, seventh US President. 'Old Hickory', as he was nicknamed, was one of the generals who fought the British in 1812 and later became the first Governor of Florida. He became President in 1828, serving two terms before retiring in 1837.

ARTS

1946 David Wall, English principal dancer with the Royal Ballet before becoming Director of the Royal Academy of Dancing.

POP

1941 Mike Love, US singer, member of the Beach Boys. His fascination with Transcendental Meditation led the group on a near-disastrous tour with the Maharishi Mahesh Yogi.

1961 Terence Trent d'Arby, US singer who settled in Britain and had hits with 'If You Let Me Stay' (1987) and 'Sign Your Name' (1988).

DIED THIS DAY

1898 Sir Henry Bessemer, English metallurgist, pioneer of mass-produced steel.

1975 Aristotle Onassis, Greek shipping tycoon.

1983 Dame Rebecca West (Cecily Isabel Fairfield), English author.

1984 Tommy Cooper, zany English comedian, of a heart attack while performing on the stage of Her Majesty's Theatre, London, for a live television show during Sunday peak viewing time. Almost 20 million viewers saw his last moments as he collapsed before the commercial break. He was rushed to hospital, but found dead on arrival.

ON THIS DAY

1820 Maine became the 23rd state of the Union.

1869 The Cincinnati Red Stockings became the first all-pro baseball team.

1877 The first cricket test between England and Australia was played at Melbourne with victory going to the home team by just 45 runs.

1907 The Finns elected the very first women members of parliament, while in Britain women had not yet been given the vote.

1909 The American, G. S. Selfridge, opened the store that bears his name in London; Britain's first American-style department store.

1917 Nicholas II, Tsar of Russia, abdicated as the Revolution reached a climax. The following day, Kerensky's socialist revolutionaries took control.

1933 Hitler proclaimed the Third Reich, which he said would endure for a thousand years. The Nazi flag would fly side by side the German Imperial flag. Left-wing newspapers and kosher meat were banned.

1937 America's first central blood bank was set up by Bernard Faustus, who coined the term 'blood bank'.

1956 The first performance of *My Fair Lady* with Julie Andrews and Rex Harrison on Broadway.

1964 Elizabeth Taylor married Richard Burton in Montreal.

1982 The director of *The Romans in Britain*, Michael Bogdanov, went on trial for presenting an 'indecent' production, but the next day the Attorney-General stopped the trial in the public interest.

1988 A man with a gun tried to rob a bank in Montpellier, France, the home of nougat. The would-be robber lost his nerve at the crucial moment and ate his gun. It was made of nougat.

1990 Farzad Bazoft, a journalist with the *Observer*, was hanged as a spy by the Iraqis. Daphne Parish, a British nurse who gave the reporter a lift to a military establishment, was sentenced to 15 years' imprisonment.

16 MARCH

BORN THIS DAY

HISTORY

1751 James Madison, fourth US President, elected 1809. He retired at the end of his second term in 1817.

1774 Matthew Flinders, English explorer who circumnavigated Australia. The Flinders River in Queensland and the Flinders Range in South Australia are named after him.

ENTERTAINMENT

1920 Leo McKern, Australian-born actor who excels playing formidable character roles on the stage, screen and television, especially as Rumpole in John Mortimer's *Rumpole of the Bailey*.

1926 Jerry Lewis (Jospeh Levitch), US film comedian who, in 1946, whilst a relatively unsuccessful cabaret and stage comedian, met an equally unsuccessful entertainer, Dean Martin. The two teamed up and went on to make a long and successful series of Hollywood comedies, including *Artists and Models* (1955) before going their separate ways.

1940 Bernardo Bertolucci, Italian film director who, in 1972, caused controversy with *Last Tango in Paris*.

SCIENCE

1787 Georg Simon Ohm, German physicist who researched electricity and gave his name to the measurement of resistance, the ohm.

DIED THIS DAY

1878 William Banting, London undertaker who pioneered slimming to reduce his own obesity. 'Banting' is the term used for abstaining from sugars, starches and fats.

1892 Aubrey Beardsley, English illustrator who, with Oscar Wilde, was one of the 'Decadents' of the 1890s, of consumption in France.

1930 Miguel Primo de Rivera y Orbaneja, Marqués de Estella, Spanish general and virtual dictator.

1937 Sir Joseph Austen Chamberlain, British statesman.

1963 William Henry, first Baron Beveridge of Tuggal, British social services pioneer.

ON THIS DAY

1802 The famous US Military Academy at West Point, was established.

1815 William of Orange was proclaimed King of the Netherlands and became William I.

1872 The first Football Association Cup Final was played. The venue was the Kennington Oval, London. The teams were the Wanderers, who beat the Royal Engineers 1–0. The gate: just 2,000.

1888 The first recorded sale of a manufactured motor car was to Émile Roger of Paris, who bought a petrol-driven car from Karl Benz's new factory.

1900 Sir Arthur Evans revealed the ancient city of Knossus, Crete, which he began excavating in 1899. The site was orginally offered to Schliemann, the German archaeologist and discoverer of Troy, who turned it down believing it showed little promise.

1912 Lawrence Oates, a member of Scott's ill-fated South Pole expedition who was suffering serious frostbite and hampering the progress of his companions, left the tent saying, 'I am just going outside and may be some time.' 'A very gallant gentleman,' Scott recorded. His body has never been found.

1918 The famous 'stuttering' song, 'K-K-K-Katy' was published, words and music by Canadian Geoffrey O'Hara.

1926 The first rocket propelled by liquid oxygen and gasoline was successfully fired by Dr Robert H. Goddard of Massachusetts. The rocket was just four feet high.

1935 Hitler renounced the Versailles Treaty and introduced conscription, the next step in his military build-up.

1968 Three platoons of US troops entered the village of Mai Lai in Vietnam. There were no Vietcong there, but the soldiers tossed grenades and shot at anything that moved – women, children and old people – killing 175 villagers. (*See* 29.3.1971)

1973 The Queen opened the new London Bridge. (The old one was sold to a US oil tycoon for £1m and rebuilt piece-by-piece in the US.)

17 MARCH

St Patrick's Day, the patron saint of Ireland.

Also the Feast Day of Gertrude of Nivelles, patron saint of the recently dead, who would help them on their way to the other world.

In the Middle Ages, this was also reckoned to be the day Noah entered the Ark as the great Flood began.

BORN THIS DAY

HISTORY

1873 Margaret Grace Bondfield, British Labour politician who became chairman of the TUC in 1923 and Minister of Labour in 1929, the first woman to hold office in the Cabinet.

ARTS

1787 Edmund Kean, who became the leading English actor of his time.

1846 Kate Greenaway, English illustrator of children's books.

1938 Rudolf Nureyev, Russian-born ballet dancer and choreographer who defected to the west in 1961. Considered one of the finest male dancers this century, his partnership with Margot Fonteyn at Covent Garden was an enormous success. He also appeared in films, including the lead in *Valentino*.

ENTERTAINMENT

1917 Nat(aniel Adams) 'King' Cole(s), legendary US singer and pianist who dominated the popular music scene with the King Cole Trio before the rock 'n' roll era. In 1956, a gang of white men dragged him off a stage in Alabama while singing to a white audience.

1918 Mercedes McCambridge, US actress who first made her reputation as one of the best radio actresses. She won an Oscar for best supporting actress in *All the King's Men* (1949) her first film.

1954 Leslie Ann Downe, English actress, who made her name in the television serial *Upstairs, Downstairs*.

SPORT

1902 Bobby Jones, US golfer who, in 1926, was the first amateur to win the Open at Lytham St Annes. He went on to win it three times and, in 1930, he completed the grand slam, winning the Open in June and the US amateur golf championship in September. He retired the following month, aged 28.

ENGINEERING

1834 Gottlieb Daimler, German engineer who improved the internal combustion engine and who, in 1885, designed one of the earliest cars. He went on to found the Daimler Automobile Company.

DIED THIS DAY

1782 Daniel Bernoulli, Swiss mathematician.

1853 Christian Doppler, Austrian physicist who described the Doppler effect, the apparent change in the frequency of a wave.

1958 Sir George Hubert Wilkins, Australian polar explorer whose ashes were taken to the North Pole, where they were scattered to the wind.

1988 Takeo Miki, former Japanese Prime Minister.

ON THIS DAY

1337 The Duchy of Cornwall was created when Edward the Black Prince was made the first Duke.

1845 Elastic bands were patented by Stephen Perry of a London rubber company.

1897 Bob (Robert Prometheus) Fitzsimmons, the only British boxer to win a world heavyweight title, who was born in England and reared in New Zealand, took the title off Jim Corbett in Carson City, Nevada and held it until 1899. The fight was filmed by the Veriscope Company of New York on the first widescreen process using 70mm film.

1899 The classic Neopolitan song 'O Sole Mio!' was published. The composer was E. di Campna with words by G. Capurro.

1899 The first radio distress call was sent from a lightship off Kent to the nearest lighthouse on the coast, summoning a lifeboat to assist a merchant ship which ran aground on the Goodwin Sands.

1921 The first birth control clinic run by Dr Marie Stopes, author of *Married Love*, opened in London.

1968 A huge demonstration in London's Grosvenor Square against the continuance of US involvement in the Vietnam War led to violent confrontation with 91 police casualties and over 200 demonstrators arrested.

1969 Golda Meir became the Prime Minister of Israel.

1978 The oil tanker *Amoco Cadiz* ran aground on the coast of Brittany. Over 220,000 tons of crude oil seeped out of the crippled ship, causing serious pollution to the coastline.

1979 Wales beat England 27–3 at Cardiff to win the Triple Crown for the fourth successive year under captain J.P.R. Williams.

1980 Britain's first woman stationmaster took charge of Burgess Hill station, Sussex. She was economics graduate, Penny Bellas.

18 MARCH

BORN THIS DAY

HISTORY

1609 Frederick III, King of Denmark and Norway, whose reign involved him in war with Sweden.

1837 Stephen Grover Cleveland, who was elected 22nd President of the US in 1885. He was defeated when standing for a second term, but won again in 1892 to become the 24th President.

1869 Arthur Neville Chamberlain, who became British Prime Minister in 1937. His appeasement policy towards Hitler led to his downfall in 1940, when he handed over to Churchill.

1889 Lavrenti Pavlovich Beria, chief of the Russian secret police, one of the most powerful and feared men in the Soviet Union.

ARTS

1842 Stéphane Mallarmé, French Symbolistic poet who used free verse and obscure words, meanings and symbols in his poetry. Best known for 'L'Après-midi d'un faune'.

1844 Nikolai Andreievich Rimsky-Korsakov, Russian composer whose career began as a sailor. He taught himself music in secret before becoming inspector of naval bands. His works include *Sheherazade* (1888).

1893 Wilfred Owen, English poet who was killed in action at the age of 25 on the western front during the First World War.

1932 John (Hoyer) Updike, US award-winning novelist of *Rabbit, Run* (1960).

ENTERTAINMENT

1905 (Friedrich) Robert Donat, English actor who took elocution lessons to overcome a stutter and became one of the most distinguished actors of his time on both stage and screen. He won an Oscar for his role in *Goodbye Mr Chips* (1939). Throughout his career he suffered from chronic asthma.

POP

1941 Wilson Pickett, US rhythm-and-blues and soul singer who had most of his successes in the 60s including 'In the Midnight Hour'.

SPORT

1949 Alex 'Hurricane' Higgins, Irish snooker player and one-time British champion, noted for his wild behaviour, from head-butting a referee to drug taking. The nickname describes his speedy approach to each shot.

1952 Pat Eddery, four times champion British jockey.

ENGINEERING

1858 Rudolf Diesel, German engineer who worked on the first compression ignition motor after devising ways to inject fuel into the cylinder head against enormous pressures. Born just a day after Daimler's 24th birthday, these two engineers pioneered modern engines.

DIED THIS DAY

978 Edward the Martyr, king of England from 975, murdered at Corfe Castle, Dorset at the instigation of his step-mother who wanted the crown for her son Ethelred.

1455 Fra Angelico (Guido di Pietri), Italian painter.

1584 Ivan IV, the first Tsar of Russia, known as 'Ivan the Terrible'. He is said to have died in sorrow for his son, whom he killed in a fit of rage three years before.

1745 Robert Walpole, first Earl of Orford, Britain's first Prime Minister.

1768 Laurence Sterne, Irish-born clergy-man and author of *Tristram Shandy* (1759), in poverty in London.

1913 King George I of Greece, assassin-ated as he was taking a walk.

1933 Duke of the Abruzzi, Luigi Ama-deo, Italian explorer and climber.

EXILES EXIT In 1965, Farouk I, King of Egypt until 1952 when he was sent into exile, died in Italy. Two years earlier, in 1963, King Umberto II of Italy who began his exile in 1946, died in a Geneva clinic.

ON THIS DAY

ON THE BUSES In 1662, the first public buses ran in Paris. Louis XIV intended them for use by the poor of the city who could not afford carriages, but they were taken up by the fashionable who crowded out the less fortunate. The poor decided that buses were not for them, and when the Parisian 'tren-dies' got bored, the service was discontinued. Over two hundred years later, in 1895, the first petrol-driven motor bus, a five-h.p. Benz, in the North Rhineland, went into service. It was capable of carrying between six and eight passengers.

1834 The 'Tolpuddle Martyrs', six Dorset farm labourers, were sentenced to be transported to a penal colony for form-ing a trade union.

1850 The American Express Company was set up in Buffalo, New York.

1871 The Communards began their uprising in Paris, which would lead, in May, to the first socialist government in history.

1922 Gandhi was sentenced to six years imprisonment for sedition, accused of stirring up disaffection against the exist-ing government in India.

1925 Two floors of the Madame Tussauds waxworks in London were destroyed by fire.

1931 Electric razors were first manufac-tured by Schick Incorporated, Stan-ford, Connecticut.

1932 Sydney Harbour bridge was opened. It was the world's longest single-arch bridge.

1935 The 30 m.p.h. speed limit in built-up areas was introduced into Britain and has remained in force ever since.

1947 The Queen's husband, Prince Philip, became a naturalized Briton.

1949 NATO (the North Atlantic Treaty organization) was set up with Britain and seven other European countries.

1958 Young English ladies of class and/or money (the latter being rather impor-tant to pay for ballgowns, expensive parties, etc.) were presented to the Queen for the last time at Buckingham Palace. But despite official lack of recognition, débutantes continued to survive and gather annually for a season of parties and balls.

1965 Lt Col Aleksey Arkhipovich Leanor left the spacecraft *Voskod II*. Connected only by a nylon cord, he floated in space for 12 minutes nine seconds, during which time he travelled around 3,000 miles at a speed of 17,500 m.p.h.

1967 The *Torrey Canyon* ran aground off Land's End, Cornwall. When the oil tanker's cargo began to seep out, the RAF were called in to napalm bomb the slick to reduce the risk of coastline pollution.

CLOSING SENTENCES In 1978, Pakistan Prime Minister Bhutto was found guilty of ordering the assassination of a political opponent and sentenced to hang. The same day, former Italian Prime Minister Aldo Moro was kidnapped by the Red Brigade. Two months later his body was found in the boot of a small Renault in central Rome.

1989 Britain's first National Fat Women's conference was held. More than 150 overweight ladies planned to establish associations throughout the country to urge fat women to stop worrying about their weight.

19 MARCH

The Feast Day of Joseph, patron saint of fathers, carpenters, procurators and bursars.

BORN THIS DAY

HISTORY

SOURCE OF THE NILE Born 1813, Dr David Livingstone, Scottish missionary and explorer who was the first European to discover the Victoria Falls of the Zambesi. While at Ujiji, on an expedition to find the source of the Nile, he became ill and it was here that newspaper man Stanley found him. Livingstone never did find the source; it was found instead by Sir Richard Francis Burton, English scholar, translator of the *Arabian Nights* and traveller, born 1821.

1848 Wyatt Earp, US lawman who was involved in five gunfights in Tombstone, Arizona including the Gunfight at the O.K. Corral. He is said to have survived by wearing a bullet-proof vest.

1906 Adolf Eichmann, Nazi colonel in the SS who played a key role in the 'Final Solution', the extermination of millions of Jews, political opponents and other 'undesirable' minorities within Europe. In April 1961 he was finally confronted by some of the few survivors of the death camps, in a Jerusalem court.

ARTS

1593 George de la Tour, French painter. Some of his paintings were for a time wrongly believed to be works by followers of Caravaggio.

1721 Tobias George Smollett, Scottish physician-turned-author, who wrote satirical novels, including *Roderick Random* (1748).

1933 Philip Roth, US author whose novels include *Portnoy's Complaint* (1969).

ENTERTAINMENT

1928 Patrick McGoohan, American-born British actor best known for his cult television series *The Prisoner*, as well as *Danger Man*.

1936 Ursula Andress, Swiss actress who

made her name in the Bond movie, *Dr No* (1962).

SAXOPHONISTS Born 1930, Ornette Coleman, US saxophonist and composer influenced by Parker. He often took improvisation 'to the edge of possibility'. He later explored other styles including jazz funk. His birthday is now shared by a remarkable English saxophonist, Courtney Pine, born 1964.

SPORT

1915 Norman Yardley, former Yorkshire and England cricket captain.

DIED THIS DAY

1930 Arthur James Balfour, first Earl, British Prime Minister 1902–6.

1950 Edgar Rice Burroughs, US author of the Tarzan stories.

1965 Alan Badel, English actor.

ON THIS DAY

721BC The first eclipse ever recorded was observed by the Babylonians, according to Ptolomy.

1920 The US Senate voted against joining the League of Nations, fearing they would have to go to war again if another member state was invaded.

1931 Alka-Seltzer was first marketed in the US.

1958 Britain's first planetarium opened at Madame Tussaud's, London.

1969 British paras and Marines were landed on the island of Anguilla and found no resistance from the 'Republican Defence Force' set up by 'President' Ronald Webster. The population welcomed the troops and the 40 London policemen sent out later to keep order. They spent most of their time sunbathing and swimming in the warm Caribbean sea.

DOUBLE EXPOSURE In 1976, Princess Margaret separated from her photographer husband, Lord Snowdon, after 15 years of marriage. Ten years to the day in 1986, marriage and the Royals were back in the news. Buckingham Palace announced the engagement of Prince Andrew and Sarah Ferguson.

20 MARCH

BORN THIS DAY

HISTORY

1938 Brian Mulroney, Prime Minister of Canada.

ARTS

43BC Ovid (Publius Ovidius Naso), Latin poet who wrote 'Medea' and 'Epistolae', imaginary love letters from ladies to their lords.

1823 Henrik Ibsen, Norwegian poet and playwright of realistic social dramas including *A Doll's House* (1879) and *Hedda Gabler* (1890). He influenced many writers with his themes and treatment, including Bernard Shaw.

1890 Beniamino Gigli, Italian tenor who made his debut in 1914 and within little over a decade was recognized as one of the world's greatest tenors, particularly in the works of Verdi and Puccini.

ENTERTAINMENT

1908 Sir Michael (Scudamore) Redgrave, English actor whose parents and grandparents were actors. He played Hamlet at the Old Vic and at Elsinore in 1949, and also starred in many modern plays and films, including *The Lady Vanishes* (1938) and *Mourning Becomes Electra* (1947), which won him an Oscar nomination. He married actress Rachel Kempson in 1935 and the Redgrave dynasty continues with daughters Vanessa and Lynn and son Corin.

1917 Dame Vera Lynn (Vera Welch), English singer who became the 'Forces Sweetheart' during the Second World War with songs like 'We'll Meet Again' and 'The White Cliffs of Dover'.

DIED THIS DAY

1413 King Henry IV of England, son of John of Gaunt, in Westminster Abbey.

1549 Thomas Seymour, Lord High Admiral of England, who married King Henry VIII's widow, Catherine Parr. When she died, he planned to marry the Princess Elizabeth, but was arrested for treason and executed on this day.

1727 Sir Isaac Newton, English scientist; buried at Westminster Abbey.

1894 Lajos Kossuth, Hungarian patriot.

1925 George Nathaniel Curzon, first Marquis, Viceroy of India.

1929 Ferdinand Foch, Marshal of France and Commander-in-Chief of the Allied forces in France; buried near Napoleon in the Invalides six days later.

1945 Lord Alfred Douglas ('Bosie'), one-time intimate of Oscar Wilde and the cause of his downfall.

1964 Brendan Behan, Irish playwright and novelist.

ON THIS DAY

1602 The Netherlands government formed the Dutch East India Company. It became one of the most powerful companies in the world during its 96-year history.

1780 James Watt began manufacturing the first duplicator, which he had invented to help with the burden of office work generated by his steam engine business.

1806 The foundation stone of Dartmoor prison in Devon was laid. It opened three years later to house French prisoners of war, but by 1850 the first convicts were being imprisoned.

1815 After his banishment to Elba, Napoleon returned to take power once more in France. It was to be his last 'Hundred Days', leading to his defeat at Waterloo and his exile to St Helena, where he would die.

1819 The famous and still very elegant and exclusive Burlington Arcade opened in London.

1852 *Uncle Tom's Cabin*, Harriet Beecher Stowe's anti-slavery novel, was published.

1926 Scotland beat England at Twickenham for the first time to win rugby's prized Calcutta Cup. In 1937, it was England's turn to beat the Scots on their famous Murrayfield turf to win the Calcutta Cup, International Championship and Triple Crown for the first time.

1934 Radar was first demonstrated in Kiel Harbour, developed by Dr Rudolf Kuhnold, Chief of the German Navy's Signals Research Department.

KIDNAPPERS In 1974, an attempt was made to kidnap Princess Anne in the Mall by a gunman who fired six shots, then tried to drag her out of the car. He fled as passers-by joined her bodyguard and police to foil the attempt, and was later caught. Ian Ball, who was charged with attempted murder claimed he did it to highlight the lack of mental care facilities. On the same day in 1976, Patricia Hearst, the newspaper heiress who had been kidnapped by the Symbionese Liberation Army, was found guilty of helping her former kidnappers in an armed robbery and was given a seven-year jail sentence. (See 5.2.1974)

21 MARCH

BORN THIS DAY

HISTORY

1801 Benito Pablo Juàrez, Mexican President who suspended Mexico's foreign debt to try and stabilize his impoverished country. This brought military pressure from debtor nations, including Britain and France, who set up Maximilian, brother of the Austrian emperor, in his place. When Maximilian was shot by a firing squad, Juàrez was again elected President.

ARTS

1685 Johann Sebastian Bach, German composer and organist from a family which had produced 53 organists, cantors and town musicians over 300 years. Besides chamber music and works for the keyboard, he composed 250 cantatas, including the *St Matthew Passion* (1729). Despite his vast output, less than a dozen of his compositions were published during his life, and his genius was not recognized until half a century after his death. Wagner called Bach's work, 'the most stupendous miracle in music'.

1839 Modest Petrovich Mussorgsky, Russian composer whose famous opera *Boris Godunov* (1868) was first rejected by the Imperial Theatre. When it was performed, it was well-received by the audience, but hated by musicians unfamiliar with its unconventionalities.

1914 Paul Tortelier, French cellist, conductor and composer with the world's leading orchestras. His year in Israel produced his *Israel Symphony* for two cellos.

ENTERTAINMENT

1862 Albert Chevalier, English composer and singer of cockney songs. He wrote 'My Old Dutch' and 'Knocked 'em in the Old Kent Road'.

1869 Florenz Ziegfeld, US impresario who staged his first Ziegfeld Follies, which were lavish shows with beautiful girls and extravagant sets in 1907, and presented an annual revue until 1931, attracting great stars and composers including Jerome Kern and Irving Berlin.

1925 Peter (Stephen Paul) Brook, English stage and film director who demonstrated his originality at his first Stratford season in 1947. He also directed operas at Covent Garden, including *Salome* with sets by Dali.

1944 Timothy Dalton, Welsh actor who made his name in classical stage roles before becoming the fourth James Bond following Roger Moore's retirement from the role.

POP

1936 Roger Whittaker, Kenyan-born singer and songwriter.

SPORT

1935 Brian Clough, English footballer and manager who despite, or because of his outspokenness, commands fierce loyalty. In 1973, the Derby team demonstrated when he was sacked.

DIED THIS DAY

1156 Thomas Cranmer, who was the first Protestant Archbishop of Canterbury. Condemned for treason, he recanted all forced confessions before being burned at the stake as a heretic.

1843 Robert Southey, English poet laureate from 1813.

1958 Michael Todd (Avram Goldenbogen), US film producer and third husband of Elizabeth Taylor.

1982 Harry H. Corbett, English actor who played Harold Steptoe in the *Steptoe and Son* television series.

1985 Sir Michael (Scudamore) Redgrave, English actor, the day after his 77th birthday.

ON THIS DAY

1829 The Duke of Wellington, aged 60, fought a bloodless duel with the Earl of Winchelsea. The reason for the duel was the Duke's support of Catholic emancipation. Wellington was both Prime Minister and leader of the Tory Party at the time.

1908 Henri Farman, the French aviator, took up the first passenger and flew over Paris. The official first air passenger was the Wright brother's mechanic who flew in Kitty Hawk on 14 May 1908.

1933 The ceremonial opening of the first Parliament of Nazi Germany with Hitler as Chancellor, was held at the Garrison Church, Potsdam, on the same day as Bismark opened the first parliament of the newly founded German Reich in 1871.

1946 In Britain, Aneurin Bevan announced the government's proposals for a National Health Service, but the doctors immediately announced the setting-up of a fighting fund to oppose legislation, fearing a loss of earnings.

1952 Dr Kwame Nkrumah was elected the first African Prime Minister south of the Sahara, when he won the Gold Coast (later renamed Ghana) elections.

1960 In South Africa, a peaceful demonstration in Sharpeville against the government's oppressive pass laws turned into a massacre. The 75 policemen in the local police station panicked as a crowd of 15,000 converged on them, suddenly opening fire and killing 56 and injuring 162.

1963 This was the last night at Alcatraz Prison in San Francisco Bay for the convicts. In its 29 years as a penitentiary, it had housed Al Capone as well as the famous 'Birdman of Alcatraz'.

1969 John Lennon and new wife Yoko Ono staged their 'Beds in Peace' at the Amsterdam Hilton; Yoko's idea to get over their peace message while on honeymoon.

1989 Australia's Prime Minister, Bob Hawke, cried on television after confessing to adultery. He said in a national broadcast that he had stopped womanizing and thanked his wife for her understanding.

1990 A massive poll tax demonstration in Trafalgar Square turned into a riot. 417 people were injured, 341 arrested.

22 MARCH

BORN THIS DAY

HISTORY

1459 Maximilian I, German Emperor who did much to foster the arts while at the same time playing a game of European 'Monopoly' with the various states and nations, using his relations as tokens to acquire more territory and power.

1930 Sir Lynden Pindling, first black Prime Minister of the Bahamas following independence from Britain and elections in 1967.

ARTS

1599 Sir Anthony van Dyke, Flemish artist who became the court portrait painter in England, eventually marrying the daughter of the Earl of Gowrie. He had been a student of Rubens and was influenced by his style. Charles I knighted him in 1632.

1842 Carl August Nicolas Rosa (Rose), German impresario and violinist who came to London and, in 1873, founded the Carl Rosa Opera Company; he made the important breakthrough of having not only operas written by English composers, but also sung in English.

1910 Nicholas Monsarrat, English author of *The Cruel Sea* (1951).

1923 Marcel Marceau, French mime artist who founded his mime company in 1964. He created the popular character, the white-faced Bip.

1931 Leslie (John) Thomas, Welsh-born novelist whose many best-sellers include *The Virgin Soldiers* (1966).

ENTERTAINMENT

1913 Karl Malden (Malden Sekulovich), US actor whose films include *On The Waterfront* (1954). He was later seen in the television series, *The Streets of San Francisco*.

TWO OF A KIND In 1930, Stephen (Joseph) Sondheim, US composer and lyricist. He wrote lyrics for *West Side Story* (1957), and *Gypsy* (1959), and composed and wrote the words for *A Little Night Music* (1973) and *Sweeney Todd* (1979). His *Follies* was given a rapturous reception when revived in 1987. His birthday is shared by English composer Andrew Lloyd Webber, born 1948, whose musicals *Jesus Christ Superstar* (1971), *Evita* (1978), *Cats* (1981) and *Phantom of the Opera* (1987) have turned the tables on US domination of the musical.

1931 William Shatner, Canadian-born film and television actor, best known as Captain Kirk of the *Starship Enterprise* in *Star Trek*.

SCIENCE

1868 Robert Andrews Millikan, US physicist and Nobel prize winner (1923) who in 1925 discovered cosmic rays.

DIED THIS DAY

1687 Jean Baptiste Lully, French composer who made French opera popular. He died as a result of a gangrenous abcess on his foot caused by striking it with the long stick he used to conduct his *Te Deum*, written to celebrate Louis XIV's recovery from illness.

1772 John Canton, English physicist who made the first artificial magnets.

1896 Johann Wolfgang von Goethe, German poet, novelist and playwright.

1896 Thomas Hughes, English reformer, author of *Tom Brown's Schooldays*.

ON THIS DAY

1774 *Tommy Thumb's Song Book*, a collection of English nursery rhymes which included 'Baa, baa, black sheep', was published by Mrs Mary Cooper.

1824 The British Parliament voted to

spend £57,000 to purchase 38 pictures from John Julius, to establish a British national collection. The exisiting building in Trafalgar Square opened in 1838.

1859 In Melbourne Ben Douglas, a plasterer, became chairman of the Political Labour League of Victoria, the first 'Labour Party'.

1888 The English Football League was formed by representatives from 12 clubs meeting at an hotel in Fleet Street, London.

1895 The first celluloid film presented publicly on a screen was a short film by Auguste and Louis Lumière in Paris. It showed workers leaving the Lumière factory at Lyons at the start of their lunch hour.

1903 Due to a drought, the US side of the Niagara Falls ran short of water.

1904 The first colour picture appeared in a newspaper, the *Daily Illustrated Mirror* in the US.

1906 The first rugby international between France and England in Paris ended with a 35–0 victory to England.

1907 The first cabs with taxi meters began operating in London.

1933 Dachau concentration camp, a former First World War munitions factory near Munich, opened.

1942 The BBC began the first morse code broadcasts to the French Resistance.

1945 The Arab League was formed in Cairo, and, exactly one year later, the former British protectorate, Jordan became independent.

TOO MUCH OF A BAD THING In 1978, Karl Wallenda, one of the great high-wire acrobats, plunged to his death while promoting a touring circus in Puerto Rico. 16 years earlier, on the same day in 1962, his nephew and son-in-law, also part of 'The Great Wallendas', had been killed when their human pyramid act collapsed, and in 1972, Richard Guzman accidentally touched a live wire while climbing a pole to join his father-in-law, Karl Wallenda, during a performance. The shock made him lose his grip and he also plunged to his death.

1988 The first official mercy killing took place in Australia when a life-support system of a terminally ill patient was turned off by doctors at a Melbourne hospital.

23 MARCH

The National Day of Pakistan; on this day in 1956, it was declared an Islamic Republic.

BORN THIS DAY

HISTORY

1860 Horatio William Bottomley, English journalist and financier who wanted a life of luxury but whose grandiose business schemes kept leading to bankruptcy. When found guilty of fraud for a third time, he was sentenced to seven years in jail. The founder of the journal *John Bull*, Horatio Bottomley had been a Member of Parliament, and gone through millions of pounds when he died in poverty in 1933.

RECORD BREAKERS In 1921, Donald Malcolm Campbell, son of former world land and water speed holder, Sir Malcolm. Much in awe of his father, he was determined to carve his own name as a world speed record-breaker which he managed in 1955. Also born this day in 1929, Sir Roger Bannister, neurologist and Master of Pembroke College, Oxford, where as a student in 1954, he ran the world's first four-minute mile.

ARTS

1887 Juan Gris (José Victoriano González), Spanish painter. A 'synthetic Cubist', he exibited in Paris, and designed ballets for Diaghilev.

ENTERTAINMENT

1908 Joan Crawford (Lucille Fay Le Sueur), US film actress who started in the chorus line on Broadway, was talent-spotted and came to Hollywood where she survived for 45 years making films such as *Mildred Pierce* (1945), for which she won an Oscar, and *Whatever Happened to Baby Jane* (1962).

1910 Akira Kurosawa, Japanese film director who made the award winning *Rashomon* (1950). His *Seven Samurai* (1954) inspired the Hollywood copy *The Magnificent Seven*. In 1990 he won a Special Oscar for his contribution to the cinema.

1920 Jimmy (James Keith O'Neill) Edwards, English comedian who appeared mainly on radio in series such as *Take It From Here*.

ENGINEERING

1912 Wernher (Magnus Maximillian) von Braun, German rocket engineer who designed and developed the V1 and V2 rockets of the Second World War. He became a US citizen soon after its conclusion to work for NASA on US rocketry, mainly for the space programme.

DIED THIS DAY

1369 Pedro the Cruel, King of Castile and Leon, who murdered one brother, was finally slain by Henry, his other brother.

1842 Stendhal (Marie Henri Beyle), French novelist.

1877 Bishop John D. Lee, executed by firing squad in Utah for his part in the massacre of settlers at Mountain Meadows by members of the Mormon Church on 18 September 1857.

1921 E(dward) W(illiam) Hornung, English novelist who created *Raffles*, the gentleman thief.

1953 Raoul Dufy, French painter.

1964 Peter Lorre (Laszlo Lowenstein), Hungarian-born US film actor who appeared in gangster and horror films.

1981 Field Marshal Sir Claude John Auchinleck, who was made a scapegoat for set-backs during the North African campaign during the Second World War.

1981 Mike Hailwood, England and nine times world motor cycling champion, died in a car crash with his nine-year-old daughter when his car collided with a lorry two miles from home.

ON THIS DAY

1752 The *Halifax Gazette*, the first Canadian newspaper, was published.

1765 The Stamp Act came into force requiring the stamping (or taxing) of all publications and legal documents in British colonies provoking the American colonies to claim 'no taxation without representation'. Although repealed the following year, the War of Independence was growing nearer.

1861 London's first tram cars began operating from Bayswater. The cars were designed by a Mr Train from New York.

SHELL SHOCK In 1918, 'Big Bertha', the giant German gun, began shelling Paris from 75 miles away, while in London at the Wood Green Empire, Chung Ling-soo (William E. Robinson, US-born magician) was about to perform his 'Defying Bullets' trick which required him to 'catch' two bullets fired at him from separate guns. Because of a mechanical failure of one of the guns, the bullet was actually discharged and pierced his lung. He managed to cry 'Lower the curtain', and died the following morning in hospital.

1919 Italian Socialist journalist, Benito Mussolini, formed the Fascists to fight liberalism and communism.

1923 'Yes, We Have No Bananas' with words and music by Frank Silver and Irving Conn, was published.

1925 Tennessee state banned the teaching of Darwin's theory of evolution. One teacher later disobeyed and sparked off one of the most bizarre court cases ever, known as the 'Monkey Trial'.

1933 Hitler became dictator of Germany.

1962 The world's first nuclear merchant vessel, the *Savannah*, was launched at Camden, New Jersey.

1966 The first official meeting for 400 years between the Catholic and the Anglican churches took place in Rome between the Pope (Paul) and Dr Ramsey, the Archbishop of Canterbury.

1984 Sarah Tisdall, the young British civil servant who tipped off the *Guardian* newspaper that Cruise missiles were on their way to Britain, was sent to jail for six months.

1985 Ben Hardwick, Britain's youngest liver transplant patient at just three years old, died in hospital; he inspired a national fund raising campaign.

24 MARCH

BORN THIS DAY

ARTS

1834 William Morris, English craftsman, poet and socialist. In association with the Pre-Raphaelites, he changed house decoration and furnishings in England.

ENTERTAINMENT

1887 Roscoe 'Fatty' Arbuckle, US silent film comedian who in 1921 was involved in a sex scandal that ruined his career. Although he was acquitted by the courts of raping and killing a young actress during a party that developed into an orgy, he never worked again.

1901 Ub Iwerks, US animator who played a key role in the creation of Walt Disney's Mickey Mouse. Disney was never a great artist, he was a conceptual producer. It was Iwerks who developed Mickey and other Disney characters in 1928. Three years later he sold his interest in the Disney company for just $2,920.

1909 Tommy Trinder, English comedian in the old music hall style, who proved a popular radio comedian during the 40s and 50s.

1930 (Terence) Steve(n) McQueen, US film actor whose first stage appearance was as a walk-on in a New York Yiddish theatre! His films made him one of the most popular and highly-paid stars in Hollywood and include *The Thomas Crown Affair* (1968) and *Papillon* (1973).

SPORT

1947 Archie Gemmill, Scottish international footballer.

DIED THIS DAY

1603 Elizabeth I of England died at Richmond Palace.

1776 John Harrison, English watchmaker and inventor of the marine chronometer.

1801 Paul I, the demented Tsar of Russia, strangled by his officers in a scuffle, following their efforts to persuade him to abdicate.

1882 H(enry) W(adsworth) Longfellow, US poet of 'The Song of Hiawatha'.

1905 Jules Verne, French science fiction pioneer.

1909 J(ohn) M(illington) Synge, Irish playwright.

1944 Orde Charles Wingate, British general who organized the Chindits in Burma as jungle-fighters, in a plane crash in the Assam jungle.

1953 Queen Mary, wife of George V.

1962 Auguste Piccard, Swiss physicist, deep-sea and stratosphere explorer.

1976 Bernard, Viscount Montgomery of Alamein, British Army Field Marshal.

ON THIS DAY

1603 James I, son of Mary, Queen of Scots, united the English and Scottish crowns when he acceded to the throne following the death of Elizabeth I.

1877 The Oxford and Cambridge Boat Race ended in a dead heat for the first and only time.

1911 Denmark abolished capital punishment.

1922 The Grand National at Aintree saw only three of the 32 horses finish. The winner was Music Hall.

1926 Marian B. Skaggs started the first Safeways supermarket in Maryland in the US.

1953 A Jamaican tenant at 10 Rillington Place, Notting Hill Gate, London made a ghoulish discovery while examining wallpaper in the kitchen. It concealed a wardrobe. Inside was the naked body of Mrs Ethel Christie. (*See* 31.3.1953)

1976 Isabel Perón was deposed as President of the Argentine in a bloodless coup.

1978 The tanker *Amoco Cadiz* split in two off Brittany spilling 50,000 tons of crude oil which polluted the French coastline.

1980 Gunmen burst into the small chapel of a nuns' hospital and shot dead Mgr Oscar Romero, Archbishop of San Salvador, as he was saying mass. They were believed to be in the pay of right-wing fanatics headed by Major Roberto d'Aubuisson.

1988 Mordechai Vanunu was sentenced by an Israeli court to 18 years in prison for disclosing Israel's nuclear programme to *The Sunday Times* in London.

1989 A claim by Professor Stanley Pons of Utah University and Professor Martin Fleischman of Southampton University that their Anglo-American collaboration had produced controlled nuclear fusion in a test tube was greeted with scepticism by the scientific community and later Harvard University said they were unable to replicate the experiment.

25 MARCH

National Day of Greece, marking this day, 1924, when it became a republic after King George of Greece was deposed.

BORN THIS DAY

HISTORY

1133 Henry II, King of England.

1769 Joachim Murat, French field

marshal who was made 'King of Naples' by Napoleon, whose sister he married.

ARTS

1867 Arturo Toscanini, Italian conductor who, because he was short-sighted, invariably conducted from memory. He refused to conduct in Italy whilst the Fascists were in power or in Germany whilst it was ruled by the Nazis.

1881 Béla Bartók, Hungarian composer who was not much appreciated in his native land. He collected old Hungarian folk songs, and folk music was integrated into much of his work.

1906 Professor A(lan) J(ohn) P(ercival) Taylor, popular English historian and broadcaster.

ENTERTAINMENT

1908 David Lean, English film director who worked his way up from clapperboy to editor to director. His films include *Brief Encounter* (1945) and *Bridge on the River Kwai* (1957) which won him an Oscar, as did *Lawrence of Arabia* (1962) and *Passage to India* (1987).

1921 Simone Signoret (Kaminker), German-born actress of French parents, who won an Oscar for *Room at the Top* (1958).

1944 Paul Michael Glaser, US actor best known for his role in the television series *Starsky and Hutch*.

POP

1942 Aretha Franklin, US singer who started in gospel with her father, a well-known evangelist. She eventually moved into more commercial recordings with 'I Never Loved a Man the Way I love You'. After a period of both marital and alcohol problems, she made a return to gospel singing.

1947 Elton John (Reginald Kenneth Dwight), English songwriter, pianist and singer, who trained at the Royal Academy of Music, London. His outlandish costumes and spectacles and his talent for writing and performing songs like 'Goodbye Yellow Brick Road' (1973) have served him well for over 20 years.

DIED THIS DAY

1914 Frédéric Mistral, French poet, winner in 1904 of the Nobel prize for Literature.

1918 (Achille) Claude Debussy, French composer.

1975 King Faisal of Saudi Arabia, assassinated by his mentally deranged nephew, Prince Museid.

ON THIS DAY

1306 Robert the Bruce was crowned King of the Scots. His reign would last until 7 June 1329.

1609 English navigator, Henry Hudson, undertook his third (and last voyage) of exploration, this time for the Dutch East India Company. He was trying to find the North West Passage, believing it to be the shortest route to the spice islands of the east. He discovered the great bay that bears his name.

1807 The British parliament abolished the slave trade, largely as a result of the campaigning of Wilberforce supported by the Quakers.

1876 The first Scotland v. Wales football match took place at Glasgow. The home team won 4–0.

1929 Mussolini claimed to have won 90

per cent of the vote in the Italian elections.

1949 *Hamlet* became the first British film to win an Oscar. There was also an Oscar for its star, Laurence Olivier.

1957 Six nations signed the Treaty of Rome to establish the EEC (European Economic Community). They were Belgium, France, West Germany, Italy, Holland and Luxembourg.

1989 A father and son celebrated a double wedding in Okehampton, Devon. Barrie Hall, a divorcee and his son, Christopher, married Caroline and Teena Atherton, sisters in the same pub skittles team.

26 MARCH

BORN THIS DAY

HISTORY

1840 George Smith, English Assyriologist who studied cuneiform inscriptions in the British Museum. A former banknote engraver, he eventually deciphered the Chaldean account of the Deluge at about the time of Noah.

1990 Princess Eugenie of York, second child of Prince Andrew and Sarah, Duchess of York.

ARTS

1859 A(lfred) E(dward) Houseman, English scholar and poet best known for 'A Shopshire Lad' (1896).

1874 Robert (Lee) Frost, US poet who first made his reputation in Britain, encouraged by Rupert Brooke, before returning to the US. He won the Pulitzer prize three times.

1914 Tennessee Williams (Thomas Lanier Williams), US playwright, screenwriter and novelist who wrote some of the most disturbing and haunting plays of the century. Usually set in the Deep South they include *The Glass Menagerie* (1944) and *A Streetcar Named Desire* (1947).

1925 Pierre Boulez, French conductor and composer who introduced avant-garde music and many new composers to an international audience.

ENTERTAINMENT

1891 Chico (Leonard) Marx, US comedian, the second eldest of the famous Marx Brothers. Chico was the pistol-fingered pianist.

1931 Leonard Nimoy, US actor who played Mr Spock in the long-running cult television and later film series, *Star Trek*.

1934 Alan Arkin, US actor who played the deaf-mute in *The Heart is a Lonely Hunter* (1968), which won him an Oscar nomination.

1939 James Caan, US actor who made his name in *The Godfather* (1972).

POP

1944 Diana Ross, US singer who made her name with the highly successful Motown group, The Supremes, before going solo with hits including 'Ain't No Mountain High Enough' (1970). She also played Billie Holiday in the film *Lady Sings The Blues* (1972).

DIED THIS DAY

1726 Sir John Vanbrugh, English playwright and architect.

1827 Ludwig von Beethoven, German

composer, in Vienna. His funeral was a national day of mourning.

1892 Walt Whitman, US poet.

1902 Cecil (John) Rhodes, English-born South African statesman and gold and diamond mine chairman, in Cape Town. He was buried in Rhodesia (now Zimbabwe), which was named after him.

1923 Sarah Bernhardt, legendary French actress.

1945 David Lloyd George, Welsh-born British statesman and Liberal Prime Minister.

1959 Raymond (Thornton) Chandler, US crime writer, creator of Philip Marlowe.

1973 Sir Noël (Pierce) Coward, English playwright, actor, singer, entertainer, composer, lyricist and director, known as 'The Master'.

ON THIS DAY

1780 The first Sunday newspaper in Britain was published; the *British Gazette and Sunday Monitor*.

1863 The first steeplechase under National Hunt rules was run at Market Harborough, when Mr Goodman on Socks was the winner.

1885 'A lady well-known in literary and scientific circles' was the only clue *The Times* gave to the identity of the woman who was cremated by the Cremation Society in Woking, Surrey. She was the first person to be officially cremated in Britain.

1898 The Sabi Game Reserve was offically designated in South Africa to become the world's first game reserve.

1920 The 'Black and Tans', so-called special constables from Britain, arrived in Ireland. Their nickname came from the colours of their uniform.

1924 Bernard Shaw's *St Joan*, starring Sybil Thorndike, was performed for the first time at the New Theatre, London.

1936 New Zealand radio began broadcasting the first parliamentary broadcasts.

1964 The first performance of *Funny Girl* on Broadway with Barbra Streisand. It established her as a star.

1973 After 171 years, the first woman stockbroker, Mrs Susan Shaw was able to set foot on the floor of the London Stock Exchange; she was one of ten women elected as members.

1979 Prime Minister Begin for Israel and President Sadat for Egypt signed a peace treaty at the White House, witnessed by President Jimmy Carter.

27 MARCH

BORN THIS DAY

HISTORY

1785 Louis XVII, King of France, second son of Louis XVI. He would only live ten years and was poisoned.

1809 Baron Georges Eugène Haussmann, French financier and town planner who made sweeping changes to Paris, widening streets and laying out boulevards and parks.

1912 Leonard James Callaghan (Lord Callaghan of Cardiff), Labour Prime Minster, 1976–9.

ARTS

1917 Mstislav (Leopoldovitch) Rostropovich, Russian cellist, pianist and conductor. His artistry led to works being specially written for him by Prokofiev, Britten and others. He was deprived of his Soviet citizenship for his public support of dissidents, especially Solzhenitsyn.

ENTERTAINMENT

1898 Gloria (Josephine Mae Swenson) Swanson, US actress who landed her first roles in films because her actor husband, Wallace Beery, would only be contracted to Mack Sennett if his wife was given parts too. A great self-publicist, she soon became popular with audiences. She is probably best known for her role as a silent movie queen in *Sunset Boulevard* (1950), which won her an Oscar nomination.

1942 Michael York, English actor who was first seen in the television serial *The Forsyte Saga*. He co-starred in the film *Cabaret* (1972).

JAZZ

1924 Sarah Vaughan, US singer, one of the great jazz singers of all time, who was popular for the middle-of-the-road songs she performed and recorded during the late 40s and 50s.

SCIENCE

1845 Wilhelm Konrad von Rontgen, German physicist who discovered electric-magnetic rays (X-rays), for which he won the Nobel prize in 1901. (*See* 5.1.1896)

ENGINEERING

1863 Sir (Frederick) Henry Royce, English engineer who founded Royce Limited in 1884 to make mechanical and electrical engines. He and C. S. Rolls formed the partnership that led to the setting up of Rolls-Royce in 1904. (*See* 4.5.1904)

SPORT

1957 Duncan Goodhew, bald-headed English Olympic swimmer who claimed the breaststroke gold medal at the 1980 Games in Moscow.

DIED THIS DAY

1770 Giovanni Battista Tiepolo, the last of the great Venetian painters.

1878 Sir George Gilbert Scott, English architect who designed many fine buildings, and also the Albert Memorial in Hyde Park.

1923 Sir James Dewar, Scottish inventor of the thermos flask.

1931 (Enoch) Arnold Bennett, English novelist who wrote the 'Clayhanger' trilogy.

1968 Yuri (Alekseyevich) Gagarin, USSR cosmonaut, killed in a plane accident near Moscow. He was buried in the Kremlin Wall reserved for Soviet heroes.

1975 Sir Arthur Bliss, English composer and Master of the Queen's Musick.

1983 Anthony Blunt, former Surveyor of the Queen's Pictures, and Russian spy who was the Fourth Man with Burgess, Maclean and Philby. He died of a heart attack in London.

ON THIS DAY

1794 The US Navy was officially created.

1871 The first international rugby match between Scotland and England took place at Edinburgh with a victory for the hosts.

1880 The Salvation Army uniform was authorized, but the distinctive bonnets for women did not appear until June.

1914 The first successful blood transfusion took place in a Brussels hospital.

1942 British commandos destroyed the U-boat base at St Nazaire. The destroyer *Campbeltown* rammed the dock gates at 20 knots with five tons of explosives on board. She put out the main dry dock on the Atlantic coast. A German ship trying to cut off the British commandos as they made their getaway in fast launches was sunk by German guns in error.

1958 Nikita Krushchev toppled Marshal Bulganin to become the Soviet leader.

1961 The first women traffic wardens began ticketing in Leicester.

1964 Six months after the 'Great Train Robbery' in Buckinghamshire, 20 of the gang were still at large, but the ten who were arrested were found guilty of stealing more than £2.6m from mailbags. They included Ronnie Biggs. Sentences totalled 307 years in jail.

1977 Two jumbo jets collided on the ground at Tenerife airport killing 574 people. The world's worst air disaster was caused by a misunderstanding about which aircraft was taking off, and was not helped by fog. A Pan-Am taxied on to the runwaway while a KLM jumbo began its take-off without clearance.

1980 A mine lift cage at the Vaal Reef gold mine in South Africa plunged 1.2 miles, probably the longest fall by any lift, killing all 23 passengers.

1989 In the first elections for the Soviet parliament, the voters dealt a devasting blow to the Soviet old guard. In Moscow, the Communist party leader and his deputy were defeated.

28 MARCH

BORN THIS DAY

HISTORY

1515 St Teresa of Ávila, Spanish founder of the reformed Carmelites who originally came from an aristocratic Castilian family. In 1970, she was declared a Doctor of the Church, the first woman saint to be so honoured.

1660 George I, King of England from 1714, in Hanover.

1862 Aristide Briand, French statesman and Nobel Peace prize winner who was Prime Minister 11 times between 1925–32.

1942 Neil Kinnock, Welsh-born leader of the Labour Party.

ARTS

FRIENDS In 1472, Fra Bartolommeo di Pagholo (Baccio della Porta), Florentine painter mainly of religious subjects. A close friend of Raphael, he is believed to have completed some of the younger painter's unfinished works. Raphael (Raffaello Santi or Sanzio) was born in 1483. He decorated the papal chambers at the Vatican, and Leo X asked him to take over as architect of St Peter's in 1514. Soon after he was busy with the cartoons for the tapestry to adorn the Sistine Chapel.

1849 Maxim Gorky (Aleksei Maksimovich Peshkov), Russian novelist and playwright.

ENTERTAINMENT

1902 Flora Robson, English actress who was noted for her historical roles, both on stage and in films such as *Fire Over England* (1937), in which she played Queen Elizabeth.

1924 Freddie Bartholomew (Llewelyn), British-born child actor who appeared on the London stage aged three. On a visit to the US, he was offered the starring role in *David Copperfield* (1935). He also made *Little Lord Fauntleroy* (1936).

1921 Dirk Bogarde (Derek Van Den Bogaerde), English actor and writer whose good looks confined him initally to light romantic roles until he was able to show his ability in films such as *The Servant* (1963) and *Death in Venice* (1971). He has also proved a successful writer of both autobiography and fiction.

1935 Michael Parkinson, English journalist, television and radio presenter.

1943 Richard Stilgoe, British entertainer, musician and lyricist of the Lloyd Webber musicals *Starlight Express* and *Phantom of the Opera*.

1943 Richard Eyre, British director of the National Theatre.

JAZZ

1891 Paul (Samuel) Whiteman, US bandleader who was a violinist with both the Denver and San Francisco symphony orchestras before forming his large orchestra in 1920 to play 'symphonic jazz'. Members included many top musicians such as Bix Beiderbecke and Tommy Dorsey. Whiteman commissioned Gershwin's *Rhapsody in Blue* which he performed first in February 1924.

DIED THIS DAY

1868 The Earl of Cardigan, who led the charge of the Light Brigade to disaster at Balaclava in the Crimean War, now best remembered for the woollen garment named after him.

1881 Modest Petrovich Mussorgsky, Russian composer, from alcoholism.

1941 Virginia Woolf (Adeline Virginia Stephen), English novelist who took her own life. She is believed to have drowned in the River Ouse near her home in Sussex, although her body was never found.

1943 Sergei Vassilievich Rachmaninov, Russian composer, in California.

1985 Marc Chagall, French painter.

1969 Dwight David Eisenhower, US General and President.

ON THIS DAY

1910 The first seaplane, designed by Henri Fabre, took off near Marseilles.

UNIVERSITY WETS In the 1912 University boat race, both the Oxford and Cambridge boats sank in the Thames and the race had to be rerun. On this same day in 1925, Cambridge won as Oxford sank. Oxford sank again in 1951, but it was not until 1978 that the Cambridge boat sank.

1913 The first Morris Oxford left the Cowley, Oxfordshire factory.

1917 The Women's Army Auxiliary Corps, Britain's first women's service unit, was formed.

1920 Douglas Fairbanks and Mary Pickford, the King and Queen of Hollywood, married.

1930 Constantinople had its name changed to Istanbul by Kemal Atatürk, and the town of Angora (where the wool comes from) was changed to Ankara, the new capital of Turkey.

1939 The Spanish Civil War ended as

Franco and his Nationalist troops took Madrid.

1941 British naval forces destroyed seven Italian warships off Crete without a single loss at the Battle of Cape Matapan.

1945 The last German V2 rocket fell on Britain.

1964 Radio Caroline, Britain's first pirate broadcasting station began transmitting from the Channel just outside British waters.

1973 Marlon Brando refused his Oscar for *The Godfather* in protest at Hollywood's portrayal of American Indians.

1979 A crippled reactor at the Three Mile Island nuclear power station in Pennsylvania threatened disaster to a wide area, but authorities decided against evacuation. The building was badly contaminated. Defective equipment and operating errors are thought to have been the cause of the accident.

1989 The San Diego Yacht Club was stripped of the America's Cup for violating the rules, according to a court judgement. The Cup was to be returned to the New Zealand Mercury Bay Boating Club, whose mono-hull *New Zealand* had been no match for the US *Stars and Stripes*, a catamaran, and therefore the race had not been 'evenly matched'. The US club subsequently won an appeal, continuing the saga.

29 MARCH

An old folk belief claimed this to be a 'borrowed day', since it was believed the last three days of March had been taken from April.

BORN THIS DAY

HISTORY

1790 John Tyler, tenth US President, who was involved in the annexation of Texas.

ARTS

1902 Sir William (Turner) Walton, one of the leading English composers this century. The poems of Edith Sitwell, his patron, were featured in his first major work, *Façade* (1921). Other works include the dramatic cantata, *Belshazzar's Feast*, as well as music for films, including *Hamlet* (1948).

1914 Chapman Pincher, British journalist and author of books on the secret services.

ENTERTAINMENT

1915 George Chisholm, Scottish jazz trombonist.

1918 Pearl Bailey, US jazz singer who won a Tony for her performance in the all-black *Hello Dolly* on Broadway.

1945 Julie Goodyear, English actress best known for her part as the glamorous Bet Gilroy in the long-running television soap opera *Coronation Street*.

POP

1935 Ruby Murray, Irish pop singer who set a UK record by having five songs simultaneously in the Top 20 in March 1955, the only time this has been achieved by a solo female artiste.

INVENTIONS

1853 Elihu Thomson, English-born US inventor who joined with Edison to form the General Electric Company. He made major contributions in electrodynamics, and invented the high-frequency dynamo and transformer.

1912 Frederick Mackenzie, Scottish printer who invented Letraset dry printing with K. J. Reed in the 1950s.

ARCHITECTURE

1869 Sir Edward Landseer Lutyens, English architect who designed Whitehall, the Roman Catholic Cathedral at Liverpool and the Cenotaph.

DIED THIS DAY

1751 Thomas Coram, English philanthropist who established a home for foundling children. The effort and other good works left him poverty-stricken. It was the artist Hogarth and others who raised an annuity of £161 in 1745 which saw him through the last six years of his life.

1772 Emanuel Swedenborg, Swedish religious philospher who believed the Last Judgement had taken place in 1757, and established the New Church with himself as the prophet.

1788 Charles Wesley, English evangelist, brother of the founder of Methodism, and writer of over 5,500 hymns.

1891 George-Pierre Seurat, French painter.

1891 Robert Falcon Scott, Antarctic explorer, returning from the South Pole. His final entry in his log book read 'For God's sake, look after our people'. The journal was found on 12 November with the bodies of Scott, Wilson and Bowen.

1957 Joyce Cary (Arthur Joyce Lunel Cary), Irish-born English author.

1970 Vera Brittain, English author and peace campaigner.

1970 Joseph Arthur, first Baron Rank, English miller who became Britain's first movie mogul.

1980 Annuzio Paolo Mantovani, Anglo-Italian conductor and arranger.

ON THIS DAY

1461 Edward VI secured the crown of England by a victory over the Lancastrians in the War of the Roses at Towton, North Yorkshire. It is believed to be the bloodiest battle ever fought on British soil with the loss of over 28,000 men.

1871 The Royal Albert Hall was opened by Queen Victoria, and, in 1904, her son Edward VII, opened Richmond Park to the public.

1886 Coca-Cola, invented by Dr John Pemberton of Atlanta, Georgia, was launched as an 'Esteemed Brain Tonic and Intellectual Beverage'. It was not until 1894 that mass production bottling began.

1918 Marshal Foch was made Commander-in-Chief of the Allied Armies in France.

1920 Sir William Robertson, who enlisted in 1877, became a field marshal in the British Army, the first man to rise to this rank from private.

SPEED MERCHANTS In 1927, Sir Henry Segrave beat Malcolm Campbell's land speed record in his *Mystery* car on the Daytona Beach, clocking 203.841 m.p.h.; in Italy, the first Mille Miglia was won by Ferdinando Minoia and Giuseppe Morandi.

1951 The first performance on Broadway of *The King and I* with Yul Brynner and Gertrude Lawrence.

1971 Major William Calley, the US lieutenant who allowed the Mai Lai massacre of Vietnamese civilians to take place, was found guilty of murder and sentenced to life. Two years later to the day in 1973, US troops finally left Vietnam.

1974 US *Mariner 10* took close-ups of the planet Mercury.

1982 David Puttnam's *Chariots of Fire* won the Oscar for best film.

1987 The 'Iron Lady', Mrs Thatcher, visited Moscow and received a warm reception, led by Mr Gorbachev.

1988 Ian Botham plus elephants began a fund-raising trek across the Alps in Hannibal's footsteps. On the same day, he learned his contract with Queensland Cricket Association had been cancelled because of his behaviour. It still had two years to run.

1988 Lloyd Honeyghan became the first British boxer to regain a world title since Ted 'Kid' Lewis, 71 years before. Honeyghan knocked out Jorgé Vaca of Mexico in the third round at the Wembley Arena, London.

30 MARCH

BORN THIS DAY

HISTORY

1135 Maimonides (Rabbi Moses ben Maimon), Jewish philosopher born in Cordoba, Spain, who migrated with his family to Egypt, where he became Saladin's physician. His contribution to Jewish thought in a number of commentaries rates him second to Moses.

1882 Melanie Klein (Reizes), Austrian-born child psychologist who settled in London. She made important contributions in analysing children's behaviour and published several books including *Narrative of a Child Analysis* (1961).

ARTS

1746 Francisco José de Goya y Lucientes, Spanish painter who was made First Court Painter to Charles IV in 1799.

1820 Anna Sewell, English author of *Black Beauty* (1877), who was an invalid for most of her life.

1844 Paul Verlaine, French poet whose bisexuality led him and his poetry into self-analysis. First he favoured a 16-year-old girl, but when he finally married her he realized he was homosexual. Eventually, he met the young poet Rimbaud and settled with him. When Rimbaud decided to leave, Verlaine shot him in the wrist and was jailed for two years. His final affair was with a young male pupil who died of typhus five years later.

1853 Vincent (Willem) van Gogh, Dutch Post-Impressionist painter who was virtually unrecognized in his day. Religious yearnings began as a result of an unrequited love affair when he was sent by a firm of art dealers to work as an assistant in their shop in London. It was as an assistant master at an Isleworth school that he began unsuccessfully to train as a Methodist preacher. His life back in Holland, and later in France was full of despair. Only Theo, his devoted brother, supported him through the years. He was advised and influenced by many painters including Gauguin, Toulouse-Lautrec and Seurat.

1884 Sean O'Casey, Irish playwright whose plays *Shadow of a Gunman* (1923) and *Juno and the Paycock* (1924) were written for the Abbey Theatre.

1928 Tom Sharpe, English novelist and historian. A period out in South Africa as a social worker, then teacher produced *Riotous Assembly* (1971) and *Indecent Exposure* (1973).

ENTERTAINMENT

1930 Rolf Harris, Australian entertainer who demonstrates his versatility on stage and television with his speed-painting and songs, including his hit 'Tie Me Kangaroo Down'.

1937 Warren Beatty, US film actor and director, brother of Shirley MacLaine, who made his name playing opposite Natalie Wood in *Splendor in the Grass* (1961) and went on to make *Bonnie and Clyde* (1967).

POP

1913 Frankie Laine (Frank Paul Lo Vecchio), US singer who had 16 Golden Records to his credit, including 'Answer Me' (1954) and 'A Woman In Love' (1956) and the title song for 'Gunfight at the O. K. Corral' (1957).

1945 Eric Clapton, English blues guitarist, considered the finest of his generation, who has played with many leading groups including the Yardbirds and Cream.

1963 Tracey Chapman, US singer whose hits include 'Fast Car' (1988).

DIED THIS DAY

1840 George Bryan 'Beau' Brummell, English dandy who fled to Calais to avoid his debts, as a pauper in a lunatic asylum.

1925 Rudolf Steiner, Austrian founder of schools for maladjusted children.

1949 Friedrich Karl Rudolf Bergius, German research chemist who invented a process to convert coal into oil and wood into sugar.

1950 Léon Blum, French Prime Minister.

1979 Airey (Middleton Sheffield) Neave, British parliamentarian, killed when a bomb planted by the IRA in his car exploded as he was driving away from the House of Commons.

1986 James Cagney, US film actor.

1987 Maria von Trapp, whose autobiography *The Trapp Family Singers* inspired the musical *The Sound of Music*.

ON THIS DAY

1842 Ether was used an an anaesthetic for the first time by Dr Crawford Long in Jefferson, Georgia, to remove a cyst from the neck of a student.

1858 Hyman Lipman of Philadelphia, patented a pencil with an eraser attached to one end.

1867 'A lot of dollars for an awful lot of ice,' critics cried when US Senator William H. Seward bought Alaska from the Russians for $7.2m – approximately two cents an acre. No one knew about the oil.

1893 The first US ambassador to Britain, Thomas Francis Bayard, took up his post.

1943 The first performance of the Rodgers and Hammerstein musical destined to be a landmark, *Oklahoma!*, on Broadway.

1951 Julius Rosenberg (a US Army signals corps engineer) and his wife, Ethel, were found guilty of passing atomic secrets to the Russians and sentenced to death. (*See* 19.6.1953)

1960 Having outlawed all black political movements following the Sharpville massacre, the South African government declared a state of emergency.

1978 The Tory Party, led by Margaret

Thatcher, called in the advertising agency, Saatchi and Saatchi to give their image and new leader a face-lift.

1981 In Washington, John Hinkley III shot and wounded President Reagan as well as several of his entourage as he walked from a hotel. The bullet lodged in Reagan's left lung.

1984 Britain's heaviest man, Peter Yarrall, 59 stone (826 lb/ 374.73kg), who suffered from a glandular disorder, died in his flat in London's East Ham. Ten firemen took five hours to demolish the bedroom and winch his body to the street using a crane.

1988 A former paratrooper bit off the ear of his sister's boyfriend after an 'unprovoked attack' following a heavy drinking session, an Exeter court was told. The attacker laughed as he bit off half of the left ear, chewed and swallowed it in front of the victim and said 'Yum, yum'. At the police station, the accused had said, 'His nose was next'.

1989 US actor Kurt Russell proposed marriage to actress Goldie Hawn on stage at the Oscar award ceremony which was televised to 1.5 billion people in 91 countries. She was not amused.

31 MARCH

BORN THIS DAY

HISTORY

1596 René Descartes, French philosopher and mathematician who is considered the 'father of modern philosophy'.

1872 Arthur Griffith, Irish nationalist and President of the Irish Free State when it signed the peace treaty with Britain.

ARTS

1732 Franz Joseph Haydn, Austrian composer, considered the best of his age. He encouraged the young Mozart, but was less enthusiastic about his pupil, Beethoven. Haydn composed 104 symphonies, 50 concertos and 84 string quartets, as well as stage works, masses and chamber and choral works.

1809 Edward Fitzgerald, English translator of the 'Rubáiyát of Omar Khayyám', then a little-known work by a Persian astronomer and poet.

1809 Nikolai Vasilievich Gogol, Russian novelist and playwright. His comedy, *The Inspector-General* (1836) is still much performed, while his *Dead Souls* (1837) is considered one of the world's most important novels.

1872 Sergei Pavlovich Diaghilev, Russian impresario. His famous Ballets Russes company was founded in 1911 with Cecchetti as ballet master. Dancers included Pavlova and Nijinsky and he attracted many young composers and artists who would become famous, such as Stravinsky.

1926 John Fowles, English novelist of *The French Lieutenant's Woman* (1969).

ENTERTAINMENT

1935 (George) Richard Chamberlain, US actor who established himself on television as *Dr Kildare*.

1934 Shirley Jones, US actress who starred in the film versions of *Oklahoma!* (1955) followed by *Carousel* (1956).

INVENTION

1693 John Harrison, English horologist who invented the marine chronometer, winning the first prize in a competition sponsored by the British government to determine longitude accurately.

1811 Robert Wilhelm Bunsen, German physicist and chemist who, besides inventing the Bunsen burner, also invented the galvanic battery and an ice calorimeter while sharing the discovery of spectrum analysis.

POP

1935 Herb Alpert, US musician who with his Tijuana Brass had hits in the 60s, including 'Spanish Flea' (1965).

SPORT

1872 Jack Johnson, known as 'Galveston Jack', first US negro world heavyweight boxing champion.

DIED THIS DAY

1631 John Donne, English poet.

1837 John Constable, English landscape painter.

1837 Charlotte Brontë, author of *Jane Eyre*, in pregnancy.

1980 Jesse (James Cleveland) Owens, US athlete, winner of three gold medals at the Berlin Olympics when Hitler snubbed him because he was a negro.

ON THIS DAY

1836 Charles Dickens' *Pickwick Papers* appeared as a monthly-part work, his first major break. Three weeks later, Dickens married Catherine Hogarth.

1854 Japan opened its ports to US traders after the signing of a treaty.

1889 The 985ft (359.06m) high Eiffel Tower, costing £260,000 at the time, was officially opened by French Premier Tirard. Designed by Gustave Eiffel, it had taken two years to erect.

1892 The world's first fingerprinting bureau was formally opened by the Buenos Aires Chief of Police, although it had been operating unofficially since 1891.

1896 Whitcomb L. Judson, a Chicago inventor, patented the first zipper, but it had too many imperfections, and it would not be until 29.4.1913 that a Swede living in New Jersey would produce the zipper as we know it today.

1901 The Daimler factory turned out its first car.

1915 D. W. Griffith's *Birth of a Nation* had its first US screening and provoked a storm of criticism regarding its favourable attitude towards the Klu Klux Klan; it presented the hooded riders as heroes.

1920 In London, Parliament passed the Irish 'Home Rule' bill.

1924 The first British national airline, Imperial, was founded at Croydon Airport.

1934 The most wanted man in the US, John Dillinger, blasted his way out of a police trap after escaping from prison in Indiana using a fake wooden pistol.

1950 Norwegian Thor Heyerdahl published his account of the 'Kon-Tiki Expedition', which he undertook to demonstrate that the Polynesians came originally from South America. To do this, he built a balsa wood raft similar to those used by the Polynesians, and, with a Scandanavian crew, took 101 days to travel the possible route.

1953 John Halliday Christie was arrested after a manhunt. As well as that of his wife, Ethel, the bodies of seven women were found hidden in the house and garden at 10 Rillington Place. (*See* 24.3.1953) Three were found together in a secret alcove in the small kitchen. The dull-witted Timothy Evans, another tenant in the house, had been convicted three years previously of the murder of his wife, Beryl Evans, and her 14-month-old daughter, Geraldine, and hanged. Christie had kept all the press cuttings of the murder, which he probably committed.

1959 The Dalai Lama fled Tibet following Chinese repression, and sought asylum in India.

1978 Red Rum won the Grand National for the third consecutive year and was retired.

1986 A fire damaged the south wing of Hampton Court Palace. A woman died and there was extensive damage to the building.

APRIL

May you live in interesting times
(Old Chinese curse)

1 APRIL

All Fool's Day (April Fools Day).

BORN THIS DAY

HISTORY

1815 Prince Otto Edward Leopold von Bismarck (Schönhausen), Prussian statesman, known as the 'Iron Chancellor'.

1885 Clementine Ogilvy Spencer-Churchill (Hozier), wife of Sir Winston Churchill, whom she married in 1908.

ARTS

1697 Abbé Prévost (Antoine François Prévost d'Exiles), French novelist best remembered for *Manon Lescaut* (1731).

1868 Edmond (Eugène Alexis) Rostand, French playwright who wrote *Cyrano de Bergerac* (1897).

1873 Sergei (Vassilievich) Rachmaninov, Russian composer of the popular *Prelude in C minor* (1892). He settled in the US in 1917, where he composed his famous *Rhapsody on a Theme of Paganini* in 1934.

1875 Edgar (Richard Horatio) Wallace, English thriller writer and journalist who was found abandoned when nine days old and brought up by a Billingsgate fish porter. His prolific output includes *The Four Just Men* (1905) and the play *The Ringer* (1926).

ENTERTAINMENT

1883 Lon (Alonso) Chaney, US actor whose parents were deaf mutes; he had to communicate with them by mime. In Hollywood, he specialized in playing bizarre characters and was known as 'The Man of a Thousand Faces'. His films include *The Hunchback of Notre Dame* (1923) and *The Phantom of the Opera* (1925).

1885 Wallace Beery, US film actor who co-starred with his wife, Gloria Swanson in some of his early comedies with Mack Sennett. He flourished when sound arrived, playing the lead in *The Champ* for which he shared an Oscar for best actor (1931) with Frederick March (the only time actors have tied for the award).

1893 Dame Cecily Courtneidge, Australian-born actress who appeared in shows with her husband Jack Hulbert. A lady of considerable energy and enthusiasm, she introduced the song 'Vitality' which she made her own.

TWO OF A KIND Born 1929, Jane Powell (Suzanne Burce), US actress and singer, who was the leading lady in many MGM musicals including *Seven Brides for Seven Brothers* (1954). She shares her birthday with (Mary Frances) Debbie Reynolds, born 1932, who was also signed to MGM, where she made *The Unsinkable Molly Brown* (1964).

1938 Ali MacGraw, US actress who starred in *Love Story* (1970).

1943 Carol White, English actress who made her name in the controversial television documentary drama on the homeless, *Cathy Come Home* (1966).

SCIENCE

1578 William Harvey, English physician who explained the circulation of the blood in a treatise in 1628.

SPORT

1948 J. J. Williams, Welsh rugby international.

1957 David Gower, England cricketer

and captain of England, 1984 and 1989. His highest test score was 215 against Australia in 1985.

DIED THIS DAY

1204 Eleanor of Aquitaine, who married Louis VII of France in 1137, but divorced him in 1152, and married the future Henry II of England.

1406 Robert III of Scotland, who died when news came that his younger son, James, had been on a vessel captured by the English.

1917 Scott Joplin, US ragtime composer and pianist.

1922 Former Emperor Karl Joseph of Austria, who had abdicated in 1918.

1952 Ferenc Molnàr, Hungarian playwright, in New York.

1976 Max Ernst, German painter and sculptor, founder of the Dada group, the day before his 85th birthday.

ON THIS DAY

1766 From about this date, William Reeves, the English supplier and maker of artists' materials, began to sell the first paintboxes with watercolour tablets.

1875 The British preoccupation with the weather was given the additional benefit of the first weather chart published by *The Times*. Appropriately, the US chose this day, 1960, to launch their first weather satellite.

1891 The telephone link between London and Paris began operating.

1899 The first time British troops fought alongside US troops was at Apia in the Samoan Campaign.

1908 The Territorial Army, a force of volunteer soldiers mainly for home defence, was formed in Britain.

1909 The first double-decker buses in Britain began running in Widnes, Cheshire.

1918 The Royal Naval Air Service and the Royal Flying Corps merged to become the Royal Air Force.

1924 Adolf Hitler was sentenced to five years imprisonment for his abortive beer hall *putsch* in Munich the previous November. The intimidated court agreed to him being paroled within six months.

1945 The US forces invaded Okinawa. The battle with the Japanese lasted until 6 June.

1948 The Berlin blockade began with Soviet troops enforcing road and rail blocks between Berlin and the Allied Western Zone. To solve the problem, the Allies mounted a massive airlift.

1967 Britain's first ombudsman, Sir Edward Compton, began work.

1979 Ayatollah Khomeini declared Iran an Islamic republic.

1984 US singer Marvin Gaye was shot dead by his father during a violent row, on the eve of his 45th birthday.

1989 Despite threats of non-payment and other protests, the Community Charge or Poll Tax was introduced in Scotland.

1990 The longest prison riot in British history began at Strangeways Prison, Manchester and lasted until the 25th. One remand prisoner died.

2 APRIL

BORN THIS DAY

HISTORY

742 Charlemagne, French Holy Roman Emperor who was crowned by the Pope on Christmas Day, AD800.

1838 Léon (Michel) Gambetta, French politician who escaped from Paris during the Franco-Prussian War in a hot-air balloon. He went to Tours, where he continued as dictator of France and, in 1871, founded the Third Republic.

ARTS

1805 Hans Christian Andersen, Danish author. The son of a poor shoemaker, his lack of education proved an obstacle when he tried to get work in the theatre. He also tried his luck as a singer, but eventually found success as a writer, and is remembered for his fairy stories, 'The Emperor's New Clothes', 'The Snow Queen' and 'The Ugly Duckling'.

1827 William Holman Hunt, English Pre-Raphaelite painter whose work includes *The Light of the World*.

1840 Émile (Édouard Charles Antoine) Zola, French writer who used realism to highlight human and social problems in novels which include *Thérèse Raquin* (1867) and *Nana* (1880).

1891 Max Ernst, German Surrealist painter and sculptor who worked mostly in France, where he was an active Dadaist and founder in 1924, of the Surrealist movement.

1925 George Macdonald Fraser, Scottish author of the 'Flashman' novels.

ENTERTAINMENT

1891 Jack Buchanan, Scottish-born actor, singer and dancer who appeared in many London revues and on Broadway with Beatrice Lillie and Gertrude Lawrence.

1914 Sir Alec Guinness (Alec Guinness de Cuffe), versatile English actor whose roles have ranged from playing Shakespeare to appearing in the film *Star Wars*. In *Kind Hearts and Coronets* (1949), he played eight parts. He won an Oscar for *The Bridge On the River Kwai* (1957).

1940 Penelope Keith, English actress best known for the television comedy series *The Good Life* and *To the Manor Born*.

POP

1939 Marvin Gaye, US singer and multi-instrumentalist from the Tamla-Motown stable, who was the first black artist to make a 'concept' album, *What's Going On* (1971).

1948 Emmylou Harris, US singer whose range covers both country and pop. She got a gold award for her album, *Elite Hotel* (1976).

SPORT

1926 Sir Jack Brabham, Australian world champion motor racing driver, who won the crown in 1966 in a car he built himself. He continued with car construction after his retirement in 1970.

DIED THIS DAY

1791 Honoré Gabriel Riquetti, Vicomte de Mirabeau, French politician, orator and writer.

1872 Samuel (Finley Breese) Morse, US inventor of the telegraph.

1966 C(ecil) S(cott) Forester, English novelist of the Horatio Hornblower stories.

1974 Georges Pompidou, President of France.

ON THIS DAY

1792 The US mint was established in the nation's capital, then Philadelphia.

1801 The British Fleet with Nelson on board the *Elephant*, engaged the Danish Fleet in the Battle of Copenhagen. When Admiral Parker signalled Nelson to end the attack, Nelson, who was Second-in-Command, pressed the telescope to his blind eye, claimed he could see no order and continued the action until the Danish Fleet were totally subdued.

1860 The first parliament in Italy met at Turin.

1873 Almost 14 years after the US, British trains were fitted with toilets, but only for sleeping cars. Day carriages were fitted in 1881. Third class passengers weren't able to spend a penny until 1886.

1877 At West's amphitheatre in London, Zazel became the first 'beautiful lady fired from a monstrous cannon'.

1884 The London debtors' prison, the notorious Fleet Prison, now in an appalling state, was finally closed.

1905 The Simplon Tunnel under the Alps linking Switzerland and Italy was officially opened.

1921 The IRA took delivery of their first consignment of 'Tommy' guns (their nickname derived from their potentential targets, British 'Tommies'), which were designed for them by Oscar Payne and Theodore Eickhoff of Hartford, Connecticut.

1939 The Spanish Civil War officially ended.

1977 Charlotte Brew on Barony Fort became the first woman to ride in a Grand National. Her mount fell at the 27th fence. The winner was Red Rum, scoring his third win, the only horse ever to achieve this.

1979 Israeli Prime Minister Begin met President Sadat in Cairo, and became the first Israeli leader to visit Egypt.

1982 Argentina invaded the Falkland Islands.

3 APRIL

BORN THIS DAY

HISTORY

1367 Henry IV, son of John of Gaunt, first Lancastrian king of England.

1866 J(ames) B(arry Munnik) Hertzog, South African statesman and nationalist Prime Minister. He founded the Nationalist Party and opposed entering the First World War to aid the British. When he declared neutrality at the outbreak of the Second World War, he was defeated and retired soon after.

1898 Henry (Robinson) Luce, US publisher born in China, founder of *Time* (1923), *Fortune* (1930) and *Life* (1936) magazines.

1930 Helmut Kohl, West German chancellor from 1982, leader of the Christian Democratic Union. He was re-elected chancellor in 1987.

ARTS

1783 Washington Irving, US historian and essayist whose collection of stories, *Sketch Book of Geoffrey Crayon*, included 'Rip van Winkle'.

1881 Daisy (Margaret Mary Julia) Ashford, English author who was only nine when she wrote *The Young Visiters* (1919), a classic of innocent humour.

ENTERTAINMENT

1924 Marlon Brando, US actor whose 'Method' style was ideally suited to film acting. His parts have ranged from the brutish Terry Malloy in *On The Water-*

front (1954), which won him an Oscar, to Brutus in *Julius Caesar* (1953). He also won an Oscar for *The Godfather* (1972), but refused to accept it in protest at the way Red Indians were portrayed by Hollywood.

1924 Doris Day (Doris von Kappelhof), US actress who was originally a vocalist with the Bob Crosby Band. With her 'girl-next-door' image, she proved a popular star in films such as *Pillow Talk* (1959) and *That Touch of Mink* (1962). Her third husband died having embezzled her of around $20m.

1961 Eddie Murphy, US black comedian who starred in the film *Trading Places* (1983).

DIED THIS DAY

1682 Bartolomé Esteban Murillo, Spanish painter.

1862 Sir James Clark Ross, English polar explorer who has the Ross Barrier, Sea and Island named after him.

1897 Johannes Brahms, German pianist and composer.

1901 Richard d'Oyly Carte, English impresario who built the Savoy Theatre. He is best remembered as the man behind Gilbert and Sullivan.

1950 Kurt Weill, German composer associated with Brecht.

1986 Peter Pears, English tenor mainly associated with Benjamin Britten, and co-founder with him of the Aldeburgh Festival; he took the lead role in the original *Peter Grimes*.

1990 Sarah Vaughan, US singer.

ON THIS DAY

RETURN TO SENDER In 1860 the Pony Express started its regular run of almost 2,000 miles (3218km) from St Joseph, Missouri to San Francisco. It took about ten days, at a speed of around 8m.p.h and only operated for 18 months, until the first transcontinental telegraph line was completed. In 1882, St Joseph would feature again in the history of the West. Jesse James, the legendary US outlaw, was shot in the back here by one of his own gang, Robert Ford. He was 35.

1913 Emmeline Pankhurst, English suffragette, was found guilty of inciting supporters to place explosives at the London residence of David Lloyd George. She was sentenced to three years' imprisonment. The Home Secretary banned all future public meetings of suffragettes.

1922 Stalin was appointed as General Secretary of the Communist Party.

1947 BUPA, the private medical care service, was founded in Britain.

1975 Anatoly Karpov, at 23, became world chess champion when Bobby Fischer failed to show up for their match in Manila.

1981 The Brixton riots began. Mobs of youths, both black and white, went on the rampage. Police harassment over a long period was given as the cause.

1987 The late Duchess of Windsor's jewels fetched £31,380,197 at auction.

4 APRIL

BORN THIS DAY

ARTS

1758 Pierre Paul Prud'hon, French painter who became the court painter to the empress Joséphine, Napoleon's wife. He also designed furniture and interiors.

1896 Robert Emmet Sherwood, US playwright and editor of *Life* magazine. He won four Pulitzer Prizes for his plays including *Abe Lincoln in Illinois* (1939).

1928 Maya Angelou (Marguerite Johnson) US novelist, poet and playwright whose autobiographical *I Know Why The Caged Bird Sings* (1970) describes life as a black woman growing up in the South.

ENTERTAINMENT

1932 Anthony Perkins, US actor destined always to be associated with his role as Norman Bates in *Psycho* (1960).

POP

1915 Muddy Waters (McKinley Morganfield), US blues singer who recorded 'Rollin' Stone' and 'Hoochie Coochie Man'.

INVENTION

1823 Sir William Siemens, German-born metallurgist and inventor who came to Britain to demonstrate his process for electro-gilding and stayed. He was naturalized in 1859. His other inventions, made by his Siemens Brothers firm, include a cable-laying steamship, a water-meter and pyrometer.

DIED THIS DAY

1617 John Napier, Scottish inventor of logarithms.

1774 Oliver Goldsmith, English playwright.

1841 William Henry Harrison, ninth US President.

1929 Karl Benz, German automobile engineer.

1941 André Michelin, French tyre manufacturer.

ON THIS DAY

1581 Francis Drake returned to England having circumnavigated the world in *The Golden Hind*. Queen Elizabeth I knighted him on board his ship.

LOADSAMONEY In 1720, the House of Lords passed the South Sea Bill to allow the South Sea Company a monopoly of South American trade in return for a loan of £7m to ease the country's French War debt. Expecting to get rich quickly, investors flocked to buy shares until the 'South Sea Bubble' burst. The promoters fled, corruption in high places was exposed and many people faced bankruptcy. On this same day in 1896, the discovery of gold in the Yukon was reported and the gold rush began. In 1974, financier Bernie Cornfield was released on bail of £700,000 in Geneva, where he faced fraud charges over the collapse of his Investors Overseas Services. He was eventually cleared of all charges in 1979.

1904 Britain and France signed the Entente Cordiale, a mutual recognition of each other's colonial interests.

1922 The man who betrayed Nurse Edith Cavell to the Germans, Armand Jeanns, was sentenced to death by a Brussels court.

1946 Dr Marcelle Pétiot was sentenced to death in Paris for the murder of 27 people (although he admitted killing 63). Posing as a Resistance member, his victims thought he could arrange their escape. He gave them an injection, claiming it was necessary for where they were going, but instead they died in agony. He kept their possessions and is said to have made over £1m from his crimes. He was guillotined on 26 May.

1949 Eleven countries signed the North Atlantic Treaty in Washington.

1968 At 6.01 p.m., US civil rights leader and Nobel Peace prize winner Dr Martin Luther King was leaning over the balcony on the second floor of a motel in Memphis, Tennessee, talking to colleagues on the ground floor when he was shot dead by James Earl Ray. His assassin escaped, but was later caught in London. Ray pleaded guilty and was given a 99-year sentence.

1979 Ex-President of Pakistan, Zulfikar Ali Bhutto, was hanged in Rawalpindi Central Jail. It was alleged that he had inspired the killing of a political opponent, but many believed it was the new regime's way of ridding themselves of their greatest threat.

1981 An emotional Aintree saw Bob Champion win the Grand National on Aldaniti. Champion, suffering from cancer, had been given eight months to live, while Aldaniti, who had led all the way, had been plagued with tendon problems and a broken hock.

1981 Susan Brown, Oxford's first woman cox, made sure her crew won the annual Boat Race by eight lengths.

1988 The long-running television soap opera *Crossroads* ended after 24 years.

5 APRIL

BORN THIS DAY

HISTORY

1588 Thomas Hobbes, English philosopher, born prematurely when his mother heard that the Armada was approaching. His political philosophy, that absolute authority should be vested in government, was expounded in his masterpiece, the *Leviathan* (1651).

1649 Elihu Yale, US-born English official who became the governor of Madras. When in 1701 he sold some of his US effects, he stipulated that the money should go towards the establishment of a collegiate school which, in 1718, became Yale College. It expanded to become Yale University in 1887.

1724 Giovanni Jacopo Casanova, the world's best known lover.

1827 Joseph Lister, first Baron, English surgeon and pioneer of antiseptics which revolutionized modern surgery.

ARTS

1732 Jean Honoré Fragonard, rococo French painter and engraver.

1837 Algernon Charles Swinburne, English poet who shocked puritan taste with uninhibited poems.

1908 Herbert von Karajan, Austrian conductor whose career after the Second World War suffered a set-back because of his Nazi affiliations. Within a few years, however, he was conducting at Bayreuth and the Berlin Philharmonic Orchestra.

1920 Arthur Hailey, English-born novelist who settled in Canada before the success of blockbusters such as *Hotel* (1965) and *Airport* (1968) led him to California and then to the Bahamas.

ENTERTAINMENT

1875 Mistinguett (Jeanne Marie Bourgeois), popular French comedienne and beauty who took her stage name from the song 'Miss Tinguett'.

1894 Chesney Allen, English comedian, partner to Bud Flanagan and member of the famous Crazy Gang, best remembered for his gravel-voiced accompaniment to the song they made their own, 'Underneath the Arches'.

1900 Spencer Tracy, US actor who appeared first on Broadway before beginning a long, illustrious career in films. He won Oscars for *Captains Courageous* (1937) and *Boys Town* (1938), making him the only male actor to win two years in succession, as well as Oscar nominations for seven other films.

1908 Bette (Ruth Elizabeth) Davis, US actress who won her first Oscar in 1935 for *Dangerous*. Her films include *All About Eve* (1950) and *Whatever Happened to Baby Jane?* (1962).

1916 Gregory Peck, US actor who won an Oscar for his performance in *To Kill A Mockingbird* (1962). Much involved in political and charitable work, he has received a number of awards for his humanitarian work.

1929 Nigel Hawthorne, English actor best known for his portrayal as Sir Humphrey in the award-winning television series *Yes, Minister*.

1946 Jane Asher, English actress who made her first film, *Mandy*, at five. She was later involved in the pop scene as Paul McCartney's girlfriend.

POP

1950 Agnetha 'Anna' Faltskög, Swedish singer, former member of Abba.

SPORT

1884 John Wisden, Sussex cricketer and compiler of the cricketer's bible.

1922 Tom Finney, Preston North End footballer who was in England's first World Cup team. He was voted Footballer of the Year in 1957, and played 76 internationals.

DIED THIS DAY

1649 John Winthrop, the Puritan govenor of the Massachusetts Bay Company.

1794 Georges Jacques Danton, French revolutionary leader, guillotined by those whom he had once led and inspired. 'Show my head to the people,' he told the executioner. 'It is worth the trouble.'

1811 Robert Raikes, English philanthropist and founder of the Sunday School movement.

1946 Vincent (Miller) Youmans, US composer and songwriter of 'Tea for Two'.

1964 Douglas MacArthur, US general and Second World War commander in the Pacific.

1975 Chiang Kai-shek, soldier and Chinese leader.

1976 Howard Hughes, US multimillionaire recluse, who had broken aviation records, built aircraft, made movies and designed Jane Russell's bra, on board his private aircraft taking him to his doctor in Houston, Texas. He left an estate worth $1.5 billion.

1984 Sir Arthur Travers Harris, Baronet, 'Bomber Harris', former chief of Bomber Command.

ON THIS DAY

1874 The first performance in Vienna of *Die Fledermaus* by Johann Strauss II.

1895 Oscar Wilde was arrested at the Cadogan Hotel, Sloane Square, London, for offences arising from his friendship with Lord Alfred Douglas, son of the 8th Marquis of Queensbury, whom Wilde had tried to sue for criminal libel. Even before the trial started, Wilde was ruined. Shops withdrew his books, and his plays at the St James and Haymarket Theatres closed.

1902 The stand at Ibrox Park stadium in Glasgow collapsed during an England v. Scotland match killing 20 and injuring over 200. History repeated itself on 2.1.1971.

1910 Kissing was banned on French railways because it could cause delays.

1915 Jack Johnson, 'Galveston Jack', the first black world heavyweight boxing champion, finally lost his title, which he won in 1908, to Jess Willard, 'the great white hope' from Iowa. The contest in Havana was a scheduled 45 rounds, but a tiring Johnson was knocked out in the 26th.

1920 On the anniversary of the Easter Uprising in Dublin, 120 police stations and 22 tax offices were set ablaze in Ireland.

1955 A frail Churchill resigned as Prime Minister, handing over to Anthony Eden.

1960 *Ben Hur* won a record ten Oscars.

1982 The British Task Force sailed from Southampton for the Falklands following the invasion of the 'Malvinas' by Argentina.

1989 Sex Aid was launched by the London-based Marie Stopes charity. Couples were asked to contribute 25p each time they had sex to help Third World countries.

6 APRIL

BORN THIS DAY

HISTORY

1758 Maximilien François Marie Isidore Robespierre, French revolutionary who became the virtual ruler of France until his enemies finally succeeded in having him guillotined.

1890 Anthony Herman Gerard Fokker, Dutch aircraft designer and engineer who built his first plane in 1911. The Fokker factory in Germany built many of the aircraft for the German airforce during the First World War.

ARTS

1906 Sir John Betjeman, popular English poet and Poet Laureate, and defender of British landmarks from developers.

1929 André Previn, US conductor, pianist and composer who was born in Berlin.

ENTERTAINMENT

1874 Harry Houdini (Erich Weiss), US escapologist who performed daring and baffling escapes from ropes and handcuffs.

1900 Leo Robin, lyricist of hit Broadway musicals including *Gentlemen Prefer Blondes* (1949). He wrote the songs 'Thanks for the Memory' and 'Diamonds Are a Girl's Best Friend'.

1938 Paul Daniels, English magician, entertainer and game show host on television.

SCIENCE

1928 James Watson, US-born scientist who with Englishman Francis Crick, built the first model DNA molecule and made discoveries concerning genetic coding. He shared the 1962 Nobel prize with Crick.

POP

1945 Peter Tosh (Winston Hubert McIntosh), Jamaican reggae musician, one-time partner of Bob Marley.

DIED THIS DAY

1199 Richard I, Coeur de Lion, King of England, killed in battle while besieging the castle of Chaluz during the Crusades.

1520 Raphael (Rafaello Santi), Italian Renaissance painter.

1528 Albrecht Dürer, German artist and engraver.

1961 Jules (Jean Baptiste Vincent) Bordet, Belgian bacteriologist and Nobel prize winner who discovered the whooping cough microbe.

1971 Igor Stravinsky, Russian-born composer, in New York.

1986 Lt Commander Bill Boaks, English eccentric who stood for parliament 30 times, losing his deposit each time. He became more famous than many of those who won. His one-man Public Safety Democratic Monarchist White Resident party had the slogan, 'Vote for Bill Boaks, the sailor with the navy-blue eyes'.

ON THIS DAY

1580 An earthquake damaged many of London's churches, including St Paul's, the Norman building that replaced the original Saxon St Paul's.

1652 Jan van Riebeck arrived at the Cape, South Africa to establish the trading station for the Dutch East India ships *en route* to the east.

1789 George Washington became the first Chief-magistrate or President of the 12 American states which formed the government following the War of Independence.

1830 The Church of Jesus Christ of the Latter Day Saints, whose adherents are known as Mormons, was founded by Joseph Smith at Fayette, New York. Smith claimed Mormon was an ancient saint who wrote *The Book of Mormon* which was delivered into his hands on the night of 22.9.1827.

1843 William Wordsworth was appointed Poet Laureate.

1896 The first modern Olympic Games, revived by Baron de Coubetin, was held in Athens. US athlete James Connolly won the first gold in the Triple Jump.

1909 US Commander Robert Peary reached the North Pole, the first to do so, accompanied by Matthew Henson and four Eskimos.

1917 The US entered the First World War.

1944 PAYE (Pay As You Earn income tax) was introduced in Britain.

1965 *Early Bird*, the first commercial communications satellite was launched by the US.

1968 Pierre Trudeau succeeded the retiring Lester Pearson as Canada's Prime Minister.

1984 The 17-year-old South African barefoot long- and middle-distance runner, Zola Budd, who was brought by the *Daily Mail* to Britain in March of this Olympic year, was granted British citizenship by Home Secretary, Leon Brittan, after only a matter of weeks, provoking considerable controversy.

7 APRIL

BORN THIS DAY

HISTORY

1506 St Francis Xavier, Spanish priest, who was ordained in Venice.

1891 Ole Kirk Christiansen, Danish toy maker who, in 1932, formed the company Lego, from the Danish *leg godt* which means 'play well'. After seeing his Lego bricks become one of the most successful toys of all time, Christiansen later discovered that *Lego* is also Latin for 'I put together'.

ARTS

1770 William Wordsworth, English Romantic poet who set up home with his sister Dorothy after the conclusion of an affair in France which produced an illegitimate daughter. Although his poetry dealing with nature is best known, his *Intimations of Immortality* is probably his masterpiece.

1891 Sir David Alexander Cecil Low, New Zealand-born British cartoonist and caricaturist who worked originally for several New Zealand and Australian newspapers before joining the *Star* in London. He created Colonel Blimp, now included in the Oxford Dictionary as 'a pompous, obese, elderly figure, popularly interpreted as a die-hard'.

1920 Ravi Shankar, Indian sitar player who introduced Indian music to modern Western audiences.

ENTERTAINMENT

1893 Irene Castle, US actress and dancer who, with her husband, Vernon created and performed some of the famous ballroom dances of the 30s, including 'The Castle Walk' and 'The Turkey Trot'.

1897 Walter Winchell, US journalist and broadcaster who wrote satirical pieces for the *New York Mirror* which were syndicated nationally.

1928 Alan J. Pakula, US film director and producer of *All The President's Men* (1976).

1928 James Garner, US actor best known for his television series, including *Maverick*, the first genuinely humorous western series, and *The Rockford Files*.

1930 Andrew Sachs, German-born British actor, known to millions as 'Manuel', the down-trodden Spanish waiter in the television series *Fawlty Towers*.

1939 David Frost, English television presenter and producer whose career began as the 'anchorman' in the first satirical television series, *That Was the Week That Was*.

1939 Francis Ford Coppola, US film director and writer who made his fame and fortune with *The Godfather* (winner of eight Oscars in 1972).

JAZZ

1915 Billie Holiday (Eleanora Fagan), US blues singer who overcame an unhappy childhood in the black ghetto of Baltimore to become 'Lady Day', the finest jazz singer of her age. She made 'Night and Day' and 'The Man I Love' unforgettable, but drug addiction led to arrests and her eventual crack-up.

SPORT

1930 Cliff Morgan, Welsh and Lions rugby player, and former head of BBC television outside broadcasting.

DIED THIS DAY

1739 (Richard) Dick Turpin, English highwayman, hanged in York for the murder of an innkeeper in Epping.

1891 Phineas Taylor Barnum, US showman.

1947 Henry Ford, US motor car manufacturer; the first to use mass-production techniques.

1955 Theda Bara (Theodosia Goodman), silent movie star.

1965 (James) Jim Clark, Scottish motor racing driver, twice world motor racing champion, killed when his Formula Two Lotus Cosworth skidded and crashed at the Hockenheim circuit, West Germany.

ON THIS DAY

1779 A former footman who became a deacon in the Church of England shot and killed the Earl of Sandwich's mistress, Margaret Reay, as she left the Covent Garden Theatre. The Rev James Hackman had fallen in love with Margaret when he was a footman to the Earl, but she had always rejected his advances. He was sentenced to death and rejected help from the Earl for clemency saying he wanted to die.

1827 The first matches were sold, invented by John Walker, a chemist in Stockton-on-Tees, Co. Durham. The first known purchaser was a local solicitor who paid one shilling (five new pence) for 100 matches and a further two pennies (one new pence) for the tin tube in which to store them.

1832 Joseph Thompson, a farmer, came to Carlisle to sell his wife, both having agreed to part. A large crowd gathered as he offered her for 50 shillings. After an hour, the price was knocked down to 20 shillings, together with a Newfoundland dog. The practice of wife selling, although illegal in Britain, was not unknown in rural areas.

1862 In the US Civil War, despite great losses and a relatively unprepared force, General Ulysses Grant forced the Confederate troops to retreat at the Battle of Shiloh.

1902 The Texas Oil Company, better known as Texaco, was formed.

1906 Mount Vesuvius erupted, killing more than 100 people.

1943 LSD (lysergic acid diethylamide) was first synthesized by Albert Hoffman in his Swiss laboratory.

1948 WHO, the World Health Organization, was set up in Geneva.

1949 *South Pacific* by Rodgers and Hammerstein, opened on on Broadway.

1951 Only three horses out of 36 finished in the Grand National, which was won by Nickel Coin. (*See also* 4.3.1922)

1953 Dag Hammarskjöld of Sweden was elected Secretary-General of the United Nations Organization.

1958 An Easter march to the Atomic Weapons Research Establishment, Aldermaston attracted 3,000 anti-atomic bomb marchers and a further 12,000 members of the new CND movement (Campaign for Nuclear Disarmament).

1985 Pop duo Wham! performed two concerts in China to somewhat bemused audiences.

1988 The first Yorkshire Pudding Birthday Lunch was held near Hull. The famous pudding's earliest known reference is in Hannah Glasse's *The Art of Cookery Plain and Easy* (1747).

8 APRIL

BORN THIS DAY

HISTORY

1875 Albert I, King of the Belgians.

1919 Ian (Douglas) Smith, Rhodesian Prime Minister who advocated white supremacy and unilaterally declared independence (UDI) from Britain in 1965. After the transfer of power to the black majority in 1979, he was elected a member of parliament in the government of Robert Mugabe.

ARTS

1889 Sir Adrian (Cedric) Boult, English conductor.

ENTERTAINMENT

1893 Mary Pickford (Gladys Smith), Canadian-born US film actress known as 'America's Sweetheart' who entered the silent movie business when stars were not given billing or clearly identified, for fear they would want high fees. A clever businesswoman, she progressed from studio to studio, securing ever more lucrative contracts before forming her own company in 1919, United Artists.

1898 E. Y. 'Yip' Harburg (Isidore Hochberg), US lyricist who won an Oscar for his lyrics for *The Wizard of Oz*.

1928 Eric Porter, English actor who played Soames in the television drama series *The Forsyte Saga*.

1930 Dorothy Tutin, leading English actress.

1944 Hywel Bennett, Welsh-born actor who established himself in the 1966 film *The Family Way* and as *Shelley* in the television comedy series.

SCIENCE

1818 August Wilhelm Hofmann, German chemist who discovered formaldehyde and extracted aniline from coal products.

SPORT

1912 Sonja Henie, Norwegian ice skater who won the World and Olympic titles, which she won three consecutive times, before becoming an actress.

DIED THIS DAY

217 Caracalla (Marcus Aurelius Antonius) Roman emperor, assassinated after a reign of terror; he had only ascended the throne by murdering his brother.

1492 Lorenzo de'Medici, 'the magnificent', Florentine statesman.

1861 Elisha Graves Otis, US inventor of the safety lift.

LEGENDS IN THEIR LIFETIME In 1950, Vaslaj Nijinsky, Russian dancer who died in London after many years of insanity, and in 1973, Pablo Picasso, Spanish painter and sculptor who pioneered Cubism and was still working right into his 92nd year.

1981 Omar (Nelson) Bradley, US general who led the invading armies through France in the Second World War.

ON THIS DAY

1838 The day before his 32nd birthday, Isambard Kingdom Brunel's 236ft steamship *Great Western* sailed from Bristol on her maiden voyage to New

York. She would become the first steamship to make regular Atlantic crossings.

1898 Lord Kitchener captured the Mahdi at Atbara River, after defeating his Sudanese army.

1925 The Australian government, together with the British Colonial Office, agreed to make available low-interest loans to enable around half a million Britons to emigrate to Australia.

1953 In Kenya, Jomo 'Burning Spear' Kenyatta was sentenced to seven years imprisonment for his involvement with the Mau-Mau.

1986 Clint Eastwood was elected Mayor of Carmel, California.

1988 Britain's first self-extinguishing armchair was unveiled with its own heat detector-activated sprinkler system.

1989 The longest single-movement work in Western musical history, the symphony *Odyssey* by Nicholas Maw, received its first complete performance in London; 100 minutes punctuated by resonating 'time-chords' inspired by the composer's grandfather clock.

1990 British golfer Nick Faldo won his second successive US Masters after a play-off. (*See* 11.4.1989)

9 APRIL

BORN THIS DAY

HISTORY

1649 James Scott, Duke of Monmouth, claimant to the English throne, who led a failed rebellion against James II which cost him his head. His 320 accomplices were sentenced to death by Judge Jeffreys.

1835 Leopold II, King of the Belgians.

1872 Léon Blum, first French Socialist and Jewish Prime Minister in 1936. Imprisoned for being both a Jew and a 'Red' by the Vichy government, he survived Buchenwald and Dachau to become Prime Minister of the provisional government after the War.

1906 Hugh (Todd Naylor) Gaitskell, English politician and leader of the Labour Party.

ARTS

1909 Sir Robert Helpmann, Australian ballet dancer and choreographer who joined Pavlova's company in 1929. He came to Britain in 1931 to study under Dame Ninette de Valois and was the first male dancer of the newly-founded Vic-Wells ballet in 1933 later renamed the Sadler's Wells Theatre Ballet.

1906 Anatole Dorati, Hungarian-born conductor who was probably the most prolifically recorded of all conductors, with the widest repertoire.

ENTERTAINMENT

1898 Paul Robeson, US actor and singer who starred in two O'Neill plays before making his reputation as both a fine bass and actor in Kern's *Show Boat* which included the song that is always identified with him, 'Ole Man River'. His strong left-wing views and his civil rights activities on behalf of fellow blacks during the US anti-communism era, led him to renounce his US citizenship.

1926 Hugh Heffner, US publisher of *Playboy*.

1928 Tom Lehrer, US songwriter and mathematician who wrote and sang satirical songs on atomic bombs and drugs, making him one of the voices of the 60s.

1933 Jean-Paul Belmondo, French actor who made his name in Godard's *Breathless* (1960).

SPORT

1957 Sevériano Ballesteros, Spanish golfer who, at 23, was the youngest player to win the US Masters. (*See* 13.4.1980)

POP

1932 Carl Perkins, US rock 'n' roller who sang the original 'Blue Suede Shoes'.

ENGINEERING

1806 Isambard Kingdom Brunel, English engineer who built the Clifton Suspension Bridge in Bristol and the *Great Western* steam ship.

1920 Alexander Moulton, English bicycle and coach designer who devised a folding bike suitable to be carried.

DIED THIS DAY

1483 Edward IV, King of England, suddenly, as a result of excessive debauchery.

1553 François Rabelais, French satirical writer.

1626 Francis Bacon, Viscount St Albans, English statesman and writer, as a result of stuffing a fowl with snow in order to observe the effect on its flesh. This early experiment in deep-freezing brought on a severe cold and he died soon after.

1882 Dante Gabriel Rossetti, English Pre-Raphaelite painter and poet.

1940 Mrs Patrick Campbell (Beatrice Stella Tanner), English actress.

1945 Dietrich Bonhoeffer, German theologian and anti-Nazi, in a concentration camp.

1959 Frank Lloyd Wright, controversial US architect.

ON THIS DAY

1483 The young Edward V acceded to the throne on the death of Edward IV. The boy was murdered in the Tower 75 days later (25.6.1483)

1747 The Jacobite, Lord Lovat, became last prisoner to be beheaded in England, a form of execution which had been reserved for the nobility.

1865 At Appotomax, General Robert E. Lee surrendered to General Ulysses S. Grant in the US Civil War.

1869 The Hudson Bay Company agreed to cede its considerable territorial rights to Canada.

1940 The German invasion of Norway and Denmark began.

1960 A 52-year-old white man, David Pratt, fired two wounding shots at South African Prime Minister, Dr Hendrik Verwoerd. Pratt claimed he'd done it because he was refused a visa to visit his second wife in Holland.

1966 In Paris, Sophia Loren married Carlo Ponti, who was still married to his wife in Italy.

1969 Concorde 002 made its maiden flight from Filton, near Bristol, with Brian Trubshaw in charge of the flight deck.

1970 Paul McCartney issued a writ in the High Court to dissolve the Beatles' business partnership.

1983 Corbierre won the Grand National, the first winner trained by a woman (Jenny Pitman).

10 APRIL

BORN THIS DAY

HISTORY

1512 James V, King of Scotland, who was still an infant when he inherited the crown.

1755 Christian Friedrich Samuel Hahnemann, German physician who founded homeopathic medicine.

1829 William Booth, founder of the Salvation Army, which he began in 1865 while performing mission work to the poor in London's East End. It was only named in 1878, when he took the title 'General'.

ARTS

1778 William Hazlitt, English essayist and critic who was unlucky in love. He married Sarah Stoddart in 1808, but divorced her in Edinburgh in 1822. He developed a passion for his landlord's daughter, but in the end married a widow with a generous £300 a year to her name. They went off to Italy where she left him on the return journey.

1827 Lewis Wallace, US novelist and author of the famous religious novel *Ben Hur* (1880), twice filmed.

1847 Joseph Pulitzer, US newspaper proprietor who also instituted the Pulitzer prize for journalism, novels, plays and other writings.

1903 Clare Boothe Luce, US playwright, wife of *Time/Life* publisher Henry Luce. She was elected to the House of Representatives, standing as a Republican, and, in 1952, was the US Ambassador to Italy.

1941 Paul (Edward) Theroux, US writer of novels and travel books.

ENTERTAINMENT

1868 George Arliss (George Augustus Andrews), English actor who specialized in playing famous historical characters and was the first British star to win an Oscar, in 1929 for his role as *Disraeli*.

1929 Max von Sydow, Swedish actor who worked with Ingmar Bergman in *The Seventh Seal* (1957) and later appeared in US films, including *The Exorcist* (1973).

1932 Omar Sharif (Michael Shalhoub), Egyptian-born actor whose first English-speaking film was *Lawrence of Arabia* (1962). He went on to star in many films including *Dr Zhivago* (1965).

1940 Gloria Hunniford, Irish-born broadcaster and chat show presenter.

SPORT

1937 Stan Mellor, English racehorse trainer who was the first National Hunt jockey to ride 1,000 winners.

DIED THIS DAY

1954 Auguste Marie Louis Lumière, French cine pioneer.

1962 Michael Curtiz (Mihaly Kertesz), Hungarian-born film director best remembered for *Casablanca* (1942).

1962 Stu Sutcliffe, original bassist with John Lennon's 'Silver Beatles' died of a brain haemorrhage in Hamburg.

1966 Evelyn (Arthur St John) Waugh, English novelist.

ON THIS DAY

1633 Bananas were displayed in the London shop window of Thomas

Johnson. The fruit had never before been seen in Britain.

1710 The Copyright Act (1709) came into effect in Britain, allowing the author to hold exclusive rights to his or her work for up to 50 years after their death.

1820 The first British settlers arrived at Algoa Bay in the eastern Cape Province, South Africa.

1841 The *New York Tribune* was first published. It later became the *Herald Tribune*.

1849 The safety pin was patented in the US by Walter Hunt of New York, but he later sold the rights for $400. On 12 October, a British inventor, Charles Roweley, also patented his safety pin, unaware of the earlier US patent.

1860 *The Mill on the Floss* by George Eliot (Marian Evans) was published.

1864 The Archduke Maximilian of Austria became the Emperor of Mexico.

1919 Mexican rebel leader Emiliano Zapata was killed by government troops.

1921 Sun Yat-sen was elected President of China.

1924 The first crossword puzzle book was published in New York.

1932 In the German elections, Paul von Hindenburg was elected president with 19 million votes to Hitler's 13 million.

1960 The US Senate passed the Civil Rights Bill.

1974 Golda Meir resigned as Israeli Prime Minister over differences with her Labour Party colleagues and Yitzhak Rabin became the new party leader (on 22 April).

1988 Probably for the first time ever, a dog died as a result of watching a television programme, in China. In a violent scene in an East German film, a long-haired man leapt out of bushes with a shotgun; the dog howled with fear, ran about in all directions and finally died of a heart attack.

1989 Nick Faldo became the first Englishman to win the the US Masters in a dramatic sudden death play-off. (*See* 8.4.1990)

11 APRIL

BORN THIS DAY

ARTS

1819 Sir Charles Hallé, German-born British pianist and conductor who came to England and settled in Manchester, where in 1858 he founded the famous orchestra that bears his name.

ENTERTAINMENT

1930 Ronald Fraser, Scottish character actor who played a variety of roles in the West End as well as in films and on television.

1932 Joel Grey (Joel Katz), US actor and singer who had his greatest success as the Master of Ceremonies in the musical *Cabaret* (1966) which he also recreated in the film version.

1937 Jill Gascoine, English actress best known for her role in the television thriller series, *Cat's Eyes*.

SCIENCE

1775 James Parkinson, English physician and palaeontologist who discovered Parkinson's disease (1817), and was the first to realize that a perforated appendix could cause death.

DIED THIS DAY

1142 Peter Abelard, French theologian who taught at Notre Dame where he fell in love with with beautiful 17-year-old Héloïse. She secretly married the 38-year-old Abelard and bore him a child, but denied the marriage to protect him. Eventually, the church separated them and she became a nun. He became a monk and died this day on his way to Rome to face charges of heresy. They were finally reunited in their graves in the Père Lachaise cemetery, Paris.

1514 Donato Bramante, Italian architect, while still working on the rebuilding of St Peter's in Rome.

1906 James Anthony Bailey, US circus owner; the other half of Barnum and Bailey.

1934 Sir Gerald du Maurier, English actor-manager.

1960 Sir Archibald McIndoe, New Zealand-born plastic surgeon.

1970 John (Henry) O'Hara, US novelist.

1975 Josephine Baker, black US-born French dancer and singer at the *Folies Bergère*.

1988 John (Thompson) Stonehouse, former British cabinet minister who was involved in a fake suicide after a failed financial venture, eventually turning up in Australia with his girlfriend. He was jailed in England, where he suffered a heart attack after serving half his seven-year sentence. Paroled, he then suffered a final attack.

ON THIS DAY

1689 William III and Mary II were crowned joint monarchs of Great Britain by the Bishop of London. The Archbishop of Canterbury refused to officiate.

1713 Gibraltar and Newfoundland were ceded to Britain by France in the Treaty of Utrecht.

1814 Napoleon abdicated and was banished to the island of Elba.

1902 Fred Gaisburg of the Gramophone Company made the first recordings of Caruso, who received the unheard of advance of £100. Caruso eventually made over £1m from his recordings, the first artist to achieve this.

1913 French aviator Gustave Hamel made a record double Channel crossing from Dunkirk to Dover and back in 90 minutes.

1919 The International Labour Organization was founded.

1929 Popeye made his first appearance as a supporting character in a cartoon strip in Hearst's New York newspapers.

1935 Severe dust storms hit Kansas, Colorado, Wyoming, Oklahoma, Texas and New Mexico, destroying crops and making many homeless. Tornadoes followed, killing 26 people and injuring 150 in Mississippi.

1951 President Truman dismissed General Douglas MacArthur from all his posts, including UN forces in Korea, for publicly criticizing his Korean policy.

1951 The Stone of Scone, stolen from Westminster Abbey by Scottish nationalists who wanted it returned to Scotland, turned up this day, 107 days later, at an abbey in Forfar, Angus.

1957 *The Entertainer*, by John Osborne, starring Sir Laurence Olivier as the music hall comedian Archie Rice, opened at the Royal Court Theatre, London.

1957 Singapore was granted self-government by Britain.

1961 Adolf Eichmann's trial began in Jerusalem, after he had been traced and captured in Argentina by the Israelis. He was found guilty on 15 December and later hanged.

1967 Tom Stoppard's first play *Rosencrantz and Guildenstern Are Dead* opened at the National Theatre.

1981 Bobby Sands, IRA hunger striker in the Maze Prison, won the Fermanagh and Tyrone by-election, but he died on 5 May.

1983 Richard Attenborough's *Gandhi* received eight Oscars, the most any British film has ever won.

1988 Sir Kenneth MacMillan's ballet, *Élite Syncopations*, based on the music by Scott Joplin, was performed at the Bavarian State Opera in Munich, accompanied by only two pianos, after the orchestra had won the right not to play music written by a black man under a 1937 Nazi law. Sir Kenneth banned any further productions of his work in Munich.

12 APRIL

BORN THIS DAY

HISTORY

1777 Henry Clay, US statesman and orator who was the speaker of the House of Congress from 1811. A founder of the Republican Party, he failed three times to become president.

ARTS

1692 Giuseppe Tartini, Italian violinist and composer who invented a new type of bow.

1913 Lionel Hampton, US bandleader and first vibraharpist to play true jazz on the instrument.

1923 Maria Callas (Cecilia Sophia Anna Maria Kalogeropoulos), New York-born Greek soprano whose dramatic singing and acting ability won her enormous international acclaim, particularly for her roles as Norma, Tosca and Violetta. Her private life attracted publicity, and her affair with Onassis ended in rejection when he married Jackie Kennedy.

ENTERTAINMENT

1949 Alan Ayckbourn, prolific English playwright of sharp contemporary farces such as *Absurd Person Singular* (1973) and *The Norman Conquests* (1974) which examine class behaviour in Britain.

SPORT

1941 (Robert Frederick) Bobby Moore, West Ham United captain who played for England 108 times and captained the victorious England World Cup team at Wembley in 1966.

DIED THIS DAY

1817 Charles Joseph Messier, French astronomer who published the first list of the nebulae.

1945 Franklin Delano Roosevelt, 32nd US President.

1962 Antoine Pevsner, French constructionist sculptor.

BEATEN BY THE BELL Two of America's great world boxing champions died this day. In 1981, Joe Louis (Joseph Louis Barrow), 'The Brown Bomber', US and world heavyweight boxing champion, and in 1989, 'Sugar' Ray Robinson (Walker Smith,

Jr), unbeaten welterweight champion and five times winner of the middleweight title.

ON THIS DAY

1204 The Fourth Crusade, which had more to do with finance and lands than religion, was diverted by the Venetians to the riches of Constantinople, sacked this day.

1606 The Union Jack became the official flag of England.

1709 The *Tatler* magazine was first published in Britain.

1838 English settlers in South Africa won the Battle of Tugela against the might of the Zulus, who were led by their chief, Dingaan. The fact that the settlers had guns and the Zulus only spears probably had some bearing on the outcome.

1861 The American Civil War began when the Confederate Army under General Pierre Beauregarde besieged Fort Sumter in South Carolina.

1914 George Bernard Shaw's *Pygmalion* opened in London, with Mrs Patrick Campbell as Eliza Doolittle, and Sir Herbert Tree as Professor Higgins.

1954 Bill Haley and the Comets recorded 'Rock Around the Clock'.

1961 The USSR put the first man in space when Yuri Gagarin was launched in Vostok I for a single orbit of the earth. The flight lasted 108 minutes before he landed safely back on earth.

1989 Lloyd Webber's *Cats* was performed for the 3,358th time at the New London Theatre, Drury Lane, making it Britain's longest running musical. Steven Wain who played one of the cats, was the only member of the original cast still in the show after eight years. Seats are booked to the end of 1999.

1990 A routine check by British Customs officers uncovered the planned shipment to Iraq of what appeared to be sections of a 'supergun', which initiated an international investigation.

13 APRIL

BORN THIS DAY

HISTORY

1732 Frederick North, 2nd Earl of Guildford, who, as Lord North, levied the tax on tea that so incensed the American colonists and provoked the 'Boston Tea Party'.

1743 Thomas Jefferson, third US President who was the original drafter of the Declaration of Independence and the founder of the Democrat Party.

1892 Sir Arthur Travers Harris, Royal Air Force Bomber commander, nicknamed 'Bomber Harris', who instituted the mass bombing raids over Germany, including the controversial blanket bombing of Dresden.

1902 Baron Philippe de Rothschild, wine producer who invited leading artists such as Picasso and Warhol to design his famous Château Mouton labels. He was also a poet, translator, Bugatti racing-driver, champion yachtsman and theatre lover.

ARTS

1906 Samuel Beckett, Irish playwright who worked as James Joyce's secretary in Paris. His first major play, *Waiting for Godot* (1956) was written in French. He won the Nobel prize for Literature in 1969.

1922 John (Gerard) Braine, English novelist who wrote his first novel, *Room at the Top* (1957) while recovering from tuberculosis.

ENTERTAINMENT

LUCKY SEVEN Born 1919, Howard Keel (Harry Clifford Leek), US singer and actor who made his name in stage musicals such as *Oklahoma*. He went on to make many Hollywood musicals, including *Kiss Me Kate* (1953) and *Seven Brides for Seven Brothers* (1954), which was directed by Stanley Donen, who was also born this day in 1924. Donen began his film career as a chorus boy and assistant choreographer before working as Gene Kelly's co-director on *On The Town* (1949).

1937 Edward Fox, English actor, brother of actor James Fox, who created the definitive Edward VIII for the television series *Edward and Mrs Simpson*.

INVENTION

1771 Richard Trevithick, English engineer and mechanic who developed the first practical steam locomotive in his native Cornwall where he started as a mining engineer. He developed the first steam carriage, which he demonstrated in London running from Leather Lane through Oxford Street to Paddington in 1803. He also developed the first steam locomotive to successfully run on rails the following year.

BUSINESS

1852 Frank Winfield Woolworth, US chain store pioneer. A former farm labourer and shop assistant, he persuaded his employers to back his idea for a store that would sell everything for five cents or less. When it failed, he tried again offering items up to ten cents. It succeeded famously, setting off a chain of similar stores, the first in Britain in 1910.

SPORT

1963 Gary Kasparov, Russian grandmaster and world chess champion in 1985, when he finally beat the holder, Antatoly Karpov.

DIED THIS DAY

1605 Boris Feodorovich Godunov, Tsar of Russia, better known as the subject of an opera by Mussorgsky.

1695 Jean de La Fontaine, French writer of fables.

1966 Abdul Salam Arif, President of Iraq, killed in a helicopter crash.

ON THIS DAY

193 Marcus Diderius Salvius Julianus was proclaimed Emperor of Rome, but 49 days later he was put to death by order of the Senate.

1668 John Dryden was appointed the first Poet Laureate and Royal Historiographer.

1741 The Royal Military Academy was established at Woolwich. It was transfered to Sandhurst, Berkshire in 1946.

1742 First performance of Handel's *Messiah*, in Dublin.

1821 Friday the 13th proved to be John Horwood's unlucky day. He was hanged at Bristol for the murder of Eliza Balsam. While the crime is now of little interest, Horwood's claim to immortality is as a result of the usual practice of allowing criminal's bodies to be used for anatomical purposes. Not one scrap of Horwood was wasted, even his skin was used to bind the anatomist's account of the post-mortem which may be found on the shelves of Bristol's record office.

1882 The founding of the Anti-Semitic League and the presentation to Bismarck of a petition demanding restrictions on the liberty of Prussian Jews.

1912 The Royal Flying Corps was formed.

1919 The Amritsar massacre took place in the Punjab when British troops led by Brigadier-General Dyer opened fire on an unlawful demonstration on an open wasteland in the Holy City of the Sikhs.

1935 Imperial Airways and QANTAS inaugurated their London to Australia air service.

1964 For his role in *Lillies of the Field*, Sydney Poitier became the first black actor to win an Oscar.

1980 Four days after his 23rd birthday, Sevériano Ballesteros won the US Masters, the youngest winner ever.

14 APRIL

BORN THIS DAY

HISTORY

1527 Philip II of Spain, who, in 1588, tried to conquer England, but sent his ill-fated Armada to destruction.

1527 Ortelius (Abraham Oertel), Dutch cartographer and engraver who produced the first atlas.

1889 Arnold Toynbee, English economic historian who coined the phrase 'Industrial Revolution' in his book covering that period in Britain.

1897 Barbara Wootton, Baroness Wootton of Abinger, English politician who became the first woman to sit on the woolsack as deputy speaker of the House of Commons.

1907 François Duvalier ('Papa Doc'), president of Haiti, virtual dictator who created his own murderous private army, the Tonton Macoute.

1925 Bishop Abel Muzorewa, Prime Minister of Zimbabwe (Rhodesia) for six months in 1979 before the election of Robert Mugabe.

1939 Trevor Locke, policeman who was taken hostage while on guard duty outside the Iranian Embassy in London (*see* 5.5.80). He tackled the terrorist leader as the SAS stormed the building, saving the life of the first SAS man on the scene.

ENTERTAINMENT

1904 Sir John Gielgud, English actor, great grand-nephew of actress Ellen Terry, who made his debut at the Old Vic in 1921. Blessed with an exceptional voice for speaking both poetry and conversational dialogue, he was outstanding as both Romeo and Hamlet. Besides his many Shakespearian and classical roles, he won an Oscar for his role as a butler in *Arthur* (1981).

1917 Valerie Hobson, Northern Ireland-born actress who made her debut aged 16 and played Estella in *Great Expectations* (1946). Her second husband, John Profumo was the British minister involved in the famous 60s sex scandal, but she stood by him and played an important part in his rehabilitation.

1925 Rod(ney Steven) Steiger, US actor who won an Oscar for best actor in 1967 for his part as the police officer in *In The Heat of the Night*.

1940 Julie Christie, English actress born in India on her father's tea plantation. Her first lead was in *Billy Liar* (1963), and she won an Oscar for *Darling* (1965).

SCIENCE

1629 Christiaan Huygens, Dutch physicist and astronomer who built the first pendulum clock, on Galileo's suggestion, discovered the ring and fourth satellite of Saturn, improved the water-pump, discovered polarization and developed the micrometer.

DIED THIS DAY

1759 George Frederick Handel, German composer who had previously had a stroke and gone blind, in London, where most of his music making had been done.

1915 Alexander Scriabin, Russian composer and pianist.

1917 Dr Lazarus Ludwig Zamenhof, Polish occulist who invented the international language, Esperanto.

1951 Ernest Bevin, English Labour politician, Minister of Labour in the coalition government during the Second World War.

ON THIS DAY

1471 The Yorkists defeated the Lancastrians at the Battle of Barnet. Richard Neville, Earl of Warwick, 'the Kingmaker', was slain in the battle. He had put Henry VI on the throne, but Edward IV returned from exile in Holland to reclaim the crown.

1828 Noah Webster published his *American Dictionary of the English Language*.

1865 On this Good Friday, at Ford's Theatre, Washington, actor John Wilkes Booth shot Abraham Lincoln, the US president. Lincoln died the following day. Booth, who injured his leg escaping from the theatre, was later cornered in a barn and shot dead. (*See* 26.4.1865)

1900 The French President, M. Loubet, opened the Paris International Exhibition, the biggest of its kind in Europe.

1903 In New York Dr Harry Plotz discovered the typhus vaccine.

1906 The term 'muckraking' entered the language when President Roosevelt criticized the press for writing about business ethics – or the lack of them. He quoted Bunyan, '... never looking at the stars, but steadily plied his rake in the muck.'

1931 Spain became a republic when King Alfonso abdicated.

1931 The British Ministry of Transport issued the Highway Code.

1932 Violent riots erupted in New Zealand when civil servants were told of major pay cuts.

1950 The British comic strip hero Dan Dare made his first appearance in the first edition of the *Eagle*, drawn by Frank Hampson.

1954 In Canberra, Soviet diplomat Vladimir Petrov asked for political asylum. His defection exposed a vast spy ring in Australia and first confirmed that Burgess and Maclean were spying for the Russians.

1965 Robert E. Hickok and Perry E. Smith, murderers of the Clutter Family featured in Truman Capote's *In Cold Blood*, were hanged at Kansas State Penitentiary.

1983 The first cordless telephone, capable of operating up to 600 feet from base, was introduced. It was made by Fidelity and British Telecom and sold for £170.

1989 Police in Huddersfield, Yorkshire, revealed that violent prisoners were being put into a bright pink cell which seemed to have a calming effect. The colour was named Baker-Miller Pink after the police chief and psychologist who thought up the idea.

15 APRIL

BORN THIS DAY

HISTORY

1800 Sir James Clark Ross, English explorer, nephew of Scottish explorer John Ross, who attempted to find the Northwest Passage. James discovered the North magnetic pole in 1831. The Ross Barrier, Sea and Island are named after him.

ARTS

1843 Henry James, US novelist who settled in England in 1869 and formed a close friendship with H. G. Wells. His novels include *Washington Square* (1880) and *The Ambassadors* (1899).

1940 Jeffrey Archer, English author, playwright and politician who wrote his first novel, *Not a Penny More, Not A Penny Less* (1975) after a financial disaster, adequately recouping his losses.

ENTERTAINMENT

1939 Claudia Cardinale, Italian film actress born in Tunis.

SCIENCE

1772 Etienne Geoffroy Saint-Hilaire, French zoologist who began the great collection at the Jardin des Plantes.

1793 Friedrich Georg Wilhelm Struve, German astronomer who constructed an observatory near St Petersburg and made important observations of double stars. His son, both grandsons and a great grandson were all astronomers.

RELIGION

1469 Nanak, founder of Sikhism, a blend of Brahmanism and Islam. He was a Hindu by birth, but later denounced many of their practices.

POP

1939 Marty Wilde, English rock singer who shone briefly in the late 50s and now manages his daughter, Kim.

1966 Samantha Fox, English topless model and singer who had a series of hits in 1987–8, including 'Nothing's Gonna Stop Me Now'.

JAZZ

1894 Bessie Smith, the 'Empress of the Blues', US singer who was taken on tour by another great blues singer, 'Ma' Rainey, when she was only 13.

SPORT

1901 Joe Davis, world snooker and billiards champion 1927–46. His style, skill and personality helped establish the modern game.

DIED THIS DAY

1764 Jeanne Antoinette Poisson, Marquise de Pompadour, who became Louis XV's mistress and virtually took over the affairs of state.

1888 Matthew Arnold, English educationist and poet.

1925 John Singer Sargent, US painter

who worked mainly in England.

1949 Wallace Beery, US film actor.

1980 Jean-Paul Sartre, French philosopher and writer.

1982 Arthur Lowe, English actor, best remembered for his role as Capt. Mainwaring in the television series *Dad's Army*.

1990 Greta Garbo (Greta Lovisa Gustafsson), legendary Swedish-born actress.

ON THIS DAY

1755 Dr Samuel Johnson published his *Dictionary*; in it he defined 'lexicographer' as 'a harmless drudge'.

1793 The Bank of England issued the first five-pound notes.

1793 At Spithead in the Solent, off Portsmouth, British naval personnel mutinied over poor conditions and pay.

1852 The first screw-top bottles were patented by François Joseph Belzung of Paris.

1865 Andrew Jackson was sworn in as US President following the death this day of Abraham Lincoln. Lincoln had been shot at Ford's Theatre the previous evening.

1901 A motor hearse was used for the first time at a British funeral. The special 6 h.p. Daimler was used for a funeral in Coventry.

1912 The *Titantic* struck an iceberg and sank with the loss of 2,206 passengers and crew on her maiden voyage. Three millionaires escaped in the first lifeboat, but John Jacob Astor, the US multimillionaire and William Thomas Stead, the English journalist and editor, perished. There were 732 survivors. This was also the first time radio was used to call a fleet of vessels to a sea rescue.

1923 At the Rialto Theatre, New York, Lee De Forest screened a selection of musical short films demonstrating his Phonofilm process. These were the first sound films to be presented using the sound-on-film method, and the first to be shown to a paying audience. They were the supporting programme of the silent main feature, *Bella Donna*, starring Pola Negri.

1925 Sir James Barrie donated the copyright fee of his play, *Peter Pan*, to the Great Ormond Street Hospital for Sick Children in London.

1942 The entire population of the tiny island of Malta was awarded the George Cross for the gallantry they showed during the pounding they took from both the German and Italians during the Second World War.

1945 Art treasures looted by the Nazis were discovered down an Austrian mine. Amongst the find were paintings by Rubens, Leonardo da Vinci, Goya, Raphael and Michelangelo's famous Ghent altarpiece.

1964 Ian Smith became Prime Minister of Rhodesia.

1970 The first hand-held electronic pocket calculator was announced by Canon Business Machines of Japan.

KIDNAPPING CONTRADICTIONS In 1974, Patty Hearst, carrying a gun, took part in a bank raid with her kidnappers. This suprise appearance was captured by the bank's video cameras and she was later convicted for the crime. On the same day in 1978, attractive US blonde Joyce McKinney was accused in London of kidnapping and sexually abusing a young male Mormon missionary, but she disappeared before coming to trial, much to the dismay of the tabloid press.

1988 The British nuclear submarine *Talent* became the last boat to be launched down a conventional slipway at Barrow-in-Furness. In future, new craft will be lowered by crane into the water.

1988 The North Korean President, Kim Il-Sung, celebrated his 76th birthday and received 43,000 gifts, including a car. Other gifts included an Arabic translation of his book, *The Non-Aligned Movement is a Mighty Anti-Imperialist Revolutionary Force of our Times*.

1989 Britain's worst football disaster took place at the Hillsborough ground in Sheffield at the start of the the FA Cup semi-final between Liverpool and Nottingham Forest. When around 3,000 supporters were suddenly let into the stadium to relieve pressure outside, they forced spectactors against the perimeter barriers. 94 died and over 200 were injured.

1989 Sylvie Guillem, the brilliant 23-year-old French ballerina, made her debut as principal guest artist with the Royal Ballet to great acclaim.

16 APRIL

BORN THIS DAY

HISTORY

1661 Charles Montague, 1st Earl of Halifax, founder of the Bank of England.

1867 Wilbur Wright, US aviation pioneer who with his younger brother Orville developed the first real powered aircraft while running their cycle business in Dayton.

1940 Queen Margrethe II of Denmark.

OLD AND NEW In 1646, Jules Hardouin-Mansart, French architect who designed the Galerie de Glaces at Versailles and, in 1895, Sir Ove Arup, English structural engineer of Danish parents, who was educated in Denmark. He built the Sydney Opera House and worked with Sir Basil Spence on Coventry Cathedral.

ARTS

1696 Giovanni Battista Tiepolo, Italian painter whose canvases of baroque figures adorn many leading galleries and museums.

1703 Caffarelli (Gaetano Majorano), Italian castrato who was once imprisoned for making obscene gestures to his audience. Nevertheless, he was much in demand and retired a wealthy man, able to afford a dukedom, an estate and a palace.

1844 Anatole France (Anatole François Thibault), French novelist who wrote the satirical *Penguin Island* (1908). He won the Nobel prize for Literature in 1921.

1871 J(ohn) M(illington) Synge, Irish playwright and poet who wrote *Playboy of the Western World* (1907).

1887 Nadia-Juliette Boulanger, French composer who was also one of the most influential teachers. Her pupils included Copland and other distinguished 20th-century composers.

1922 Kingsley Amis, English novelist who made his name with his new type of comic hero, *Lucky Jim* (1954). His other novels include *The Old Devils* which won the 1986 Booker prize.

ENTERTAINMENT

1889 Sir Charles Spencer Chaplin, English-born comedian, writer, composer, director and producer who began as a child performer in British music halls. He went to the US in 1910, where he was spotted by Mack Sennett and began to make films for Keystone. The bowler hat and baggy trousers appeared in his second film, but it took around three dozen films before the character of the tramp emerged in the film *The Tramp* (1915). Chaplin's classics include *The Goldrush* (1925), *City Lights* (1931) and *Modern Times* (1936). In 1927, he was awarded a Special Oscar. In 1952, as a result of his left-wing views, his return visa was withdrawn while he was on his way to visit Europe, and he only returned to Hollywood in 1972, to accept a second special Oscar. He received a rapturous welcome.

1918 Spike Milligan, Indian-born humorist who revolutionized British comedy. He wrote the scripts for the highly innovative *Goon Shows* which ran on BBC radio for nine years, also playing many of the celebrated roles, including the idiot Eccles.

1921 Peter (Alexander) Ustinov, English actor and writer who began in revues. His plays include *Romanoff and Juliet* (1956). He won an Oscar for his performance in *Spartacus* (1960) and again in 1964 for *Topkapi*.

1924 Henry Mancini, US composer of 'Moon River' and scores for numerous films including *The Pink Panther*.

1943 Ruth Madoc, Welsh actress, best known for her role in the television series, *Hi Di Hi*.

SCIENCE

1660 Sir Hans Sloane, Irish-born English physician and naturalist whose home and library was the basis of the British Museum and British Library.

POP

1940 Dusty Springfield (Mary Isobel Catherine Bernadette O'Brien), English singer of Irish parents. She had ten Top Ten hits in the UK, including 'You Don't Have To Say You Loved Me' (1966), which went to No. 1.

DIED THIS DAY

1446 Filippo Brunelleschi, Italian architect, painter and writer.

1689 Aphra Behn, the only English woman writer to be buried in Westminster Abbey. She was an agnostic.

1828 Francisco José de Goya y Lucientes, Spanish painter.

1850 Marie Tussaud (née Grosholtz), Swiss wax modeller who, during the French Revolution, made death masks from the severed heads. She toured her exhibition around Britain before setting up at a permanent site in Baker Street, London in 1835.

1879 St Bernadette of Lourdes (Bernadette Soubirous), French saint.

ON THIS DAY

238 The Senate in Rome appointed two emperors, D. Caelinus Balbinus to run civil affairs, and M. Clodius Pupierus Maximus to command the Legions.

1746 The Duke of Cumberland's forces defeated the Jacobite Scots at the Battle of Culloden near Inverness. The bloody battle earned the Duke the name 'Butcher Cumberland'. The Young Pretender Charles Stuart escaped and was later helped by Flora Macdonald to flee the country.

1883 Paul Kruger became the President of the South African Republic. The seeds of the Boer war were sown.

1902 A rally in Dublin Park attracted over 20,000 people protesting against the British government's harsh legislation.

1912 Harriet Quimby became the first woman to fly the English Channel, and on this day in 1964, Geraldine Monk of West Germany became the first woman to complete a solo round-the-world flight.

1953 The Royal yacht, *Britannia*, was launched.

1975 Cambodia fell to the Communist Khmer Rouge when the capital, Phnom Penh, surrendered.

17 APRIL

BORN THIS DAY

HISTORY

1837 John Pierpont Morgan, US financier, son of the founder of the international banking house of Morgan. He helped raise the huge loans for Britain during the First World War.

1880 Sir (Charles) Leonard Woolley, English archaeologist who carried out the excavations at Ur in Mesopotamia.

1894 Nikita Sergeyevich Khrushchev, USSR leader best remembered for his shoe banging performance at the United Nations during a speech by British Prime Minister, Harold Macmillan.

1916 Mrs Sirimavo Bandaranaike, Prime Minister of Sri Lanka 1960–65, and again 1970–77; the world's first woman prime minister. She was re-elected for a third time in 1988.

ARTS

1897 Thornton (Niven) Wilder, US playwright and novelist whose award-winning plays included *Our Town* (1938) and *The Skin of Our Teeth* (1942). He also wrote *The Matchmaker* (1954) which was later adapted as the musical *Hello Dolly* in 1964.

1923 Lindsay Anderson, Indian-born son of a Scottish major-general, who became a film and theatre director, film critic and documentary writer. His first feature film was *This Sporting Life*, (1963). His other films include the disturbing *If...* (1968) and *O Lucky Man* (1973).

ENTERTAINMENT

1929 James Last, internationally successful Dutch bandleader, composer and arranger.

1951 Olivia Hussey, English actress born in Buenos Aires, who made her debut when only 17 in Zeffirelli's *Romeo and Juliet* (1968).

SPORT

1911 Mikhail Moiseyevich Botvinnik, Russian world chess champion in 1948. At the age of 14 he had defeated world champion Capablanca in a game at an exhibition.

1946 Clare Francis, English yachtswoman who, in 1976, became the fastest across the Atlantic, taking 29 days in the Observer Royal Western Single-handed Transatlantic Race. She wrote her first novel, *Come Hell or High Water*, in 1977.

DIED THIS DAY

1790 Benjamin Franklin, US author, scientist and diplomat.

1960 Eddie Cochran, US rockstar, while on tour with Gene Vincent in England. Both were involved in a major car crash when Cochran's car blew a tyre at Chippenham. Cochran was killed and Vincent seriously injured.

ON THIS DAY

1421 At Dort, Holland, the sea broke through the dykes and an estimated 100,000 people were drowned.

1521 Martin Luther was excommunicated by the diet at Worms.

1860 The first international boxing match between a US boxer, John C. Heenan and a British boxer, champion Tom Sayers, at Farnborough, Hampshire took place. Despite being 46lb lighter, Sayers forced a draw after 42 rounds of bare-knuckle brawling.

1956 Harold Macmillan's budget speech introduced Premium Bonds to Britain with prizes of up to £1,000.

1963 British businessman, Greville Wynne, was charged in Moscow with spying. Found guilty, he was sentenced to three years in prison and five years in a labour camp.

1982 The Queen signed an act transferring sovereignty of the 1867 Canadian Constitution from Britain to Canada.

1984 WPC Yvonne Fletcher was shot dead during an anti-Gaddafi protest outside the Libyan Peoples Bureau in London. Her killer escaped under the cloak of diplomatic immunity.

1986 El Al security officials at Heathrow Airport, London foiled an attempt to smuggle a bomb on board an airliner with 360 passengers. The bomb was found in the baggage of a pregnant Irish woman duped by her Jordanian boyfriend. He was arrested the following day.

18 APRIL

BORN THIS DAY

HISTORY

1480 Lucrezia Borgia, illegitimate daughter of Pope Alexander VI. She married aged 12, but this was annulled when she was 13 so that she could marry once more to advance her father's position. She married a third time at 18, but her husband was murdered on the orders of her brother, Cesare, with whom she was suspected of having committed incest. She married a final time in 1501.

1797 Louis Adolphe Thiers, President of France who put down the Paris Commune.

ARTS

1882 Leopold Antoni Stanislaw Stokowski, English-born conductor and composer who had a Polish father and an Irish mother, and eventually became a US citizen. He conducted the Philadelphia Symphony Orchestra and was musical advisor for Disney's *Fantasia* (1940).

1946 Hayley Mills, English actress, daughter of Sir John Mills and writer Mary Hayley Bell, who first appeared in the film *Tiger Bay* (1959), aged 13, directed by her father.

SPORT

1958 Malcolm (Denzil) Marshall, West Indian and Hampshire cricketer who was born in Barbados and grew up to be a devastating bowler.

DIED THIS DAY

1689 Judge George Jeffreys, the infamous 'hanging judge', who as chief justice of the king's bench tried many of James II's critics. He was responsible for hanging a vast number of people, and for having others transported, whipped or fined. When King James was forced to flee, he was put in the Tower for his own safety, where he died.

1955 Albert Einstein, German-born US physicist who formulated the theory of relativity.

1964 Ben Hecht, US playwright, journalist and screenwriter.

1986 Marcel Desault, French aircraft designer and manufacturer.

1988 James E. Olson, chairman of the American Telephone and Telegraph Company who began with the company as a manhole digger. He once said, 'I didn't start at the bottom, I started below ground.'

ON THIS DAY

1775 Paul Revere made his famous ride from Charlestown to rouse the minutemen (civil militia prepared to turn out in a minute) on the eve of the War of Independence. Revere had been one of the party that threw the tea into Boston harbour.

1881 The Natural History Museum in London was opened.

1906 At 5.12 a.m. the first rumblings of the San Francisco earthquake were felt. Enrico Caruso was in the city to sing in *Carmen* with the Metropolitan Opera. He survived the destruction, but swore never to return. Four square miles, 514 blocks of 28,000 buildings were destroyed by the earthquake, which killed over 450 people.

1909 Joan of Arc was beatified at the Vatican.

1917 Pacific Aero products changed its name to the Boeing Airplane Company.

1934 The first launderette or 'washeteria' was opened in Fort Worth, Texas.

1942 US aircraft bombed Tokyo for the first time, using the aircraft carrier, *Hornet*, as their base.

1949 The Republic of Ireland Act came into force, and with it the establishment of Eire.

1949 The first Scouts' Bob-a-Job week was held.

1954 Colonel Nasser became Prime Minister and military governor of Egypt having seized power while President Neguib was away from the capital.

1964 Joe Orton's *Entertaining Mr Sloane* opened at the Royal Court, London.

1980 Robert Mugabe became Prime Minister of Zimbabwe as the Union Jack was lowered in the dying seconds of a nation called Rhodesia. On this day in 1982, Salisbury became Harare.

1986 Guinness, the giant brewery business, won their battle to take over the equally large spirits combine, the Distillers Group. The manner of the takeover was later investigated by the Director of Public Prosecutions and led to arrests of top financial figures including the Guinness chief executive, James Saunders.

1988 'Ivan the Terrible', John Ivan Demanjanuk, a Polish-born former SS camp guard was found guilty in Jerusalem of operating the Treblinka gas chambers and murdering 870,000 Jews in 1943. He was sentenced to hang ten days later, but he appealed against the verdict.

1988 In the House of Commons, the 16th-century symbol of the Speaker's authority, the Mace, was damaged by

Ron Brown, Labour MP for Leith, when he flung it to the floor during a debate. It was described by his own supporters as 'a childish stunt'.

1989 The Spanish tenor, José Carreras, gave a recital at the Royal Opera House, Covent Garden, his first for three years because of his leukaemia.

19 APRIL

BORN THIS DAY

HISTORY

1905 (James Allan) 'Jim' Mollison, Scottish aviator who flew from Australia to England in 1931 in eight days, 19 hours and 28 minutes. He married aviator Amy Johnson, and together they made the first east-west crossing of the North Atlantic and several other pioneering flights.

ARTS

1900 Richard (Arthur Warren) Hughes, English author of *High Wind in Jamaica* (1929).

ENTERTAINMENT

1933 Jayne Mansfield (Vera Jane Palmer), big-bosomed US actress who made her name on Broadway and then in the film version of *Will Success Spoil Rock Hunter?* (1957).

1935 Dudley Moore, English actor who started as one of *Beyond the Fringe* satire team on the London stage, and was soon invited to appear with Peter Cook on television. In Hollywood, despite being so short, he became a sex symbol when he played opposite Bo Derek in *10* (1979).

1946 Tim Curry, English actor mainly associated with *The Rocky Horror Picture Show* (1975).

POP

1928 Alexis Korner, French-born guitarist who was a major influence on the British jazz and blues scene. His Blues Incorporated had Charlie Watts and Mick Jagger in the line-up.

1942 Alan Price, English composer, singer and pianist, who was originally a member of the Animals who, for a time, rivalled the Beatles and the Rolling Stones, with their hit 'The House of the Rising Sun' (1964). He also wrote and performed the title song for the film *O Lucky Man*.

CRIME

1903 Eliot Ness, famous US government agent who fought US Mafia gangsters and had more success than most.

SPORT

1933 Harold 'Dickie' Bird, England cricket umpire; probably the best known test umpire in the world.

1954 Trevor Francis, who became the first British £1m footballer when Brian Clough bought the 24-year-old for Nottingham Forest in February 1979 from Birmingham City.

DIED THIS DAY

1588 Paolo Veronese (Cagliari), Italian painter.

1689 Queen Christina of Sweden who, in 1654, abdicated to further her intellectual pursuits and who embraced Catholicism. She tried unsuccessfully in 1660 to reinstate herself as queen and spent the remainder of her life in Rome.

1824 Lord Byron (George Gordon Noel Byron), English poet, of marsh fever, at Missolonghi, with the Greek insurgents fighting the Turks.

1881 Benjamin Disraeli, Earl of Beaconsfield, British Prime Minister and author. Queen Victoria sent a wreath of primroses to the funeral, his favourite flowers.

1882 Charles (Robert) Darwin, English biologist who wrote *The Origin of Species by Means of Natural Selection*.

1906 Pierre Curie, French physicist who worked with his wife on magnetism and radioactivity, run over and killed by a car in Paris.

1967 Konrad Adenauer, West German statesman, Chancellor from 1940–63.

ON THIS DAY

1637 Amye Everard became the first English woman to be granted a patent for her tincture of saffron and essence of roses.

1775 The American Civil War began when General Gage fired into a crowd at Lexington, Massachusetts.

1883 At a meeting in Liverpool to establish a home for dogs, the proposer, T. F. Agnew suggested it should perhaps be turned into a home for children. He had seen the work of the New York Society for the Prevention of Cruelty to Children. The evening of this day, the Liverpool Society for the Prevention of Cruelty to Children was formed. Later, it would become the National Society (NSPCC).

1917 The US *Mongolia* fired the first shots to enter the First World War when she sank a German submarine.

1927 Mae West was found guilty of 'indecent behaviour' in her Broadway production of *Sex*. She was sentenced to ten days in prison and a $500 fine.

1947 When a fire on board a French ship loaded with high explosives in Texas City harbour ignited a chemical plant by the dockside, it set off massive explosions at the neighbouring oil refinery, killing 714 people.

1951 Eric Morley, Publicity Officer with Mecca Ltd, devised the first Miss World beauty contest to coincide with the Festival of Britain. Of the 30 contestants, only five came from overseas, but that produced the winner, Kiki Haakonson, a Stockholm policeman's daughter.

1956 Prince Rainier of Monaco married his dream princess, film star Grace Kelly.

1958 Paul Raymond's *Festival of Erotica* opened in London's Soho. It became the second-longest running show in London, beaten only by *The Mousetrap*.

1959 The Dalai Lama, fleeing from Tibet and the Chinese invasion, was offered sanctuary in India.

1961 US-backed Cuban exiles invaded their former homeland at the Bay of Pigs. Castro's forces were supported by the threat of Soviet missiles. There was talk of a Third World War, but the invasion failed and both the US and the USSR pulled back from the brink.

1966 An advance party of 4,500 Australian troops sailed from Sydney to join with US troops in Vietnam.

1971 The USSR launched the Salyut space station.

1988 China radio began broadcasting western pop music for the first time, ranging from Glenn Miller to Madonna. 'Roll Over Beethoven' was banned as being disrespectful to the composer.

20 APRIL

BORN THIS DAY

HISTORY

1808 Napoleon III, whose efforts to emulate his uncle's previous military glories, led to the collapse of his empire and defeat by the Prussians, whom he had goaded into war. During his reign, corruption flourished, and this fed republican and socialist opposition.

1889 Adolf Hitler, German dictator, whose real name was Schicklgrüber and whose original ambition was to be a painter. He sold postcard sketches in Vienna and drifted into politics, ranting against money lenders and trade unions, revealing his philosphy in *Mein Kampf* (1925). In 1933, he came to power in a Germany weakened by its defeat in the First World War. His 'Third Reich', which he claimed would last 1,000 years, ended after twelve years when he died in a Berlin bunker in 1945.

ARTS

1893 Joán Miró, Spanish Surrealist painter who injected a degree of humour into many of his works.

ENTERTAINMENT

1893 Harold Lloyd, US film comedian who found success when he tried the revolutionary idea of wearing ordinary clothes and a pair of horn-rimmed glasses.

1902 Sir Donald Wolfit, the last of the English actor-managers. His company performed mainly Shakespeare, both in London and the provinces. He was considered one of the finest Lears ever.

1941 (Patrick) Ryan O'Neal, US film actor who beat 300 other hopefuls to get his first starring role in *Love Story* (1970) which won him an Oscar nomination. He starred with his daughter, Tatum, in *Paper Moon* (1973), which won her an Oscar for best supporting actress.

1961 Nicholas Lyndhurst, English actor best known for his role as the 'Plonker' in the television series, *Only Fools and Horses*.

DIED THIS DAY

1768 Canaletto (Antonio Canale), Italian painter.

1769 Pontiac, Chief of the Ottawa Indians, who was murdered by an Illinois Indian.

1883 Édouard Manet, French painter.

1912 (Abraham) Bram Stoker, English actor-manager, author of *Dracula* (1897).

ON THIS DAY

1653 Oliver Cromwell dissolved the Long Parliament which had governed during the Civil War.

1657 The British Admiral Blake destroyed the Spanish fleet in the harbour of Santa Cruz.

1841 *The Murders in the Rue Morgue* by Edgar Allan Poe, considered the first modern detective story, was published in *Graham's* magazine in the US.

1887 The first motor race was held in Paris. Only one driver took part, Georges Bouton in his four-seater steam quadricycle. The following year he had just one rival to beat.

1902 At an exhibition in Paris, 'Art Nouveau' was introduced.

1913 The dancer Isadora Duncan's two

children, one by theatre designer, Gordon Craig, and the other by sewing machine magnate, Paris Singer, were the passengers in a chauffeur-driven car with their nurse when it stalled on a hill. When the chauffeur got out to crank the car, it began to roll downhill, finally crashing into the Seine, drowning Deidre, aged seven, and Patrick, aged five and their nurse.

1929 The first parliament made up exclusively of Fascists led by Benito Mussolini, was opened by King Victor Emanuel III of Italy.

1981 Steve Davis became the world snooker champion at 23 years old, beating Doug Mountjoy at Sheffield.

1988 The world's largest termite mound, around 21ft high, was found in the Australian outback, it was claimed this day. The mound was located at Hayes Creek, 105 miles south of Darwin.

21 APRIL

BORN THIS DAY

HISTORY

1634 Jan van Riebeck, Dutch naval surgeon who was put in charge of the Dutch East India Company's refuelling station at the Cape of Good Hope and was the founder of Cape Town.

1926 Queen Elizabeth II of England.

ARTS

1816 Charlotte Brontë, eldest of the three Brontë sisters and author of *Jane Eyre* (under the name of Currer Bell, 1847). She was mainly responsible for the sisters finding a publisher, although her first effort, the publication of poems by all three sold only two copies. Her other novels include *Shirley* (1849) and *Villette* (1852).

1913 Norman Parkinson, English photographer of celebrities and royalty, and inventor of the 'Parky' deluxe sausage, whose birthday is the same as one of his most frequent sitters, Queen Elizabeth II.

ENTERTAINMENT

1915 Anthony Quinn, Mexican-born actor of Irish-Mexican parents. After a long stint as a bit-part player, he played a supporting role in *Viva Zapata* (1952) which won him an Oscar.

1923 John Mortimer, QC, English author and playwright of the acclaimed *A Voyage Around My Father* (1970). His television series, *Rumpole of the Bailey* began its run in 1978, with Leo McKern as the unconventional barrister.

POP

1947 Iggy Pop (James Jewel Osterberg), US performer associated with wild antics when he performed with David Bowie.

SPORT

1932 Angela Mortimer, English tennis champion who won the Wimbledon finals playing another Briton, Christine Truman in the first all-British final since the very early days of the championship.

EDUCATION

1782 Friedrich Froebel, German educational pioneer who developed the kindergarten system.

DIED THIS DAY

1109 St Anselm, Archbishop of Canterbury and English saint, canonized in

1494. He was buried at Canterbury.

1509 King Henry VII, at Richmond, Surrey.

1699 Jean Baptiste Racine, French playwright.

1910 (Samuel Langhorne Clemens) Mark Twain, US novelist.

1946 John Maynard Keynes, 1st Baron, English economist, advisor to the Treasury who pioneered the theory of full employment.

1952 Sir (Richard) Stafford Cripps, British statesman, economist and chemist who was Chancellor of the Exchequer in the Labour government in 1947.

1971 François Duvalier, 'Papa Doc', dictator of Haiti.

1990 Erte (Romain de Tirtoff), Russian-born artist and designer (*Folies Bergère, Ziegfeld Follies*).

ON THIS DAY

753BC According to the historian Varro, this was the day that Romulus founded Rome.

1509 The accession of Henry VIII to the throne.

1836 The Mexicans were defeated by the Texans at the Battle of San Jacinto.

1894 Bernard Shaw's *Arms and the Man* was performed for the first time in London.

1901 The French sculptor Rodin shocked Paris with his semi-nude 'Victor Hugo' when it was exhibited at the Grand Palais.

1916 Roger Casement, the Irish-born British consular official, landed in Ireland from a German submarine prepared to lead the Sinn Fein rebellion, but was arrested this day as the 'Easter uprising' took place. The rebellion against the British in Dublin reached its worst level as Irish republicans took over sections of the city, while a Royal Navy gunboat bombarded them from the River Liffey.

1917 The Canadians finally took Vimy Ridge after a battle which started on 9 April.

1918 Baron Manfred von Richthofen, the legendary German ace pilot, known as the 'Red Baron' because of his distinctive red Fokker tri-plane, was shot down by an RAF fighter. He died from the crash behind British lines, but not before he had shot down 80 Allied aircraft.

1923 At the Birmingham Repertory Theatre, Sir Barry Jackson's production of Shakespeare's *Cymbeline* was staged entirely in modern dress, the first such production.

1945 Ivor Novello's musical *Perchance to Dream* opened at the London Hippodrome with his now-classic song, 'We'll Gather Lilacs'. The show ran 1,022 performances.

1959 Ballerina Dame Margot Fonteyn was jailed for a day in Panama City while Panamanian police hunted for her husband, Dr Roberto Arias, former ambassador to Britain who was accused of planning a coup to overthrow his government. Dame Margot was released and flown to New York, and was reunited with her exiled husband in June.

1960 Brasilia was inaugurated as the new capital of Brazil.

1962 The US Bell Telephone Company introduced radio paging.

1964 BBC television launched *Playschool* as the opening programme of their second channel. BBC2 actually opened a day late due to a major power failure the previous day.

1989 Over 100,000 Chinese students poured into Peking's Tiananmen Square, ignoring government warnings of severe punishment.

22 APRIL

BORN THIS DAY

HISTORY

1724 Immanuel Kant, German philosopher who wrote the *Critique of Pure Reason*, a classic work. He was very much a person of order and method. People could set their watches by his constitutional walk, it was said.

LEFT, CENTRE AND RIGHT OUT The first two leaders of Russia after the Revolution were born exactly 11 years apart; in 1870, Lenin (Vladimir Ilyich Ulyanov), leader of the Bolshevik Revolution, who prepared the way for the acceptance of the doctrines of Marx and Engels, mainly in exile, and in 1881, Alexander Feodorovich Kerensky. A few days after the Tsar was deposed, in April 1917, Lenin was sent in a sealed train by arrangement with the Germans back to Petrograd, to organize the overthrow of the moderate provisional government led by Kerensky. Deposed by Lenin and his Bolsheviks, Kerensky fled to Austria. In 1940, he went to Australia, moving six years later to the US.

ARTS

1707 Henry Fielding, English novelist, author of *Tom Jones* (1749).

1766 Madame de Staël (Anne Louise Germaine Necker), Baronne de Staël-Holstein, probably the most famous French woman writer, who surrounded herself with the famous of her age on both the Continent and in England, where she stayed during the French Revolution. She wrote several novels including *Delphine* (1802). She was the first to use the word 'romanticism'.

1889 Vladimir Vladimirovich Nabokov, Russian-born US novelist, poet and lepidopterist. His controversial *Lolita*, in which the word 'nymphet' was coined, was published in 1955.

1906 Dr Eric Fenby, English organist, composer and teacher who went out to France when he was 22 years old to act as amanuensis to the blind and paralysed English composer, Delius. He laboriously took down the music dictated by the ageing composer and, after his death, arranged some of his music.

1912 Kathleen (Mary) Ferrier, English contralto who rose from a telephone switchboard operator to become one of Britain's finest singers. She died tragically young in 1953, shortly after her final appearance at Covent Garden in *Orfeo*.

1916 Yehudi Menuhin, US-born violinist who, as a child prodigy, gave his first recital aged six. In 1934 he played concerts in 73 cities, and during the Second World War gave concerts for the troops. He settled in England after the War, where he later established his famous school for highly talented musicians from all over the world. He was awarded an honorary knighthood in 1965.

1917 Sir Sidney (Robert) Nolan, Australian painter, known for his famous 'Ned Kelly' paintings.

ENTERTAINMENT

1925 George Cole, English actor who played either silly young men or spivvy roles on radio and in films, including the St Trinian's comedies, but is best known for his role as a more mature 'spiv', Arthur Daley, in the long-running and highly successful television series, *Minder*.

SCIENCE

1904 (Julius) Robert Oppenheimer, US nuclear scientist who was the director of the Los Alamos laboratory that developed the first atomic bomb. He advocated joint control of the bomb by both the US and USSR, and he was later suspended when it was thought he had become a security risk.

JAZZ

1922 Charlie Mingus, US bass, composer, arranger and bandleader who was one of the great jazz innovators influencing a whole generation of musicians.

POP

1950 Peter Frampton, English pop guitarist and singer who worked with the Herd before forming Humble Pie. In 1971, he began his solo career and had a hit with 'Show Me the Way' (1976).

SPORT

1938 Alan Bond, Australian business tycoon and yachtsman who both financed and directed the Australian team that won the America's Cup in 1983 in *Australia II*, the first yacht to beat the US crews for 132 years.

1960 Lloyd Honeyghan, English boxer who became world welterweight boxing champion when he beat Don Currie of the US in 1986.

DIED THIS DAY

1778 James Hargreaves, English inventor of the spinning jenny.

1827 Thomas Rowlandson, English cartoonist.

1908 Sir Henry Campbell-Bannerman, Scottish statesman and British Liberal Prime Minister in 1905–8, resigning on 4 April 1908, 18 days before his death.

1933 Frederick Henry Royce, motor car pioneer.

ON THIS DAY

1500 Pedro Alvarez Cabral discovered Brazil and claimed it for the King of Portugal.

1760 The first known pair of roller-skates were worn by a young Belgian musical instrument maker who rolled into a London party while playing a violin, finally crashing into a mirror.

1769 Madame du Barry became Louis XV's official mistress.

1838 The first steamship to cross the Atlantic to New York from England was the British packet steamer, *Sirius*. The journey took 18 days and ten hours.

1915 The Germans used chlorine (poison gas) for the first time on the Western front at Ypres, blinding French Canadian troops and French Zouaves.

1952 South African Prime Minister Daniel F. Malan introduced legislation to make parliament the highest court in the land and so passed the apartheid bill which had been previously invalidated by the South African Supreme Court.

1964 British businessman Greville

Wynne, imprisoned by the Russians for spying, was swapped for the Russian spy Gordon Lonsdale, who was jailed by the British for his role in the Portland espionage ring in 1961.

1969 British lone-yachtsman, Robin Knox-Johnston completed his solo non-stop circumnavigation of the world in just 312 days in his 32ft ketch, *Suhaili*.

1983 £1 coins were introduced into Britain, replacing paper money.

23 APRIL

St George's Day, the national day of England.

St George slayed the dragon in Libya in the third century, and became the patron saint of England when he appeared as an apparition in the sky while the Crusaders were fighting their Muslim enemy.

BORN THIS DAY

HISTORY

1791 James Buchanan, US Democrat statesman who became the 15th President during the run-up to the Civil War.

1861 Henry Hyman, Viscount Allenby, British Field Marshal during the First World War, who crushed the Turks at Megiddo in Palestine in 1918.

1897 Lester (Bowles) Pearson, Canadian Prime Minister (1963–8), and Nobel Peace prize winner for his work in establishing the United Nations Emergency Force.

ARTS

1564 William Shakespeare, English playwright, poet and actor, born Stratford-upon-Avon. This is the traditional date of both his birth and his death (in 1616). He wrote his first major play, *Love's Labour's Lost*, in 1588, but it was only staged in 1594. His first performed play was *Henry VI Part I*, around 1589, and his last, *Henry VIII*, was staged in 1613. He married Anne Hathaway in 1582. They had three children, including twins.

1775 Joseph Mallard William Turner, English landscape painter, etcher and watercolourist who was one of the greatest British artists, advancing painting with his Pre-Impressionistic sunset skies and stormy seas. Almost illiterate, he also lived a secretive life. He produced over 300 oil paintings and 20,000 watercolours, which he bequeathed to the nation.

1858 Dame Ethel (Mary) Smythe, English composer and active campaigner for women's suffrage. She composed 'March of the Women' which she conducted while in Holloway Jail using a toothbrush to direct her fellow imprisoned suffragettes.

1891 Sergei Sergeyevich Prokofiev, Russian composer who wrote his first opera aged nine. He wrote much film and ballet music, including *Cinderella* (1940). One of his most popular works is *Peter and the Wolf*, composed in 1936.

1899 Dame Ngaio (Edith) Marsh, New Zealand novelist who wrote *Enter a Murderer* (1935) and other outstanding detective novels featuring Roderick Alleyn.

1926 J(ames) P(atrick) Donleavy, US novelist who studied microbiology in Dublin and whose first novel, *The Ginger Man* (1955), was hailed as a comic masterpiece.

ENTERTAINMENT

1911 Ronald Neame, English film director of *Tunes of Glory* (1960) and *The Prime* *of Miss Jean Brodie* (1969), who began as assistant camerman on Hitchcock's *Blackmail* (1929).

1928 Shirley Temple (Black), US child star, who later became the US Ambassador to Ghana, but along the way starred in a series of 'cute' films as a precocious under-ten which made her the top box office attraction of the late 30s. She won a special Oscar for her 'outstanding contribution to screen entertainment', but her career did a fast fade as she entered her teens and, in the late 60s, she entered politics.

1942 Lee Majors, US film and television actor who became a star in the long-running television series, *The Six Million Dollar Man*.

SCIENCE

1858 Max Karl Ernst Planck, German theoretical physicist who revolutionized physics when he developed the quantum theory for which he was awarded the Nobel prize in 1918.

POP

1936 Roy Orbison, US singer and songwriter who had 15 major hits in the 60s including 'Pretty Woman' and 'Only the Lonely'.

DIED THIS DAY

TO DIE, TO SLEEP In 1616, three years after his last play was first performed, William Shakespeare died in Stratford-upon-Avon, where he had retired in 1610. On this same day, the great Spanish author of *Don Quixote* and some 20 or 30 plays, Miguel de Cervantes (Saveedra), also died. Two other British poets also died this day: in 1850, William Wordsworth and in 1915, Rupert Brooke, one of 'the lost generation' of young, talented men who died during the First World War, from blood poisoning, on the Greek island of Skyros on his way to the Dardenelles.

1986 Otto Preminger, US film director.

1986 Jim Laker, England cricketer.

1990 Paulette Goddard (Marion Levy), US actress who made her name in *Modern Times* (1936).

ON THIS DAY

1661 Charles II was crowned king of England, and this day in 1702 saw the coronation of Queen Anne.

1879 The first Shakespeare Memorial Theatre opened in Stratford-upon-Avon, and in 1932 the New Shakespeare Memorial Theatre was opened by the Prince of Wales. The opening performances were *Henry VI Parts 1 and 2*, Shakespeare's first plays.

1924 King George V and Queen Mary opened the British Empire Exhibition at Wembley Stadium.

1935 The official opening by Stalin of the Moscow Underground railway took place.

1962 Stirling Moss crashed at the Goodwood circuit at 110 m.p.h. He was rushed to hospital with a broken rib and leg, and serious head injuries.

1968 The first decimal coins appeared in Britain. They were the five- and ten-pence pieces which replaced the old 1/- (one shilling) and 2/- (two shilling) coins.

1969 In the US, Sirhan Bishara Sirhan was found guilty of the assassination of Robert F. Kennedy and was sentenced to die in the gas chamber.

1980 Saudi Arabia threatened to break off diplomatic relations with Britain following the screening on television of the documentary *Death of a Princess*, which described the events leading to the death of a Saudi princess for infidelity.

1984 The US announced the discovery of the AIDS virus.

1988 A Greek myth relates that on this day Daedalus flew from the island of Crete across the Aegean Sea to the island of Santorini, a distance of 74 miles. This day, a Greek cycling champion, Kanellos Kanellopoulos pedalled an extra-lightweight flying machine called *Daedalus* through the air over the same route, setting a record for man-powered flight. He crashed into the sea, just yards from the shore, and swam safely to land.

1990 The 'silent man of the Great Train Robbery' (8.8.1963), Charlie Wilson, was shot dead at his home near Marbella, Spain.

24 APRIL

St Mark's Eve, on which apparitions of those to die in the coming year are said to appear at midnight in churchyards.

BORN THIS DAY

HISTORY

1533 William I, the Prince of Orange, in Germany. He was known as 'William the Silent' because of his ability to keep a secret. He helped free the Netherlands from Spanish domination.

1856 (Henri) Philippe (Omer) Pétain, French statesman and Army marshal who tried to make terms with the Germans during the Second World War and established a collaboratist government in Vichy. After the War, he was imprisoned for life as a traitor.

1882 Lord Dowding (Hugh Caswall Tremenheere, 1st Baron), British Air Force Commander-in-Chief in the Battle of Britain, which he directed from Bentley Priory.

1889 Sir (Richard) Stafford Cripps, British statesman, economist and chemist who became the Chancellor of the Exchequer in the 1947 Labour government. The ravages of war left him no alternative but to introduce an austerity programme, but his style produced a positive public reponse; trade unions imposed a voluntary wage freeze.

1906 William Joyce, US-born British traitor who collaborated with the Nazis, broadcasting propaganda to Britain from Germany during the Second World War in a curious English accent which earned him the nickname 'Lord Haw-Haw'.

ARTS

1815 Anthony Trollope, English novelist who wrote the Barsetshire series.

1846 Marcus Andrew Hislop Clarke, British-born Australian author of *For the Term of His Natural Life* (1874), a history of the penal settlements.

1905 Robert Penn Warren, US poet and award-winning author of *All the King's Men* (1943), as well as volumes of verse and short stories.

1931 Bridget Riley, British artist who made an impact in the 60s with Op Art, which involved optical illusions and effects.

ENTERTAINMENT

1892 Jack Hulbert, English actor who played opposite his wife, Cecily Courtneidge in 13 musicals.

1934 Shirley MacLaine (Shirley MacLean Beatty), US actress and dancer (Warren Beatty's sister), who got her break on Broadway when leading lady Carol Haney broke her leg shortly after the opening night of the musical *The Pajama Game* giving her understudy the chance of success that would soon lead to Hollywood. Her main films include three Oscar-nominated performances in *Some Came Running* (1959), *The Apartment* (1960) and *Irma La Douce* (1963).

1936 Jill Ireland, English actress and former Monte Carlo Ballet dancer married to US actor Charles Bronson, with whom she appeared in several films. She wrote two books about her fight against breast cancer from which she died in 1990.

1942 Barbra (Barbara Joan) Streisand, US actress and singer who starred on Broadway in *Funny Girl* in 1964, playing Fanny Brice. This led immediately to Hollywood, where she played the role in the film, and won an Oscar which she shared with Katharine Hepburn.

INVENTION

1743 Edmund Cartwright, English inventor who was a rector in an agricultural area of Leicestershire. He visited Arkwright's cotton-spinning mills in 1784 which led to him inventing the power loom the following year, but it was not initially welcomed for fear of job losses. He also invented wool combing machines and even became involved with Robert Fulton in developments in steam navigation.

POP/JAZZ/CLASSICAL

1941 John Williams, Australian guitarist who studied with Segovia. He has covered the full range from classical to pop and jazz with Sky, the group he founded.

SPORT

1928 Tommy Docherty, controversial football manager with Manchester United.

DIED THIS DAY

1731 Daniel Defoe, English author of *Robinson Crusoe*.

1986 Wallis, Duchess of Windsor, the former Mrs Simpson.

ON THIS DAY

1792 This night, and into the early hours of the morning, Claude Rouget de Lisle composed the French national anthem, the *Marseillaise*.

1895 Captain Joshua Slocum, in his sloop *Spray*, set sail from Boston to circumnavigate the world single-handed. He would return on 27 June 1898.

1930 Amy Johnson landed her Gypsy Moth *Jason* in Darwin, Australia, the first woman to fly solo from England. Her departure 19 days earlier had not attracted much attention, but her courage in braving sandstorms and forced landings made her an international heroine.

1932 A mass trespass by thousands of ramblers took place on Kinder Scout in the Peak District to establish public right of access on the moors and mountains which were privately owned for grouse shooting.

1939 Robert Menzies became Australian Prime Minister, aged 44.

1949 One of the great days in any British child's life – if they were born during the war years – sweets and chocolate were no longer rationed!

1967 The first space tragedy occurred: Vladimir Komarov, aged 40, was killed when the Russian *Soyuz I* crashed to earth after leaving orbit.

1989 Peter Scudamore became the first National Hunt jockey to ride 200 winners in a season over jumps when he won at Towcester with Gay Moore.

25 APRIL

Anzac Day, commemorating the landing at Gallipoli in 1915 of the heroic Australian and New Zealand troops. It was first celebrated in 1916.

BORN THIS DAY

HISTORY

1214 St Louis IX, King of France who led a crusade to Egypt. Defeated, he was captured and ransomed in 1250. Eventually he returned to France, where he reorganized the courts and authorized new laws before heading off on another crusade, in 1270, from which he would not return.

1284 King Edward II, who became the first heir-apparent to bear the title Prince of Wales. King from 1307, he ruled during a period of pestilence, famine, defeats at the hands of the Scots and intrigues, and was eventually murdered.

1559 Oliver Cromwell, Protector of England who led his 'Ironsides' in the English Civil War against the 'Roundheads' of King Charles I. Cromwell's victories enabled him to have the King tried and beheaded, after which he established a republic.

ARTS

1873 Walter de la Mare, English poet and novelist.

1906 Edward (Egbert Roscoe) Murrow, US broadcaster, journalist and director of the US Information Agency, who made many broadcasts from London during the Second World War prior to the US involvement, winning much US support for Britain.

1915 The Reverend Marcus (Harston) Morris who, as a 30-year-old parson, had only ever edited the parish magazine but nevertheless launched the comic, the *Eagle* (14.3.1950). He later became managing director of the National Magazine Company, which included *Cosmopolitan* and *Good Housekeeping*.

1939 Patrick Lichfield (the Earl of Lichfield), English photographer of the fashionable and the famous.

JAZZ

1918 Ella Fitzgerald, US jazz singer whose first hit was 'A-tisket, A-tasket' (1938). She graduated from jazz clubs to glamorous nightspots and concert halls, singing with Duke Ellington's band and the Oscar Peterson Trio. It was her jazz interpretation of Gershwin and Cole Porter songs that earned her the reputation of being one of the greatest singers ever.

ENTERTAINMENT

1939 Al(berto) Pacino, US actor who made his name in his third film, *The Godfather* (1972), which won him an Oscar nomination.

INVENTION

1874 Guglielmo Marconi, Italian pioneer in wireless telegraphy who came to

England, where he conducted several successful transmissions, eventually setting up the Marconi Wireless Telegraph Company. He won the Nobel prize for Physics in 1909.

SCIENCE

1900 Wolfgang Pauli, Austrian-born US physicist and Nobel prize winner for his work on atomic structure. He was the first to postulate the existence of the neutrino.

CHESSSMEN Born 1945, Bjorn Ulvaeus, one of the founders of the internationally successful Swedish pop group, Abba. When the group split up, in 1985, he co-composed the music for the musical, *Chess* with British lyricist, Tim Rice, and another ex-Abba member, Benny Andersson. Born 1955, Dr Michael Nunn, the British chess grandmaster who has helped make Britain a major force on the international chess scene.

SPORT

1872 C(harles) B(urgess) Fry, the great all-round English sportsman and one-time holder of the world long jump record.

1947 Johann Cruyff, great Dutch international footballer.

1957 Eric Bristow, 'The Crafty Cockney', English world darts champion.

DIED THIS DAY

1744 Anders Celsius, Swedish astronomer who devised the centigrade thermometer.

1800 William Cowper, English poet.

1878 Anna Sewell, English author of the most famous of horse novels, *Black Beauty* (1877).

1952 Gertie Millar, English musical comedy actress.

1955 Constance Collier (Laura Constance Hardie), English actress.

1976 Sir Carol Reed, English film director.

1982 Dame Celia Johnson, English actress who, coincidentally, appeared in Sir Carol Reed's *A Kid for Two Farthings* (1955).

1988 Clifford Simak, US journalist and science-fiction author of *The Visitors* (1979).

1990 Dexter (Keith) Gordon, US tenor saxophonist who was nominated for an Oscar for his role in *Round Midnight* (1986).

ON THIS DAY

1660 Ironically, on the 63rd anniversary of the birth of Oliver Cromwell, a Convention parliament in London voted for the restoration of Charles II.

1719 The publication in London of Daniel Defoe's *Robinson Crusoe*.

1792 Although in use since the Middle Ages, Dr Guillotin much improved the device for beheading people. On this day, his new model was used in Paris to remove the head of a highwayman.

1848 The first Royal yacht, *Victoria and Albert*, was launched at Pembroke Docks, after suffering serious damage when first floated.

1859 Ferdinand de Lesseps saw his great plan initiated when work began on the 100-mile Suez Canal. He supervised the project until its opening on 16.11.1869.

1920 Percy Toplis, who had led a mutiny in the British Army, and then deserted, shot and killed a taxi driver near Salisbury Barracks. He followed this crime with a succession of robberies, until he was finally captured after one of the biggest manhunts of its time, which ended with him dying in a hail of police bullets.

1926 Toscanini conducted the first performance of Puccini's last opera, *Turandot*. The composer had died before completing his masterpiece, and it was left to Franco Alfano to write the final missing section based on the composer's notes.

1945 The United Nations Organization (UNO) was planned at a meeting of 46 nations at the Paris Opera.

1953 The British monthly magazine *Nature* published an article by US genetic researcher, James Dewey Watson, and an English geneticist, Francis H. C. Crick, introducing their work on DNA.

1956 Rocky Marciano, US world heavyweight champion since 1952, retired unbeaten.

1964 The head of the famous Little Mermaid statue in Copenhagen harbour was sawn off and stolen.

1969 The 21-year-old BBC radio serial *Mrs Dale's Diary* ended.

1980 The US made a disastrous attempt to rescue hostages from the US Embassy in Tehran. A helicopter collided with a fuel tanker aircraft when they landed secretly near the city, and the covert mission had to be aborted.

1983 In Germany, *Stern* magazine published the first extracts from the so-called *Hitler Diaries*, which were also published by the *Sunday Times* in Britain. Sir Hugh Trevor-Roper said they were authentic, but they were later found to be forgeries by Konrad Kujau.

1988 In Israel, a monkey and his owner were arrested by police after they both got drunk on cocktails in a hotel bar. The owner bought the drinks.

1989 Italian MP, Ilona Staller, better known as La Cicciolona, a former striptease artiste, released a symbolic white dove to mark the departure of Soviet tanks from Hungary, but the bird perched on the road and was run over by the leading tank.

1990 The Hubble Space Telescope was launched from the space shuttle *Discovery* and began sending back pictures on 20 May 1990.

26 APRIL

BORN THIS DAY

HISTORY

AD121 Marcus Aurelius, Roman Emperor who was trained as a philosopher. He proved a noble, civilized emperor despite ruling through difficult times. He found time to write his *Meditations*, revealing his loneliness, and founded chairs of philosophy.

1711 David Hume, Scottish philosopher and historian who wrote the *Treatise of Human Nature*. As an atheist, he was barred from a professorship at Edinburgh, so he taught a mentally deranged nobleman until he became the keeper of a library in the city.

1812 Alfred Krupp, German armaments manufacturer who succeeded to the business begun by his father, making the firm the biggest supplier of arms to the world. The firm later supported Hitler's rise to power.

1875 Syngman Rhee, the founder of South Korea in 1948, when he was elected President.

1894 (Walther Richard) Rudolf Hess, Nazi leader, who was imprisioned with Hitler in the 20s, when Hitler dictated

Mein Kampf to him. When the Nazis came to power, he was made deputy to the Fuhrer, but early in the War he flew to Scotland to try to arrange a peace treaty (*see* 10.5.1941) and was imprisoned in Britain. At Nuremberg, he was sentenced to life imprisonment. He hanged himself in Spandau Prison. (*See* 17.8.1987)

NATURAL HISTORY

1785 John James Audubon, US naturalist and artist who published *Birds of North America* having toured Europe to raise money for this project in 1826.

ARTS

1452 Leonardo da Vinci, Italian painter, sculptor, architect, musician, engineer, scientist and inventor; the complete Renaissance man. Painter of the *Mona Lisa* and *The Last Supper*, he also drew scientific anatomical drawings, designed an autogyro and created 'aerial perspectives'.

1798 Ferdinand Victor Eugene Delacroix, French painter who broke away from the conventions of his day to produce often violent paintings such as *Massacre at Chios* with colours and style that pre-dated Impressionism.

1880 Michel (Mikhail Mikhailovich) Fokine, Russian choreographer for the Ballets Russes and Diaghilev, who created many modern ballets, including *The Dying Swan* for Pavlova, *Les Sylphides* (1907) and *The Firebird* (1910).

1893 Anita Loos, US screenwriter, novelist and playwright, best known for her novel *Gentlemen Prefer Blondes* (1925), which she adapted for both the stage and screen.

1949 Peter Shaufuss, Danish ballet dancer and artistic director of the London Festival Ballet until he was fired in 1990 over a policy disagreement.

ENTERTAINMENT

1898 John Grierson, Scottish film producer, director and documentary film pioneer. He invented the term 'documentary' and made some memorable examples, including *The Night Mail* (1936), with verse commentary by W. H. Auden.

1936 Carol (Creighton) Burnett, US comedienne.

1914 Charlie Chester, English comedian who was known as 'Cheerful Charlie Chester' and appeared on both radio, during its 'golden age', and stage.

1956 (Kathleen) Koo (Dee Anne) Stark, English model, erotic film actress and libel-case winner over her alleged relationship with Prince Andrew.

SPORT

1918 Fanny Blankers-Koen, Dutch athlete who became the first woman to win four Olympic gold medals (in London, 1948). More remarkable was the fact that she was 30, and the mother of two children, but she still set three Olympic and one world record.

1926 David Coleman, English radio and television commentator, immortalized by the satirical magazine *Private Eye* for his 'Colemanballs', nonsensical remarks made by him, and later other commentators, in the heat of the moment.

POP

1938 Duane Eddy, US rock guitarist who is best known for his hits 'Rebel

Rouser' and 'Peter Gunn', which was revived in 1983.

DIED THIS DAY

1865 John Wilkes Booth, the assassin of Abraham Lincoln on 14 April, was finally trapped by troops in a farmhouse some distance from Washington. He was shot dead, while his accomplice, Harrald, was captured alive.

1970 Gypsy Rose Lee (Rose Louise Hovick), described as an 'ecdyasiast' – one who sheds her outer covering, as a snake discards its skin.

1976 Sid(ney) James, South African-born English comedian of stage, screen, radio and television, after collapsing on stage while performing at Sunderland.

1980 Dame Cecily Courtneidge, English actress.

1984 William 'Count' Basie, US jazz pianist and bandleader.

ON THIS DAY

1876 The town of Deadwood, Arizona was officially laid out. The locals included 'Wild Bill' Hickok, Calamity Jane, Wyatt Earp and later, 'Doc' Holliday.

1895 At the Old Bailey the trial of Oscar Wilde for homosexuality, which was then a crime, began. Wilde was released on bail.

1900 A huge fire in Ottawa and Hull, Canada, destroyed vast areas, making 12,000 homeless in just 12 hours.

1921 The first motor cycle police patrols went on duty in London.

1923 The Duke of York (the future King George VI) and Lady Elizabeth Bowes-Lyon were married at Westminster Abbey.

1931 The first (private) performance was given by the Carmargo Society, London, of the ballet *Façade* by Frederick Ashton, with music by William Walton, based on poems by Edith Sitwell. The first public performance was on 4 May, staged by the Ballet Rambert, London.

1937 German bombers, under the command of Franco's forces, made the first raid on a civilian population during the Spanish Civil War when they attacked Guernica, the spiritual home of the Basques. This atrocity was later captured on canvas by Picasso.

1975 Portugal held its first free elections for 50 years, with a victory for Mario Soares.

1986 The world's worst nuclear accident occurred at Chernobyl. The area around the power station near Kiev, USSR, was evacuated, but radioactive levels increased over a huge area, even affecting Welsh sheep. It was four days before the Soviets admitted the disaster.

1988 Mick Jagger was cleared of pirating a song by an unknown reggae musician and recording it as 'Just Another Night'. The judgement came after a two-day hearing in the US.

1989 Naas, County Kildare, in Ireland held their first annual pig race watched by over 7,000 people. One punter won £200 on the favourite, Porky's Revenge, and the bookies handed the remainder of their money to the charity People in Need. The organizers plan to invite competitors from as far afield as the US and USSR.

27 APRIL

BORN THIS DAY

HISTORY

1822 Ulysses (Simpson) Grant, American general with the Union Army and 18th US President.

1927 Sheila (Christine) Scott, English aviator who broke 104 light aircraft records and was the first to fly solo over the North Pole. Despite this, she failed her driving test three times. Her flying endeavours were always under-financed and when funds ran out, she was left to a sad and lonely retirement.

1932 Pik Botha, South African Minister for Foreign Affairs, and one of the more enlightened members of the Nationalist Party and government.

ARTS

1737 Edward Gibbon, English historian who wrote *The Decline and Fall of the Roman Empire*. The first of six volumes appeared in 1776.

1759 Mary Wollstonecraft (Godwin), English author and feminist pioneer who caused a stir with her book, *A Vindication of the Rights of Women* (1790). After a failed love affair, she married the philosopher William Godwin. Her daughter Mary, born soon after, would marry the poet Shelley and be the equally remarkable author of *Frankenstein*.

1904 C(ecil) Day-Lewis, Irish-born English poet and novelist who became Poet Laureate, 1968–72. A left-wing poet like his contemporaries Auden and Spender, he helped influence a generation of British poets. He also wrote detective novels under the pseudonym, Nicholas Blake.

SPORT

1840 Edward Whymper, English mountaineer who was the first to climb the Matterhorn (1865) and helped popularize mountain climbing as a sport.

ENTERTAINMENT

1932 Anouk Aimée (Françoise Sorya Dreyfus), French actress who achieved international success in *La Dolce Vita* (1960) and won an Oscar nomination for her role in *A Man and a Woman* (1966). Her fourth husband was Albert Finney.

1939 Judy Carne, English actress who made her name in the US in the television comedy series, *Rowan and Martin's Laugh In*.

INVENTION

1791 Samuel (Finley Breese) Morse, US inventor who first came to England to study painting. Back in the US, he studied chemistry and electricity. In 1833, he devised a magnetic telegraph. He later developed Morse code to send messages using the telegraph.

1896 Wallace Corothers, US chemist and developer, with his research team at the US chemical company E. I. du Pont de Nemours, of nylon which was patented on 24.2.1938.

POP

1959 Sheena Easton, Scottish singer who made the big time in a BBC television programme called *The Big Time* which followed her from audition to cutting her first record. She subsequently became even more successful in the US, with songs such as 'Nine to Five' which went to No. 1.

DIED THIS DAY

1521 Ferdinand Magellan, Portuguese navigator, killed by natives on the island of Mactan in the Philippines while on his round-the-world voyage with a fleet of five ships. His ship was taken safely on to Spain, completing the circumnavigation.

1882 Ralph Waldo Emerson, US philosopher and poet.

1972 Kwame Nkrumah, former Ghananian Prime Minister and President, in Bucharest.

ON THIS DAY

1828 The London Zoological Gardens in Regents Park, London, were opened.

1888 The oil company Esso was established in London.

1932 Imperial Airways began its service from London to Cape Town.

1943 English-born Judy Johnson rode Lone Gallant in a steeplechase in Baltimore to become the first woman jockey to ride as a professional.

1950 The British Government recognized the state of Israel.

1968 Abortion was legalized in Britain as a result of the Abortion Act presented by Liberal MP, David Steel. This was the eighth attempt over the years to get the Act on the statute books.

1970 US actor Tony Curtis was fined £50 in London for being in possession of cannabis.

28 APRIL

BORN THIS DAY

HISTORY

1442 King Edward IV, son of Richard, Duke of York, who beat the Lancastrians at Mortimer's Cross and St Albans to enter London and take the crown.

1758 James Monroe, US Republican statesman and fifth President, elected first in 1816. His popular 'Monroe Doctrine', which said that no European power would colonize any part of the American continent, won him a second term.

1795 Charles Sturt, English explorer who headed three major Australian expeditions. With Hume, he discovered the River Darling. He also charted the Murray to its source near Adelaide, suffering great hardships along the way. Another area he explored, the Sturt desert, is named after him.

1801 Anthony Ashley Cooper, Lord Shaftesbury, 7th Earl, who introduced the Coal Mines Act in 1842 which prohibited the employment of women and children underground.

1889 António de Oliviera Salazar, Portuguese Prime Minister and dictator from 1932–68.

1912 Odette Hallowes, British secret agent in wartime France who was captured and tortured by the Gestapo. She later woh the George Cross.

1924 Kenneth (David) Kaunda, first President of Zambia who was imprisoned in 1958 for founding the Zambia African National Congress. Later released, he became the first Prime Minister of Northern Rhodesia in 1964, before becoming President of a one-party state in 1973.

ENTERTAINMENT

1878 Lionel Barrymore (Lionel Blythe), US actor, eldest of the famous Barrymores, who was a leading man on Broadway and became one of the first major legitimate actors to go to Hollywood.

1941 Ann-Margret (Ann-Margaret Olsson), Swedish actress, singer and dancer who was raised in the US from the age of five. Her films include *Carnal Knowledge* (1971).

SPORT

1942 Mike Brearly, Middlesex and England cricket captain.

DIED THIS DAY

1936 Fuad I, King of Egypt. He was succeeded by his son Farouk.

1976 Richard Hughes, English author of *A High Wind in Jamaica* (1929).

ON THIS DAY

1770 Captain James Cook in *Endeavour* landed at Botany Bay. It was first named Sting Ray Bay, but this was changed to Botany Bay when it was found to be a botanist's paradise. Two years later, in 1772, the world's most travelled goat died in London. She had circumnavigated the world twice, first on *Dolphin* under Captain Wallis, then on Cook's *Endeavour*. The Lord of the Admiralty signed a document admitting her to the privileges of an in-pensioner, but she died soon after.

1788 Maryland became the seventh state of the Union.

1789 The crew of the *Bounty*, led by Fletcher Christian, mutinied against the harsh life at sea under Captain Bligh. They were on the return journey from Tahiti where they had spent six months gathering breadfruit trees. Bligh and 17 others were cast adrift in a small boat without a chart. While the mutineers eventually colonized Pitcairn Island, Bligh managed to sail the small craft 3,618 miles to Timor, near Java, arriving there on 14 June.

1923 The first FA Cup final was held at Wembley Stadium. Before the game started, the huge crowd spilled out on to the pitch, but a single policeman astride a white horse managed to get the crowd off the playing area. Bolton Wanderers won 2–1 against West Ham in front of a crowd of 126,000 people and another 75,000 who had scaled the walls.

1930 John Gielgud opened at the Old Vic as Hamlet.

1945 In Milan, Mussolini (*Il Duce*) and his mistress, Clara Petacci, were caught by Italian partisans and shot. Their bodies were strung upside down from the rafters of a petrol station.

1953 Japan was allowed self-government following its defeat at the end of the Second World War in 1945.

1969 De Gaulle resigned when the response to his referendum for major government reforms was '*Non*'.

1977 In Germany, the Baader-Meinhof terrorists, Andreas Baader, Gudrun Ensslin and Jan Raspe were jailed for life, plus 15 years.

1987 It was announced that some 3,000 toads had passed through a special toad tunnel at Henley-on-Thames during the first six weeks. This crossing between woods had reduced the death toll by 95 per cent as it was now unnecessary for toads to risk life and limb crossing the road.

1988 The first woman conductor at the Royal Opera House, Covent Garden took up the baton this day. Sian Edwards, a 28-year-old from Manchester made her debut with a new production of Sir Michael Tippett's *The Knot Garden*.

1990 *A Chorus Line* closed on Broadway after a record-breaking 15 years.

29 APRIL

National Day of Japan.

BORN THIS DAY

HISTORY

1769 Arthur Wellesley, Duke of Wellington, in Ireland. Known as the Iron Duke, he defeated Napoleon at Waterloo. He was Tory Prime Minister from 1828–30, becoming unpopular when he conceded Roman Catholic emancipation. His London house had its windows smashed by an angry mob on the anniversary of the Battle of Waterloo.

1818 Alexander II, Tsar of Russia who emancipated the serfs in 1861. The Russian Empire grew during his reign, and despite being a liberal ruler, there was severe repression of political opposition which would lead to his assassination on 13.3.1881.

1863 William Randolph Hearst, US newspaper magnate who introduced banner headlines and other techniques to sensationalize news.

1901 Emperor Hirohito of Japan, the first crown prince to visit Europe. He became emperor in 1926, but after defeat in the Second World War, he formally renounced his divinity and the racial supremacy of the Japanese.

1929 (John) Jeremy Thorpe, British Liberal Party leader, who resigned in 1976 following allegations of a homosexual relationship with Norman Scott. He was later acquitted of conspiracy and incitement to murder Scott.

ARTS

FOUR OF A KIND Clearly a very good day to be born if you want to be an orchestral conductor. Born 1879, Sir Thomas Beecham, English conductor and impresario who founded the New Symphony orchestra with the backing of the Beecham patent medicine business. He also staged the first performances at Covent Garden of Strauss's *Elektra* and Delius's *A Village Romeo and Juliet*, and became involved in leading British and some US orchestras. A legendary and controversial figure, he was famous for his outspoken and often witty remarks. This day also marks the birth in 1895, of an equally flamboyant and brilliant conductor, Sir (Harold) Malcolm (Watts) Sargent, nicknamed 'Flash Harry', who became the chief conductor of the Sir Henry Wood Promenade Concerts from 1948 until his death in 1967. On the same day in 1905, Rudolf Schwarz was born in Vienna. The Second World War temporarily ended his career when he was interned in Belsen concentration camp, but he came to Britain after the War and became the chief conductor of the BBC Symphony Orchestra. Lastly, in 1936, Zubin Mehta, the Indian conductor and violinist who won the coveted Liverpool International Conductors prize in 1958, was born.

1889 (Edward Kennedy) 'Duke' Ellington, US composer, bandleader and pianist who was the first to experiment and successfully extend jazz with his 30s compositions, 'Creole Rhapsody',

'Mood Indigo' and 'In a Sentimental Mood'.

ENTERTAINMENT

1907 Fred Zinnemann, US film director, born in Vienna, who is best known for *High Noon* (1952) and *From Here To Eternity* (1953), for which he won an Oscar.

1919 Celeste Holm, US actress who scored a success on Broadway as Ado Annie in *Oklahoma!* (1943). In her third film, *Gentleman's Agreement* (1947) she won an Oscar for best supporting actress.

1924 Zizi (Renee) Jeanmaire, French dancer and actress who became prima ballerina for husband Roland Petit's company.

1949 Anita Dobson, English actress who made her name in the BBC soap opera, *EastEnders*.

1957 Daniel Day-Lewis, Irish-born actor who won an Oscar for best actor in *My Left Foot* (1989).

POP

1931 Lonnie Donegan, British skiffle king who had his first UK and US hit in 1956 with 'Rock Island Line'.

1933 Rod McKuen, US author and composer with over 200 record albums to his credit.

SPORT

1930 Alfred Lewis Valentine, all-round West Indian cricketer, in Jamaica.

1941 Jonah Barrington, British squash champion who was also world champion for six years from 1966 to 1973. He was the first Briton to win both the American and Open titles.

1947 Johnny Miller, US golfer who won the US Open in 1973, and the British Open in 1976.

DIED THIS DAY

1937 Wallace Hume Corothers, US chemist who developed nylon. Suffering from depression, he committed suicide in a Philadelphia hotel room, just two months after patenting nylon (16.2.1937).

1980 Sir Alfred (Joseph) Hitchcock, English film director of *Psycho* (1960).

ON THIS DAY

1376 The first Speaker of the House of Commons, Sir Peter de la Mare, took office.

1696 There were many attempts on the life of William III, King of England, who attracted opposition in part because he was a foreigner. This day, three would-be assassins, Rookwood, Lowick and Cranbourne, were executed for an attempt that failed.

1842 The Corn Bill received Royal Assent. The law was designed to ensure an adequate supply of corn for domestic use and a fair price for the producers.

1885 Women were granted permission to be admitted to Oxford University examinations.

1913 The zipper that zipped was finally patented by a young Swedish engineer, Gideon Sundback. Previous patents were not for the zip as we know it today.

1930 The UK to Australia telephone service was inaugurated.

1933 The FA Cup Final match between Everton and Manchester City was the first in which players wore numbered shirts – from 1 to 22. Everton, who wore 1 to 11, won 3–0.

1935 Just one year after their invention by Percy Shaw of Yorkshire, 'cat's eyes' were being inserted into British roads.

1945 The Nazi concentration camp of Dachau, on the outskirts of Munich, was relieved by US troops.

1967 Muhammed Ali was stripped of his world heavyweight title for refusing to be drafted into the US Army to fight in the Vietnam War.

1976 The first consignment of British North Sea crude oil was exported to Germany.

1977 For the first time since 1936, trade unions were declared legal in Spain.

1977 Britsh Aerospace was founded.

1981 Peter Sutcliffe admitted he was the 'Yorkshire Ripper' who had killed 13 women over four years. The 34-year-old lorry driver from Bradford appeared at the Old Bailey, and two of his victims who had survived were there to confront him.

1987 A unique night at the theatre. The musical revival *Cabaret* was performed without music. The orchestra went on strike at the Strand Theatre, London after five of its members had been sacked. The show was performed for a further two performances without music before being suspended until the dispute was settled.

1990 Stephen Hendry of Scotland, aged 21, became the youngest ever Embassy World Snooker Champion.

30 APRIL

National day of the Netherlands.
Walpurgisnacht in Germany – the Witch's Sabbath held in the Harz Mountains, during which bonfires are lit. This is considered a time of great evil, yet events recorded below seem to indicate quite the contrary.

BORN THIS DAY

HISTORY

1651 Jean Baptiste, Abbé de la Salle, the canon of Rheims who founded the Christian Brothers.

1770 David Thompson, London-born Canadian explorer who explored much of western Canada, including the Columbia River.

1893 Joachim von Ribbentrop, Hitler's Foreign Minister. The British captured him at the end of the Second World War, and the tribunal at Nuremberg sentenced the former wine merchant to death.

1909 Juliana, Queen of the Netherlands who passed her final exam in international law in 1930. She married Prince Bernhard in 1937. During the war, she escaped to Britain and later resided in Canada. Her mother, Queen Wilhelmina abdicated this day in 1948 and she became queen on her 39th birthday.

ARTS

1870 Franz Lehar, Hungarian composer of *The Merry Widow* (1905).

1883 Jaroslav Hašek, Czech novelist and short story writer who wrote the great satire on military life, *The Good Soldier Schweik*. Hašek was in the Austrian army during the time Austria ruled his country, but deserted to Russia where he wrote satirical attacks about both sides.

ENTERTAINMENT

1944 Jill Clayburgh, US actress nominated for an Oscar for her role in *An Unmarried Woman* (1978).

SCIENCE

1777 Johann Karl Friedrich Gauss, German mathematician and astronomer who developed new theories about numbers as well as work in the field of magnetism and electricity. The term 'degauss', for countering magnetic mines, originated from his name and was later used in electronic equipment.

POP

1943 Bobby Vee, US pop singer whose best-known hit was 'Take Good Care of My Baby'.

DIED THIS DAY

1883 Édouard Manet, French Impressionist painter.

1885 Jens Peter Jacobsen, Danish poet and novelist.

1936 A(lfred) E(dward) Housman, English poet who wrote *A Shropshire Lad* (1896).

1968 Frankie Lymon, US pop star who had a hit aged 14, 'Why Do Fools Fall In Love?', of a heroin overdose.

1983 George Balanchine, Russian-born US choreographer.

ON THIS DAY

311 Galerius Valerius Maximianus issued the edict of Nicomedia which meant the Roman Empire legally recognized Christianity.

1772 John Clais of London patented the first dial weighing machine.

1789 General George Washington was inaugurated as the first President of the United States. John Adams was the first Vice-President.

1803 Louisiana and New Orleans were purchased from the French by the US.

1821 The first iron steamship, *Aaron Manby*, named after the proprietor of the Staffordshire ironworks at which it had been made, was completed, having been assembled at Rotherhithe.

1900 Hawaii, a republic, ceded itself to the US.

1900 John Luther 'Casey' Jones, an engineer on Illinois Central Railroad's *Canonball Express* from Chicago to New Orleans, ran down the train warning everyone to jump as the train was about to the smash into a stalled freight train. As a result, only one person died.

1905 The French psychologist, Alfred Binet, explained his new 'intelligence tests'.

1925 The Distillers whisky and spirit group was formed.

1925 Field Marshal Paul von Hindenburg was elected the first President of Germany.

1945 In his underground bunker in besieged Berlin, Hitler first poisoned his wife of a day, Eva Braun, then stuck a revolver in his mouth and pulled the trigger.

1948 The first Land-Rover, made by the Rover company, went on show at the Amsterdam Motor Show.

1975 There was panic in and around the US Embassy in Saigon as pro-US Vietnamese tried to flee the country before the city fell to the North Vietnamese forces. The Vietcong would rename it Ho Chi Minh City.

THE PAN BOOK OF DATES

MAY

When I want to understand what is happening today or to try and decide what will happen tomorrow, I look back
(Oliver Wendell Holmes)

1 MAY

May Day, originally a Roman festival which began on 28 April and lasted several days to mark the commencement of summer. In England, middle and lower classes would gather flowers – 'go a maying' – and the prettiest village maid was crowned Queen of the May, celebrated with dancing around the maypole.

Labour Day, the annual Labour movement holiday, held on the first Monday each May, and linked to 1 May, became an official bank holiday in England from 1976. (In the US, Labor Day is celebrated on the first Monday in September).

BORN THIS DAY

HISTORY

1218 Rudolf I of Hapsburg, King of Germany who was the founder of the Imperial Hapsburg dynasty.

ARTS

1672 Joseph Addison, English poet and essayist who was a co-founder of the *Spectator* in March 1711.

1929 Joseph Heller, US novelist of the highly successful satirical novel, *Catch-22* (1955).

ENTERTAINMENT

1916 Glenn Ford (Gwyllyn Samuel Newton Ford), Canadian-born US actor whose family moved to California when he was five. His films include *The Blackboard Jungle* (1955).

1937 Una Stubbs, English actress and dancer, best known for her appearances on television, including the series *Till Death Us Do Part* as Alf Garnett's daughter.

1946 Joanna Lumley, English actress who made her name in the internationally successful television thriller series, *The New Avengers*.

SCIENCE

1839 Hilaire, Comte de Chardonnet, French chemist who pioneered artificial silk, which he patented in 1885 and manufactured in 1892. It was not like rayon, invented in England in 1898, and was therefore unsuitable for woven goods.

POP

1945 Rita Coolidge, US pianist and singer.

SPORT

1960 Steve Cauthen, record-breaking US jockey who came to ride in Britain when he was just 17 years old.

DIED THIS DAY

1700 John Dryden, English poet and Poet Laureate.

1859 John Walker, English chemist who invented the first friction matches, which were later nicknamed 'lucifers'.

1873 David Livingstone, Scottish missionary and explorer, in Old Chitambo (now Zambia). The locals embalmed his body and carried it to the coast to be shipped back to Britain, where he was buried in Westminster Abbey.

1904 Antonin Dvořák, Czech composer.

1907 Neil Brodie, Canada's dirtiest man, who only bathed when ordered to do so by the law.

1945 Joseph Goebbels, Nazi propaganda chief who followed the example set by Hitler the previous day, and committed suicide in his bunker after first killing his wife and six children.

1952 William Fox (Wilhelm Fried), Hungarian-born US film impresario who formed the Fox Corporation, later 20th Century-Fox.

1968 Sir Harold (George) Nicholson, English diplomat and biographer.

1988 Ben Lexcen (Robert Clyde Miller), Australian yacht designer of Alan Bond's America's Cup winner, *Australia II*. After a business break up he changed his name, using a computer to find a six-letter surname that was unique.

ON THIS DAY

1707 The Union with Scotland and England was proclaimed.

1840 The first Penny Black stamps with Queen Victoria's head went on sale five days before the official issue date. They are now worth at least £65,000 each.

1841 The London Library, founded by Thomas Carlyle, Gladstone, Lord Macauley and others, opened.

1851 Queen Victoria opened the Great Exhibition in the Crystal Palace in Hyde Park, which ran until 11 October. The glass Crystal Palace was so popular it was rebuilt in south London.

1889 In Germany, the Bayer company introduced aspirin in a powder form.

1912 The first performance of *L'Après midi d'un faune*, music by Claude Debussy and starring Nijinsky, was given in Paris. All performances sold out as controversy over its eroticism became the talk of the city.

1925 Cyprus became a British colony, having originally been annexed in 1914 when Turkey supported Germany during the First World War.

1927 Imperial Airways served the first hot meals on a flight from London to Paris. The galley could only provide meals for 18 passengers.

1931 President Hoover opened the Empire State Building in New York, then the world's tallest (1250ft high, with 102 floors).

1937 Picasso began work on his most political painting, *Guernica*, which depicted the agony of the Basque town which had been bombed only days before (26.4.1937).

1939 Batman, the creation of Bob Kane, made his debut (as *The Batman*) in the May edition (No. 17) of Detective Comics.

1945 The German Army in Italy surrendered to the Allies.

1952 TWA introduced 'Tourist Class' air travel.

1955 Stirling Moss became the first British driver to win the Mille Miglia. His Mercedes Benz finished 30 minutes ahead of the second car, driven by the legendary Italian, Fangio.

1960 The USSR shot down the US U-2 spy aircraft piloted by Gary Powers. He was captured and later put on trial which ended with a ten-year sentence.

1961 Betting shops became legal in Britain.

1967 Elvis Presley married his childhood sweetheart, Priscilla Beaulieu, and held a lavish reception in Las Vegas.

1968 Legoland Family Park, the Danish toy maker's answer to Disneyland, opened at Billund. It began as a permament display of Lego models, but developed to become Denmark's most popular tourist attraction after the Tivoli Gardens.

1981 Billy Jean King admitted she had had an affair with Marilyn Barnett, a former hairdresser who became the US tennis star's secretary. Barnett claimed they had an oral contract and sought lifetime support and a Malibu beach house. The married tennis champion fought the case in court, winning both enormous public sympathy and support, and the case against her.

2 MAY

BORN THIS DAY

HISTORY

1729 Catherine II (the Great), Empress of Russia, whose infidelities led her to be banished to another residence before her husband, Peter, was first dethroned and then murdered. As Empress, she embarked on enlarging the Russian Empire.

1860 Theodor Herzl, founder of Zionism. As an Austrian journalist, he was sent to cover the Dreyfus affair in Paris. The resultant anti-semitism convinced him that a national homeland was needed for Jews, and he outlined his views in a book, *Jewish State* (1896). He became the first President of the World Zionist Organization in 1897.

1892 Baron Manfred von Richthofen, former German cavalry officer who later joined the German Air Force and became the commander of the 11th Chasing Squadron, 'Richthofen's Flying Circus'. British pilots nicknamed him the 'Red Baron' because he flew a red Fokker during his many First World War aerial battles. He shot down 80 aircraft before he was finally brought down.

1935 Faisal II, King of Iraq who was educated at Harrow. He succeeded his father, King Ghazi, who was killed in a car accident in 1939. The entire royal family and their household were assassinated in 1958, when Iraq became a republic.

ARTS

1859 Jerome K(lapka) Jerome, English humorous novelist and playwright who wrote *Three Men in a Boat* (1889).

ENTERTAINMENT

1887 Vernon Castle (Vernon Blyth), English ballroom dancer who teamed up with his wife, Irene, and became internationally famous with their dances the Castle Walk, the Turkey Trot and the tango.

1895 Lorenz (Milton) Hart, US lyricist who worked with Richard Rodgers, a collaboration which produced such classic songs as 'The Lady is a Tramp' and 'My Funny Valentine'.

1904 Bing (Harry Lillis) Crosby, US crooner and actor, whose career began as a vocalist with the Paul Whiteman Band in the late 20s. He set a style which produced some of the world's biggest hits including his recording of 'White Christmas', 1942, probably the biggest selling single ever. In films, he first starred in light comedy roles, and, in 1940, began the hugely popular *Road* series with Bob Hope. He could also play dramatic roles, winning an Oscar for his role as the Catholic priest in *Going My Way* (1944).

1921 Satyajit Ray, Indian film maker.

CHILD CARE

1903 Dr Benjamin (McLane) Spock, US child care specialist who wrote the influential book *Common Sense Book of Baby and Child Care* (1946). He was also involved in politics and was the

People's Party candidate for the Presidency in 1972.

DIED THIS DAY

1857 Louis Charles Alfred de Musset, French playwright, aged 47, of a heart attack brought on by his lifestyle and an extraordinarily passionate affair with George Sand.

REDS UNDER THE BEDS In 1957, Joseph Raymond McCarthy, US politician, described by Truman as 'pathological character assassin', who chaired the Permanent Subcommittee on Investigations that carried out the Communist witch-hunts of the 1950s. In 1972, J(ohn) Edgar Hoover, director of the FBI, who served under nine US presidents. In his latter years he, too, seemed to fit Truman's description of McCarthy, as he turned from hunting gangsters to communists real and imaginary, yet US Presidents were reluctant to remove him.

1964 Nancy, Viscountess Astor, first woman member of the British parliament.

ON THIS DAY

1670 The Hudson Bay Company was incorporated as 'The Governor and the Company of Adventurers of England trading into Hudson Bay'.

1923 The first non-stop flight across the US, lasting 27 hours, was made from Long Island to San Diego by Lieutenants Kelly and Macready in a Fokker T-2.

1923 At the BBC's new studio (opened the previous day) at Savoy Hill, London the first *Woman's Hour* programme was broadcast on radio.

1936 The Emperor Haile Selassie and his family fled from the Abyssinian capital, Addis Ababa, three days before it fell to Italian forces.

1965 The first satellite television programme *Out of this World* linked nine countries and over 300 million viewers. The first colour programme was satellited on the 17 May by NBC for US viewers. It was called *A New Look at Olde England*.

1973 The Lebanese Civil War began when 29 died as the army clashed with Palestinian refugees.

1982 The Argentinian battleship *General Belgrano* was torpedoed by the submarine *Conqueror* during the Falklands War. The crew of 362 seamen perished and there was considerable criticism in Britain as the ship was sailing outside the 200-mile exclusion zone at the time.

3 MAY

BORN THIS DAY

HISTORY

1469 Niccolo di Bernardo dei Machiavelli, Italian author and statesman who wrote *The Prince* (1532), which insisted that all means are acceptable to achieve the maintenance of authority.

1874 François Coty (Francesco Giuseppe Spoturno), Corsican-born perfume manufacturer.

1898 Golda Meir (Goldie Meyerson, née Mabovitch), Israeli Prime Minister 1969–73. Born in Kiev, she was educated in the US, but settled in Palestine in 1921, where she worked on a kibbutz with her husband. She became Prime Minister when aged 70.

ARTS

1844 Richard D'Oyly Carte, English impresario and producer of Gilbert and Sullivan operas. Their success enabled him to build the Savoy Theatre (1881).

1896 Dodie Smith, English author of the children's book, *The One Hundred and One Dalmatians* (1956).

1913 William Inge, US playwright of *Come Back Little Sheba* (1952), *Picnic* and *Bus Stop* (1956), all adapted by Inge for the screen.

ENTERTAINMENT

1906 Mary Astor (Lucille Vasconcellos Langhanke), US film actress whose own life reads like a film scenario: divorces, stormy love affairs, suicide attempts and alcoholism. She is best remembered as the murderess in *The Maltese Falcon* (1941).

POP

1919 Pete Seeger, US folk singer.

1936 Engelbert Humperdink (Arnold George Dorsey), in Madras. Like Tom Jones, he made his career in the US in the 70s when ballad singing gave way to rock. His last big hits in the UK were 'Release Me', six weeks at No. 1 and 'The Last Waltz', five weeks at No. 1, both in 1967.

SPORT

CHAMPS Born 1920, 'Sugar' Ray Robinson (Walker Smith), US world middleweight and welterweight champion. He won back his middleweight title no less than five times after first winning it in 1951, when he moved up from welterweight. He lost it to British champion, Randolph Turpin, in a surprise defeat in July of that year, but in September he reclaimed his crown. Also born this day, 1934, Henry Cooper, British Empire and Commonwealth heavyweight champion from 1959, when he beat Brian London. His two clashes with Cassius Clay (Muhammed Ali) ended in defeat, but not before he had floored Clay in the first encounter.

1948 Peter Oosterhuis, English golfer who topped the European Order of Merit from 1971–5, winning the French Open twice.

1952 Allan Wells, Scottish athlete, who won the 100 metres gold at the Moscow Olympics.

DIED THIS DAY

1606 Henry Garnet, English priest, originally a Protestant, who became a Jesuit. Aware of the Gunpowder Plot, he was found guilty of treason, and hanged.

1958 Henry Cornelius, South African-born film director of such classics as *Passport to Pimlico* (1948).

1990 David Rappaport, English dwarf who starred in *The Time Bandits (1981)* and was appearing in television's *L.A. Law* when he committed suicide in Los Angeles.

ON THIS DAY

1494 Columbus on his second expedition, discovered Jamaica.

1500 The Portuguese explorer, Pedro Alvarez Cabral, claimed Brazil for his nation.

1788 The first daily evening newspaper, the *Star and Evening Advertiser*, was published in London.

1808 The first duel fought from two hot-air balloons took place above Paris. The shots were carefully aimed, and a Monsier Le Pique was killed.

1810 Lord Byron swam the Hellespont (Dardanelles) in Turkey which separates Europe from Asia. He took one hour ten minutes.
1951 King George VI opened the Festival of Britain on London's South Bank, brightening the drab post-war scene.
1952 Newcastle United became the first team since 1891 to win two FA Cups in succession by beating Arsenal 1–0.
1968 The first heart transplant operation was carried out in Britain on a 45-year-old man at the National Heart Hospital in Marylebone by a team led by Dr Donald Ross.
1977 The first World Badminton Championships were held in Malmoe. The men's singles championship was won by the Dane, Flemming Delfs.

4 MAY

The Feast Day of Florian, patron saint of blacksmiths and firemen.

BORN THIS DAY

HISTORY

1827 John Hanning Speke, English explorer who joined Richard Burton's African expedition. When Burton fell ill, Speke went on and became the first European to see Lake Victoria (1858), which he claimed was the source of the Nile. Burton disputed this, even after a second expedition. (The remotest head-stream is further south in Burundi, but the Nile proper does indeed begin from Lake Victoria.)
1852 Alice Liddell, the inspiration of Lewis Carroll's *Alice in Wonderland* (1865). She died in 1934.
1882 (Estelle) Sylvia Pankhurst, English painter and suffragette who was the third member of her family to fight for votes for women. Unlike her mother and sister who believed the vote should be for middle-class women, she wanted it for women of all classes.
1928 Muhammed Hosni Mubarak, President of Egypt.

ARTS

1655 Bartolommeo di Francesco Cristofori, harpsichord maker who made the first pianoforte.

ENTERTAINMENT

TWO OF A KIND Born 1923, Eric Sykes, English comedian and writer who established himself on radio before moving to television and films, as did Terry Scott, English comedian, born this day in 1927, who is best known for the long-running television comedy series *Terry and June*.

1929 Audrey Hepburn (-Ruston), Belgium-born actress and dancer, daughter of an English father and Dutch mother. A chance meeting with the author, Colette led to her playing the title role in her classic, *Gigi*, on Broadway in 1951. Later films included *Roman Holiday* (1953), which won her an Oscar.
1942 Tammy Wynette, US country and western singer, best known for her 1975 hit, 'Stand By Your Man'.

SCIENCE

1825 Thomas Henry Huxley, English naturalist and humanist who championed Darwin's theory of evolution. The author of *Man's Place in Nature* (1863), he coined the word 'agnostic' in his works on scientific humanism. His grandsons include writer Aldous, biologist Julian, and Andrew, winner of the Nobel prize for Medicine.

1900 Sir Archibald Hector McIndoe, New Zealand-born plastic surgeon who won fame during the Second World War for his work on severely injured airmen; their faces and limbs were skilfully remodelled by his team at the Queen Victoria Hospital, East Grinstead, Sussex.

BULLFIGHTING

1936 El Cordobe (Manuel Benitez Pérez), Spain's most celebrated bullfighter during the 60s who was also the highest paid torero in history.

DIED THIS DAY

1969 Sir Osbert Sitwell, English author.

1980 Josip Broz Tito, President of Yugoslavia.

1984 Diana Dors (Fluck), English actress, of cancer.

1989 Christine Jorgensen (George Jorgensen), former US Army private who shocked the world in 1952 by having the first sex change operation. She died of cancer, aged 62.

ON THIS DAY

1780 The first Epsom Derby was won by Charles Bunbury's Diomed.

1839 The Cunard Shipping Line was founded by Sir Samuel Cunard.

1863 The Maori uprising against the British began in New Zealand.

1896 The first edition of the half-penny *Daily Mail* was published.

1904 A provisional agreement was signed in Manchester's Midland Hotel by the Hon. Charles Rolls, seller and repairer of motor cars, and Henry Royce, electrical engineer and builder of a single motor car. Together they would produce Rolls-Royce cars. Rolls had driven a car at a world record 93 m.p.h. at Dublin's Phoenix Park the previous year.

1926 The first General Strike in British history called by the TUC began. Troops were called in to man essential services and public volunteers helped on the buses and with the mail. Troops and armoured cars were out in all cities in case of trouble, but the strike lasted just nine days.

1970 Two girls and two male students were shot dead and 11 injured by US National Guards at Kent State University, Ohio, during an anti-war demonstration against Nixon's decision to send troops into Cambodia.

1976 'Waltzing Matilda' was adopted as the Australian national anthem, but was replaced by 'Australia Fair' in 1986.

1979 Margaret Thatcher became Britain's first woman Prime Minister following the Conservative Party's election win.

1982 HMS *Sheffield* was sunk by an Exocet missile during the Falklands war. 21 died, many others suffered appalling burns.

1989 Former marine Colonel Oliver North was convicted of three charges and had nine others dismissed in the US District Court regarding his action in supplying arms to the Contras from money made by selling arms to Iran.

5 MAY

BORN THIS DAY

HISTORY

1800 Louis Hachette, French bookseller, publisher and editor.

1813 Soren Aaby Kierkegaarde, Danish philosopher and theologian. A deformed Jew who converted to Christianity, he came into conflict with the Church over his views on existentialism.

1818 (Heinrich) Karl Marx, German author and founder of international Communism. With Engels, he co-wrote the *Communist Manifesto* (1848). Using the resources of the British Museum reading room to study economics and political thought, he produced *Das Kapital* (1867), although he didn't live to complete the final volume.

1867 Nellie Bly (Elizabeth Cochrane), legendary US news reporter who pioneered modern investigative journalism with exposés on the treatment of the mentally ill, slum life and divorce. She was also famous for her stunts. (*See* 14.11.1889)

ARTS

1815 Eugène Martin Labiche, French playwright who wrote over 100 comedies, farces and sketches.

1846 Henryk Sienkiewicz, Polish novelist, author of the best-selling *Quo Vadis* (1896).

SPORT

1904 Sir Gordon Richards, English jockey, who was champion jockey 26 times during his career. He rode 4,500 winners from 1925–52.

ENTERTAINMENT

1913 Tyrone (Edmund) Power, US actor who usually played romantic leads in films such as *The Mark of Zorro* (1940).

1943 Michael Palin, English writer, comedian, actor and member of the Monty Python team.

1944 Roger Rees, English actor who made his name on both the London and Broadway stage playing the title role in the Royal Shakespeare Company production of *Nicholas Nickleby* (1981).

DIED THIS DAY

1821 Napoleon Bonaparte, Emperor of France, in exile on the Atlantic island of St Helena.

1949 Count Maurice (Polydore Marie Bernard) Maeterlinck, Belgian playwright of *The Blue Bird* (1908).

ON THIS DAY

1760 The first hanging took place at Tyburn in London; Earl Ferrers was executed for murdering his steward.

1865 The first train robbery took place, near North Bend, Ohio.

1952 The third verse of 'Deutschland Über Alles' was adopted as the national anthem of West Germany. On the same day in 1955, West Germany became a sovereign state with Dr Konrad Adenauer as first Federal Chancellor.

GOING UP In 1961, the US put astronaut Alan B. Shepard in space for a sub-orbital flight and President J. F. Kennedy promised that the US would be the first to get a man on the moon. In 1963, Britain's first satellite,

Ariel III was launched from Vandenburg Air base in California.

1968 Rioting students led by Daniel Cohn-Bendit erected barricades in Paris as they clashed with police in violent confrontations. Over 1,000 were injured and French workers added their support to bring the country to a virtual standstill.

1980 Millions in Britain watched live on television as the SAS stormed the Iranian embassy in London, freeing 19 hostages held by five terroists. Four gunmen were killed, the first shot by one of the hostages, PC Lock, as the first SAS man entered, probably saving his life.

1988 The first live television broadcast from the summit of Mount Everest was transmitted by Japanese television.

2000 On this day, the next conjunction of the Sun, Moon, Mercury, Venus, Mars, Jupiter and Saturn will take place.

6 MAY

BORN THIS DAY

HISTORY

1758 Maximillien (François Marie Isidore de) Robespierre, leader of the French Revolution. A great manipulator of the mob, he became virtual dictator of France, but his popularity waned and the overworked guillotine finally caught up with him on 28.7.1794.

1856 Sigmund Freud, Austrian psychiatrist and father of modern psychology and psychoanalysis, who stressed the relationship between sexual repression and neuroses. In 1938, as the Nazis entered Austria, he fled to London.

1856 Robert Edwin Peary, US polar explorer who was the first to reach the North Pole (6.4.1909) on his seventh attempt.

ENTERTAINMENT

1895 Rudolph Valentino (Rodolfo Alfonzo Guglielmi di Valentina d'Antonguolla), Italian silent film actor who migrated to the US. His first roles in Hollywood films were as an exotic dancer, and his break came with *The Four Horsemen of the Apocalypse* and *The Sheikh*, both in 1921. He became a sensation at the box office and the sex idol of women throughout the world before his tragic death from a perforated ulcer in 1926, aged 31.

1902 Max Ophuls (Maximillian Oppenheimer) German director who only entered films after having directed over 200 stage productions. He left Germany as Nazi power increased, but he only went to Hollywood in 1941. His films include the highly successful *La Ronde* (1950).

1913 Stewart Granger (James Stewart), English film actor who changed his name to avoid confusion with the famous US actor. Granger became a US citizen in 1956 although many of his best films were made in Britain including *The Man in Grey* (1943).

1915 Orson Welles, US actor, writer, film director and *enfant terrible* who directed and starred in one of the world's greatest films, *Citizen Kane* (1941), and played the role of Harry Lime in *The Third Man* (1949).

DIED THIS DAY

1862 Henry David Thoreau, US poet and essayist.

1919 (Lyman) Frank Baum, US author of *The Wizard of Oz*.
1952 Maria Montessori, Italian educationalist and teacher, in Holland.

ON THIS DAY

1626 A Dutch settler, Paul Minuit, bought what is now Manhattan Island from the local Red Indians for a handful of trinkets worth no more than $25.
1642 Montreal was officially established under its original name 'Ville Marie'.
1733 The first international boxing match took place at Figg's Amphitheatre, London, when Bob Whittaker beat Italy's Tito di Carni.
1840 The first postage stamps, the 'Penny Black' and two-penny 'blues', which were the brainchild of Roland Hill, officially went on sale in Britain. (Some had been sold four days before and are now valued at not less than £65,000 each.)
1851 US inventor, Linus Yale, patented his Yale lock.
1875 The first Kentucky Derby was run for three-year-olds at Churchhill Downs track, Louisville, Kentucky, and has been run on the first Saturday in May ever since.
1882 In Dublin's Phoenix Park, the Fenian 'Irish Invincibles' murdered Lord Cavendish, Chief Secretary for Ireland, and Thomas Henry Burke, Irish Under-Secretary.
1910 Following the death this day of King Edward VII, George V acceded to the throne. He celebrated his Silver Jubilee with Queen Mary in 1935.
1937 The German airship, *Hindenburg* arrived at Lakehurst, New Jersey, after its flight from Frankfurt. A radio commentator for WLS, Herb Morrison, began to describe the scene when the airship struck the landing mast and suddenly exploded. Within seconds, it was a ball of fire. Morrison's now classic broadcast heard him sob, 'Oh, the humanity, all the passengers, I don't believe it.' Amazingly, only 36 of 97 on board perished, but it was the end of airships for another 50 years. Ironically, this very day back in 1919 the British Admiralty had recommended that helium, a non-inflammable, lighter-than-air gas was a safe substitute for hydrogen-filled balloons and airships.
1954 At the Iffley Road track in Oxford, in a meeting between the University and the Amateur Athletic Association, Roger Bannister, with university pacemakers, Chris Chattaway and Chris Brasher, became the first to break the four-minute mile, winning in three minutes 59.4 seconds.
1959 The Cod War between Britain and Iceland over fishing rights intensified when Icelandic gunboats fired live ammunition at British trawlers.
1960 Princess Margaret married Anthony Armstrong-Jones (Lord Snowdon) at Westminster Abbey.
1961 The first football team to achieve the double, (FA Cup and League champions), was Tottenham Hotspur led by Danny Blanchflower when they beat Leicester City 2–0 to win the Cup at Wembley.
1966 The Moors Murderers, Ian Brady and Myra Hindley, were sentenced for the murders of several children including Lesley Ann Downey and John Kilbride, both aged ten, who, like the other victims, were buried on the Pennine moors. Brady was given three concurrent life sentences, and Hindley two.
1974 The German Chancellor Willy

Brandt resigned when it was revealed that his closest aide was working for the Communists.

1987 In Belgrade, Niroslav Milhailovic began a 54-hour joke-telling marathon claiming he knew 287,000 jokes.

1988 Zimbabwe-born cricketer, Graeme Hick, playing for Worcester, scored 405 in a single innings, the first since 1895 when Archie MacLaren scored 424 on the same ground at Taunton, Somerset.

1990 London telephone codes changed to 071 and 081 (replacing 01).

7 MAY

BORN THIS DAY

HISTORY

1919 Maria Eva Duarte Perón (née Ibarguren), 'Evita', legendary Argentinian who was born the illegitimate daughter of a cook. Singing in a Buenos Aires nightclub, she met Juan Perón, then Minister of Labour. He married her a year later when she was just 16. After he became President, her popularity increased, despite her involvement in corruption and torture. However, she did achieve many reforms and became the heroine of 'the shirtless ones'.

ARTS

1812 Robert Browning, popular Victorian English poet who secretly married Elizabeth Barrett Browning and went to live in Italy. He returned after her death in 1861. Although his innovative poetry was sometimes considered obscure, poems such as *The Pied Piper of Hamelin* and *Home Thoughts From Abroad* were well received.

MUSIC MAKERS Born 1833, Johannes Brahms, German composer and pianist of the Concerto No. 1 in D Minor (1857) and four great symphonies. Seven years later on this day in 1840, Piotr Ilyich Tchaikovsky, the Russian composer who is best known for his ballet music including *Swan Lake* (1875), *Sleeping Beauty* (1888) and *The Nutcracker* (1891), was born.

1892 Archibald McLeish, US poet who was Assistant Secretary of State 1944–5, and helped draft the consitution of UNESCO.

1927 Ruth Prawer Jhabvala, German-born screenplay writer and author of Polish-Jewish descent who became an Indian by marriage, closely associated with film maker James Ivory.

ENTERTAINMENT

1901 Gary Cooper (Frank James Cooper), US actor who received his early education in England. He started as an extra in Westerns before being given a chance in *The Winning of Barbara Worth* (1926). He won Oscars for *Sergeant York* (1942) and *High Noon* (1952).

INVENTION

1909 Edwin (Herbert) Land, US physicist and inventor of the Polaroid camera and process (1947). His birth was on the 21st anniversary of Eastman patenting his Kodak camera (*see* ON THIS DAY).

DIED THIS DAY

1890 James Nasmyth, Scottish engineer, inventor of the steam hammer.

1925 William Lever (Lord Leverhulme), English manufacturer, founder of the giant Lever Brothers enterprise.

1940 George Lansbury, British Labour Party leader.

1957 Eliot Ness, US Goverment agent who investigated Al Capone.

ON THIS DAY

1663 The Theatre Royal, Drury Lane, built by Thomas Killigrew, opened under a charter granted by Charles II with a performance of Beaumont and Fletcher's *The Humorous Lieutenant*.

1763 Pontiac, chief of the Ottawa Indians, rose up against the English garrison at Detroit and laid siege to it for five months.

1823 The deaf Beethoven conducted the first performance of his *Ninth Symphony* in Vienna.

1832 Greece was proclaimed an independent kingdom.

1888 George Eastman patented his Kodak box camera, a name he felt would be easy to remember.

1907 The first Isle of Man TT Race was held. The winner was Charles Collier on a Matchless, at an average speed of 38.22 m.p.h.

1915 A German submarine torpedoed the Cunard liner, *Lusitania*, without prior warning and around 1,400 of the 1978 men, women and children on board were drowned off the Irish coast, including 128 US citizens and the multi-millionaire, Alfred Vanderbilt.

1921 Crown Prince Hirohito (later the Emperor of Japan) arrived on an official visit to Britain.

1926 Womens suffrage in Britain was lowered from the age of 30 to 21 years and over.

1945 The Germans surrendered to Generals Montgomery and Bedell-Smith. German Chief-of-Staff Jodl signed the instrument of unconditional surrender in a small schoolhouse in Rheims.

1960 Leonid Brezhnev became head of the USSR.

1988 The first gathering of people claiming to have been abducted by aliens met in Boston.

8 MAY

BORN THIS DAY

HISTORY

1828 Jean Henri Dunant, Swiss founder of the Red Cross (29.10.1863). It was while he was at the Battle of Solferino (1859) that he saw the agony of war and determined to establish an international organization accepted by all nations.

1884 Harry S. Truman, 33rd President of the US who took over on Roosevelt's death (1945) and gave the orders for the atomic bombs to be dropped on Japan bringing the Second World War to an end.

1904 John Snagge, English broadcaster. A veteran BBC sports commentator, he was best known for his University Boat Race commentaries.

1926 Sir David Attenborough, English broadcaster and naturalist who has presented many award-winning television series, including *Life on Earth*.

ARTS

1940 Peter Benchley, US author, son of the humorist Robert Benchley, and writer of the bestseller *Jaws* (1974).

ENTERTAINMENT

1946 Candice Bergen, US actress, daughter of US ventriloquist, Edgar Bergen, she was a successful model before appearing in films.

POP

1944 Gary Glitter (Paul Gadd), English rock star known for his energetic performances in glittering costumes, who had a No. 1 (for four weeks) with 'I'm The Leader of the Gang (I Am)'.

SPORT

1932 Sonny (Charles) Liston, US heavyweight boxer who became world champion when he knocked out Floyd Patterson in the first round in 1962.

1936 Jack Charlton, English football international and club manager, older brother of the legendary Bobby.

DIED THIS DAY

1854 Captain Barclay-Allardice, English long-distance walker who covered 1,000 miles in 1,000 hours. £10,000 was staked on the challenge, which began at Newmarket at midnight on 1 June and ended at 3 p.m. on 12 July.

1873 John Stuart Mill, English political and economic philosopher and reformer.

1876 Truganini, the last Tasmanian Aborigine.

1880 Gustave Flaubert, French novelist of *Madame Bovary*, as a result, so rumour has it, of a stroke in the arms of his servant Suzanne.

1947 Harry Gordon Selfridge, US department store pioneer who left only £1,544 in his will.

1986 Baron Shinwell (Manny Shinwell), former Labour MP and minister, who died aged 101.

1988 Robert Anson Heinlein, US science fiction writer, one of the pioneers of the genre.

1990 Cardinal Tomas O'Fiach (Tomas Seamus Fee), Cardinal Archbishop of All Ireland, while on a visit to Lourdes.

ON THIS DAY

1794 Antoine Lavoisier, the French chemist who identified oxygen as a result of Priestley's previous work, was guillotined because he had once accepted the office of farmer general of taxes.

1849 The first international yacht race was won by *Pearl* of Bermuda when she beat the US yacht, *Brenda*.

1902 Volcanic activity had begun in April near St Pierre, Martinique, forcing over 100 fer-de-lance snakes to invade the town's mulatto quarter. Over 50 people and many animals died before these six-foot long snakes were finally killed by the town's giant street cats. On this day, however, the volcano erupted violently and within minutes St Pierre was destroyed. Of the 30,000 inhabitants only two survived.

1921 Sweden abolished capital punishment.

CRICKET, LOVELY CRICKET In 1896, the highest county championship innings score, 887, was achieved by Yorkshire against Warwickshire at Edgbaston. In 1923, Jack Hobbs, the Surrey and England opening batsman made his 100th century in first-class cricket. In 1953, Gloucester wicketkeeper

Arthur Wilson held a record ten catches in an innings against Hampshire.

1924 Afrikaans became the official language of South Africa.

1945 VE Day (Victory in Europe) was celebrated.

1961 George Blake, a former British diplomat, was jailed for 42 years for spying for Russia. The former Vice Consul in Seoul had been captured by the Communists and held for three years, during which time he may have been brainwashed. He escaped from Wormwood Scrubs in 1966.

1962 The London trolley buses ran for the last time.

1977 The trial of Pieter Menten, the Dutch art dealer and Nazi collaborator, began in Amsterdam. Accused of murdering Polish Jews in 1941 in order to obtain their art treasures and other possessions, he was sentenced to 15 years, but he appealed to the Supreme Court and was released on a technicality, sparking off demonstrations. He was retried in 1980, but only served a third of his ten year sentence.

1984 The Thames Barrier, designed to prevent the river flooding central London, was opened.

1988 Nancy Reagan's reliance on an astrologer and its influence on President Reagan was revealed when *Time* magazine published the first extract of former ex-chief of staff, Donald Regan's memoirs. The astrologer was an heiress, Joan Quigley, who confirmed her services had been used since 1981.

9 MAY

National Day of Czechoslovakia.

BORN THIS DAY

HISTORY

1800 John Brown, US abolitionist who married twice and had twenty children. His anti-slavery campaign was ruthless – he attacked a US armoury at Harper's ferry in Virginia – and was eventually arrested and tried for insurrection.

1873 Howard Carter, English Egyptologist who discovered the tomb of Tutankhamun in the Valley of the Kings.

ARTS

1860 Sir J(ames) M(atthew) Barrie, Scottish playwright best known for *Peter Pan* (1904), but his plays include *Quality Street* and *The Admirable Crichton*, both 1902.

1874 Lilian (Mary) Baylis, founder of the Old Vic Shakespeare company in 1914. Decades later, it evolved into the National Theatre. She also managed the Sadler's Wells Theatre, where she presented opera and ballet.

1920 Richard Adams, English author of the classic *Watership Down* (1972), and a former civil servant in the Department of the Environment.

1934 Alan Bennett, English playwright and actor, much influenced by his northern England roots. His work has been seen both on the stage and television. His films include *A Private Function* (1984).

ENTERTAINMENT

TWO OF A KIND Two of Britain's leading actors, both from the north of England and both of working class parents, were born this day in 1936 – Albert Finney, son of a Salford bookie, who established himself on the stage before appearing in films such as *Saturday Night and Sunday Morning* (1960) and *The Dresser* (1985), and Glenda Jackson, a Merseyside bricklayer's daughter, who won Oscars for *Women In Love* (1969) and *A Touch of Class* (1972).

SPORT

1928 (Richard Alonzo) Pancho Gonzáles, US tennis player of Mexican-American parents, who won the US men's singles eight times, including seven consecutively, between 1953 and 1959. At Wimbledon in 1969, he took five hours 20 minutes to beat Charlie Pasarell, the longest match ever played there.

1936 Terry Downes, British and former world middleweight boxing champion who won the title after a punishing nine rounds in 1961 against a much older Paul Pendar from the US.

WALKIES

1910, Barbara Woodhouse, Irish-born dog trainer who became a national celebrity in her late sixties with her television dog training programme and her bossy commands to both animals and human students.

DIED THIS DAY

1657 William Bradford, Pilgrim Father, Governor of Plymouth Colony, Massachusetts.

1805 Johann Christoph Friedrich von Schiller, German romantic poet and playwright.

1903 (Eugène Henri) Paul Gauguin, French Post-Impressionist painter after a long illness, alone in his small house on the tiny Polynesian island of Hiva Oa, where he was buried.

1976 Ulrike Meinhof, German terrorist, was found dead in her cell in a Stuttgart jail. (*See* 16.6.1972)

ON THIS DAY

1671 Colonel Thomas Blood, the Irish adventurer, gained entry to the Tower of London disguised as a parson, and befriended one of the keepers of the Royal Regalia. This night, together with several accomplices armed with pistols and daggers, he stole the crown jewels. The gang managed to make their way out of the Tower, but were soon apprehended by a Captain Beckman. Tried and found guilty, Blood convinced King Charles I that his death would set off a revolution, so was granted a pardon.

1785 Joseph Bramah patented the beer pump handle.

1887 *Buffalo Bill's Wild West Show* opened at West Brompton, London, as part of the America Exhibition.

1896 The first Horseless Carriage Show opened to the motor trade, with ten models on show at London's Imperial Institute.

1901 The first Federal parliament met in Melbourne, Australia, and on this day, 1927, the Duke of York opened the Parliament House in Canberra, replacing Melbourne as the capital.

1944 The first eye bank opened at the New York Ear, Nose and Throat Hospital.

1946 Victor Emmanuel III, Italian monarch since 1900, abdicated as Italy became a republic.

1949 Britain's first launderette opened at

184 Queensway in London for a six-month trial.

1956 John Osborne's *Look Back in Anger* opened at the Royal Court Theatre, London and launched an era of 'angry young men'.

1978 The body of former Italian Prime Minister Aldo Moro was found in the boot of a small Renault in central Rome, a victim of the Red Brigade.

10 MAY

BORN THIS DAY

HISTORY

1760 Claude Joseph Rouget de Lisle, French army officer who wrote and composed the *Marseillaise*. Originally called 'Chant de l'armeé du Rhin', it was sung by troops from Marseilles.

1838 John Wilkes Booth, failed US actor and assassin of Abraham Lincoln.

1915 Dennis Thatcher, English businessman and husband of the British Prime Minister.

ARTS

1894 Dimitri Tiomkin, Russian composer who settled in the US, where he wrote major film scores such as *High Noon* (1952).

ENTERTAINMENT

1899 Fred Astaire (Frederick Austerlitz) US dancer, actor and singer. His career with his sister, Adele, began in vaudeville and despite an initial unfavourable screen test he went on to make several successful films with Ginger Rogers. He also partnered Rita Hayworth, Eleanor Powell and Cyd Charisse.

1902 David O(liver) Selznick, US film producer of *Gone With the Wind* (1939). He was also responsible for bringing Hitchcock to Hollywood.

1910 Arthur Marshall, English journalist, author and perfomer, one-time schoolmaster with a voice like a girl's public school headmistress, who first made his name as a performer of humorous monologues.

1946 Maureen Lipman, English actress who, despite her many television and stage roles including her one-woman show, *Re-Joyce* (1988) which celebrates the work of Joyce Grenfell, has become nationally known as the very Jewish lady in the enormously popular British Telecom television commercials.

SCIENCE

1788 Augustin Jean Fresnel, French physicist who made contributions in the study of polarized light and lenses.

POP

1946 Donovan (David Leitch), Scottish guitarist, singer and songwriter who had hits with 'Catch the Wind', 'Mellow Yellow' and 'Sunshine Superman' which was No. 1 in the US charts in 1966.

1957 Sid Vicious (John Beverly), English punk bassist with the Sex Pistols, whose brief life seems to have lived up to his stage surname.

BUSINESS

1850 Sir Thomas (Johnstone) Lipton, Scottish errand boy who rose to be a multimillionaire grocer by the time he was 30 by such innovative methods as putting tea in tea bags.

DIED THIS DAY

1566 Leonhard Fuchs, German botanist after whom fuchsias are named.

1774 Louis XV, King of France, of smallpox.

1798 George Vancouver, English navigator and explorer, who sailed with Cook on his second and third voyages. He carried out surveys of Australia and New Zealand, as well as the West Coast of North America, including the island named after him, Vancouver.

1818 Paul Revere, American hero, immortalized by Longfellow's poem.

1863 Thomas Jonathan ' Stonewall' Jackson, American Confederate general, from his wounds after being shot in error by his own troops returning from a reconnaisance trip.

1904 Sir Henry Morton Stanley (the illegitimate Welsh-born John Rowlands who took his name from a man who befriended him in the US), journalist and explorer who went in search of, and found, Livingstone.

1920 John Wesley Hyatt, US inventor of celluloid.

1977 Joan Crawford (Lucille Fay Le Seuer), US film actress.

ON THIS DAY

1655 The English captured Jamaica from the Spanish.

1857 The Sepoy Rebellion broke out in Meerat, triggering the Indian mutiny against British rule.

1865 Jefferson Davis, President of the Confederacy was taken prisoner by the Union forces at Irvinsville, Georgia, during the American Civil War.

1869 The Central Pacific and Union Pacific railroads met at Promontory, Utah, where the lines were linked to complete the transcontinental railroad.

1886 The FA Council approved football international caps.

1907 Mother's Day was first celebrated, initiated by Miss Anna Jarvis of Philadelphia, as part of her women's suffrage and temperance movement.

1922 Dr Ivy Williams became the first woman to be called to the English Bar.

FIRE WARNING In 1933, the Nazis began burning books by 'unGerman' writers, including those by Heinrich Mann, Upton Sinclair and Erich Maria Remarque, author of *All Quiet on the Western Front.* At the same time in New York, Nelson Rockefeller fired the Mexican painter Diego Rivera from completing his mural for the new RCA building because he refused to remove a portrait of Lenin. The mural was destroyed.

1940 Churchill took over as Prime Minister from the discredited Chamberlain.

1941 The worst of the London Blitz occurred when 550 German bombers dropped 100,000 incendiaries. This night, 1915, the Zeppelins had first bombed London.

1941 Rudolf Hess, Hitler's deputy, parachuted into Scotland from a Messerschmitt, in an effort to negotiate a peace settlement, but was arrested and imprisoned for the remainder of the war. He was tried at Nuremberg Tribunal, found guilty of war crimes and imprisoned in Spandau Prison until his death in 1987.

1942 The German and Italian warplanes stopped their blanket bombing of Malta after 11,000 missions.

1981 François Mitterand became President of France, at the third attempt.

1988 In New York State, rescue workers had to cut a hole in a bedroom wall to extract a man needing hospital care for acute bronchitis. He weighed 70 stone.

1990 Robert Maxwell launched the first European weekend newspaper, *The European*.

11 MAY

BORN THIS DAY

HISTORY

1720 Baron von Karl Friedrich Hieronymus Münchhausen, German hunter and soldier who fought with the Russians against the Turks and returned to tell the most exaggerated tales.

ARTS

1893 Martha Graham, US dancer, choreographer and pioneer of modern dance, who established her own company. Her best known ballet is *Appalachian Spring* (1958).

1904 Salvador Dali, Spanish Surrealist painter. A neurotic man, he revealed his phobias in pictures which contain startling psychological images, and are painted with a masterly technique. He was involved in two major films: Buñuel's Surrealist *Chien Andalou* which he co-wrote, and Hitchcock's *Spellbound*, for which he created an unforgettable dream sequence.

ENTERTAINMENT

1888 Irving Berlin (Israel Baline), Russian-born US composer and lyricist who, although self-taught, produced some of the most famous songs of the century including 'Easter Parade', 'God Bless America', 'Alexander's Ragtime Band', 'There's No Business Like Show Business' and 'White Christmas'.

1892 Dame Margaret Rutherford, English actress who specialized in eccentric roles which she played to perfection in films such as *Blithe Spirit* (1945).

1912 Phil Silvers (Philip Silversmith), US comedian who will for ever be 'Sergeant Bilko'.

SCIENCE

1918 Richard Feynman, US physicist, who shared the Nobel prize for Physics with Shinichero Tomonaga in 1965 for the work they did separately on attempting to merge Einstein's theory of relativity with the new science of quantum mechanics.

INVENTION

1854 Ottmar Mergenthaler, German inventor who settled in the US where he patented the Linotype printing machine in 1884.

POP

1941 Eric Burdon, English rock singer, who, together with Alan Price, formed the Animals, probably the top blues band of the 60s. They had hits including 'House of the Rising Sun' (1964) before Burdon went solo.

1942 Ian Dury, English rock singer who, usually backed by his Blockheads, formed part of the 'New Wave', with offerings such as 'Sex and Drugs and Rock and Roll' (1977).

SPORT

1924 (John) Jackie Milburn, English footballer, known as 'Wor Jackie' to his Newcastle fans.

DIED THIS DAY

1610 Matteo Ricci, Italian Jesuit missionary who worked in China.

1686 Otto von Guericke, German physicist who demonstrated the vacuum.

1708 Jules Hardouin-Mansart, French architect who designed the Galérie de Glaces at Versailles.

1778 William Pitt (the Elder), first Earl of Chatham.

1848 Tom Cribb, English prize fighter who retired unbeaten.

1871 Sir John Herschel, British astronomer royal.

1927 Juan Gris, French painter.

1935 Edward Herbert Thompson, US explorer who excavated several Mayan cities.

1981 Bob Marley, who, with his Wailers, popularized reggae, of brain cancer in Miami.

1988 'Kim' Philby, former British intelligence officer who spied for Russia.

ON THIS DAY

868 The first printed book, known as the *Diamond Sutra*, was published in China. It was found in 1900.

1811 The original Siamese twins, Chang and Eng, were born of Chinese parents in Siam. Joined from breastbone to navel, they settled in the US, where they were exhibited and where they married, and fathered several normal children.

1812 Spencer Perceval, the British Prime Minister, was shot and killed by a bankrupt Liverpool broker, John Bellingham, as he entered the House of Commons.

1858 Minnesota became the 32nd US state.

1904 Australian diva, Nellie Melba, signed a contract with the Gramophone Company. The records, which were to have a distinct mauve label, would be sold for one guinea, a far higher price than anything else on sale at this time, and she would receive an advance of £1000 and a five-shilling (25%) royalty. The first records reached the shops in July and were sold out within days.

1949 Siam changed its name to Thailand.

1960 The world's longest liner, SS *France* was launched at St Nazaire by General de Gaulle.

1964 (Sir) Terence Conran opened the first Habitat shop in London's Fulham Road.

1981 The first performance of Lloyd Webber's musical *Cats*, based on T. S. Eliot's *Old Possum* poems, opened in London.

1985 A fire at Bradford City football ground killed 40 and injured 150 spectators.

12 MAY

BORN THIS DAY

HISTORY

1765 Lady Hamilton (Emma Lyon) was baptized this day; her date of birth is somewhat obscure. The daughter of a blacksmith, she became a courtesan. One of her lovers, Sir William Hamilton, then married her. Nelson first met her in 1793 and their romance flourished. She gave him a daughter, Horatia. He left Emma £2,000 a year when he died, but she still managed to run up massive debts and eventually fled to Calais, where she later died in poverty.

1820 Florence Nightingale, English hospital reformer who attended to the wounded during the Crimean War. 'The Lady of the Lamp' had over 10,000 under her care in appalling and unsanitary conditions. Determined to remedy the suffering she had experienced, she raised £50,000 to establish nurses' training in Britain.

1880 Lincoln Ellsworth, US explorer and civil engineer who surveyed the routes and helped build the Canadian transcontinental railway.

ARTS

1812 Edward Lear, English artist and humorous poet, whose *Book of Nonsense* (1846), which was written for the grandchildren of his patron, the Earl of Derby, completely overshadowed his accomplishments as a painter, particularly of Italian landscapes.

1828 Dante Gabriel Rossetti, English poet and Pre-Raphaelite painter, the son of an Italian poet and writer who settled in London. He married his model, who features in many of his paintings, but two years later she died from an overdose of laudanum. The only manuscript of his poems was placed in her coffin, but later, in 1869, he arranged for them to be exhumed.

MUSIQUE Two French composers were born this day: in 1842, Jules (Émile Frédéric) Massenet, who is best known for his opera *Manon* (1884), and in 1845, Gabriel (Urbain) Fauré, composer, organist and director of the Conservatoire, who is best remembered for his *Requiem* (1888).

1907 Leslie Charteris (Leslie Charles Bowyer Yin), creator of the 'Saint' thrillers, in Singapore, of a Chinese surgeon father and English mother.

ENTERTAINMENT

1903 Wilfred Hyde-White, English character actor with an impish quality which endeared him to audiences on both sides of the Atlantic on stage and screen. His films include *Two Way Stretch* (1960).

1937 Dr Miriam Stoppard, English physician, writer and broadcaster, wife of playwright Tom.

1942 Susan Hampshire, English actress who is still remembered as Fleur in the television series *The Forsyte Saga*. Dyslexic, she has to memorize her entire part by the first rehearsal.

SCIENCE

1803 Justus, Baron von Liebig, German chemist who discovered chloroform.

POP

1929 Burt Bacharach, US composer, with Hal David, of songs such as 'Walk On By', 'What's New, Pussycat?' and 'Raindrops Keep Fallin' on My Head'.

SPORT

1945 Alan Ball, former international England footballer, member of the victorious World Cup team of 1966.

DIED THIS DAY

1860 Sir Charles Barry, English architect who won the competition to rebuild the Houses of Parliament after it was burnt down in 1834.

1884 Bedřich Smetana, Czechoslovakian composer of *The Bartered Bride* (1866).

1925 Amy (Lawrence) Lowell, US poet.

1957 Erich von Stroheim, German-born film actor and director.

1967 John Edward Masefield, English poet and, from 1930, Poet Laureate.

ON THIS DAY

1861 'John Brown's body lies a-mouldering in the grave' was played for the first time at a flag-raising ceremony at Fort Warren, near Boston. The words and music were by C. S. Hall about John Brown, a sergeant at the Fort, and not the anti-slavery campaigner as is popularly believed, although the song was used later to parody the famous abolitionist.

1870 The Red River Colony, now called Manitoba, was purchased from the Hudson Bay Company by Canada and became a province.

1870 The London Swimming Association drafted the rules of water polo.

1906 The first edition of Horatio Bottomley's magazine, *John Bull* was published. In 1912, the first edition of *Pravda* was published.

1926 The General Strike ended. It lasted only nine days.

1935 Alcoholics Anonymous was founded by 'Bill W' (William Wilson) in Akron, Ohio.

1937 The BBC transmitted its first outside television broadcast of King George VI's coronation procession.

1949 The Russian blockade of Berlin ended after 11 months. It had cost the Allies $200m to fly in food and essential supplies.

1951 The first H-bomb test on Eniwetok Atoll in the mid-Pacific proved it was possible to destroy a city over 100 times the size of Hiroshima and Nagasaki.

1969 The minimum voting age was reduced to 18 years in Britain.

13 MAY

BORN THIS DAY

HISTORY

1717 Maria Theresa, Queen of Hungary and Bohemia, who reigned for 40 years, during which she made many changes both financial and cultural, and raised Austria to the status of a major power.

1828 Josephine (Elizabeth) Butler, English social reformer who campaigned for women's rights in the 1860s and 1870s, promoting education for women and the Married Women's Property Act.

ARTS

1842 Sir Arthur (Seymour) Sullivan, English composer associated with the librettist, W.S. Gilbert. Their 16 operettas include *The Gondoliers* and *The Pirates of Penzance*. He also composed the hymn, 'Onward Christian Soldiers'.

1882 Georges Braque, French Cubist painter who worked for six years with Picasso. He also designed sets for Diaghilev's ballets.

1907 Dame Daphne du Maurier (Lady Browning), granddaughter of novelist George, daughter of actor-manager Gerald, English novelist who is best known for her novel *Rebecca* (1938).

1927 Clive Barnes, English-born US drama critic of the *New York Post*; one of the 'butchers' who can make or break a Broadway production.

1940 Bruce Chatwin, English author whose novel *Utz* (1988), nominated for the Booker prize, was written while he had a period of remission from a rare bone marrow disease from which he died the following year.

ENTERTAINMENT

1941 Joe Brown, English actor and singer who was once in the backing band during Eddie Cochran's fateful 1960 UK tour.

1946 Tim Pigott-Smith, English actor who made a major debut in television's *The Jewel in the Crown* in 1984.

POP

1950 Stevie Wonder (Steveland Morris Hardaway), US singer who made his first Motown recording when he was 12 years old. The following year he had his first No. 1 ('Fingertips Pt.II') in the US charts. Other hits include 'Uptight' (1966), 'I Just Called To Say I Love You' (1984) which was five weeks in the UK chart at No. 1, three weeks as US No. 1.

SPORT

1914 Joe Louis (Joseph Louis Barrow), US world heavyweight boxing champion. Known as 'The Brown Bomber', he first won the title in 1937 and held it for 12 years. After 25 successful defences, he retired in 1949. He made the mistake of coming back out of retirement, and it was only in 1951, when Marciano knocked him out, that he hung up his gloves.

DIED THIS DAY

1835 John Nash, English architect and town planner. London's Regent's Park and Regent Street are two of his contributions.

1883 James Young, Scottish industrial chemist who was the first to produce paraffin oil and solid paraffin on a commercial scale.

1884 Cyrus Hall McCormick, US inventor of the mechanical harvester.

1930 Fridtjof Nansen, Norwegian Arctic explorer, zoologist, statesman, ambassador in London and Nobel Peace prize winner.

1961 Gary Cooper (Frank James Cooper), US film actor and twice Oscar winner.

ON THIS DAY

1607 The first permanent English settlement in America was established with the landing of soldiers from three ships on the Virginian coast at Jamestown.

1868 A team of Aboriginal cricketers arrived in England to play 47 matches. They preceded a white Australian team by more than ten years.

1981 Pope Paul II was shot in St Peter's Square by a Turkish gunman, Mehmet Ali Agca, witnessed by a crowd of 20,000 people. The Pope survived four bullets, and some bystanders were also injured.

1986 Legal history was made in Britain when Leo Abse, a member of parliament and a solicitor, appeared in proceedings in the High Court in his professional role, the first solicitor able to do so following changes in court rules.

14 MAY

National Day of Paraguay, marking this day, 1811, when she proclaimed her independence from Spain.

BORN THIS DAY

HISTORY

1905 Dr Hastings (Kamuzu) Banda, President of Malawi (formerly Nyasaland) from 1966, and Life President from 1971.

ARTS

1727 Thomas Gainsborough, English painter, who was a founder of the English School of portrait and landscape painting. He painted the famous of his time, including the popular *Blue Boy*, but preferred painting landscapes.

1885 Otto Klemperer, German conductor who became the chief conductor of the Los Angeles Orchestra from 1933 after fleeing Germany. From 1959, he became conductor of the New Philharmonia Orchestra of London. He went on to conduct at many great opera houses and with leading orchestras.

ENTERTAINMENT

1926 Eric Morecambe, English comedian, one half of Morecambe and Wise, who became not merely the top comedy duo in Britain, but a national institution. Their television shows attracted vast audiences and guest stars included many top stars such as André Previn and Glenda Jackson who was offered her first major comedy role as a result of being seen on the show.

1934 Sian Phillips, Welsh actress who has played many leading roles in classical and contemporary plays, the film *Goodbye Mr Chips* and the television serial, *I, Claudius*.

NAVIGATION

1940 Chay Blyth, English yachtsman who circumnavigated the world solo.

POP

1936 Bobby Darin (Robert Cassotto), US singer who had hits with 'Splish Splash' and 'Mack the Knife'.

JAZZ

1897 Sidney Bechet, US saxophonist, born in New Orleans where he played with many of the jazz greats. Acclaimed by classical and jazz musicians alike, he died on his 62nd birthday in 1959.

DIED THIS DAY

1610 Henry IV of France, assassinated by a Jesuit fanatic, François Ravailac.

1912 August Strindberg, Swedish playwright of *Miss Julie* (1888).

1925 Sir Henry Rider Haggard, English author of *King Solomon's Mines* (1885).

1936 Edmund Allenby, Viscount, British military commander.

ON THIS DAY

1643 Louis XIV, aged four, became King of France on the death of his father, Louis XIII. He reigned for 72 years.

1767 The British government imposed a tax on importing tea into America which would lead to the 'Boston Tea Party' and the start of the American War of Independence.

1796 Edward Jenner carried out his first successful vaccination against smallpox, inoculating a boy called Phipps with fluid from a pustule in the hand of a young woman, Sarah Nelmes, who had been infected by her master's cows.

1842 The first edition of the *London Illustrated News* was published.

1847 HMS *Driver* arrived back at Spithead, the first steamship to circumnavigate the world.

1856 The trial of William Palmer, doctor and poisoner began at the Old Bailey. Palmer's victims were poisoned with strychnine and included creditors, at least four of his 14 illegitimate children, his mother-in-law, his wife who had brought him a large dowry, and other relations. Palmer was found guilty and executed in his native Staffordshire.

1940 The British Local Defence Volunteers was formed. It would later become known as the Home Guard, with civilians providing a last-ditch defence against a possible German invasion.

1948 The state of Israel was born with David Ben-Gurion as its first Prime Minister and Chiam Weizman as President of the provisional government.

1948 Atlantic Records was founded by Ahmet Ertegun, son of the Turkish ambassador to the US. He nurtured many famous artists from Ray Charles and Aretha Franklin to rock stars Led Zeppelin, the Bee Gees and Mick Jagger.

1955 The Eastern bloc signed the Warsaw Pact.

1965 The field at Runnymede, the site of the signing of the Magna Carta, was dedicated by the Queen as a memorial to the late John F. Kennedy, US President.

1973 The first US space station *Skylab I* was launched, followed on the 25th by the crew to board and man the station.

1977 At the end of of his 1,000th professional football match, England international Bobby Moore retired.

1987 A state of emergency was declared in Fiji as troops led by Lt Col Sitveni Rabuka entered parliament. The conflict was a power struggle between native Fijians and the now larger Indian community who were still considered immigrants.

1989 Leading British theatre and film stars began a vigil at the site of the freshly excavated Rose Theatre on London's south bank, the only remains of an Elizabethan theatre where Shakespeare probably performed, now threatened by developers.

15 MAY

The Feast Day of Dympna, patron saint of the insane, thought to have been an Irish princess who was slain by her incestuous father.

BORN THIS DAY

HISTORY

1773 Prince Clemens Lothar Metternich, Prince of the Austrian Empire.

1981 Zara Phillips, daughter of Anne, the Princess Royal and Mark Phillips.

ARTS

1856 (Lyman) Frank Baum, US children's author, best remembered for *The Wonderful Wizard of Oz* (1900).

1890 Katherine Anne Porter, US short story writer and novelist, best known for *Ship of Fools* (1962).

1926 Anthony and Peter (Levin) Shaffer, English playwrights. Anthony is best known for his clever detective plays such as *Sleuth* made into a film (1972). Twin brother Peter has written *Five Finger Exercise* (1958), *Royal Hunt of the Sun* (1964) and *Equus* (1973), all of which have been filmed.

ENTERTAINMENT

1905 Joseph Cotton, US actor who started with Orson Welles's Mercury Theatre, performing on the radio. He was in the *War of the Worlds* broadcast (30.10.1938), and later starred with Katherine Hepburn on Broadway in *The Philadelphia Story* (1939). In 1941 he played a leading role in Welles's film masterpiece, *Citizen Kane*. He was also in *The Magnificent Ambersons* (1942) and *The Third Man* (1949).

1909 James Mason, English actor who qualified as an architect before changing his career. It was his twentieth film, *The Man in Grey* (1943), that truly established him as a star. He made numerous films, the best of which include *Odd Man Out* (1947), *Lolita* (1962) and *The Boys From Brazil* (1978).

SCIENCE

1859 Pierre Curie, French physicist who abandoned his own work to assist his wife Marie with her research into the nature of uranium rays in 1898. (*See* 7.11.1867)

POP

1948 Brian Eno, English singer and multi-instrumentalist, co-founder of Roxy Music, who also worked with David Bowie and Talking Heads.

1953 Mike Oldfield, English composer and multi-instrumentalist, best known for 'Tubular Bells' which was used for the film *The Exorcist*.

SPORT

1892 Jimmy Wilde, Welsh boxer known as the Mighty Atom, who became the British flyweight boxing champion.

1935 E(dward) R(alph) 'Ted' Dexter, former Sussex and England cricket captain, manager of the England cricket squad from 1988.

DIED THIS DAY

1833 Edmund Kean, English actor.

1886 Emily Elizabeth Dickinson, whose thousands of poems remained unpublished until after her death.

1895 Joseph Whitaker, English publisher of *Whitaker's Almanac* which first appeared in 1869.

1977 Herbert Wilcox, English film producer, husband of Dame Anna Neagle, who made many of her films.

1987 Rita Hayworth (Margarita Carmen) US actress and dancer.

ON THIS DAY

1718 The machine gun was patented by a London lawyer, James Puckle. He began to manufacture it in London in 1721.

MISSED! In 1800, James Hatfield attempted to assassinate George III at Drury Lane Theatre. The mad king had many enemies, but he survived another 20 years. In the US in 1972, 172 years later, a white gunman fired five shots at George Wallace, Governor of Alabama in Laurel, Maryland. Several others were also hit. Wallace survived this assassination attempt, but a bullet damaged the

spinal cord, paralysing him from the waist down.

1862 The first baseball stadium was opened at Union Grounds, Brooklyn.

1897 A Gay Lib society was formed in Munich by Max Spohr and others.

1918 The world's first regular airmail service began between New York and Washington, operated for the US Post Office by the US Army.

1928 The Australian Flying Doctor service was started by Dr Vincent Welsh, at Australian Inland Mission, Cloncurry in Queensland.

1929 In the first football international, England lost to Spain 4–3 in Madrid.

1930 The 11 passengers travelling on United Airlines tri-motor Boeing 80A from Oakland, California to Cheyenne, Wyoming were greeted by the world's first air hostess, Mrs Ellen Church, a Registered Nurse. (First British air hostess, *see* 16.5.1936.)

1940 Nylon stockings went on sale in the US. All competing brands went on sale simultaneously under an agreement between the manufacturers.

FAST AND MUCH FASTER In 1936 Amy Johnson arrived in England after a record-breaking 12-day 15-hour flight from London to Cape Town and back, while seven years later in 1941, Frank Whittle's jet-propelled Gloster E28/39 aircraft, Britain's first, made its first top secret flight from RAF Cranwell.

1957 Britain's first H-bomb was dropped on Christmas Island in the Indian Ocean. The effect of the radiation on some of the British soldiers who watched the test only came to light years later.

1963 Tottenham Hotspur beat Atletico Madrid 5–1 to become the first British winners of the European Winners Cup, and in 1977, Liverpool won the League Championship for a record tenth time.

1989 The Guardian Angels (British chapter), began patrolling selected London Underground trains after being established and trained by US leaders.

1990 Miss Whiplash, retired brothel madam Lindi St Clare, lost her 15-year battle against the Inland Revenue who demanded back taxes. She had appealed against them on the grounds that they would be living off immoral earnings.

16 MAY

BORN THIS DAY

ARTS

1892 Richard Tauber (Ernst Seiffert), Austrian tenor and conductor who made his first appearance in England in 1931 in Lehar's *Land of Smiles*. He settled in England where he appeared in other light operas.

1912 Studs Terkel, US writer and broadcaster who converted his tape recorded conversations to produce books such as *Hard Times* about the Depression, and *The Good War* about the Second World War.

ENTERTAINMENT

1905 Henry Fonda, US actor whose career started when asked by a family friend (Marlon Brando's mother) to play the leading role in an amateur production. It gave him the taste for acting that would lead eventually to Broadway and Hollywood. His films include *The Grapes of Wrath* (1940) and *Mr Roberts* (1955) which he also played on Broadway. His last film, in which his daughter Jane also starred, was *On Golden Pond* (1980) which won him a posthumous Oscar.

1919 Liberace (Wladsiu Valentino), flamboyant US pianist and entertainer who commanded a huge following at his peak. In 1956, he sued the *Daily Mirror* during one British tour for calling him 'the biggest sentimental vomit of all time'. He was awarded £8000 damages.

1936 Roy Hudd, English comedian, actor, writer and music hall enthusiast.

1955 Hazel O'Connor, English singer and actress who starred in *Breaking Glass* (1980).

INVENTION

1831 David Edward Hughes, English-born US inventor of the telegraph typewriter (teleprinter) in 1855, and the microphone in 1878. His vast fortune was left to London hospitals when he died.

JAZZ

1913 Woody Herman (Woodrow Charles) US jazz clarinettist, and bandleader when he was only 23. Soloists with his famous Herd band included Lester Young and Stan Getz.

SPORT

1955 Olga Korbut, waif-like USSR gymnast whose technique and showmanship made her a major star at the 1972 Munich Olympics. She won two gold medals and one silver.

DIED THIS DAY

1703 Charles Perrault, French fairy-tale writer whose stories include *Sleeping Beauty* and *Red Riding Hood*.

1984 Irwin Shaw, US author of *The Young Lions*, among others.

1990 Sammy Davis Jr, US entertainer from age five, from throat cancer. When asked what his golf handicap was, he quipped, 'Who needs a handicap? I'm a one-eyed coloured Jew.'

1990 Jim Henson, US creator of the Muppets.

ON THIS DAY

1763 Dr Johnson and James Boswell met for the first time, at Tom Davie's bookshop in Russell Street.

1770 The Dauphin of France (later Louis XVI) married Marie Antoinette.

1888 Emile Berliner gave the first demonstration of flat disc recording and reproduction before members of the Franklin Institute, Philadelphia.

1929 The first Academy Awards ceremony was held – the name 'Oscar' was only coined in 1931 – and went to *Wings* for Best film, to Emil Jannings for Best Actor, and to Janet Gaynor for Best Actress.

1936 The first British air hostess, Daphne Kearley, flew from Croydon to Le Bourget.

1938 The Women's Voluntary Service (WVS) was started by the Marchioness of Reading. It was granted a royal charter in 1966.

1943 The famous 'Dam Busters' raid by the 617 Squadron of Lancaster bombers led by Wing Commander Guy Gibson breached the Mohne, Eder and Sorpe dams in Germany using the 'bouncing' bombs developed by Dr Barnes Wallis. The Eder was Europe's largest dam, and massive damage and loss of life were caused by flood water, as well as a serious loss of hydroelectric power for the German industrial area of the Rhine.

1952 The British parliament voted in favour of equal pay for women.

1956 Jim Laker of Surrey took all ten Australian wickets for 88 in 46 overs at the Oval, London.

1975 Junko Takei from Japan became the first woman to scale Everest.

1980 Dr George Nickopoulos was indicted on 14 counts of overprescribing drugs to Elvis Presley, Jerry Lee Lewis and others.

1983 Wheel clamps were first used in London on cars parked in the Chelsea, Kensington and Westminster areas.

1989 The first successful hole-in-the-heart operation was performed on an adult, Eileen Molyneaux, aged 66, from Kent at the Brook Hospital, Greenwich.

1990 Van Gogh's *Portrait of Dr Gachet* was sold at Christies, New York for $82.5 million (£50m) – the most expensive painting in the world.

17 MAY

National Day of Norway.

BORN THIS DAY

HISTORY

1900 Ayatollah Ruhollah Khomeini, Iranian religious leader who was exiled for opposing the Shah in 1964. When the Shah was deposed in 1979, he returned to impose a strict fundamentalist Islamic republic.

ARTS

1866 Erik (Alfred Leslie) Satie, French composer born of Scottish parents. He became a café pianist, and wrote music for the music hall before producing his delightful and influential *Gymnopedies*, *Sarabandes* and his ballet *Parade*.

1918 Birgit Nilsson, Swedish opera singer, who made her debut in 1946. The following year she became a member of the Royal Swedish Opera. Her international career has shown her to be outstanding in Wagnerian roles.

1935 Dennis Potter, English playwright, author and journalist who has established himself as a major writer using television as his main medium for plays such as the *The Singing Detective*, *Blackeyes* and the award-winning *Pennies from Heaven*.

ENTERTAINMENT

1911 Maureen O'Sullivan, Irish-born US actress who was Jane to Johnny Weissmuller's Tarzan in six movies. In between, she was in films such as *The Thin Man* (1934) and *Pride and Prejudice* (1940).

1936 Dennis Hopper, US actor and director (and co-author) with Peter Fonda of *Easy Rider* (1969) which opened the Hollywood floodgates for 'youth' films.

1955 Grace Jones, Jamaican-born US singer whose hits have included 'Slave to the Rhythm' and 'La Vie en Rose', but who is equally well known for striking the late Russell Harty during a live interview on his BBC chatshow.

SCIENCE

1749 Edward Jenner, English surgeon and pioneer of vaccination. In 1775 he began examining cowpox, convinced it could be a protection against smallpox (*see* 14.5.1796). Besides the many honours he received, he was also given grants of £30,000 to continue his research.

1836 Joseph Norman Lockyer, English astronomer and co-discoverer of helium, which he detected in the sun's chromosphere.

SPORT

1956 'Sugar' Ray Leonard, US boxer, and world champion at welterweight, light-middleweight and middleweight.

DIED THIS DAY

1163 Héloïse, the secret wife of Abelard, finally laid to rest in the cemetery of Père Lachaise in Paris in 1817. Not long after, the body of Abelard (who died on 11.4.1142) was reburied next to her.

1510 Sandro Botticelli (Alessandro di Mariano dei Filipepi), Italian painter.

1935 Paul Abraham Dukas, French composer of *The Sorcerer's Apprentice* (1897).

ON THIS DAY

1620 The first merry-go-round is referred to in records as being set up at a fair in Philippolis, Turkey.

1861 The first package holiday arranged by Thomas Cook set off for Paris. A party from a Working Men's club went with coupons for pre-paid hotel accommodation inclusive of meals.

1890 The first weekly comic paper, *Comic Cuts*, was published by Alfred Harmsworth, in London.

1900 Mafeking, a small town in the northern Cape was relieved after a 217-day siege by the Boers. Robert Baden-Powell became a national hero for refusing to surrender and for the innovative way he kept spirits up during the siege. The man who later started the Scout movement had, in retrospect, achieved a trivial success and should never have been trapped in Mafeking in the first place.

1916 The Daylight-Saving Act ('Summer Time') was passed in Britain.

1937 Dizzy Gillespie was featured for the first time in a recording made in New York by Teddy Hill and the NBC Orchestra of 'King Porter Stomp'.

1938 The Marquess of Bute sold half the city of Cardiff for £20m in the biggest British property deal ever. It included theatres, farmlands, villages, 20,000 houses, 1,000 shops and 250 pubs.

1969 Tom McClean from Dublin rowed from Newfoundland to Blacksod Bay, Co. Mayo, completing the first transatlantic solo crossing in a rowing boat.

1978 Charlie Chaplin's coffin turned up ten miles from its original Swiss cemetery, after being stolen on 2 March.

18 MAY

BORN THIS DAY

HISTORY

1868 Nicholas II, the last Russian Tsar, who was forced to abdicate at the start of the Revolution.

1872 Bertrand (Arthur William) Russell, 3rd Earl Russell, Welsh-born philosopher and mathematician who was imprisioned during the First World War for his outspoken pacifism, where he wrote his *Introduction to Mathematical Philosophy* (1919). He won the Nobel Literature prize in 1950 and was one of the founders of the Committee of 100 advocating nuclear disarmament.

1883 Walter Adolph Gropius, German architect who was a founder of the Bauhaus in Berlin; a movement that tried to combine all the visual arts in a single concept. When the Nazis came to power he left for the US, where he became professor of architecture at Harvard.

1920 Pope John Paul II (Karol Jozef Wojtyla), the Polish archbishop who became the first non-Italian pope in 450 years.

ARTS

1919 Dame Margot Fonteyn de Arias (Peggy Hookham), English ballerina who, in 1934, joined the Vic-Wells (which became the Sadler's Wells, then Royal) Ballet. She danced most of the major roles and her partnership near the end of her dancing years with Nureyev produced legendary performances. She married Roberto Emilia Arias, the Panamanian ambassador, in London in 1955.

ENTERTAINMENT

1897 Frank Capra, US screenwriter, director and producer, born in Italy. He made films such as *It Happened One Night* (1934), *Mr Deeds Goes to Town* (1936) and *You Can't Take It With You* (1938), all Oscar winners.

1912 Richard Brooks, US film director and screenwriter of *Key Largo* (1948), *The Blackboard Jungle* (1955) and *Elmer Gantry* (1960). He married Jean Simmons in 1961.

1912 Perry Como, US crooner with hits in the 50s including 'Magic Moments' and 'Wanted'. He appeared in a number of films, and *The Perry Como Television Show* in the US was an important showcase for new talent.

SPORT

1909 Fred Perry, probably the finest English tennis player ever, winner of the Wimbledon men's singles title three times in the mid 30s, and the US and Australian Open. He later established himself as an indispensable member of the BBC tennis commentating team.

1942 N.P. 'Nobby' Stiles, English footballer who was in the victorious England World Cup team in 1966.

DIED THIS DAY

1909 George Meredith, English novelist and poet.

1909 Isaac Albéniz, Spanish pianist and composer.

1911 Gustav Mahler, Czech-born Austrian composer and conductor.

1917 John Nevil Maskelyne, English illusionist who performed his magic for 31 years in London's Egyptian Hall. He made major contributions to the conjuror's repertoire and effectively exposed spiritualist frauds prevalent at the time.

1981 William Saroyan, US poet, playwright and novelist who is best remembered for his play *The Time of Your Life* (1939).

ON THIS DAY

1804 Napoleon Bonaparte was proclaimed Emperor of France.

1827 William Corder murdered Maria Marten in the Red Barn, Polstead, Sussex. Corder wanted to break off his affair with the mole catcher's daughter and pretended to arrange their marriage. They met secretly in the Red Barn where he killed her. The murder became the subject of ballads and melodramas.

1830 Edwin Budding of Gloucestershire signed an agreement for the manufacture of his invention, the lawn mower. The first customer was Regent's Park Zoo.

1901 Alexandra Palace in London was opened to the public.

1910 Halley's Comet passed the sun, and despite predictions of tidal waves, plagues and other disasters, nothing happened.

1936 Jasmine Bligh and Elizabeth Cowell became the BBC's first women announcers.

1951 Britain's first four-engined jet bomber, the Vickers Valiant, made its maiden flight.

1953 In London, the police exhumed the body of Beryl Evans and her baby following the arrest of Christie. Timothy Evans, who once shared the house with the mass-murderer, had been found guilty and hanged for the murder of his wife and child. At Christie's trial the evidence suggested that Evans might have been innocent.

1955 The first Wimpy Bar opened in London, beginning the fast-food invasion.

1960 Real Madrid won their fifth consecutive European Cup beating Eintracht Frankfurt 7–3 at Hampden Park, Glasgow.

1969 Britain's champion motor racing driver, Graham Hill, won his fifth and record-breaking Monaco Grand Prix.

1979 Karen Silkwood, a worker in a US nuclear plant won $10.5m for suffering nuclear contamination.

19 MAY

The Feast Day of Dunstan, the Anglo-Saxon saint and Archbishop of Canterbury who died in 908.

BORN THIS DAY

HISTORY

1879 William Waldorf Astor, 2nd Viscount, English politician and proprietor of the *Observer* newspaper, whose American wife Nancy became the first woman to take her seat in the House of Commons.

1890 Ho Chi Minh, 'the Enlightener', North Vietnam revolutionary leader who fought against the French for independence and became President and Prime Minister in 1954.

1926 Malcolm X (Malcolm Little), US Black Muslim leader who split from the Black Muslims to form his own group in 1964. He was assassinated the following year.

1933 Dr Edward de Bono, born in Malta, English doctor of medicine who developed thinking as a curriculum subject in schools. His concept of lateral thinking boiled down to thinking around a problem instead of confronting it, and attracted a vast public for his books and study courses.

ARTS

1848 Dame Nellie Melba (Helen Porter Mitchell), Australian operatic soprano whose marriage enabled her to further her career by coming to London and Paris to study. She became one of the world's leading singers, particularly in demand to sing Donizetti's 'Lucia'. Peach Melba – half a peach served with vanilla ice-cream, Melba Sauce and wafer thin Melba toast – is named after her.

ENTERTAINMENT

1924 Sandy Wilson, English composer, lyricist and librettist of the musical *The Boyfriend*.

1926 David Jacobs, pioneer British DJ.

1939 James Fox, English actor, brother of Edward, who began his career as a child actor. In the 70s, he abandoned acting to join a religious sect. His films include *The Servant* (1963) and *Performance* (1970).

1942 Robert Kilroy-Silk, English television presenter, former Labour member of parliament.

1953 Victoria Wood, English comedienne, writer and songwriter whose regular and often award-winning appearances on both stage and television have established her as a major talent.

POP

1945 Pete Townshend, English guitarist and guitar smasher with the Who. He wrote 'My Generation', which became one of their biggest hits.

DIED THIS DAY

1536 Anne Boleyn, second wife of Henry VIII, mother of Elizabeth I, who was accused of incest with her brother Lord Rochford, and adultery with four commoners. She was beheaded at Tower Green, allowing Henry to marry Jane Seymour the following day.

1715 Charles Montague, 1st Earl of Halifax, politician, poet and founder of the Bank of England.

1795 James Boswell, biographer of Dr Johnson.

1864 Nathaniel Hawthorne, US novelist and short-story writer, author of *The Scarlet Letter* (1850).

1898 William Ewart Gladstone, British statesman, who was Liberal Prime Minister on four occasions.

1935 T(homas) E(dward) Lawrence, 'Lawrence of Arabia', died six days after a motor cycle crash in a Dorset lane.

1954 Charles (Edward) Ives, US composer and founder of modern US music.

1958 Ronald Colman, English actor.

1971 (Frederick) Ogden Nash, ingenious US humorous versifier.

1984 Sir John Betjeman, Poet Laureate from 1972.

1987 Wilberforce, tabby cat, resident at No. 10 Downing Street, originally invited to stay to solve the mice problem, who shared the premises with four prime ministers during his 14 years.

ON THIS DAY

1657 Devoted entirely to advertising, *Publick Advertiser* first appeared in London with classified advertisements.

1802 Napoleon instituted the *Légion d'honneur* to be awarded for civil and military distinction of the highest order.

1900 Tonga, 'The Friendly Islands', were annexed by Britain.

1909 The Simplon rail tunnel between Switzerland and Italy was officially opened.

1958 Harold Pinter's *The Birthday Party* opened in London. It initially flopped, but was later recognized as a major development in British drama.

1974 Timothy Davey, a London schoolboy, now 17, was released from a Turkish jail. (*See* 1.3.1972)

1980 The previously dormant Mount St Helens in the north west US, erupted killing eight people and sending ash 60,000 feet up into the air which drifted hundreds of miles.

1982 Sophia Loren, jailed for one month for tax evasion, started her sentence in a Naples women's prison.

1989 A woman about to be cross-examined on allegations of fraud at Cardiff Crown Court had a note passed to the judge which read: 'Your honour, I, Patricia Morgan, have superglued my mouth to draw the public's attention to the mis-trial and injustice in this court.'

20 MAY

BORN THIS DAY

HISTORY

1364 Sir Henry Percy, known as Harry Hotspur, supporter of Henry IV, who was the model for Shakespeare's Hotspur in *Henry IV*.

1806 John Stuart Mill, English philosopher, political economist and radical reformer. His father taught him from a tender age. He was proficient at Greek by the age of three, arithmetic at eight and logic at 12. Best remembered for his essay *On Liberty* (1859), which proposed a form of liberal socialism and women's suffrage.

1818 William George Fargo, US founder, with Henry Wells and Daniel Dunning of Wells Fargo which carried freight swiftly west beyond Buffalo. Through its success, he was invited to become the President of the newly-formed American Express Company in 1868.

1881 Wladyslaw Sikorski, Polish statesman and soldier who was Commander-in-Chief of the Free Polish forces during the Second World War and Premier of the Polish government in exile in London, from 1940.

1915 Moshe Dayan, Israeli military commander, statesman and archaeologist who led Israel's civilian army to victory in the 'Six-day War' (1967) and recaptured Jerusalem to turn it into a free city.

ARTS

1759 William Thornton, US architect of the Capitol building, Washington.

1799 Honoré de Balzac, French novelist who would write for 15 to 18 hours each day, producing 85 novels in 20 years. His main work, *The Human Comedy*, which was to cover every aspect of contemporary French life in 143 volumes, was never completed. Always burdened by debt, he earned only a modest income for all his labours.

1904 Margery (Louise) Allingham, English crime novelist who first created the amateur detective, Albert Campion in *The Crime at Black Dudley* (1928).

ENTERTAINMENT

1908 James Stewart, US actor whose hesitant drawl made him universally popular in films such as *Mr Deeds Goes to Town*, *The Philadelphia Story* (1940) for which he won an Oscar, and

Anatomy of a Murder (1959). He was in both the film and stage productions of *Harvey*, about an invisible rabbit – an appropriate subject for someone who was a talented amateur magician.

1945 Cher (Cherilyn Sakasian La Pierre) US singer, songwriter and actress who first made her name with Sonny Bono as Sonny and Cher with hits including 'I Got You Babe' (1965). She was nominated for an Oscar for her role in *Moonstruck* (1987).

SCIENCE

1537 Hieronymous Fabricius (Girolamo Fabriel), Italian anatomist and physician who had Harvey as one of his pupils at Padua, where he was professor of anatomy.

POP

1944 Joe Cocker, English singer and drummer, first with the Grease Band, then on his own, producing the LP *Sheffield Steel.*

DIED THIS DAY

1506 Christopher Columbus, Italian navigator who made four voyages of discovery, in poverty in Valladolid, Spain.

1834 Marie Joseph Gilbert de Motier, Marquis de Lafayette, French soldier and statesman.

1956 Sir Max (Henry Maximilian) Beerbohm, English caricaturist and writer, author of *Zuleika Dobson* (1912).

1975 Dame (Jocelyn) Barbara Hepworth, English sculptor, killed in a fire in her studio at St Ives, Cornwall.

ON THIS DAY

1347 Rome was established as a republic by Cola di Rienza, tribune of the people who had driven out the nobles and senators.

1498 Vasco da Gama arrive at Calicut, southern India, after discovering a route via the Cape of Storms, later named Cape of Good Hope, Southern Africa.

1777 A pleasure craft launched on Yorkshire's River Foss was the first iron boat in the world, reported ten years before the official first iron boat *Trial*.

1867 Queen Victoria laid the foundation stone for the Royal Albert Hall.

1882 The first performance of Ibsen's *Ghosts* was staged, not in Norway, but in Chicago, to an audience of Scandinavian immigrants.

1895 Income tax was declared unconstitutional in the US.

1913 The first Chelsea Flower Show in the grounds of the Royal Hospital was held, attracting around 200,000 visitors. The show started in 1827, moving to larger venues until it settled in Chelsea.

1939 Pan-American Airways started regular commercial flights between the US and Europe.

1941 German airborne troops invaded Crete.

1956 The US dropped the first H-bomb over Bikini Atoll in a test.

1959 The first person to be arrested through an identikit picture was Guy Trebert in Paris.

1970 In the World Cup, Bobby Charlton scored his record 49th goal for England in the match against Columbia.

1979 Helen Smith, a 23-year-old nurse from Leeds working in Jedda, was found dead having apparently fallen from the sixth floor balcony of a flat where an illegal drinks party was being held by British surgeon Richard Arnot and his wife, Penny. Helen's father, ex-policeman Ron, was convinced it was murder and began a personal – some say obsessional – pursuit of the truth.

1980 Quebec voted against a move to take the French-speaking province out of the federation.

1987 Harvey Proctor, member of the British parliament, admitted sex sessions with rent boys.

21 MAY

BORN THIS DAY

HISTORY

1763 Joseph Fouché, Duc d'Otranto, French revolutionary who became head of the police after proving himself a bloodthirsty member of the National Convention, voting for the execution of Louis XVI during the Revolution.

1780 Elizabeth (Gurney) Fry, English Quaker and prison reformer who visited Newgate Prison, London in 1813 where over 300 women and their children were living in filthy, overcrowded conditions. From this time, she devoted herself to improving conditions, providing hostels for the homeless and establishing various charitable organizations to help the poor.

1884 Sir Claude John Eyre Auchinleck, English field marshal who was replaced during the North African campaign against Rommel despite having paved the way to the success of El Alamein. He was sent as Commander-in-Chief to India and Pakistan in 1947.

1930 Malcolm Fraser, Australian Liberal politician and millionaire sheep farmer, and Prime Minister from 1975–83.

ARTS

1471 Albrecht Dürer, German painter and engraver who drew his own portrait looking into a mirror when he was 13, creating the earliest known self-portrait in European art. A major German artist, he eventually became court painter for Charles V.

1688 Alexander Pope, English poet and satirist who wrote *The Rape of the Lock* (1712). He also translated Homer's *Iliad* and *Odyssey*.

1844 Henri Rousseau, French painter who was known as 'Le Douanier' as he was a customs officer. His primitive, naïve paintings, now in many major galleries and museums, are exotic landscapes with wild animals and surrealistic portraits, all vividly coloured.

1916 Harold Robbins (Francis Kane), US best-selling author of novels including *The Carpet Baggers* (1961).

SCIENCE

NOBELMEN Born 1860, Willem Einthoven, Dutch physiologist who invented the string galvonometer which advanced the use of electrocardiography. He won the Nobel prize for Medicine in 1924. Nobel Peace prize winner in 1965 was Andrei (Dmitrievich) Sakharov, Soviet physicist, born 1921, known as the father of the Russian H-bomb. A civil rights campaigner, he was sent into exile in Gorky in 1980, finally freed in 1986.

JAZZ

1904 (Thomas) 'Fats' Waller, US pianist and composer, best known for 'Ain't Misbehavin'' and 'Honeysuckle Rose'.

DIED THIS DAY

1542 Hernando de Soto, Spanish explorer of South America and Mississippi area where he died from a fever. To hide his body from hostile Indians, it was lowered into the river he had discovered.

1619 Hieronymous Fabricius, Italian physician, died one day after his 82nd birthday.

1786 Carl Wilhelm Scheele, Swedish chemist who, independent of Priestley, showed that the atmosphere consisted of two main gases.

1865 Christian Thomsen, Danish archaeologist who divided human prehistory into various ages, from Stone to Iron.

1926 Ronald (Arthur Annesley) Firbank, English writer, author of *Valmouth* (1918).

1929 Lord Roseberry, 5th Earl, Liberal Prime Minister, 1894–5.

1935 Hugo de Vries, Dutch botanist.

ON THIS DAY

1471 Henry VI, King of England was murdered in the Tower of London where he had been imprisoned by Edward.

1502 The remote island of St Helena in the Atlantic, was discovered by the Portuguese explorer, Joao de Nova.

1804 The cemetery of Père Lachaise, the burial ground of the famous, opened in Paris.

1840 New Zealand was proclaimed a British colony.

1856 The first eight-hour working day was achieved by Australian stonemasons in Victoria.

1894 Queen Victoria opened the Manchester Ship Canal.

1904 FIFA – the Football Federation's international body – was established.

1916 The clocks and watches in Britain went forward one hour for the first daylight-saving day.

1924 Two rich Chicago teenagers, Richard Loeb and Nathan Leopold, murdered 14-year-old Bobby Franks and pretended to be kidnappers, demanding a ransom. They were eventually arrested and went on trial in July in a sensational 'murder for kicks' trial. Both were sentenced to 99 years. Loeb died in a prison brawl in 1936, Leopold served 33 years before being paroled in 1958. He died in Puerto Rico in 1971.

SOLO FLYERS In 1927, 'World acclamation goes to Lindbergh for epochal non-stop flight to Paris' ran the headline of one US newspaper which summed up the excitement created by Charles Lindbergh's flight from Roosevelt Field, Long Island, New York to Le Bourget airfield, Paris in 33 hours 30 minutes in his monoplane, *The Spirit of St Louis*. He won $25,000, and became an international hero. Then, appropriately, in 1932, Amelia Earhart landed in Londonderry, Ireland having flown solo from Newfoundland in just under 15 hours, a record solo transatlantic flight.

1966 Cassius Clay (Muhammad Ali) ended Henry Cooper's hopes of winning the world heavyweight crown for Britain, in Round 6, in London.

1967 A fire at the Brussels department

store, L'Innovation, killed 322 people.

1979 Elton John became the first rock star to perform in the USSR with a concert in Leningrad, totally sold out. He ended with the Beatles' 'Back In The USSR'.

22 MAY

BORN THIS DAY

HISTORY

1874 Dr Daniel François Malan, architect of South Africa's apartheid policy, which he introduced when he became Premier in 1948. He first instituted the Group Areas Act which divided the country into separate residential areas for different races, black and white.

1880 Sir Ernest Oppenheimer, South African mining industrialist and philanthropist who formed the Anglo-American Corporation of South Africa in 1917 which by the 1950s controlled 95 per cent of the world's diamond industry.

1943 Betty Williams, Northern Irish peace campaigner and joint Nobel prize winner with Mairead Corrigan, founders of the Ulster Peace Movement.

ARTS

1813 (Wilhelm) Richard Wagner, German composer who was admired blindly by some, and greatly critized by others. His operas include *The Flying Dutchman* (1843), the *Ring* (*Walkure*, *Siegfried*, *Gotterdammerung* and the *Rheingold*) in 1836.

1859 Sir Arthur Conan Doyle, Scottish-born novelist of Irish parents, who created the detective Sherlock Holmes in *A Study in Scarlet* (1887). He wrote several historical novels which have been completely overshadowed by the success of his fictional detective who he tried to 'kill off', but had to bring back in *The Return of Sherlock Holmes*.

1907 Georges Remi, better known as Hergé, Belgian cartoonist and creator of 'Tintin' when he was 21. The adventures are printed in 30 languages.

ENTERTAINMENT

1907 Laurence (Kerr) Olivier (Lord Olivier), English actor, producer and director, considered to be the most dynamic, versatile actor of this century. His films, *Henry V* (1944) and *Hamlet* (1948) collected a crop of Oscars. His stage, screen and television performances spanning a long and illustrious career were rewarded by his being made a peer of the realm, the only actor ever to be so honoured.

1924 Charles Aznavour (Shanour Varenagh Aznavourian), French singer, songwriter and actor, of an Armenian father. He had a major hit in 1974 with 'She' and films include *Shoot the Piano Player* (1960).

1931 Kenny Ball, English jazz trumpeter and bandleader.

INVENTION

1783 William Sturgeon, English shoemaker's apprentice who became a physicist and built the first moving-coil galvanometer and the first practical electromagnet.

SPORT

1946 George Best, highly talented Irish footballer who played for Manchester United, who also had a talent for self-destruction which put an end to his career. He was frequently in trouble with referees and in his private life.

DIED THIS DAY

337 Constantine the Great, Roman emperor who converted to Christianity.

1885 Victor (Marie) Hugo, French author of *Les Misérables*.

1932 Augusta, Lady Gregory, Irish poet, playwright and co-founder of the Abbey Theatre.

1972 Cecil Day-Lewis, Poet Laureate from 1968 until his death.

1990 Major Pat Reid, author of *The Colditz Story* (1952) about his experiences as the escape officer at the infamous German war prison.

1990 Max Wall (Maxwell George Lorimer), the last of the great British music hall clowns, who excelled in Beckett's *Waiting for Godot*.

ON THIS DAY

1455 The Lancastrians defeated the Yorkists in the first battle in the War of the Roses, at St Albans.

1795 The Scottish explorer, Mungo Park, set sail on his first voyage to Africa which he would relate in his book *Travels in the Interior of Africa*.

1908 The Wright brothers patented their flying machine, and the following year, on 23 May, the British Aeronautical Society presented them with its gold medal for achievement.

1915 The worst rail disaster in Britain took place when a troop train collided with a passenger train at Gretna Green in Scotland, killing 227 people.

1927 The world's first 'open plan' zoo, Whipsnade, opened in Bedfordshire.

1972 Richard Nixon became the first US President to visit Russia, where he signed a pact with Leonid Brezhnev to reduce the risk of military confrontation. This day, one year later, Nixon admitted the Watergate cover-up by the White House following the Senate Select committee's hearings which began on the 17th. (On 30 May, 1975 he was warned he could be impeached for not surrendering the Watergate tapes.)

1981 Peter William Sutcliffe known as the Yorkshire Ripper, was found guilty at the Old Bailey of the murder of 13 women and the attempted murder of seven others. A plea of insanity was dismissed and he was sentenced to 30 years minimum and sent to Parkhurst. In 1984, he was transferred to Broadmoor suffering from paranoid schizophrenia.

1990 New Zealand yacht *Steinlager 2* captained by Peter Blake, won the Whitbread Round the World Race. New Zealanders also came second and third. (*See also* 28.5.1990)

23 MAY

BORN THIS DAY

HISTORY

1848 Otto Lilienthal, German aviation pioneer who built gliders and other heavier-than-air flying machines based on bird flight. He inspired the Wright brothers by his many short unpowered flights, one which ended in his death.

ARTS

1795 Sir Charles Barry, English architect who designed the Houses of Parliament.

1799 Thomas Hood, English poet, journalist and humorist who wrote *Song of the Shirt*. He produced his annuals such as *Whims and Oddities*, featuring 'picture-puns' which he first devised, and later *The Gem*.

ENTERTAINMENT

1883 Douglas Fairbanks (Douglas Elton Ullman), US actor who became an established Broadway star before being invited to Hollywood. Later he formed his own company and, after marrying Mary Pickford, they joined with Chaplin and others to form United Artists. He and Mary separated in 1933 and later divorced. His films include *The Black Pirate* (1926).

1890 Herbert Marshall, English actor, equally successful in the US where he appeared in *The Razor's Edge* (1946) and *The Secret Garden* (1949).

MUSIC MAKERS In 1906, Libby Holman, US torch singer with a dark sultry voice who was the first to sing 'Body and Soul', 'Something to Remember You By' and 'You and the Night and the Music'. In 1910, Artie Shore (Arthur Jacob Arshawsky), US jazz clarinettist who recorded 'Begin the Beguine' in 1938. Humphrey Lyttleton, English trumpet player, band leader and journalist was also born this day, 1921, and in 1934, Richard Moog, US inventor of the Moog synthesizer.

1928 Nigel Davenport, English actor with a long list of credits in the theatre, in films such as *A Taste of Honey* (1961) and *A Man for All Seasons* (1966) and on television, where he was in the long-running *Howard's Way* playing an aristocratic tycoon.

1928 Rosemary Clooney, US singer and actress who had a big hit with 'Come-on-a-my-House' before appearing in films such as *White Christmas* (1954). She later suffered from mental problems from which she eventually recovered.

1933 Joan Collins, English actress whose most popular films were *The Stud* (1978) and *The Bitch* (1979) until Hollywood offered her the role of Alexis in *Dynasty* to adorn television screens in a multitude of countries.

SCIENCE

1707 Carl Linnaeus (Carl Linne), Swedish botanist who was the founder of modern botany, producing major works on classification of the species.

1734 Franz Mesmer, Austrian physician, who developed the technique of 'mesmerism' or hypnosis. His demonstrations in Paris caused a sensation and brought offers of vast sums of money to reveal his secret, which he refused.

SPORT

1918 Denis Compton, English international cricketer and footballer, one of the stars of England's post-war cricket fortunes, scoring over 100 centuries. His batting played an important part in England regaining the Ashes in 1953.

1951 Anatoly Karpov, Russian chess champion, and former world champion.

DIED THIS DAY

1498 Girolamo Savonarola, Italian religious and political reformer, strangled and burnt at the stake.

1783 James Otis, American lawyer and leader of the resistance against the British.

1868 Kit (Christopher) Carson, American frontiersman.

1906 Henrik (Johan) Ibsen, Norwegian playwright of *Hedda Gabler* (1890).
1925 Sir Edward Hulton, British publishing magnate, after a fall from a penny-farthing bicycle.
1937 John D(avison) Rockefeller, US multimillionaire, monopolist and philanthropist.
1945 Heinrich Himmler, Hitler's Minister of the Interior, by suicide.
1960 Georges Claude, French engineer and devisor of a process for liquefying air.
1990 (Cuthbert) Ted Tinling, English dress designer, best known for his creations for tennis stars.
1990 Rocky Graziano, US boxer and world middleweight champion (1946–8).

ON THIS DAY

1533 Henry VIII divorced Catherine of Aragon to marry Anne Boleyn, wife number two. The result was a break with the church in Rome despite Henry's title as 'Protector of the Faith'.
1701 'Captain' William Kidd, Scottish privateer-turned-pirate, was hanged with three others at London's Execution Docks.
1706 Marlborough defeated the French at the Battle of Ramillies in Belgium, the British allied with the Dutch and Danish armies.
1797 A cartoon by Gillray was published which gave the Bank of England its nickname, 'The Old Lady of Threadneedle Street'.
1887 The French crown jewels went on sale and raised six million francs.
1901 Gaetano Brecci, assassin of Italian King Humbert, committed suicide in a Rome prison.

GETTING THEIR MAN ... AND WOMAN In 1873, the men who always get their man, The North West Mounted Police were formed in Canada. In 1920, they became the Royal Canadian Mounted Police. In 1934, Bonnie (Parker) and Clyde (Baron), the young US outlaws, died in a hail of bullets on a lonely stretch of road in Louisiana where they were trapped by the police. During their four-year partnership, they killed at least 12 people as they robbed banks, petrol stations and diners.

1948 The *Empire Windrush* sailed from Jamaica with the first West Indian immigrants to help with Britain's severe manpower shortage following the Second World War.
1960 Adolf Eichmann, Nazi wanted for war atrocities, was found living in Argentina under the name Ricardo Klement by an Israeli kidnap squad. Assisted by the Argentine secret service, they flew him out on an El Al Britannia flight to Tel Aviv this night to face trial in Israel.
1988 Possibly the first underwater marriage took place; two Danish tourists married on an underwater reef in Mauritius. Fleming Koch and Nina Tolgard used divers language to make their vows to a Mauritian civil servant conducting the service in a glass-bottomed boat. The couple's diving instructor served as the underwater witness.

24 MAY

BORN THIS DAY

HISTORY

1743 Jean Paul Marat, Swiss-born French revolutionary leader, doctor and journalist who won the support of the Paris mob. He had many enemies and was once forced to hide in the sewers where he contracted a painful skin disease which he found could only be eased by sitting in a bath, which is where he did most of his writing and where he was finally murdered. (*See* 13.7.1793)

1819 Victoria, Queen of England on the death of William IV in 1837 and Empress of India in 1876. She married Prince Albert in 1840 and had four sons and five daughters. After Albert's death in 1861, she went into virtual retirement which stirred up resentment with some sections of the population; at one time republicanism threatened. She returned to public life for her diamond jubilee (1897).

1870 Jan Christian Smuts, South African soldier, statesman and Prime Minister who studied at Cambridge. He was a Boer commander in the Cape during the conflict with Britain. He worked for reconciliation between English-speaking and Afrikaaner communities, and was Prime Minister from 1919–24 and again during the Second World War.

ARTS

1855 Sir Arthur Wing Pinero, English playwright who is best remembered for *The Second Mrs Tanqueray* (1893), and *Trelawney of the Wells* (1898) but he wrote around 50 plays and was one of the most popular playwrights of his time.

1928 William Trevor (Cox), Irish novelist, short story writer and playwright, author of *The Old Boys* (1964). Many of his short stories were adapted for television, some in his collection *Lovers of Their Time* (1979).

1932 Arnold Wesker, English playwright who scored a notable success with his early plays, *Chicken Soup with Barley* (1957) and *Roots* (1959).

SCIENCE

1686 Gabriel Daniel Fahrenheit, German physicist who invented the mercury thermometer. He fixed the freezing point at 32 degrees, giving his name to the scale.

POP

1941 Bob Dylan (Robert Allen Zimmerman), US singer who took his name from his favourite poet, Dylan Thomas. His recordings and live performances built up an enormous following worldwide, with songs which include 'Blowing In The Wind', 'Lay Lady Lay' and 'Like a Rolling Stone'.

SPORT

1899 Suzanne Lenglen, French tennis champion, six times Wimbledon women's singles champion. She first won in 1919 wearing a loose, short, sleeveless dress and became the first non-English-speaking champion.

DIED THIS DAY

1543 Nicolas Copernicus, Polish astronomer.

1844 William Crockford, English fishmonger and gambler who opened the famous gambling club Crockfords in 1827.

1959 John Foster Dulles, US Secretary of State who warned of conflict between the West and Communist bloc.

1974 Edward Kennedy 'Duke' Ellington,

US jazz pianist, composer and band-leader.

ON THIS DAY

1738 John Wesley first attended even-song at St Paul's Cathedral, London, then went on to a meeting at Aldersgate where he experienced his conversion. This was the start of Wesley's Methodism, and over 250 years later there are 54 million Methodists in 60 countries.

1809 Dartmoor Prison opened to house French prisoners-of-war. Only in 1850 were the first convicts imprisoned.

1844 Samuel Morse transmitted the first message of the US Telegraph line from Washington to Baltimore in Morse code: 'What God hath wrought'.

1856 John Brown, the US anti-slavery campaigner led the Free-Staters to massacre pro-slavers at Pottawatamie Creek.

1862 London's Westminster Bridge opened, as did Brooklyn Bridge over the East River this day in 1883.

1920 President Deschamel of France fell from a sleeper train and was found wandering along the line in his pajamas.

1941 The German battleship, *Bismarck*, sank HMS *Hood* off the Greenland coast. Almost all of her 1,421 crew perished. (*See* 27.5.1941)

1956 The first Eurovision Song Contest was held at Lugano, Switzerland. The winner, Lys Assia (Switzerland) sang 'Refrains'.

1959 The former Empire Day, first celebrated this day back in 1902, was renamed Commonwealth Day.

1988 Snow fell on the Syrian desert and Damascus had ten hours of snowfall for the first time in 50 years.

25 MAY

BORN THIS DAY

HISTORY

1879 William Maxwell Aitken, 1st Baron Beaverbrook, British newspaper magnate born in Canada. Lloyd George made him Minister of Information, an appropriate post for the owner of *Daily Express* and the *Evening Standard*. Churchill made him Minister of Supply during the Second World War, a task he fulfilled brilliantly to produce sufficient aircraft to meet the German challenge.

1892 Marshal Tito (Josip Broz), Yugoslavian leader who became Prime Minister of the Federal republic, 1946 and President-for-life, 1974.

1913 Richard Dimbleby, award-winning English broadcaster and journalist who became the BBC's first war correspondent (1939) and later became famous for memorable commentaries on historic occasions.

ARTS

1803 Ralph Waldo Emerson, US poet and essayist who was influenced by Carlyle in England.

1926 Miles (Dewey, Jr.) Davis, legendary US jazz trumpeter, composer and pioneer of jazz-rock fusion and other innovations. Considered one of the major jazz musicians, his influential work grew progressively complex.

1929 Beverley Sills, US opera singer and director who was a dramatic soprano, particularly renowned for her role in *La*

Traviata. She retired from singing in 1980 and became director of New York City Opera.

THE CHAMPS Born 1826, Tom Sayers, English pugilist, around middleweight, who was beaten only once. He ended his fighting days in a 37-round match lasting over two hours, with the Bernica Boy in 1860. The result was a draw. In 1898, James Joseph Tunney, better known as Gene Tunney, was born in the US and became world heavyweight champion in 1926, when he beat Jack Dempsey. In the controversial return, he was knocked down in the seventh, but because Dempsey failed to retire to a neutral corner, the count started late allowing him to recover.

ENTERTAINMENT

1878 Bill 'Bojangles' Robinson, US tap dancer with a casual, effortless style which he demonstrated to best advantage in *Blackbirds of 1928* and *The Hot Mikado*. He's appeared in several Shirley Temple films and played the lead in *Stormy Weather* (1943).

1939 Ian McKellen, English actor of both classical and contemporary parts. He was an acclaimed Coriolanus at the National Theatre, 1984, and was equally moving as the mentally retarded *Walter* on television.

INVENTION

1889 Igor Ivanovich Sikorsky, Russian-born US aeronautical engineer and inventor of the helicopter who emigrated to the US in 1919 and founded the Sikorsky Aero Engineering Corporation. In 1939 he built the first practical helicopter.

POP

1958 Paul Weller, English singer, first with the Jam, then with the Style Council.

DIED THIS DAY

1675 Gespard (Dughet) Poussin, French landscape painter.

1934 Gustav (Theodore) Holst, English composer of Swedish origin who is best known for his suite *The Planets* (1914–17).

ON THIS DAY

1660 King Charles II of England rowed ashore from the *Royal Charter* at Dover, ending his nine-year exile and, with it, Puritanism.

1768 Captain Cook set sail on his first voyage in the *Endeavour* which circumnavigated New Zealand and surveyed the east coast of Australia.

1787 The Philadelphia Convention met under George Washington to draw up the US constitution.

1833 The first flower show in Britain was held at the Royal Horticultural Society in Chiswick, west London.

1840 The first drama school in Britain opened. Miss Kelly's Theatre and Dramatic School in Dean Street later became a theatre.

1850 The first hippopotamus arrived in Britain destined for Regent's Park Zoo.

1871 The House of Commons passed the Bank Holiday Act creating the now-established public holidays of Easter Monday, Whit Monday and Christmas Day.

1882 The first mutton from New Zealand arrived in Britain.

1925 The 'Monkey Trial' began in a small

town in Tennessee when a school teacher, John Scopes defended by one of the top US defence lawyers, Clarence Darrow, was charged for teaching Darwin's theory of evolution. Brought by Bible fundamentalists claiming it was blasphemous, the trial attracted wide press interest.

1935 On this Saturday in Michigan in a period of 45 minutes, the US athlete Jesse Owens broke five world records and equalled a sixth.

1951 Guy Burgess and Donald Maclean, British Foreign Office officials, disappeared and were later discovered to have spied for Russia.

1962 The new Coventry Cathedral was consecrated. Architect Sir Basil Spence had recreated the bombed cathedral with new stained glass by John Piper and a huge tapestry by Graham Sutherland.

1965 Cassius Clay (Muhammed Ali) knocked out Sonny Liston in the first round of their fight at Lewiston, Maine.

1967 Jock Stein's Celtic football club, the Scottish champions captained by Billy McNeill, became the first British football club to win the European Cup by beating Internazionale 2–1 in Lisbon.

1982 The electronics firm, Philips, introduced Laservision – laserdiscs and player unit.

1986 Bob Geldof's 'Race Against Time' had 30 million people on the run for Sport Aid to raise money for the starving in Africa.

1989 The satirical magazine *Private Eye* faced bankruptcy after a record High Court libel damages judgement of £600,000 and £100,000 costs, for alleging that the estranged wife of the Yorkshire Ripper exploited her husband's notoriety. The award was later reduced in an appeal to £60,000.

26 MAY

BORN THIS DAY

HISTORY

1650 John Churchill, the Duke of Marlborough, English general and statesman who started as a page to the Duke of York. With the help of influential people and his wife Sarah, who became the lady-in-waiting to Queen Anne, he advanced his career. He proved a skilled general with a concern for the welfare of his troops.

1867 Queen Mary (born Princess Mary of Teck), wife of King George V.

1874 Henri Farman, French aircraft designer and pioneer aviator who, with his brother Maurice, produced the first bi-plane in 1909.

1912 Janos Kadar, Premier of Hungary who changed his anti-Stalinist approach after the entry of Russian tanks into his country, and helped to crush any revolution.

ENTERTAINMENT

1886 Al Jolson (Asa Yoelson), US singer and entertainer who billed himself as 'the world's greatest entertainer'. He was the most popular singer of his day introducing songs such as 'Mammy', 'Sonny Boy', 'April Showers' and 'Toot, Toot, Tootsie, Goodbye!', and starring in the first (part-)sound film, *The Jazz Singer* (1927).

1904 George Formby, English entertainer and ukulele player. Son of a music hall artist of the same name, he also learnt his art in the music hall to become one of Britain's most popular entertainers on stage, screen, radio and recordings. His risqué songs sung in his broad Lancashire accent included 'Cleaning Windows' and 'Mr Wu', accompanied on the ukulele.

1907 John Wayne (Marion Michael Morrison), US actor known as 'the Duke' who played the tough hero in over 250 films. A fiercely patriotic man, his political stance was pro-McCarthy during the witch-hunts of that era, and pro-Vietnam War. He won an Oscar for *True Grit* (1969), and other notable films include *The Alamo* (1960) and his last film, *The Shootist* (1976).

1908 Robert Morley, English actor and playwright. His play, *Edward, My Son* (1949), written in collaboration with Noel Langley, was a major success. Besides many stage appearances, mainly in comedy, he appeared in *The African Queen* (1952) and *Those Magnificent Men in their Flying Machines* (1965).

1913 Peter Cushing, English actor best known for his roles in horror films who actually made his screen debut in Olivier's *Hamlet*. His Hammer period includes *The Curse of Frankenstein* (1958), and *The Brides of Dracula* (1960).

1923 James Arness (Auerness), US actor best remembered for the television series *Gunsmoke*.

ONE-MAN SHOW OFFS Both British actors born this day in 1925 have acclaimed one-man stage shows: Roy Dotrice, formerly with the Royal Shakespeare Company presented *Brief Lives* as Aubrey, which ran 213 performances in 1969, setting a world record; Alec McCowen, also with the RSC in the award-winning *Hadrian the Seventh*, later presented *The Gospel According to St Matthew* (1978).

JAZZ

1920 Peggy Lee (Norma Delores Egstrom), US singer, songwriter and actress who was a vocalist with the Benny Goodman band before making her name in nightclubs and later in films and recordings. She sang and wrote the lyrics for songs in the Disney film *Lady and the Tramp* (1955) and she was nominated for an Oscar for her role in *Pete Kelly's Blues* (1955).

SPORT

1909 Sir Matt Busby, Scottish international footballer and Manchester United manager at the time of the Munich disaster. (*See* 6.2.1958)

1966 Zola Budd, South African-cum-British athlete who attracted international attention when she broke Mary Decker's 5,000 metres world record, running barefoot in South Africa. The 17-year-old country girl from the Orange Free State was suddenly propelled into the international scene by the *Daily Mail* who managed to organize a British passport for her in 13 days so she could run for Britain in the Olympics and beat the ban on South African athletes.

DIED THIS DAY

604 Augustine, the first Archbishop of Canterbury who originally came to Britain to convert the Anglo-Saxons to Christianity.

735 The Venerable Bede, English monk, scholar and writer of the most important history of ancient Britain; just after completing a translation of St John into Anglo-Saxon, and buried at Jarrow.

1703 Samuel Pepys, English Admiralty official and diarist.

ON THIS DAY

1733 John Kay, Richard Arkwright's assistant and a former clockmaker, patented the Flying Shuttle to operate on Arkwright's spinning frame.

1805 Napoleon was crowned King of Italy, in Milan Cathedral.

1865 The Confederate General Kirby Smith surrendered in Texas to end the American Civil War.

1868 Michael Barrett, an Irish nationalist who was responsible for the Clerkenwell Outrage, which left 13 dead, was hanged outside Newgate Prison in London, the last public execution in England.

1908 The first major oil strike in the Middle East was made in Persia.

1923 The first Le Mans 24-hour race took place and was won by two French drivers, Lagache and Leonard at an average speed of 57.2 m.p.h. covering 1,373 miles in the 24 hours.

1940 Operation Dynamo began – the evacuation of the trapped British Expeditionary Forces on the beach at Dunkirk. Besides the efforts of the Royal Navy, 700 little ships set off from Britain to rescue 385,000 soldiers over the following nine days.

1975 Evel Knievel, the US stuntman, suffered serious spinal injuries in Britain when his car crashed, attempting to leap 13 buses.

1988 Andrew Lloyd Webber's *Cats* opened in Moscow with a British and US cast.

1989 The BBC broadcast the 10,000th episode of the daily radio serial *The Archers*, with Terry Wogan as a guest.

27 MAY

BORN THIS DAY

HISTORY

1815 Sir Henry Parkes, Australian statesman, in England. He emigrated in 1839 and became a leading Sydney journalist and a member of the colonial parliament in 1884 before becoming Prime Minister from 1872, an office he held a number of times.

CAMPAIGNERS Two women who fought for women's rights and left behind them words which have entered the chronicles of history, were both born in New York this day. In 1818, Amelia (Jenks) Bloomer was born. This US woman's rights campaigner designed, in 1849, the knee-length skirt and trousers called 'bloomers', as part of her attempts at dress reform. One year later in 1819, Julia Ward Howe was born, US suffragette who is best known for 'The Battle Hymn of the Republic' (1861) sung to the tune of 'John Brown's Body'.

1837 James Butler 'Wild Bill' Hickok, US frontiersman, sharpshooter and scout during the Civil War for the Union army. He became a US marshal and is credited with the deaths of a number of outlaws.

1923 Dr Henry Kissinger, US Secretary of State, born in Germany, who emigrated to the US in 1938. He set up the visits of Nixon to both Russia and China and shared the Nobel Peace prize in 1973 with Le Duc Tho for helping to negotiate an end to the Vietnam War.

ARTS

1867 (Enoch) Arnold Bennett, English novelist, born in Hanley, one of the Five Towns he was to immortalize in *Anna of the Five Towns* (1902). He also wrote the trilogy commencing with *Clayhanger* (1910).

1878 Isadora Duncan, US dancer who introduced a new style of dancing which influenced modern dance. She established schools in Europe and scandalized society with her private life and loves.

1915 Herman Wouk, US author of *The Caine Mutiny* (1951) and *Marjorie Morningstar* (1955).

ENTERTAINMENT

GOTHIC HORRORS Two men who have frightened millions and been well paid for the pleasure, born 1911, Vincent Price, US actor, art and food expert. He is best known for the *The House of Wax* (1953), *The Fly* (1958) and *The Pit and the Pendulum* (1961); born 1922, Christopher Lee, English actor who dripped blood in films such as *The Curse of Frankenstein* (1957) and *Dracula* (1958). Yet both actors had also played serious dramatic roles – Price as Prince Albert in the London production of *Victoria Regina* (1935) and Lee in a part in the film version of *Hamlet* (1948).

1943 Cilla Black (Priscilla White) singer and presenter on television of *Surprise, Surprise*. Like the Beatles, she came from Liverpool and had hits with songs like 'Love of the Loved' (1963), given to her by John Lennon and Paul McCartney, and 'Anyone Who had a Heart' (1964), followed by 'You're My World' which also went to No. 1.

SCIENCE

1897 Sir John Douglas Cockcroft, English physicist who worked with Rutherford at Cambridge where they split the atom for the first time (1932) and were jointly awarded the Nobel prize.

SPORT

1912 Sam Snead, US golfer, one of the greatest international golfers who won 135 tournaments between 1936 and 1965 including the US Masters (in 1949, 1952, 1954) and the British Open (1946). He won six PGA Senior and World Senior's titles.

1956 John Conteh, English boxer who became world lightweight champion in 1973, and world light heavyweight champion the following year, the first to hold the title since Freddie Mills.

1957 Duncan Goodhew, English swimmer, bald-headed Olympic breaststroke champion at Moscow in 1980.

1965 Pat Cash, Australian tennis champion who beat Lendl to win the Wimbledon men's singles crown in 1987.

DIED THIS DAY

1564 John Calvin, French theologian who promoted the Protestant Reformation.

1840 Nicolo Paganini, Italian virtuoso violinist and composer who had syphilis and was prescribed mercury to swallow. Over the years this took away his ability to play and changed his character. When told by another doctor that he had tuberculosis and one year to live, he increased the dose and probably died of mercury poisoning, not TB, as Australian Dr J.G. O'Shea claimed in an article in the *Journal of the Royal Society of Medicine* (1988).

1910 Robert Koch, German bacteriologist who discovered the bacillus of tuberculosis.

1914 Sir Joseph (Wilson) Swan, English physicist, chemist and inventor of the incandescent filament electric lamp.

1964 Jawaharlal Nehru, first Indian Prime Minister and father of Indira Gandhi.

ON THIS DAY

1679 The Habeas Corpus Act, which demands that the prisoner must be brought before the courts, not unlawfully detained, was passed in Britain.

1703 Tsar Peter the Great proclaimed St Petersburg the new Russian capital.

1851 The first Chess International Masters tournament was held in London and was won by Adolf Anderssen of Germany.

1878 'Demon bowler' Frederick Spofforth of Australia took 11 wickets for 20 runs against the MCC.

1900 Belgium became the first country to elect a government by proportional representation.

1905 Japan's Admiral Togo led his fleet to a victory at Tsushima Straits, destroying 32 Russian vessels. Only three escaped.

1919 The first aircraft to fly across the Atlantic from New York to Lisbon arrived after 44 hours and several stops.

1931 Auguste Piccard and Charles Kipfer reached the stratosphere (52,462 feet) in a special aluminium gondola before landing safely on an Austrian glacier.

1935 Alma Rattenbury and her lover, George Percy Stoner, went on trial at the Old Bailey for the murder of her husband. Alma was 25 years younger than her husband, who was 63, and she began an affair with the young Stoner. He became wild when Alma and her husband were to stay at friends and once more share a bed, and beat Rattenbury with a mallet. He was found guilty and sentenced to death, which was commuted to life. Alma was found not guilty, but committed suicide soon after.

1936 The first open prison in Britain was opened at New Hall, Yorkshire.

1936 The *Queen Mary* sailed on her maiden voyage from Southampton via Cherbourg to New York.

1937 The world's longest suspension bridge, the 4,200ft Golden Gate Bridge in San Francisco was opened.

1941 The German battleship, *Bismark* was sunk by aircraft from the *Ark Royal,* and HMS *Rodney*, *Prince of Wales* and *King George V*.

1958 Jerry Lee Lewis cut short his UK tour after just two concerts when a storm broke out about his 13-year-old wife.

1963 Jomo Kenyatta was elected Kenya's first Prime Minister, and in 1974, Jacques Chirac became Premier of France.

1988 In Canada, a man was acquitted of murdering his mother after he said he had been sleepwalking when he drove 14 miles to her home, hit her with an iron bar and then stabbed her.

28 MAY

BORN THIS DAY

HISTORY

1738 Joseph Ignace Guillotin, French physician and revolutionary who suggested a decapitating machine which bears his name. Adopted in 1791, it was not a new invention. Similar instruments of execution were used in other countries including Scotland.

1759 William Pitt the Younger, English statesman, who was Prime Minister from 1783–1801. He was England's youngest prime minister ever. He was elected again in 1804–6.

1884 Eduard Beněs, founder of modern Czechoslovakia who was President of the republic from 1935. During the Second World War, he ran the government in exile from London. He was President again from 1945, resigning shortly before his death in 1948.

1930 Edward Seaga, Prime Minister of Jamaica in 1980–89.

1934 The Dionne Quintuplets, to Mrs Oliva Dionne in Ontario: Emilie, Yvonne, Cecile, Marie and Annette.

ARTS

1779 Thomas Moore, Irish-born poet who managed to get 3,000 guineas from his publishers for his *Lalla Rookh* in 1817, which then was the largest advance given to a poet.

1908 Ian (Lancaster) Fleming, English novelist who worked in naval intelligence during the Second World War and only started writing in 1952. His hero, James Bond, was initially condemmed by critics for his life style, attitudes and violence. The books, all filmed, include *Casino Royale* (1953) and *On Her Majesty's Secret Service* (1963), made the year before he died.

1912 Patrick (Victor Martindale) White, Australian novelist, born in England of Australian parents who settled in Australia after the Second World War. His award-winning novel, *Voss* (1957), was followed by other well-received novels, including *The Eye of the Storm* (1973), the same year he received the Nobel prize.

ENTERTAINMENT

1912 Rachel Kempson (Lady Redgrave), English actress, wife of Sir Michael, mother of Vanessa, Lynn and Corin, a leading actress at Stratford-upon-Avon from 1933, who appeared in the film *Jane Eyre* (1944).

1918 Thora Hird, English actress who played character roles on both stage and screen, including the film *A Taste of Honey* (1961).

1968 Kylie Minogue, Australian actress in television's *Neighbours*, and pop star with hits including 'I Should Be So Lucky' (1988).

DIED THIS DAY

1805 Luigi Boccherini, Italian cellist and composer.

1843 Noah Webster, US lexicographer, publisher of *Webster's Dictionary*.

1849 Anne Brontë, who, as Acton Bell, wrote *The Tenant of Wildfell Hall* (1848).

1900 Sir George Grove, English engineer and first director of the Royal College of Music, editor of the *Dictionary of Music and Musicians*.

1937 Alfred Adler, Austrian psychiatrist and psychologist.

1972 Edward VIII, Duke of Windsor, former king of England.

1984 Eric Morecambe (Eric Bartholomew), English comedian who with Eric Wise formed a popular comedy duo performing on both stage and television.

ON THIS DAY

1588 The Spanish Armada set sail from Lisbon under the command of the Duke of Medina Sidonia to invade England. The fleet of 130 vessels was the mightiest ever assembled.

1742 The first indoor swimming-pool in England opened in London. The entrance fee was one guinea.

1891 The first world weightlifting championships were held at the Café Monico, Piccadilly.

1858 Tonic water was patented by Erasmus Bond of London.

1932 The world's largest sea dam was completed in Holland. It stretched 2,000m across the mouth of the Zuider Zee creating a new inland lake, the IJsselmeer.

1951 The first *Goon Show* was broadcast by the BBC. Peter Sellers, Spike Milligan (who also wrote the script) and Harry Secombe brought to life Henry Crunn, Major Bloodnock, Minnie Bannister, Bluebottle, Neddy Seagoon and Eccles. British comedy would never be the same – or sane – again.

1967 Francis Chichester, a 65-year-old English yachtsman, sailed into Plymouth to a huge welcome at the end of his solo circumnavigation of the world in *Gypsy Moth IV*.

1982 Diego Maradona of Argentinos Juniors was bought by Barcelona football club for a record £5m.

1987 Mathias Rust, a 19-year-old West German flew his small aircraft through Soviet air space from Helsinki to Moscow, landing right in Red Square.

1990 The *Maiden* arrived in Southampton, completing the Whitbread around-the-world yacht race (*see* 22.5.1990). The first ever all-woman crew was skippered by Tracy Edwards.

29 MAY

Oak Apple (or Royal Oak) Day, commemorating King Charles II finding safety in an oak tree in the grounds of Boscobel House, Shropshire after the Battle of Worcester (1651), because it was too dangerous for him to remain in the house while Parliamentary troops searched for him.

BORN THIS DAY

HISTORY

1630 Charles II, King of England, crowned at Scone in Scotland in 1650. He attempted to invade England, but Cromwell defeated him at Worcester. Only in 1660 was he able to regain the throne. (*See* ON THIS DAY)

1880 Oswald Spengler, German philosopher who came to the conclusion that the west was in decline which, in 1918, was not far off the mark.

1917 John F(itzgerald) Kennedy, 35th US President. He was both the first Roman Catholic and the youngest president to be elected.

ARTS

1860 Isaac Albéniz, Spanish composer and infant prodigy, both composing and as a pianist. When only seven, his pasadoble was performed by a military band in Paris.

1874 G(ilbert) K(eith) Chesterton, English author, journalist and humorous illustrator who wrote *The Man Who was Thursday* (1908) and popular crime novels featuring Father Brown, the

Roman Catholic priest-detective. Chesterton, an agnostic, converted to Catholicism in 1922.

1906 T(erence H(anbury) White, English novelist, born in India who wrote *The Sword and the Stone* (1939).

ENTERTAINMENT

1894 Joseph von Sternberg, Austrian film director and actor who was ahead of his time. His early films, made for MGM and even Chaplin, were either remade, completed by other directors or not released because they were considered too sophisticated. Eventually he succeeded with films such as *The Blue Angel* made in Germany with Marlene Dietrich in 1929 and *Shanghai Express* made in Hollywood in 1932. He came to Britain in 1937 to direct Charles Laughton in *I, Claudius*. When Merle Oberon, who was playing the female lead, was involved in a car accident, filming had to stop and mysteriously was never resumed. What was shot – and much later screened by BBC – shows it would have been a masterpiece.

1903 Bob Hope (Leslie Townes Hope), in England. He went to the US as a child, where he later became popular on radio, and this led to Hollywood and a long list of classic comedies that made him internationally famous and the wealthiest entertainer ever. His theme song, 'Thanks for the Memory' was sung in his first film, *The Big Broadcast of 1938*. The 'Road' films with Bing Crosby (*Road to Singapore* was first of seven) were highly successful, and other films include *The Lemon-Drop Kid* (1951). He won five special Oscars and made many appearances for US troops.

1939 Nanette Newman, English actress, married to Bryan Forbes. She has appeared on stage, television and films such as *The Stepford Wives* (1975). She has also written books for children.

INVENTION

STRIKE A LIGHT In 1769, Philippe Lebon, French chemist and inventor who developed gas illumination, and in 1781, Dr John Walker, English inventor of the friction match, which he sold at his shop in Stockton-on-Tees.

SCIENCE

1902 Sir Leonard (George Holden) Huxley, English scientist who developed radar, blind bombing and anti-submarine detection systems. After the war he became Professor of Physics at Adelaide, and from 1960, vice-chancellor of the Australian National University, involved in the plan to build a large optical telescope in Australia.

SPORT

1935 Alvin Schokemohle, champion German showjumper.

DIED THIS DAY

1500 Bartolomeu Diaz, Portuguese explorer, drowned at sea during a storm while on a voyage with Cabral, the discoverer of Brazil.

1829 Sir Humphrey Davy, English chemist and inventor of the miners' safety lamp.

1911 Sir W(illiam) S(chwenk) Gilbert, librettist and playwright, drowned in his own lake, at Grim's Dyke. He was swimming there with two young ladies, one of whom got into difficulties; Gilbert went to the rescue, but suddenly sank, dying of a heart attack.

1942 John Barrymore (Blythe), US actor.

1951 Fanny Brice (Fannie Borach), US comedienne.

1979 Mary Pickford (Gladys Mary Smith) US actress, 'America's Sweetheart'.

ON THIS DAY

1453 Constantinople fell to the Turkish army after a year's siege.

1660 On his 30th birthday, Charles II entered London to be restored as King of England.

1795 In the Virginia Assembly, the eloquent patriot Patrick Henry challenged the proposed taxing of the American Colonies by the Stamp Act.

1848 Wisconsin became the 38th state of the Union.

1879 On this Monday, Britain enjoyed the first Bank Holiday.

1884 The first steam cable tramway began operating in London's Highgate.

1913 *The Rites of Spring*, danced by Nijinsky, opened in Paris. Its sensuality and the disturbing music by Stravinsky caused the audience to riot.

1914 The *Empress of Ireland*, a Canadian Pacific liner, was wrecked in the St Lawrence River. Over 1,000 people perished.

1922 Liberal MP Horatio Bottomley was sentenced to seven years for fraud. His so-called Victory Bonds had attracted money from thousands of people with small savings, who were swindled of a total of £150,000.

1953 Sir Edmund Hillary and Sherpa Tenzing became the first two climbers to reach the summit of Everest. The news broke on Coronation day (2 June).

1977 Nigel Short of England, aged 11, qualified as the youngest ever competitor in a national chess championship. He had already beaten Viktor Korchnoi during an exhibition game. The Cuban player, Capablanca was 12 when he first played in a national contest.

1979 Bishop Abel Muzorewa became Rhodesia's first black Prime Minister. On 1 June, the country changed its name to Zimbabwe.

1982 Pope Paul II became the first Pope in 450 years to step on to British soil, and the first to pray side by side with the Archbishop of Canterbury in Canterbury Cathedral.

1985 Heysal Stadium, Belgium was the scene of the worst football riot in Europe when Liverpool fans clashed with Juventas fans as a wall collapsed during the European Cup Final, killing 41 and injuring 350, mostly Italians.

30 MAY

The Feast Day of Joan of Arc, patron saint of soldiers, who was burnt at the stake in Rouen in 1431. She was canonized by Pope Benedict XV in 1921 on the anniversary of her death.

BORN THIS DAY

HISTORY

1814 Mikhail Alexandrovich Bakunin, Russian anarchist who took part in the German revolutionary movement. He was condemned to death, but was handed back to Russia and sent to Siberia. He escaped and eventually made his way to England, later returning to play a part in the Communist

International Congress before he was expelled.

1859 Pierre Marie Felix Janet, French psychologist who made a significant contribution to the understanding of hysteria.

ARTS

1846 Peter Carl (Karl Gustavovich) Fabergé, Russian goldsmith who was educated in several countries including France and England. He inherited his father's business and began making exotic objects, including his bejewelled Imperial Easter eggs, for Tsar Alexander.

ENTERTAINMENT

1908 Mel Blanc, US cartoon voice-over specialist who was the voice of Bugs Bunny and Daffy Duck.

1909 Benny (Benjamin David) Goodman, bandleader, clarinettist and child prodigy, making his debut aged 12. He played with the Ben Pollack band in 1926–9, forming his own band soon after. Called 'The King of Swing', his was the first genuine jazz band to visit the USSR on this day, 1962, attended by Soviet leader, Kruschev.

1932 Ray Cooney, English actor, playwright, director and producer of comedies with his Theatre of Comedy, specializing in farces such as *One For the Pot* with Terry Hilton (1961) and *Chase Me Comrade* (1964) which ran over 1,000 performances.

SPORT

1906 Leslie (Smokey) Dawson, English motor cycle designer and racer who invented a number of motor cycle innovations including telescopic front suspension. He was also the man who supplied Aircraftsman Shaw – T.E. Lawrence – with the motorcycle he was riding when killed.

1949 Bob Willis, former England cricket captain and fast bowler who took eight Australian wickets for 43 in the historic test in 1981 when Australia had to score only 130 to win.

DIED THIS DAY

1593 Christopher Marlowe, English playwright who greatly influenced Shakespeare, killed in a tavern brawl, possibly because he was promoting atheistic opinions.

1640 Peter Paul Rubens, Flemish painter.

1744 Alexander Pope, English poet and satirist.

1788 Voltaire (François Marie Arouet de), French philosopher, historian, playwright and novelist who wrote *Candide*.

1912 Wilbur Wright, US aviation pioneer.

1960 Boris Leonidovich Pasternak, Russian poet and author of *Dr Zhivago*.

1967 Claude Rains, British-born film actor who featured in *Casablanca*.

1985 Roy Plomley, English broadcaster and devisor of the prestigious and long-running radio programme *Desert Island Discs*, which he started in 1941 on the BBC.

ON THIS DAY

1498 Christopher Columbus set sail on his third voyage of discovery which would take him to discover the South American mainland.

1536 Jane Seymour became Henry VIII's

third wife 11 days after he had separated Anne Boleyn's head from her body.

1656 The Grenadier Guards were formed in the British Army.

1842 Jon Francis attempted to assassinate Queen Victoria as she rode in her carriage with Prince Albert.

1911 The first Indianapolis 500 motor race was won by Ray Harroun at an average speed of 74.59 m.p.h.

1959 The first experimental hovercraft, designed by Sir Christopher Cockerell and built by Saunders-Roe, was launched at Cowes, Isle of Wight.

1959 The Auckland Harbour bridge was officially opened on New Zealand's North Island.

1978 Liverpool won the European Cup for the second year running, beating FC Bruges of Belgium 1–0, the lone goal scored by Kenny Dalglish.

31 MAY

The National Day of South Africa.

BORN THIS DAY

HISTORY

1923 Prince Rainier of Monaco (Rainier Louis Henri Maxence Bertrand de Grimaldi), who married US film star Grace Kelly.

1939 Terry Waite, Anglican emissary, held prisoner in Lebanon after he was kidnapped on a visit to negotiate the release of hostages. (*See* 20.1.1987)

ARTS

1819 Walt(er) Whitman, influential US poet who wrote *The Leaves of Grass* (1855), employing blank verse to reveal explicit emotions. It grew from a modest volume to 440 pages.

1860 Walter (Richard) Sickert, English painter who was born in Munich. He is best known for his paintings of London music halls which show the influence of Degas.

1872 William Heath Robinson, English cartoonist and illustrator who gave his name to a ramshackle device following his ingenious and often hilarious drawings of absurd devices to perform simple tasks.

ENTERTAINMENT

1922 Denholm Elliott, English actor who was in the films *The Boys From Brazil* (1978), *Defence of the Realm* (1985) and *A Room with a View* (1987), among others.

1930 Clint Eastwood, US actor, director and former mayor of Carmel who made his name in spaghetti Westerns such as *The Good, the Bad and the Ugly* (1964) before moving on to films like *Play Misty for Me* (1971) which he also directed. He was back in tough guy roles in *Dirty Harry* (1971) and in a comedy *Every Which Way But Loose* (1978). Since turning director, he has directed notable productions including *Heartbreak Ridge* (1987).

1965 Brooke Shields, US actress and child model who starred in *Pretty Baby* (1978) playing a child prostitute. She was also in *The Blue Lagoon* (1980).

DIED THIS DAY

1594 Tintoretto (Jacopo Robusti) Italian painter and boy genius who painted *The Last Judgement*.

1809 Franz Joseph Haydn, Austrian composer.

1837 Joseph Grimaldi, English clown and comic actor who appeared at Drury Lane when only two years old. Known as Joey, all clowns since have been called 'Joey'. Another Grimaldi was born on the 86th anniversary of his death, but no relation (*see* BORN THIS DAY). Joey would certainly have been able to get a laugh out of that.

1910 Elizabeth Blackwell, English physician, officially the first woman doctor to qualify professionally (in the US) and later practised in England.

1942 Reinhard Heydrich, Nazi and deputy chief of the Gestapo, the 'protector of Bohemia and Moravia' who was assassinated by Czech resistance fighters. Nazi reprisals were violent; the village of Lidice was razed and all the men shot.

1983 Jack Dempsey, US boxer and former world heavyweight champion.

ON THIS DAY

1669 Samuel Pepys stopped writing his diary because of failing eyesight. He spent two months abroad, saving his eyesight, but lost his wife who died later that year.

1838 The last battle on English soil took place at the Battle of Bosendon Wood, when 40 peasants and a Cornish wine merchant, known as Sir William Percy Honeywood Courtenay, King of Jerusalem, led an armed uprising of Kentish peasants. His real name was John Nichols Tom and he settled in Kent and became a champion of the workers. He was killed by one of the 100 soldiers sent to put down the insurrection.

1859 Big Ben began telling the time from this day.

1889 A painting of a small dog listening to a phonograph was shown to William Barry Owen, the general manager of the Gramophone Company in Maiden Lane, London by the painter, Francis Barraud. It was of his dog, Nipper. Owen asked for the phonograph to be painted out and a gramophone substituted. He paid £50 for the picture and £50 for the copyright of 'His Master's Voice', which soon became the Company's famous trade mark. Nipper died in 1895 and was buried under a mulberry tree in Kingston-upon-Thames, now covered by a car park.

1891 Construction began of the Trans-Siberian Railway.

1902 The Boer War ended with the signing of the Treaty of Vereeniging. On this same day in 1910, the Act of Union created the Union of South Africa, and on its anniversary in 1961, South Africa declared itself a republic independent of the Commonwealth.

1910 Lord Baden-Powell's sister, Agnes, announced the formation of the Girl Guides.

1916 In the Battle of Jutland during the First World War, the Royal Navy under Jellicoe and Beatty lost one battleship, one cruiser and five destroyers. The Germans under Scheer and von Hipper lost one battleship, one cruiser and one destroyer. At the end of the day, 2,545 men were dead.

1938 US boxer Henry Armstrong, known as 'Homicide Hank' or 'Perpetual Motion', won the world welterweight title. He went on to take the lightweight crown on 17 August.

1938 The BBC's first television panel game, *Spelling Bee* was broadcast.

1940 Sir Oswald Moseley, the British fascist, was interned with other aliens and fascist sympathizers.

1956 Len Hutton, the England cricketer was knighted.

1957 US playwright, Arthur Miller was convicted for contempt of Congress for refusing to name other celebrities as likely communist supporters to the House of Representives Un-American Activities Committee. His conviction was dismissed the following year.

1965 Jim Clark, the Scottish world motor racing champion became the first non-US driver to win the Indianapolis 500.

1970 The great British steeplechaser Arkle was put down.

1984 Viv Richards made the highest one day score of 189 not out for the West Indies against the host country.

1988 A Norwegian soldier won the right to wear ear-rings on parade. Two women judges declared it would be sexual discrimination to order him to take them off.

THE PAN BOOK OF DATES

JUNE

It may be those who do most, dream most
(Stephen Leacock)

1 JUNE

BORN THIS DAY

ARTS

1878 John (Edward) Masefield, English poet, Poet Laureate, novelist and playwright who wrote *The Box of Delights* (1935).

1882 John Drinkwater, English poet and playwright whose interest in theatre led to the founding of the Pilgrim Players which eventually became the famous Birmingham Repertory Theatre. He was also the first to broadcast poetry (6.3.1924) on the BBC.

1936 Gerald Scarfe, English cartoonist and illustrator who was born on the 121st anniversary of the death of another great English caricaturist, James Gillray (*see* DIED THIS DAY).

ENTERTAINMENT

1857 Joseph Pujol, 'Le Petomane', who performed at the Moulin Rouge, 1906-10. He had a most unusual act, described as 'an extraordinary musical anus'. Not only did he perform simple tunes, but one of his tricks was to blow out a candle from his rear. He was the sensation of Paris attracting many leading celebrities to his audience. The Medical Faculty offered 25,000 francs to examine his corpse.

1926 Marilyn Monroe (Norma Jean Mortensen) US actress who had a deprived childhood, but became a Hollywood legend. To make a living she did photographic modelling, including the famous nude calendar picture. She got $150 for the session; the calendar company made $750,000 profit. Eventually she began to get the parts that established her as a star, in *The Seven Year Itch* (1955), *Bus Stop* (1956) and *Some Like It Hot* (1959). Her husbands included Jo DiMaggio and Arthur Miller. Her suicide (5.8.62) is still clouded in mystery.

1928 Bob Monkhouse, English comedian.

1930 Edward Woodward, English actor who is best known for his successful television series, *Callan* and *The Exterminator*.

1934 Pat Boone, US actor and singer who projected a wholesome image.

1944 Robert Powell, English actor who played Jesus in the television series, *Jesus of Nazareth*.

1947 Jonathan Pryce, English actor who starred in *The Ploughman's Lunch* (1983) and *Miss Saigon* (1989).

1950 Gemma Craven, English actress and singer who starred in Dennis Potter's television production of *Pennies from Heaven*.

SCIENCE

1796 Nicolas Léonard Sadi Carnot, French physicist and founder of thermodynamics.

1907 Air Commodore Sir Frank Whittle, English inventor of the modern jet engine (1930).

POP

1968 Jason Donovan, Australian television actor and singer, best known for his part in the soap opera *Neighbours*.

RELIGION

1801 Brigham Young, US Mormon leader who succeeded Joseph Smith, the founder of the Mormons, and led the migration to set up their colony at Salt Lake City, Utah.

1793 Henry Francis Lyte, Scottish hymn writer who wrote 'Abide With Me'.

DIED THIS DAY

1815 James Gillray, English caricaturist of leading politicians of the day.

1868 James Buchanan, 15th US President.

1879 Eugène Louis Jean Napoleon, Prince Imperial of France, who escaped to England, trained at Woolwich Academy and was killed in the Zulu Campaign in South Africa.

1944 Lizzie Borden, the US Sunday school teacher and alleged axe murderer whose trial began in Massachusetts this same day, 1893. She was acquitted on 4 June 1893. (*See* 19.7.1860)

1946 Ion Antonescu, Romanian dictator executed for bringing his country into the Second World War on the side of Germany.

1959 Sax Rohmer (Arthur Sarsfield Ward), English author, creator of the inscrutable Dr Fu Manchu, first published in 1913.

1968 Helen (Adams) Keller, US blind and deaf social worker and author. (*See* 27.6.1880)

ON THIS DAY

1792 Kentucky became the 15th state of the union, and this day 1796, Tennessee became the 16th.

1831 The magnetic North Pole was located by Sir James Clark Ross on his Arctic exploration expedition with Admiral Parry.

1874 The first Pullman cars in Britain were introduced on the Midland railway on the London to Bradford route.

1910 Captain Robert Falcon Scott set off to reach the South Pole, sailing from London's East India Dock in the *Terra Nova*.

1911 The first electric trolley buses in Britain began running in Leeds and Bradford.

1913 French heavyweight, Georges Carpentier, only 19, knocked out British challenger for the European title, Bombadier Billy Wells in the fourth round. Carpentier was already European welter-, middle- and light-heavyweight champion.

1927 The BBC broadcast a commentary on the Derby at Epsom.

1935 The use of L-plates for British learner drivers became compulsory.

1938 Superman made his first flight in a DC Comic, created by Joe Shuster and Jerry Siegal, two US college students.

1939 In Liverpool Bay, while carrying out trials, the Royal Navy submarine *Thetis* leaked carbon monoxide, poisoning 70 crew; four escaped through a hatch. The Admiralty were criticized for delaying the rescue operation.

1946 Television licences were first issued in Britain at a cost of £2, which included a percentage for radio services.

GETTING A LEG UP In 1953, Gordon Richards became the first jockey to be knighted. Six days later he won the Derby at his 28th attempt. On this day in 1977 and 1983, Lester Piggott won his eighth and ninth Derbys.

1957 ERNIE selected its first £1,000 premium bond winner.

1966 Bob Dylan had purist fans booing at the Royal Albert Hall when he used an electric guitar for the first time on his British tour.

1967 The Beatles *Sergeant Pepper's Lonely Hearts Club Band* album was released.

1973 Greece became a republic.

1979 Rhodesia became Zimbabwe.

1988 Prisoners inside Oregon prison began walking the exercise yard in the first sponsored walk to take place in a prison. They were raising money for organ transplants and walked 3,400 miles.

1989 Dustin Hoffman played his first Shakespearian role on stage when he opened in London as Shylock in *The Merchant of Venice*, directed by Sir Peter Hall.

2 JUNE

The Feast Day of Erasmus, patron saint of sailors; also known as St Elmo's Day.

BORN THIS DAY

HISTORY

1740 Comte Donatien Alphonse François de Sade, known as Marquis de Sade, French writer and 'sadist' (the term derived from his name) who was imprisoned in the Bastille for his sexual perversions, where he wrote *Justine* (1791) and other novels of sexual fantasy. He died in the asylum of Charenton.

1940 King Constantine II of the Hellenes, who was deposed by a military coup in June 1973.

ARTS

1840 Thomas Hardy, English novelist who wrote *Far From the Madding Crowd* (1874), *Tess of the D'Urbervilles* (1891) and *Jude the Obscure* (1896) as well as the epic *The Dynasts* (1903–8). His Wessex novels secured him a place as a major British novelist, while his poetry was popular with readers, but less so with some critics.

1857 Sir Edward (William) Elgar, English composer who wrote his *Enigma Variations* in 1899 and set Cardinal Newman's *The Dream of Gerontius* to music (1900). His *Pomp and Circumstance* marches added to his popularity.

1899 Lotte Reiniger, German film animator who made the world's first full-length animated film *The Adventures of Prince Achmed* (1926) using silhouette animation. She settled in England in 1930.

ENTERTAINMENT

1903 (Peter John) Johnny Weissmuller, US swimming champion who won five gold medals at the 1924 and 1928 Olympics. He played Tarzan in 11 films from 1932. He had difficulty finding his own 'Jane', with five divorces and six marriages.

1920 Johnny Speight, English scriptwriter of the award-winning television series *Till Death Do Us Part*.

1938 Sally Kellerman, US actress who was nominated for an Oscar playing Hotlips Houlihan in the film version of *M*A*S*H* (1970).

1941 (Walter) Stacy Keach, US actor who made his first film, *The Heart is a Lonely Hunter*, in 1968, and consolidated his reputation with *The Life and Times of Judge Roy Bean* (1972) and *Conduct Unbecoming* (1975).

1944 Marvin Hamlisch, US composer of the hit musical *A Chorus Line* and songs and film scores for *The Sting* and *The Way We Were*, both in 1974, who became the first person to win three Oscars in one night; for the score of each movie and for the title song of the second.

POP

1941 Charlie Watts, English drummer with the Rolling Stones.

BUSINESS

1850 Sir Jesse Boot, 1st Baron Trent who took over his father's herbalist shop in Nottingham and studied pharmacy. In 1877, he opened his first chemist's shop, and by 1883 had ten branches. In 1892, he began the mass production of drugs and by the end of the century, he had the biggest pharmaceutical manufacturing and retailing operation in the world with over 1000 High Street branches. He died 13 June 1931.

DIED THIS DAY

1882 Giuseppe Garibaldi, Italian nationalist leader.

1962 Victoria (Mary) Sackville-West, English writer of the novel, *All Passion Spent* (1931).

1970 Bruce McLaren, New Zealand motor racing driver, killed in an accident.

1985 George Alfred, Baron George Brown, English statesman, deputy leader of the Labour Party and a larger-than-life politician.

ON THIS DAY

1780 Lord George Gordon led the 'No Popery' or 'Gordon Riots' in protest at the ending of penalties against Roman Catholics.

1868 The Trades Union Congress was first held in Manchester. It concluded on 6 June.

1909 The ballet *Les Sylphides* was performed for the first time in Paris with choreography by Fokine to music by Chopin, and the leads danced by Nijinsky and Pavlova.

1896 Guglielmo Marconi patented his broadcasting system using electromagnetic waves and, in 1924, the first radio conversation between England and Australia was relayed by Marconi's stations in Cornwall and Sydney.

1910 The Hon C.S. Rolls became the first Briton to fly across the Channel travelling from Dover to Sangatte and back in a Short-Wright biplane. The following year on this day, the Air Navigation Act came into force to control the requirements of both pilots and machines.

NOT FOR CHILDREN, NOT FOR ADULTS In 1937 the day was shared by the first performance of Alban Berg's erotic opera of Wedekind's play, *Lulu*, in Zurich, while in London's Regent's Park, Robert and Edward Kennedy opened the Children's Zoo, the first of its type in the world.

1953 The coronation of Queen Elizabeth II, the first to be televised, was watched by millions.

1954 At age 18, Lester Piggott won his first Derby on the 33–1 horse Never Say Die, the first US horse to win the Derby since Iroquois in 1881.

1962 Britain's first legal casino opened at the Metropole, Brighton.

1964 The PLO (Palestine Liberation Organization) was formed in Jerusalem.

1979 Pope John Paul II returned on a visit

to his homeland, Poland, becoming the first pope to visit a communist country.

1985 English football clubs were banned indefinitely from playing in Europe, following continued hooliganism by British fans abroad.

1987 Lindy Chamberlain, the mother in the Australian 'Dingo' murder case, was pardoned. (*See* 13.9.1982)

3 JUNE

BORN THIS DAY

HISTORY

1726 James Hutton, Scottish physician and geologist who wrote *Theory of the Earth* in 1785, which became the basis of modern geology.

1804 Richard Cobden, English political reformer and Liberal politician who fought to repeal the Corn Laws.

1808 Jefferson Davis, president of the Confederate States of America. He proclaimed a form of 'humane' slavery and when the Confederacy surrendered at the end of the Civil War was arrested and imprisoned for two years.

1853 Sir William Matthew Flinders Petrie, English egyptologist who excavated at the pyramids and temples of Gizeh.

1865 George V, King of England from 1910 to 1936 who married Princess May of Teck (Queen Mary) in 1893. He ruled during the First World War and changed the family name from Saxe-Coburg-Gotha to Windsor in 1917.

ARTS

1877 Raoul Dufy, French painter.

1926 Allen Ginsburg, US poet of the 'beat' generation who wrote *Howl and Other Poems*.

ENTERTAINMENT

1911 Paulette Goddard (Marion Levy), US actress who began as a Ziegfeld Girl when only 14 years old. In 1936, she married Charles Chaplin in secret. She co-starred with him in *Modern Times* (1936) and *The Great Dictator* (1940).

1925 Tony Curtis (Bernard Schwartz), US actor who appeared in such films as *The Sweet Taste of Success* (1957) and *Some Like It Hot* (1959).

POP

1950 Suzi Quatro, US rock singer and actress who starred in the UK revival of *Annie Get Your Gun*.

DIED THIS DAY

1657 William Harvey, court physician to James I and Charles I who published his theory of the circulation of blood in 1628.

1838 Jonathan Martin, English religious extremist who set fire to York Minster in 1829. He spent the remaining nine years of his life in an asylum.

1875 Georges (Alexandre Césare Léopold) Bizet, French composer of the opera *Carmen*.

1898 Samuel Plimsoll, English politician and reformer.

1899 Johann Strauss the Younger, Austrian composer, violinist and conductor who wrote *The Blue Danube* waltz.

1924 Franz Kafka, Czech author who wrote the novel, *The Trial* (1925).

1963 Pope John XXIII (Angelo Giuseppe Roncalli).

1986 Dame Anna Neagle, English actress.

1989 Ruhollah Khomeini, Iranian religious leader who returned from exile in France after the overthrow of the Shah in 1979.

ON THIS DAY

1665 The Duke of York defeated the Dutch Fleet off the coast of Lowestoft.

1837 The Hippodrome opened in London's Bayswater to run steeple-chase horse races.

1931 The Baird Company televised the Epsom Derby, which was transmitted by the BBC.

1937 The Duke of Windsor, the former king of England, married Wallis Simpson privately in a château near Tours, France.

1946 The first 'bikini' bathing suit was unveiled in Paris, invented by Louis Reard, a former motor engineer. He named it after Bikini Atoll where the first peacetime atomic bomb tests were being held because he thought the two-piece bathing costume would be 'highly explosive'.

1956 Third-class travel on British Railways came to an end.

1965 Major Edward White became the first US astronaut to walk in space. He spent 14 minutes outside *Gemini 4*.

1971 *No Sex Please, We're British* opened in London, with Michael Crawford in the cast. When it closed (*see* 5.9.1987), it had become the world's longest running comedy.

1972 Sally Priesand was ordained at the Isaac M. Wise Temple, Cincinatti, Ohio as the first woman rabbi.

1975 Brazilian super footballer, Pélé, signed a three-year contract with New York Cosmos for a $7m fee.

1981 The Aga Khan's horse Shergar won the Derby by a record ten lengths.

4 JUNE

BORN THIS DAY

HISTORY

1738 George III, King of England from 1760. There was continual friction between him and his Prime Minister, Pitt, who was highly popular with the people. During his reign he mishandled the conflict with the American colony, which led to the War of Independence. He went insane in 1811 and the Prince of Wales was appointed Regent.

1867 Baron Carl (Gustav Emil) von Mannerheim, Finnish military commander. He secured the independence of Finland from Russia in 1918 just after the Revolution and became Regent; he was later elected President in 1944.

ENTERTAINMENT

1826 Stephen (Collins) Foster, US composer of popular minstrel songs including 'The Old Folks at Home' and 'Swanee River'.

1908 Rosalind Russell, US actress who starred on Broadway in dramas and musicals. In Hollywood, she received Oscar nominations for four films: *My Sister Eileen* (1942), *Mourning Becomes Electra* (1947), *Aunt Mame* (1958), which she had also performed on Broadway, and *Gypsy* (1962), when she played Baby June's ambitious mother, Rose.

1927 Geoffrey Palmer, English actor,

seen in many television series including *Butterflies* and *Hot Metal*.

INVENTIONS

1910 Sir Christopher (Sydney) Cockerell, English inventor of the hovercraft in 1953.

SPORT

1948 Bob Champion, English jockey who was given eight months to live in 1979 when cancer was diagnosed, but confounded the doctors and returned to racing to win the 1981 Grand National.

DIED THIS DAY

1798 Giovanni Casanova, Italian romantic, author and librarian at the castle of Waldstein in Bohemia, where he was was also buried.

1926 Frederick Robert Spofforth, Australia cricketer who was known as 'the demon bowler'.

1941 Wilhelm II, former German Emperor, in exile in the Netherlands.

1988 Sir Douglas Nicholls, former boxer, footballer and first Aborigine to become a state governor (South Australia), and to receive a knighthood.

ON THIS DAY

1805 The first Trooping the Colour ceremony took place at the Horse Guards Parade, London.

1831 Prince Leopold became the first King of Belgium.

1913 At the Epsom Derby, suffragette Emily Davison threw herself in front of the King's horse, Amner, and was seriously injured as the horse fell and rolled over her. She died on the 8th and thousands of suffragettes marched across central London at her funeral, accompanied by ten bands.

1937 The first supermarket trolleys were wheeled in an Oklahoma supermarket, one of the Standard Supermarket chain owned by Sylvan Goldman.

1940 The evacuation of Dunkirk which had begun on 27 May, was completed. Thousands of little ships captained by British yachtsman, fishermen and other civilians, under heavy German attack, picked up trapped British Expeditionary Forces soldiers from the beaches of Dunkirk and returned to the English south coast with 338,226 men.

1944 Rome was liberated by the Allies.

1946 Juan Perón became President of Argentina.

1963 London's most fashionable nightclub, Annabel's in Berkeley Square, was opened by Mark Birley and named after his sister.

1973 The Russian supersonic airliner that looked suspiciously like Concorde and was nicknamed Concordski, exploded while performing at the Paris Airshow, killing the six crew and 27 people on the ground.

1989 Tanks rolled into Beijing's (Peking) Tiananmen Square and soldiers fired on the thousands of unarmed students and workers who had been peacefully protesting for democratic reforms. Thousands were massacred, machine-gunned or crushed by tanks.

5 JUNE

National Day of Denmark.

BORN THIS DAY

HISTORY

1723 Adam Smith, Scottish political economist who wrote *The Wealth of Nations*, baptized on this day.

1819 John Couch Adams, English mathematician and astronomer who discovered the planet Neptune on 3.7.1841.

1878 Francisco Pancho Villa, Mexican revolutionary who led one of the factions against the autocratic Porfirio Díaz, 1910–17.

ARTS

1884 Dame Ivy Compton-Burnett, English novelist whose works include *Brothers and Sisters* (1929) and *Daughters and Sons* (1937).

1898 Federico García Lorca, probably the most important Spanish poet and playwright this century, best known for his trilogy of plays including *Blood Wedding* (1933).

1939 Margaret Drabble, English author of *The Waterfall* (1969) and other novels.

1947 David Hare, English playwright whose plays include the award-winning *Pravda* (1985) and *Plenty*, which became a successful film (1985).

ENTERTAINMENT

1922 Sheila Sim, English actress and wife of Sir Richard Attenborough.

1928 Tony Richardson, English theatre and film director who directed the first stage production of *Look Back in Anger*. Films include *Tom Jones* (1953), which won him an Oscar.

POP

1926 Bill Hayes, US singer who had an international hit in 1955 with 'The Ballad of Davy Crockett' that encouraged an epidemic of Crocket-type fur hats on thousands of heads.

DIED THIS DAY

755 St Boniface, English missionary who went to Germany to establish Christianity and was murdered by unbelievers.

1826 Carl Maria Friedrich Ernst, Baron von Weber, German composer, in London, where he was conducting performances of his opera *Oberon*.

1900 Stephen Crane, US poet and novelist, author of *The Red Badge of Courage* (1895).

1910 O. Henry (William Sydney Porter), US short story writer.

1915 Henri Gaudier-Brzeska, French abstract sculptor, in combat during the First World War.

1916 Horatio Herbert, the first Earl Kitchener of Khartoum, lost at sea when the HMS *Hampshire* carrying him from England to Russia struck a mine and sank. There were no survivors.

1921 Georges Léon Jules Marie Feydeau, French playwright of farces such as *A Flea in Her Ear* (1907).

1983 Harry James, US trumpeter and bandleader.

ON THIS DAY

1944 The Café Gondrée was the first place to be liberated from the Germans on the eve of the D-Day landings when paratroopers from the 6th Brigade dropped on the town of Benouville to seize the vital canal bridge.

1947 US Secretary of State, George Marshall announced the Marshall Plan to help Europe recover from near-bankruptcy following the war.

1963 John Profumo, British Secretary of State for War, resigned after admitting to the House of Commons that he had lied over his relationship with Christine Keeler, who he met at the flat of osteopath Dr Stephen Ward. Miss Keeler was also seeing the Soviet naval attaché, Eugene Ivanov, but Mr Profumo said there had been no breach of security. The big sex scandal of the 1960s was to gather momentum and almost bring down the Conservative government of Harold Macmillan.

1967 The Six-day War began between Israel and her Arab neighbours Egypt, Jordan and Syria.

1968 Senator Robert Kennedy, destined to be the next president of the US, was shot by Palestinian Sirhan Sirhan, as he entered the Ambassador Hotel, Los Angeles. He was rushed to hospital, but died the following day.

1972 The Duke of Windsor, the former Edward VIII, was buried at Frogmore, Windsor.

1975 The Suez Canal was reopened after eight years by the President of Egypt, Anwar Sadat.

1988 Lone yachtswoman Kay Cottee sailed into Sydney Harbour to a huge welcome, becoming the first woman to circumnavigate the world non-stop. It had taken her six months.

1989 In Poland, Solidarity defeated the Communists in the first free elections since the end of the Second World War.

6 JUNE

National Day of Sweden.

BORN THIS DAY

HISTORY

1755 Nathan Hale, American revolutionary who spied on the British and was caught. Before he was hanged, he is alleged to have said, 'I regret I have only one life to lose for my country.'

1868 Captain Robert Falcon Scott, English naval officer and Antarctic explorer who set out on a second expedition to reach the South Pole in 1910, which turned out to be an ill-fated race to beat Amundsen.

1901 Sukarno, leader of the Indonesian independence movement who struggled to remove the Dutch from his country, suffering imprisonment then banishment before achieving his goal.

ARTS

1599 Diego Rodriguez de Silva y Velazquez, Spanish painter, baptized on this day. In 1623 he became court painter to Philip IV.

1606 Pierre Corneille, French playwright best remembered for his tragi-comedy, *Le Cid* (1636).

1799 Aleksandr Sergeyevich Pushkin, Russian poet, novelist, playwright and short-story writer who is considered the founder of modern Russian literature. His work includes the play *Boris Godunov* (1824) and the novel *The Queen of Spades* (1834).

1862 Sir Henry John Newbolt, English poet and naval historian who wrote *The Song of the Sea* (1904).

1875 Thomas Mann, German novelist who wrote *Death In Venice* (1912).

With the rise of Nazism, he left for the US where he became a citizen in 1944.

1898 Dame Ninette de Valois (Edris Stannus), Irish dancer, choreographer, teacher and founder of the Royal Ballet.

1903 Aram Ilyich Khachaturyan, Russian composer who wrote the popular *Sabre Dance*.

ENTERTAINMENT

1900 Arthur (Bowden) Askey, 'Big Hearted Arthur', English comedian who made his mark during the golden age of radio in comedy shows such as *Much Binding In the Marsh* with partner, Richard 'Stinker' Murdoch.

1932 Billie Whitelaw, English actress who has played leads on stage, screen and television. Her films include *Charlie Bubbles* (1968).

SPORT

1943 Asif Iqbal Razvi, Pakistan cricket captain in 1979 and outstanding batsman.

1956 Bjorn (Rune) Borg, Swedish tennis player and five-times Wimbledon champion. One of the richest and most successful players of all time, he also won the French Open six times before he suddenly retired in 1982 to concentrate on his business interests.

1957 Mike (Michael William) Gatting, Middlesex and England cricket captain who lost his job after a disastrous tour of Pakistan in 1988 when he had a serious confrontation with an umpire. He subsequently led the infamous rebel tour of South Africa, abandoned halfway through due to controversy.

DIED THIS DAY

1861 Count Camillo Benso di Cavour, Italian statesman who played a leading role in unifying Italy.

1891 Sir John Alexander Macdonald, first Prime Minister of Canada.

1941 Louis Chevrolet, US motor racer and car designer.

1956 Hiram Bingham, US archaeologist and senator who located the Inca city of Machu Picchu.

1961 Carl Gustav Jung, Swiss psychiatrist and pioneer psychoanalyst who worked with, but became increasingly critical of, Freud.

1976 Jean Paul Getty, US oil billionaire.

1990 Rex (Reginald Carey) Harrison, English actor, in New York, aged 82.

ON THIS DAY

1683 The first public museum, the Ashmolean, was opened by Elias Ashmole in Oxford. Exhibits included stuffed animals and a dodo, and visitors were charged for the length of stay.

1727 The first title fight took place in London between James Figg and Ned Sutton who was defeated. Figg was undisputed champion for around 15 years and made England the leading country in this sport.

1844 George Williams founded the YMCA at 72 St Paul's Churchyard, London.

1844 The first baseball match took place between the New York Nine and the Knickerbocker Club at Elysian Fields, Hoboken, New Jersey.

1907 Persil, the first household detergent, was marketed by Henkel et Cie of Dusseldorf.

1933 There was room for the occupants of 400 cars to watch the first drive-in movie in Camden, New Jersey when it was opened by Richard Hollingshead.

1936 Gatwick Airport opened in Surrey. Half a century later, it became Britain's second biggest international airport, and one of the world's busiest.

1944 D-Day: Allied troops landed on the beaches of Normandy in the biggest land, sea and air operation ever seen, under the command of General Dwight D. Eisenhower.

1949 *Nineteen Eighty-Four*, George Orwell's prophetic novel of a world ruled by Big Brother, was published.

1954 The Eurovision television network was launched, linking Britain, France, Italy, Belgium, Switzerland, Holland and Denmark.

1966 The first *Till Death Us Do Part* was televised by the BBC.

1984 Indian troops stormed the Golden Temple at Amritsar, the Sikhs' holiest temple, to arrest Sikh militants who had occupied the holy place. The attack resulted in 90 soldiers and 712 extremists being killed.

1988 Three giant snapping turtles turned up inside a Bronx sewage treatment plant. Each weighed about 50lbs and had probably been unwanted pets, flushed down the loo when quite small.

7 JUNE

BORN THIS DAY

HISTORY

1778 George Bryan 'Beau' Brummell, English dandy who inherited a large fortune, was a leader of fashion and a friend of the Prince Regent until they quarrelled. A great gambler, Brummell also accumulated large debts and was forced to flee to Calais in 1816. He was later imprisoned for debt, and died in a charitable asylum.

1879 Knud Johan Victor Rasmussen, Danish explorer who made the longest dog-sledge journey ever recorded across the American Arctic, making a study of the Eskimo tribes.

1896 Imre Nagy, Hungarian leader who led the revolt against Soviet domination of his country in 1956, for which he was executed two years later.

ARTS

1811 Richard Doddridge Blackmore, English novelist who wrote *Lorna Doone* (1869).

1848 (Eugène Henri) Paul Gauguin, French Post-Impressionist painter who left his job as a stockbroker in 1883 to become a full time painter. He visited van Gogh in Arles and was influenced by him before going to the islands of the South Pacific, where he produced some of his most important paintings.

1899 Elizabeth Bowen (Elizabeth Dorothea Cole), Irish novelist and short-story writer who was educated in England. Her work includes *The Death of the Heart* (1938).

1910 Pietro Annigoni, Italian painter best known for his portrait of the Queen at the National Portrait Gallery.

ENTERTAINMENT

1907 T(homas) E(rnest) B(ennett) Clarke, English screenwriter best remembered for *The Lavender Hill Mob* (1951) for which he won an Oscar.

1909 Jessica Tandy, English-born US

actress who was the original Blanche du Bois in Tennessee Williams' *A Streetcar Named Desire* on Broadway. In 1990, when she was 80, she became the oldest recipient of the Oscar for Best Actress for her part in *Driving Miss Daisy*.

1917 Dean Martin (Dino Paul Crocetti), US singer and actor who started as the straight man to Jerry Lewis in 16 films. After their partnership was dissolved he went on to perform solo in clubs and films.

1928 James Ivory, US film director who worked in India with Ismail Merchant and writer Ruth Prawer Jhabvala to make *Shakespeare Wallah* (1965). This remarkable partnership has continued to produce award-winning films including *A Room With A View* (1986) from the novel by E.M. Forster who died this day (*see* DIED THIS DAY).

1931 Virginia McKenna, English actress who will always be associated with her role in *Born Free* (1966).

POP

1940 Tom Jones (Thomas Jones Woodward), Welsh singer who had a No. 1 hit in 1965 with his still-popular 'It's Not Unusual'.

1960 Prince (Rogers Nelson) US singer who became a cult figure with the release of both the film and album, *Purple Rain* (1984) and with the hit single 'When Doves Cry'. 'Kiss' was his No. 1 hit in 1986.

ENGINEERING

1761 John Rennie, Scottish civil engineer who built old Waterloo Bridge and Southwark Bridge across the Thames, and New London Bridge which was sold in the 1960s to a US consortium who removed it brick by brick and rebuilt it in Arizona.

DIED THIS DAY

1329 Robert the Bruce, who seized the throne in 1306 to become King of Scotland. He died of leprosy and was buried in Dunfermline Abbey.

1886 Richard March Hoe, English-born rotary press inventor who emigrated to the US where he established his printing company.

1937 Jean Harlow (Harlean Carpenter), the 26-year-old US actress, of cerebral oedema.

1954 Alan (Mathison) Turing, English mathematician and computer pioneer who cracked the German codes in the Second World War. He committed suicide after a prosecution for alleged indecency.

1970 E(dward) M(organ) Forster, English novelist whose works include *A Passage to India* (1924).

1980 Henry (Valentien) Miller, US author of *Tropic of Cancer* (1934).

1988 Peter Hurkos, US 'telepathic detective' who helped the police with various celebrated cases, including that of the Boston Strangler.

ON THIS DAY

1566 Sir Thomas Gresham laid the foundation stone of the first Royal Exchange in London.

1905 Norway refused to recognize the Swedish king and declared its independence.

1929 The Papal State, which had not existed since 1870, was revived, and the Vatican City was established in Rome.

1929 Mrs Margaret Bondfield became the

first woman cabinet minister in the Labour government as Ramsay Macdonald's Minister of Labour.

1933 *The Seven Deadly Sins* was performed in Paris for the first time, choreographed by Georges Balanchine, with music by Kurt Weill, libretto by Bertold Brecht and songs sung by Lotte Lenya, Weill's wife.

1942 In the Battle of Midway in the Pacific, the US Navy sank two Japanese aircraft carriers and damaged 12 other warships.

1945 Benjamin Britten's *Peter Grimes* was performed for the first time, at Sadler's Wells Theatre.

1950 The first episode of the BBC's radio serial of the lives of the farming folk of Ambridge, *The Archers*, created by Godfrey Baseley, was broadcast.

1973 The Chancellor of West Germany, Willy Brandt, began a historic and emotional visit to Israel.

1977 Queen Elizabeth II's Jubilee celebrations began to mark her 25 years on the throne.

1988 An ailing parrot in a southern Brazilian zoo regained its appetite after a dentist fitted it with a plastic beak. The parrot's lower beak had split, preventing it from eating.

8 JUNE

BORN THIS DAY

HISTORY

1652 William Dampier, English explorer who became a buccaneer after exploring part of the Australian coastline. His piracy, mainly off the South American coast, netted £200,000 worth of booty in only two voyages. His ship's log describes what is believed to be the earliest record of a typhoon encountered by a European.

BRIGHT LIGHTS Born 1724, John Smeaton, considered the founder of English civil engineering, who built the all-masonry Eddystone lighthouse in 1756–9 at the same time developing cement which could be used underwater. Born 1772, Robert Stevenson, who built Bell Rock lighthouse, the first in Scotland.

ARTS

1810 Robert (Alexander) Schumann, German composer who had to give up his piano career when he injured his hand in a mechanical contrivance which he had invented to strengthen his fingers; he was compensated by marrying Clara Wieck, a brilliant pianist. Schumann ended his days in an asylum, suffering from hallucinations.

1829 Sir John (Everett) Millais, English painter, who was one of the founders of the Pre-Raphaelite Brotherhood, who achieved great popularity with *The Boyhood of Raleigh* (1870) and *Bubbles* (1886), famous as the Pear's soap poster.

1869 Frank Lloyd Wright, influential US architect whose work includes the Guggenheim Museum in New York.

ENTERTAINMENT

1934 Millicent Martin, English actress and singer who first made her name in the musical, *Expresso Bongo* in London (1958) and the weekly satirical television show, *That Was the Week That Was*.

SCIENCE

1916 Professor Sir Francis Crick, English biologist and Nobel prize winner with

J.D. Watson for their work in discovering the structure of DNA.

POP

1940 Nancy Sinatra, US singer, oldest daughter of Frank who recorded 'These Boots Are Made for Walking' which was No. 1 in February 1966.

SPORT

1932 Ray(mond) Illingworth, English cricketer who played for Yorkshire, Leicestershire and England where he reached the top ten of international wicket takers.

1947 Derek (Leslie) Underwood, English cricketer who played for Kent and took 2,420 wickets in first class matches between 1963 and 1986.

DIED THIS DAY

632 The Prophet Muhammad, founder of Islam, in Mecca, having united most of Arabia and established a springboard to spread the faith.

1376 Edward the Black Prince, one of the outstanding commanders of the Hundred Years War.

1809 Thomas Paine, English radical who wrote *The Rights of Man* (1791–2).

1845 Andrew Jackson, seventh US President.

1865 Sir Joseph Paxton, English architect who designed the Crystal Palace.

1876 George Sand (Amandine Aurore Lucie Dupin), French novelist.

1889 Gerard Manley Hopkins, English poet.

1929 Starr Faithfull, US nymphomaniac. She was found dead on Long Beach clad only in a silk dress. Starr's story was retold in the novel and film *Butterfield 8* by John O'Hara. She had kept a diary of her sex life and heavy drinking. A victim of the Roaring Twenties, no one could prove she had been murdered.

1969 Robert Taylor, US actor.

1974 Katherine Cornell, leading US actress.

1979 Sir Norman Hartnell, dressmaker to the Royals.

1979 Michael Wilding, English actor.

1988 Russell (Frederick) Harty, English journalist and broadcaster who died from hepatitis which he caught while filming his BBC television series *The Grand Tour*.

ON THIS DAY

FIRST NIGHTS, LAST NIGHT In 1914, the first performance outside Russia of *Prince Igor* by Borodin was sung by the great Chaliapin in London. In 1925, Noel Coward's comedy *Hay Fever* opened, making three Coward plays running simultaneously in London. *The Vortex* had opened earlier this year, followed by *Fallen Angels* with the playwright in the lead. In 1926, Dame Nellie Melba gave her farewell performance at Covent Garden. The audience, which included the Royal family, heard the 65-year-old diva sing a selection of her favourite arias.

1942 Japanese bombers made Australia their target attacking Sydney and Newcastle.

1968 James Earl Ray, wanted for the murder of Martin Luther King, was arrested in London travelling under an assumed name with a Canadian passport.

1969 Spain closed the frontier with Gibraltar hoping to cripple its economy following Britain's refusal to hand over the colony to Spain.

1978 Naomi James completed her round-the-world voyage, sailing solo, beating the record held by Sir Francis Chichester by two days.

1985 Barry McGuigan won the WBA featherweight title when he beat Panama's Eusébio Pedroza.

EYE DEFECT This day in 1988, Japan's Nippon Airways said that it had cut midair collisions with birds by 20 percent by painting huge eyeballs on its jet engines, and the East German authorities said that an 11-year-old dog belonging to Brigitte Bornschein, who had defected to West Germany earlier in this year, would not be allowed to join her.

9 JUNE

BORN THIS DAY

HISTORY

1672 Peter the Great, Tsar of Russia from 1689, who visited Holland and England before reorganizing Russia along western lines, building a fleet and restructuring the legal and education systems.

1836 Elizabeth Garrett Anderson, English physician who was refused admission to medical schools, so studied privately and was licensed to practise in 1865. She created a medical school for women which became the New Hospital for Women, later named the Elizabeth Garrett Anderson Hospital. She also became the first woman mayor of Aldeburgh.

1913 Patrick Christopher Steptoe, English obstetrician and gynaecologist who faced enormous ethical problems and much criticism pioneering 'test-tube' babies as a way of overcoming infertility.

ARTS

1853 Walter Weedon Grossmith, English humorous writer and comedian, who with his actor brother George, wrote *The Diary of a Nobody* which was published weekly in Punch.

ENTERTAINMENT

1893 Cole (Albert) Porter, US composer and lyricist who wrote Broadway hit musicals including *Anything Goes* (1934), *Kiss Me Kate* (1948) and *Can-Can* (1953). His best-remembered songs would fill the page, but just a small selection must include 'You Do Something to Me', 'Night and Day', 'I Get a Kick Out of You', 'Let's Do It', 'I Love Paris' and 'Begin the Beguine'.

INVENTION

1781 George Stephenson, English locomotive designer who learnt mathematics from his son, Robert, whom he managed to send to school in Newcastle. Stephenson's *Blucher* hauled coal for the first time and he won the contract for the first locomotive for the Stockton to Darlington run, while his *Rocket* was chosen as the first locomotive on the Liverpool-Manchester railway.

BUSINESS

1943 Charles Saatchi, advertising boss and art collector, in Bagdad, who together with older brother Maurice Saatchi (*see* 21.6.1946) runs advertising agency Saatchi and Saatchi.

DIED THIS DAY

1441 Jan van Eyck, Dutch painter.
1870 Charles (John Huffham) Dickens, English novelist, of a brain haemorrhage.
1874 Conchise, Apache chief and leader of the Apache and Navajo wars of 1860–86.
1964 William Maxwell Aitken, 1st Baron Beaverbrook, newspaper magnate.
1976 Dame Sybil Thorndike, English actress.

ON THIS DAY

1549 The Church of England adopted *The Book of Common Prayer* compiled by Thomas Cranmer.
1898 Britain took a 99-year lease on Hong Kong from China.
1899 In the 11th round, James Jackson Jeffries, US heavyweight boxing champion, knocked out Britain's Bob Fitzsimmons to become the world heavyweight champion, a title he would safely defend until his retirement in 1905.
1902 The first automat opened in the US, in Philadelphia.
1908 King Edward VII visited Tsar Nicholas II. The controversial meeting on board the Royal yacht, anchored in the Baltic Sea, was the first between a Russian tsar and a British monarch. But the British parliament was divided, with the less enthusiastic claiming that the Tsar was a murderer and a persecutor of the Jews.
1933 Baird demonstrated high definition television at his Long Acre studio in London, showing the difference between the previous 30-line picture and the new 120-line tubes.
1953 Randolf Turpin, British boxing champion, won the world middleweight crown when he beat Charles Hunez of France on points at White City.
1959 The US launched the *George Washington*, first nuclear submarine equipped with Polaris missiles.
1975 A live broadcast from the House of Commons was relayed by both the BBC and LBC (London Broadcasting).

10 JUNE

Time Observance Day in Japan, when people are supposed to be especially punctual.

BORN THIS DAY

HISTORY

1688 James Edward Stuart, the Old Pretender, son of the deposed Roman Catholic monarch James II, who was once thought to have been an imposter slipped into the Queen's bed in a warming pan to provide a Catholic successor to the throne.
1844 Carl Hagenbeck, German animal dealer and trainer who demonstrated that it was possible to control wild animals by kindness, not fear, and that they had suprising intelligence. He also created an open air zoo near Hamburg which was the prototype for the safari parks of the future.
1921 Prince Philip, the Duke of Edinburgh and husband of Queen Elizabeth II of Great Britain.
1923 Robert (Ian) Maxwell, chairman of the Mirror Group, who was born in

Czechoslovakia. He was also a Labour Member of Parliament (1964–70).

ARTS

REALISTS Born 1819, Gustave Courbet, French painter and leader of the Realist movement who rebelled against the Romantic painting of his day to paint everyday subjects, and in 1880, André Derain, French painter who turned from the abstract to Realism, finding inspiration in the old masters. He also designed sets for the Ballets Russes.

1911 Sir Terence (Mervyn) Rattigan, English playwright who was a superb craftsman with plays such as *French Without Tears* (1936), *The Winslow Boy* (1943) and *Separate Tables* (1945), as well as screenplays including *Goodbye, Mr Chips* (1968).

1915 Saul Bellow, Canadian-born US author of *Henderson the Rain King* (1959) and *Herzog* (1964), who won the Nobel prize in 1976.

1928 Maurice Sendak, US writer and book illustrator, arts which come together in *Where the Wild Things Are* (1963) and *Outside Over There* (1981).

ENTERTAINMENT

WORDS AND MUSIC Two contributors to the musical were born this day in 1901. One is now little known, the other remembered for his major successes. Eric Maschwitz, English lyricist, librettist and BBC executive wrote shows including *Love From Judy* (1952) and the words for songs like 'These Foolish Things' and 'A Nightingale Sang In Berkeley Square'. Frederick Loewe, US composer born in Berlin, wrote the music with Alan Jay Lerner for *Brigadoon* (1947), *Paint Your Wagon* (1951), *My Fair Lady* (1956) and *Gigi* (1963), including songs such as 'I Could Have Danced All Night' and 'Almost Like Being In Love'.

1922 Judy Garland (Frances Ethel Gumm) US singer and actress, charismatic star of *The Wizard of Oz* (1939), *Meet Me in St Louis* (1944) and *A Star Is Born* (1954).

1926 June Haver (June Stovenor), US actress who was groomed to take over from Betty Grable, but when her films including *I'll Get By* (1950) failed to make much impact, she retired, entered a convent, and became a nun.

INVENTIONS

1832 Nikolaus August Otto, German inventor of the four-stroke internal combustion engine in 1876 which was highly successful. More than 30,000 were sold but his patent was revoked in 1886 when an earlier patent by French engineer Alphonse Beau de Rochas came to light.

DIED THIS DAY

1190 Frederick Barbarossa, Holy Roman Emperor who led the third crusade against Saladin.

1727 George I, King of England, in Osnabrück on his way to Hanover, which he much preferred to London.

1836 André Marie Ampère, French physicist.

1924 Giacomo Matteotti, Italian socialist leader, assassinated by Mussolini's Fascists.

1926 Antonio Gaudi i Cornet, Catalan architect of the famous unfinished, surreal church of the Sagrada Familia in Barcelona.

1934 Frederick (Theodore Albert) Delius, English composer.

1946 Jack Johnson, US boxer and the first black world heavyweight champion, in a car crash in North Carolina.

1967 Spencer Tracy, Oscar-wining US actor.

ON THIS DAY

1692 The first of 19 people – 14 women and five men – were hanged at Salem at the end of the hysterical witch-hunt trials conducted by Judge Jonathan Corwin. One other accused person was crushed to death under weights for refusing to plead.

1793 The first public zoo, the Jardin des Plantes, opened in Paris.

1829 The first Oxford and Cambridge boat race took place from Hambledon Lock to Henley Bridge, a distance of 2¼ miles, and was won by Oxford.

1865 The first performance of Wagner's *Tristan and Isolde* took place in Munich.

1909 The Cunard liner SS *Slavonia* sent out the first SOS signal when she was wrecked off the Azores. The signals were picked up by vessels close by who took part in the rescue operation.

1931 Toscanini was allowed to leave Italy with his wife after his passport had been confiscated and they had both been attacked in Bologna because of his refusal to conduct the Fascist anthem at a concert. Two years later he again refused to conduct, this time at the Bayreuth Wagner Festival, in protest against the Nazis.

1943 Lazlo Biró, a Hungarian hypnotist, sculptor and journalist, patented his ballpoint pen, which he first devised in 1938.

1948 The first heart operations to unblock valves were carried out on three female patients aged between 11 and 23, called 'blue babies' because of the lack of oxygen in their blood which turned them that colour from birth. The surgeon who carried out the successful operations was Mr R.C. Broch at Guy's Hospital, London.

1965 A BEA (now BA) de Havilland jet airliner from Paris made the first automatic landing (relying entirely on instruments) at Heathrow.

1967 The Six-day War ended when Israel agreed to observe the UN ceasefire.

1983 Mrs Thatcher won her second term as British Prime Minister.

1985 Claus von Bulow was found not guilty at the end of his second trial of murdering his millionaire wife, 'Sunny', by injecting her with an overdose of insulin. But the battle for her $75m fortune continued.

1986 Bob Geldof, an Irish citizen, and John Paul Getty II, a US citizen, were made honorary knights by the Queen.

1988 A US clergyman claimed that the cartoon character Mighty Mouse had been shown snorting cocaine. Producers CBS denied the claim and said he was only sniffing flowers.

1989 The body of France's celebrated thief, Albert Spangiari who led 20 men through the sewers of Nice to steal £5m from a bank in 1976, was secretly delivered to his mother's house. He had been in hiding and apparently died from natural causes.

11 JUNE

BORN THIS DAY

HISTORY

1895 Nikolai Aleksandrovich Bulganin, Russian Premier from 1955–8 and former secret service officer.

ARTS

1572 Ben Jonson, English, poet and playwright, who wrote such masterpieces as *Every Man in His Humour* (1599) and *Volpone* (1606). He also created masques for the court with elaborate scenery devised by Inigo Jones.

1776 John Constable, English landscape painter of some of the most important and popular pictures of the 19th century. They include *Hay Wain* (1821) and other beautiful views of Suffolk.

1864 Richard Strauss, German composer of operas such as *Salome* (1905) and *Der Rosenkavalier* (1911), and the symphonic poem, *Don Juan* (1899).

1927 Beryl Grey, English prima ballerina who made her debut in 1941 with the Sadler's Wells Ballet. In 1968 she became artistic director of the Festival Ballet, until 1979.

1932 Athol Fugard, leading South African playwright and director who achieved international acclaim with plays such as *Boesman and Lena* (1974).

ENTERTAINMENT

1919 Richard Todd (Richard Andrew Palethorpe-Todd), actor, born in Dublin, whose films include *The Hasty Heart* (1949) and *The Story of Robin Hood* (1952). He also played Sir Walter Raleigh in *The Virgin Queen* (1955), the same year he made *The Dam Busters*.

1935 Gene Wilder (Jerry Silberman), US actor who had some of his training at the Bristol Old Vic. His most hilarious films include *The Producers* (1968), which won him an Oscar nomination, and *Young Frankenstein* (1974).

SCIENCE

1910 Jacques Yves Cousteau, French underwater explorer who was the commander of *Calypso* which travelled extensively to investigate the oceans. He was the director of the Oceanographic Museum of Monaco from 1957. The inventor of the Aqualung diving apparatus and a process for underwater television, he was able to produce popular and educational films such as *The Living Sea* (1963), which promoted conservation.

SPORT

1939 Rachel Heyhoe Flint, captain of England's women's cricket team (1966–77), broadcaster and journalist.

1939 Jackie Stewart, Scottish racing driver and world champion from 1969–73. He quit after winning the title for the third time (7.9.1973) making him one of the most successful Formula 1 drivers ever.

1946 Jenny Pitman, English racehorse trainer; the first woman to train a Grand National winner. (*See* 9.4.1983)

DIED THIS DAY

1847 Sir John Franklin, English naval officer and Arctic explorer who perished with his men trying to find the North West Passage. Their ship became trapped in the ice and they were not discovered again until 1859. In 1984 the bodies of two members of the expedition were found perfectly preserved in their icy graves.

1970 Aleksandr Fyodorovich Kerensky, a moderate Russian socialist who emigrated to the US after the Bolsheviks seized power from his government. He died in New York City.

1979 John Wayne (Marion Michael Morrison), US actor known as 'the Duke', who appeared in over 250 films.

1982 Gala Dali, wife of the famous Spanish surrealist painter who had said that if she died before him, he would eat her. She was buried without so much as a nibble.

ON THIS DAY

1509 Henry VIII married for the first time. Catharine of Aragon proved a good wife and queen until Henry's desire for a male successor led to divorce.

1727 Following the death of George I on 10.6.1727, his son George II acceded to the throne.

1903 Harry Vardon, the Jersey-born golfer, won his fourth Open golf championship at Prestwick.

1940 Mussolini declared war on the Allies.

1952 Denis Compton hit his 100th century, and on this day in 1953 Len Hutton became the first professional to captain England.

1955 Three cars travelling at 150 m.p.h. crashed and ploughed into spectators at Le Mans, killing 80 people and injuring over 100 in the worst accident in motor racing history. The race was not stopped and Britain's Mike Hawthorn was declared the winner.

1977 Dutch marines stormed a train at Assen where South Moluccan terrorists had held 55 hostages for 20 days. Six terrorists were killed and two hostages died in the action that followed.

1981 The musical *Barnum* opened at the London Palladium, starring Michael Crawford who personally performed all the stunts and acrobatics and was insured for £3m.

12 JUNE

BORN THIS DAY

HISTORY

1897 (Robert) Anthony Eden, 1st Earl of Avon, who was British Prime Minister, 1955–7. At the time of the Suez crisis, he sent in British troops ahead of the Israeli invasion. The bitter controversy that this stirred up internationally, and the failing health of a man considered one of the ablest statesmen in the world, led to his resignation.

1924 George Bush, US President, 1989–, who was Vice-President to Ronald Reagan. Dubbed a 'wimp', he finally produced a gutsy campaign to beat Michael Dukakis for the White House.

ARTS

1819 Charles Kingsley, English clergyman and author of *The Water Babies* (1863), a children's book which influenced Victorian society, and especially the working classes, to think about nature. His other novels include *Westward Ho!* (1855) and *Hereward the Wake* (1866).

1897 Leon Goosens, English oboist whose virtuosity pioneered the oboe as a solo instrument, encouraging composers to write special works. In 1962 he suffered severe damage to his mouth and teeth in a car crash, but managed to master a new technique to resume his career.

1929 Anne Frank, diarist, who was born in Germany before her family moved to Amsterdam. She was 13 years old when she began her diary describing the daily life of her family and four other Jews who were living in the backroom office and warehouse of her father's business to avoid deportation by the Nazis. Her father found her hidden diary after the war and published it in 1947.

ENTERTAINMENT

1920 Peter Jones, English actor, best known for his much-imitated narration of the cult radio serial-cum-comic novel, *The Hitch-Hiker's Guide to the Galaxy*.

1928 Vic Damone (Vito Farinola), US singer, who was in a number of films in the 50s and 60s including *Kismet* (1955). His recording of 'The Street Where You Live' from *My Fair Lady* got to No. 1 in 1958.

JAZZ

1941 Chick Corea (Armando Anthony Corea), US composer and pianist who worked with Miles Davis before forming his own group playing his strongly Latin-flavoured compositions including 'Return to Forever'.

SPORT

1945 Pat Jennings, Northern Ireland goalkeeper who in 1983 became the first player in England to appear in over 1,000 first class matches.

FASHION

1901 Sir Norman Hartnell, English designer and purveyor of clothes to the Royals and others.

DIED THIS DAY

1842 Dr Thomas Arnold, English educational reformer and headmaster of Rugby school.

1980 Sir Billy (William Edmond) Butlin, South African-born holiday camp promoter.

1982 Dame Marie Rambert (Mariam Rambach), born Warsaw, British ballet dancer, teacher and founder of the Ballet Rambert.

1983 (Edith) Norma Shearer, Canadian-born actress who starred in *The Barretts of Wimpole Street* (1934).

ON THIS DAY

1458 Magdalen College, Oxford, was founded.

1667 Jean-Baptiste Denys of Montpellier University and personal physician to Louis XIV carried out a successful blood transfusion using sheep's blood. The patient was a 15-year-old boy. Although claimed as the first successful transfusion, the Incas practised successful blood transfusions much earlier than European doctors.

1839 Abner Doubleday invented baseball at Cooperstown, New York.

1922 Leigh Mallory and two British climbers reached a height of 25,800 ft up Everest without the aid of oxygen; the highest point ever achieved. Two years later, this same month, Mallory made another attempt with Andrew Irvine. Less than 1,000 feet from the summit, they were trapped by bad weather and were never seen again.

1930 Germany's Max Schmeling became the first heavyweight boxer to win the world title as a result of a disqualification. Jack Sharkey of the US was disqualified in the fourth round for a foul.

1978 David Berkowitz, the New York killer called 'Son of Sam' was given life imprisonment for each of the six people he killed.

1979 A man-powered aircraft was 'pedalled' across the Channel by Bryan Allen from the US to claim the £100,000 prize.

1987 Princess Anne was made Princess Royal, the title awarded to the monarch's eldest daughter.

1987 Mrs Thatcher started her third term as Prime Minister.

13 JUNE

BORN THIS DAY

HISTORY

1910 Mary Whitehouse, English cofounder of 'Clean up TV campaign' and Honorary General Secretary of the National Viewers' and Listeners' Association.

ARTS

1752 Fanny Burney (Madame d'Arblay), English novelist and diarist who observed and recorded society which she used in her novel, *Evelina* (1778). It caused a sensation when it was published and the then anonymous author received praise from Dr Johnson and Sir Joshua Reynolds.

1865 W(illiam) B(utler) Yeats, Irish poet and playwright who was one of the founders of the Abbey Theatre, Dublin. His poem 'Easter 1916' deals with the Irish rebellion.

1885 Elizabeth Schumann, German-born US operatic soprano best remembered for her interpretation of the music of Mozart and Richard Strauss.

1893 Dorothy L(eigh) Sayers, English detective story writer whose Lord Peter Wimsey first appeared in *Whose Body?* (1923) then in novels such as *Hangman's Holiday* (1933) and *The Nine Tailors* (1934).

ENTERTAINMENT

1892 Basil Rathbone, South African-born English actor who played Sherlock Holmes in 14 films in the 1940s.

1943 Malcolm McDowell, English actor who played the lead in *If...* (1968), and in *The Clockwork Orange* (1971), but probably had his best success in *O Lucky Man* (1973).

SPORT

1897 Paavo (Johannes) Nurmi, Finnish distance runner who won six gold medals in three Olympic Games in 1920, 1924 and 1928. He was the world record holder for the mile (4 minutes 10.4 seconds) for eight years.

1915 (John) Don(ald) Budge, US tennis champion who was the first amateur to win the 'grand slam': the singles championship in Australia, France, Britain and US in 1938. He won the 1937 and 1938 Wimbledon men's singles and doubles championships (with Gene Mako) and mixed doubles (with Alice Marble). He turned professional in 1939.

1958 Peter Scudamore, English champion jockey who became only the third National Hunt jockey to ride over 1,000 winners and was well on the way to becoming the champion of champions.

EDUCATION

1795 Dr Thomas Arnold, English educationalist and reformer of the Public School system while headmaster of Rugby School. (*See* 12.6.1842)

DIED THIS DAY

323BC Alexander the Great, following an illness in Babylon after a long banquet accompanied by heavy drinking. He had conquered half the world and would have been 33 years old in eight days (suggested date).

WATERY GRAVES In 1886, Ludwig II, the certified insane King of Bavaria, committed suicide by drowning in the Starnberger Sea. Also perished, his psychiatrist Bernhard von Gudden, attempting to save his life. In 1930, Sir Henry Segrave, English land- and water-speed breaker, killed when his speedboat capsized on Lake Windermere, travelling at 98 m.p.h. The superstitious might note his attempt had been made on a Friday.

1986 Benny (Benjamin David) Goodman, US bandleader and clarinettist, called 'the king of swing'.

ON THIS DAY

1381 Wat Tyler led the first popular rebellion in English history called the Peasant's Revolt. (*See also* 15.6.1381)

1842 Queen Victoria travelled by train for the first time, from Slough (near Windsor Castle) to Paddington, accompanied by Prince Albert. A special coach had been built earlier, but the Queen had been reluctant to try this new form of travel. On her first journey, the engine driver was assisted by the great civil engineer, Isambard Kingdom Brunel.

1893 The first Women's Golf Championship, held at Royal Lytham, was won by Lady Margaret Scott.

1900 The Boxer Rebellion began in China to end the domination and exploitation of the country by foreigners. The Boxers were a secret society, originally formed to promote boxing.

1944 The first V-1 flying bomb landed in England. Hitler's 'secret weapon' hit a house in Southampton, killing three people.

1951 Princess Elizabeth laid the foundation stone on London's South Bank of the National Theatre.

1956 The first European Cup was won by Real Madrid in Paris when they beat Stade de Reims 4–3.

1988 The first Miss Moscow was Maria Kalinina who won amidst much controversy. Prizes included a television set, publicity contracts and a Mediterranean cruise.

14 JUNE

BORN THIS DAY

HISTORY

1928 Che Guevara (Ernesto Guevara de la Serna), legendary Cuban revolutionary born in Argentina. He joined Fidel Castro's revolutionary forces in 1956, but in 1966 he suddenly appeared in Bolivia after vanishing for a year. It was here, while training and fighting with guerrillas, that he was captured and executed.

ARTS

1811 Harriet Beecher Stowe, US novelist who wrote *Uncle Tom's Cabin* (1852), which was not only a huge success, but did much to direct public sympathy to the emancipation of slaves. The book was translated into 23 languages. When adapted as a stage play, it proved equally successful, becoming the longest-running US play.

ENTERTAINMENT

1909 Burl Ives, US folk singer and actor who won an Oscar for his supporting role in *The Big Country* (1958), the same year as his most memorable role as Big Daddy in *Cat on a Hot Tin Roof*.

1919 Sam Wanamaker, US actor, director and producer who came to Britain in the late 1940s when he feared he would be blacklisted in Hollywood during the McCarthy hysteria. He was also responsible for organizing both opinion and finance to rebuild Shakespeare's Globe as close to the original site on the South Bank as possible.

POP

1961 Boy George (George O'Dowd), English lead singer with Culture Club whose female attire and appearance made him a magnet for the media. He achieved notable hits with 'Do You Really Want to Hurt Me' (1982) and 'Karma Chameleon' (1983).

SPORT

1969 Steffi Graf, German tennis champion who at age 19, won the Wimbledon women's singles, and also a gold medal at the 1988 Olympics. In 1989, she successfully defended her Wimbledon crown and made it a double victory for Germany with Boris Becker winning the men's singles.

DIED THIS DAY

1801 Benedict Arnold, US soldier and traitor, who offered his services after the Revolution to the British in return for £20,000. He came to England in 1781 where he received a small pension. Ostracised and in ill-health, he died in London.

1927 Jerome K(lapka) Jerome, English humorous writer, author of *Three Men in a Boat* (1889).

1928 Emmeline Pankhurst (Goulden), English women's rights champion.

1936 G(ilbert) K(eith) Chesterton, English author, remembered for his Father Brown detective stories.

1946 John Logie Baird, Scottish television pioneer.

1986 Alan Jay Lerner, US lyricist and playwright, best remembered for *My Fair Lady*.

ON THIS DAY

1645 Cromwell's Parliamentarians (Roundheads) defeated the Royalists (Cavaliers) under Prince Rupert, defending King Charles I, at the Battle of Naseby, Northamptonshire.

1755 Dr Johnson's *Dictionary* went on sale, priced £4/10s for both volumes.

1777 The US Congress adopted the 'Stars and Stripes' as the official flag.

1800 The Battle of Marengo, in north-west Italy, ended with Napoleon and the French army crushing the Austrians during the French Revolutionary Wars.

1839 The first Henley Regatta was held. The annual event has since become an international festival for rowers and imbibers of Pimms No. 1.

1917 The first German bombs dropped by airplanes as opposed to Zeppelins killed over 100 and injured 400 people in the London's East End.

1919 At 14.13 GMT, Captain John Alcock and Lt Arthur Whitten-Brown took off from Newfoundland on the first non-stop transatlantic flight to Galway, Ireland, in a Vickers Vimy. They landed safely 16½ hours later, on the 15th.

1940 German troops entered Paris and the Swastika flew from the Eiffel Tower. Eight days later, on the 22nd, the armistice was signed and the Vichy government was set up.

1964 Nelson Mandela was sentenced to life imprisonment and sent to Robben Island, seven miles off Cape Town, sparking off international protests.

1982 The Argentinian troops on the Falkland Islands surrendered when General Menendez agreed to an armistice.

BEAR FACTS Hot-air balloonists flying over Stockholm Zoo in 1988 startled a bear cub, which fell from its tree perch and died. Authorities said they would ban further flights. While this was happening, over in New Jersey students in a school were kept in an extra 45 minutes by a six-foot black bear that had wandered into the playground. They kept it at bay by tossing out peanut butter sandwiches until the game warden arrived to take him away.

15 JUNE

BORN THIS DAY

HISTORY

1330 Edward the Black Prince, eldest son of Edward III, who got his popular title because he wore black armour in battle. He married his cousin Joan, 'The Fair Maid of Kent', who gave him two sons, one of whom was the future Richard II.

1913 Father Trevor Huddleston, English president of the Anti-Apartheid Movement, chairman of International Defence and Aid Fund for Southern Africa, and author of *Nought for Your Comfort* (1956).

ARTS

1843 Edvard (Hagerup) Grieg, Norwegian composer whose Scottish father (formerly Greig) was the British consul at Bergen who married Gesine Harup of a well-established Norwegian family. His music, heavily influenced by Norwegian folk music, won him awards and honours not only from his native land, but from many countries. Besides his popular Piano Concerto (*Opus 16*), he wrote the incidental music to *Peer Gynt* (1876).

ENTERTAINMENT

1884 Harry Langdon, US silent film comedian with the distinctive baby face who appeared in a string of comedies. He was once rated one of the four top Hollywood comedians until he fired his writers and directors and decided to take on these roles too. It was downhill all the way to bankruptcy in 1931.

1945 Nicola Pagett, English actress.

1949 Simon Callow, English actor of both stage and screen, whose films include

Amadeus (1985) and *Room with a View* (1987).

JAZZ

1923 (Louis) Erroll Garner, US jazz pianist and composer who is best known for 'Misty', composed in the late 50s.

POP

1941 Harry (Edward) Nilsson, US singer and songwriter who began in the 60s with 'This Could Be The Night'; he continued to sing his own songs, but his big success came in England in 1972 when he recorded 'Without You', a song he didn't write, which stayed No. 1 for four weeks.

DIED THIS DAY

1381 Wat Tyler, English poll tax rebel, beheaded at Smithfield. (*See* 13.6.1381)

1888 Frederick III, Emperor of Germany.

ON THIS DAY

1215 The Magna Carta was sealed by King John at Runnymede, near Windsor.

1752 Benjamin Franklin flew a kite with a metal frame during a storm as part of his experiments with electricity, to prove lightning is attracted to metal.

1825 The foundation stone of the New London Bridge was laid by 'the grand old' Duke of York. It now spans an artificial lake in Arizona.

1836 Arkansas became the 25th state of the Union.

1844 Charles Goodyear patented his vulcanized rubber process in the US, which made possible the commercial use of rubber.

1846 The 49th parallel was established as the border between Canada and the USA.

1860 Florence Nightingale started her School for Nurses at St Thomas's Hospital, London.

1883 Germany's prince and chancellor, Bismarck instituted the first Health Insurance Act.

1887 Carlisle D. Graham shot Niagara Falls in a barrel for the second time, and survived.

1937 The first performance of *Checkmate*, the ballet by Ninette de Valois with music by Arthur Bliss, was staged by the Vic-Wells Ballet (later renamed the Sadler's Wells Ballet) in Paris.

1970 Olivier was made a Life Peer, the first actor to be thus honoured.

1977 Adolfo Suarez won the first democratic elections in Spain for 41 years.

1988 Yasser Arafat, the leader of the Palestinian Liberation Organization, was asked by ultra-orthodox Rabbi Moshe Hirsch to intervene to close down a Jerusalem sex shop. The Rabbi, himself an anti-Zionist, turned to Arafat to end the sale of porn videos and inflatable Chinese dolls in the Holy City.

16 JUNE

BORN THIS DAY

HISTORY

1858 Gustav V, king of Sweden from 1907 to 1950, the longest reign in Sweden's history. A popular king, he managed to keep his country neutral during two world wars.

1922 Enoch Powell, English politician and classicist who was once tipped as a future British Prime Minister, but fell out with the Conservative Party over their Northern Ireland policy and over immigration, warning that the influx of black people from Commonwealth countries was sowing the seeds for a bloody confrontation between black and white.

ENTERTAINMENT

1890 Stan Laurel (Arthur Stanley Jefferson), English-born comedian in US films (the thin one) with his partner Oliver Hardy (the fat one).

1892 Lupino Lane (Harry Lupino), English actor, singer, dancer and choreographer who introduced 'The Lambeth Walk' in the musical *Me and My Girl* (1937).

SPORT

1927 Tom (Thomas William) Graveney, England cricketer awarded the OBE who was an elegant and high scoring batsman for both his country, and clubs Worcester and Gloucester, (he also played for Queensland). With an average 44.91 in first class cricket, he is rated one of the top ten English batsmen of all time.

DIED THIS DAY

1722 John Churchill, first Duke of Marlborough, an outstanding British general.

1869 Charles Sturt, English explorer who led one of the most important expeditons in Australian history.

1930 Elmer Ambrose Sperry, US inventor of the gyroscopic compass and other devices.

1958 Imre Nagy, former Prime Minister of Hungary, hanged following a secret trial for his part in the 1956 revolution.

1969 Earl Alexander of Tunis, British field marshal and later Governor-General of Canada.

1971 Sir John Charles Reith, first Baron Reith of Stonehaven, first director-general of the BBC.

1977 Wernher von Braun, German rocket pioneer who went to work on the US space programme after the war.

ON THIS DAY

1794 The first stone was laid of the world's biggest grain windmill in Holland. Known as 'De Walvisch' (the whale) it is still in existence.

1880 The distinctive Salvation Army ladies bonnets were worn for the first time when they marched in procession in Hackney in London's East End.

IN THE BEGINNING In 1903, Henry Ford formed his motor manufacturing company. He retained 25 per cent of the shares and was made Vice-President and Chief Engineer. On the same day, a company just one year old registered its trade name, Pepsi-Cola.

1904 The entire novel *Ulysses* by James Joyce takes place on this day, now known and celebrated in Dublin, where the novel is set, as Bloomsday, after the leading character, Leopold Bloom.

1929 Bentleys took the first four places at the Le Mans 24-hour endurance race.

1935 Roosevelt's 'New Deal' was passed by the US Congress to start a recovery programme to beat the Depression.

1948 Chinese bandits hijacked a Cathay Airways Catalina flying boat; the captain, experiencing the first hijacking of an aircraft ever, refused to take their orders. There was gunfire and the plane crashed, killing all but the bandit leader.

1958 Yellow 'No Waiting' lines were introduced to British streets.

1961 Rudolf Nureyev defected to the West while at Le Bourget Airport, Paris as the Kirov Ballet prepared to fly to London on the next stop of their tour.

1963 Valentina Tereshkova in *Vostok 6* became the first woman to travel in space. She made 48 orbits of the earth before returning safely to earth.

1972 German police captured the last member of the notorious Baader-Meinhof 'Red Army Faction' when they arrested Ulrike Meinhof in Hanover. (*See* 9.5.1976)

1976 The people of the huge black township of Soweto near Johannesburg rebelled against the enforced teaching of Afrikaans in their schools. Over 1,000 people died before security forces crushed the uprising. It has now become Soweto Day for blacks in South Africa.

1978 The electronic 'Space Invaders' game was demonstrated by Taito Corporation of Tokyo.

17 JUNE

BORN THIS DAY

HISTORY

1239 Edward I, King of England (1272–1307) who invaded Wales in 1277 and ended the autonomy of the principality. He was less successful with Scotland where there was unrest and rebellion.

1703 John Wesley, English evangelist who initiated the Methodist societies and brought about an evangelical revival not only in England, but also in North America.

ARTS

1818 Charles François Gounod, French composer, best known for his opera *Faust* produced in 1859. He came to London in 1870 where he formed a choir which later became the Royal Choral Society.

1882 Igor (Fyodorovich) Stravinsky, Russian composer and one of the leading figures in 20th-century music, who first composed for the Ballets Russes including *The Firebird* (1910) and *The Rite of Spring* (1913). He also composed the vocal work, *Oedipus Rex* (1927). At the outbreak of the Second World War he moved to the US where he continued to compose symphonies and the opera *The Rake's Progress* (1948).

ENTERTAINMENT

1920 Beryl Reid, English actress who moved from a comedienne in revues and on radio and television, to a stage actress with her award-winning role in *The Killing of Sister George* which opened on her 45th birthday, and which she repeated in the 1968 film.

1936 Ken Loach, English television and film director whose work includes the award-winning television production *Cathy Come Home*, which highlighted the problems of Britain's homeless and gave the fledgling charity, 'Shelter', such a successful start. His films include *Poor Cow* (1967).

POP

1946 Barry Manilow, US singer who had hits with 'Mandy' (1975), 'I Write the Songs' (1976) and 'It Looks Like We Made It' (1977).

SPORT

1930 (John) Brian Statham, England and Lancashire fast bowler.

1932 Derek Ibbotson, English athlete who won back the world mile record in 1957 in 3 minutes 57.2 seconds at White City in London.

DIED THIS DAY

1719 Joseph Addison, English poet and essayist, co-founder of the *Spectator*.

1898 Sir Edward Coley Burne-Jones, English-born romantic painter of Welsh parents.

1963 John Cowper Powys, English-born novelist and poet of Welsh parents.

ON THIS DAY

1579 Sir Francis Drake anchored the *Golden Hind* just north of what would one day be San Francisco Bay, and named the area New Albion.

1775 The Battle of Bunker Hill took place, one of the earliest battles of the US War of Independence during the Siege of Boston. Although the British eventually took the hill, the resistance displayed by the American 'rebels' had a marked effect on the war.

1823 Charles Macintosh patented the waterproof cloth he was to use in making raincoats.

MEDICAL FIRSTS In 1867, Joseph Lister amputated a cancerous breast from his sister Isabella using carbolic acid as an antiseptic. The operation in the Glasgow Royal Infirmary was the first under antiseptic conditions. In Chicago in 1950, the first kidney transplant was carried out on a woman patient by surgeon Mr R.H. Lawler.

1929 Hitchcock's *Blackmail* was premièred at the Royal, Marble Arch, London. The first reel was shot before the studio was equipped for sound, and has only sound effects and music; the dialogue begins in reel two, although the leading lady, Czech actress Anny Oudra spoke little English and her voice was dubbed by Joan Barry.

1944 Iceland became an independent republic.

1959 The *Daily Mirror* paid £8,000 libel charges to Liberace after columnist Cassandra had implied he was a homosexual when he wrote that Liberace was 'a fruit-flavoured, mincing, ice-covered heap of Mother Love'.

1970 Edwin Land patented his Polaroid camera.

1972 Five men were arrested at the Watergate complex in Washington attempting to bug the Democratic National Committee offices.

1982 Following the collapse of the Banco Ambrosiano, Roberto Calvi, its head who had links with the Vatican Bank and the unofficial P2 masonic lodge, was found hanging under Blackfriars Bridge, London. It was suicide, the court decided. It seemed to others a long way to come to hang oneself.

1988 Dennis Loban, a reggae poet and street vendor, was found guilty of the murder of reggae star Peter Tosh in Kingston, Jamaica. He was sentenced to hang.

1989 France celebrated the 100th birthday of the much-loved Eiffel Tower, the symbol of Paris which a century before had had critics claiming it was ugly, unsafe or both.

18 JUNE

BORN THIS DAY

HISTORY

1769 Viscount Castlereagh, 2nd Marquis of Londonderry. British statesman born in Ireland who, as foreign secretary to Lord Liverpool, organized the coalition against Napoleon; Europe enjoyed 40 years of peace due to his efforts.

1884 Édouard Daladier, three times French Premier, each for a short term.

ENTERTAINMENT

1901 Jeanette MacDonald, US actress and singer who teamed up with Nelson Eddy to form the most successful and popular film singing partnership ever until their style went out of fashion in the 1940s. Films include *Rose Marie* (1936) and *Maytime* (1937).

1920 Ian Carmichael, English actor who played light comedy roles on stage and screen, including *The Lady Vanishes* (1979). He played Lord Peter Wimsey, the bumbling detective on television.

1927 Paul Eddington, English actor with a solid stage career and highly successful on television as Jim Hacker in *Yes, Prime Minister*.

1978 Garfield, the world's favourite fat cat, created by Jim Davis. Now the fastest-growing comic strip ever, Garfield can be seen in more than 2,000 newspapers in 37 countries and in 12 languages. The name comes from Davis' grandfather, James A. Garfield Davis.

POP

1942 Paul McCartney, former Beatle, still one of the top writer-performers in the world, probably the most successful of all time with 20 No. 1 hits with the Fab Four, nine with his own group Wings or with other artists such as wife Linda and Michael Jackson. He has written more hits than any other contemporary, over 30 including Beatles' classics such as 'A Hard Day's Night' (1964) and 'Yesterday' (1965). He also wrote 'Live and Let Die' (1973) for the Bond movie.

1961 Alison Moyet, English singer who won acclaim with her album *Alf* (1984) with the single 'All Cried Out'.

DIED THIS DAY

1902 Samuel Butler, English novelist, essayist, critic and author of the autobiographical novel, *The Way of All Flesh* published posthumously in 1903.

1928 Roald Amundsen, Norwegian explorer who beat Scott to the South Pole, but lost his life in a plane crash when flying to rescue Umberto Nobile, with whom he had previously made the first flight over the North Pole in a dirigible.

1936 Maxim Gorky (Aleksei Maksimovich Peshkov), Russian novelist and short story writer.

1958 Douglas Jardine, former England cricket captain at the centre of the controversial body-line bowling drama during a 30s tour of Australia.

1959 Ethel Barrymore (Ethel Mae Blythe), US actress and sister of actors

John and Lionel, who has a Broadway Theatre named after her.

1971 Libby Holman, US 'torch' singer who introduced many new songs including 'You and the Night and the Music'.

ON THIS DAY

1583 The first Life Insurance policy was sold (according to records in London), and it was also the first to be disputed by the insurance company who refused to pay out on the death of the insured, but the court ruled against and payment was eventually made.

1815 The combined forces led by Wellington and Blucher defeated Napoleon at the Battle of Waterloo. Two years later, on the anniversary of the famous battle, London's Waterloo Bridge was opened.

1928 Amelia Earhart became the first woman to fly the Atlantic when she and her two male companions landed safely in Wales.

1963 Henry Cooper floored Cassius Clay (Muhammad Ali) in round four at Wembley Stadium, London, but by the sixth, with Cooper badly cut, the fight was stopped and Clay remained world heavyweight boxing champion.

1975 The first North Sea oil came ashore from a Liberian tanker which berthed at BP's Isle of Grain refinery.

1979 President Carter and USSR's Brezhnev signed the SALT (Strategic Arms Limitation Treaty) in Vienna.

19 JUNE

BORN THIS DAY

HISTORY

1556 James I, King of England and Scotland, son of Mary Queen of Scots and Lord Darnley, who was proclaimed king in 1567 when his mother was forced to abdicate.

1623 Blaise Pascal, French mathematician and philosopher who invented the first calculating machines. Other research led to the invention of the syringe and hydraulic press and with it, Pascal's law of pressure.

1861 Douglas, 1st Earl Haig, British field marshal, born in Scotland, who during the First World War took charge of the army on the western front succeeding Sir John French. His war of attrition led to eventual victory, but at a terrible price. After the war, he devoted himself to the care of ex-Servicemen.

1896 Bessie Wallis Warfield, Duchess of Windsor, born in the US where she first married a naval officer in 1916. She married Ernest Simpson, a US-born Englishman in 1928. They mixed in high society and in 1936 she met the Prince of Wales. She divorced Simpson that same year, and when Edward, now King, told Prime Minister Baldwin he intended marrying a twice-divorced woman, he met fierce government opposition. They eventually settled in Paris in a luxurious exile; the king who abdicated, the queen who never was.

1917 Joshua Nkomo, Zimbabwean politician, leader of ZAPU, who served in Mugabe's cabinet despite their fierce rivalry.

ARTS

1947 Salman Rushdie, British novelist who wrote among others, *The Satanic Verses*, the book which caused Iranian Ayatollah Khomeini to issue his infamous death threat against the author.

ENTERTAINMENT

1877 Charles Coburn, US actor who specialized in tough businessmen with soft centres winning an Oscar for *The More the Merrier* (1943).

1933 Thelma Barlow, English actress who has played Mavis in *Coronation Street* since 1971.

SCIENCE

1906 Ernst Boris Chain, British biochemist born in Berlin who worked with Florey at Oxford to purify penicillin discovered by Fleming. They shared the 1945 Nobel prize.

SPORT

1903 Walter Reginald Hammond, England and Gloucester cricket captain and one of the great batsman. He and the legendary Bradman are the only batsmen to have passed 900 runs in a single test series. He also scored the fastest triple century in Test cricket against New Zealand (1933), reaching his 300 in 288 minutes.

DIED THIS DAY

1815 William Combe, English writer of satirical books and poems including his *Tour of Dr Syntax in Search of the Picturesque* (1812) which was 19th-century bestseller in England.

1820 Sir Joseph Banks, English explorer and naturalist who travelled around the world with Cook and collected plant and natural history specimens.

1937 Sir J(ames) M(atthew) Barrie, Scottish playwright who wrote *Peter Pan*.

ON THIS DAY

1829 Sir Robert Peel established the London Metropolitan Police by an Act of Parliament passed this day.

1846 The first official game of baseball was played at the Elysian Fields, Hoboken, New Jersey by the New York Nine and the Knickerbocker Club.

1910 Father's Day was instituted in the US by Mrs John Bruce Dodd of Spokane, Washington.

1953 Ethel and Julius Rosenberg went to the electric chair in Sing Sing at 8 p.m. guilty of spying for the USSR. They were the first married couple to be executed for espionage in the US. Demonstrations took place in the US and Europe to protest at the sentence of death during peacetime. (*See* 30.3.1951)

1957 ITV began screening *The Army Game* with Alfie Bass and Bill Fraser.

1960 Daimler was acquired by Jaguar Motors.

1970 *Soyuz 9* landed safely after a record 17 days in space.

20 JUNE

BORN THIS DAY

ARTS

1819 Jacques Offenbach (Jakob Levy Eberst), French composer, born Cologne, who created a genre of comic opera at his own theatre in Paris, Bouffes parisiens, including *Orpheus in the*

Underworld (1859). He also composed several pieces for cancan dancers, but he died in 1880 before finishing his only grand opera, *The Tales of Hoffmann*.

1887 Kurt Schwitters, German Dada artist and poet, best known for his collages assembled from everyday objects including train tickets, string and postage stamps. Even his poems were created this way, with newspaper headlines and other printed ephemera. He came to work in England in 1940, after the Nazis had declared his work decadent.

1906 Catherine Cookson, popular and prolific English author who wrote the Mallen novels amongst many others.

ENTERTAINMENT

1909 Errol Flynn, Tasmanian-born swashbuckling actor on screen and in real life. The athletic Flynn starred in costume dramas such as *The Adventures of Robin Hood* (1938) and *The Sea Hawk* (1940); he appeared to win the war single-handed in films like *Objective Burma!* (1946), but was turned down for military service because he had a heart defect, recurring malaria and a mild form of tuberculosis. His heavy drinking, womanizing and increasing debts drove him out of Hollywood and his career ended prematurely.

1934 Wendy Craig, English actress who was at her best in Carla Lane's television series *Butterflies*, playing a frustrated suburban middle-class housewife.

POP

1949 Lionel (Brockman) Richie, US singer and songwriter who had the most successful Motown single ever with 'Endless Love' which he wrote and performed with Diana Ross. It reached No. 1 on 15 August 1981 and stayed there for nine weeks. He had a string of hits, including 'Say You, Say Me' (1985) from the movie *White Nights* which also won him an Oscar for the Best Original Song.

SPORT

1954 Allan (Joseph) Lamb, England cricketer, born in South Africa where he played for Western Province. In England, he joined Northampton. He is one of only five players to have ever batted on each day of a five-day test (against the West Indies at Lords in 1984).

DIED THIS DAY

1597 Willem Barents, Dutch explorer, in the Arctic searching for the north-east passage from Europe to Asia. His ship became trapped in ice, and he and his party tried to find safety by sailing in open boats. They perished within a week. The Barents Sea is named after him.

1837 William IV, British king (*see* ON THIS DAY).

1923 Francisco Pancho Villa (Dorteo Arango), Mexican revolutionary, assassinated on his farm several years after he retired from politics.

ON THIS DAY

1756 The 146 captured defenders of Calcutta, all from the East India Company's garrison were imprisoned by the Nawab of Bengal in the Company's lock-up for petty offenders known as the Black Hole. Only 23 survived.

1819 The paddle-wheel steamship *Savannah* arrived at Liverpool after a voyage lasting 27 days 11 hours, the first steamship to cross the Atlantic.

1837 Queen Victoria, just 18 years old, ascended the throne following the death of her uncle, William IV.

1887 On Queen Victoria's Golden Jubilee, Buffalo Bill Cody staged a Royal Command performance of his famous Wild West Show and four European kings attending boarded the original Deadwood coach driven by Cody.

1887 Britain's longest railway bridge over the River Tay was opened. The first bridge had collapsed in 1879 while the Edinburgh to Dundee train was crossing, killing over 90 people.

1949 'Gorgeous Gussie' Moran, US tennis player, caused a sensation at Wimbledon wearing lace-trimmed panties under her short skirt, designed by Teddy Tinling.

1960 Half way through the fifth round, Floyd Patterson of the US floored Sweden's Ingemar Johansson to become the first boxer to regain a world heavyweight title.

1963 The White House and the Kremlin agreed to set up the 'hot line'.

1966 Mohamet Yusuf Daar, formerly of Kenya, became PC 492 in Coventry, the first black policeman in Britain.

1969 The discovery of high-grade crude oil deposits in the North sea was announced, ten years after the first natural gas was found.

1987 The All Blacks won Rugby's first World Cup when they beat France.

21 JUNE

BORN THIS DAY

HISTORY

1002 Leo IX, the pope who brought the conflict between Rome and the eastern Church to a head in 1054, ending with the Patriarch of Constantinople being excommunicated and the creation of the Schism.

1884 Field Marshal Sir Claude Auchinleck, British general who revived the flagging Eighth Army to go back on the offensive against the German army under Rommel in the Middle East, but who was later replaced. History has reassessed his skills and judgement.

1953 Benazir Bhutto, Prime Minister of Pakistan, elected in 1988 after the military regime had agreed to free elections following the death of President Zhia.

1982 Prince William, eldest son of Prince Charles and Princess Diana.

ARTS

1850 Enrico Cechetti, Italian dancer and choreographer noted for his brilliant technique. He created several major roles including the Bluebird for *Sleeping Beauty*, but it is as a teacher that he made his major contribution with pupils including Pavlova, Nijinsky and Karsavina and with schools using his method in many parts of the world.

1905 Jean-Paul Sartre, French existentialist philosopher, novelist and playwright, author of *Being and Nothingness* (1943). He lived with writer Simone de Beauvoir and jointly edited a monthly review, *Les Temps Modernes*. He also wrote screenplays including the adaptation of Millers' *The*

Crucible as *The Witches of Salem* (1957).

MEMORIES Born 1912, Mary McCarthy, US novelist who wrote her first book, *The Company She Keeps* at 30. Her autobiography, *Memories of a Catholic Childhood*, was published in 1957. Born 1935, Françoise Sagan (Françoise Quoirez), French novelist who had written two novels before she was 20: *Bonjour Tristesse* (1954) and *Un Certain Sourire* (tr. *A Certain Smile*) published in 1956, which reflected her memories of a Catholic childhood.

ENTERTAINMENT

1921 Jane Russell (Ernestine Jane Geraldine Russell), US actress who had to prove she was more than just a 38-inch bust in films such as *The Outlaw* (1943), for which Howard Hughes personally designed her bra. Her chance came in later films when she played cynical females, and in 1971 she replaced Elaine Stritch on Broadway in the musical *Company*.

SPORT

1937 John (Hugh) Edrich, England and Surrey cricketer who is the only batsman to have scored 57 boundaries in a single innings, making 310 not out for England against New Zealand at Headingly, Leeds (1965).

BUSINESS

1946 Maurice Saatchi, chairman of Saatchi and Saatchi. (*See* 9.6.1946)

DIED THIS DAY

1377 Edward III, King of England.

1527 Niccolo Machiavelli, Italian writer and statesman, author of *The Prince* (1532).

1652 Inigo Jones, English architect and designer of some of the finest buildings in London, including the Banqueting House, Whitehall.

1852 (Wilhelm August) Friedrich Froebel, German educationalist and founder of the kindergarten system.

1876 Antonio López de Santa Anna, Mexican revolutionary, the general who beat the Texans at the Battle of the Alamo and President of Mexico, blind and in poverty.

1908 Nickolai Andreievich Rimsky-Korsakov, Russian composer.

1969 Maureen Connolly, US tennis champion nicknamed Little Mo, from cancer, aged 34.

ON THIS DAY

1675 Work began to rebuild St Paul's Cathedral in London by Sir Christopher Wren, replacing the old building which had been destroyed by the Great Fire.

1788 The US Constitution came into force on the same day as New Hampshire became the ninth state of the Union.

1843 The Royal College of Surgeons was founded from the original Barber-Surgeons Company.

1854 The first VC was awarded to Charles Lucas, an Irishman and mate aboard the HMS *Hecla* for conspicuous gallantry at Bomarsrund in the Baltic. The medal was made from metal from a canon captured at Sebastopol.

1868 The first performance of Wagner's opera *Die Meistersinger* took place in Munich.

1876 The first gorilla arrived in Britain.

1919 German sailors scuttled 72 warships

at Scapa Flow in the Orkneys even though Germany had surrendered. It was the greatest act of self-destruction in modern military history.

1937 Wimbledon was televised for the first time.

1942 Tobruk fell to Rommel with the capture of 25,000 Allied troops.

1948 The first successfully produced microgroove (long-playing) records were unveiled by Dr Peter Goldmark of Columbia Records.

1970 Tony Jacklin became the first British golfer to win the US Open for 50 years, and with his British Open victory eleven months earlier, he became only the third golfer to accomplish this double within a 12-month period.

1975 Captained by Clive Lloyd, West Indies won the first World Cup Cricket series, beating Australia by 17 runs at Lords.

1978 The Lloyd Webber/Rice musical *Evita* starring Elaine Page opened at the Prince Edward Theatre, London.

1988 The youngest person to bite a snake to death? An 18-month-old Bangladeshi boy is reported to have done just this.

22 JUNE

BORN THIS DAY

HISTORY

1757 George Vancouver, explorer who carried out surveys of North America and after whom Vancouver Island and Vancouver, British Columbia are named.

1805 Giuseppe Mazzini, Italian thinker and writer who worked passionately for Italian unity only to find that it resulted in a kingdom instead of a republic.

ARTS

1856 Sir H(enry) Rider Haggard, English writer best known for *King Solomon's Mines* (1885).

1898 Erich Maria Remarque, German novelist who wrote the anti-war *All Quiet on the Western Front* (1929) based on his war experiences. His pacifist views were not to the liking of the Nazis. Stripped of German citizenship, he became a US citizen.

1912 Katherine Dunham, US dancer and choreographer who founded her own school and company in 1945.

ENTERTAINMENT

1906 Billy Wilder (Samuel Wilder), Austrian-born US film director and writer who came to the US to escape Nazi persecution. His partnership with Charles Brackett led to a string of successes as director and co-scriptwriter, with Hackett producing such films as *Sunset Boulevard* (1950). He later collaborated with I.A.L.Diamond on the Oscar-winning *The Apartment* (1960). Other films include *Some Like It Hot* (1959).

1907 Michael Todd (Avram Goldenbogen), film producer and one of the major promoters of the wide screen with shares in Cinerama, and later his own Todd-AO process which included the production of *Around The World in 80 Days* (1956). He was killed in 1958 when his private plane, *Lucky Liz*, named after his wife, Elizabeth Taylor, crashed near Minneapolis. They had been married one year.

1921 Joseph Papp, US producer of free

performances of Shakespeare and contemporary plays in Central Park and in his Public Theatre, where in 1967 he first produced *Hair* and in 1975 *A Chorus Line*.

1932 Prunella Scales, English actress who played the domineering wife in the classic television comedy series, *Fawlty Towers*, and who has had a successful stage career.

1936 Kris Kristofferson, US singer, songwriter, actor and former Rhodes scholar who starred in the 1976 version of *A Star is Born*.

1949 Meryl Streep, US actress who followed her stage career with equal success in films such as *The Deer Hunter* (1978), which won her an Oscar nomination, *Kramer v Kramer* (1979) which won her an Oscar for best supporting actress, and *Out of Africa* (1985). *Sophie's Choice* (1982) won her the Oscar for best actress.

1940 Esther Rantzen, television presenter and producer, and promoter of Childline, the telephone counselling service for sexually and physically abused children.

SCIENCE

1887 Sir Julian Sorrell Huxley, English biologist and son of the famous humanist Thomas, and the first Director-General of UNESCO.

SPORT

1910 John Hunt, Baron, leader of the successful British Everest expedition in 1953.

DIED THIS DAY

1956 Walter de la Mare, English poet and novelist.

HAVE RAINBOW, WILL DANCE Two showbiz legends died this day. In 1969, Judy Garland (Frances Ethel Gumm), US actress and singer, in her London flat from an overdose of pills and booze. In 1987, Fred Astaire (Frederick Austerlitz), actor, dancer and singer, aged 88.

ON THIS DAY

1377 Richard II ascended the English throne following the death of his grandfather, Edward III, the previous day.

1611 Henry Hudson, English navigator, with his son and seven others was cast adrift in a small boat in arctic conditions in the bay that later bore his name, after the crew mutinied. It was the last time they were seen alive.

1814 The first match at the new Lord's cricket ground was played between the MCC and Hertfordshire.

1921 King George V opened the Northern Ireland Parliament; pleading for peace and reconciliation.

1937 'The Brown Bomber', Joe Louis, became world heavyweight champion when he knocked out James J. Braddock in the eighth round in Chicago. Exactly one year later, he avenged a previous defeat before becoming champion, by knocking out Germany's Max Schmeling in the first round.

1979 Jeremy Thorpe, the former Liberal leader was found not guilty of plotting to murder Norman Scott who alleged he had a homosexual relationship. Several key Liberals were also accused of being involved and were also found not guilty.

1984 The first Virgin Atlantic flight left Gatwick for New York, with tickets priced £99.

23 JUNE

BORN THIS DAY

HISTORY

1763 Empress Joséphine, on the island of Martinique, as Marie Rose Joseph Tascher de la Pagerie, who married Napoleon two years after her first husband, Beauharnais, was guillotined during the French Revolution. The childless marriage was dissolved on 16 December 1809, but she was allowed to retain the title Empress.

1894 Edward, Duke of Windsor who became King Edward VIII from 20 January to 10 December 1936 before abdicating to marry twice-divorced Mrs Wallis Warfield Simpson. (*See* 19.6.1896)

1894 Dr Alfred (Charles) Kinsey, US zoologist and director of the Institute for Sex Research. He was the author of *Sexual Behaviour in the Human Male* (1948) and the companion volume on the female (1953), based on 18,500 personal interviews. They caused a sensation, but later were criticized as being unsatisfactorily sampled.

1912 Alan (Mathison) Turing, English mathematician, logician and computer pioneer. During the Second World War he served in the Code and Cypher School and was responsible for cracking German codes.

ENTERTAINMENT

1927 Bob Fosse (Robert Louis Fosse), US actor, choreographer and director who danced and acted in several films and stage musicals before concentrating on choreography and direction for hits such as *Sweet Charity* (1966). He won an Oscar for directing and choreographing the film version of *Cabaret* (1972) and directed and co-scripted the semi-autobiographical *All That Jazz* (1979).

1940 Adam Faith (Terence Nelhams), English pop singer, actor and business consultant who had hits in the 1960s beginning with 'What Do You Want' in December 1959. He starred in the highly successful television series *Budgie*, but decades later when he backed and starred in a musical version, it flopped.

SPORT

1910 Ted Tinling, English sportswear designer who is best known for his distinctive, and sometimes daring designs for the stars of Wimbledon.

1916 Sir Leonard Hutton, England and Yorkshire cricketer who captained England 23 times and was the first professional to do so. He made 364 against Australia at the Oval (1938), the highest score by an English batsman.

DIED THIS DAY

1537 Pedro de Mendoza, Spanish explorer and one-time governor of the Rio de la Plata region of Argentina. He was on his way back to Spain, suffering from syphilis, and was buried at sea.

1839 Lady Hester Lucy Stanhope, English traveller in the Middle East who was treated as a prophetess by the tribes she settled with. She died in poverty as a result of her excessive generosity.

1980 Olivia Manning, English novelist who wrote *Friends and Heroes* (1965).

ON THIS DAY

1757 British troops under Clive overthrew the Nawab of Bengal at the Battle of Passey, which made him the virtual ruler of Bengal and prepared the way for the British Empire in India.

1848 Adolphe Sax was awarded a patent for the saxophone.

1956 General Nasser became the first President of Egypt in an unopposed election.

1980 Sanjay Gandhi, son of the Indian Prime Minister and 'heir apparent', was killed while performing aerobatics in a light plane which went out of control and crashed.

1985 Sikh terrorists planted a bomb in an Air India Boeing 747 from Canada which exploded over the sea 120 miles off Ireland, killing 325 people.

1987 The US Supreme Court backed the use of hypnosis to obtain testimony. The first to be affected was Mrs Vickie Lorene Rock who had shot her husband when he tried to prevent her leaving the house to buy a hamburger. Under hypnosis, she said her finger was not on the trigger and that the gun went off accidentally. The judge was unimpressed. He said hypnosis was unreliable, but the Supreme Court overruled him.

24 JUNE

BORN THIS DAY

HISTORY

1850 Horatio Herbert, Earl Kitchener, British field marshal, born in County Kerry. He achieved notable victories in foreign parts fighting for the Empire, and was Secretary of State for War at the outbreak of hostilities in 1914, mounting a major recruitment campaign and appearing on posters to exhort 'Your country needs you!'

ARTS

1915 Professor Fred Hoyle, English astronomer and author of both non-fiction, with books such as *The Nature of the Universe* (1950), and science fiction, *The Inferno* (1973).

ENTERTAINMENT

1930 Claude Chabrol, French film director of *Les Biches* (1968).

POP

1947 Mick Fleetwood, English founder of Anglo-US pop group Fleetwood Mac (with John McVie) who had hits with 'Albatross' (1961) and their album *Rumours*, which sold over 15 million copies (1977).

SPORT

1895 Jack Dempsey (William Harrison Dempsey), US world heavyweight boxing champion, known as the 'Manassa Mauler' (b. Manassa, Colorado), who held the title from 1919 to 1926. The most popular boxer of his time, he was the first to command a 'million dollar gate' (attendance receipts).

1911 Juan (Manuel) Fangio, Argentinian

motor racing driver, who dominated the sport during the 1950s winning the world driving championship in 1951, 1954, 1956 and 1957 while driving for Alfa Romeo, Mercedes-Benz, Ferrari and Maserati.

BUSINESS

1825 W(illiam) H(enry) Smith, English newsagent and bookseller, who joined his father's newsagent business and took full control in 1846. Taking advantage of improving communications with new raiiways and eventually motor transport, he built up the biggest chain of newsagents in Britain before going into politics.

DIED THIS DAY

79AD Vespasian (Titus Flavius Sabinus Vespasianus), Roman emperor who stabilized the empire after the death of Nero.

1519 Lucrezia Borgia, Duchess of Ferrara, member of the infamous family, and sister of Cesare.

1908 (Stephen) Grover Cleveland, 22nd and 24th US President.

1968 Tony Hancock, exceptionally gifted English comedian, by suicide, in a Sydney hotel.

1985 Keith Castle, Britain's longest surviving heart transplant patient, six years after receiving his replacement heart.

ON THIS DAY

1314 Robert the Bruce defeated the English troops under Edward II at the Battle of Bannockburn.

1509 Henry VIII's coronation took place.

1717 The Grand Lodge of English Freemasons was formed in London.

BEARING HIS CROSS Henri Dunant, a Swiss businessman travelling through Italy this day in 1859, saw the aftermath of the Battle of Solferino and was inspired to found the International Red Cross. On this same day in 1857, the Red Cross assisted with the formation of the St John's Ambulance Brigade, under its original name, the Ambulance Association.

1901 Picasso's first Paris Exhibition had critics predicting a bright future for the young artist.

1948 The Berlin Airlift began when the USSR blockaded Berlin, requiring the Allies to fly in food and other essential supplies.

1953 Jacqueline Bouvier announced her engagement to John F. Kennedy, US senator.

1973 Eamon de Valera resigned as Ireland's President, aged 90, the world's oldest statesman.

1983 The first US spacewoman, Sally Ride, joined four other crew members aboard *Challenger* for the launch.

25 JUNE

BORN THIS DAY

HISTORY

1870 Robert Erskine Childers, Irish author and nationalist who resigned as a clerk in the House of Commons to promote Irish Home Rule. He was elected as a Sinn Fein member to the Dail (Irish assembly) and joined the IRA which eventually led to his arrest and execution for being in possession of unauthorized weapons. He was also the author of the spy novel, *The Riddle of the Sands* (1903)

1900 Louis (Francis Albert Victor), 1st Earl Mountbatten of Burma who was Commander-in-Chief for the Royal Navy in South East Asia during the Second World War, and later Viceroy of India during the transfer of power from Britain to that country.

ARTS

1903 George Orwell (Eric Arthur Blair), English novelist and essayist born in Bengal who worked in England in a book shop while he wrote his first books including *Burmese Days* (1934). He fought with the Republicans in the Spanish Civil War and returned wounded and disillusioned to write *Homage to Catalonia* (1938). Other books include *The Road to Wigan Pier* (1937), and his two most famous novels, *Animal Farm* (1945) and *Nineteen Eighty-Four* (1949) published shortly before his death.

ENTERTAINMENT

1906 Roger Livesey, Welsh-born actor who played leads in both stage and film productions, including *The Life and Death of Colonel Blimp* (1943) and *A Matter of Life and Death* (1946).

POP

1945 Carly Simon, US singer and songwriter of the hits 'You're So Vain' (1973) subject to much speculation about who the song was aimed at, and 'Nobody Does Does It Better' for the James Bond film *The Spy Who Loved Me* (1977).

1963 George Michael (Panos), English singer who teamed up with friend Andrew Ridgeley to form the Executives before changing the name to Wham! Both with the group and solo, George has had several No. 1s on both sides of the Atlantic including 'Faith' (1987), and 'One More Try' (1988).

DIED THIS DAY

1976 Johnny (John Hendon) Mercer, US composer, lyricist and singer who wrote Broadway and Hollywood musicals including *Seven Brides For Seven Brothers.*

ON THIS DAY

1788 Virginia became the tenth US state.

1797 At 2 p.m. during the battle off Santa Cruz, Admiral Nelson was wounded in the right arm by grapeshot and had it amputated that afternoon.

1867 Barbed wire was patented by Lucien B. Smith of Kent, Ohio.

1876 Custer's last stand took place at Little Bighorn, Montana. The Sioux Indians, led by Chief Crazy Horse, killed Colonel George Armstrong Custer and all 264 soldiers of his 7th US Cavalry. Whether Custer was a hero or a glory-seeker, his failure to wait for the arrival of General Terry's men to attack the Sioux led to the disaster for his men.

1903 Marie Curie presented her thesis at the University of Paris announcing the discovery of radium.

1932 India played their first test against England at Lords which they lost by 158 runs.

1950 North Korea invaded South Korea, crossing the 38th parallel border. The US and other allies, including Australia, said they would come to the aid of the non-communist south.

1953 John Reginald Halliday Christie was sentenced to death for the murder of four women, including his wife, in west London. His plea of insanity was dismissed. He is believed to have killed three other women including Beryl Evans and her daughter in 1950, for which Timothy Evans was found guilty and hanged.

MARITAL PROBLEMS In 1962, Sophia Loren and Italian film producer Carlo Ponti were charged with bigamy in Rome because Ponti's Mexican divorce from his first wife was not recognized by Italy. In 1987, Joan Collins won a 45-second divorce from Swedish businessman Peter Holm, and claimed she did not want any more husbands.

1969 Wimbledon saw the longest men's singles match ever when Charlie Passarell was beaten by Pancho Gonzalez 22–24, 1–6, 16–14, 6–3, 11–9. (*See* 2.7.1954)

26 JUNE

BORN THIS DAY

HISTORY

1898 Willy Messerschmitt, German aircraft designer who built the first jet fighter to go into combat, his Me-262, in 1944. A former glider and sailplane designer, he developed a major aircraft business.

ARTS

1892 Pearl S(ydenstricker) Buck, US novelist who moved to China with her missionary parents, which provided the material for her second novel, *The Good Earth* (1931).

1914 Laurie Lee, English poet and author of the autobiographical *Cider With Rosie* (1959) and *As I Walked Out One Midsummer Morning* (1969).

ENTERTAINMENT

1904 Peter Lorre (Lazlo Loewenstein) Hungarian-born actor who worked in German films before moving to Hollywood where he was cast mainly as a menacing or maniacal foreigner in films such as *The Maltese Falcon* (1941) and *Casablanca* (1942), but he was probably at his best in *Arsenic and Old Lace* (1940) playing a Peter Lorré-type character.

SCIENCE

1710 Charles Messier, French astronomer who was called a comet ferret by King Louis XV, and was the first to anticipate the return of Halley's Comet.

1824 William Thomson, 1st Baron Kelvin, Irish physicist and inventor who was a brilliant mathematician in his teens. He became a rich man with his invention of a receiver for the submarine telegraph and was knighted by Queen Victoria.

POP

1910 'Colonel' Tom Parker, US concert impresario and later Elvis Presley's manager and a very powerful father-figure to the pop superstar. He first booked Presley for one of his own shows, The Hank Snow All-Star Jamboree on 1 May 1955, putting him low down the bill.

1943 Georgie Fame, English musician and composer who had his first hit with the Blue Flames in 1965. 'Yeh Yeh' was No. 1 in the UK charts for two weeks, and in 1968 he was back with 'The

Ballad of Bonnie and Clyde', before moving to jazz.

DIED THIS DAY

BLOOD ON THE SAND This day AD363, Julian the Apostate, Roman emperor, died of wounds inflicted by a spear in battle with the Persians and in 1541 Francisco Pizarro, conqueror of Peru, was assassinated by rivals in Lima, the city he founded. He died a protracted death. Before his final breath, he drew a cross on the ground with his own blood, kissed it and cried, 'Jesus'. The conqueror of the Inca empire was dead, aged about 66.

1810 Joseph Michel Montgolfier, French pioneer balloonist.

1827 Samuel Crompton, English inventor of the spinning mule who was too poor to patent his invention. Eventually, a Bolton merchant persuaded him to disclose the invention on the promise that a general subscription from businessmen would compensate him. Big business made fortunes from the spinning mule and Crompton ended up with a few thousand pounds.

1830 George IV, King of England (1820–30).

1836 Claude Joseph Rouget de Lisle, author and composer of the *Marseillaise*.

1939 Ford Madox Ford, English novelist and poet.

1971 Inia Te Wiata, New Zealand opera and concert singer.

1984 Carl Foreman, US film director, screenwriter and producer, whose films include *The Guns of Navarone* (1961).

1984 George Horace Gallup, US opinion poll organizer.

ON THIS DAY

1830 Following the death of George IV, his brother William VI ascended the throne.

1857 The first investiture ceremony of Victoria Crosses took place at Hyde Park. Queen Victoria awarded 62 service men the highest military honour.

1862 Kent bowler Joseph Wells, the father of H.G. Wells, became the first man in cricketing history to take four first-class wickets with four successive balls against Sussex.

1906 The first Grand Prix took place at Le Mans. The Hungarian Ferenc Szisz was the winner, driving a Renault at an average speed of 63 m.p.h.

1909 Edward VII opened the Victoria and Albert Museum in London.

1913 Emily Dawson was appointed the first woman magistrate in Britain.

1917 The first contingent of the American Expeditionary Force arrived in France under General Pershing.

1959 Ingemar Johansson knocked out Floyd Patterson in New York to become Sweden's first world heavyweight boxing champion.

1959 Queen Elizabeth and President Eisenhower inaugurated the St Lawrence Seaway.

27 JUNE

BORN THIS DAY

HISTORY

1462 Louis XII, King of France from 1498 until his death in 1515. A popular king, he was known as 'the Father of the People', and retained the support of the people despite a disastrous invasion of Italy.

1550 Charles IX, King of France during the Wars of Religion, who ordered the Massacre of the Huguenots on St Bartholomew's Day (*see* 24.8 1572), pressured by his mother, Catherine de' Medici.

1846 Charles Stewart Parnell, Irish nationalist leader who was Member of Parliament for Meath and later leader of the Nationalist Party supporting a policy of violence which led to imprisonment in 1881. His career ended when he was cited as the co-respondent in a divorce case and was dumped by his party.

1880 Helen Adams Keller, US blind, deaf and mute scholar and teacher who was taught by Anne Sullivan. She was the first person with these handicaps to not merely overcome her afflictions, but achieve such academic and international status with books and articles.

DIED THIS DAY

1816 Samuel, 1st Viscount Hood, brilliant English admiral whose strategies served later as a model to Nelson.

1829 James Lewis Macie Smithson, English scientist and founder of the Smithsonian Institute, Washington, DC, in Genoa. In 1904, his remains were brought to the US under escort (one was Alexander Graham Bell) and interned in the original Smithsonian building.

1844 Joseph Smith, founder of the Mormons (Church of Jesus Christ of Latter Day Saints), who, with his brother Hyrum, was imprisoned in Carthage city jail, Illinois, charged with treason for calling out troops to protect his Mormon city of Nauvoo from a mob agitating against his sect and their polygamy. The mob gained access to the prison where he and his brother were both murdered. It assured his martyrdom and resulted in the church splitting with Brigham Young leading a migration to Salt Lake City.

1957 (Clarence) Malcolm Lowry, English novelist and short story writer, author of *Under the Volcano* (1947) which only received acclamation when reissued in 1962, five years after his death.

ON THIS DAY

1693 The *Ladies' Mercury*, the first magazine for women, was published.

1743 The last British king to lead his troops into battle was George II, who led the Pragmatic Army made up of British, Hanoverian and Hessian troops. At the Battle of Dettingen, he was victorious over the French.

1900 The Central Line (Railway), now part of London Underground, began a service between Shepherd's Bush and Bank.

1905 A mutiny erupted on board the Russian battleship *Potemkin* in the Black Sea when sailors were shot for complaining about bad food. The mutineers eventually overpowered the officers and raised the Red Flag with the ship anchored off Odessa.

1939 Sheer luxury took to the air on the first scheduled transatlantic airline service. Using Boeing 314 luxury-class flying boats, Pan Am operated the service from Newfoundland to Southampton.

1954 The first nuclear power station was opened in Obninsk, 55 miles from Moscow.

1967 The first cash dispenser in Britain became operational at Barclays Bank, Enfield, London.

1968 Maggie Wright, playing Helen of Troy in *Dr Faustus* in the Royal Shakespeare Company production in London, became the first actress in Britain to appear nude on the 'legitimate' stage.

1971 The first National Scrabble competition ever held was staged in London and won by Stephen Haskell, a young schoolteacher. Invented by Alfred Butt, a former US architect in 1932–3, he first called the game Lexico. In 1940, he thought he might have more luck by calling it Criss Cross Words, but in 1946 it was marketed as Scrabble. From 1946 to 1953 it sold an average 8,000 per annum, but its popularity suddenly grew and between 1953 and in 1955 Butt's game sold 4½ million sets!

1971 The Fillimore East, the legendary rock club in New York City run by Bill Graham, closed. Every major rock star had performed there over the past decade.

1976 Six Palestinians hijacked an Air France Airbus after it took off from Athens with 280 passengers on board, and forced the pilot to fly to Entebbe where they were sure of support from Uganda's Idi Amin for their demands for the release of 33 Palestinians imprisoned in Israel.

1988 Dave Hurst and Alan Matthews, both from England, became the first blind climbers to reach the summit of Europe's highest mountain, Mont Blanc, which is 15,781ft high.

28 JUNE

BORN THIS DAY

HISTORY

1491 Henry VIII, King of England, second son of Henry VII, who married six times, beheaded two wives, broke away from the Catholic church to form the Church of England, executed Catholics who failed to recognize his church and Protestants who complained he should execute more Catholics, and still managed to remain a popular king.

1712 Jean Jacques (Henri) Rousseau, French philospher who was born in Geneva. His concept of the 'noble savage' and his *Social Contract* (1762) influenced the leaders of the French Revolution.

1883 Pierre Laval, French politician who was Prime Minister once, 1931–2 and again 1935–6. During the war, he was made head of the Vichy government on Hitler's orders and played a major role in deporting French labour to Germany. After the war, he was tried for treason and shot.

ARTS

1577 Sir Peter Paul Rubens, Flemish artist who was one of the oustanding painters of all time. Charles I of England was not only impressed with his international reputation as an artist, but also as a skilful ambassador. Rubens painted the portraits of the king and queen, and many other paintings while in England, including the ceiling of Inigo Jones' royal Banqueting House, and was knighted by the king.

1867 Luigi Pirandello, Italian playwright and novelist who is best remembered for his play, *Six Characters in Search of an Author*, still popular since its first performance in 1921. He was awarded the Nobel prize for Literature in 1934.

1871 Luisa Tetrazzini, Italian operatic singer, one of the finest coloratura sopranos, who toured extensively, including Russia and Mexico. She was, by all accounts, a superb technician but a poor actress.

ENTERTAINMENT

1902 Richard (Charles) Rodgers, US composer and lyricist who collaborated with Lorenz Hart, Oscar Hammerstein II (the longest and most fruitful partnership) and later, Stephen Sondheim. No Broadway composer has had a longer and more distinguished career from the 20s to the 70s, with some of the greatest musicals ever, including *Oklahoma!* (1943), *South Pacific* (1949), *The King and I* (1951) and *The Sound of Music* (1959).

1926 Mel Brooks, US actor, writer, producer and director of comedies including the hilarious *The Producers*, in 1968, and *Blazing Saddles* and *Young Frankenstein*, both in 1974.

SCIENCE

1873 Alexis Carrel, French surgeon and biologist who won the Nobel prize in 1912 for his investigations into the preservation of tissues outside the body. A strain of chick heart tissue was kept alive for over 30 years. His work later played an important part in tissue transplant.

DIED THIS DAY

1836 James Maddison, fourth US President.

1861 Robert O'Hara Burke, Australian explorer who was born in Ireland and made the south to north crossing of Australia with William Wills. Both died on the return journey.

1961 William Wyler, US film director of *Ben Hur* (1959).

ON THIS DAY

1838 Queen Victoria's coronation took place in Westminster Abbey. She was 19 years old.

1841 The ballet *Giselle* opened in Paris.

WAR STORIES In 1914, a 19-year-old student assassinated the heir to the Austro-Hungarian throne, the Archduke Franz Ferdinand and his morganatic wife, the Duchess of Hohenburg, who were out in their carriage in the streets of Sarajevo on the 14th anniversary of their marriage. Gavrilo Princep's shots killed them both, and was the spark needed to ignite the First World War when Austria declared war on Serbia. The war over, it was on this day in 1919 that the Germans finally and reluctantly agreed to sign the Treaty of Versailles. The financial demands made by the Allies on the defeated Germans of 20 billion gold marks would drag the nation down and allow the Nazis to appear as saviours. The Second World War was just two decades away.

1935 Roosevelt requested a building to hold all federal gold to be built at Fort Knox, Kentucky.

1950 The football 'shock, horror' story of the century in the World Cup in Brazil: England 0, the US 1 in the first round. The novice US team beat a side which included Billy Wright and Tom Finney.

1984 After 104 years, the British magazine *Tit Bits* stopped publishing.

1988 The longest trial in Spanish legal

history ended after 15 months. 1,500 witnesses, including the former Prime Minister and two cabinet members, were cross-examined to decide who was responsible for poisoning 25,000 Spaniards in the toxic olive oil case. More than 600 died from the cheap olive oil, and thousands more were left partially paralysed or suffering from other afflictions in one of the worst public health disasters in modern history.

29 JUNE

The Feast Day of St Peter, patron saint of fishermen.

BORN THIS DAY

HISTORY

1858 George Washington Goethals, US army engineer who built the Panama Canal and became the first governor of the Canal Zone.

1886 Robert Schuman, French statesman who proposed the Schuman Plan for European unity which advocated the setting up of the European Coal and Steel Community (achieved in 1952).

1911 Prince Bernhard of the Netherlands, husband of Queen Juliana, founder president of the World Wildlife Fund International.

ARTS

1798 Conte Giacomo Leopardi, Italian poet who wrote his best verse before he was 21 and was considered the finest Italian poet after Dante. A hunchback, his was a lonely life with failed love affairs.

1900 Antoine Marie Roger de Saint-Exupéry, French aviator and author who became a pilot in 1922 flying airmail routes over northern Africa. He flew reconaissance flights during the Second World War despite injuries from previous flying accidents. His writings include *Flight to Arras* (1942) and *The Little Prince* (1944).

1914 Rafael Kubelik, Czech conductor and composer who was for a time principal conductor with Bayerischer Rundfunk, in Munich. He has written two operas including *Veronika* (1947) as well as symphonies, concertos and other works.

ENTERTAINMENT

1901 Nelson Eddy, singer and actor who was the other half of the successful partnership with Jeanette MacDonald in film operettas that earned them the title of the 'Singing Sweethearts'. (*See also* 18.6.1901)

1910 Frank Loesser, US composer and lyricist of Broadway hits including *Guys and Dolls* (1950) and *How To Succeed in Business Without Really Trying* (1961).

1928 Ian Bannen, Scottish stage, screen and television actor. He was in the television version of Le Carré's *Tinker Tailor Soldier Spy*, and his films include *The Flight of the Phoenix* (1965) which won him an Oscar for best supporting actor.

SCIENCE

1861 William James Mayo, surgeon and co-founder of the Mayo Clinic, one of the famous Mayo family, all distinguished US surgeons.

DIED THIS DAY

1861 Elizabeth Barrett Browning, English poet.

1882 Joseph Aloysius Hansom, English architect and promoter of the hansom cab.

1895 Thomas Henry Huxley, English biologist and defender of Darwin's theory.

1921 Lady Randolph Churchill (Jennie Jerome), US-born mother of Winston Churchill.

1940 Paul Klee, Swiss semi-abstract painter.

1941 Ignace Jan Paderewski, celebrated Polish pianist and Prime Minister.

1967 Jayne Mansfield (Vera Jayne Palmer), US actress killed in a car crash on her way to a television engagement.

1982 Pierre Alexandre Balmain, French fashion designer.

1983 Raymond Massey, Canadian actor, star of *Dr Kildare*.

1983 (James) David (Graham) Niven, Scottish-born actor and author.

ON THIS DAY

48BC Julius Caesar defeated Pompey at Pharsalus to become the absolute ruler of Rome.

1613 During a performance of *Henry VIII* by William Shakespeare at the Globe Theatre, London, a cannon was set off to mark the King's entrance, which accidently set fire to the thatched gallery roof. The theatre was totally destroyed, but rose again in June 1614, this time with a tiled roof.

1801 The first census in Britain was carried out revealing a population totalling 8,872,000.

1829 The first policeman to be murdered in Britain was Constable William Grantham in Somers Town, London who went to the aid a woman involved in a fight between drunken Irishmen. When he fell, all three proceeded to kick him to death.

LATEST NEWS In 1838, to mark Queen Victoria's coronation the previous day, the *Sun* published its entire issue in gold ink. This day 1855, saw the first edition of the *Daily Telegraph* in London, and in 1868 the Press Association was founded in London.

1864 Samuel Crowther, the Bishop of Niger was consecrated at Canterbury, the first black Church of England bishop.

1871 An Act of Parliament made British unions legal.

1887 A lady called Miss Cass was wrongfully charged by PC Endacott at Marlborough Police Station. The magistrate said she had done nothing wrong, and warned her not to do it again.

1905 The AA (Automobile Association) was formed in Britain to counter police harrassment and to warn of speed traps.

1913 Norway granted women equal electoral rights.

1916 Sir Roger Casement was found guilty of treason in a Dublin court and sentenced to death.

1956 Arthur Miller, US playwright, married Marilyn Monroe in London.

1966 Barclaycard was introduced by Barclays Bank, the first credit card in Britain.

1967 Mick Jagger and Keith Richard were sentenced to three months and one year respectively for drug offences, but after an appeal court hearing, their sentences were quashed.

1974 Isabel Perón, second wife of Juan Perón, was sworn in as President of Argentina, as a result of his illness.

1980 Vigdis Finnbogadottir became Iceland's first woman president.

1986 Richard Branson's Virgin Atlantic *Challenger II* powerboat made a record-breaking Atlantic crossing, but there was strong objection to it claiming the Blue Ribband.

30 JUNE

BORN THIS DAY

HISTORY

1893 Harold (Joseph) Laski, English politician and economist who campaigned for social reforms. He became chairman of the Labour Party in 1945.

1893 Walter Ulbricht, Communist and East German leader who fled Germany during the Nazi rise to power. When the German Democratic Republic was formed in 1949, he became Deputy Prime Minister, assuming full control in 1960.

ARTS

1685 John Gay, English poet and playwright famous for his *Beggar's Opera*. The sequel to this satirical comedy was *Polly* but this was banned by the Lord Chamberlain. The text was printed and, like most banned books, became a best-seller. When it was allowed to be produced in 1777, it was only a modest success.

1891 Sir Stanley Spencer, leading English artist best known for his paintings set in his native Cookham, where contemporary figures are featured in the chuchyard of his *Resurrection*.

1911 Ruskin Spear, English painter, mainly of portraits including one of Olivier as Macbeth.

ENTERTAINMENT

1918 Susan Hayward (Edythe Marrener), US actress who won five Oscar nominations for films including *I'll Cry Tomorrow* (1956). The previous year she had tried to commit suicide over a legal battle for custody of her twin sons from her first husband, Jess Barker, but she won her Oscar for *I Want To Live* (1958).

1939 Tony Hatch, English pianist, composer and arranger, who married Jackie Trent to become known as 'Mr and Mrs Music', writing and performing several hits and theme music for television, including the popular soap opera, *Crossroads*, and more recently, the successful Australian soap, *Neighbours*.

JAZZ

1917 Lena Horne, US singer who worked in the chorus of the famous Cotton Club before becoming a popular blues and ballads singer. She appeared in several films including *Stormy Weather* (1943) in which she sang the title song.

1917 Buddy (Bernard) Rich, US drummer (one of the greatest ever in jazz history), and bandleader who began performing at 18 months with his parents, vaudevillians Wilson and Rich. Later he was the drummer with several major bands including Harry James and Artie Shaw. When the big bands went out of fashion, he formed his own with a clever repertoire and skilled musicians. It toured Britain, Australia, Japan and other countries scoring a huge success.

SPORT

1966 Mike Tyson, US and world heavyweight boxing champion who is probably the fastest boxer in this class since Muhammad Ali. At aged only 20, he won the WBC crown in just two rounds from Trevor Berbick in 1986. The following August, he became the undisputed champion when he beat Tony Tucker. The formidable Iron Man took on the challengers and usually ended their dreams within the first minutes. The same fate was predicted for Britain's Frank Bruno, but he survived until the fifth in 1989. Then came James 'Buster' Douglas... (*See* 11.2.1990)

DIED THIS DAY

1520 Montezuma II, the last Atzec emperor who had been taken prisoner by Cortés and his Spanish soldiers. He was allowed to talk to his people, but according to Cortés, they were disillusioned with the emperor and stoned him to death. Some commentators believe the Spaniards murdered Montezuma.

1660 William Oughtred, English mathematician and inventor of the slide rule.

1919 Lord Rayleigh, English physicist and co-discoverer of the inert gas Argon.

1966 Margery (Louise) Allingham, English crime novelist.

1984 Lillian Hellman, US playwright of *The Children's Hour* (1934).

ON THIS DAY

1837 Punishment by pillory was finally abolished in Britain.

1859 The great tightrope walker, Blondin, crossed Niagara Falls from the US to Canada in just eight minutes. The rope was stretched 1,100ft (335.28m) and suspended 160ft (48.76m) above the Falls. Over 25,000 people watched him make the return with a tripod camera, stop midway and photograph the crowds. Many fainted.

1893 In South Africa's Orange Free State, the finder of a 971.75 carat diamond was awarded £500 plus a horse with bridle and saddle.

1894 London's Tower Bridge was officially opened to traffic.

1926 During this month, the first pop-up toasters went on sale, marketed by McGraw Electric Company of Minneapolis.

1934 This was the Night of the Long Knives in Germany as Hitler eliminated all political critics, including the leader of the Brown Shirts and former close friend, Ernst Roehm.

1936 *Gone With The Wind* by Margaret Mitchell was published.

1948 Doctors John Barden and Walter Brittain demonstrated the transistor at Bell Telephone Laboratories in New Jersey.

1956 'I'm Walking Backwards For Christmas', written and performed by arch-Goon Spike Milligan, entered the British singles chart six months after Christmas.

1960 The blood ran in the shower for the first time to a paying audience with the première of Hitchcock's *Psycho* in New York.

1971 After a record-breaking 24 days in space, the crew of three Russian astronauts were found dead after landing safely. An oxygen failure in the final moments was the cause.

1974 Mikhail Baryshnikov, Soviet-born ballet dancer, defected while on tour in Canada with the Bolshoi Ballet.

JULY

Hold Infinity in the palm of your hand/And Eternity in an hour
(William Blake)

1 JULY

National Day of Canada. In 1867 the Dominion of Canada was established.

BORN THIS DAY

HISTORY

1534 Frederick II, King of Denmark and Norway, an enlightened monarch who guided Denmark to prosperity. A patron of the arts and sciences, he granted the astronomer Tycho Brahe an island where he founded his observatory.

1872 Louis Blériot, French aviator who used the money he made as an inventor of motor car lights and accessories to develop airplanes, one of which he flew across the English Channel (25.7.1909).

1903 Amy Johnson, English aviator who flew solo from England to Australia. She married aviator Jim Mollison with whom she flew across the North Atlantic in 1933 and made other pioneering flights before their marriage was dissolved in 1938.

1961 Lady Diana Spencer (later the Princess of Wales). Her future husband, Prince Charles, was invested as the Prince of Wales on her eighth birthday.

ARTS

1804 George Sand (Amandine Aurore Lucie Dudevant), French romantic novelist who adopted her masculine pseudonym for the novel *Indiana* (1832). While her novels are now neglected, she is remembered for her long list of lovers including Chopin, with whom she lived for eight years.

1926 Hans Werner Henze, West German composer who incorporated jazz in some of his later work. One of the leaders of modern music, he has written operas, ballets and orchestral works.

ENTERTAINMENT

1899 Charles Laughton, English actor who made his professional debut on the stage in 1926. His film career included memorable performances in *The Private Life of Henry VIII* (1933), which won him an Oscar, *Mutiny on the Bounty* (1935) and as Quasimodo in *The Hunchback of Notre Dame* (1939).

1902 William Wyler, German-born US film director and producer who studied violin in Paris. He went to Hollywood and worked in a variety of jobs from prop man to director of such films as *The Best Years of Our Lives* (1946) which won him one of three Oscars and *Funny Girl* (1968).

1916 Olivia de Havilland, actress born in Tokyo of US mother who divorced her English father when she was three and moved to California together with her sister, Joan Fontaine. Her Oscar winning performances include *The Heiress* (1949).

1931 Leslie Caron, French actress and dancer who was spotted by Gene Kelly while dancing with Roland Petit's Ballet de Champs-Elysées. She co-starred with him in *An American in Paris* (1951) and went on to make both musicals and films. *The L-Shaped Room* (1962) won her an Oscar.

1934 Jean Marsh, English actress best known as Rose in the television serial, *Upstairs, Downstairs*.

1934 Sydney Pollack, US film director of *They Shoot Horses, Don't They?* (1969) and *Three Days of the Condor* (1975).

SPORT

1961 Carl Lewis, US athlete who dominated the 1984 Olympics in Los Angeles by winning gold in 100m, 200m, and with the relay team in the 4 x 100m and the long jump. The previous Olympics saw him claim gold in all these events other than the 200m. In 1988, he came second in the 100m in the Olympics in Seoul, until Ben Johnson's sensational disqualification when he failed a drug test.

DIED THIS DAY

1782 Charles Watson Wentworth, 2nd Marquis of Rockingham, English statesman and twice Prime Minister.

1860 Charles Goodyear, US inventor of a process to make rubber commercially viable, but infringements of his patents left him $200,000 in debt when he died.

1896 Harriet Beecher Stowe, US author of *Uncle Tom's Cabin*.

1925 Erik (Alfred Leslie) Satie, former café pianist and highly influential French composer.

1974 Juan Domingo Perón, Argentine President.

ON THIS DAY

1690 William III of Great Britain defeated the forces of the Roman Catholic James II supported by the French at the Boyne, Ireland and opened the way to a reconquest of the Irish.

1837 The first Register of Births, Deaths and Marriages was begun in Britain.

1838 Charles Darwin presented a paper on his theory of the evolution of the species to the Linnean Society in London, together with the naturalist, Alfred Russel Wallace. His *The Origin of Species* was not published until 24.11.1859.

1847 In the US the first adhesive stamps (five cents and ten cents) went on sale.

1863 The Battle of Gettysburg began with Confederate General Robert E. Lee attacking the North, but it ended in retreat and huge scale losses on both sides after three days.

1912 The first Royal Variety Command Performance took place at the Palace Theatre, London.

1912 The British Copyright Act came into force protecting authors' works for 50 years after their death.

1916 Coca-Cola adopted its distinctive contoured-shaped bottle to fend off competitors.

1929 The cartoon character Popeye the sailor was created by Elzie Segar in the US.

1937 Dial 999 for Emergency Services came into operation in Britain. It was the first of its type in the world.

1941 The first television commercial was shown on WNBT in New York. It showed a Bulova clock for 20 seconds while a voice-over gave the sales message to no more than 4,700 viewers. It cost the advertisers $9. (First UK commercial: 22.9.1955.)

1967 BBC 2 began colour television in Britain.

1969 The investiture of Prince Charles as Prince of Wales took place at Caernarvon Castle. (*See also* Lady Diana Spencer, born today.)

1974 Laura Ashley opened her first US shop, in San Francisco.

1977 Virginia Wade, at age 31, won the women's singles championships at Wimbledon in the Queen's Jubilee year and Wimbledon's Centenary Year.

1984 Argentina's football star Diego Maradona was signed by Naples for £1m.

2 JULY

BORN THIS DAY

HISTORY

1489 Thomas Cranmer, Henry VIII's first reformed Archbishop of Canterbury, who was responsible for the *The Book of Common Prayer* (1549).

1903 King Olaf V of Norway, born in England, who became king in 1957 succeeding Haakon VII, his father. In the 1928 Olympics, he represented his country as a yachtsman.

1903 Sir Alec Douglas Home, Tory Prime Minister briefly from 1963 succeeding Macmillan. He renounced his title as 14th Earl of Home in 1964 to fight the general election, which he lost.

1938 Dr David Owen, British leader of the SDP (the Social Democratic Party) who was a former Foreign Minister in the Labour government.

ARTS

1714 Christoph (Willibald) Gluck, German composer who is best known for his operas *Orfeo ed Euridice* (1762) and *Alceste* (1767) which influenced the development of opera.

ENTERTAINMENT

1892 Jack Hylton, popular English bandleader and impresario who presented seven 'Crazy Gang' shows and *Salad Days*, and brought ten Broadway musicals to London.

DIED THIS DAY

1566 Nostradamus (Michel de Notredame), French physician and astrologer whose predictions still intrigue. Did the man who cast horoscopes for Catherine de' Medici's children know he would die this day?

1778 Jean Jacques Rousseau, Swiss-born French philosopher who gave the world the slogan 'Liberty, Equality, Fraternity'. He died insane and lies buried next to Voltaire in the Panthéon, Paris.

1843 Christian Friedrich Samuel Hahnemann, German physician and founder of homeopathy.

1850 Sir Robert Peel, English statesman, twice Prime Minister, founder of the British police force, who was thrown from a horse on 29 June and died this day from injuries.

1961 Ernest (Miller) Hemingway, US novelist of *A Farewell to Arms* and Nobel prize winner. Fearing ill-health would cripple him, he turned a shotgun on himself and committed suicide.

1973 Betty Grable (Elizabeth Ruth Grable), US actress, singer and the possessor of the most expensive legs in the world.

1977 Vladimir (Vladimirovich) Nabokov, novelist (*Lolita* in 1959 and *Pale Fire* in 1962).

ON THIS DAY

1644 Oliver Cromwell's Roundheads defeated the Royalist Cavaliers under Prince Rupert at the Battle of Marston Moor near York. It turned the tide of the Civil War.

1865 At a revivalist meeting at Whitechapel, London, William Booth formed the Salvation Army.

1900 The Zeppelin made its maiden flight from Lake Constance near Friedrichshafen, Germany.

1937 In an attempt to fly around the world, US pilots Amelia Earhart and Fred Noonan took off on the leg from New Guinea to Howland Island in the central Pacific and were never seen again.

1938 Helen Wills Moody (US) won her record eighth Wimbledon women's singles title. In 1954, the longest ever final at Wimbledon was fought out by Jaroslav Drobny who finally beat Australia's Ken Rosewall 13–11, 4–6, 6–2, 9–7, despite a bad knee. (*See also* 25.6.1969)

1951 The worst floods in US history hit Kansas and Missouri; 41 died and 200,000 were left homeless.

PALPABLE HITS Pop history was made this day in 1956 with Elvis Presley recording 'Hound Dog' and 'Don't Be Cruel' in RCA's New York studio, and Buddy Holly's first record 'Love Me' being released. Presley's got to No. 1, but Holly, with the Crickets, (probably the most influential pop musicians ever), didn't get their No. 1 until the following year with 'That'll Be The Day'.

1964 President Johnson signed the US Civil Rights Bill prohibiting racial discrimination.

3 JULY

BORN THIS DAY

ARTS

1728 Robert Adam, Scottish architect and designer who created the elegant Adam style both for buildings and for interiors, with features such as the Adam staircase. Important commissions included Syon House, Middlesex and Kenwood House, London.

CZECHMATES Three artists from Czechoslovakia were born this day spanning 84 years. In 1854: Leoš Janáček, composer who is best known for his operas *Jenufa* (1904) and *The House of the Dead* (1938). In 1883: Franz Kafka, poet and playwright, constantly ill and depressed as a result of tuberculosis, which finally killed him when he was 41. His most famous work *The Trial* (1937) influenced 20th-century European fiction and drama. In 1937: Tom Stoppard (Thomas Straussler), Czech-born English playwright whose widowed mother brought him to England via India in 1946. His highly successful *Rosencrantz and Guildenstern Are Dead* (1967) established his reputation. This was consolidated by plays including *Jumpers* (1972) and *Travesties* (1974).

ENTERTAINMENT

1927 Ken Russell, controversial English film director who made his name with imaginative film biographies of composers such as Delius for the BBC's famous arts programme *Monitor*, before going on to make features including *Women In Love* (1969).

SPORT

1951 Richard (John) Hadlee, New Zealand captain and Nottinghamshire all-rounder, one of the world's finest players who is the New Zealand cricketer to have taken the most wickets in a test innings and in a test match (11 for 58), and best bowling in a Test (7 for 23 against India). He has also taken all ten wickets in three Tests, and is the first New Zealander to take the 'double': 100 Test wickets and 1,000 Test runs in 1984.

DIED THIS DAY

1642 Marie de' Medici, Queen of France.

1904 Theodor Herzl, Zionist leader, in Austria, 43 years before his dream of an independent Jewish state came true.

1908 Joel Chandler Harris, US writer, creator of Uncle Remus and Brer Rabbit.

THE DOORS CLOSE Drowned in his swimming pool at his Essex home, 1969, Brian Jones, member of the Rolling Stones. Drugs and alcohol were found in his bloodstream. In 1971, Jim Morrison, US lead singer and writer with the Doors, died of a heart attack in Paris, where he was buried.

1986 Rudy Vallee, US singer and actor.

ON THIS DAY

1608 French explorer, Samuel de Champlain founded Quebec.

1898 Captain Joshua Slocum sailed into Newport, Rhode Island in his fishing boat *Spray* to become the first to sail around the world solo. It took him just over three years (set off 24.4.1895).

1905 Russian troops killed over 6,000 people in Odessa to restore order during a general strike.

1916 One of the most devastating battles of modern times began. The Battle of the Somme during the First World War saw 100,000 killed on the first day in the British and French offensive against the Germans. The British went 'over the top' (of their trenches) in waves and were cut down by the enemy.

1920 William Tilden became the first US tennis player to win the men's singles title at Wimbledon.

1928 The first colour transmission was demonstrated at John Logie Baird's studio in Long Acre, in London's Covent Garden.

1938 In Britain, the Mallard reached 126 m.p.h. to set a world speed record for steam locomotives.

1940 Churchill reluctantly ordered the destruction of the French fleet in Miers-el-Kebr, Algeria, following the German invasion of France, to prevent the ships falling into enemy hands. Over 1,000 French sailors died.

1954 Rationing finally ended in Britain, nearly nine years after the end of the Second World War.

1962 French President de Gaulle signed the declaration granting Algeria independence.

1976 In a daring night raid, Israeli commandos rescued 103 hostages held in Entebbe Airport, Uganda, after their Air France airliner had been diverted there by Palestinian hijackers expecting and getting help from Idi Amin. The commandos flew 2,500 miles and landed in three large transport planes in the dark. In just 35 minutes, they killed all the hijackers and 20 Ugandan troops helping them guard the hostages. Three hostages and one commando were killed in cross fire. The Israelis also destroyed 11 Russian Mig aircraft on the ground before taking off for Nairobi, where they refuelled before the flight to Tel Aviv.

1987 Now aged 73, Klaus Barbie, former SS officer, was sentenced to life for war crimes committed in France.

1988 The US *Vincennes* patrolling in the Gulf during the Iraq-Iran conflict, mistook an Iranian civil airliner for a bomber and shot it down killing all 290 people on board.

4 JULY

This day has a special place in US history. Not only is it US Independence Day when, in 1776, the American Congress voted for independence from Britain, with Thomas Jefferson later signing the Declaration of Independence, but it is also the birthday, in 1872, of John Calvin Coolidge, 30th US President. It is also the anniversary of the deaths of three US Presidents; John Adams, 2nd US President, 1826 and Thomas Jefferson, 3rd US President, died on the same day. Both men wanted to live until the 50th anniversary of the Declaration. Jefferson died at one o'clock on the afternoon of the 4th, Adams a few hours later. Five years later to the day, James Monroe, the 5th President made it three.

BORN THIS DAY

HISTORY

1753 Jean Pierre Blanchard, French balloonist who only turned to this mode of flight after failing to build a flying machine. He made the first Channel crossing (7.1.1785) and, during a balloon flight, tested the parachute by dropping one with a dog attached to it. He later made several successful jumps and demonstrated his balloons in Europe and in North America.

1807 Giuseppe Garibaldi, Italian patriot who fought to make a single, unified nation. With his 1,000 Redshirts he retook Naples and Sardinia in 1860 for the new Italian kingdom.

1845 Thomas John Barnardo, Dublin-born philanthropist who, in 1867, started homes for some of London's many destitute children. They became known as Dr Barnardo's Homes, although he never qualified as a medical doctor.

ARTS

1804 Nathaniel Hawthorne, one of the first major US novelists, who wrote *The Scarlet Letter* (1850) and *The House of the Seven Gables* (1851).

ENTERTAINMENT

1826 Stephen Collins Foster, US songwriter and composer, mainly of sentimental and minstrel songs. He wrote over 200, but he made little money from them. 'Oh, Susanna' was sold for $100, and made its publisher $10,000. Among the classics he composed are 'Swanee River', 'Jeannie with the Light Brown Hair' (written to his wife who left him in 1861) and 'Beautiful Dreamer'. His last years were dogged by debt and alcoholism.

1847 James Anthony Bailey, US circus proprietor who is best remembered for his association with Barnum, making it the most successful circus ever, touring both the US and Europe.

1878 George M(ichael) Cohan, US actor, composer, lyricist, librettist, director and producer of vigorous shows whose titles are probably forgotten, but whose songs are not: 'The Yankee Doodle Boy' and 'Give My Regards to Broadway'.

1885 Louis B. Mayer (Eliezar [Lazar] Mayer), Russian-born US film mogul who came to the US as a child and made his money from junk. Like other early film moguls, he bought a run-down movie house and ended up with a cinema chain, and naturally, a studio to make films to screen in them, taking control of MGM (Metro-Goldwyn-Mayer).

1898 Gertrude Lawrence (Getrud Alexandra Dagmar Lawrence Klasen), English actress, singer and dancer who was a star on both sides of the Atlantic. She worked with Noël Coward in his *London Calling* (1923) introducing 'Parisian Pierrot', and in *Tonight at 8.30* (1936). In 1951 she played her last role in *The King and I*.

1900 (Daniel) Louis 'Satchmo' Armstrong, legendary US virtuoso jazz trumpeter, bandleader and inventor of 'scat' singing whose career began in New Orleans in 1918. He appeared in many films, *High Society* (1956) and *Hello Dolly* (1969) in which he sang the title song he had recorded five years earlier and made No. 1 in the hit parade.

1927 Gina Lollobrigida, popular Italian actress and sex symbol known as 'La Lollo'. Her films include *Trapeze* (1956) and *Buona Sera, Mrs Campbell* (1969).

1927 Neil Simon, highly successful US playwright who wrote *The Odd Couple* (1965) and *The Sunshine Boys* (1972), just two of a long list of hits on both the stage and screen.

DIED THIS DAY

1761 Samuel Richardson, one of the first major English novelists with *Pamela* (1741).

1934 Marie Curie (Marja Sklodowska), Polish-born discoverer of radium and twice winner of the Nobel prize; one for Physics, the other for Chemistry.

1938 Suzanne Longlen, French tennis star, winner of 15 Wimbledon titles between 1919 and 1925, who died of leukaemia aged 39.

1943 Wladyslaw Sikorski, Polish Prime Minister, killed in an aircrash shortly after taking off from Gibraltar. There were those who believed at the time that his death was engineered by the Allies fearful that his open hostility to the Soviets could cause problems during this sensitive period of the Second World War.

ON THIS DAY

1817 Work began on the Erie Canal and, in 1904, on the 40-mile long Panama Canal.

1829 The first regular horse-drawn buses went into service in London between Marylebone Road and Bank.

1840 The Cunard Line began its first Atlantic crossing when the paddle steamer *Britannia* sailed from Liverpool. The voyage would take just over 14 days.

1848 *The Communist Manifesto* was published.

1892 James Keir Hardie standing in the general election for Holytown, Lanarkshire became the first Socialist to win a seat in the British Parliament.

HEAVIES In 1910 in Reno, 'the Great White Hope', John Jeffries came out of retirement to try and take away the world heavyweight title from first black champion, Jack Johnson. Jeffries nose was broken in the 15th and the fight was stopped, leading to racial violence in many parts of the US. In 1919, Jack Dempsey, known as the Manassa Mauler, beat Jess Willard, world heavyweight boxing champion for the preceding four years. The fight should have lasted only one round as Willard was down seven times, but the referee let it continue until the fourth.

1946 The US gave the Philippine islands their independence. Manuel Roxas became the first President.
1969 After 14 attempts, Britain's Ann Jones, aged 30, became Wimbledon women's singles champion when she beat Billie-Jean King.

5 JULY

National Day of Venezuela. In 1811 Simón Bolívar (see 24.7.1783) declared its independence from Spain.

BORN THIS DAY

HISTORY

1853 Cecil John Rhodes, English colonialist and financier, noted for his commercial exploitation of southern Africa where he gained control of the world's major diamond and gold mines. His part in the infamous Jameson Raid, an attempt to overthrow the Boers in the gold-rich Transvaal, led to his resignation as Prime Minister. His expansion north led to the formation of Rhodesia, named after him.
1911 Georges (Jean Raymond) Pompidou, French Premier from 1962–8 and President from 1969 until his death in 1974.
1948 Jean Murray, on the stroke of midnight in Ashton-in-Makerfield, near Wigan, the first baby born on the National Health.

ARTS

1889 Jean Cocteau, French poet, novelist, painter and film director best known for his play *Orpheus* (1926), his novel *Children of the Game* (1955) and his film *Beauty and the Beast* (1945).

ENTERTAINMENT

1755 Mrs Sarah Siddons, English actress, daughter of a travelling theatre family who by 1782 was considered the leading actress on the British stage, performing at Drury Lane and Covent Garden.
1810 P(hineas) T(aylor) Barnum, US showman who was one of the fathers of 'hype', promoting everything from dubious freaks to the 'Swedish Nightingale', Jenny Lind. He only became involved in the circus business when he was over 60, when he joined with Bailey (*see* 4.7.1847) to stage the most spectacular circus seen in the US.

FASHION

1953 Elizabeth Emmanuel, English dress designer who with her husband rose to fame when they designed Princess Diana's wedding dress and subsequent outfits.

SPORT

1879 Dwight Filley Davis, founder of the Davis Tennis Cup who was a leading US tennis player and doubles champion for three consecutive years (1899–1901) before concentrating on politics and serving as Secretary of War in President Hoover's administration.

DIED THIS DAY

1826 Sir Thomas Stamford Raffles, who as a British East Indian administrator was the founder of Singapore (1819).
1974 Georgette Heyer, English historical and detective novelist who wrote *Penhallow* (1942).

ON THIS DAY

1791 The first British ambassador to the US, George Hammond was appointed.

1817 The first gold coin sovereigns were issued in Britain.

1865 A 2 m.p.h. speed limit was imposed in Britain under the Locomotives and Highways Act. This was the first speed limit in the world covering all steam-driven vehicles as well as petrol vehicles. In 1865 there were only two cars in Britain!

1888 Three match girls were sacked at the Bryant and May match factory in London for giving Annie Besant information about working conditions. The other 672 women workers came out on strike, which became a landmark for women workers in Britain.

RACKETEERS In 1919 the great Suzanne Longlen of France became women's singles champion at Wimbledon for the first time; the first non-English-speaking winner. She set a new style with a startling sleeveless 'short' dress. In 1952 'Little Mo' (Maureen Connolly) from the US, aged 17, won the women's singles title at Wimbledon, but she was not the youngest. In 1887, Lottie Dod, England won the championship, aged 15 years. This day in 1975, Arthur Ashe of the US beat countryman Jimmy Connors to become Wimbledon's first black men's singles champion. 1980, Bjorn Borg, the 'ice cool' Swede won the men's singles championship for the fifth consecutive time, the only player this century to achieve this. In 1987, Martina Navratilova beat Steffi Graf to win the Wimbledon crown for a record sixth time.

1945 Having led Britain throughout the Second World War, Churchill was defeated in the general election, and the Labour Party under Attlee swept in with 393 seats to 213 Tories, 12 Liberals and 22 Independents.

1965 Maria Callas gave her last stage performance singing *Tosca* at Covent Garden. She was 41.

1967 Israel annexed Gaza.

1969 The Rolling Stones gave a free concert in Hyde Park to an audience of 250,000, three days after Brian Jones' death.

1977 Pakistan Prime Minister Zulfikar Ali Bhutto was arrested by General Zia ul-Huq, in a military coup.

1979 The Isle of Man celebrated 1,000 years of its 'Tynewald' or Parliament.

1989 Former Marine colonel Oliver North was fined $150,000 (£95,000) and given a suspended prison sentence for his involvement in the Iran-Contra affair.

6 JULY

BORN THIS DAY

HISTORY

1832 Maximilian, Archduke of Austria and Emperor of Mexico who accepted the throne believing he had the full support of the people and unaware of the deals that had preceded it.

1935 Dalai Lama, the 14th spiritual leader of Tibet, who fled to India in 1959 following a failed uprising of his people against the Chinese communist troops occupying his country.

1921 Nancy Reagan, former US actress who played opposite Ronald Reagan in less-than-exciting films and who got her first real juicy role as First Lady of the US to Ronald Reagan's President.

ARTS

1937 Vladimir Ashkénazy, acclaimed Russian pianist and conductor who was joint winner of the Tchaikovsky Competition with John Ogden in 1962.

ENTERTAINMENT

1936 Dave Allen, Irish comedian who has been equally successful in cabaret and on television in Britain and Australia with his blend of religious jokes and wry observations of human nature.

1946 Sylvester Stallone, US film actor and director, who wrote the screenplay of *Rocky* in three days. It won Oscars for best film of 1976, best director and best editing. Stallone won an Oscar nomination for best actor and screenplay.

POP

1925 Bill Haley (William John Clifton Hayley), US pioneer rock musician who had his first hit in the 9 July 1955 edition of *Billboard*. '(We're Gonna) Rock Around the Clock' with his Comets, and was No. 1 for eight weeks, the first rock 'n roll record to make it to the top.

SPORT

1939 Mary Peters, Northern Ireland athlete and Olympic pentathlon gold medallist in Munich in 1972.

DIED THIS DAY

1189 Henry II, French-born King of England, in Tours.

1535 Sir Thomas More, English Lord Chancellor, executed on Tower Hill for refusing to accept Henry VIII as the head of the Church of England. He was later canonized for this act.

1553 Edward VI, King of England, only legitimate son of Henry VIII, of tuberculosis.

1893 (Henry René Albert) Guy de Maupassant, French author, master of the short story, in an asylum, after going insane as a result of syphilis.

1931 Edward Goodrich Acheson, US chemist and inventor who worked with Edison.

19[illegible] Kenneth Grahame, English children's author of *The Wind in the Willows* (1908).

1960 William (Harrison) Faulkner, US novelist and Nobel prize winner, author of *As I Lay Dying* (1931).

1960 Aneurin Bevan, British politician responsible for introducing the National Health Service which celebrated its 12th anniversary the previous day.

1971 (Daniel) Louis Armstrong, 'Satchmo', US jazz trumpeter and bandleader, two days after his 71st birthday.

1973 Otto Klemperer, leading German conductor who was recommended by Mahler for his first major appointment.

ON THIS DAY

1189 On the death of his father, Henry II, Richard the Lionheart (Richard I) became king.

1553 Mary I acceded to the throne, the first queen to rule in England in her own right. She was later called 'Bloody Mary' because of her persecution of the Protestants.

1886 The first box numbers were used in classified advertising by the *Daily Telegraph*.

1892 Britain's first coloured MP was

elected when Dadabhai Naoraji won the Central Finsbury seat.

1907 The world's first purpose-built motor racing track opened at Brooklands, Surrey.

1919 The British airship R34 became the first to cross the Atlantic, from Edinburgh to New York in 108 hours.

1928 The first feature-length all-sound film, *The Lights of New York* was premièred (no, *The Jazz Singer* was only *part* 'talkie').

1952 The last of London's trams ran for the last time.

1957 Althea Gibson (US) became the first black player to win the women's singles title at Wimbledon. Eleven years later, the first Wimbledon Open was won by Australia's Rod Laver as the men's champion, and Billie-Jean King as the women's.

1964 The Beatles' *A Hard Days Night* premièred in London, attended by Princess Margaret and Lord Snowdon. Seven years earlier on this day (1957) John Lennon, aged 17, and his Quarrymen were appearing at a church fête when a friend introduced him to a 15-year-old called Paul McCartney.

1988 The worst off-shore oil rig disaster in history took place in the North Sea when an explosion aboard Piper Alpha killed 167 men. Some of the bodies were never recovered.

7 JULY

BORN THIS DAY

HISTORY

1752 Joseph Marie Jacquard, French silk weaver and loom inventor who started the textile technology revolution. Napoleon granted him a patent and a medal. The loom was made public property with a royalty on each machine paid to Jacquard, but silk weavers, fearing for their jobs, burned the new looms. Nevertheless, by 1812 11,000 were in use in France. It incorporated punch cards to control the pattern, the same system that English computer inventor Charles Babbage later used to store data.

ARTS

1860 Gustav Mahler, Austrian composer and conductor who composed ten symphonies and six songs for orchestra including 'The Song of the Earth'.

1887 Marc Chagall, Russian painter and designer who settled in Paris, famous for his dreamlike pictures of Russian folklore.

1911 Gian-Carlo Menotti, Italian composer best known for his popular operas *Amahl and the Night Visitors*, the first opera composed specifically for television in 1951, and *The Saint of Bleecker Street* (1954).

ENTERTAINMENT

1899 George Cukor, US film director of many classic films. He was fired as director of *Gone with the Wind* after only ten days. His films include *The Philadelphia Story* (1940) and *My Fair Lady* (1964) which won him an Oscar.

1901 Vittorio de Sica, Italian film director who can claim four Best Foreign Film Oscars amongst his moving neo-realistic films which include *The Bicycle Thieves* (1948) and *The Garden of the Finzi-Continis* (1971).

1919 Jon Pertwee, English comedy actor best known as one *Dr Who* in the television series, and later as *Worzel Gummidge*.

1941 Bill Oddie, English comedy writer, comedian and birdwatcher, best known for being one of *The Goodies*.

POP

1940 Ringo Starr (Richard Starkey), former Beatles drummer who proved there was life after the Fab Four disbanded. He wrote and recorded several hits including 'It Don't Come Easy' (1971), 'Back Off Boogaloo' (1972) and 'Photograph' (1973).

FASHION

1922 Pierre Cardin, French fashion designer and leader in ready-to-wear fashion who was born in Venice. He also pioneered high fashion for men.

SPORT

1944 Tony Jacklin, English golfer, Ryder team captain and winner of the US and British Open in 1969–70, the first Briton to hold both titles at the same time.

DIED THIS DAY

1307 Edward I, King of England, on his way to subdue a rebellion in Scotland.

1573 Giacomo da Vignola, one of the greatest Italian architects who introduced many new ideas which were copied for centuries.

1816 Richard Brinsley Butler Sheridan, Irish-born playwright of *School for Scandal* (1777) who became the manager of the Drury Lane Theatre as well as a politician. When the Drury Lane burned down, he found himself in financial difficulties and eventually died in poverty.

1854 Georg Simon Ohm, German physicist after whom the 'ohm' (the measure of resistance) and 'Ohm's Law' (which governs electrical current) are named.

1930 Sir Arthur Conan Doyle, English author, creator of Sherlock Holmes.

1970 Sir Allen Lane, English publisher, founder of Penguin where he initiated the modern paperback.

1984 Dame Flora Robson, English actress on stage and screen who played Queen Elizabeth in two of her many films.

ON THIS DAY

1814 Sir Walter Scott's historical novel *Waverley* was published.

1853 US naval officer Matthew Perry sailed into the Japanese harbour of Uraga with two frigates and two other vessels, and announced that he would not leave until the government met his delegation. The Japanese had no defence and agreed to meet with him, if only to buy time. This historic meeting opened the way to trade with Japan and ended her isolation.

1950 The Farnborough Airshow was held – the first real airshow.

1967 Using Sir Francis Drake's sword, the Queen knighted Francis Chichester who had sailed solo around the world in *Gypsy Moth IV*.

1982 An intruder, Michael Fagan, asked the Queen for a cigarette while sitting on the end of her bed in Buckingham Palace. The incident revealed a serious flaw in Palace security.

1985 Live Aid, the pop extravaganza organized by Bob Geldof to aid the starving millions in Ethiopia, was beamed to 160 countries and raised over £50m.

1985 Boris Becker, the unseeded 17-

year-old, became the youngest ever men's singles champion at Wimbledon.

1988 An 11-year-old Californian boy took off from San Diego. He landed at Le Bourget, Paris on 13.7.1988 to become the youngest pilot to ever fly the Atlantic.

8 JULY

BORN THIS DAY

HISTORY

1836 Joseph Chamberlain, English politician and social reformer who consolidated the British Empire by a system of preferential tariffs.

1838 Ferdinand Adolf August Heinrich, Count von Zeppelin, German soldier and builder of rigid dirigibles which were named after him. During the US Civil War, he served as a military observer for the Union Army where he made his first ascent in a balloon.

1839 John D(avison) Rockefeller, US multimillionaire, founder of Standard Oil Company (1870) who built his first refinery in 1863 and devoted his later years to philanthropy. His grandson, Nelson (Aldrich) Rockefeller, was born on the same day in 1908. He was first elected governor of New York in 1958.

1851 Sir Arthur John Evans, English archaeologist who excavated the ruins of the ancient city of Knossos in Crete.

ARTS

1882 Percy (Aldridge) Grainger, Australian composer who was befriended by Grieg. This association influenced Grainger to collect folk songs. The Grainger Museum for Australian music was built in Melbourne in 1935.

SPORT

GLOVES OFF Born 1781, Tom Cribb, English pugilist who was a highly popular champion bareknuckle boxer. While he was never world champion, he defeated the best North American boxers of that time. His birthday coincides with the last bareknuckle world heavyweight boxing match which took place in 1889 in Richburg, Mississippi when John L. Sullivan defeated Jake Kilrain in the 75th round!

DIED THIS DAY

1822 Percy Bysshe Shelley, English poet, drowned off Leghorn while sailing his small schooner *Ariel* to his home on the Gulf of Spezia.

1933 Anthony Hope, English writer, author of *The Prisoner of Zenda* (1894).

1939 Henry Havelock Ellis, English physician and author of *Studies in the Psychology of Sex* (1897–1928).

1967 Vivien Leigh, English actress, star of *Gone With the Wind*, of tuberculosis aged 53.

1970 Dame Laura Knight, English painter of circus and gypsy life.

1979 Michael Wilding, English stage and screen actor.

ON THIS DAY

1497 Portuguese navigator Vasco da Gama set sail from Lisbon with four vessels in search of a sea route to India.

1892 Inspector Éduardo Alvarez found a number of bloody fingermarks at the scene of a murder in La Plata, Buenos Aires Province. The prints were compared with those of the suspect, and the mother of the two murdered children who claimed her neighbour was the murderer. The fingerprints matched hers and she confessed, the first person to be convicted on the evidence of fingerprints.

1907 Ziegfeld's *Follies of 1907* opened, his first, and like the others that followed, containing 13 characters in the title for good luck.

1918 National Savings stamps went on sale in Britain.

1943 Jean Moulin, the French Resistance leader known as 'Max', was executed after being tortured by the Gestapo.

1961 The first all-England women's singles final took place at Wimbledon between Christine Truman and Angela Mortimer who was beaten in three sets. In 1963, the first Australian to win that title was Margaret Smith.

1965 Horse racing starting gates were first used in Britain, at Newmarket for the Chesterfield Stakes.

1988 A London double-decker bus parked in Orville Road, Battersea, which had been converted into a luxury home to overcome rising property prices in the capital, was offered for sale at £40,000.

9 JULY

National Day of Argentina commemorating its declaration of independence from Spain in 1816.

BORN THIS DAY

HISTORY

1916 Edward (Richard George) Heath, British Prime Minister, 1970–74, who took Britain into the European Economic Community in 1972.

ARTS

1901 Barbara Cartland, English queen of romantic novels, with almost 500 books to her credit. Her longevity and energy must be the best advertisement that health foods and vitamins – which she enthusiastically promotes – have ever had.

1937 David Hockney, English painter who first established himself in the pop-art scene before working in several other styles. His Californian swimming pool paintings (1965–7) and his later portaits, have established him as a leading international artist.

ENTERTAINMENT

1935 Michael Williams, British actor who, among other roles, appeared with his wife Dame Judi Dench in the television series *A Fine Romance*.

INVENTION

1819 Elias Howe, US inventor of the sewing machine which proved suitable for garment factories and who was granted a patent in 1846.

DIED THIS DAY

1440 Jan van Eyck, Flemish painter, famous for his many religious paintings.

1797 Edmund Burke, British statesman and orator.

1850 Zachary Taylor, 12th US President.

ON THIS DAY

1877 The first Wimbledon Lawn Tennis championship was held.

1887 The first paper napkins were introduced by stationery manufacturers John Dickenson at their annual dinner at the Castle Hotel, Hastings.

1900 The Royal Assent was given to the act creating a federal Commonwealth of Australia.

THE YOUNG ONES In 1922, US swimmer (and later one of Hollywood's better Tarzan's) Johnny Weismuller, then 18, swam the 100m in under a minute (58.6 seconds). In 1925, 22-year-old Miss Oonagh Keogh became the first female member of a stock exchange when she was admitted to the floor of the Dublin Stock Exchange, forty years before a woman was allowed to join a British stock exchange. In 1954, Australia's Peter Thomson, 24, became the youngest ever winner of the British Open golf championship.

1938 Gas masks were first issued to the civilian population of Britain in anticipation of the Second World War. Some 35 million went into the shops this day.

1969 The first rhino in captivity gave birth in an Irish zoo.

1984 A bolt of lightning set fire to York Minster. The 700-year old building suffered serious damage to the south transept, but the famous Rose Window survived.

10 JULY

BORN THIS DAY

ARTS

1792 Captain Frederick Marryat, English novelist on life at sea and other adventure stories, including in 1847 the children's English Civil War classic, *The Children of the New Forest*.

1802 Robert Chambers, Scottish author and publisher who wrote one of the best *Book of Days* (1888).

1830 Camille Pissaro, French Impressionist painter who was born in the Danish West Indies and who, despite serious eye problems, produced over 1,600 works.

1834 James (Abbott) McNeill Whistler, US painter and etcher who spent some years of his boyhood in Russia and attended the US military academy at West Point before coming to study painting in Europe, where he stayed. His paintings of London and Venice are rich in atmosphere, and stunning full-length portraits were highly innovative. His *Mother* hangs in the Louvre.

1871 Marcel Proust, French author of *Remembrance of Things Past* (1917–25), one of the greatest novels ever written. After a life in society and artistic salons, he became a virtual recluse after the death of his parents, suffering from hypochondria and crippling asthma.

1895 Carl Orff, German composer best known for his secular oratorio *Carmina Burana* (1943–53) and the opera *Prometheus* (1968).

1917 Reg Smythe, English cartoonist who created the legendary Andy Capp strip of a working-class anti-hero.

ENTERTAINMENT

1900 Evelyn Laye, English actress and singer who made her name in operettas and with the revivals of *The Merry Widow* and *Madame Pompadour*. On Broadway, she starred in *Bitter Sweet*.

POP

1947 Arlo Guthrie, US singer, son of the legendary Woody, who had hits with his album *Alice's Restaurant* (1967) and the single 'The City of New Orleans' (1972).

RELIGION

1509 John Calvin, French theologian and a leading Protestant reformer. His followers promoted Calvinism which particularly influenced John Knox, the Scottish Reformer.

SPORT

1927 Don Revie, former Leeds and England football manager.

DOUBLES Born 1943, Arthur Ashe, US tennis star and the first black Wimbledon men's singles tennis champion which he won (5.7.75) a few days before his 32nd birthday. Born 1945, Virginia Wade, finally became Wimbledon women's singles champion (1.7.77), just over a week to her 32nd birthday.

1949 Sunil Gavaskar, former Indian cricket captain who was the first to score over 10,000 runs in test cricket.

DIED THIS DAY

AD138 Hadrian (Publius Aelius Hadrianus), Roman emperor who built a wall across England's northern border to keep out the Scots.

1099 El Cid (Rodrigo Díaz de Vivar), somewhat overrated Spanish hero who recaptured Valencia from the Moors. It was retaken after his death.

1806 George Stubbs, English painter of animals, especially horses.

1851 Louis Jacques Mandé Daguerre, French photographic pioneer.

1884 Karl Richard Lepsius, Egyptologist and founder of modern scientific archaeology.

1923 Albert Chevalier, English actor and music hall entertainer, known as the 'costers' laureate' because of his cockney songs such as 'My Old Dutch'.

1941 (Ferdinand) Jelly Roll Morton, ragtime composer and pianist, one of the great jazz pioneers.

1978 Giorgio de Chirico, Italian painter who was one of the founders of the modern 'Metaphysical School'.

1989 Mel Blanc, US actor who was the voice of Bugs Bunny, Woody Woodpecker, Daffy Duck, Tweety Pie, Sylvester, the Road Runner and Elmer Fudd, of emphysema.

1989 (Thomas Edward) Tommy Trinder, English comedian and actor.

ON THIS DAY

1890 Wyoming became the 4th state of the Union.

1900 The Paris Metro opened.

1958 The first parking meters in Britain were installed in Mayfair.

1962 *Telstar I* was launched. The following day it transmitted a special television inaugural programme to mark the first communications satellite.

1970 David Broome became the first British rider to win the World Showjumping Championship, held in France.

1976 The Italian town of Sveso was covered by a poisonous cloud as a result of an explosion at a chemical factory, leading to mass evacuation. Crops and 40,000 animals died, and the number of abnormal births rose dramatically.

1985 The Greenpeace ship, *Rainbow Warrior*, was badly damaged by an explosion in Auckland harbour. Nine people escaped, but a photographer died. French agents were arrested after the incident. They had tried to prevent the ship sailing to protest in a French nuclear testing area in the Pacific.

1989 Footballer Maurice Johnston had to have a police guard after he was transferred to Scotland's Rangers FC for £1.5m. He was the first Catholic to play for the club that had been exclusively Protestant.

11 JULY

BORN THIS DAY

HISTORY

1274 Robert the Bruce, King of Scotland, who seized the throne in 1306, beat the English at Bannockburn in 1314 and united the clans.

1657 Frederick I, first King of Prussia from 1701–13, who established his new kingdom making it both politically and culurally important.

1767 John Quincy Adams, 6th US President (1825–9) who campaigned against slavery.

1916 (Edward) Gough Whitlam, Australian Prime Minister (1972–5) combining it with Minister of Foreign Affairs for the first term of his office.

1754 Thomas Bowdler, English doctor, man of letters and 'bowdlerizer' of Shakespeare, taking out all the naughty bits to produce his *Family Shakespeare*.

ENTERTAINMENT

1915 Yul Brynner (Youl Bryner), US film actor who was born at Sakhalin, off Siberia and made baldness sexy when he played the lead in the stage musical, *The King and I* (1951) and in the film version (1956). The one-time balalaika player and trapeze artiste went on to play strong, masculine roles in such films as *The Magnificent Seven* (1960).

SPORT

1944 Peter de Savary, international entrepreneur, owner of Land's End and head of Britain's America's Cup yachting challenge.

1953 Leon Spinks, US boxer who became the first to take away Muhammad Ali's crown on 15 February 1978, but Ali won it back that September.

DIED THIS DAY

66BC Nero, mentally unstable Roman emperor who was condemned to death by the Senate, fled Rome and is believed to have committed suicide.

1935 Alfred Dreyfus, French soldier and central figure of one of France's most traumatic scandals.

1937 George Gershwin (Jacob Gershvin), US composer and songwriter whose shows included *Porgy and Bess*.

1941 Sir Arthur John Evans, English archaeologist, three days after his 90th birthday.

1950 Buddy (George Gard) DeSylva, US lyricist, librettist and director who wrote the words for many Broadway shows including the song 'April Showers'.

1957 The Aga Khan III, spiritual head of the Ismaili Muslim sect. He was succeeded by his grandson.

1989 Laurence Olivier (Lord Olivier), the greatest actor of his generation, aged 82, in his sleep. The lights went out for an hour outside West End theatres and leading actors made speeches of tribute at the Royal Shakespeare Company and the National Theatre Company.

ON THIS DAY

1776 Captain Cook set off from Plymouth on his third and final voyage of exploration.

1789 In France Lafayette presented his draft *Rights of man and the Citizen* to the revolutionary National Assembly.

1950 BBC television first transmitted the children's programme, *Andy Pandy*.

1975 China's great terracotta army was uncovered near the ancient Chinese capital of Xian. Over 6,000 life-sized warriors were made around 206BC to guard the tomb of the first Ch-in emperor.

1977 One of the rare blasphemy trials took place in Britain when Gay News was find £1,000 for publishing a poem about a homosexual Jesus.

1979 The 79-ton US Skylab returned to earth after six years. As it reached the earth's atmosphere, it burned up and shattered over Western Australia providing a spectacular fireworks show.

1986 British newspapers were banned from printing extracts from Peter Wright's *Spycatcher*.

12 JULY

BORN THIS DAY

HISTORY

100BC Gaius Julius Caesar, the most famous general in Roman history, who became a dictator. When he was born, the month was called *Quintilis*, but was renamed in his honour.

1730 Josiah Wedgwood, English pottery designer and manufacturer, baptized this day in Burslem, Staffordshire where he worked in the family pottery business at Churchyard Works. When his right leg was affected by smallpox and had to be amputated, he spent the time recovering in research and experimentation which led to Wedgwood becoming prized worldwide.

1817 Henry David Thoreau, US author and naturalist who went and lived in the woods, which he described in many of his books including *Early Spring in Massachusetts* (1881).

ARTS

1884 Amedeo Modigliani, Italian painter and sculptor, influenced by Cézanne, whose series of nudes was banned from being exhibited in 1917.

1895 Kirsten Flagstaff, Norwegian operatic soprano who was considered the finest Wagnerian singer of this century, excelling in roles such as Brunhilde in *The Ring*, which she sang in Bayreuth, London and the US.

ENTERTAINMENT

1895 Oscar Hammerstein II, US librettist, lyricist, producer and director, one of the greats of showbiz who worked with various composers from Jerome Kern to Richard Rodgers. With them, he wrote shows ranging from *The Desert Song* (1926), *Show Boat* (1927), *Oklahoma* (1943) to *South Pacific* (1949), *The King and I* (1951) and *The Sound of Music* (1959).

1908 Milton Berle (Mendel Berlinger), US comedian from vaudeville, where he made the transition to television, appearing in television films such as *The Legend of Valentino*.

1928 Sir Alistair Burnet, award-winning doyen of British television newsreaders, and head of Independent Television News.

1937 Bill Cosby, top US comedian with his top-rated television show, *The Cosby Show*, who was first seen in the series *I Spy* when he became the first black actor to get equal billing and won three Emmys.

DOUBLE EXPOSURE Born 1854, George Eastman, US photographic pioneer who founded Kodak, a name he chose because it was easy to remember. He was born on the third anniversary of the death of another great photographic pioneer in 1851, Frenchman Louis Daguerre.

DIED THIS DAY

1705 Titus Oates, English Anglican priest responsible for the fabricated 'Popish Plot' of 1678 which caused a reign of terror in London. After being expelled from the church, he died in obscurity.

1910 The Hon Charles Stewart Rolls, aviator and car manufacturer (of Rolls-Royce fame), killed in an aircraft crash near Bournemouth. He was the first pilot to be killed in British aviation history.

ON THIS DAY

1543 Henry VIII married for the sixth and final time at Hampton Court. His wife was Catherine Parr, who would outlive him.

1845 The first performance of *Pas de Quatre*, the most celebrated divertissement in ballet history, was staged at a Royal Command Peformance for Queen Victoria in London.

1878 Cyprus was ceded to British administration by Turkey.

1920 President Wilson opened the Panama Canal.

1930 The great Australian batsman Don Bradman hit 309 runs in a record-breaking single day in the Test at Headingly, Leeds to finally reach a record-breaking score of 334.

1969 Tony Jacklin became the first British golfer to win the British Open since 1951.

1989 A shouting woman, convicted in a Cleveland, Ohio court for stealing jewellery, was ordered to have her mouth taped shut by the judge.

13 JULY

BORN THIS DAY

HISTORY

1527 John Dee, English alchemist and mathematician who was astrologer to Mary Tudor, but was imprisoned for performing magic feats. He was soon back in favour, casting horoscopes for Elizabeth I and advising navigators and explorers. He named the best day for Elizabeth's coronation, but by far his most serious work was encouraging an interest in mathematics, although he seems to have been more popular touring European courts performing magical tricks.

1859 Sidney James Webb, English social reformer with his wife, Beatrice. Leading lights of the Fabian Society, they also founded the London School of Economics and the socialist journal, the *New Statesman*.

ARTS

1811 Sir George Gilbert Scott, English architect responsible for the Gothic revival, the man to blame for the Albert Memorial.

1933 David (Malcolm) Storey, English novelist of *This Sporting Life* (1960) and playwright of *Home* (1969), which starred John Gielgud and Ralph Richardson, and *The March on Russia* (1989).

ENTERTAINMENT

1942 Harrison Ford, US actor who starred in *Star Wars* (1977) and *Raiders of the Lost Ark* (1980). There was a previous dashing screen hero in silent films called Harrison Ford (1892–1957) who was no relation.

DIED THIS DAY

1793 Jean Paul Marat, French revolutionary leader, stabbed to death by Charlotte Corday while in his bath. Suffering from a painful skin disease, he would spend hours in a warm bath. (*See also* 17.7.1793)

1951 Arnold Schonberg, Austrian composer who created atonal music, in California.

1980 Sir Seretse Khama, President of Botswana, in a London hospital.

ON THIS DAY

1837 Queen Victoria moved into Buckingham Palace, the first monarch to live there.

1911 A suffragette hid in a broom cupboard in the House of Commons during the night of the 1911 census so she could record her address as The House of Commons, 'thus making my claim to the same right as men'.

1923 A bill banning the sale of alcohol to people under 18 was passed by the British Parliament.

1930 The World Cup football competition was inaugurated in Montevideo, Uruguay. The hosts beat 13 other countries to be the first winners. British teams had declined to participate because of the long sea voyage and the costs.

1939 Frank Sinatra made his first record, 'From the Bottom of My Heart', with the Harry James Band.

1947 Europe accepted Marshall Aid, the US financial package to aid European recovery after the Second World War and to prevent some countries going bankrupt.

1955 Night club hostess Ruth Ellis became the last woman to be hanged in Britain, when the sentence for the murder of her lover was carried out at Holloway Prison.

1973 The Everly Brothers parted on stage in California when Phil smashed his guitar and stormed off, leaving Don to finish the gig.

14 JULY

Bastille Day, National Day of France; in 1789 the hated Bastille, the state prison in Paris, was stormed and razed to the ground as the French Revolution began.

The National Day of Iraq. In 1958, King Faisal of Iraq was assassinated in a military coup led by General Kassem. Iraq became a republic.

BORN THIS DAY

HISTORY

1858 Emmeline Pankhurst, English suffragette who fought a 40-year campaign with her daughters Christabel and Sylvia. The struggle included imprisonment and hunger strikes.

1913 Gerald (Rudolph) Ford (Leslie Lynch King), 38th US President whose parents were divorced when he was an infant. His mother later married Gerald Ford, Sr., and adopted the boy. Ford was Vice-President to Richard Nixon and took over after his resignation.

ARTS

1903 Irving Stone (Irving Tennenbaum), US bestselling author of biog-novels including *Lust for Life* (about van Gogh) and *The Agony and the Ecstasy* (about Michelangelo).

ENTERTAINMENT

1911 Terry Thomas (Thomas Terry Hoar Stevens), English actor and comedian who specialized in upper-class characters in such films as *Carlton Browne of the F.O.* (1959) and *Those Magnificent Men in their Flying Machines* (1965). Afflicted by Parkinson's disease, he was forced to abandon his highly successful career that had also spanned the stage, radio and television.

1912 Woody Guthrie (Woodrow Wilson Guthrie), legendary US folk singer, guitarist and composer of classics such as 'So Long (It's Been Good to Know Yuh)' and the song adopted by the Civil Rights movement, 'This Land is Our Land'.

1918 Ingmar Bergman, Swedish film and stage director whose films have a distinctive introspective quality. They include *Smiles of a Summer Night* (1955) and the award-winning *The Seventh Seal* (1957). His films introduced leading Swedish actors such as Max von Sydow and Liv Ullman to a wide audience.

1918 Arthur Laurents, US playwright, librettist and director, who wrote the play *Home of the Brave* (1946), which was later filmed, and the book for *West Side Story* (1957) and *Gypsy* (1959).

1931 Robert Stephens, English actor on stage, television and in films such as *Travels With my Aunt* (1972) playing opposite his second wife, Maggie Smith.

1946 Sue Lawley, English television news reader, interviewer and presenter.

DIED THIS DAY

1867 Alfred Krupp, German munitions manufacturer.

1904 (Stephanus Johannes) Paul(us) Kruger, the Boer leader known as 'Oom Paul' (Uncle Paul), President of the Transvaal, in exile in Switzerland.

1907 Sir William Henry Perkin, English chemist and inventor of aniline dyes.

1959 Grock (Karl Adrien Wettach), famous Swiss clown.

1965 Adlai (Ewing) Stevenson, US politician and diplomat, UN ambassador, in London, of a heart attack.

ON THIS DAY

1865 On his seventh attempt, English climber Edward Whymper led the first climbers to reach the 14,690ft summit of the Matterhorn in the Alps. In 1965 on the centenary of this achievement, the first woman to climb the Matterhorn, Mademoiselle Vaucher made it to the summit.

1867 Alfred Nobel demonstrated dynamite for the first time at a quarry in Redhill, Surrey.

1902 The famous bell tower of Venice, the Campanile of St Mark's Cathedral, suddenly collapsed during a safety inspection.

1930 The BBC transmitted its first television play, an adaptation of Pirandello's *The Man with a Flower in His Mouth*. (*See also* 19.1.1937)

1959 The first nuclear warship, 14,000-ton cruiser USS *Long Beach* was launched.

1972 Gary Glitter and the Glittermen played their first gig in Wiltshire. The backing group later called themselves the Glitter Band.

15 JULY

St Swithun's Day. This Anglo-Saxon saint asked to be buried outside Winchester Cathedral where he was bishop. He said he wanted to be exposed to 'the feet of passers-by and the drops falling from above' which led to the meteorological superstition that if it rains on 15 July it will rain for 40 days.

BORN THIS DAY

HISTORY

1865 Alfred (Charles William) Harmsworth, 1st Viscount Northcliffe, Irish-born English journalist and newspaper proprietor who was one of the pioneers of the tabloid press with his *Daily Mail* and later the *Daily Mirror*, he proved also to be one of the saviours of *The Times* when he took over the declining newspaper in 1908.

ARTS

1573 Inigo Jones, first great English architect and theatre designer who arranged the masques of Ben Jonson. He designed and built many royal buildings, as well as laying out Covent Garden.

1606 Rembrandt (Harmenszoon van Rijn), Dutch painter, one of the great masters who was influenced by Italian art. His *Night Watch* and some of his later masterpieces proved unpopular at the time, and he went bankrupt, but he continued to paint, producing over 650 oil paintings, 2,000 drawings and 300 etchings.

1933 Julian (Alexander) Bream, English virtuoso guitarist and lutist.

1934 Harrison Birtwistle, English composer of the chamber opera *Punch and Judy* (1967) and his piece for electronic music, *Chronometer* (1972), based on the ticking of a clock.

1913 (Ralph) Hammond Innes, English author of bestsellers such as *Campbell's Kingdom* (1952) and *The Mary Deare* (1956).

1919 Dame Iris Murdoch, Irish-born novelist and philosopher, author of many novels, including *Under the Net* (1954) and her Booker prize winning *The Sea, the Sea* (1978).

ENTERTAINMENT

1898 Noël Gay, English composer of London's longest running musical of the 30s, *Me and My Girl* (1937) with the famous song, 'The Lambeth Walk'. A revival of the show in the 80s has enjoyed enormous success and seems likely to exceed the original 1,646 performances.

POP

1946 Linda (Maria) Rondstadt, US singer and actress who scored a hit in 1975 with 'You're No Good' and starred in *The Pirates of Penzance* in New

York, which opened on her 34th birthday in 1980.

DIED THIS DAY

1685 James Scott, Duke of Monmouth, illegitimate son of King Charles II and his mistress Lucy Walter, beheaded in London for leading an unsuccessful rebellion against the new King James II.

1883 General Tom Thumb (Charles Sherwood Stratton), US dwarf who became an international celebrity when promoted by P.T. Barnum.

1904 Anton Chekhov, Russian playwright and short-story writer, who wrote *The Cherry Orchard* (1904).

1929 Hugo von Hofmannsthal, Austrian poet, playwright and essayist who also wrote the libretti for Strauss operas including *Der Rosenkavalier* (1911).

1976 Paul William Gallico, US author of *The Snow Goose* (1941).

ON THIS DAY

1099 Jerusalem was captured by the Crusaders with troops led by Godfrey and Robert of Flanders and Tancred of Normandy. The Muslim governor surrendered in the Tower of David.

1795 The *Marseillaise* written by Rouget de Lisle, was officially adopted as the French national anthem.

1857 The Massacre of Cawnpore took place at an Indian frontier station where British troops including women and children were massacred, their bodies thrown in a well which has since become a memorial.

1869 Hippolyte Mege Mouries patented margerine in Paris.

1881 Billy the Kid, the notorious US outlaw (William H. Bonney), who killed his first man at 12, and murdered another 21 people before he was shot dead this day in New Mexico by Sherrif Pat Garrett while trying to escape rearrest after a jail break.

1912 Lloyd George's social insurance scheme came into force in Britain.

TAKING OFF In 1916, William Edward Boeing formed his Pacific Aero Products, while in 1933, US aviator Wiley Post took off on the first solo round-the-world flight in *Winnie Mae*. After ten refuelling stops he completed the flight on the 22 July. Five years later, in 1938, 32-year-old Howard Hughes did the same thing, setting a record of three days 19 hours 14 minutes. Not surprising, then, that the first Boeing 707 jetliner, made its maiden flight from Seattle this same day, 1954.

1948 The British branch of Alcoholics Anonymous began, 13 years after the original was formed in the US.

1949 Jaroslav Drobny defected to the west two weeks after winning the men's singles title at Wimbledon.

16 JULY

The traditional starting day of the Islamic Era in AD*622 when a persecuted Muhammad fled from Mecca to Medina, and known as the* hegira, *Arabic for 'flight'.*

BORN THIS DAY

HISTORY

1872 Roald Amundsen, Norwegian explorer who was the first to reach the

South Pole (14.12.1911), just weeks before Scott.

1896 Trygve Lie, Norwegian statesman and first Secretary-General of the United Nations.

ARTS

1486 Andrea del Sarto (Andrea Domenico d'Angnolo di Francesco), leading Florentine painter whose religious frescos decorate many major churches.

1723 Sir Joshua Reynolds, English portrait painter who was elected first President of the Royal Academy in 1768. He was so successful that he virtually ran a portrait factory, with assistants completing the paintings like an assembly line.

1938 Anita Brookner, English novelist and art historian, who won the Booker prize for her novel *Hotel du Lac* (1984).

ENTERTAINMENT

1907 Barbara Stanwyck (Ruby Stevens), who was one of the most workman-like, non-temperamental actresses in Hollywood in films such as *Double Indemnity* which made her the highest paid actress in the US in 1944.

1911 Ginger Rogers (Virginia Katherine McMath) who played leads in Broadway musicals including *Girl Crazy*, when she introduced the song, 'Embraceable You'. While she is linked with Fred Astaire in ten incomparable musicals including *Top Hat* (1935), she won an Oscar for her dramatic performance in *Kitty Foyle* (1940).

SPORT

1942 Margaret Court, Australian tennis player who in 1970 won the Grand Slam, which comprises Wimbledon, the US, French and Australian championships.

RELIGION

1821 Mary Baker Eddy, US religious leader who founded the Christian Science movement. The inspiration for this came from Phineas P. Quimby of Maine who performed feats of healing without medication. She believed he had discovered the healing powers of Christ.

DIED THIS DAY

1557 Anne of Cleves, the fourth of Henry VIII's wives whose marriage was declared null and void after six months.

1827 Joseph Spode, English potter whose bone china work bears his name.

1953 (Joseph) Hilaire (Pierre) Belloc, English writer of verses, and books on the French Revolution.

1989 Herbert von Karajan, leading Austrian-born conductor.

ON THIS DAY

1661 The Bank of Stockholm issued the first banknotes in Europe.

1867 Reinforced concrete was patented by Joseph Monier of Paris.

1885 Louis Pasteur treated a nine-year-old boy from Alsace for rabies, the first such successful treatment.

1918 The last Russian Tsar, Nicholas II, along with his entire family, family doctor, servants and even the pet dog, was shot by the Bolsheviks in a cellar in a house in Ekaterinburg.

1935 The first parking meters appeared in Oklahoma City, invented by Carlton Magee.

1936 The would-be-assassin of King Edward VIII, a Scottish journalist,

George Andrew MacMahon, was arrested before he could fire the first shot.

1945 The atomic age began officially when the first atomic bomb developed by Robert Oppenheimer and his team at Los Alamos was detonated in New Mexico.

1948 The Vickers Viscount, the first turbo-prop aircraft, flew for the first time.

1950 The largest crowd to ever attend a football match, 205,000 people saw the Brazil-Uruguay World Cup match in Rio de Janeiro which Brazil lost 1–2.

1969 *Apollo II* was launched with US astronauts Neil Armstrong, Edwin Aldrin and Michael Collins on board.

1970 The first state of emergency in Britain since 1926 was called by Prime Minister Edward Heath as the dockers went on strike.

HOLIEST AND SMALLEST In 1988 thousands of Sri Lankans gathered at a Buddhist temple in Kandy to mourn the death of Raja, a holy elephant and 'national treasure' who died aged 81. Meanwhile in England, the cousin of the Queen, Lord Harewood, had to call in police to investigate the theft of his 27-inch high Shetland stallion, Pernod, believed to be the world's smallest horse.

17 JULY

BORN THIS DAY

HISTORY

1876 Maxim Litvinov, Soviet statesman who represented the Bolshevik government in Britain in 1917 before it was recognized, when he was arrested for propaganda activities. He was later swapped for British journalist Robert Bruce Lockhart who had been held while on a special mission to the Soviet Union.

1909 Hardy Amies, dressmaker to the Queen.

ARTS

1889 Earle Stanley Gardner, US author and lawyer who created Perry Mason who first appeared in 1933 in *The Case of the Velvet Claws*. Gardner used to write 200,000 words a month as well as devoting two days a week to his law practice; he wrote almost 100 mystery novels.

1948 Wayne Sleep, English ballet dancer and actor who concentrated his exceptional talent on character roles, several of which were specially created for him.

ENTERTAINMENT

1899 James Cagney, US actor and song and dance man before going to Hollywood to play tough guy roles, although he was able to use his musical talents in *Yankee Doodle Dandy* (1942) which won him an Oscar. He is best remembered for his 'dirty rat' roles in films such as *The Public Enemy* (1931) and *Angels with Dirty Faces* (1938).

1917 Phyllis Diller, US comedienne who made her debut aged 40 with her stand-up one-line comedy routine. She has continued to make guest appearances on both US and British television.

1931 Ray Galton, other half of the English scriptwriting team Galton and Simpson who wrote the classic television series *Hancock's Half Hour* and *Steptoe and Son*.

1935 Donald Sutherland, Canadian actor who trained in London. His films include *M*A*S*H* (1970), *The Eagle*

Has Landed (1976) and *A Dry White Season* (1990).

DIED THIS DAY

1790 Adam Smith, Scottish economist and author of *Wealth of Nations* (1776).

1903 James (Abbott) McNeil Whistler, US-born painter.

1959 Billie Holiday ('Lady Day'), US jazz singer, probably the greatest of them all, who was arrested on her death bed in hospital for possession of narcotics.

ON THIS DAY

1790 Thomas Saint of London, patented the first sewing machine, but there is no record of it ever being produced.

1793 Charlott Corday was guillotined for the murder of Marat, the French Revolutionary (13.7.1793). The executioner held up her severed head for the crowd to see and slapped her face. The cheeks reddened and 'her countenance expressed the most unequivocal marks of indignation' according to a doctor who witnessed the execution. It seemed that the head lived on briefly after it was speedily and cleanly removed from the body.

1841 The first edition of *Punch* was published in London.

1917 The British royal family changed their name from 'Saxe-Coburg-Gotha' to the decidedly more English 'Windsor'.

1945 The Potsdam Conference began with world leaders Truman, Stalin and Churchill planning for the future peace at the conclusion of the Second World War.

1951 The famous Abbey Theatre in Dublin burned down. The play that evening closed with soldiers on stage singing, 'Keep the Home Fires Burning'.

1968 *Yellow Submarine*, the animated film with the Beatles sound track, was premièred.

1969 Opening night in New York of the 'daring' sex revue that typified the 'Swinging Sixties', *Oh! Calcutta!* devised by theatre critic Ken Tynan with contributions from several leading writers including Joe Orton. But another leading critic, Clive Barnes, said the show gave pornography a dirty name.

1975 An international space link-up between US astronauts and Soviet astronauts took place when they crossed over from the docked spacecraft and shook hands 140 miles above Britain's south coast.

18 JULY

National Day of Spain.

BORN THIS DAY

HISTORY

1887 Vidkun Quisling (Abraham Lauritz Jonsson), Norwegian army officer who formed a fascist party in 1933 and who urged the Nazis to occupy Norway in 1940. After the war he was tried for treason and executed (24.10.1945). His name has become a synonym for 'traitor'.

1918 Nelson (Rolihlahla) Mandela, South African lawyer and politician, a leader of the banned African National Congress (ANC) who was dubbed the Black Pimpernel while on the run from police in 1961. He was eventually arrested and tried for plotting to overthrow the government, was imprisoned in 1964 and was not released until 11.2.1990.

1921 John (Herschel) Glenn, the first US astronaut to orbit the earth (20.2.1962).

ARTS

1811 William Makepeace Thackeray, English novelist and poet, born in India and who settled in London in 1815, best known for his popular *Vanity Fair* (1847–8) and *The History of Pendennis* (1848–50).

1935 Edward Bond, English playwright and director who created a stir in 1965 with his play *Saved*, which had a symbolic scene of the violent killing of a baby.

SCIENCE

1635 Robert Hooke, English physicist whose experimental work made possible the inventions of the steam engine, the quadrant, Gregorian telescope and microscope.

1720 The Rev Gilbert White, English naturalist and author of *The Natural History and Antiquities of Selborne* (1789), the first work on natural history which has become a classic and is still reprinted in many countries.

JAZZ

1938 Dudu Pukwana (Mtutuzel), South African-born alto and soprano sax player and composer who has performed with many groups in the US and Britain including his own, Assegai, which has had an important influence on British jazz.

SPORT

1848 Dr William Gilbert Grace, bearded English cricketer, doctor of medicine and great all-rounder who scored 54,896 runs and took 2,876 wickets. He was also in the first Test in Australia in 1880. He scorned training and usually had a large scotch and soda in the lunch break.

1948 David Hemery, English athlete who won the gold in the 400 metres hurdles at the Mexican Olympics in 1968.

1949 Dennis Lillee, Australian cricketer and one of the finest fast bowlers ever with over 350 wickets. He was also the first to take five wickets in a one-day international.

1957 Nick (Nicholas Alexander) Faldo, champion English golfer who first won the British Open in 1987 and the Augusta Masters in 1989, and was one of the key players in the great British golf renaissance.

BUSINESS

1950 Richard Branson, English entrepreneur and managing director of the Virgin Group, who has a penchant for adventure which also creates publicity such as his abortive attempt to balloon across the Atlantic following his record-breaking crossing in a power boat.

DIED THIS DAY

1610 Michelangelo Merisi da Caravaggio, Italian painter who fled to Malta after killing a man in a quarrel. On his return to Rome, he had all his baggage stolen and was wounded in a fight. He finally caught fever and died by a river bank.

1721 Jean Antoine Watteau, French painter who came to London for treatment for tuberculosis, but finally died from the illness shortly after his return to France.

1762 Tsar Peter III, strangled by conspirators planning to place his wife (Catherine II) on the throne.
1792 John Paul Jones, Scottish-born American naval officer who defeated the English fleet during the War of Independence.
1817 Jane Austen, English novelist who wrote *Pride and Prejudice*.
1872 Benito Pablo Juárez, Mexican President and national hero.
1892 Thomas Cook, English travel agent and pioneer of the package holiday.

ON THIS DAY

64BC Rome burned, but contrary to the legend, Nero did not fiddle while the fire destroyed two thirds of the city. The mentally unbalanced emperor rebuilt Rome, one of his few positive achievements.
1870 The Vatican Council proclaimed the dogma of Papal infallibity as regards faith and morals.
1877 Edison carried out his first successful experiment in recording and storing the human voice, but decided more work was needed before he would demonstrate his invention to an excited crowd at the office of the *Scientific American* journal early in 1878.
1919 The Cenotaph in London's Whitehall was unveiled. The First World War memorial was designed by Sir Edward Lutyens and would later do double-duty for the Second World War.
1925 *Mein Kampf* (My Struggle), which Adolf Hitler wrote while in jail, was published.
1936 The Spanish Civil War began when the army, led by General Francisco Franco revolted against the Republican government. It would last over three years.
1955 Disneyland opened at Anaheim, California – Walt Disney's 160 acres of fantasy and fun which cost $17m.
1969 An Oldsmobile driven by Senator Edward Kennedy crashed into the Chappaquidick River near Martha's Vineyard on America's east coast. Kennedy escaped, but his companion, Mary Jo Kopechne drowned. What caused the real stir was his failure to report the incident for almost ten hours. He was later found guilty of leaving the scene of the accident and given a two-month suspended sentence.
1979 Joyce McKinney, 29, a former Miss Wyoming and a central figure in the 'sex-in-chains' kidnapping case, was arrested in the US after fleeing Britain shortly before her Old Bailey trial. While in England, she allegedly kidnapped a 21-year-old Mormon missionary, Kirk Anderson, and chained him to a bed for sexual purposes.
1984 A security guard who said he hated Mondays, walked into a McDonalds in San Ysidro, California and randomly opened fire, killing 20 and wounding 16 people, before a police marksman shot him. This was the largest death toll by a gunman in a single day in US crime history.

19 JULY

BORN THIS DAY

HISTORY

1814 Samuel Colt, US inventor of the six-shot revolver which he made of wood during his time at sea and patented in 1835. The gun was not an instant success, and his manufacturing business faltered. He also invented the first remotely controlled naval mine, by which time his guns were proving popular. He ended up a rich man with progressive ideas about the welfare of his workers.

1860 Lizzie Borden, alleged US axe murderess of her father and stepmother whose bodies were found on 4 August 1892 in their locked house in the small Massachusetts town of Fall River. After a 13-day trial, the Sunday-school teacher and an active Christian Endeavour Society member was acquitted, the case unsolved.

1865 Charles Horace Mayo, US surgeon and one of the three brothers who co-founded the Mayo Clinic.

ARTS

1834 Edgar Degas (Hilaire Germaine Edgar Degas), leading French Impressionist painter, also admired for his pastel work, particularly of dancers.

1896 Dr A(rchibald) J(oseph) Cronin, Scottish novelist who used his experience as a medical man and later, as inspector of coal mines investigating occupational diseases in his acclaimed and successful novels which include *The Citadel* (1937) and *The Keys of the Kingdom* (1944).

SPORT

1946 Ile Nastase, Romanian tennis player who was banned for three months in 1978 for bad behaviour which earned him the nickname 'Nasty' after losing in the early stages of the men's singles at Wimbledon.

DIED THIS DAY

1814 Matthew Flinders, English navigator who explored and charted much of the Australian coastline.

1965 Sygman Rhee, Korean President.

ON THIS DAY

THREE SHIPS In 1545, the pride of Henry VIII's battle fleet, the *Mary Rose* keeled over in the Solent and sank, with the loss of 700 lives. The ship was raised 437 years later (11.10.1982). In 1837 Brunel's *Great Western* steamship was launched at Bristol, and on the same day in 1843, the first all-metal liner, *Great Britain*, also designed by the great Brunel was launched from Wapping Dock. With an appropriate sense of occasion, the old vessel was brought back to Britain this day in 1970, from the Falkland Islands where it had been rusting away.

1821 George IV was crowned King of Great Britain, while his wife Caroline, from whom he had separated soon after their loveless marriage, returned from Italy to claim her rights and was restrained from attending the coronation. Any problems she might have caused were solved with her death on 7 August, this year.

1848 At a convention in Seneca Falls, New York State, female rights campaigner Amelia Bloomer introduced 'bloomers' to the world, which she described as 'the lower part of a rational dress'.

1877 Spencer Gore became the first ever Wimbledon men's singles champion.

1903 Maurice Garin became the first winner of the Tour de France cycle race, devised and promoted by a journalist, Henri Desgranger.

20 JULY

The former feast day of Margaret, patron saint of women in childbirth. She was a third-century saint who is said to have been swallowed by a dragon, from which she escaped by bursting through its belly.

BORN THIS DAY

HISTORY

1889 Sir John (Charles Walsham) Reith, 1st Baron, born in Scotland, an engineer in the field of radio communication who became the first General Manager of the British Broadcasting Corporation (BBC) in 1922 and its Director-General from 1927–38. His aspirations for radio produced the high standard of programmes that established the BBC's international reputation.

1919 Sir Edmund (Percival) Hillary, New Zealand mountaineer and Antarctic explorer who was the first to reach the summit of Everest with Sherpa Tenzing (29.5.1953). He was later New Zealand High Commissioner to India.

ENTERTAINMENT

1938 Diana Rigg, English actress who established herself as a leading Shakespearian actress before reaching a larger audience on television as the mistress of martial arts, Emma Peel, in *The Avengers*. She went on to make films, but also returned to play classical roles in the theatre.

DIED THIS DAY

1912 Andrew Lang, Scottish author of *The Blue Book of Fairy Tales*.

1937 Guglielmo Marconi, Italian physicist who was the inventor and pioneer of modern radio telegraphy.

1951 King Abdullah of Jordan, shot outside a mosque. A member of the King's guard then shot dead the assassin.

1973 Bruce Lee, US martial arts star whose films created an international kung-fu craze, tragically in Hong Kong, aged 32, of cerebral oedema.

1989 Harry Worth (Illingsworth), endearing English comedian.

ON THIS DAY

1588 The Spanish Armada set sail from Corunna after its initial setback on 19 June when the fleet was dispersed by a severe storm.

1837 The first railway station in London, Euston was opened.

1871 The Football Association proposed that there should be an FA Challenge Cup competition. On the same day, four years later in 1875, professional football was legalized in England.

1940 The first singles charts were published in the US journal, *Billboard*. No. 1 was 'I'll Never Smile Again' by the Tommy Dorsey Band, vocal by Frank Sinatra.

1941 The 'V for Victory' campaign was launched in Britain with the opening notes of Beethoven's Fifth symphony which sounds like dot-dot-dot-dash also used on the BBC's overseas broadcasts.

1944 Claus Graf (Schenk) von Stauffenberg, German army officer, was summarily executed in Berlin after leading the unsuccessful attempt on Hitler's life this day. The bomb he had placed under the table of a meeting room in Hitler's Rastenburg headquarters failed to kill the Führer, and a simultaneous coup in Berlin also proved abortive, leading to the execution of around 1,000 people of which von Stauffenberg was the first.

1957 'Let's be frank about it. Most of our people have never had it so good,' said the British Prime Minister, Harold Macmillan, at a meeting in Bradford, repeating it in the House of Commons on the 25th. It became a derisory slogan as did his nickname, 'Supermac'.

1968 Actress Jane Asher broke off her engagement with Paul McCartney in a BBC television interview, which meant the Beatle learned the news at the same time as the millions watching.

1976 The US Viking spacecraft made a soft landing on Mars and sent back television pictures of the rock-strewn Gold Plain.

1982 An IRA bomb exploded killing two guardsmen and seven army horses, and injuring 17 spectators, en route to Horse Guards Parade for the changing of the guard.

21 JULY

National day of Belgium. In 1831 Belgium became a separate kingdom after breaking from the Netherlands. Prince Leopold was proclaimed Leopold I of Belgium.

BORN THIS DAY

HISTORY

1620 Jean Piccard, French astronomer who was the first to compute the size of the earth. His data was used by Newton to verify his theory of gravitation.

1816 Paul Julius von Reuter who formed a company in his native Germany to transmit commercial information by telegraph. In 1851 he made London the headquarters of Reuters and began including general news items.

ARTS

1899 (Harold) Hart Crane, US poet whose collection of poems on New York life, *The White Buildings* (1926), is his major work.

1899 Ernest (Miller) Hemingway, US novelist and short-story writer whose experiences in the First World War provided much of the material of his first important novel, *A Farewell to Arms* (1929). His style was to influence generations of writers, and his macho stance made him a cult figure.

ENTERTAINMENT

FOUR OF A KIND No less than four directors of stage and screen were born this day. In 1888, Jacques Feyder (Frederix), French film director who changed his name because his family objected to him going on the stage. He eventually turned to film directing during the First World War, but it was much later, with his award-winning *Carnival in Flanders* (1935) that he consolidated his career. The Canadian Norman Jewison, born 1926, began as an actor and writer with BBCTV. In Hollywood he directed a score of successes including *The Thomas Crown Affair* (1968) and *Fiddler on the Roof* (1971). Karel Reisz, born the same year in Czechoslovakia, came to England aged 12. He began directing in the 50s, but his big successes were *Saturday Night and Sunday Morning* (1960) and *Morgan: A Suitable Case for Treatment* (1966). Born 1934, Jonathan Miller, English theatre, opera and television director who trained as a doctor and once went back to medicine only to return to make television programmes including *The Body In Question* and to produce *The Beggar's Opera* starring pop star Roger Daltry.

POP

1922 Kay Starr (Katherine La Verne Starks), US singer who had a hit with 'Rock and Roll Waltz' in 1956.

DIED THIS DAY

1403 Sir Henry Percy, known as Hotspur, killed in a battle near Shrewsbury with the forces of King Henry IV while attempting to join with others to overthrow the King.

1796 Robert Burns, Scotland's national poet, aged 37.

1809 Daniel Lambert, English fatty who weighed 739lbs at his death.

1928 Dame Ellen (Alicia) Terry, English actress, leading lady to Sir Henry Irving.

1964 Tottenham Hotspur's international inside right, John White, was killed when lightning struck the tree he was sheltering under while out playing golf.

1967 Albert John Luthuli, African leader, Nobel Peace prize winner, killed when he was hit by a train at a railway bridge.

1967 (Philip St John) Basil Rathbone, South African-born English actor who played Sherlock Holmes in 14 films.

1984 The man who popularized jogging, James F. Fixx, 52, had a heart attack and dropped down dead while jogging in Vermont.

ON THIS DAY

1798 After invading Egypt, Napoleon defeated the Mamelukes at the Battle of the Pyramids.

1861 The Confederates won the Battle of Bull Run, the first of two engagements during the American Civil War.

1897 The Tate Gallery opened on the site of the Millbank Prison, London.

1904 A 13.5 ltr Gobron-Brillie driven by Louis Rignolly of Ostend, became the first car to go faster than 100 m.p.h., reaching 103.56 m.p.h.

1904 The Trans-Siberian railway was finally completed. The 4,607 miles of track had taken 13 years to lay.

1960 Francis Chichester, a 58-year-old former lung cancer patient docked in New York in *Gypsy Moth II*, setting a new record of 40 days for a solo Atlantic crossing.

1960 Mrs Sirimavo Bandaranaike, widow of the assassinated Prime Minister of Sri Lanka, took office and so became the first woman prime mininster in the world.

1966 Gwynfor Evans became the first Welsh Nationalist member of parliament.

1969 'That's one small step for a man, one giant leap for mankind,' said Neil Armstrong as the US astronauts stepped out of *Apollo II* onto the Moon. Watched on television by much of planet Earth, at 3.56 a.m. BST, Armstrong and Edwin 'Buzz' Aldrin began their first exploratory walk.

1988 The first known case of a bull attacking and being killed by a jet was recorded when an Indian Airlines Boeing 737 was charged while landing at Baroda Airport, western India. None of the 90 passengers were injured. The bull, who tried to take the jet by the horns, died.

22 JULY

National day of Poland.

BORN THIS DAY

HISTORY

1478 Philip I, King of Spain, who married the accurately named Joan the Mad. When his father-in-law was forced to give up his control of Castile, Philip became King.

1844 The Rev William Archibald Spooner, Anglican clergyman and warden of New College, Oxford, who was the originator of 'spoonerisms'. As a result of nervousness, he sometimes transposed the initial letters or syllables of a word, so, for example, 'a half-formed wish' becomes 'a half-warmed fish'.

1890 Rose Kennedy, US matriarch, wife of Senator Joseph Kennedy, one-time Ambassador to Britain, mother of nine children including a US president (John F.), and an attorney-general of the US (Robert) who were both assassinated, and a senator (Edward) who was tipped to be president until scandal struck.

ARTS

1898 Stephen Vincent Benet, US poet and short-story writer who wrote the award-winning poem about the Civil War, 'John Brown's Body' (1928) and the story, *The Devil and Daniel Webster* (1937) which was later adapted for film.

ENTERTAINMENT

1926 Bryan Forbes, English film director, author and bookseller who began as an actor in films such as *The Small Back Room* (1948). His first screenplay was *Cockleshell Heroes* (1955) and he made his directing debut with *Whistle Down the Wind* (1961).

1940 Terence Stamp, English actor who won an Oscar for best supporting actor in *Billy Budd* (1962), his first film.

SCIENCE

1784 Friedrich Wilhelm Bessel, German astronomer and mathematician who was the first to measure the positions of some 50,000 stars.

1822 Gregor Johann Mendel, Austrian monk and botanist who failed botany when trying to obtain a certificate, and began his experiments in the monastery garden at Brunn in 1856. His book, *Experiments with Plant Hybrids* (1866) laid the basis for the study of genetics.

1888 Selman Abraham Waksman, Ukrainian-born US biochemist and Nobel prize winner who discovered the antibiotic streptomycin, the first effective treatment for tuberculosis.

SPORT

1928 Jimmy Hill, English footballer and later television presenter and commentator.

DIED THIS DAY

1932 Florenz Ziegfeld, US impresario.

1950 (William Lyon) Mackenzie King, three times Canadian Prime Minister.

1976 Sir (Robert Eric) Mortimer Wheeler, English archaeologist who popularized history on radio and television.

ON THIS DAY

1284 Legend has it that this was the day the Pied Piper appeared in Hamelin, Brunswick, struck his bargain to rid the town of rats and took his revenge when the burghers refused to pay.

1917 Alexandr Kerensky became Prime Minister of the Russian provisional government following the overthrow of the Tsar.

1934 As the crowds came out of the Biograph Cinema, Chicago, plain clothes men were waiting to arrest John Dillinger, 'public enemy No. 1', the bank robber for whose capture J. Edgar Hoover, FBI chief, had offered a $10,000 reward, dead or alive. A Chicago brothel madame had tipped off the agents that the man beside her, as they came out of the Biograph, would be Dillinger. When he appeared and seemed to go for a gun, the FBI squad shot him dead. But was it the end of an era? There are those who believe from US Naval records of Dillinger's description while a crewman, that he may not have been the man shot dead.

23 JULY

The National days of Ethiopia and the United Arab Republic.

BORN THIS DAY

HISTORY

1883 Alan Francis Brooke, 1st Viscount Alanbrooke, British field marshal who was Chief-of-Staff from 1941. He stirred controversy with his criticism of US strategy and Eisenhower's ability as a military commander.

1892 Ras Tafari Makonnen, Haile Selassie, Emperor of Ethopia who modernized his country. When the Italians invaded in 1936, he went into exile, but he resumed full authority after Ethiopia was liberated by British and Ethiopian forces in 1941.

1913 Michael Foot, Labour Party leader from 1980–83 until replaced by Neil Kinnock after his party suffered a severe reversal at the general election.

ARTS

1888 Raymond (Thornton) Chandler, US novelist who was educated in England but went to work in the US. He only turned to writing when he was 44 after being fired from an oil company for his alcoholic excesses. His novels which he wrote for 'the pulps' include *The Big Sleep* (1939) and *Farewell, My Lovely* (1940).

1933 Richard Rogers, English architect who designed the Pompidou Centre in Paris and the Lloyd's building, London.

ENTERTAINMENT

1912 Michael Wilding, English actor who was popular on both the stage and screen. His films include *An Ideal Husband* (1947) and *Lady Caroline Lamb* (1972), in which he made his last appearance.

1913 Coral Browne, Australian actress who became a leading lady on the London stage and also appeared in films including *Theatre of Blood* (1973) with her husband, Vincent Price.

1947 David Essex (David Cook), English singer and actor who began his career as the lead in the London production of *Godspell* in 1971.

SPORT

1931 Victor Korchnoi, Russian chess grandmaster who defected to the west in 1978, but failed to beat Russian champion, Anatoly Karpov for the world title, claiming the Russians were using parapsychological techniques to unsettle his mind during the contest.

1953 Graham (Alan) Gooch, Essex and England cricketer who made his test debut in 1975 and was the first to bowl both left- and right-handed in a Test (against India at Calcutta in 1981). By captaining the English rebel team against South Africa in 1982 he was banned from Test cricket for three years. In 1990 he led the first England side to win a test in the West Indies for 16 years.

DIED THIS DAY

1757 Domenico Scarlatti, Italian composer and harpsichordist.

1875 Isaac Merritt Singer, US sewing machine inventor, who retired to Torquay, Devon.

1885 Ulysses Simpson Grant, American general and 18th US President.

1916 Sir William Ramsay, Scottish chemist and Nobel prize winner who discovered helium, argon and other inert gases.

1930 Glenn (Hammond) Curtiss, US aircraft pioneer who eventually merged his company with the Wright Company.

1948 D(avid) W(arck) Griffith, US film director of *The Birth of a Nation*, one of the greatest silent films ever made.

1951 Marshal Pétain, French army marshal and head of Vichy France (1940–4), in prison, aged 95.

1973 Eddie Rickenbacker (Edward Vernon Rickenbacker), the First World War ace fighter pilot.

1988 Jahangir Khan, Pakistan cricketer who came from one of his country's great cricketing families. His nephew is Imran Khan, Pakistan captain. In an MCC – Cambridge match at Lords in 1932, he struck a sparrow dead in mid-flight with one of his deliveries. The bird has been stuffed and is mounted on a cricket ball at Lords.

ON THIS DAY

WHAT A WAY TO GO In 1884, a yacht sailing from Britain to Sydney, with its Australian owner and a crew of four, had to abandon ship when the small pump failed to cope in a storm. Their food and drink all gone, the cabin boy drank sea water and went insane and the others decided to kill and eat him this day. When finally rescued, they made no secret of the murder and were later tried and sentenced to death, but on a wave of public sympathy, were reprieved to serve six months in prison. In 1943 in Essex, a wheelchair bound tyrant who concentrated his wrath on his son, Eric, was out in his wheelchair escorted by a resident nurse when there was a huge explosion. While the nurse survived, there was little or no trace of either the wheelchair or the cantankerous occupant. Eric, who was in the army, was charged with murder when it was discovered a grenade mine designed to blow up tanks, had been placed under the seat. He was found guilty, but insane.

1940 The Local Defence Volunteers were renamed by Winston Churchill as the Home Guard.

1967 In the heat of the mountain stage in the Tours de France, British cyclist Tony Simpson, 29, collapsed and died.

1986 Prince Andrew married Lady Sarah Ferguson at Westminster Abbey.

24 JULY

BORN THIS DAY

HISTORY

1783 Simón Bolívar, South American liberator who gained independence for six republics. He first played a major role in Venezuela's independence from Spain. Bolivia is named after him.

1775 Eugène François Vidocq, French petty thief who eventually organized the Brigade de Sûreté, the world's first detective force. Accused of masterminding a theft, he was dismissed and started the world's first private detective agency. Among his friends was Alexandre Dumas, with whom he shares the same birthday.

1898 Amelia Earhart, US aviator who was the first woman to fly solo over the Atlantic (21.5.1932). She made other pioneering flights which not only encouraged future commercial flights, but also established a role for women in the new world of aviation.

ARTS

1802 Alexandre Dumas *père* (Davy de la Pailleterie), French author who first made his reputation as a playwright before publishing *The Three Musketeers* (1844) and *The Count of Monte Cristo* (1844–5) which made him a fortune; however he spent his earnings freely and extravagantly, and had to rely on his son for support.

1864 Frank Wedekind, German playwright best known for his plays about the amoral Lulu, *Earth Spirit* (1895) and *Pandora's Box* (1904), which inspired Alban Berg's opera and influenced Bertold Brecht.

ENTERTAINMENT

1929 Peter Yates, English film director who made his debut with *Summer Holiday* (1963) and went on to make more dramatic films such as *Breaking Away* (1979) and *The Dresser* (1984).

DIED THIS DAY

1862 Martin van Buren, eighth US President.

1883 Captain Matthew Webb, English swimmer who was the first to swim the Channel (25.8.1875), but drowned trying to swim the rapids above Niagara Falls, aged 35.

1957 Sacha (Alexander) Guitry, French actor and playwright.

1965 Constance Bennett, US actress, of a cerebral haemorrhage.

1974 Sir James Chadwick, English physicist and Nobel prize winner who discovered the neutron.

1980 Peter Sellers, English actor, enjoyed a reunion lunch with fellow Goons Spike Milligan and Harry Secombe at the Dorchester Hotel, Park Lane on 22 July. As he left, he had a heart attack and was rushed to hospital where he died this day.

ON THIS DAY

1701 Antoine de la Mothe Cadillac, administrator in French North America, founded a fur trading post he named Fort-Pontchartain du Detroit which became the city of Detroit.

1704 Admiral Sir George Rooke, with Sir Cloudesley Shovel, captured Gibraltar from the Spaniards.

1824 The first public opinion poll was conducted in Wilmington, Delaware on voting intentions in the forthcoming US

Presidential election. It was published in the *Harrisburg Pennsylvanian* showing Andrew Jackson ahead of John Quincy Adams.

1925 Six-year-old Patricia Cheeseman was successfully treated with insulin at Guy's Hospital, London – a first.

1965 Former champion British boxer and now nightclub owner, Freddie Mills, was found shot dead in his car in Soho. Was it murder or suicide? He was known to be in financial difficulties.

1987 Author Jeffrey Archer won a libel action against the *Star* over his alleged pay-off to prostitute Mary Coghlan. He was awarded £500,000 because the newspaper claimed he had 'consorted with a prostitute'.

25 JULY

BORN THIS DAY

HISTORY

1848 Arthur James Balfour, 1st Earl, British Prime Minister (1902-5), born in Scotland. He was Foreign Secretary from 1916-19 when he made his famous Balfour Declaration, promising the Zionists a homeland in Palestine.

1978 Louise (Joy) Brown, born at Oldham General Hospital, who was the world's first test-tube baby, courtesy Patrick Steptoe and Robert Edwards, whose research made it possible for Mrs Lesley Brown to have her baby. An embryo planted in her womb was fertilized in a test-tube with the sperm of her husband.

ENTERTAINMENT

1894 Walter Brennan, US film actor who played character parts in over 100 films and was the first to win three Oscars for best supporting actor. His films include *The Westerner* (1940) and *Rio Bravo* (1959).

JAZZ

1907 Johnny 'Rabbit' Hodges (Cornelius Hodge), US pioneer alto saxophonist who was playing for Duke Ellington by the age of 18. In 1951 he formed his own band which made numerous recordings including 'Such Sweet Thunder' (1957). His nickname came from his love of lettuce and tomato sandwiches.

1930 Annie Ross (Annabel Short Lynch), singer and actress, born in London of Scottish parents, who wrote and performed 'Twisted'. The Lambert, Hendricks and Ross vocal trio were considered one of the greatest vocalizing jazz groups ever, with Annie being described as 'technically the most remarkable female vocalist since Ella Fitzgerald'.

DIED THIS DAY

1834 Samuel Taylor Coleridge, English poet who wrote 'The Rime of Ancient Mariner'.

1843 Charles Macintosh, Scottish chemist who invented waterproof clothing.

1865 Dr James Barry (Jane Barry), on Corfu. She had become the first woman doctor, although only by masquerading as a man. This enabled her to rise to Inspector General in the British army having qualified in 1812. In 1819, while stationed in Cape Town, Barry not only introduced vaccinations, but was also involved in a duel which threatened to end her military and medical career. She had several affairs and an illegitimate child. Only on her death was it officially admitted that she was a woman.

1887 Henry Mayhew, founder of *Punch*.

1934 Englebert Dollfuss, Chancellor of Austria, shot in Vienna by Austrian Nazis, who bled to death as the assassins, led by Otto Planetta, bargained for their freedom.

ON THIS DAY

1554 Mary I of England ('Bloody Mary'), married Philip II of Spain. It was not a popular move.

1888 At a contest in Cincinnati Frank McGurrin, the official stenographer of the Salt Lake City Federal Court, beat typing instructor Luis Taub at speed-typing. McGurrin demonstrated touch-typing for the first time, while his opponent used four fingers and had to look at the keyboard.

CHANNEL FIRSTS In 1909 Louis Blériot flew the Channel in a Blériot XI, landing in Dover after 43 minutes. He won the £1,000 offered by the *Daily Mail* to the first man to fly the Channel either way. In 1959, half a century to the day, the first of (Sir) Christopher Cockerell's Hovercrafts, the experimental SRN1 made the crossing in 50 minutes.

1917 Margaretha Geertruida Zelle, the Dutch spy known as 'Mata Hari', was sentenced to death. (*See* 7.8.1876)

1943 Fascism was outlawed in Italy after Mussolini was deposed. King Victor Emmanuel assumed control and the anti-fascist Marshal Badoglio became Prime Minister.

1957 Tunisia became a republic with Habib Bourguiba as first President.

1989 Authorities in southern Norway put up road signs with a symbol of a ghost, to warn motorists of a supernatural hazard. Locals claimed this to be the cause of numerous accidents.

26 JULY

The National Day of Liberia, the first African colony to gain independence in 1847.

BORN THIS DAY

HISTORY

1875 Carl Gustav Jung, Swiss psychologist and psychiatrist who was the founder of analytical psychology. The idea of extrovert and introvert character types was first proposed by him.

1908 Salvador Allende Gossens, Chile's first Marxist president from 1970 to his death when he was overthrown by a military coup in 1973.

ARTS

1782 John Field, Irish pianist and composer who developed the nocturne which influenced Chopin. He settled in Russia where he first went to demonstrate pianos.

1796 Jean Baptiste Camille Corot, French landscape painter who influenced the Impressionists. He would sketch using oils, and these have become as valuable as the finished paintings.

1856 George Bernard Shaw, Irish-born journalist, music and drama critic, pamphleteer and playwright. A failed novelist, Shaw was 36 before his first play, *Widower's Houses*, was performed just twice; it caused a sensation with its social realistic portrayal of slum housing and exploitation. He went on to establish himself with plays including *Caesar and Cleopatra* (1901), *Major Barbara* (1905) and *St Joan* (1923). Much of his work was filmed, and two became musicals: *Arms and the Man* was turned into *The Chocolate Soldier* and *Pygmalion* was adapted as *My Fair Lady*.

1885 André Maurois (Emile Salomon Wilhelm Herzog), French author who served with the British army in the First World War and became interested in things British. His first novel *The Silence of Colonel Bramble* (1918) was based on war experiences and he wrote several biographies of Englishmen.

1893 Georg Grosz, German artist whose caricatures earned him the title Cultural Bolshevist No. 1 by the Nazis. He took the hint and went to the US in 1932 where he did magazine cartoons.

1894 Aldous (Leonard) Huxley, English novelist, who was a member of the distinguished family which included his famous grandfather Thomas. *Brave New World* (1932) preceded Orwell's *1984* by 17 years, and his other novels included *Eyeless in Gaza* (1936). He also wrote on mysticism and the paranormal in *The Doors of Perception* (1956).

1895 Robert (Ranke) Graves, English poet, novelist and critic, author of the historical novel *I, Claudius* (1934) and his autobiographical *Goodbye to all That* (1929), just two of over 100 books he wrote.

1897 Paul (William) Gallico, US writer who made his name with his highly successful short novel, *The Snow Goose* (1941).

1928 Bernice Rubens, English novelist and director of documentary films who won the Booker prize in 1970 with her novel *The Elected Member*.

ENTERTAINMENT

1882 André (Eugène Maurice) Charlot, French producer, director who made his reputation with sophisticated revues in London which included Beatrice Lillie, Gertrude Lawrence and a young Noël Coward.

1922 Blake Edwards, US film director, producer and screenwriter whose films include *The Tamarind Seed* (1974) with his wife Julie Andrews in the lead, and *The Return of the Pink Panther* (1979).

1928 Stanley Kubrick, US film director who made many of his major films in Britain, such as *Dr Strangelove* (1964) and *2001: A Space Odyssey* (1968). Twenty years later, he proved he was still in command with *Full Metal Jacket* (1987).

1946 Helen Mirren, English actress on stage and television playing both Shakespearian and contemporary roles including *Blue Remembered Hills* on television.

1950 Susan George, English actress who played leads in films including *The Looking-Glass War* (1970).

JAZZ

1924 Louie Paul Bellson (Louis Balassoni), US jazz drummer with big bands such as Benny Goodman and Tommy Dorsey. He formed his own band which toured with Pearl Bailey shortly after their marriage in London in 1952.

POP

1943 Mick (Michael Phillip) Jagger, lead singer and founder member of the Rolling Stones. Besides enormous international success with '(I Can't Get No) Satisfaction' (1965) and 'Jumping Jack Flash' (1968), the former London School of Economics student went on to act in films, including *Ned Kelly* (1970).

DIED THIS DAY

1863 Sam(uel) Houston, US soldier and twice President, (1836–8, 1841–4).

1939 Ford Maddox Ford (Hermann Hueffer), English author of *The Good Soldier* (1915).

1952 Evita (Maria Eva Perón), Argentina's First Lady, of cancer, aged 33.

1969 Frank Loesser, US composer of musicals including *Guys and Dolls*.

ON THIS DAY

1745 The first recorded woman's cricket match took place at Gosden Common near Guildford, Surrey with neighbouring village Hambledon against Bramley.

1788 New York became the 11th state of the Union.

1845 The *Great Britain* sailed from Liverpool on her maiden voyage, the first iron ship designed by Brunel and the first liner fitted with a screw propeller.

1908 The FBI (Federal Bureau of Investigation) was formed in Washington, DC.

1948 Freddie Mills (GB) beat Gus Lesnovich (US) at White City, London on points to become the world light heavyweight boxing champion.

1952 King Farouk of Egypt was forced to abdicate by General Neguib.

1956 President Nasser of Egypt nationalized the Suez Canal which would trigger off confrontation with Britain, France and Israel.

1974 Military rule ended in Greece when 'the Colonels' announced they would entrust civilians to run the government.

1987 Steve Roche won the Tour de France, the first Irishman and only the second cyclist not from continental Europe to win.

1989 A turnip killed a man when it was thrown from a passing car in east London. It knocked 56-year-old Leslie Merry off his feet. He broke a rib and ruptured his spleen. Respiratory failure finally killed him. Two months earlier, a jogger received internal injuries after being hit in the stomach by a cabbage thrown from a vehicle.

27 JULY

BORN THIS DAY

ARTS

1824 Alexandre Dumas *fils*, French playwright, illegitimate son of Alexandre (*père*). He wrote the novel *La Dame aux Camélias* (1848), then adapted it as a highly successful play, *Camille*, which was performed in 1892, and on which Verdi based his opera, *La Traviata*.

1867 Enrique Granados, Spanish pianist and composer, best known for his romantic *Goyescas* (1911-13) based on some of Goya's paintings.

1870 (Joseph) Hilaire Belloc, English author who wrote *The Bad Child's Book of Beasts* (1896) and a series of books on the French Revolution.

1904 Anton Dolin (Patrick Healey-Kay), dancer, choreographer and director who founded the Markova-Dolin company with his partner, Alicia Markova. In 1950, they founded London's Festival Ballet.

1929 Jack Higgins (Harry Patterson), English author of *The Eagle Has Landed* (1975) who was a senior lecturer in education for mature students at a Leeds college.

POP

1944 Bobbie Gentry (Roberta Lee Streeter), US singer best known for her 1967 hit which she both wrote and sang, 'Ode to Billy Joe' which was recorded on 10 July of that year and won her three Grammys.

SPORT

1955 Allan (Robert) Border, Australian cricket captain and scorer of over 6,000 runs in Test cricket.

1958 Christopher Dean, English ice-skater who, with his partner Jayne Torvill, won the European ice dancing title in 1981, and in 1984, skating to Ravel's *Bolero*, they won the Olympic gold with maximum points for artistic impression.

DIED THIS DAY

1844 John Dalton, English chemist and physicist who developed the atomic theory of matter.

1942 Sir William Matthew Flinders Petrie, English Egyptologist who excavated the temples of Gizeh.

1946 Gertrude Stein, US novelist and poet.

1970 António de Oliviera Salazar, Portuguese Prime Minister and dictator.

1980 Mohammad Reza Pahlavi, Shah of Iran, exiled in Egypt.

1984 James Mason, English actor.

1986 Sir Osbert Lancaster, English cartoonist and writer.

ON THIS DAY

1921 At the University of Toronto, Canadians Sir Frederick Banting and Charles Best isolated insulin, the first effective treatment for diabetes.

1949 The de Havilland Comet, the world's first jet airliner, made its maiden flight, flown on his 32nd birthday by Group Captain John Cunningham, (*b*. 1917), former British Second World War night fighter hero and now chief test pilot for de Havilland.

1953 The Korean armistice was signed in Panmunjom, ending three years of war which killed 116,000 UN troops including 54,000 US troops. 1.5 million North Koreans and Chinese were killed or wounded.

1988 National pole vault record holder Jeff Gutteridge became the first British athlete to be banned for life for taking anabolic steroids.

28 JULY

National day of Peru, when in 1821, San Martin's soldiers liberated the country and declared its independence from Spain.

BORN THIS DAY

HISTORY

1929 Jacqueline (Kennedy) Onassis, (née Bouvier), widow of the assassinated US President, John F. Kennedy, who married multimillionaire Aristotle Onassis after he had literally cleared the decks of his luxury yacht of Maria Callas.

ARTS

1844 Gerard Manley Hopkins, English poet and Jesuit, who wrote 'The Wreck of the Deutschland' one year after the event took place in 1875, when five Franciscan nuns were amongst the passengers who drowned.

1866 (Helen) Beatrix Potter, English children's author and illustrator who created Peter Rabbit, Squirrel Nutkin and Jemima Puddleduck – just some of the immortal characters in her children's books which she wrote and illustrated in her Lake District home from 1902.

1887 Marcel Duchamp, French painter who is best known for his *Nude Decending a Staircase No. 2* (1912) and his 'readymades' whereby everyday objects are quickly turned into works of art, as, for example, when a bicycle wheel is attached to a kitchen chair. This gave him the title of anti-artist.

1909 (Clarence) Malcolm Lowry, English novelist and short story writer, who wrote *Under the Volcano* (1947) which he began in 1936.

1941 Riccardo Muti, Italian conductor who has been principal conductor with the London Philharmonia Orchestra (1973–83) and artistic director of La Scala, Milan since 1986.

ENTERTAINMENT

1901 Rudy (Herbert Prior) Vallee, popular US singer who used a hand megaphone. He was the first to be called a 'crooner' prior to the Bing Crosby era, and appeared in films both as a singer and light comedian, including *The Vagabond Lover* (1929) which was also the title of one of his most successful songs.

CRIME

1925 John (Thompson) Stonehouse, English politician, former Labour Postmaster General who had everyone believing he had drowned off a Miami beach in 1974, then turned up at Christmas in Australia to be met by his mistress, Sheila Buckley. Police were investigating the affairs of the Bangladesh Bank in London with which he was involved and he was extradited in 1975 and received a seven-year sentence for fraud, deception and forgery.

SPORT

1936 Sir Garfield Sobers, in Barbados. West Indies cricket captain who was one of the great all-rounders. He scored a record 365 runs in the West Indies-Pakistan Test during the 1957–8 series.

DIED THIS DAY

1540 Thomas Cromwell, Earl of Essex, Chancellor to King Henry VIII, who fell from grace when he advised Henry to marry the unpopular Anne of Cleves, and ended up accused of being a heretic and traitor. Condemned without a hearing, he was executed.

1655 (Savinien de) Cyrano de Bergerac, large-nosed French poet and soldier, and one of the first science fiction writers.

1741 Antonio Lucio Vivaldi, Italian priest, composer and violinist.

1750 Johann Sebastian Bach, German composer.

1794 Maximilien François Marie Isidore de Robespierre, revolutionary leader of the Jacobins, together with his loyal supporter, Louis Antoine Léon Florelle de Richebourg de Saint-Just, went to the guillotine.

1944 Otto Hahn, German nuclear physicist.

ON THIS DAY

1586 The first potatoes arrived in Britain from Columbia, brought by Sir Thomas Harriot when he docked at Plymouth.

1858 Fingerprints were used for the first time as a means of identification by William Herschel. In the Indian Civil Service, he got a local contractor to give him a print. He followed this up by establishing a fingerprint register.

1937 The former Rector of Stiffkey, Harold Davidson forced to earn a living as a showground attraction, was mauled by a lion at an amusement ground at Skegness when, as part of the act, he put his head into the lion's mouth. He died two days later.

1945 A B-25 light bomber flying in fog, crashed into the 78th floor of the Empire State building killing 11 people and the three crew in the plane. Fortunately, the accident took place on a Saturday when the offices were closed.

1959 Post codes were introduced into Britain by the Postmaster-General together with new postal sorting machines.

1966 Florence Nagle took the Jockey Club to court for not allowing her or any woman to hold a licence to train horses. Although she and other women were training horses in Britain, they had to run under the names of the head lads. The 71-year-old won her case this day, but she had to wait another year for her first winner.

1986 Suzy Lamplugh, a 25-year-old executive working for a London estate agent, left her Fulham office at 12.40 p.m. this Monday to meet a 'Mr Kipper' and show him a house. She was never seen again. Her car was later found abandoned.

1987 Laura Davis, at 23 became the first British golfer to win the US Women's Open.

1988 A father and son saved each other from leukaemia. In 1980, Alan Lack donated bone marrow to his son. Eight years later, 19-year-old Stuart Luck made medical history when he donated marrow to his father to save him from the disease.

29 JULY

The Feast Day of Martha, patron saint of housewives.

BORN THIS DAY

HISTORY

1801 George Bradshaw, English publisher and originator of the railway guides.

1805 Alexis Henri Maurice Charles de Tocqueville, French historian and politician who spent nine months in the US. This resulted in his book *Democracy in America* (1835). Back in France after the Revolution, he helped write the constitution of the Second Republic.

1883 Benito Amilcare Andrea Mussolini, Italian founder of the Fascist Party who became dictator with the support of his Fascist militia. He allied his country with Hitler during the Second World War which led to Italy's defeat, his expulsion from office and ultimate death.

1905 Dag Hjalmar Hammarskjold, Swedish economist and statesman, who became the second Secretary-General of the UN. His work raised the status of the organization and he was posthumously awarded the Nobel Peace prize in 1961.

1913 Jo(seph) Grimmond, Lord Grimmond, Scottish-born leader of the Liberal Party from 1956–67.

ARTS

1869 (Newton) Booth Tarkington, US author *The Magnificent Ambersons* (1918).

ENTERTAINMENT

1887 Sigmund Romberg, Hungarian-born composer who settled in New York in 1909 and who is best remembered for *The Student Prince* (1924), *The Desert Song* (1926) and songs 'Lover, Come Back to Me' and 'Deep in My Heart'.

1938 Dennis the Menace, the popular character in the Beano comic, was born.

DIED THIS DAY

1833 William Wilberforce, English campaigner for the abolition of the slave trade in the British Empire.

ESCAPE FROM THE MAD HOUSE
Robert (Alexander) Schumann, German composer who went insane and threw himself into the Rhine in 1854, was admitted to an asylum near Bonn where he died this day in 1856. In 1890, Vincent van Gogh, the Dutch painter suffering from schizophrenia, died two days after shooting himself in the chest while painting in a wheat field in Arles.

1966 Edward Gordon Craig, English theatre designer and director.

1970 Sir John (Giovanni Battista) Barbirolli, English conductor.

1974 Cass Elliot, US singer known as Mama Cass of the Mamas and Papas pop group, died aged 32, after choking on a sandwich at the flat of singer Harry Nilsson in London. The actual cause of death of this overweight lady was a heart attack.

1983 (James) David (Graham) Niven, Scottish-born actor, from a muscle-wasting disease.

1983 Raymond Massey, Canadian actor.

ON THIS DAY

1565 Mary, Queen of Scots married her cousin, Lord Darnley.

1588 Sir Francis Drake, playing bowls on Plymouth Hoe was told that the Spanish Armada had been sighted and to put to sea with the British Fleet. He finished the game first.

1900 King Umberto I of Italy was shot dead by anarchist Angelo Bresci. He was succeeded by the Prince of Naples, Victor Emmanuel.

1907 Baden-Powell officially formed the Boy Scouts following the success of his first camp on Brownsea Island, off Poole, Dorset.

1948 The 14th Olympic Games, the first for 12 years and the first after the war, opened at Wembley Stadium.

1949 The BBC began broadcasting their first weather forecasts.

1966 Bob Dylan crashed his motor cycle and suffered serious injuries. He would not return to performing for a year.

1981 Prince Charles married Lady Diana Spencer at St Paul's, watched by over 700 million on television.

30 JULY

BORN THIS DAY

ARTS

1511 Giorgi Vasari, Italian painter, architect and art historian noted for his great fresco cycles in the Palazzo Vecchio, Florence. He was also the architect of the Uffizi in Florence.

1818 Emily (Jane) Brontë, English novelist, one of the three famous sisters, who wrote her single masterpiece *Wuthering Heights* under the name of Ellis Bell in 1846, published 1847.

1898 Henry (Spencer) Moore, probably the most important English sculptor this century. The son of a Yorkshire coal miner, he also became an official war artist. His drawings of air-raid shelter scenes in the London Underground are amongst the most important produced during this period.

1909 Professor Cyril Northcote Parkinson, English author and professor of history who invented Parkinson's law (published 1957): 'Work expands so as to fill the time available for its completion.' His books included *In Laws and Outlaws* (1962).

ENTERTAINMENT

1939 Peter Bogdanovich, US stage and film director who also co-scripted *The Last Picture Show* (1971) and directed *Paper Moon* (1973).

INVENTION

1863 Henry Ford, US motor car engineer and manufacturer who produced his first car in 1893. The Ford Motor Company was formed in 1903 and his mass-production assembly line techniques were used to produce his famous Model T in 1908. By 1928 over 15 million had been made.

1940 Sir Clive Sinclair, English inventor of electronic products from pocket-sized television sets to highly-affordable computers. He came a cropper though, when he brought out the C5 electric car.

POP

1941 Paul Anka, Canadian singer and songwriter who became an international success at age 15 with 'Diana' (1957). His other hits include 'Puppy Love', 'Put Your Head on My Shoulder' and Sinatra's theme song, 'My Way' (1968), which he adapted from a French ballad.

1958 Kate Bush, English singer and songwriter whose first hit was 'Wuthering Heights' (1978).

SPORT

1958 Daley Thompson, one of the greatest modern British athletes, son of a Nigerian father and a Scottish mother. He began to dominate the decathlon event from 1978 when he won the gold at the Commonwealth Games, did the same at the Moscow Olympics in 1980, (the first Briton to win the event at an Olympics), became world champion in 1983 and struck gold again in 1984 at the Los Angeles Olympics.

DIED THIS DAY

1718 William Penn, English Quaker leader who founded Pennsylvania.

1771 Thomas Gray, English poet who wrote 'Elegy in a Country Churchyard'.

1898 Otto von Bismark, German Chancellor.

ON THIS DAY

1930 Uruguay beat Argentina 4–2 in the first World Cup final.

1935 The first Penguin was published, starting the paperback revolution. *Ariel*, a life of Shelley by André Maurois was the first title selected by Sir Allen Lane, produced at a price to suit all pockets.

1949 HMS *Amethyst* arrived at Hong Kong after fleeing from the advancing Communist troops with food and fuel supplies running out, and being shelled from the banks of the Yangtze River.

1963 'Third Man' Kim Philby turned up in Moscow after escaping arrest in Britain for spying.

1966 England beat West Germany to win the World Cup in extra time. The 4–2 victory at Wembley with Alf Ramsey's England team led by Bobby Moore, with Banks in goal, the Charlton brothers, and the Germans led by Beckenbauer, saw three goals scored by Geoff Hurst, the highest total scored by any player in any World Cup.

1968 The 17-stone (238lb) Californian state public defender, Don Jones of Ventura County, was fined for being too fat.

1973 The Thalidomide Case, taken up by the *Sunday Times* on behalf of the victims ended after 11 years with compensation of £20m.

1984 Holly Roffey, 11 days old, became the world's youngest heart transplant patient, but she died in England on 17 August 1984.

1990 Ian Gow, MP and close friend of Margaret Thatcher, was killed by the IRA when his car blew up in the driveway of his home.

31 JULY

BORN THIS DAY

HISTORY

1912 Professor Milton Friedman, US monetarist who argued against income tax or a guaranteed income to overcome bureaucratic social welfare services.

ARTS

1927 Peter Nichols, English playwright for both stage and television including *Forget-Me-Not Lane* (1975).

1929 Lynne Reid Banks, English author of *The L-Shaped Room* (1960).

ENTERTAINMENT

1944 Geraldine Chaplin, US actress, first daughter from Chaplin's marriage to Oonagh O'Neil. She trained at the Royal Ballet School before deciding against a dancing career to appear in films including *Roseland* (1977).

1944 Jonathan Dimbleby, English television presenter and journalist, brother of David. Programmes include *This Week* and *First Tuesday*.

SCIENCE

1718 John Canton, English scientist, who was the first to make artificial magnets.

1800 Friedrich Wohler, German chemist who discovered calcium carbide from which he could derive acetylene.

SPORT

1902 (Sir George Oswald Browning) 'Gubby' Allen, former England cricket captain until aged 46 (1948), the second oldest in first class cricket history. (W.G. Grace packed in the captaincy just short of 51). A brilliant bowler, he took all ten wickets in a single innings in a first class match.

1951 Evonne (Goolagong) Crawley, Australian tennis player and Wimbledon women's singles champion on 2 July 1971, beating fellow Australian, Margaret Court, the number one seed.

DIED THIS DAY

1556 St Ignatius Loyola, founder of the Jesuit Order.

1875 Andrew Johnson, 17th US President, 1865–9.

1886 Franz Liszt, Hungarian pianist and composer.

1964 Jim Reeves, US country singer, in an air crash near Nashville, Tennessee.

ON THIS DAY

1498 Columbus changed from a parallel course with the mainland on 28 July, hoping to discover the Amazon. Instead, this part of his third voyage of exploration took him to an island which he named Trinidad.

1910 Wanted for the murder of his wife, Dr Hawley Crippen and his mistress, Ethel Le Neve, disguised as a boy, were arrested on board the SS *Montrose* which sailed from England to Canada. The Captain Henry Kendall had become suspicious of the relationship of the two passengers and radioed London; it was the first arrest made using radio. Chief Inspector Walter Drew, came aboard disguised as the pilot, when the ship entered the St Lawrence River.

1917 The third Battle of Ypres (Passchendaele) began.

1919 The Weimar Republic was established in post-war Germany.

1950 Britain's first self-service store, Sainsburys, opened in Croydon.

1964 The US *Ranger 7* sent back the first close up pictures of the moon's surface, and in 1971, James Irwin and David Scott went for a ride on the moon in their Lunar Roving Vehicle (Lunar Buggy) watched by millions on earth on colour television, but they were both later reprimanded for smuggling philatelic souvenirs to the moon and back.

1965 Cigarette commercials were banned on British television.

1990 Graham Gooch completed a record-breaking 333 and 123 in the first Test against India at Lords. The game saw 1,603 runs made by both teams in exactly 1,603 minutes.

THE PAN BOOK OF DATES

AUGUST

We live in reference to past experience and not to future events,
however inevitable
(H.G. Wells)

1 AUGUST

The National Day of Switzerland.

BORN THIS DAY

HISTORY

10BC Claudius I (Tiberius Claudius Drusus Nero Germanicus), in Lyons (then called Lugdunum), Roman emperor who invaded Britain in 43 and made it a province.

ARTS

1779 Francis Scott Key, US poet, attorney and author. He wrote 'The Star-spangled Banner' which became the official US national anthem in 1931.

MAKING WAVES In 1815, Richard Henry Dana, US author who wrote the famous sea novel *Two Years Before the Mast* (1840). He worked as a sailor before making a career as a lawyer and politician. In 1819, Herman Melville, one of the greatest US novelists; who wrote *Moby Dick* (1851), the classic sea novel in which the hunt for a whale by an obsessed man is used as an allegory. It was initially received with little enthusiasm and only gained its status after 1920.

ENTERTAINMENT

1838 Jules Leotard, French acrobat who devised the Flying Trapeze and the costume (the leotard) adopted by all trapezists. His debut at the Cirque d'Ête in Paris without a safety net (12.11.1859) was a sensation.

1930 Lionel Bart (Lionel Begleiter), English composer and lyricist who played a major part in the renaissance of the British musical as an exportable commodity with *Fings Ain't Wot They Us'd T'Be* (1959) and *Oliver!* both 1960. *Oliver!* was also filmed and several songs proved memorable, such as 'As Long As He Needs Me' and 'Food, Glorious Food'.

SCIENCE

1774 Jean Baptiste (Pierre Antoine) de Lamark, French zoologist who created the terms vertebrate and invertebrate.

SPORT

1921 Jack Kramer, US tennis champion and Wimbledon men's singles champion in 1947, who later became a highly successful tennis promoter.

FASHION

1936 Yves (-Mathieu) Saint-Laurent, Algerian-born French couturier who became Christian Dior's protégé when just 17, and went on to take over the business on Dior's death in 1957. In 1962 he opened his own fashion house.

DIED THIS DAY

1137 Louis VI, King of France, called Louis le Gros (the Fat) who did much to consolidate the role of the monarch.

1714 Queen Anne, the last Stuart sovereign who reigned as Queen of England from 1702 to her death as a result of chronic ill health, aged 49.

1834 Robert Morrison, first English missionary to China who translated the Bible into Chinese.

1973 Walter Ulbricht, East German leader.

1989 John Ogdon, English concert pianist who suffered from schizophrenia, died from pneumonia.

ON THIS DAY

1714 With the death of Queen Anne, George Louis, Elector of Hanover, was proclaimed King George I of Great Britain.

1716 The Doggett's Coat and Badge race, the first competitive rowing event, took place on the Thames.

SONGS Two famous songs were introduced this day. In 1740, 'Rule Britannia' was sung for the first time, in Thomas Arne's masque, *Alfred*. In 1859, Gounod's 'Ave Maria' was published.

1774 Sir Joseph Priestley discovered oxygen, or as he first called it 'a new species of air', although it seems a Swedish chemist, Carl Wilhelm Scheele, probably made the discovery the previous year.

1778 The first savings bank opened, in Hamburg.

1798 At the Battle of the Nile, Nelson destroyed the French fleet, cutting off Napoleon's supply route to his army in Egypt.

1831 New London Bridge was opened by King William IV and Queen Adelaide. Old London Bridge was built in 1209.

1873 The Clay Street Hill Railroad, San Francisco's cable car system, began running.

1876 Colorado became the 38th state of the Union.

1928 Morris Motors launched the Morris Minor.

A MARS A DAY In 1932 the first Mars Bar, made in Slough, Berkshire, went on sale. On its 37th anniversary, the first pictures of Mars (the planet) were beamed back to earth by the US *Mariner 6* unmanned spacecraft. If it had not been sheer coincidence, it would have been one of the greatest publicity stunts of all time!

1936 The XIth Olympics opened in Nazi Germany. It was to be the last for 12 years.

1939 Glen Miller and his band recorded 'In The Mood' which became his theme tune.

1960 Football's first European Cup-winners' Cup match was played in Berlin between ASK Vorwaerts and Red Star Brno.

1975 The Helsinki Agreement was signed by the Western powers and the USSR to uphold human rights.

2 AUGUST

BORN THIS DAY

ARTS

1881 Ethel M(ary) Dell, English romantic author who achieved enormous popularity with her novels, such as *Storm Drift* (1930), which featured physically unattractive heroes.

1891 Sir Arthur (Edward Drummond) Bliss, English composer and Master of the Queen's Music from 1953 whose work includes music for the ballet *Checkmate* (1937) and film music.

1924 James Baldwin, US author born in Harlem whose novels explore black contemporary society. His work includes *Another Country* (1962) and the play *The Amen Corner* (1955).

ENTERTAINMENT

1905 Myrna Loy (Myrna Williams), US actress who is best known for her light comedy roles opposite William Powell in *The Thin Man* (1934) and Frederick March in *The Best Years of Our Lives* (1946).

1932 Peter O'Toole, Irish actor who grew up in Leeds. His performance in the film *Lawrence of Arabia* won him an Oscar nomination in 1962. He had great success in the play *Jeffrey Bernard is Unwell* in 1989.

SPORT

1954 Sammy McIlroy, Irish international footballer.

DIED THIS DAY

1100 King William II (William Rufus), son of William the Conqueror, accidentally killed by an arrow fired by Walter Tirrel, while out hunting in the New Forest. It could have been intentional on orders of the King's younger brother (Henry I), who seized the throne on receiving the news.

1788 Thomas Gainsborough, English painter.

1799 Jacques Étienne Montgolfier, French ballonist, while travelling by road from Lyons to his home in Annonay.

1876 'Wild Bill' Hickok (James Butler), US frontier scout and law enforcer known as 'the fastest gun in the West', shot in the back by Jack McCall who was hiding behind the bar in the saloon in Deadwood, South Dakota. Hickok slumped over the poker table and died. McCall was later hanged.

1921 Enrico Caruso, the great Italian tenor, from peritonitis, aged 48. 50,000 attended his funeral in Naples.

1923 Warren (Gamaliel) Harding, 29th US President, while in office. Calvin Coolidge took over the remaining term.

1934 Paul (von Beneckendorff und) von Hindenburg, German military leader and statesman. His death gave Hitler the chance to assume the title 'Führer'.

1936 Louis Blériot, French pioneer aviator and manufacturer.

1945 Pietro Mascagni, Italian opera composer of *Cavalleria Rusticana*.

1976 Fritz Lang, German film director of *Metropolis*.

ON THIS DAY

1865 *Alice's Adventures in Wonderland* by Lewis Carroll was published, but it was soon withdrawn because of bad printing. Only 21 copies of the first edition survive, making it one of the rarest 19th-century books.

1875 The Belgravia Roller Skating Rink opened in London, the first in Britain.

1894 Death duties were introduced into Britain.

1973 Summerland, 'the family fun centre' on the Isle of Man, caught fire. 30 people, including ten children, were killed and 80 were injured. Many were either suffocated or trampled to death as the perspex-type roof (not permitted on mainland Britain) created a roaring inferno.

1980 Right-wing terrorists exploded a bomb in the crowded Bologna Railway Station, northern Italy, killing 84 people.

1987 For the first time in the history of the Corrida, a matador entered a Spanish bullring with advertising displayed on his suit. Luis Reina shocked purists when he appeared in the ring 130 miles west of Madrid advertising on behalf of Japanese electronics firm, Akai.

1990 Iraq invaded Kuwait causing an international crisis.

3 AUGUST

BORN THIS DAY

HISTORY

1867 Stanley Baldwin, English Prime Minister from 1923–9 during the General Strike of 1926. He served a third time in 1935–7, at the time of Edward VIII's abdication.

1872 King Haakon VII of Norway from 1905, who refused to surrender when the Germans invaded in 1940.

1811 Elisha Graves Otis, US safety lift inventor.

ARTS

1801 Sir Joseph Paxton, English architect, designer and landscape gardener of Crystal Palace.

1887 Rupert (Chawner) Brooke, English poet who was one of 'the lost generation' as a result of the First World War. His war poems and his evocative 'The Old Vicarage, Grantchester' (1912) are his best known works. His early death (23.4.1915) contributed to his legendary status.

1904 Clifford D(onald) Simak, US sci-fi writer who was the first to write pastoral science fiction, including *Where the Evil Dwells* (1982).

1920 P(hyllis) D. James, English crime novelist who has established herself as the new queen of crime, continuing the tradition of literary craftmanship established by Margery Allingham and others with novels such as *Death of an Expert Witness* (1977) and *Innocent Blood* (1980).

1921 Richard Adler, US composer and lyricist, who wrote the musicals *The Pyjama Game* (1954) and *Damn Yankees* (1955).

1924 Leon Uris, US author of *Exodus* (1958), about the creation of Israel, and *Topaz* (1967), about Cuban espionage.

ENTERTAINMENT

1926 Tony Bennett (Angelo Benedetto), US singer who made 'I Left My Heart in San Francisco' his theme song.

1940 Martin Sheen (Ramon Estevez), US actor who made his name in films such as *Catch-22* (1970) and *Apocalypse Now* (1979).

1938 Terry Wogan, Irish-born radio DJ turned thrice-weekly BBC chat show host, presenter at award ceremonies and close to becoming a British institution.

JAZZ

1907 Lawrence Brown, US trombonist with the Duke Ellington Orchestra from 1932.

SPORT

1953 Osvaldo Ardiles, popular Argentinian footballer who came to play for Tottenham Hotspur and came back again after the Falklands War.

DIED THIS DAY

1460 James II, King of Scotland, killed by the English during the siege of Roxburgh Castle.

1792 Sir Richard Arkwright, English inventor of the spinning frame.

1881 William George Fargo, US co-founder of the famous Wells-Fargo Express Company.

1916 Sir Roger Casement, British diplomat and Irish nationalist, hanged for high treason at Pentonville Prison, London.

1924 Joseph Conrad (Teodor Josef

Konrad Korzeniowski), Polish-born author who wrote *Heart of Darkness* and *Lord Jim*.

1954 (Sidonie-Gabrielle) Colette, French novelist who wrote *Gigi* (1944).

1966 Lenny Bruce, biting US comedian, from an overdose of drugs.

ON THIS DAY

216 At the Battle of Cannae, Hannibal seized the large Roman army supply depot after defeating the numerically superior Roman infantry.

1492 Christopher Columbus set sail from Palos de la Frontera in Andalucia, Spain on the first voyage of discovery in the *Santa Maria*, accompanied by the *Pinta* and the *Niña*.

1778 The La Scala Opera House in Milan opened.

1914 The first ships passed through the Panama Canal.

1926 Traffic lights were installed at Piccadilly Circus, the first in Britain.

1936 Hitler's attempt to prove Aryan superiority were seriously dented by the great black US athlete, Jesse Owens, who won gold medals in the long jump, the 100m and 200m from this day to the 5th at the Berlin Olympics.

1955 Samuel Beckett's now-acknowledged classic, *Waiting for Godot* was performed for the first time in London at the Arts Theatre. The performance was punctuated throughout with the clatter of seats as half the audience walked out.

1957 John Charles became the first British footballer to be transferred to a foreign club. Juventus paid Leeds the £65,000 transfer fee.

1963 The Beatles played The Cavern in Liverpool for the last time. 'Please, Please Me' had just been released.

4 AUGUST

BORN THIS DAY

HISTORY

1900 Queen Elizabeth, the Queen Mother (Elizabeth Angela Marguerite Bowes-Lyon).

1942 David Russell Lange, who became Prime Minister of New Zealand (1984–9), a year after becoming leader of the Labour Party. He instituted a non-nuclear defence policy.

ARTS

1792 Percy Bysshe Shelley, English romantic poet who was expelled in 1811 from Oxford for writing a pamphlet on atheism. With his second wife Mary, he settled in Italy where he wrote 'Prometheus Unbound' in 1818.

1908 Sir Osbert Lancaster, English artist, cartoonist and writer who produced a daily satirical cartoon for the *Daily Express*.

ENTERTAINMENT

1870 Sir Harry Lauder (Maclennan), Scottish music-hall comedian who achieved international success with his songs such as 'I Love a Lassie' and 'Roamin' in the Gloamin''. He also toured the US, Australia and South Africa.

DIED THIS DAY

1875 Hans Christian Andersen, Danish fairy-tale writer.

1973 Eddie Condon, US jazz guitarist, of a bone disease.

1987 Pola Negri, German silent movie star who was rumoured to be romantically linked to Hitler and later, in Hollywood, to Valentino. She was known as the Vamp and her erotic performances had to be toned down.

1988 Ellin Berlin (Ellen Mackay) US short story writer and wife of Irving Berlin who was the inspiration for the songs 'What'll I Do?' and 'Always', the royalties of which he gave her as a wedding present.

ON THIS DAY

1870 The Red Cross Society was founded in Britain.

1914 The First World War began with Britain declaring war on Germany.

1954 The P-1 English Electric Lightning, Britain's first supersonic fighter, made its maiden flight from Boscombe Down.

1966 John Lennon claimed on a local US radio station that the Beatles were probably more popular than Jesus Christ. Beatles records were banned in many US states and in South Africa.

1984 Zola Budd accidentally tripped Mary Decker, US champion, during the 3,000m in the Los Angeles Olympics to cause one of the most dramatic upsets ever.

5 AUGUST

BORN THIS DAY

HISTORY

1815 Edward John Eyre, English administrator in Jamaica where he put down a negro uprising with brutality, and also explorer of Australia – Lake Eyre and the Eyre Peninsula are named after him. Despite the Jamaican incident, he became a magistrate and protector of the Aborigines, learning their language and customs and earning their respect.

1908 Harold (Edward) Holt, Australian Prime Minister (1966–7) who succeeded Menzies; he backed US intervention in Vietnam, sending Australian troops to the war.

1930 Professor Neil Armstrong, first man on the moon (21.7.1969) who in 1955 became a civilian research pilot for NASA.

ARTS

1850 (Henri René Albert) Guy de Maupassant, French author of *Bel-Ami* (1885), but better known for his short stories mainly about brothels and prostitution.

1910 Jacquetta Hawkes, English archaeologist and author, second wife of J. B. Priestley. She wrote *A Land* (1951).

ENTERTAINMENT

1906 John Huston, US film director who once sang for pennies on the streets of London, ended up scriptwriting and making a long list of greats including, *The Maltese Falcon* (1941), the Oscar winning *The Treasure of the Sierra Madre* (1948), *The African Queen* (1952) and *The Misfits* (1961), which was Marilyn Monroe's last film.

1906 Joan Hickson, English actress best known for her wholly convincing Agatha Christie detective in the television series *Miss Marple*.

1911 Robert Taylor (Spangler Arlington Brugh), US actor who played leading roles in *Magnificent Obsession* (1935) and *Ivanhoe* (1952).

POP

1951 Bob Geldof, Irish musician, member of the Boomtown Rats, and international fund raiser who was nominated for the Nobel Peace prize following his organization of the Live Aid pop extravaganza to raise funds for Ethiopian famine victims in 1987. He was also awarded an honorary knighthood by the Queen.

DIED THIS DAY

1729 Thomas Newcomen, English inventor of the first 'automatic' steam engine.

1792 Lord Frederick North, British Prime Minister from 1770 to 1782 whose indecisive leadership led to the loss of the American colonies.

1799 Robert Howe, English admiral who led the fleet in a decisive victory at the Battle of the First of June (1794).

1895 Friedrich Engels, German co-author with Marx of the Communist Manifesto, who also died in London.

LEGENDS In 1962, Marilyn Monroe (Norma Jean Baker) US actress and legendary sex symbol, was found naked on her bed having died from an overdose of sleeping pills, aged 36. In 1984, Richard Burton (Richard Jenkins), Welsh actor who became a Hollywood legend mainly through his extravagances while married to Elizabeth Taylor, died in Geneva of a stroke, aged 58.

ON THIS DAY

1858 The laying of the first transatlantic cable was completed by Cyrus Field and opened by Queen Victoria at the British end, exchanging greetings with President Buchanan in the US.

1891 The first traveller's cheque, devised by American Express, was cashed.

1914 The first electric traffic lights were installed, in Cleveland, Ohio.

1950 Florence Chadwick, US swimmer set a new record for swimming the English Channel in 13 hours 23 minutes, over an hour faster than the previous record.

1962 Nelson Mandela, African Nationalist leader, was given a life sentence for attempting to overthrow the South African government.

1970 Penalty kicks were used for the first time as a tie breaker in an English first-class football match. With Hull City and Manchester United 1–1 after extra time, the game was won by United by 4–3 on penalties.

6 AUGUST

National day of Bolivia when it freed itself from 300 years of Spanish rule in 1825.

BORN THIS DAY

HISTORY

1504 Matthew Parker, second Protestant Archbishop of Canterbury.

1775 Daniel O'Connell, Irish leader called 'the Liberator', who forced the government to grant Catholic emancipation.

1916 Dom(inic) Mintoff, Prime Minister of Malta from 1971–9 who negotiated the removal of British and other foreign bases from the island.

ARTS

1809 Alfred, Lord Tennyson, English poet and Poet Laureate from 1850 succeeding Wordsworth, who is best known for 'The Lady of Shalott', 'In Memoriam' (on the death of his friend Arthur Hallam) and 'The Charge of the Light Brigade'.

ENTERTAINMENT

1910 Charles Crichton, English film director of such classic comedies as *The Lavender Hill Mob* (1951) and *A Fish Called Wanda,* 37 years later in 1988.

1911 Lucille Ball, US comedienne in films and television including the long-running and most successful *I Love Lucy* with her first husband, Desi Arnaz. Her many films include *Mame* (1974).

1917 Robert Mitchum, US actor with the sleepy eyes who began as a bit player in 'Hopalong Cassidy' westerns. He later starred in films such as *The Friends of Eddie Coyle* (1973) and *The Big Sleep* (1978).

1926 Frank Finlay, Scottish actor best known for his television roles as *Casanova* and in the award-winning *Bouquet of Barbed Wire.*

1937 Barbara Windsor, English comic actress who specialized in big-bosomed chirpy cockney roles, exposed to best advantage in the 'Carry On' films.

SCIENCE

1881 Alexander Fleming, Scottish bacteriologist who discovered penicillin in 1928 at St Mary's Hospital, Paddington, London, when green mould appeared on a culture dish. Scientists normally discarded these, but Fleming decided to make a close examination. In 1945, he shared the Nobel prize for Medicine with Chain and Florey who both developed the production of penicillin.

BUSINESS

1922 Sir Freddie Laker, English pioneer of cheap airflights whose Laker Airlines went bust in 1982 as a result of a combination of factors, gaining him much public sympathy. Richard Branson's Virgin Airlines took over where Sir Freddie was forced to leave off.

POP

1923 Jack Parnell, English bandleader who was Ted Heath's drummer before leading bands for countless television shows, but who recharged his batteries by playing jazz in clubs and concerts.

DIED THIS DAY

1623 Anne Hathaway, Shakespeare's wife.

1637 Ben(jamin) Jonson, English playwright who had Shakespeare in the original cast of one of his plays.

1660 Diego Velazquez, Spanish painter.

1973 Fulgencio Batista y Zaldivar, Cuban dictator overthrown by Castro.

1978 Pope Paul VI (Giovanni Battista Montini), aged 80.

ON THIS DAY

1859 'Worth a guinea a box' appeared on Beechams Powders' packets and advertising material to promote the British patent medicine. It was the first known advertising slogan.

1889 London's Savoy Hotel was opened.

PLACE OF EXECUTION In 1890, in Auburn Prison, New York, murderer William Kemmler became the first to die in the electric chair devised by Harold P. Brown, who tested his macabre invention by electrocuting a large number of animals. From all accounts, it took Kemmler eight minutes to die. In 1949, John George Haigh was sent to the gallows. Convicted of murder, he had tried to destroy the remains of his victims in an acid bath (see 18.2.1949), and was hanged at Wandsworth Prison, south London.

1926 Gertrude Ederle of the US became the first woman to swim the English Channel, in a time of 14 hours 34 minutes. (*See* 5.8.1950)

1945 The US Boeing B-29 bomber *Enola Gay* dropped the first atomic bomb. Seconds later the Japanese city of Hiroshima was devastated.

1988 Ballerina Natalia Makarova danced with the Kirov (in London) for the first time in 18 years since she defected to the West. She danced the role of Odette in *Swan Lake*, which made her famous with the Kirov, and was given a 35-minute standing ovation.

7 AUGUST

BORN THIS DAY

HISTORY

1876 Mata Hari (Margaretha Geertruida Zelle), exotic Dutch spy who passed secrets to the Germans during the First World War. When she separated from her husband in 1905, she began to dance professionally in Paris. Dancing semi-nude, she was soon a success, taking numerous lovers, mainly military officers. The French arrested her in 1917 and she met her death by firing squad (15.10.1917).

1903 Louis Seymour Bazett Leakey, British archaeologist, in Kenya, where he made his discoveries of huge animal fossils, and, with his wife Mary, found ancient human remains which were about 20 million years old.

1904 Ralph Johnson Bunche, US diplomat and Nobel prize winner for his efforts to bring peace to Palestine (1950). A grandson of a slave, he became UN under-secretary (1954–67).

ARTS

1831 Dean (Frederick William) Farrar, English clergyman born in Bombay, who wrote sentimental school stories including *Eric, or Little By Little* (1858) which became a bestseller of its time.

ENTERTAINMENT

1885 Billy Burke (Mary William Ethelbert Appleton Burke), US actress who made her debut on the London stage. Her film appearances include Glinda, the Good Fairy in *The Wizard of Oz* (1939).

1924 Kenneth Kendall, English television broadcaster, former BBC newsreader, later in the Channel 4 adventure game show, *Treasure Hunt*.

1952 Alexei Sayle, English alternative comedian, known to a television audience through programmes such as *The Young Ones* and *Whoops Apocalypse*.

JAZZ

1936 (Rahsaan) Roland Kirk, blind US tenor saxophonist, flautist and composer who could play three different saxes at a time producing three-part harmony by trick fingering. One of the great improvisers, he toured extensively.

SPORT

1948 Greg(ory Stephen) Chappell,

former Australian cricket captain who has scored a record 380 runs in a Test match (Australia v. New Zealand in 1973), and his total runs in test cricket exceeds a record 7,000. His catching was also remarkable – he took 122 catches in his Test career. One of the most successful Australian captains, he won 21 of the 48 tests he captained.

1961 Walter Swinburn, Irish jockey who won the Derby in 1981 with the famous Shergar.

DIED THIS DAY

1657 Robert Blake, British naval commander who captured the Spanish treasure fleet off Santa Cruz.

1931 Bix (Leon) Beiderbecke, legendary US jazz musician and composer who played cornet and piano. His style and technique changed and influenced jazz and trumpet players and he was the first white jazz musician to be admired by his black colleagues. He died aged 28 from a combination of pneumonia and alcoholism.

1938 Konstantin (Sergeyevich Alekseyev) Stanislavsky, revolutionary Russian stage director and teacher.

1957 Oliver (Norvell) Hardy, US comedian, fat half of the famous Laurel and Hardy film comedy duo.

ON THIS DAY

1556 A UFO or Flying Saucer appeared over the city of Basle in Switzerland and was captured as an illustration on a woodcut.

1711 Ascot became 'Royal' with the attendance of Queen Anne at the horse races.

1840 The British parliament passed an act prohibiting the employment of climbing boys as chimney sweeps.

1913 The US aviator Samuel Cody was killed when his aircraft crashed at Farnborough. It was Britain's first air tragedy.

1926 The first British Grand Prix was run at Brooklands. The winning car, a Delage, averaged 71.61 m.p.h.

1990 At 12hr 34min 56secs on this day 7.8.90, the sequence of numbers runs from 1 to 0; which occurs once each century.

8 AUGUST

In 1988, this became the luckiest day of the century according to the Chinese, because the date is a palindrome – 8.8.88. In Kentucky, a town called Eighty-Eight with only 300 inhabitants, was visited by 6,000 people who wanted to buy postcards to have 8.08 a.m. stamped on them with an 88 postmark, and one couple drove to the town to be married at eight minutes past eight on the church's eighth step. The town was named by one of the founders who discovered he had only 88 cents in his pocket.

BORN THIS DAY

HISTORY

1988 Beatrice, first child of Andy and Fergie, (Prince Andrew and the Duchess of York).

ARTS

1876 Frank Richards (Charles Harold St John Hamilton), English author who created the the most famous fat schoolboy in the English-speaking world, Billy Bunter. His stories appeared in

The Gem (1906–39) and *The Magnet* (1908–40).

1896 Marjorie Kinnan Rawlings, US author who wrote *The Yearling* (1938), about a boy and his pet fawn, which was also filmed.

1900 Victor Young, US composer and conductor, mainly of film scores including *Three Coins in the Fountain* (1954) and *Around the World in 80 Days* which won him an Oscar.

ENTERTAINMENT

1919 Dino de Laurentiis, Italian film producer behind many Oscar winning films such as *La Strada* (1954) and later went to Hollywood to make films including *Serpico* (1973).

1923 Esther Williams, US actress and former champion swimmer who is best remembered for a series of MGM musicals with lavish underwater ballets.

1934 Keith Barron, popular English actor in the television comedy series *Duty Free*, but equally good in dramas.

1937 Dustin Hoffman, US actor whose first success was in *The Graduate* (1967) which won him an Oscar nomination as did several other films including *Midnight Cowboy* (1969) and *Kramer v. Kramer* (1979). His performance in *Rain Man* (1989) won him an Oscar. He made his first stage appearance that year in Britain as Shylock in Peter Brook's production of *The Merchant of Venice*.

SCIENCE

1901 Ernest Orlando Lawrence, US physicist and inventor of the cyclotron, the first subatomic particle accelerator (1936). He also invented and patented a colour television picture tube. In 1939, he won the Nobel prize for Physics.

JAZZ

1907 Benny (Bennett Lester) Carter, US jazz multi-instrumentalist, composer and bandleader. He wrote the music for films including *Snows of Kilimanjaro* (1952) as well as many television series including *Ironside*.

1911 Jimmy (James) Witherspoon, US blues singer who after a successful career as a solo performer was encouraged to make a comeback by British singer Eric Burdon which resulted in several international tours.

SPORT

1954 Nigel Mansell, British champion motor racing driver who moved to the Ferrari stable in 1989 hoping to win the world crown which he had narrowly missed on two occasions.

DIED THIS DAY

1827 George Canning, English statesman who became Prime Minister for just three months in 1827, through ill health, at the Duke of Devonshire's Chiswick house.

1884 Sir William James Erasmus Wilson. English dermatologist who was also a keen Egyptologist and used some of his personal wealth to bring 'Cleopatra's Needle' to London where it stands on the Thames embankment.

1902 Jean Joseph Jacques Tissot, French painter and illustrator.

1919 Ernst Heinrich Haeckel, German naturalist who formulated the recapitulation theory of evolution (i.e. that stages in the embryological development of an individual reflect stages in the evolution of the species).

1919 Frank Winfield Woolworth, US chain store founder.

1975 (Julian Edwin) 'Cannonball' Adderley, leading US saxophonist.

1978 James Gould Cozzens, US author of *By Love Possessed*.

1979 Nicholas (John Turney) Monsarrat, English author of *The Cruel Sea* (1951).

ON THIS DAY

117 Hadrian became emperor of Rome following the death of his father Trajan.

1576 Tycho Brahe began work in the first purpose-built observatory at Uraniborg, Denmark.

1588 England's final naval engagement with the Spanish Armada took place. Medina Sidonia's ships engaged the British in a nine-hour battle off Gravelines. One Spanish ship sunk and two were disabled, but by now the British had once again run out of shot. Meanwhile, the wind was forcing the Spanish away from Flanders and out into the North Sea.

1786 The man responsible for the sport of mountain climbing, a Swiss scientist, Horace Benedict Saussure, offered a prize for the first person to climb Mont Blanc, Europe's tallest peak. The prize was won this day by a doctor, Michel Gabriel Piccard, and his porter, Jacques Balmat.

1834 In Britain the Poor Law Amendment Act was passed, which abandoned the system of outdoor relief by which parishes look after their poor via a rate for poor relief; in place of this the workhouse for those requiring assistance was instituted.

1900 The first Davis Cup, presented by Dwight Filley Davis, began on the tennis courts at Brookline, Massachusetts, and was won two days later by the US team.

1944 In Germany, a field-marshal and four generals were hanged by piano wires for a failed attempt on Hitler's life. This slow and agonizing execution was photographed for the Führer who is said to have gloated over the pictures.

1963 The US, Britain and the USSR signed the Test Ban Treaty in the Kremlin.

1963 The Great Train Robbery took place at Cheddington, Buckinghamshire, when a gang of 15 men including Ronnie Biggs and Buster Edwards, changed the signals to stop the Royal Mail train on a quiet stretch of line, and stole in excess of £2.6m.

1974 Richard Nixon became the first US President to resign from office in the face of threats to impeach him for his part in the Watergate affair.

9 AUGUST

BORN THIS DAY

HISTORY

1757 Thomas Telford, Scottish civil engineer who designed and built the Menai suspension bridge in Wales (1825) spanning 177m; one of the first suspension bridges in Britain.

1905 Dame Elizabeth Lane, English High Court judge who managed to break down the barriers to become the first woman barrister to appear in the House of Lords on a murder case, as well as the first part-time judge and the first High Court judge. (*See* 12.8.1965)

ARTS

1593 Izaak Walton, English author of the classic *The Compleat Angler* (1633) which established the concept of the sport of angling as a gentle, philosophical pastime.

1896 Leonide (Fedorovich) Massine (Miassin), Russian dancer and choreographer who created more than 50 ballets for Diaghilev including *La Boutique fantasque* and *The Three-Cornered Hat*, both in 1919. He also danced in the films *The Red Shoes* (1948) and *The Tales of Hoffman* (1951).

1902 Solomon (Cutner), English pianist who was one of the greatest this century. He made a spectacular debut at the age of eight and performed for the first time in a Promenade Concert when just 12. He made over 100 recordings until his career ended when a stroke lost him the use of one hand.

1922 Philip (Arthur) Larkin, English poet and novelist whose collections include *The Less Deceived* and the *Whitsun Weddings*. He succeeded Yeats as editor of the *Oxford Book of Twentieth-Century English Verse.*

ENTERTAINMENT

1918 Robert Aldrich, US film director who made films including *Whatever Happened to Baby Jane?* (1962) and *The Choirboys* (1977).

SPORT

1938 Rod(ney George) Laver, Australian tennis champion, one of the outstanding players of the 60s and only the second player in the game's history to win four major titles in one year. In 1962 he claimed the men's singles title at Wimbledon, Australia, France and the US, and was the first to repeat this in 1969.

DIED THIS DAY

1653 Maarten Harpertzoon Tromp, Dutch admiral who with his admiral son Cornelis (*b.*9.9.1629/ *d.*29.5.1691) played a major part in the 17th-century wars against both Spain and England. Maarten was killed this day following a battle with the English fleet off the coast of Holland.

1848 Captain Frederick Marryat, English author who wrote *Mr Midshipman Easy* (1834).

1919 Ruggiero Leoncavallo, Italian composer of *I Pagliacci*.

1975 Dmitri Shostakovich, Russian composer.

ON THIS DAY

1867 John Harrison Surratt was arrested as an alleged co-conspirator in the assassination of President Lincoln, but his alibi split the jury (eight not guilty, four guilty).

1902 The coronation of 64-year-old Edward VII took place in Westminster Abbey after a six-week delay following an emergency appendectomy.

1945 The second atomic bomb was dropped on a Japanese city. Nagasaki's devastation finally forced the Emperor to surrender to the Allies.

1963 *Ready Steady Go* was first transmitted by ITV to rival the BBC's *Top of the Pops*, and presenter Cathy McGowan became known as 'Queen of the Mods'.

1967 English playwright, Joe Orton was battered to death by his male lover who then committed suicide. His successful play *Entertaining Mr Sloane* had been about perversion and murder. His other success *Loot* centred around funeral arrangements.

1969 The bodies of actress Sharon Tate, eight months pregnant, and four others were found butchered at a Beverly Hills mansion. Members of a commune known as 'The Family' led by Charles Manson were arrested on 24 December 1969 for the crime.

1974 Gerald Ford became the first non-elected President of the US (the 38th), following Nixon's resignation the day before. Nelson Rockefeller became his vice-president while John Dean and John Erlichman were sent to jail for four and five years respectively for their part in the Watergate affair.

1979 Brighton established the first nudist beach in Britain, despite protests from those who feared great depravity.

10 AUGUST

BORN THIS DAY

HISTORY

1810 Count (Camillo Benso) Cavour, Italian statesman who was the key figure in the unification of Italy and first Prime Minister in the new kingdom.

1874 Herbert (Clark) Hoover, 31st US President who did little to alleviate the economic hardships of the Depression.

ARTS

1865 Aleksandr Konstantinovich Glazunov, Russian composer of symphonies and ballets as well as a concerto for saxophone in 1934.

ENTERTAINMENT

1928 Eddie Fisher (Edwin Jack Fisher), US crooner and actor whose career seemed to nosedive when he divorced popular Debbie Reynolds (their daughter is actress Carrie Fisher) for Elizabeth Taylor. He appeared with her in *Butterfield 8* (1960). Their marriage lasted four years until she met Richard Burton.

SPORT

1941 Anita Lonsborough (Porter), English swimmer and winner of a gold medal at the Rome Olympics in 1960 in the 200m breastroke.

DIED THIS DAY

1896 Otto Lillenthal, German aviation pioneer who influenced the Wright brothers, as a result of a glider crash the previous day.

ON THIS DAY

1675 The foundation stone of the Royal Observatory, Greenwich was laid by King Charles II.

1787 Mozart completed his popular *Eine Kleine Nachtmusik* (A Little Night Music).

1821 Missouri became the 24th state of the Union.

1846 The Smithsonian Institution was established at Washington with a bequest from English scientist, James Smithson, to foster scientific research.

1889 The screw bottle top was patented by Dan Rylands of Hope Glass Works, Barnsley, Yorkshire.

1893 Dr Rudolf Diesel's prototype 'diesel' engine was tested at Krupps, but it would take four more years before it could be commercially produced.

1895 Sir Henry Wood's first Promenade Concert was held at the Queen's Hall, London.

1897 The Royal Automobile Club (RAC)

was formed under its original name of The Automobile Club of Great Britain.

1954 Sir Gordon Richards, champion English jockey retired after 4,870 wins.

1966 The first US moon satellite *Orbiter I* was launched.

11 AUGUST

BORN THIS DAY

HISTORY

1673 Richard Meade, English physician whose patients included two British kings and a queen, as well as the prime minister. He made a significant contribution to preventative medicine writing on the treatment of smallpox, measles, the plague and scurvy.

ARTS

1876 Mary Roberts Rinehart, US mystery writer whose books include *The Circular Staircase* (1908) and *Haunted Lady* (1942).

1892 Hugh MacDiarmid (Christopher Murray Grieve), Scottish dialect poet and founder of the Scottish Nationalist Party,

1897 Enid (Mary) Blyton, English author of children's stories who published her first book, a collection of verses, in 1922. In the mid-30s she began her stories, which featured Noddy, the Famous Five and the Secret Seven. She edited *Sunny Stories* and other magazines and considered her work both educational and moral, which was not what some educationalists and librarians thought. She published over 400 books and is the most translated British author after Agatha Christie.

1913 Sir Angus Wilson (Angus Frank Johnstone Wilson), English novelist and short-story writer, former professor of English Literature at the University of East Anglia, author of *Hemlock and After* (1952) and *The Old Men at the Zoo* (1961). He had a success with his play *The Mulberry Bush* (1955) which was also filmed.

1921 Alex Haley, US author of the best-selling *Roots* which traced his ancestry from Africa to slavery in the US and was made into a major television film.

1929 Alun Hoddinott, Welsh composer, former Professor of Music, University College, Cardiff.

ENTERTAINMENT

1935 Anna Massey, English actress (daughter of Raymond and sister of Daniel) who gave a memorable performance in the television adaptation of *Hotel du Lac* (1986).

DIED THIS DAY

1519 Johan Tetzel, the monk who sold indulgences to raise money to pay for the building of St Peter's in Rome, and by doing so incensed and provoked Luther.

1890 John Henry, Cardinal Newman, English churchman and promoter of the restoration of the High Church.

1919 Andrew Carnegie, Scottish-born philanthropist who died in the US.

1956 (Paul) Jackson Pollock, US painter, killed when his car hit a tree while travelling at high speed.

ON THIS DAY

1942 Dmitri Shostakovich's Seventh Symphony, the *Leningrad*, was first performed in that city, with many members of the orchestra in their military uniforms, some on leave from the Front, many half-starving.

1952 Harrow schoolboy Crown Prince Hussein, was named to succeed his father, King Talal of Jordan, who suffered from schizophrenia.

1960 The French colony of Chad became independent.

12 AUGUST

The Glorious Twelfth in Britain, when the grouse shooting season officially opens.

BORN THIS DAY

HISTORY

1762 George IV, King of England, eldest son of the insane George III. He did little to enhance the crown 'being too fond of women and wine'. He secretly married Maria Fitzherbert, a Roman Catholic, in 1785, but the marriage was invalid and he was forced into a loveless marriage ten years later with his cousin Caroline to persuade Parliament to pay off his debts. (*See* DIED THIS DAY)

1924 Mohammad Zia ul-Haq, military general and President of Pakistan from 1978 until his death (17.8.1988). As Chief of Army Staff, he led the coup deposing Zulfikar Ali Bhutto in July 1977, whom he later had tried and hanged.

ARTS

1774 Robert Southey, English poet and Poet Laureate from 1813–43 who was one of the leaders of the romantic movement with Wordsworth and others. His poems include 'Inchcape Rock' and a verse play *Wat Tyler* (1817).

ENTERTAINMENT

1881 Cecil B(lount) De Mille, US film producer, director and screenwriter who is acknowledged as the person who did most to make Hollywood the world centre for films. A great showman, his biblical epics such as *The Ten Commandments* (1923, re-made 1956) and *Samson and Delilah* (1949) were sheer Hollywood.

1925 Norris & Ross McWhirter, British twins who founded the Guinness Book of Records, second best-selling book in the world (The Bible just beats them).

POP

1949 Mark Knopfler, English rock guitarist and composer who took over and led the group Dire Straits when brother David quit in 1980.

DIED THIS DAY

1822 Viscount Castlereagh (Robert Stewart, 2nd Marquis of Londonderry), British foreign secretary who committed suicide while under pressure by critics over his attempts to dissolve legally the marriage of King George IV and Queen Caroline. He died on the King's 60th birthday.

1827 William Blake, English poet and painter whose works include *The Songs of Innocence and Experience* (1789, 1794).

1848 George Stephenson, English engineer who built the steam locomotive *Rocket*.

1955 Thomas Mann, German author of *Death in Venice* and Nobel Literature prize winner.

1964 Ian (Lancaster) Fleming, English author, creator of James Bond.

1982 Henry Fonda, US actor.

1988 Jean-Michel Basquiat, Haitian New York subway graffiti sprayer under the name SAMO, whose life changed dramatically when a New York art dealer gave him space in her cellar to create graffiti-like paintings on old cardboard and planks which realized prices of $20,000 to $99,000. Andy Warhol became his mentor, but drugs finally ended a meteoric career when he was just 28.

ON THIS DAY

1851 The first Hundred Guinea Cup was offered by the Royal Yacht Squadron of Great Britain for a race around the Isle of Wight and the cup was won by the 100ft US yacht *America* which beat the British *Aurora*. The cup became known as the America's Cup.

ZOO STORY A day for rare animals. In 1883 the quagga died in Amsterdam Zoo, the last of this zebra-like animal in the world, while in 1980 the first giant panda born in captivity was delivered naturally in a zoo in Mexico.

1887 Thomas Alva Edison made the first sound recording when he recited 'Mary Had a Little Lamb' which was recorded on to a foil-wrapped cylinder on the Edisonphone.

1908 The first Ford Model T, affectionately known as the 'Tin Lizzie' was produced, replacing the Model A.

1944 PLUTO (Pipe Line Under the Ocean) began operating, running under the Channel to supply petrol from the Isle of Wight to the Allied forces in France.

1960 The first US communications satellite, *Echo I* was launched.

1965 Three days after her 60th birthday, Judge Elizabeth Lane became the first woman appointed to the High Court; she was still to be called 'Your Lordship'.

1988 Jiffy Condoms announced they would be including cards in their packets. Collectors would need 64 Kama Sutra cards to have a full set of all positions.

13 AUGUST

BORN THIS DAY

HISTORY

1860 Annie Oakley (Phoebe Anne Oakley Moses/ Mozee), US marksman who starred in Buffalo Bill's Wild West show, where she was nicknamed 'Little Sure Shot'. She gained her reputation when she beat national crackshot Frank E. Butler whom she later married. She is said to have been able to hit the thin edge of a playing card from 30 paces, a coin tossed in the air and the end of a cigarette held in Butler's lips. The musical *Annie Get Your Gun* was based on her life.

1913 Archbishop Makarios III (Michael Christodolou Mouskos), Cypriot priest and President who was closely identified with *enosis* (union) with Greece against the desires of the Turkish Cypriots. The British arrested him in 1956 for sedition and he was exiled to the Seychelles. After abandoning *enosis*, he was allowed to return and became President in 1959.

1927 Fidel (Ruz) Castro, Cuban leader who led a guerrilla campaign in the early 50s to rid his country of the Batista regime. With the help of Che Guevara and others, he finally came to power (1.1.1959) to institute reforms.

ARTS

1907 Sir Basil (Urwin) Spence, British architect, born Bombay, who is best known for designing the new Coventry Cathedral, and the University of Sussex.

ENTERTAINMENT

1899 Alfred (Joseph) Hitchcock, English film director who became a US citizen in 1955. He made the first British sound film – *Blackmail* (1929) – although dialogue only began in reel two as the studio was not equipped in the early sequences. The master of suspense, his many films include *Rebecca* (1940) which won him an Oscar, and *Psycho* (1960) which has become a cult film.

1913 Melvin Frank, US film director, writer and producer who made many polished films including *That Certain Feeling* (1956) and *A Touch of Class* (1973).

1935 Rod Hull, Australian entertainer who manipulates the highly aggressive Emu on stage and television.

SCIENCE

1888 John Logie Baird, Scottish television pioneer.

1902 Felix Wankel, German engine designer whose rotary engine managed to attract a great deal of investment and is said to be one of the few inventors who made a lot of money from an idea which had yet to prove its worth.

JAZZ

1919 George (Albert) Shearing, English jazz pianist and composer, blind from birth, who settled in the US where he established himself as a major recording artist especially with his 1952 success, 'Lullaby of Birdland'.

SPORT

1898 Jean Borotra, French tennis champion and the first Frenchman to win the men's singles title at Wimbledon (1924). He next won in 1926, and was a finalist on two more occasions.

1912 Ben Hogan, award-winning, money-winning, US golf champion who is only one of four players to ever have won four of the world's major titles. In 1953 he took the British as well as his fourth US Open title. He won the US Masters and the US PGA twice.

BUSINESS

1902 Lord Sainsbury, joint-president of the Sainsbury grocery chain.

DIED THIS DAY

1826 René Théophile Hyacinthe Laënnec, French physician and inventor of the stethoscope.

1896 Sir John (Everett) Millais, English Pre-Raphaelite painter.

1910 Florence Nightingale, English founder of modern nursing and the first woman to win the Order of Merit, aged 90.

1912 Jules Émile Frédéric Massenet, French composer of the opera *Manon* (1885).

1946 H(erbert) G(eorge) Wells, English writer.

1977 Henry Williamson, English author of *Tarka the Otter* (1927).

ON THIS DAY

1704 The Anglo-Austrian army, under the command of Marlborough and Prince Eugène, inflicted a decisive defeat on the French armies at Blenheim.

1814 The Cape of Good Hope was made a British colony when it was ceded by the Dutch.

1876 The first performance of Wagner's *Der Ring des Nibelungen* (*The Ring Cycle*) in its entirety was staged at Bayreuth.

1915 The 'Brides in the Bath' murderer, George Joseph Smith, who drowned his brides in a zinc bath after ensuring their finances were set up in his favour,was hanged this Friday 13th.

1952 The first recording of 'Hound Dog' by Leiber and Stoller was made by Big Mama Thornton.

1961 The Berlin Wall began to go up; at first it was barbed wire, but by the 17th, this was being replaced by a five-foot high wall. In 1962, on the wall's first anniversary, Peter Fechter was shot trying to escape from the East and bled to death trapped at the wall, helped only by West German police who threw him bandages. His death sparked off protests and he became a martyr.

1964 The last executions took place in Britain when Peter Allen at Walton Prison, Liverpool and John Walby at Manchester's Strangeways, were hanged.

1989 The worst hot-air balloon disaster in history took place ten miles south of Alice Springs, in central Australia, when two hot-air balloons collided. One remained airborne, the other plunged 600 feet to the ground, killing the pilot and 12 passengers.

14 AUGUST

BORN THIS DAY

HISTORY

1840 Baron (Richard) von Krafft-Ebing, German neuropsychiatrist who pioneered the study of sexual perversions, and published *Psychopathia Sexualis* (1886).

ARTS

1864 John Galsworthy, English novelist and playwright who wrote the *The Forsyte Saga*, a sequence of novels which began with *The Man of Property* (1906). His plays include *The Skin Game* (1920).

1892 Kaikhosru (Shapurji) Sorabji, English composer, of a Parsee father and a Spanish-Sicilian mother, who composed *Symphonic Variations for piano* which takes over seven hours to perform. All his works were later withdrawn from public performance unless he gave his permission for them to be performed.

1907 H(arford) Montgomery Hyde, born Belfast, where he was their Member of Parliament 1950–59 and wrote several biographies, including *The Trials of Oscar Wilde* (1948), which was adapted as a film.

1910 Pierre Schaeffer, French composer and originator of *musique concrète*.

1931 Frederick Raphael, English writer best known for his television serial *The Glittering Prizes*, who was described by one critic as 'jester to the British intelligentsia'.

ENTERTAINMENT

1961 Sarah Brightman, English singer and actress, wife of Andrew Lloyd

Webber and co-star of his *Phantom of the Opera*.

SPORT

1913 Fred Davis, English and twice world professional snooker champion (1948–9, 1951), and younger brother of Joe.
1914 Sydney Wooderson, English athlete; mile world record holder in 1937.

DIED THIS DAY

1778 Augustus Toplady, English clergyman who wrote the hymn, 'Rock of Ages'.

STOP PRESS Two giants of the newspaper world on either side of the Atlantic died this day: in 1922, Alfred (Charles William) Harmsworth, 1st Viscount Northcliffe, who revolutionized British journalism and founded the *Daily Mail* (1896) and the first newspaper for women, the *Daily Mirror* (1903). In 1951, William Randolph Hearst, US newspaper proprietor, king of 'yellow' (sensational) journalism whose life was as colourful as his journalists' prose.

1932 Rin Tin Tin, Hollywood star dog.
1956 Bertolt Brecht, German playwright.
1984 J(ohn) B(oynton) Priestley, English novelist and playwright.

ON THIS DAY

1893 The world's first car registration plates were introduced in France. To make sure drivers were really what they claimed, they also issued the first driving licences for passing the driving test conducted by the Chief Engineer of Mines. To complete the day, the first parking restrictions came into force.
1908 Young women paraded at the Pier Hippodrome, Folkestone, Kent in the first International Beauty Contest.
1928 The first scheduled television programmes were broadcast from WRNY, in New York.
1945 Japan surrendered unconditionally to the Allies. The Second World War was finally over. V-J (Victory over Japan) Day would be celebrated on the 15th.
1948 Probably the greatest batsman ever, Donald Bradman, went out to the pitch at the Oval to play his last innings. The Australian received a standing ovation from the spectators and England fielding side. He finally took guard...and was bowled for a duck. It was said that the tears in his eyes blinded him.
1949 Konrad Adenauer became Chancellor of West Germany.
1955 Pietro Annigoni's portrait of the Queen went on show at the Royal Academy Summer Show and attracted over 250,000 visitors.
1969 The first British troops were deployed in Northern Ireland to restore order.
1986 Benazir Bhutto was arrested by President Zia of Pakistan and held in prison for 30 days under a public order law.

15 AUGUST

BORN THIS DAY

HISTORY

1769 Napoleon I (Bonaparte), in Corsica, French military leader and Emperor, who expanded the French empire until curbed by an allied coalition which sent him into exile to the island of Elba. He returned to fight again, this time at Waterloo, which led to final exile on the remote south Atlantic island of St Helena.

1856 James Keir Hardie, Scottish politician and a founder of the British Labour Party which he led from 1906.

1888 T(homas) E(dward) Lawrence, enigmatic Welsh-born soldier and writer known as 'Lawrence of Arabia' through his legendary exploits in the Middle East during the First World War. He led an Arab revolt against Germany's ally, Turkey, which he retold in *The Seven Pillars of Wisdom* (1926).

1903 (Thomas Joseph) Tom Mboya, Kenyan independence leader and founder member of the African National Union in 1960, and a minister in Kenyatta's government.

1950 Princess Anne, the Princess Royal.

ARTS

1771 Sir Walter Scott, Scottish historic novelist and inventor of the genre with his novel *Waverley* (1814). He became one of the most popular novelists of his time.

1785 Thomas de Quincey, English essayist and critic, opium addict and author of *Confessions of an Opium Eater* (1821).

1875 Samuel Coleridge-Taylor, English composer of a West African father who deserted his son and English wife after enduring racial prejudice. The son went on to become the composer of the much acclaimed *Hiawatha's Wedding Feast* (1898) for solo voices, chorus and orchestra.

1885 Edna Ferber, US novelist and playwright who wrote *Show Boat* (1926) which became a successful musical on stage and screen. She collaborated with George S. Kaufman to write the equally successful plays *Dinner at Eight* (1932) and *Stage Door* (1938).

1924 Robert Bolt, English playwright of *A Man for All Seasons* (1960), which was also an Oscar-winning film, and other plays and screenplays, including *Lawrence of Arabia* (1962) whose birthday he shares.

1933 Rita Hunter, English opera singer with the English National Opera in 1970. She made her New York debut as Brünnhilde in *Die Walkure* in 1972.

ENTERTAINMENT

1879 Ethel Barrymore (Ethel Mae Blythe), US actress, sister of the actors John and Lionel. She won an Oscar for her supporting role in *None But the Lonely Heart* (1944).

1912 Dame Wendy Hiller, English actress who made her debut on the stage in *Love on the Dole* in 1935. In films she played Eliza Doolittle in *Pygmalion* (1938) and won an Oscar for best supporting actress in *Separate Tables* (1958).

1935 Jim Dale (James Smith), English actor and singer who trained as a ballet dancer. He appeared in several 'Carry On' films and wrote the title song *Georgy Girl* for the 1966 film, and later went to the US where he appeared in both films and on Broadway.

JAZZ

1925 Oscar (Emmanuel) Peterson, Canadian jazz pianist and composer who went to the US in 1949 and toured with 'Jazz at the Philharmonic' before forming his own trio. Amongst his compositions is *Canadiana Suite*.

DIED THIS DAY

1057 Macbeth, King of Scotland, killed in battle by Malcolm and buried on the island of Iona.

1935 Wiley Post, US aviator killed in an aircrash in Alaska with his passenger, Will Rogers (William Penn Adair Rogers), US humorist.

1967 René (Francis Ghislain) Magritte, Belgian painter.

ON THIS DAY

1842 The first regular British detective force was formed, but this division of the Metropolitan Police only assumed the name, Criminal Investigation Department (CID), in 1878.

1843 The Tivoli Pleasure Gardens were opened in Copenhagen.

1914 The Panama Canal was opened and the first ship through was the SS *Ancon*.

1938 The Queen Mary set a record for the eastbound crossing of the Atlantic. Having set a record on the westward crossing, it completed the return journey two minutes short of four days.

1947 The Union Jack was run down for the last time in New Delhi as India gained independence from Britain. Nehru became the first Prime Minister.

1965 Race riots in Watts, Los Angeles required 20,000 National Guardsmen to control the situation, which left 28 dead, including children, and 676 injured.

1967 The Marine Broadcasting Act came into force outlawing pirate radio stations broadcasting within British territorial waters.

1969 The Woodstock Music and Arts Fair began on a dairy farm in upstate New York. This now-legendary rock festival included Janis Joplin, the Who, Jimi Hendrix, Joan Baez and Jefferson Airplane. In the three days it lasted, 400,000 attended, two children were born and three people died.

1971 English showjumping champion, Harvey Smith was disqualified for making a V-sign to his critics after winning the British Showjumping Derby, but he was reinstated as the winner two days later.

1979 At Zurich, Sebastian Coe raced to his third world record in the space of just six weeks – the 1500m. He also achieved the record for the 800m and the Golden Mile.

1987 Caning was officially banned in Britain except in independent schools.

16 AUGUST

BORN THIS DAY

HISTORY

1913 Menachem Begin, Israeli Prime Minister from 1977–83, who was a former member of the extremist Irgun Zvai Leumi and later leader of the right-wing Likud. During his premiership, he made peace with Egypt and shared the Nobel Peace prize with President Anwar Sadat.

ARTS

1930 (Edward James) Ted Hughes, English Poet Laureate (1984), married to US poet Sylvia Plath who committed suicide in 1963, best known for collections *Crow* (1970) and *Cave Birds* (1978) and his children's stories and poems.

POP

1958 Madonna (Louise Veronica Ciccone), US rock singer and actress who had her first No. 1, with 'Like A Virgin' in 1984 and scored a success in her first film, *Desperately Seeking Susan*, the following year.

SPORT

1950 Jeff(rey Robert) Thompson, Australian and Middlesex cricketer who has taken over 200 Test wickets and was the first bowler to take a wicket in a limited-overs international.

1956 Dominic Erbani, French rugby football international.

1964 Nigel Redman, English rugby football international.

DIED THIS DAY

1738 Joe Miller, leading English comic.

1886 Ned Buntline (Edward Zane Carroll Judson), US adventurer, author and originator of the dime novel.

1899 Robert Wilhelm Bunsen, German chemist who invented the Bunsen burner.

1920 Sir Joseph Lockyer, astronomer and discoverer of helium.

1948 (George Herman) Babe Ruth, legendary US baseball player.

1949 Margaret Mitchell, US author of *Gone with the Wind* after being knocked down by a car two days previously.

1956 Bela Lugosi (Bela Blasko), actor who played *Dracula*, in poverty after being released from hospital as a result of drug dependency. He was buried in his Dracula cloak according to his wishes.

1977 Elvis (Aaron) Presley, US rock superstar, at his mansion Gracelands, from heart failure probably brought on by drug abuse.

1979 John George Diefenbaker, Canadian Prime Minister from 1957–63.

ON THIS DAY

1819 Troops including Waterloo veterans broke up a crowd meeting to demand Parliamentary reforms, on St Peter's Field, Manchester. Eleven died in what became known as the Peterloo Massacre.

1960 Cyprus became a republic at midnight, with Archbishop Makarios as President.

MISSING A BEAT In 1962 Pete Best, original drummer with the Beatles, was fired by Brian Epstein and replaced by Ringo Starr, and in 1975 Phil Collins, drummer with Genesis, took over as lead singer when Peter Gabriel departed.

2012 The earth will change its 'time beam' at the end of a 5,000 year cycle and enter a New Age. This is not only the belief of the Atzec, Hopi and Mayan Indians and author José Arguelles (*The Mayan Factor*), but of US actress Shirley MacLaine, high priestess of the New Age cult.

17 AUGUST

National day of Indonesia marking its independence in 1945 following Japanese occupation.

BORN THIS DAY

HISTORY

1786 Davy (David) Crockett, US frontiersman and politician, who despite little formal education during his childhood in the backwoods was eventually elected to the US Congress in 1827. Much of the legend was encouraged, but in reality he spoke reasonable English and was involved in a number of business deals. It was the Disney film in 1955 that revived the myth, with the character of the backwoodsman hunting bears and racoons wearing the famous Crockett 'coonskin' hat.

ARTS

1932 V(idiadhar) S(urajprasad) Naipaul, in Trinidad, who later settled in England. His collection of short fiction, *In a Free State* (1971), won the Booker prize.

ENTERTAINMENT

1888 Monty (Edgar Montillion) Woolley, US actor, former English instructor and drama coach at Yale, who is best remembered for his role in both the play and film as the caustic bearded *Man Who Came To Dinner* (1942).

1892 Mae West, US actress and playwright who wrote *Sex* (1926) which was closed on Broadway when she was charged with obscenity and sent to prison for ten days. She went to Hollywood and became the buxom, sexy and enduringly witty character. Sayings like 'Come up and see me sometime' made her a legend and the richest woman in the US in the mid-30s.

1920 Maureen O'Hara (FitzSimmons), Irish-born US actress who at 19, played Esmerelda in the film, *The Hunchback of Notre Dame* with Charles Laughton (1939) and went on to star in many successful films including *How Green Was My Valley* (1941).

1926 George Melly, flamboyant English jazz singer, autobiographer, journalist, critic and broadcaster.

1943 Robert de Niro, US actor who won an Oscar for his supporting role in *The Godfather Part II* (1974),and a nomination for his performance in *The Deer Hunter* (1978).

SPORT

1951 Alan Minter, English boxer who won the world middleweight title in 1980 which he held only until that September when he lost it to 'Marvellous' Marvin Hagler.

1957 Robin Cousins, English ice-skating champion who followed in the footsteps of Britain's John Curry by winning a gold medal for the men's figure skating title at the 1976 Winter Olympics, as well as the European Championships that year.

DIED THIS DAY

1786 Frederick II (the Great), who laid the foundation of Prussia's greatness.

1955 Fernand Léger, French painter associated with Cubism.

1983 Ira Gershwin (Israel Gershvin), US lyricist to his brother George; together they penned some of the greatest popular songs ever written such as 'The Man I Love' and 'Lady Be Good'.

1987 Rudolf Hess, Hitler's deputy, in Spandau Prison, aged 94 after 46 years in prison. Was it suicide? Was it murder? He was found with an electrical flex around his neck, and was buried secretly in Bavaria to avoid neo-Nazi demonstrations.

1988 President Zia ul-Haq, Pakistan's ruler, killed when the military transport plane taking him and others – including the US ambassador – back to the capital

Islamabad exploded ten minutes after take-off.

ON THIS DAY

1896 Gold was discovered at Bonanza Creek, a small tributary of the Klondike River in Canada's Yukon Territory. This led to the great gold rush of 1898 when the settlement of Dawson would grow into a city of some 25,000 inhabitants.

1896 The first pedestrian to be knocked down and killed by a motor vehicle in Britain was Mrs Bridget Driscoll of Croydon, Surrey. The car that hit Mrs Driscoll was travelling at 4 m.p.h. Apparently, she froze in panic at the oncoming vehicle.

1977 The Soviet nuclear-powered ice-breaker *Artika* became the first to reach the North Pole.

1987 In Cincinnati, Ohio, a former nurses' aide, Donald Harvey, was charged with the murder of 28 people, including 20 patients at a public hospital, and was sentenced to three consecutive terms of life imprisonment. Harvey admitted to more than 50 murders.

1989 An Australian commercial airliner became the first to fly non-stop from London to Sydney.

1989 Richard Hart, accused of theft, became Britain's first electronically-tagged suspect and was allowed home.

18 AUGUST

BORN THIS DAY

HISTORY

1587 Virginia Dare, the first child of English parents to be born in America, in present-day North Carolina, a week after Sir Walter Raleigh's second expedition landed in an attempt to set up a colony.

1774 Meriwether Lewis, American explorer, who with William Clark led the first overland expedition to the Pacific North-west.

1792 John Russell, 1st Earl Russell, British Prime Minister 1846–52 and again 1865–6 who was a champion of the Parliamentary Reform Bill.

1830 Franz Joseph I, Emperor of Austria-Hungary who invaded Serbia in 1914 and helped light the touchpaper that set off the First World War.

1908 Edgar Fauré, French Prime Minister in 1952 and 1955–6.

1917 Caspar (Willard) Weinberger, US statesman who served under Nixon and Ford and was Reagan's Secretary of Defence and was awarded an honorary KBE by the Queen.

ARTS

1922 Alain Robbe-Grillet, French novelist and scriptwriter, who scripted *Last Year at Marienbad* (1961) for Resnais, before adding direction to his credits.

1925 Brian (Wilson) Aldiss, English science fiction writer and comic novelist who wrote *Soldier Erect* (1971) and *A Rude Awakening* (1978).

ENTERTAINMENT

1913 Henry Cornelius, South African-born film director who trained in Germany and made some of the most British of British comedies including the classics, *Passport to Pimlico* (1949) and *Genevieve* (1953).

1922 Shelley Winters (Shirley Schrift), US actress who was nominated for an

Oscar for her performance in *A Place in the Sun* (1951), and won Oscars for her supporting roles in *The Diary of Anne Frank* (1959) and *The Poseidon Adventure* (1972).

1933 Roman Polanski, Polish film director whose films include *Rosemary's Baby* (1968) and *Tess* (1979).

1937 (Charles) Robert Redford, one of Hollywood's most popular actors who came from a successful Broadway and television career to films including *Butch Cassidy and the Sundance Kid* (1969), *The Sting* (1973) (which won him an Oscar nomination), and *All the President's Men* (1976) which he also produced.

1937 William Rushton, English actor, cartoonist and writer who wrote for the satirical *Private Eye* as well as turning up on television and radio from time to time in comedy and quiz shows.

SPORT

1920 (Thomas) Godfrey Evans, England and Kent wicket-keeper who was the first to make 200 dismissals which he achieved in his 80th Test with a catch (1957).

BUSINESS

1834 Marshall Field, US department store founder who opened the store in Chicago in 1868 which bears his name, offering special services for the customer, ranging from a restaurant in the store, to the privilege of being able to return goods.

DIED THIS DAY

1227 Genghis Khan, ruler of Mongolia, after a fall from his horse.

1823 André Jacques Garnerin, French balloonist and parachutist.

1988 Marie Paoleschi, known as 'Marie-la-Jolie', infamous Marseilles madam, who also kept brothels in Saigon, Buenos Aires and Paris.

ON THIS DAY

1743 The first rules of boxing, drawn up by Jack Broughton, Britain's third heavyweight champion, were confirmed this day. He later devised 'mufflers', the first form of boxing gloves.

1930 The two halves of Sydney Bridge met in the centre and were formally joined.

1939 The film *The Wizard of Oz*, starring Judy Garland, opened in New York.

1959 The first Mini Minor was unveiled by designer Alec Issigonis at the British Motor Corporation.

1960 The first oral contraceptive was marketed by the Searle Drug Company in the US.

1964 South Africa was banned from participating in the Olympics because of its racial policies.

19 AUGUST

BORN THIS DAY

HISTORY

1646 John Flamsteed, the first Astronomer Royal in Britain, at the Royal Greenwich Observatory which was founded in 1675. He catalogued thousands of stars which later proved useful to Newton.

1743 Comtesse du Barry (Marie Jeanne Becu), Louis XV's last mistress. She was dismissed from the court on his death (1774) and was later guillotined by the Revolutionary Tribunal for squandering state treasures. (*See* 8.12.1763)

1843 Charles Montague Doughty, English explorer and author who travelled extensively in Egypt, the Holy Land and Syria.

ARTS

1631 John Dryden, English poet who became Poet Laureate in 1668. His plays also proved popular including *All For Love* (1677).

1750 Antonio Salieri, Italian composer and conductor who some believed poisoned Mozart.

1902 (Frederick) Ogden Nash, US humorist whose slick lines have become immortal, such as 'Candy is dandy/But liquor is quicker'. He also wrote lyrics for musicals such as *One Touch of Venus* with Kurt Weill in 1943, which included the song 'Speak Low'.

1903 James Gould Cozzens, US novelist of *Castaway* (1934) and *By Love Possessed* (1957).

1937 Richard Ingrams, English journalist and co-founder of *Private Eye*, Britain's post-war satirical magazine.

ENTERTAINMENT

1900 Colleen Moore (Kathleen Morrison), bobbed-haired US actress who epitomized the 20s and 'flappers'. She was the first star to earn over $10,000 a week and wrote *How Women Can Make Money on the Stock Market*.

1940 Jill St John (Jill Oppenheim), US actress who was in *Tender is the Night* (1962) and *Diamonds Are Forever* (1971).

INVENTION

1808 James Nasmyth, Scottish inventor of the steam hammer which he patented in 1842. He also manufactured over 100 steam locomotives and retired, aged 48, to devote himself to astronomy.

1871 Orville Wright, US aviation pioneer who, with his older brother Wilbur ran a bicycle business while investing their efforts in powered-flight. (*See* 17.12.1903)

POP

1940 Johnny Nash, US singer and songwriter who had a big hit with his 'I Can See Clearly Now' in 1972.

1940 Ginger (Peter) Baker, English drummer who formed Cream with Eric Clapton and others. After they broke up he formed other groups including the Afro-jazz Air-Force.

SPORT

1931 Willy (William Lee) Shoemaker, US champion jockey who rode a record-breaking 7,000 winners, including three Kentucky Derby winners.

FASHION

1883 Gabrielle 'Coco' Chanel, French fashion designer who revolutionized women's fashions during the 20s, liberating them from the corset. She also manufactured the famous Chanel No. 5 perfume. Immensely wealthy, she retired in 1938, but made a comeback in the 50s.

DIED THIS DAY

AD14 Augustus, the first Roman emperor, known as Octavian, heir of his great-uncle, Julius Caesar, who was deified after his death.

1662 Blaise Pascal, French philosopher

and mathematician, inventor of the first calculating machine.

1876 George Smith, English Assyriologist who deciphered cuneiform tablets and caused a sensation when he discovered text relating to The Flood. He died of exhaustion during an excavation, aged 36 years.

1929 Sergei Pavlovich Diaghilev, founder of the Ballets Russes.

1936 Frederico Garcìa Lorca, Spanish poet and playwright of *Blood Wedding* (1933), shot by Nationalists after the outbreak of the Civil War.

1944 Sir Henry (Joseph) Wood, English conductor and founder of the Proms.

1976 Alistair Sim, Scottish actor who starred in *The Anatomist* both on stage and screen.

1977 (Julius Henry) Groucho Marx, US comedian, the fast-talking member of the famous Marx Brothers.

1981 Jessie Matthews, English actress and singer who played Mrs Dale in the long-running radio daily serial, *Mrs Dale's Diary*.

ON THIS DAY

1897 Electric-powered cabs appeared in London. With an average speed of nine m.p.h. and a range of up to just 30 miles, they proved uneconomical and were withdrawn in 1900.

1960 Gary Powers, the US U-2 spy plane pilot who was brought down by the Russians, was sentenced by a Soviet court to ten years detention.

1987 In Hungerford, Hertfordshire, Michael Ryan, 27, shot dead 16 people including his mother, wounded 14, set fire to his mother's house and finally shot himself. It was the worst civil massacre in modern British history.

1989 Poland became the first country in east Europe to end one-party rule when Solidarity's Tadeuz Mazowiecki became Prime Minister.

20 AUGUST

BORN THIS DAY

HISTORY

1833 Benjamin Harrison, 23rd US President, and grandson of the ninth President.

ARTS

1890 H(oward) P(hillips) Lovecraft, US master of the macabre story and short novel. Most of his work appeared in the magazine *Weird Tales*.

1905 Jack (Weldon John) Teagarden, US jazz trombonist, singer and leader of his own band from 1939–47, then went on to play with Louis Armstrong.

POP

1924 Jim Reeves, US country and western singer.

SPORT

1906 (H.W.) Bunny Austin, British tennis player and four-times Davis Cup winner, 1933–6.

1952 John (Ernest) Emburey, England and Middlesex cricketer. One of the finest off-break bowlers, he once took 7–6 when Middlesex played Cambridge University in 1977.

DIED THIS DAY

1912 William Booth, English founder of the Salvation Army.

1989 George Adamson, British naturalist

and conservationist, best known for his work with his wife Joy, and the lioness, Elsa, murdered by bandits in a remote game park in Kenya.

ON THIS DAY

1913 Stainless steel was first cast in Sheffield by Harry Brearley.

1913 Adolphe Pégond baled out from a Blériot airplane 700 feet above Buc in France. His parachute brought him down safely, making him the first to bale out from a plane.

1924 The British sprinter Eric Liddel refused to run in the heats of the 100m at the Paris Olympics because it fell on a Sunday and was against his religious convictions. He had been tipped as the likely winner, but he did win the 400m on a weekday, setting a new record.

1940 Leon Trotsky, the Bolshevik leader exiled by Stalin who found asylum in Mexico, was struck several blows on the head with an ice pick wielded by Ramon Mercader, who had posed as a supporter, but was actually an agent for Stalin. Trotsky died later this day.

1940 'Never in the field of human conflict was so much owed by so many to so few,' said Winston Churchill in a broadcast with reference to the Battle of Britain raging in the skies above him.

1956 The first nuclear power was generated in Britain from the Calder Hall nuclear power station in Cumberland.

1968 Russian troops invaded Czechoslovakia.

1989 A Thames pleasure boat, *The Marchioness*, with 125 party-goers on board was rammed in the stern by a barge, and sank in the early hours of the morning. 51 young people drowned.

21 AUGUST

BORN THIS DAY

HISTORY

1754 William Murdock, Scottish engineer who invented coal-gas lighting in 1792 while working with James Watt and Matthew Boulton on their steam engines. Distilling coal to produce the gas, he first illuminated his cottage and offices.

1765 William IV, King of England, known as 'the sailor king' for his service in the Royal Navy which he joined aged 13 years, and for his action during the American Revolution and close friendship with Nelson. His numerous affairs were legendary; he had ten illegitimate children by Dorothea Jordan, the Irish actress who was an enormous success at Drury Lane.

1930 Princess Margaret (Rose), younger sister of Queen Elizabeth II, born at Glamis Castle, Scotland.

ARTS

1874 Aubrey (Vincent) Beardsley, English artist who, along with Wilde, was a major figure in the Aesthetic movement. In his brief life – he died aged 25 – he was the leading illustrator in the movement, working for the quarterly *Yellow Book* and producing illustrations for the published version of Wilde's play *Salome* (1893).

1933 Dame Janet Baker, English opera and concert singer.

ENTERTAINMENT

1904 Count (William) Basie, US jazz pianist and bandleader who perfected the big band sound, attracting many leading musicians including the saxophonist Lester Young and the singer Billie Holiday.

1933 Barry Norman, English broadcaster and journalist, son of film director Leslie Norman, who presents programmes on films and the film world on television.

SPORT

1928 Chris(topher) Brasher, English athlete, journalist and one of the driving forces behind the establishment of the London Marathon. In 1956 he won an Olympic gold medal in the steeplechase.

1959 Anne Hobbs, English tennis player.

DIED THIS DAY

1951 (Leonard) Constant Lambert, English composer and conductor with the Sadler's Wells Ballet.

1959 Sir Jacob Epstein, US-born sculptor who became a British citizen and whose works include *St Michael and the Devil* at the new Coventry Cathedral.

1988 Chris Gittin, English actor who is best remembered as Walter Gabriel in the daily radio series *The Archers*, a part he played for 35 years.

ON THIS DAY

1858 Sir Sam Browne, VC, Commander of the 2nd Punjab Cavalry, invented the 'Sam Browne belt' to hold his sword and pistol after he had lost one arm in action. It soon became standard kit for two-armed British soldiers.

1901 The Cadillac Motor Company was formed in Detroit, named after the French explorer.

1911 Leonardo da Vinci's masterpiece, the *Mona Lisa – La Gioconda* – probably the world's best-known painting, was stolen from the Louvre in Paris by an Italian house-painter, Vincenzo Perruggia, angered at being called 'a macaroni eater' by Frenchmen. It was two years later that a Florence art dealer was sent a note by Perruggia telling him he had hidden the painting in a hotel under a bed. The hotel was subsequently renamed the Gioconda.

1959 Hawaii became the 50th state of the Union.

1965 Keith Peacock became the first substitute permitted by the Football League when he went on for his team, Charlton Athletic.

1976 One more battle of the sexes ended when Mary Langdon, aged 25, joined the fire brigade at Battle, East Sussex to become Britain's first female fireman; she was not called a 'firewoman' or 'fireperson'.

1983 Benigno Aquino, exiled Philippine opposition leader who had been assured a safe return by President Marcos, was shot dead in full view of the television cameras as he stepped out of the plane at Manila airport.

1988 Amended British licensing laws allowing more flexible pub opening hours came into force at midnight. Pubs could now stay open 12 hours in the day, except on Sunday.

22 AUGUST

BORN THIS DAY

HISTORY

1741 Jean François de Galaup de la Pérouse, French navigator who destroyed the forts of the Hudson Bay Company in the war against the British. On a voyage of discovery in 1785, his explorations took him to the Asian coast and Botany Bay.

ARTS

1862 Claude (Achille) Debussy, French composer who is best known for his orchestral impression *La Mer* and *Prélude à l'après-midi d'un faune*, first performed in 1894.

1891 Jacques Lipchitz, Lithuanian-born US sculptor who was an exponent of Cubism in the 30s, but moved on to bold bronzes of human figures and animals.

1893 Dorothy Parker (Rothschild), US humorist and writer whose remarks became legendary. Mainly remembered as a short-story writer for the *New Yorker* magazine, she also scripted films with her second husband, Alan Campbell. Together they wrote *A Star Is Born* (1937).

1902 Leni (Hélène Bertha Amalie) Riefenstahl, German actress, film director and photographer, she was favoured by Hitler to film the 1934 Nuremberg Party Convention which she turned into the classic documentary *Triumph of Will*. She also filmed the 1936 Berlin Olympics.

1908 Henri Cartier-Bresson, French photographer who is considered one of the greatest ever.

1920 Ray Bradbury, US poetic science-fiction writer of the classic *Martian Chronicles* (1950). Much of his work has been adapted for the screen including *Fahrenheit 451* and *The Illustrated Man*, both published 1951.

1928 Karlheinz Stockhausen, German composer and conductor who co-founded Cologne's influential electronic music studio in 1953. His work includes *Kontakte* (1959).

ENTERTAINMENT

1926 Honor Blackman, English actress who was the original Avengers girl on television in the 60s, and went on to play leads on the stage, television and in films including *Life At The Top* (1965).

1940 Valerie Harper, US actress who was first seen in *The Mary Tyler Moore Show* before starring on television in *Rhoda* and several television movies.

SPORT

1892 (George Herbert) Percy Fender, Surrey and England cricketer who scored a century against Northamptonshire in a record 35 minutes on 26.8.1926.

1957 Steve Davis, English snooker world champion in 1981, 1983, 1984, 1987 and 1989, who became the first player to win over £1m from the game which now commands huge television audiences.

DIED THIS DAY

1806 Jean Honoré Fragonard, French painter.

1889 'Lord' John Sanger, English circus owner.

1922 Michael Collins, Irish nationalist leader, killed when a bullet ricocheted during an ambush by extremist Republicans.

1940 Sir Oliver (Joseph) Lodge, English physicist who pioneered wireless telegraphy.

1942 Michel (Mikhail) Fokine, Russian dancer and choreographer.

1963 Viscount Nuffield (William Richard Morris), British car manufacturer and philanthropist.

1978 Jomo Kenyatta (Kamau), first President of Kenya.

ON THIS DAY

1485 In the last of the Wars of the Roses on Bosworth Field in Leicestershire, Henry VII led his troops to victory over Richard III (Richard Plantagenet), who was killed.

1642 The Civil War began in England when Charles I erected his standard in front of a few hundred of his Royalists or Cavaliers in Nottingham. In the south were the parliamentary party or Roundheads.

1950 The first swimming race across the Channel was won in 10 hours, 50 minutes by Lt Abdel Rehim of Egypt.

1960 *Beyond the Fringe*, one of the most influential satirical reviews staged in Britain this century, opened in Edinburgh.

1985 A British Airtours Boeing 737 burst into flames at the end of the runway at Manchester Airport when take-off was aborted. Although 80 escaped, 55 died in the flames and noxious fumes.

1989 British Telecom launched the world's first pocketphone service – small radio handsets which operated within 100 yards of a public base station, such as a remote call-box.

23 AUGUST

BORN THIS DAY

HISTORY

1754 Louis XVI, the last king of France who set in motion the Revolution with the help of his wife, Marie-Antoinette.

ARTS

1869 Edgar Lee Masters, US poet and novelist of *Spoon River Anthology* which uses free verse in the form of monologues about the fictitious town of Spoon River.

1905 (Leonard) Constant Lambert, English composer and conductor of the Sadler's Wells Ballet for whom he wrote *Horoscope* (1938).

1947 Willy Russell, English playwright with his roots firmly in Liverpool. His work includes the highly successful plays *Educating Rita* (1979) and *Shirley Valentine* (1986) which were equally acclaimed films.

ENTERTAINMENT

1912 Gene (Eugène Curran) Kelly, US dancer, choreographer, singer, actor and director who rose to fame on Broadway in the 1940 musical *Pal Joey*. In Hollywood, he starred in some of the best musicals ever produced including *Anchors Aweigh* (1945), which got him an Oscar nomination, *On The Town* (1949), *Singin' in the Rain* (1952) and his own all-dance *Invitation to the Dance* (1956).

POP

1947 Keith Moon, ill-fated drummer with the Who.

SPORT

1929 Peter Thomson, outstanding Australian golfer who won the British Open three successive times from 1954–6, and again in 1958 and 1965 to set a new record. His other successes include three wins in the Australian Open, nine in New Zealand and 25 other major victories overseas.

1949 Geoff(rey) Capes, English shot putter and strongman who was once a policeman.

DIED THIS DAY

AD93 Julius Gnaeus Agricola, Roman general renowned for his conquests in Britain, in retirement in Rome.

1305 Sir William Wallace, Scottish patriot who demanded independence for his country, was hanged, drawn and quartered at Smithfield, London.

1628 The arrogant Duke of Buckingham was assassinated at Portsmouth by John Felton, a discontented subaltern.

1926 Rudolph Valentino, 'the world's greatest screen lover'. Born in Italy as Rudolfo Guglielmi di Valentina d'Antonguolla, he died in New York, aged 31, following an operation for a ruptured appendix.

1960 Oscar Hammerstein II, US lyricist.

1987 Didier Peroni, French racing driver killed in a power boat race off the Isle of Wight with two others when the *Colibri* corkscrewed into the air after hitting the wake of an oil tanker.

ON THIS DAY

AD410 The Visigoths sacked Rome and put an end to the era of Roman civilization and influence.

1914 The Battle of Mons during the First World War was the first for the British Expeditionary Forces and the first in which the VC (Victoria Cross) was awarded for gallantry in this war.

1927 Two Italian-born anarchists living in the US, Nicola Saccho and Bartolomeo Vanzetti, were sent to the electric chair, convicted of a payroll robbery which left two dead. There was world-wide protest at the verdict, many believing the men innocent and guilty only of unpopular political views. It was revealed that the robbery was carried out by the Morelli gang, but the judge refused to reopen the case. The Governor of Massachusetts officially cleared their names in 1977, 50 years too late.

1938 Len Hutton scored a world record 364 in 13 hours and 20 minutes at The Oval in the fifth Test against Australia, making more than England's totals in each of their last ten innings. England were all out for a record 903. Church bells pealed 364 times in celebration.

1939 Germany and Russia signed a short-lived non-aggression pact which left Hitler free to attack Poland.

1939 The British driver John Cobb reached 368.85 m.p.h. at Bonneville Flats, Utah.

1940 The Blitz began as German bombers began an all-night raid on London.

1988 Morten and Anna Riis became British Airways' first husband and wife pilot recruits.

24 AUGUST

The Feast day of Bartholomew, patron saint of tanners and shoemakers.

BORN THIS DAY

HISTORY

1759 William Wilberforce, English philanthropist and anti-slavery campaigner who championed other causes, including catholic political emancipation and the French Revolution. The French made him an honorary citizen, much to his embarrassment. His battle to have the slave trade and slavery abolished in British overseas possessions achieved its first success on 25.3.1807 when a bill abolishing this trade in the British West Indies became law.

1787 James Wedell, English Antarctic explorer who was born in Ostend. He sailed south to explore the edge of the Antarctic including the South Orkneys which he named. He reached the most southern point at that time, three degrees below Cook's record.

ARTS

1591 Robert Herrick (baptized), English lyric poet, cleric, close friend of Ben Jonson and writer of 'Gather ye rosebuds while ye may'.

1724 George Stubbs, English anatomical draughtsman and painter of animals, predominantly horses. He declined into obscurity in later life and interest in his work only revived in the 1950s.

1872 Sir (Henry Maximilian) Max Beerbohm, English caricaturist, writer and wit whose only novel, *Zuleika Dobson* (1911) was also made into a musical.

1899 Jorge Luis Borges, acclaimed Argentinian writer, author of *The Book of Imaginary Beings* (1967), which he dictated having gone blind in 1955.

1903 Graham (Vivian) Sutherland, English painter best known for his magnificent tapestry for the new Coventry Cathedral and his 'warts-and-all' portraits of leading figures. These included Somerset Maugham (1949) and Winston Churchill commissioned by Parliament for the great man's 80th birthday and later destroyed by Lady Churchill because her husband had hated it so much.

SPORT

1953 Sam Torrance, Scottish golfer and member of the winning Ryder Cup team in 1985 when he hit the winning putt to give victory to the European team over the US for the first time in 28 years (15.9.1985).

DIED THIS DAY

1680 Captain Blood, Irish adventurer who tried to steal the Crown jewels from the Tower of London (9.5.1671).

BY THEIR OWN HAND In 1770 Thomas Chatterton, an unhappy English poet starving in the proverbial garret, refused food from his friends and instead took arsenic and died, aged only 22. His reputation was assured for posterity when his story was reincarnated in an Italian opera (*Chatterton* by Leoncavallo) and a popular painting by Lewis. In 1954, to avoid mounting scandals and demands that he give up power, Getulio (Dorneles) Vargas, President of Brazil, took his own life. He was 71.

1942 The Duke of Kent, youngest brother of King George VI, when his Sutherland flying boat crashed *en route* to Iceland. He was the first Royal to die on active duty, although not in action.

ON THIS DAY

AD79 Mount Vesuvius erupted and buried the cities of Pompeii and Herculaneum in hot volcanic ash.

1572 Thousands of French Huguenots were murdered in Paris by order of Catherine de' Medici and the Catholic French court, in what became known as the St Bartholomew's Day massacre.

1690 Job Charnock established a trading post on behalf of the English East India Company in the small village of Kalikata in West Bengal. This is considered the official founding of India's largest city, Calcutta.

1814 British troops under General Ross invaded Washington and set fire to the White House and the Capitol. Both were rebuilt and enlarged.

1847 Charlotte Brontë sent her manuscript of *Jane Eyre*, written under the name Currer Bell, from the little railway station at Haworth to her London publishers, Smith, Elder & Company.

1940 The *Lancet* reported the first purification of penicillin by Professor Howard Florey of Adelaide and Professor Ernest Chain.

1957 Jimmy Greaves, at age 17, made his football debut for Chelsea.

1975 Annabel Hunt sang the opening aria of *Ulysses* at Glyndebourne in the nude for a televised performance, believed to be the first nude performance in a British opera production and certainly the first on television.

1989 The British brewing company, Bass, added the US Holiday Inns chain to their other hotel groups, to become the world's biggest hotelier.

25 AUGUST

Feast day of Louis, patron saint of France and of barbers who died this day, 1270, near Tunis while leading a Crusade.

The national day of Uruguay, marking its independence from Spain in 1825.

BORN THIS DAY

HISTORY

1530 Ivan IV ('the Terrible'), crowned first Tsar of Russia in 1547. He expanded the Russian state with campaigns against the Tartars, but his debaucheries and oppression, in which over 3,000 (including the royal heir) were executed, gave him his descriptive title.

1819 Allan Pinkerton, Scottish-born US founder of the famous Pinkerton National Detective Agency, who settled in the US in 1842. In 1846 he caught a gang of counterfeiters and was made deputy sheriff of Kane County. He resigned to found his agency in 1850 which specialized in the relatively new crime of railway theft.

1919 George (Corley) Wallace, the reactionary Governor of Alabama who survived an assassination attempt that left him confined to a wheelchair, but still able to conduct the affairs of office.

ARTS

1918 Leonard Bernstein, US composer and conductor who achieved equal success in both classical and modern music. He composed music for several ballets including *Fancy Free* (1944), a number of symphonies and choral works, and musicals including *Wonderful Town* (1953), *Candide* (1956) and one of the greatest and most significant in the history of the musical, *West Side Story* (1957).

1938 Frederick Forsyth, English thriller writer who was also a former reporter for Reuters. His first novel, *The Day of the Jackal* (1970) was a world best-seller and an equally successful film. He followed this with an unfaltering succession of novels, many of which were filmed, including *The Odessa File* (1972), *The Dogs of War* (1974) and *The Fourth Protocol* (1984).

1949 Martin Amis, English author, son of Kingsley, whose novels include *The Rachel Papers* (1974), *Money* (1984) and *London Fields* (1989).

ENTERTAINMENT

1905 Clara Bow, US actress known as the 'It' girl ('it' being some extra quality and vitality) which came from her role in the film *It* (1927). It made her a symbol of the Roaring Twenties and a huge draw at the box office, but by 1933 her career was over.

1909 Ruby (Ethel Hilda) Keeler, Canadian-born US musical star who tap-danced her way from chorus girl to starring parts on Broadway and musicals in Hollywood including *42nd Street* (1933).

1916 (Charles) Van Johnson, US actor who was at his most popular in the 40s in films including *Till the Clouds Roll By* (1946) and *State of the Union* (1947). He made his first appearance on the London stage in *The Music Man* (1961).

1930 (Thomas) Sean Connery, Scottish actor, once in the chorus of *South Pacific*, became the best of the Bonds in seven films starting with *Dr No* in 1962. He won an Oscar for best supporting actor in *The Untouchables* (1987).

JAZZ

1933 Wayne Shorter, US saxophonist with Art Blakey's Jazz Messengers in 1959, moving to Miles Davis in 1964 to tour both sides of the Atlantic and Japan. Davis's repertoire included many Shorter compositions including 'ESP'. With Joe Zawini, he formed the very successful Weather Report.

POP

1954 Elvis Costello (Declan McManus), English singer and songwriter.

DIED THIS DAY

1688 Sir Henry Morgan, Welsh buccaneer who plundered Spanish possessions in the Caribbean; he died as Lieutenant-Governor of Jamaica.

POWER CUTS The deaths of two pioneers of power. In 1819 James Watt, English engineer and inventor of steam engines who has the unit of power, the watt, named in his honour, and in 1867 Michael Faraday, English chemist and physicist who invented the first electrical battery.

1822 Sir William (Frederick Wilhelm) Herschel, German-born British astronomer who discovered the planet Uranus.

1936 Gregori Yevseyevich Zinoviev (Ovsel Gershon Aronov Radomyslsky), Russian revolutionary, executed after the first great Soviet show trial which saw 15 other opponents of Stalin meet their death by firing squad.

1979 Stan(ley Newcomb) Kenton, US pianist and composer, jazz experimentalist and innovator in the field of progressive jazz.

ON THIS DAY

325 The General Council of Nicaea decided the rules for computing the date of Easter each year.

LEADING LADIES In 1804 Alicia Meynell became the first known woman jockey when she rode Vingarillo over a four-mile course at York. She was in the lead most of the way, but lost to the only other challenger. In 1830, leading British actress Fanny Kemble rode on the footplate of Stephenson's *Northumbrian*, the first woman to do so, in a trial run prior to the opening of the Liverpool and Manchester Railway. In 1841 three women graduated as Bachelors of Arts at the Oberlin Collegiate Institute, Ohio. They were the first women to be granted degrees. That would not happen in Britain until 1880 (17.11.1880).

1837 The process of producing galvanized iron was patented by Henry William Crawford of London.

1875 Captain Matthew Webb became the first person to swim the English Channel, doing the breastroke from Dover to Calais in 22 hours, having set off on the 24th.

1919 Daily flights between Paris and London began, starting the first scheduled international air service.

1928 Liverpool FC's famous Kop at their Anfield ground was opened, named after Spion Kop, the sight of a famous Boer War battle in South Africa.

1978 The Shroud of Turin went on show for the first time on the high altar at St John's Cathedral, Turin.

1989 The spacecraft *Voyager*, completing its 12-year voyage to Neptune, sent back outstanding pictures of Triton, its moon, and revealed two additional moons previously unknown to scientists.

26 AUGUST

BORN THIS DAY

HISTORY

1676 Sir Robert Walpole, lst Earl of Orford, British Whig politician regarded as the first Prime Minister, first Lord of the treasury and first Chancellor of the Exchequer.

1740 Joseph Michel Montgolfier, French hot air balloon inventor and pioneer with his brother Jacques Étienne (6.1.1745). They both inherited the family papermaking firm where their inventive minds made many improvements. Joseph invented an air pump for removing paper from moulds and a hydraulic ram.

1743 Antoine Laurent Lavoisier, French chemist who is considered the father of modern chemistry. He was also a member of the commission which recommended the introduction of the metric system into France.

1819 Prince Albert, Consort to Queen Victoria, born in Bavaria as Albert of Saxe-Coburg-Gotha. He played a valuable role behind the throne, not only by changing some of the Queen's less progressive views, but also through his interest in the arts and the organizing of the Great Exhibition of 1851 in the Crystal Palace.

1873 Lee De Forest, US radio and television pioneer and inventor of the Audion vacuum tube, patented in 1907, which made broadcasting possible and was a key component in electronic equipment until the invention of the transistor.

ARTS

1875 John Buchan, Lord Tweedsmuir, Scottish novelist and Governor-General of Canada who wrote *The Thirty-nine Steps* (1915) and *Greenmantle* (1916) as well as several other novels and biographies.

1880 Guillaume Apollinaire (Wilhelm Apollonaris de Kostrowitsky), born in Rome of a Polish mother, who wrote short stories, poems, novels and a surrealist drama which Poulenc later turned into a one-act comic opera.

1904 Christopher Isherwood, English

author who is best known for his stories of Berlin in the 30s including *Mr Norris Changes Trains* (1935) and *Goodbye Berlin* (1939). He collaborated with W.H. Auden on several verse dramas including *The Ascent of F-6* (1936).

SPORT

1941 Malcolm Pyrah, British show-jumper.

DIED THIS DAY

1850 Louis Philippe, the 'Citizen King' of France who abdicated in face of a middle-class revolt and came to live in Surrey in 1848 where he died.

1930 (Alonso) Lon Chaney, US actor known as 'the man with a thousand faces', two of which he used for *Phantom of the Opera.*

1931 Frank (James Thomas) Harris, Irish-born editor and author of the sexually explicit *My Life and Loves* in three volumes.

1958 Ralph Vaughan Williams, English composer of *Sea Symphony* (1909).

1972 Sir Francis Chichester, English round-the-world yachtsman.

1974 Charles (Augustus) Lindbergh, US aviator who flew solo to Paris to become an international hero.

1978 Charles Boyer, French actor who was everyone's idea of the great French lover; he took an overdose of barbiturates two days before his 81st birthday and two days after the death of his wife, whom he had married in 1934.

1989 Lucille Ball, US comedienne, following open heart surgery, 20 days after her 78th birthday.

ON THIS DAY

1346 The Battle of Crécy took place between Edward III of England, aided by his son Edward the Black Prince, and Philip VI of France. This was a victory for the English in the first decade of the Hundred Years War, and it was here that the infamous two-fingered insult was first used by the British.

1789 The French Assembly adopted the Declaration of the Rights of Man.

1920 The 19th Amendment to the US constitution gave women the right to vote.

1936 The BBC transmitted the first high definition television pictures introduced by its first announcer, Leslie Mitchell. Over 7,000 people queued to see the pictures from Alexander Palace in north London, on sets at the Olympia Radio Show, west London.

1940 The RAF bombed Berlin for the first time in retaliation for attacks on London.

1952 The Soviets announced that the first successful ICBM (Intercontinental Ballistic Missile) tests had taken place.

1987 A sex-crazed elephant had to be shot when it ran amok in a village north of Bangkok. Two people were killed and a radio centre flattened. The police said that the elephant 'was urgently in search of a mate'.

1988 Lynne Cox of the US swam across Lake Baikal, Siberia, covering the 11 miles in 4 hours, 20 minutes, the first ever long swim in the cold water lake.

27 AUGUST

BORN THIS DAY

HISTORY

551BC Confucius, (one suggested birthday of the great philosopher), probably China's most famous man whose sayings are still universally quoted.

1877 The Hon Charles Stewart Rolls, English aviator and motor manufacturer who formed a partnership with Henry Royce to make luxury cars in 1906. Rolls was the first to fly across the English Channel and back non-stop in June 1910 and was also a keen motorist, taking part in several classic long-distance races.

1908 Lyndon Baines Johnson, 30th US President who took over on Kennedy's assassination (22.11.1963). The following year he won the election with a huge majority but escalated the war in Vietnam, despite considerable domestic unrest at this policy.

1910 Mother Teresa of Calcutta (Agnes Gonxha Bojaxhui), Yugoslavian-born founder of the Order of the Missionaries of Charity, dedicated to the poor and the sick, particularly in India where she opened many centres including several for lepers. She was awarded the Nobel Peace prize in 1979 and the Order of Merit from the Queen in 1986.

ARTS

1871 Theodore (Herman Albert) Dreiser, US author whose first novel *Sister Carrie* (1900) had to be withdrawn because it was considered obscene. *An American Tragedy* (1925) made a major contribution to US literature.

1899 C(ecil) S(cott) Forester, English novelist, born in Cairo and educated at Dulwich College (Raymond Chandler's old school). He published *The African Queen* in 1935, and in 1937 created a series of historical novels featuring his most popular character, Captain Horatio Hornblower.

LIFE STORIES Two distinguished English biographers were born this day three years apart: in 1932 Lady Antonia Fraser, author of *Mary Queen of Scots* (1969) and *Oliver Cromwell* (1973), whose second husband is playwright Harold Pinter, and in 1935 Michael (de Courcy Fraser) Holroyd, biographer of Lytton Strachey (two volumes, 1967-8), Augustus John, (two volumes, 1974-5) and George Bernard Shaw (first volume, 1988).

ENTERTAINMENT

1882 Sam(uel Gelbfisch 'Goldfish') Goldwyn, Hollywood mogul, who arrived penniless in the US from Warsaw via England, and became one of the founders of MGM which he promptly left to go independent again. He was responsible for some of the most entertaining films reaching the screen, from the original *Ben Hur* in 1925 to *Porgy and Bess* in 1959. Like Confucius (born this day), he was famous for his sayings, and those invented by others but attributed to him, such as 'Include me out'.

SPORT

1908 Sir Don(ald George) Bradman, Australian cricket captain and batsman, one of the greatest in the history of cricket. 'The Don' scored 6,996 runs for Australia, an average of 99.94 per match. He retired in 1949 and was knighted the same year.

1954 John Lloyd, English tennis player

who never reached the heights expected of him and became better known as the husband of US and Wimbledon tennis champion, Chris Evert.

1954 Derek Warwick, English grand prix driver.

1957 Bernhard Langer, German golfer.

1959 Gerhard Berger, German Grand Prix driver.

JAZZ

1925 (Anthony John) Tony Crombie, English drummer and composer who wrote several film scores and compositions performed by the likes of Miles Davis ('So Near So Far') and 'Restless Child' recorded by Stephane Grappelli.

DIED THIS DAY

1576 Titian (Tiziano Vecelli), major Venetian painter.

1879 Sir Rowland Hill, English postal service pioneer.

1919 Louis Botha, first South African Prime Minister.

1965 Le Corbusier (Charles Edouard Jeanneret), French architect, one of the most influential figures in modern architecture.

1975 Haile Selassie, deposed emperor of Ethiopia.

ON THIS DAY

1859 The world's first oil well was drilled at Titusville, Pennsylvania by Edwin Drake.

1883 The climax of the volcanic eruption of Krakatoa on the island of Pulau in the Selat strait between Java and Sumatra was the most catastrophic ever witnessed and could be heard 2,200 miles away in Australia. The ash and debris was propelled over 50 miles into the air. Tidal waves followed as far away as Hawaii killing thousands.

1910 Edison demonstrated sound film projection with phonograph records at his laboratory in West Orange, New Jersey.

1913 The Russian Lieutenant Peter Nesterov became the first pilot to perform the loop-the-loop.

1966 Francis Chichester set sail from Plymouth in *Gypsy Moth IV* on his solo voyage around the world (returning 28.5.1967), the first official old age pensioner to accomplish this feat.

1967 The man who helped make the Beatles, Brian Epstein, died in his London home from an overdose of sleeping pills.

1979 Lord Louis Mountbatten, the Queen's cousin, was killed when the IRA exploded a remote-controlled 50lb bomb on his boat *Shadow V* off the coast of County Sligo, Ireland.

BALLOONS In 1783 balloon pioneers, the Montgolfier brothers helped Jacques Alexandre César Charles launch the first hydrogen balloon to fly. He had solved the problem of gas leaking through the porous skin by using a varnish coating. The following year to the day in 1784, James Tytler in Edinburgh made the first free flight ascent in a balloon in Britain.

MAKING PIGS OF THEMSELVES On this day 1987, a young Chinese girl who was left to live with a family of pigs and was suckled by them, was finally returned to normal life after three years special training. The girl, now 13, was taught to speak and read and sing children's songs. Meanwhile across the world, about 30,000 feet above the US, a just-married couple caused the pilot of a jetliner on a coast-to-coast flight to land in

Houston, because of their amorous behaviour. They were accused of lewd and obscene acts in the presence of a minor and faced a maximum one year in prison.

28 AUGUST

BORN THIS DAY

HISTORY

1884 Peter Fraser, Scottish-born New Zealand Prime Minister from 1940–9.

ARTS

1749 Johann Wolfgang von Goethe, German poet, novelist playwright, founder of modern German literature and leader of the Romantic *Sturm und Drang* (storm and stress) movement. His masterpiece, the play *Faust*, was written in 1808. The second part was completed only in 1831.

1828 Count Leo (Lev Nikolayevich) Tolstoy, Russian author of *War and Peace* (1863–9), considered by many as the greatest novel ever written, and *Anna Karenina* (1874–6). He led a tempestuous life and travelled extensively but eventually renounced all his property – which was considerable – and lived as a peasant.

ENTERTAINMENT

1899 Charles Boyer, French actor who played romantic roles in films such as *All This And Heaven Too* (1940). (*See* 26.8.1978)

1925 Donald O'Connor, US actor and dancer, a Peter Pan-like performer who never seemed to age, co-starring in musicals such as *Singin' In The Rain* (1952). In 1956 he decided to concentrate on composing, as well as conducting the Los Angeles Philharmonic.

1930 Ben Gazzara, US actor who starred on Broadway in *Cat on a Hot Tin Roof* and other plays before taking dramatic roles in films such as *Anatomy of Murder* (1959) and Cassavete's *Husbands* (1970).

1930 Windsor Davis, Welsh actor usually in comedy roles such as the sergeant-major in the television comedy series *It Ain't Half Hot, Mum* as well as in the theatre.

1933 Elizabeth Seal, English actress, dancer and singer, born in Italy who starred in the London production of *Irma La Douce* (1958) and played the role when the musical opened on Broadway (1960). She was in other musicals including the London production of *Damn Yankees*.

1944 David Soul (Solberg), US actor and singer who starred in television's *Starsky and Hutch*.

SCIENCE

1919 Sir Godfrey Hounsfield, English inventor of the EMI medical scanner and Nobel prize winner for Physiology in 1979.

SPORT

1913 (Arthur) Lindsay Hassett, Australian cricket captain and high scoring batsman.

1947 Emlyn Hughes, Welsh footballer who played for Liverpool and Wolves and was an England international before retiring and concentrating on his broadcasting career.

DIED THIS DAY

1967 Charles Darrow, US inventor of the world's most successful modern board game, 'Monopoly', which he first devised in 1933 and for which he filed the patent on 31 August 1935. *(See 31.12.1935)*

1988 John Huston, US film director, writer and actor whose films include *The Maltese Falcon* (1941).

ON THIS DAY

1850 The Channel telegraph cable was finally laid between Dover and Cap Gris Nez.

1850 The first performance of Wagner's *Lohengrin* was staged at Weimar.

1933 The BBC was used for the first time by the police in tracking down a wanted man by broadcasting an appeal for information on Stanley Hobday, wanted for murder.

1953 At the Lincoln Memorial in Washington over 300,000 people ended the civil rights march from the South and heard Dr Martin Luther King, Jr. make his famous 'I have a dream' speech.

1988 The worst air crash during an aerobatic display took place at an airshow at the US base in Ramstein, West Germany when three Italian Airforce jets collided above the crowd of 300,000 killing over 30 and injuring 500. West Germany banned further air displays.

1988 A new slimming technique was reported from Bangkok where overweight Thais were sticking lettuce seeds in their ears. The Yan Hee Polyclinic said that pressing the seeds in the ears ten times before meals killed hunger.

29 AUGUST

BORN THIS DAY

HISTORY

1619 Jean-Baptiste Colbert, French statesman and founder of the French Navy who was finance minister to Louis XIV. His financial reforms helped to make France once again a major European power.

1944 Rajiv Gandhi, Prime Minister of India, a former airline pilot who took over on the assassination of his mother, Indira.

ARTS

1780 Jean Auguste Dominique Ingres, French classical painter who studied under David and continued the tradition established by his master.

1809 Oliver Wendell Holmes, US physician, poet, humorist and Dean of Harvard Medical School whose writings include *The Autocrat of the Breakfast Table* (1858).

1862 Maurice (Polydore Marie Bernard) Maeterlinck, Belgian poet and playwright best known for *Pelléas et Mélisande* (1892), and his popular children's play *The Blue Bird* (1908).

1929 Thom(son William) Gunn, English poet who taught English at the University of Berkeley, California, author of *My Sad Captains* (1961).

ENTERTAINMENT

1915 Ingrid Bergman, Swedish actress whose distinguished film career began in the 30s. She starred in films which have become established favourites with each generation including *Casablanca* (1943) *Notorious* (1946), her Oscar-winning *Anastasia* (1956) and

The Inn of the Sixth Happiness (1958). Winner of three Oscars, she was also an accomplished stage actress particularly in the role of St Joan. She died on her 67th birthday of cancer in her London flat.

1923 Sir Richard Attenborough, English film actor, director and producer whose distinguished career as an actor in films such as *In Which We Serve* (1942) and *The Guinea Pig* (1949) led to producing and directing big budget films, such as *A Bridge Too Far* (1977), his Oscar-winning *Gandhi* (1982) and *Cry Freedom* (1985).

1928 Charles Gray, English actor in innumerable television and film parts from Blofeld in the James Bond *Diamonds are Forever* (1971) to providing the voice for the Jack Hawkins's parts after cancer had destroyed his vocal chords.

1938 Elliott Gould (Goldstein), US actor who was nominated for an Oscar in his second film, *Bob & Carol & Ted & Alice* (1968). He also starred in *The Long Goodbye* (1973) and *The Lady Vanishes* (1979).

1949 Richard Gere, US actor who made his mark with *Yanks* and *American Gigolo* (1979).

1958 Lenny Henry, English comedian who established himself in television's *Three of a Kind* before going on to his own *Lenny Henry Show* series and a leading light of the Comic Relief fund-raising epic.

POP

1958 Michael (Joseph) Jackson, US rock megastar who was the youngest member of the Jackson Five with a series of No. 1s in the 70s. His solo career also produced many hits, and his album *Thriller* (1983) became the best selling album of all time together with an award-winning video. More No. 1s followed, including 'Bad' (1987), backed by dynamic videos.

SPORT

1947 James Hunt, English world champion racing driver in 1976 by just one point.

DIED THIS DAY

1671 Edmond Hoyle, English writer of books which codified the rules of card and indoor games, aged 97.

1877 Brigham Young, Mormon leader in Salt Lake City which he founded.

1930 The Reverend William Archibald Spooner who gave the world spoonerisms.

1975 Eamon de Valera, three times Irish Prime Minister and President from 1959–73.

1987 Lee Marvin, US actor who won an Oscar for *Cat Ballou*, of a heart attack.

1989 Sir Peter (Markham) Scott, English naturalist and conservationist, and former chairman of the World Wildlife Fund.

ON THIS DAY

1782 The HMS *Royal George* sank off Spithead while at anchor, with the loss of 900 lives. The man who revolutionized naval signalling and communications, Admiral Richard Kempefelt, was one of those who drowned.

1831 Michael Faraday successfully demonstrated the first electrical transformer at the Royal Institute, London.

1835 John Batman and his associates bought 600,000 acres of land along the northern shores of Port Phillip Bay from the Aborigines and officially established Melbourne which received its name from Lord Melbourne, the British Prime Minister, in 1837.

1842 The Treaty of Nanking was signed by the British and Chinese to end the Opium War.

1885 The first motor cycle was patented by Gottlieb Daimler in Germany.

1895 The Rugby League was formed at a meeting of 21 clubs at the George Hotel, Huddersfield and called the Northern Union. The name Rugby League was only adopted in 1922.

1918 At midnight, over 6,000 British policemen went on strike for the first time, demanding better pay.

1966 The Beatles played their last live concert at Candlestick Park, San Francisco.

1988 Matthew Sadler, 14, from Kent, became Britain's youngest ever international chess master at a tournament in London.

30 AUGUST

BORN THIS DAY

HISTORY

1908 Ernest Rutherford (Baron Rutherford), New Zealand physicist who pioneered modern atomic science at Cambridge. He was awarded the Nobel prize for Chemistry in 1908.

1917 Dennis Healey, former Labour Chancellor of the Exchequer, and skilful photographer.

ARTS

1748 Jacques Louis David, French painter of such masterpieces as *The Rape of the Sabines* (1799). He was an enthusiastic participant in the Revolution, voting for the death of Louis XVI. Napoleon appointed him court painter.

1797 Mary Wollstonecraft Shelley, English author who was the daughter of the early feminist Mary Wollstonecraft and the second wife of the poet Percy Bysshe Shelley. In 1818 her novel *Frankenstein, or the Modern Prometheus* was published and became the best known novel of terror.

1901 John Gunther, US author and journalist who enjoyed success during the 40s and 50s with books such as *Inside USA* (1947) and *Inside Russia Today* (1958).

ENTERTAINMENT

1896 Raymond Massey, Canadian actor who starred in films and stage productions in both the US and Britain. His most famous roles were in *Abe Lincoln in Illinois* both on stage and screen, and as Dr Gillespie in the television series *Dr Kildare*.

1907 Shirley Booth (Thelma Booth Ford), US actress best known for stage and screen performance in *Come Back, Little Sheba* (1950) and the television series *Hazel*.

1908 Fred MacMurray, US actor whose film career goes back to 1934 and includes *The Caine Muntiny* (1954) and *The Apartment* (1960).

SPORT

1943 Jean Claude Killey, French ski champion who won the first World Cup in 1967 and 1968. The same year he won all three gold medals at the Winter Olympics at Grenoble; slalom, giant slalom and downhill.

DIED THIS DAY

30BC Cleopatra, Queen of Egypt, aided by an asp.

1483 Louis XI, King of France responsible for its unification after the Hundred Years War.

1884 Dr James Collis Browne, inventor of Chlorodyne, the famous patent medicine for stomach upsets developed by the good doctor while out in India, where he had plenty of scope to test the remedy on the British troops in his care.

ON THIS DAY

1860 The first trams in Britain began running, operated by the Birkenhead Street Railway.

1862 'Stonewall' Jackson led the Confederates to victory against the Union army at the second Battle of Bull Run in Virginia, during the American Civil War.

1881 The first stereo system was patented by Clement Ader of Germany, for a telephonic broadcasting service, and in 1901, Hubert Cecil Booth patented the vacuum cleaner. The canny Scot had watched a dustblowing machine in action, and so reversed the action.

1933 Air France was formed.

1939 The great evacuation of children from British cities began. With the Second World War four days away, thousands of children were moved out into the country to avoid the anticipated German bombing.

1941 The Germans laid siege to Leningrad. It would last until January 1943.

1963 The 'Hotline' between the US President and the Soviet Premier was established to reduce the risk of an accidental nuclear war.

31 AUGUST

BORN THIS DAY

HISTORY

AD12 Caligula (Gaius Caesar), Roman emperor whose name was Latin for 'Little Boots', a nickname given to him as a child, remembered for his murderous reign.

1569 Jahangir, Mogul emperor who was a heavy drinker and opium eater until his later years, but whose influence encouraged the growth of Persian culture in India.

1880 Wilhelmina (Helena Pauline Maria of Orange-Nassau), Queen of the Netherlands who won international admiration during the Second World War when she was forced to seek refuge in Britain, but continued to encourage Dutch resistance.

ARTS

1885 (Edwin) Dubose Heyward, US author of *Porgy* (1925). With wife Dorothy he dramatized his novel, while Ira Gershwin wrote the lyrics and brother George wrote the music to make what is often described as the first US opera.

ENTERTAINMENT

BEST YEARS Born 1897, Frederic March (Ernest Frederick McIntyre Bickel), US actor who won an Oscar playing the lead in *Dr Jeckyll and Mr Hyde* (1932). Born 1908, William Saroyan, US playwright and novelist of *The Human Comedy* (1943) and the play *The Time of Your Life*, a hit on Broadway in 1939 and a successful film in 1946, starring Frederic March who won his second Oscar for best actor.

1900 Roland Culver, very English actor on both stage and screen, including *The Man Who Loved Redheads* (1955).

1914 Richard Basehart, US actor whose films are as varied as Fellini's *La Strada* (1954) and *Moby Dick* (1956).

1918 Alan Jay Lerner, US librettist and lyricist who worked with Frederick Lowe on seven Broadway musicals including *Brigadoon* (1947), *Paint Your Wagon* (1951) and *My Fair Lady* (1956). The partners worked with André Previn on the film success *Gigi* in 1973.

1928 James Coburn, US actor who seemed to get better as he got older, in films such as *The Internecine Project* (1974) but probably best known for his role in James Bond spoofs starting with *Our Man Flint* (1966).

SCIENCE

1913 Sir Bernard Lovell, English astronomer and first director of the Jodrell Bank Experimental Station in Cheshire, now known as the Nuffield radio Astronomy Laboratories.

POP

1945 Van Morrison, Irish-born lead singer with Them who went solo in 1967 with the song 'Brown-eyed Girl'.

EDUCATION

1870 Maria Montessori, Italian educationist who developed the Montessori system which revolutionized the teaching of young children, encouraging initiative and physical freedom.

SPORT

1889 (William) Bombardier Billy Wells, English heavyweight boxer who revived interest in British boxing with his style and personality, but was floored by his counterpart in France, Georges Carpentier (1.6.1913).

1942 Isao Aoki, leading Japanese golfer.

1944 Clive (Hubert) Lloyd, West Indies cricket captain (1974–85) born in Georgetown, Guyana, who made his test debut in 1966. A great batsman, he scored 202 not out in 120 minutes for the West Indies against Glamorgan, 1976.

1955 Ed(win) Moses, US athlete who took the gold and made a world record at his first Olympics in 1976 in the 400m hurdles which he dominated for over a decade.

1958 Serge Blanco, French international rugby player considered one of the most talented in the world.

DIED THIS DAY

1422 Henry V, King of England, from dysentry while in France. Henry VI acceded to the throne, aged nine months.

1688 John Bunyan, English author of *Pilgrim's Progress*.

1867 Charles Pierre Baudelaire, French poet of *Les Fleurs du mal* (Flowers of Evil) (1857).

1963 Georges Braque, French Cubist painter.

1969 Rocky Marciano, US boxer and unbeaten world heavyweight champion during his reign from 1952–6, killed this day in an aircrash.

1973 John Ford (Sean O'Feeney), US film director of *Stagecoach* (1939).

1986 Henry Moore, major English sculptor.

ON THIS DAY

1888 In the early hours of this morning, in

Bucks Row, Whitechapel Mary Ann 'Polly' Nicholls, 42, a prostitute, was found disembowelled. The murderer had clamped his hand over her mouth before cutting her throat. This was the first of the murders attributed to Jack the Ripper, the most legendary sex killer of them all.

1900 Coca-Cola went on sale in Britain.

1928 The first performance of the Brecht-Weill musical *The Threepenny Opera* was staged in Berlin.

1957 Malaya, later Malaysia, achieved independence, and in 1962, Trinidad and Tobago, former British possessions, became independent.

1962 Chris Bonnington and Ian Clough became the first Britons to conquer the north face of the Eiger.

1972 US swimmer Mark Spitz won five of seven gold medals that he achieved in total at the Munich Olympics, including the 100m and 200m freestyle and the 100m and 200m butterfly.

1989 A brief statement was issued by Buckingham Palace stating that the Princess Royal, Princess Anne, was separating from her husband, Captain Mark Phillips.

THE PAN BOOK OF DATES

SEPTEMBER

All progress is based upon a universal innate desire on the part of every organism to live beyond its income
(Samuel Butler)

1 SEPTEMBER

National day of Libya, commemorating the overthrow of King Idris I by Colonel Gaddafi in 1969.

BORN THIS DAY

HISTORY

1864 Sir Roger David Casement, Irish nationalist and British diplomat. During the First World War he encouraged Irish prisoners of war in Germany in 1914 to form a brigade and take part with him in a Republican uprising. The Germans arranged for a submarine to take them to Ireland, but as they tried to land he was arrested by the British, and later tried and sentenced to death for treason.

1931 Cecil Parkinson, Secretary of State for Energy and close confidante of Prime Minister Margaret Thatcher, whose career was temporarily halted in 1983 when his affair with his secretary Sara Keays became public.

ARTS

1834 Amilcare Ponchielli, Italian composer who composed the opera *La Gioconda* (1876) and its ballet, 'Dance of the Hours'.

1854 Engelbert Humperdinck, German composer of the opera *Hansel and Gretel* (1893).

1875 Edgar Rice Burroughs, US novelist and creator of Tarzan in 1912 in a short story. *Tarzan of the Apes*, the first Tarzan novel, was published in 1914. Burroughs never visited Africa where his stories were set.

ENTERTAINMENT

1898 Marilyn Miller, US actress, dancer and singer who made her name in the Ziegfeld Follies in the 20s and starred in the musical *Sally* (1920), in which she introduced the song 'Look For A Silver Lining', and was the first to sing 'Easter Parade' in the stage production of *As Thousands Cheer* (1933).

POP

1946 Barry Gibb, English-born rock musician, eldest of the Gibb brothers (Maurice and Robin) who formed the Bee Gees in Australia where their parents had emigrated. Barry alone wrote 'Grease' (1978), the title song of the hit musical.

CHAMPS Two great boxers share a birthday. In 1866, 'Gentleman Jim' (James John) Corbett, US heavyweight boxer who became world champion on 7.9.1892 when he knocked out John L. Sullivan. He lost it in 1897 when the Cornish-born Bob Fitzsimmons knocked him out in the 11th. No such fate awaited Rocky Marciano (Rocco Marchegiano), born 1923, US heavyweight boxer and world champion from 23 September 1952 when he knocked out Jersey Joe Walcott and remained undefeated in 49 professional fights, 43 by a knockout. He retired at 32 and was killed in an airplane crash one day before his 46th birthday.

DIED THIS DAY

1159 Adrian IV (Nicholas Breakspear), the only English pope.

1557 Jacques Cartier, French explorer of North America.

1666 Frans Hals, Dutch portrait painter.

1715 Louis XIV, the Sun King, French king who was the longest reigning sovereign in Europe from 1643–1715.

1729 Sir Richard Steele, Irish-born

essayist and founder of the *Tatler* magazine, in Wales.

1963 Guy Burgess, British defector who spied for Russia.

1967 Siegfried (Lorraine) Sassoon, English poet and author, remembered for his sensitive war poems.

ON THIS DAY

1830 Sarah J. Hales published a poem in Boston, on or about this day, entitled 'Mary Had a Little Lamb'. In 1867, it was set to music and became a classic children's nursery rhyme.

1904 In the US Helen Keller, who had become both deaf and blind in infancy, graduated with honours from Radcliffe College.

1920 The state of Lebanon was created by the French, with Beirut as the capital.

1923 A huge earthquake killed over 300,000 in Japan, devastating Tokyo and Yokohama.

1933 H.G. Well's classic science-fiction novel *The Shape of the Things to Come* was published.

1939 Germany invaded Poland to start the Second World War.

1951 Britain's first supermarket opened, the Premier in Earl's Court, London.

1972 Bobby Fischer became the first American world chess champion when he beat Boris Spassky at Reykjavik.

1988 A report published by the New York Health Department stated that 8,064 people had been bitten by dogs in the past year, 1,587 people had been bitten by other people and one person had been attacked by a penguin.

2 SEPTEMBER

BORN THIS DAY

HISTORY

1726 John Howard, English prison reformer who was shocked at the conditions in Bedford jail which he inspected as high sheriff. Not only were conditions unsanitary, but prisoners fees were paid to jailers, instead of salaries. He persuaded Parliament to end many of the abuses.

1914 Lord George Brown, colourful and outspoken British statesman, who was Foreign Secretary (1966–8) during Harold Wilson's Labour government.

ARTS

1938 Michael Hastings, English playwright whose work includes *Gloo-Joo* which won the *Evening Standard* best Comedy award in 1978.

ENTERTAINMENT

1925 Russ Conway (Trevor Stanford), English pianist and entertainer who established himself in the 60s with the Billy Cotton Band Show on television, and had several successful records.

1931 Francis Matthews, English actor best known for lightweight thrillers, from the long-running 'Paul Temple' series to several adapted from Francis Durbridge stories.

SPORT

1952 Jimmy Connors, US tennis player who won his first Wimbledon singles title at age 21 in 1974. The following year he was beaten by Arthur Ashe, and from then on he was often in the finals, but never the winner.

DIED THIS DAY

1645 Lady Alice Lisle, widow of John Lisle, was beheaded. She had been sentenced to death for harbouring a Nonconformist minister, John Hickes, whom she was not aware had fought in the rebel army against King James II.

1834 Thomas Telford, Scottish engineer and canal and bridge builder, who was buried at Westminster Abbey.

1910 Henri Rousseau, French primitive painter known as 'Le Douanier' because of his job as a customs official.

1937 Baron Pierre de Coubertin, founder of the modern Olympics.

1973 J(ohn) R(onald) R(ueul) Tolkien, South African-born English author of *The Lord of the Rings* (1954–5).

1979 Felix Aylmer (Felix Edward Aylmer-Jones), distinguished English stage and screen actor who appeared as Polonius in Olivier's *Hamlet*.

ON THIS DAY

1666 The Great Fire of London started in a bakery in Pudding Lane and spread to the neighbouring warehouse which stored tar barrels, causing a sudden explosion. The fire did five times as much damage as the Blitz, destroying 13,000 buildings in four days.

1858 The song 'The Yellow Rose of Texas', by the anonymous J.K., was copyrighted in New York.

1906 Roald Amundsen completed his sailing round Canada's Northwest Passage.

1923 The Irish Free State held its first elections.

1942 The German SS destroyed the Warsaw Ghetto after several weeks of resistance. With flame throwers and grenades, they flushed out the remaining Jews, leaving 50,000 dead.

1945 As General MacArthur accepted the Japanese surrender on board the aircraft carrier *Missouri* in Tokyo Bay to end the Second World War, Ho Chi Minh became President of the new North Vietnam Republic.

1980 John Arlott, probably the most memorable and distinctive BBC cricket commentator, retired at the end of the Lord's Centenary Match after 35 years of broadcasting.

1987 Philips launched the video version of their compact disc, called CD-video, combining digital sound and high-definition video.

3 SEPTEMBER

BORN THIS DAY

SCIENCE

1728 Matthew Boulton, English engineer who with James Watt invented and manufactured steam engines.

1899 Sir Frank Macfarlane Burnet, Australian immunologist and joint winner of the Nobel prize for Physiology with Peter Medawar (1960) for their discovery of acquired immunological tolerance to foreign tissue transplants.

ENTERTAINMENT

1897 Cecil Parker (Cecil Schwabe), English actor on both stage and screen, whose films include *The Admirable Crichton* (1957) and *The Amorous Prawn* (1962).

1913 Alan Ladd, US actor who played heroic film leads from the 30s until his death in 1964, including those in *This Gun For Hire* (1942) and *Shane* (1953).

1940 Pauline Collins, English actress who appears frequently with her husband John Alderton on both stage and television, including in *Forever Green* (1989). She was nominated for an Oscar as best actress in *Shirley Valentine* (1989).

SPORT

1940 Brian Lochore, former All Black rugby football captain who was one of the leading New Zealand forwards dominating the rugby world.

DIED THIS DAY

1658 Oliver Cromwell, Lord Protector of England, from pneumonia. He was succeeded by his son Richard as Lord Protector.

1883 Ivan Sergeyevich Turgenev, Russian novelist and playwright of *A Month in the Country* (1850).

1948 Eduard Benes, Czechoslovakian President until the Communist takeover in 1948.

1962 e e cummings (Edward Estlin Cummings) US poet who wrote all his verse in lower case letters.

1963 (Frederick) Louis MacNeice, Irish-born English poet and broadcaster.

1969 Ho Chi Minh, president of North Vietnam, after a heart attack during the Vietnam war. His Communist Viet Cong called for a three-day truce to mark the death.

ON THIS DAY

1752 The Gregorian Calendar was introduced into Britain. This day – 3 September by the former Julian Calendar – now became 14 September.

1783 In Paris, Britain recognized US independence with the signing of a treaty, ending the War of Independence.

1916 The first pilot to shoot down a Zeppelin was Captain Leefe Robinson. During a raid on London, his tiny biplane attacked the airship which caught fire and crashed in Hertfordshire. The engagement was watched by thousands on the ground who cheered Leefe Robinson's victory. He was later summoned to see the King at Windsor and awarded the VC. In 1988 his medal was sold at Christie's for £99,000, sent for sale by his niece to raise money for children suffering from leukaemia.

1930 Diedonne Coste and Maurice Bellonte landed in New York after the first non-stop flight from Paris.

1935 On Bonneville Salt Flats, Utah, Malcolm Campbell reached a new world landspeed record of 301.13 m.p.h. in *Bluebird*.

1939 Britain and France declared war on Germany. The Second World War began.

1950 The first world championship of drivers was won by Nino Farina of Italy, which he clinched by winning the Monza Grand Prix.

1966 Captain John Ridgway and Sergeant Chay Blyth of the Parachute Regiment rowed into Inishmore, the isle of Aran in Eire, having crossed the Atlantic in a rowing boat, *English Rose III*. It had taken 91 days.

1967 Sweden changed from driving on the left to the right.

1976 The US spacecraft *Viking 2* landed on Mars and began sending back pictures to earth.

1980 Peter O'Toole opened as *Macbeth* at the Old Vic which proved to be the most successful flop of modern times.

Universally panned by the critics, this Bryan Forbes production played to packed houses with the audience often roaring with laughter at the quirky production.

4 SEPTEMBER

BORN THIS DAY

HISTORY

1736 Robert Raikes, English founder of the Sunday School movement.

ARTS

1824 (Josef) Anton Bruckner, Austrian composer and organist mainly remembered for his religious music.

1892 Darius Milhaud, French composer, best known for his *La Création du Monde* (1923), who was one of the famous Les Six group of leading and influential French composers.

1896 Antonin Artaud, French playwright and director of the Theatre of Cruelty which influenced Beckett.

1905 Mary Renault (Mary Challens), English author whose novels, set in ancient Greece, include *The King Must Die* (1958) and *The Bull From The Sea* (1962).

ENTERTAINMENT

1908 Edward Dmytryk, Canadian film director best known for *Crossfire* (1947) and *The Human Factor* (1975). His career was seriously affected by the Communist witch hunts in Hollywood in the 50s when he was sentenced to a year in prison.

1929 Mitzi Gaynor (Franceska Mitizi Marlene de Charney von Gerber), US actress and dancer, daughter of a Hungarian ballerina, who enjoyed some success in *The Joker is Wild* (1957), opposite Sinatra, but a lot less in *South Pacific* (1958).

1932 Dinsdale Lansden, English stage and television actor who established himself in the comedy series, *Devenish*.

SPORT

1937 Dawn Fraser, Australian swimmer and one of the greatest ever, who won gold medals in three consecutive Olympics, the first woman to perform the feat, from 1956 to 1964. She broke the world 100m freestyle record nine successive times.

1949 Tom Watson, US golfer who won the British Open five times; in 1982, he won the US Masters as well, only the fifth golfer ever to achieve this feat.

DIED THIS DAY

1907 Edvard (Hagerup) Grieg, Norwegian composer.

1963 Robert Schuman, former French Prime Minister and Foreign Minister.

1965 Albert Schweitzer, French medical missionary, organist and Nobel prize winner. He died in Lambaréné in the Gabon, where he had established his hospital, and was buried close by.

1989 Georges Simenon (Sim), Belgian novelist, creator of Maigret. He wrote over 400 books with world sale of over 500 million.

ON THIS DAY

1733 The first lioness in Britain died in the Tower of London of old age. She had produced a litter of cubs each year for several years and was looked after by the Keeper of the Lion Office.

1870 The Emperor Napoleon III, Bonaparte's nephew, was deposed and the Third republic was proclaimed.

1871 New York municipal government at Tammany Hall was accused of widespread corruption in what was known as the Tammany Frauds.

1893 Beatrix Potter sent an illustrated note to Noel Moore, aged five, son of her governess, in which for the first time she introduced Peter Rabbit, Squirrel Nutkin, Flopsy, Mopsy and Cottontail.

1909 The first Boy Scout rally was held at Crystal Palace, London.

1912 The first accident on the London Underground took place on the Piccadilly Line. 22 were injured when two trains collided.

1948 Queen Wilhelmina of the Netherlands abdicated in favour of her daughter Juliana.

1955 Kenneth Kendall and Richard Baker became Britain's first television newsreaders.

1957 Governor Orval Faubus called out Arkansas National Guard to turn away nine black students trying to enter the formerly whites-only Central High School. It provoked President Eisenhower to send in troops of the 101st Airborne division to enforce the law.

1962 The Beatles began their first recording session at EMI's famous Abbey Road studios, London with their producer, George Martin.

1964 The Forth Road Bridge in Scotland, the longest bridge in Europe, was opened.

1970 Natalia Makarova of the Kirov Ballet defected to the West.

1988 The first known attempt to smuggle drugs into Britain using a helicopter failed when Customs officers swooped on the aircraft as it landed from Holland.

5 SEPTEMBER

BORN THIS DAY

HISTORY

1638 Louis XIV, King of France, called the Sun King because of the prestige and patronage his reign brought. At his sumptuous palace at Versailles, he established himself as the greatest of the French kings.

1847 Jesse (Woodson) James, US outlaw who with his elder brother Frank, led the former Quantrill gang (a one-time Confederate guerilla unit that had descended to looting and lawlessness). They carried out daylight bank robberies which usually included murder, and were the first to stage train robberies. Two days after his 29th birthday, on 7 September 1876, eight gang members were killed trying to rob the First National Bank at Northfield, but both he and Frank escaped. A reward of $10,000 dead or alive was offered, enough to tempt a new gang member, Robert Ford, to put a bullet in the back of Jesse's head (3.4.1882). Frank died of heart disease, aged 73.

ARTS

1791 Giacomo Meyerbeer (Jakob Liebmann Beer), German composer best known for his operas *Les Huguenots* (1836) and *L'Africaine* (1864).

1831 Victorien Sardou, French playwright who wrote *Fedora* (1882), which starred Sarah Bernhardt, and *La Tosca* (1887) which was used by Puccini for his opera.

1905 Arthur Koestler, author who was born in Budapest, educated in Vienna and settled in England. His work includes *Darkness at Noon* (1940). Interested in the paranormal, he endowed the first seat for paranormal studies at Edinburgh University.

1916 Frank (Garvin) Yerby, US novelist who wrote *The Foxes of Harrow* (1946).

1937 Dick Clement, English television scriptwriter and director who wrote several now-classic comedy series with Ian La Fresnais, including *The Likely Lads* and *Porridge*.

ENTERTAINMENT

1902 Darryl F(rancis) Zanuck, US film producer and screenwriter who wrote scripts for dog star, Rin Tin Tin, but survived that to eventually become a major executive producer responsible for *Jesse James* (1939), with whom he shares his birthday, *All About Eve* (1950) and *The Longest Day* (1962).

1929 Bob Newhart, US television comedian and actor who starred in the long-running *The Bob Newhart Show* shown in many countries, and his subsequent *Newhart*.

1934 (Frederick) Russell Harty, English journalist, broadcaster and chat show host who claimed he would be remembered for being assaulted on screen by singer Grace Jones, although his programme on Dali won an international Emmy. His northern roots dictated his viewpoint and gave a distinctive quality to much of his work.

1940 Raquel Welch (Racquel Tejada), US actress who exploited her physical assets to break into films including *One Million Years BC* (1966) and *The Prince and the Pauper* (1977).

POP

1946 Freddy Mercury (Frederick Bulsara), born in Zanzibar, lead singer with the pop group Queen. This former British art student brought much of the style to the group and wrote some of its biggest hits including 'Bohemian Rhapsody' which was No. 1 in the UK charts for nine weeks in December 1975 and January 1976.

SPORT

1826 John Wisden, English cricketer and compiler of cricket records, which he first published as *Wisden's Cricketers' Almanac* in 1864 and which has become cricket's 'Bible'.

DIED THIS DAY

1569 Pieter Brueghel the Elder, Flemish painter of humorous peasant pictures and landscapes.

1969 Josh White, US blues singer.

1982 Group Captain Sir Douglas Robert Bader, British fighter pilot who lost both legs. He later devoted himself to the disabled.

ON THIS DAY

1800 French troops occupying Malta surrendered to the British.

1920 Roscoe 'Fatty' Arbuckle, one of the most lovable of the silent comedians, was alleged to have sexually assaulted Virginia Rappe at a wild drinking party he threw in a San Francisco hotel. The starlet died a few days later of a ruptured bladder said to have been caused by the comedian who weighed around 23 stone (just over 320 lbs). Arbuckle was charged with manslaughter and on his third retrial was acquitted, but by then the publicity surrounding the case had ruined his career.

1922 US aviator James Doolittle made the first US coast-to-coast flight in 21 hours 19 minutes.

1951 Little Mo – 16-year-old US tennis player Maureen Connolly – became the youngest-ever winner of the US Tennis Championships.

1963 Christine Keeler, one of the girls at the centre of the Profumo scandal, was arrested and charged with perjury.

1969 ITV, Britain's commercial television network, began broadcasting in colour.

1972 Members of the Palestinian Black September movement broke into the Olympic Village in Munich and attacked the Israeli building with submachine-guns. A coach and one athlete were shot dead and another nine taken hostage. The German authorities allowed a bus to take the gunmen and their hostages to the airport. A special squad failed to rescue the Israelis at the airport and all nine were killed. Four Arabs and one German policeman were shot dead, and three gunmen were captured.

1980 The world's longest road tunnel, the St Gotthard, was opened running ten miles from Goschenen to Airolo, Switzerland.

1987 *No Sex Please – We're British* closed after 6,671 performances over 16 years – the longest running comedy in the world. (Opened 3.6.1971.)

6 SEPTEMBER

BORN THIS DAY

HISTORY

1757 Marquis de Lafayette, French statesman and soldier who fought with the American colonists against the British in the War of Independence. During the French Revolution, he became a major figure presenting his famous Declaration of the Rights of Man to the Assembly on 11.7.1789.

1888 Joseph (Patrick) Kennedy, US founder with his wife Rose of the dynasty that spawned the first Catholic US president, an attorney-general and two senators. Joseph made his fortune in banking, and was ambassador to Britain (1937–40). He is remembered for saying in 1940 that Britain had no chance of surviving Hitler's aggression.

1915 Franz Josef Strauss, Premier of Bavaria (1978–88), who also held ministerial posts in the German parliament. His otherwise brilliant career was tainted by financial scandals which were never proved and his sympathies for certain right-wing governments in South America and for the South African regime.

ENTERTAINMENT

1899 Billy Rose (William Samuel Rosenberg), US impresario and composer of songs such as 'It's Only A Paper Moon' and 'Me and My Shadow' plus 400 others; his show successes including *Carmen Jones* (1943) and his nightclubs, such as the famous Diamond Horseshoe, were equally successful ventures. One of his marriages was to leading lady Fanny Brice.

1932 Bernie Winters, English comedian

who was a double act with older brother Mike before they split up in 1978, and who seems to have done better as a solo performer, including playing Bud Flanagan in *Bud 'n' Ches* on television.

1942 Britt Ekland (Britt Marie Eklund), Swedish actress and former model, best known as the former Mrs Peter Sellers, with whom she appeared in *The Bobo* (1967). She was also in *The Man With the Golden Gun* (1974) and other films.

SCIENCE

1766 John Dalton, English chemist and physicist who was one of the founders of modern physical science with his work developing the theory of atomic matter.

1876 John James Rickard Macleod, Scottish physiologist and co-discoverer of insulin independently of Sir Frederick Banting and Charles Best, with whom he shared the 1923 Nobel prize for Medicine.

1941 Monica Mason, South African born senior principal dancer with the Royal Ballet.

POP

1940 Jackie Trent, English singer, wife of composer Tony Hatch with whom she also formed a writing and singing partnership in the 60s which earned them the title Mr and Mrs Music. Their successes include theme music for the soaps, *Crossroads* (now ended) and the Australian *Neighbours*.

1947 Roger Waters, English bassist and founding member of Pink Floyd, and one of the originators of the film *The Wall* (1982).

DIED THIS DAY

1566 Suleiman I the Magnificent, known as the Lawgiver, he was the Ottoman ruler under whom the Ottoman Empire achieved its peak.

1952 Gertrude Lawrence, English actress and singer, during the run of *The King and I* on Broadway.

1959 Kay Kendall (Justine McCarthy), English actress in *Genevieve* (1953) and other comedies including *Once More With Feeling* (1955) with husband Rex Harrison, from leukaemia, aged 33.

ON THIS DAY

1522 After three years, under the command of Juan del Cano, the *Vittoria* sailed into San Lucar harbour in Spain with 17 surviving crew members having completed the first circumnavigation of the world. The great navigator, Ferdinand Magellan had been in command until they reached the island of Mactan in the Philippines where he was killed in a battle. Five ships had set out, only one returned (20.9.1519).

1666 The Great Fire of London was finally extinguished (started 2.9.1666.)

1852 The first free lending library in Britain opened in Manchester.

1879 The first British telephone exchange opened in Lombard Street, London.

1880 England played the Australians at The Oval, London, in the first cricket test match. There was another cricketing first on this day in 1776, when three stumps were used for the first time for a match between Coulsdon and Chertsey in Surrey.

1907 The *Lusitania* embarked on her maiden voyage to New York, arriving on the 13th in a record five days averaging 23 knots.

UNHAPPY LANDINGS In 1936, British flyer Beryl Markham flew solo across the Atlantic and crash-landed at Cape Breton Island, Nova Scotia; she was only superficially hurt. In 1952, 26 died at the Farnborough Airshow when a prototype de Havilland jet fighter exploded while breaking the sound barrier and debris fell on to the crowd below. In 1970, Palestinians hijacked three passenger jets – a British, a US and a Swiss and forced them to fly to Jordan. There, the crews and passengers were released and the aircraft blown up six days later (12.9.1970). In 1983, the Soviets shot down a Korean Airlines Boeing 747 flight 007 which had flown into its sensitive airspace despite warnings. All 269 people on board died.

1941 Nazi Germany made the wearing of the hated yellow Star of David badges compulsory for all its Jewish citizens.

1966 Dr Hendrik Frensch Verwoerd, South African Prime Minister, was stabbed to death with a stiletto by a white parliamentary messenger. He was succeeded by Johannes Balthazar Vorster who was sworn in as Prime Minster on the 13th.

1987 Indian military scientists announced they had successfully devised a long-life chapati, using a preservative which keeps the unleavened bread fresh for six months.

1987 For the first time since 1315, the historic Venice regatta was held without the city's 230 gondoliers, who were on strike as a protest against the damage caused to the city fabric by powerboats.

1988 The youngest person to swim the English Channel, 11-year-old Thomas Gregory from London, swam from France to Dover in 12 hours.

1989 A computer error resulted in 41,000 Parisians receiving letters charging them with murder, extortion and organized prostitution instead of traffic fines.

7 SEPTEMBER

The National Day of Brazil: on this day 1822, it declared itself independent from Portugal with Pedro I as its emperor.

BORN THIS DAY

HISTORY

1533 Elizabeth I, Queen of England 1558–1603 who was the daughter of Anne Boleyn and Henry VIII. The reign of the Virgin Queen, as she was called because she never married, saw a flowering of English endeavours in all fields from voyages of discovery to the theatre of Shakespeare.

1735 Thomas Coutts, Scottish banker, son of a wealthy merchant, who founded his London banking house with his brother James.

1815 John McDouall Stuart, Scottish-born explorer of Australia who made six expeditions into the interior.

1836 Sir Henry Campbell-Bannerman, Scottish Liberal statesman who became British Prime Minister (1905–8).

1895 Lt-Gen Sir Brian (Gwynne) Horrocks, English soldier and writer who served in both World Wars.

1917 Group Captain (Geoffrey) Leonard Cheshire, British airman who won the VC in the Second World War. He founded the Cheshire Foundation Home for the Incurably Sick in 1948 with his wife Sue Ryder.

1930 King Baudouin I of the Belgians, (1951–)

ARTS

1726 François André Philidor, French composer of popular operas including *Tom Jones* (1765), who was also an outstanding chess player. He came to England where he published a book on the game and received a pension from the London Chess Club.

1860 (Anna Mary Robertson) 'Grandma' Moses, US primitive painter, so nicknamed because she was 78 before she took up painting professionally.

1887 Dame Edith Sitwell, English poet and formidable eccentric best remembered for *Façade* (1923) which Walton set to music.

1932 Malcolm (Stanley) Bradbury, English author of *Eating People is Wrong* (1959) and *The History Man* (1975), who is Professor of American Studies at the University of East Anglia.

ENTERTAINMENT

1909 Elia Kazan (Elia Kazanjoglou), US stage and film director and writer, born in Turkey who emigrated with his Greek parents to the US. He became a leading Broadway director with *A Streetcar Named Desire* (1947) and *Death of a Salesman* (1949), and co-founded the Actors Studio which trained stars such as Brando, who starred in Kazan's Oscar-winning *On the Waterfront* (1954). He also directed James Dean's first film, *East of Eden* (1955).

1913 Anthony Quayle, English actor who specialized in Shakespearian roles on stage. He was the director of the Shakespeare Memorial Theatre 1948–56, and has played a variety of roles in films including Cardinal Wolsey in *Anne of the Thousand Days* (1969) which won him an Oscar nomination, and *The Guns of Navarone* (1961) and *The Eagle Has Landed* (1976).

1923 Peter Lawford, English actor who made a career in Hollywood and married Patricia Kennedy, the US President's sister. His films include *Oceans 11* (1960).

INVENTION

1677 Stephen Hales, English botanist and inventor who was the first to measure blood pressure. He invented a ventilator to bring fresh air into prisons and ships.

JAZZ

1929 (Theodore Walter) Sonny Rollins, US saxophonist and composer of the now-popular calypso, 'Don't Stop the Carnival', although most of the work which established him as a major musician was improvisation.

POP

1936 Buddy Holly (Charles Hardin Holley), US rock singer and guitarist who in his short career – he was killed in an aircrash aged 23 (3.2.1959) – produced classic hits including 'That'll Be the Day', 'Peggy Sue' and 'Oh Boy'.

DIED THIS DAY

1548 Catherine Parr, Henry VIII's sixth wife, in childbirth on the same day that his daughter Elizabeth (by Anne Boleyn) celebrated her 15th birthday.

1910 William Holman Hunt, English Pre-Raphaelite painter.

1956 C(harles) B(urgess) Fry, English cricketer, footballer, rugby player, athlete and journalist.

1978 Keith Moon, English rock drummer

with the Who, in his London flat from an overdose of drugs.

1981 Christy Brown, Irish novelist of the autobiographical *Down All Our Days* which he wrote with the toes of one foot. Cerebral palsy from birth left him severely handicapped, but he refused to allow his disabilities to dampen his creative urge.

ON THIS DAY

1812 Napoleon's forces marching to Moscow defeated the Russians at the Battle of Borodino, 70 miles west of the city.

1838 On a wild, stormy night on the cruel sea, the small steamship *Forfarshire* struck rocks near the Longstone Lighthouse on Farne Islands off the Northumberland coast. The lighthouse-keeper's daughter, Grace Darling, rowed a mile in a small boat to rescue four men and a woman, and became a British heroine and a legend.

1892 'Gentleman Jim' Corbett beat John L. Sullivan in 21 rounds at New Orleans to become the first world heavyweight champion under the Queensberry Rules, which included the introduction of gloves and three-minute rounds.

1895 The first Rugby league football matches were played under the Northern Union rules.

1901 The Boxer Rising in China ended with the signing of the Peace of Peking.

1940 From this day to 2 November 1940 London was blitzed every night by German bombers.

1943 Italy surrendered to the Allies during the Second World War.

1973 Jackie Stewart, the second Scot to become world champion racing driver, won for a third year.

1986 Bishop Desmond Tutu was enthroned as Archbishop of Capetown, the first black head of South African Anglicans.

8 SEPTEMBER

The Feast day of the Blessed Virgin Mary, observed in the West since AD600.

BORN THIS DAY

HISTORY

1157 Richard I, King of England, known as *Coeur de Lion* (the Lion Heart), who set out on a crusade in 1190 which ended with a three-year peace with Saladin.

1901 Dr Hendrik Frensch Verwoerd, born in Holland, South African Prime Minister 1958–66 who instituted the country's policy of racial separation or apartheid. South Africa became a republic during his period in office. He was stabbed to death in the parliamentary chamber two days before his 65th birthday.

ARTS

1830 Frédéric Mistral, French poet who led the revival of the Provençal language and literature which won him a Nobel prize in 1905.

1841 Antonin Dvořak, Czech composer best known for his *Slavonic Dances* and his enduringly popular *From the New World* Symphony, which he wrote while a director of the National Conservatory in New York in 1891.

1873 Alfred Jarry, French playwright who, aged 23, created *Ubu Roi* (1896), the first production of the Theatre of the Absurd, which caused a sensation

(10.12.1896). His three 'Ubu' plays were revived in a composite production by the French producer and director, Jean-Louis Barrault who was also born this day.

1886 Siegfried (Lorraine) Sassoon, English poet and author of autobiographical novels; *Memoirs of an Infantry Officer* (1930) expresses his horror of war, which he experienced at first hand in France during the First World War. He won the Military Cross for bravery.

1914 Sir Denys Lasdun, leading British architect who designed the National Theatre.

1931 Jack Rosenthal, English playwright, best known for his television plays including *The Barmitzvah Boy*, also adapted as a musical, and his successful series *London's Burning*, set in a London fire station.

1933 Michael Frayn, English humorist and playwright of biting comedies including the highly-successful *Noises Off* (1982).

1934 Sir Peter Maxwell Davies, British composer and conductor who specialized in music for the theatre as well as opera, including *Taverner* (1972).

ENTERTAINMENT

1910 Jean-Louis Barrault, French actor and director. He was director of the Comédie-Française 1940–6, and his films include *Les Enfants du Paradis* (1944) and *La Ronde* (1950).

ONCE A GOON... Two British funny men who were both involved in the changing face of British comedy and both members of the legendary Goons also share a birthday. Born 1921, Sir Harry Secombe, Welsh-born comedian and singer who also played Pickwick in the 1963 musical version of the same name; it included the song 'If I ruled the World', which he made his own. Born 1925, Peter (Richard Henry) Sellers, English actor who proved he was not only wonderful as a comedian with a variety of zany voices, but also capable of sustaining many dramatic roles, demonstrated in the films *Dr Strangelove* (1964) and *Being There* (1979). However his comedies will always be best remembered, in particular the many Pink Panther films with his manic performances as Inspector Clouseau.

1954 Anne Diamond, English television presenter.

DIED THIS DAY

1560 Amy Robsart, wife of the Earl of Leicester, from a fall down the great staircase at Cumnor Place which broke her neck. It was suspected that she was pushed, for soon after the Earl became an active suitor to Queen Elizabeth, although he failed to become her consort.

1784 Ann Lee, English-born leader of the Shakers.

1853 George Bradshaw, English publisher of the first railway guides.

1933 King Faisal I of Iraq.

1949 Richard (Georg) Strauss, German composer of *Der Rosenkavalier* (1911).

1954 André Derain, French Post-Impressionist painter.

1979 Jean Seberg, US actress driven to suicide by FBI harassment and smears because she supported the Black Panthers.

ON THIS DAY

1664 The small Dutch colony of New

Amsterdam under Governor Peter Stuyvesant surrendered to the British fleet which sailed into the harbour. In 1669 the British renamed the place New York after the Duke of York.

1886 Public diggings for gold were permitted so thousands flocked to the Witwatersrand, where a town sprang up, founded this day as Johannesburg. It became South Africa's largest city.

1888 The first English Football league matches were played.

1935 US Senator Huey Long of Louisana, who behaved like a despot, was shot by a member of a group opposed to him. The assassin was shot dead by the Senator's bodyguards, but Long died on the 10th.

1944 The first V2 'flying bombs' hit Britain, killing three people in Chiswick, west London.

1945 General Tojo, Prime Minister of Japan at the time of Pearl Harbor, tried to commit suicide by shooting himself rather than face trial as a war criminal. US medics were able to treat him and ensure he stood trial.

1968 Britain's Virginia Wade beat Billie Jean King to win the first US Open Tennis Championships.

1974 President Ford pardoned Nixon for his part in the Watergate affair.

9 SEPTEMBER

BORN THIS DAY

HISTORY

1585 Cardinal de Richelieu, French statesman and Louis XIII's Chief Minister from 1624, who crushed all opposition to the monarchy.

1754 William Bligh, English captain of the *Bounty* who sailed around the world on Cook's second voyage before taking command of his own ship in 1787, sailing for Tahiti to collect plants of the breadfruit tree. The infamous mutiny (28.4.1789) was not the end of his career; he became Governor of New South Wales in 1805.

ARTS

1873 Max Reinhardt (Goldman), leading Austrian theatre and film director who influenced many of the European actors and directors who went to Hollywood in the 30s including Preminger and Marlene Dietrich.

1877 James (Evershed) Agate, influential English theatre critic from the 20s right into the 40s, mainly writing reviews for the *Sunday Times* and the BBC.

1900 James Hilton, English novelist who wrote *Goodbye, Mr Chips* and *Lost Horizon*, both during 1933–4.

1908 Cesare Pavese, Italian poet and novelist who was considered the most important of his time. He took a strong anti-fascist stand, which led to his arrest and imprisonment in 1935. His work includes *The Moon and Bonfires* (1950).

ENTERTAINMENT

1920 Michael Aldridge, English character actor on stage and television who plays the dotty retired schoolmaster-inventor in *The Last of the Summer Wine*.

1935 Chaim Topol, Israeli stage and screen actor who played the lead in *Fiddler on the Roof* at Her Majesty's, London and won an Oscar for the film version.

SCIENCE

1737 Luigi Galvani, Italian physiologist who discovered animal electricity or galvanic electricity produced by the contractions of dead frogs legs connected to different metals, and opened the way for Volta to develop the electric battery.

POP

1941 Otis Redding, US songwriter and singer of 'Try A Little Tenderness' and 'Sittin' on the Dock of the Bay'.

SPORT

1938 Richard Sharpe, former England and British Lions rugby footballer.

1949 John Curry, Britain's first skating superstar who enhanced the sport by introducing a balletic quality. In the first three months of 1976 he won the European mens' single title, gold at the winter Olympics (the first medal of any sort Britain had ever won in this event) and the World Championships in Stockholm.

DIED THIS DAY

1087 William the Conqueror, in France, from injuries sustained when his horse stumbled.

1583 Sir Humphrey Gilbert, English explorer who established a colony on Newfoundland, drowned while on his way home to England when the frigate *Squirrel* sank off the Azores with all on board.

1901 Henri (Marie Raymond) Toulouse-Lautrec (-Monfa), French painter and lithographer, from a paralytic stroke brought on by venereal disease.

1976 Mao Tse-tung, Chinese leader who established Communist China.

ON THIS DAY

1513 James IV, King of Scotland, died at the Battle of Flodden Field, Northumberland when English troops under the Earl of Surrey defeated his troops.

1835 Modern local government came into being when the British Municipal Corporations Act came into force.

1850 California became the 31st state of the Union.

1911 The first airmail service in Britain began between Hendon and Windsor.

1948 North Korea proclaimed its independence.

1958 Race riots began in London's Notting Hill Gate. Television crews were accused of encouraging the rioting by staging reconstructions of events in the streets.

1963 Jim Clark of Scotland became the world's youngest motor racing champion at 27, driving Colin Chapman's Lotus.

1970 Palestinians tried to hijack an El Al flight but were overpowered by security guards. The plane landed at Heathrow and the Israelis reluctantly handed over the failed hijackers including Leila Khaled.

1971 Geoffrey Jackson, 'our man in Uruguay' was released by the Tupamaros who had kidnapped him eight months previously.

1971 Inmates at New York's Attica Jail took 32 guards hostage. It ended in a bloody shoot out that left altogether 42 hostages and inmates dead.

1975 Martina Navratilova, an 18-year-old Czech tennis player, defected to the West and asked the US for political asylum.

10 SEPTEMBER

BORN THIS DAY

HISTORY

1771 Mungo Park, Scottish surgeon and explorer of the true course of the Niger in Africa. His first expedition made him famous, but his second led to his death.

1855 Robert Koldewey, German archaeologist who discovered Babylon which was thought by some to be mythical. He made expeditions to southern Iraq where he began digging work which carried on with 200 workers for 18 years. He discovered the foundations of the Tower of Babel.

1914 Lord (Terence) O'Neill of the Maine, former Northern Ireland prime minister.

ARTS

1727 Giovanni Domenico Tiepolo, Italian Rococo painter and engraver who is famed for his historical and allegorical church fresco painting.

1753 Sir John Soane, English neoclassical architect who built the Bank of England (though not much of his work remains) and many fine country homes.

1903 Cyril (Vernon) Connolly, English author and critic who wrote *The Unquiet Grave* (1945).

1926 Beryl Cook, English painter of vibrantly coloured, candid pictures often varnished with gentle humour.

ENTERTAINMENT

1914 Robert Wise, US film director whose productions include the multi-Oscar-winning *West Side Story* (1961) and *Star Trek – the Motion Picture* (1979).

POP

1939 David Hamilton (David Pilditch), British DJ and presenter on both radio and television.

1945 José Feliciano, blind Spanish guitarist and ballad singer who created a stir in 1968 with his controversial recording of 'The Star-spangled Banner'.

1957 Siobhan Fahey, Irish pop singer and member of the all-girl Bananarama.

SPORT

1929 Arnold Palmer, US champion golfer, probably the most exciting the sport has ever known, with four US Masters, two British Opens and the US and Spanish Opens.

DIED THIS DAY

1938 Charles Cruft, English founder of the famous dog show that bears his name, formerly general manager of the Spratts dog-biscuit company. He organized his first dog show in 1886.

1983 Balthazar Johannes Vorster, former Prime Minister of South Africa who resigned over misuse of public funds in the so-called Muldergate Affair.

ON THIS DAY

1894 London taxi driver George Smith became the first person to be convicted for drunken driving while in charge of an electric cab in Bond Street. He was fined 20s (£1).

1942 The RAF dropped 100,000 bombs on Dusseldorf in a single raid.

1945 Vidkun Quisling who collaborated with the Germans while he was Premier of Norway during the Second World War, was sentenced to death (24.10.1945).

1962 Australian Rod Laver won the US Tennis Championships to complete the Grand Slam.

1981 Picasso's *Guernica* returned to Spain after 40 years custodianship in the US. Picasso refused to allow the painting to be shown in Spain until the restoration of democracy.

1987 A 35-year-old ban on stage hypnotists in London was lifted by the Westminster Council despite protests from doctors. Although hypnotist Andrew Newton was permitted to perform, he was not allowed to demonstrate regression – taking hypnotized people back to their childhood.

1989 Hungary opened its border to the West allowing thousands of East German refugees to leave, much to the anger of the East German government.

11 SEPTEMBER

BORN THIS DAY

HISTORY

1917 Ferdinand Marcos, former president of the Philippines who was deposed by Cory Aquino, ending a rule that was conspicuous for its corruption and his wife Imelda's extravagances.

ARTS

1700 James Thompson, Scottish poet who wrote 'Rule Britannia'.

1862 O. Henry (William Sydney Porter), US short-story writer of contrived stories with a twist in the tale. He made an impact with his first book, *Cabbages and Kings* (1904).

1885 D(avid) H(erbert) Lawrence, English coal miner's son who became one of the most controversial novelists of the 20th century with his examination of human sexuality and social conditions in industrial society with the autobiographical *Sons and Lovers* (1913), *Women in Love* (1916) and the previously banned *Lady Chatterley's Lover* (1928).

1917 Jessica Mitford, English author, one of the famous four sisters, who wrote *Hons and Rebels* (1960) and *The American Way of Death* (1963).

ENTERTAINMENT

1917 Herbert Lom (Herbert Charles Angelo Kuchacevich ze Schluderpacheru), actor born in Prague who came to train with the Old Vic in 1939. His films include *War and Peace* (1956) and, in contrast, the Pink Panther films with Peter Sellers.

SPORT

1950 Barry Sheene, British motor cycling champion.

1949 Roger Uttley, former England and British Lions rugby footballer.

DIED THIS DAY

1948 Mohammed Ali Jinnah, first Governor of Pakistan.

1950 Field-Marshal Jan Christian Smuts, soldier, founder of the United Party and twice Prime Minister of South Africa (1919–24, 1939–48).

1971 Nikita Kruschev, former Soviet Premier, in obscurity.

1987 Al Read, English comedian who began his career entertaining customers of the family sausage and pie manufacturing business. He developed the art of the monologue on both radio and stage, but was less successful on television. He gave the nation such catch phrases as

'Right, monkey' and 'You'll be lucky'.

1988 (Charles) Roger Hargreaves, English creator of the now-classic Mr Men and Little Miss characters which he first published in 1972 and have since sold in excess of 85 million copies worldwide.

1987 Peter Tosh (Winston Hubert McIntosh), Jamaican reggae star, when three armed robbers burst into his home and shot him.

ON THIS DAY

1777 At the Battle of Brandywine Creek in the American War of Independence, the British, commanded by General Howe, defeated the American troops led by George Washington.

1841 The commuter age began early for the south-east of England when the London to Brighton commuter express train began regular service taking just 105 minutes.

1895 The FA Cup was stolen from football outfitters William Shillcock in Birmingham. Only 68 years later (1963) did an 83-year-old man confess that he had melted it down to make counterfeit half-crown coins.

1914 W.C. Handy published his 'St Louis Blues' which has since been recorded almost 100 separate times.

1915 The first British Women's Institute was opened at Llanfairpwllgwyngyllgogerychwyrndrobwllllantysiliogogogoch, Anglesey, Wales.

1951 The first performance of Stravinsky's *The Rakes Progress* took place in Venice. The libretto was by W.H. Auden.

1973 A military junta with US support overthrew the elected government of Chile. President Salvador Allende was said to have shot himself, but few believed he was not assassinated.

1978 Bulgarian defector Georgi Markov was killed in London, stabbed by a poisoned umbrella point wielded by an unknown Bulgarian secret agent. The unidentified poison brought on a coma and he died on the 15th.

1987 Four men were arrested and charged with plotting to steal a £25,000 dolphin from the Marineland Oceanarium in Morecambe, Lancashire.

12 SEPTEMBER

BORN THIS DAY

HISTORY

1852 Herbert Henry Asquith, British Liberal Prime Minister who had Lloyd-George as his Chancellor of the Exchequer. He put through radical changes and introduced old age pensions.

ARTS

1880 H(enry) L(ouis) Mencken, US essayist and critic who wrote *The American Language* (1918).

1907 Louis MacNeice, poet, playwright and broadcaster, in Belfast. He was a member of the Oxford Group, with Auden, C. Day Lewis and Spender, which was determined to write socially committed poetry. He also wrote and produced plays for the BBC including the verse play *The Dark Tower* (1947) with music by Benjamin Britten.

1917 Han Suyin, doctor and author of *A Many-splendoured Thing*. Born of a Belgian mother and a Chinese father, she was educated in Brussels and London, then worked as a doctor in Hong Kong where she set this her most successful novel, later a successful film.

Other novels include *Till Morning Comes*.

ENTERTAINMENT

1888 Maurice Chevalier, legendary French entertainer and actor who began as an acrobat, and at 21 became Mistinguett's partner at the *Folies Bergère*. He also appeared in European and Hollywood films including *Gigi* (1958) singing 'Thank Heavens for Little Girls', and in *Can Can* (1960).

1931 Ian Holm (Cuthbert), English actor who concentrated on the stage until the late 60s when he gave an award-winning performance in the film *The Bofors Gun* (1968). In 1970 he played Nelson in the London production of *Bequest to the Nation*. Other films include *Alien* (1979).

INVENTION

1812 Richard Marsh Hoe, English-born US inventor of the rotary printing press which he based and greatly improved on other patents including the English-imported Napier printing press.

1818 Richard Jordan Gatling, US inventor of the Gatling gun, a crank-operated multi-barrelled gun which he patented in 1862.

SPORT

1913 (John Cleveland) Jesse Owens, US track and field athlete who caused a sensation at the Berlin Olympics in 1936 when Hitler's show of Aryan superiority was badly dented by the black athlete winning four gold medals. Hitler, who had shaken the hands of other winners, left the stadium during the medal presentations.

1937 Wesley Hall, West Indian cricketer and penetrating fast bowler.

DIED THIS DAY

1733 François Couperin, one of a family of distinguished French musicians and composers, he was known as 'le Grand' who taught and composed for the harpsichord.

1869 Dr Peter Mark Roget, compiler of his *Thesaurus*.

1972 William Boyd, US actor who played a sanitized Hopalong Cassidy in a series of Hollywood westerns.

1977 Steve Biko, South African Black Consciousness movement leader, in police custody six days after his detention. International protests and demonstrations erupted, and another martyr was added to the long list of black civil rights leaders and supporters who have mysteriously died while in the custody of South African police.

ON THIS DAY

1878 Cleopatra's Needle, the obelisk of Thothmes III, standing almost 69 feet high, was erected on London's Thames Embankment.

WEDDING BELLS In 1908 Winston Churchill married Clementine Hozier, and in 1953, John F. Kennedy married Jacqueline Lee Bouvier in Newport, Rhode Island.

1910 The Los Angeles Police Department appointed the world's first policewoman, former social worker Mrs Alice Stebbins Wells.

1935 US multimillionaire Howard Hughes achieved the first of several aviation records he established before going into self-enforced seclusion. He flew a plane of his own design at 352.46 m.p.h.

1936 Fred Perry, British tennis champion, beat Donald Budge to become the first non-US winner of the US Tennis Championships.

1953 Nikita Kruschev was elected First Secretary of the Soviet Communist Party.

1960 MOT vehicle testing came into force in Britain for all cars over two years old.

1970 Concorde landed at Heathrow for the first time to a barrage of complaints about noise.

1972 In the Cod War, Icelandic gunboats sank two British trawlers.

1974 Haile Selassie of Ethiopia, the Lion of Judah, was deposed by a military coup.

1987 Reference Point, with US jockey Steve Cauthen, won the St Leger and set a new record for trainer Henry Cecil of 147 wins in a season, ending John Day's of 146 wins in 1867. Day was former champion jockey Lester Piggott's great great great grandfather.

13 SEPTEMBER

BORN THIS DAY

HISTORY

1860 John J(oseph) Pershing, US general who commanded the US Expeditionary Force in Europe which made a major contribution to the Allied victory in the First World War. A rigid disciplinarian, he was nicknamed 'Black Jack'.

CHOCOLATE MEN This day has several connections with chocolate, starting in 1857 with the birth of Milton Snaveley Hershey, US manufacturer who in 1903, built the world's largest chocolate factory to make his Hershey Bars. He also established the Hershey Foundation in which his wealth was used for educational purposes. In 1909, the first performance of *The Chocolate Soldier*, the operetta based on Shaw's *Arms and the Man*, took place in New York, introducing songs 'My Hero' and 'Falling in Love' with music by Oscar Straus, lyrics by Stanislaus Strange. Finally, the author of the popular children's novel *Charlie and the Chocolate Factory* (1964), Roald Dahl, was born this day. (*See below*).

ARTS

1819 Clara Schumann, major German pianist, who was the wife of composer Robert and best known for her interpretation of his work and that of Chopin.

1874 Arnold Schoenberg, Austrian composer who produced some of the major work of the 20th century and introduced atonal compositions, the first being a piano piece in 1909. He also invented the 12-tone method for his opera *Moses und Aron* in 1912, which he never completed.

1876 Sherwood Anderson, US author who influenced the naturalistic school of American writing with *Winesburg, Ohio* (1921) and his novel *Dark Laughter* (1925).

1894 J(ohn) B(oynton) Priestley, English novelist and playwright who scored a popular success with *The Good Companions* (1929) and with his plays *Time and the Conways* (1937) and *An Inspector Calls* (1946).

1916 Roald Dahl, British author of Norwegian parents, who made his name with macabre stories later used in the television series *Tales of the Unexpected*. His children's books were equally successful such as *Charlie and the Chocolate Factory* (1964) as was his screenplay for the film *Chitty Chitty Bang Bang* (1968).

ENTERTAINMENT

1905 Claudette Colbert (Claudette Lily Chauchoin), French-born actress who came to the US as a child. She became a successful star of sophisticated comedy in such films as *It Happened One Night*, which won her an Oscar in 1934, and *The Egg and I* (1947).

1944 Jacqueline (Fraser) Bisset, English actress who failed to make an impression in British films such as *Casino Royale* (1967) and did better in the US with *Airport* (1970) and *The Deep* (1977).

INVENTION

1735 Oliver Evans, US inventor of high-pressure steam engines in 1790, who in 1806 pioneered automatic production and assembly lines to make his machines.

JAZZ

1925 Mel(vin Howard) Torme, US singer and accomplished musician who scored all his own arrangements for the big bands with whom he sang including Buddy Rich. After hits in the mid-40s with his Mel-Tones, he turned with equal success to jazz.

POP

1943 Maria Muldaur (Maria Grazia Rosa Domenica D'Amato) US singer best known for her hit *Midnight at the Oasis* (1973).

DIED THIS DAY

1806 Charles James Fox, English statesman who was about to introduce a bill abolishing slavery when he was taken ill and died at his home in Chiswick, London. He is buried in Westminster Abbey.

1944 William Heath-Robinson, English artist whose surname has now become the term for an ultra-complex machine which performs simple tasks, as demonstrated in his drawings and many popular models.

ON THIS DAY

490BC The Greeks defeated the Persians under Darius at the Battle of Marathon. Philippides had run 150 miles in two days in a futile attempt to ask the Spartans to assist the Greek army, but in the end their help was not required.

1759 Two opposing military leaders died in battle. General Wolfe, the British commander, defeated the French under Montcalm on the Plains of Abraham, defending Quebec close by. While Wolfe was killed in battle, Montcalm died the following day from his wounds.

1788 New York became the federal capital of the US.

1845 The Knickerbocker Club, the first baseball club, was founded in New York.

1955 Little Richard recorded 'Tutti Frutti' in Los Angeles with cleaned-up lyrics.

1957 *The Mousetrap* became Britain's longest running play, reaching its 1,998th performance.

1970 In Mexico for the World Cup, England captain Bobby Moore was accused of stealing a diamond bracelet from a shop. After being kept under house arrest, he was finally released and all charges were dropped.

1970 Australia's Margaret Court became only the second tennis player to win the

Grand Slam: the US, Australian and French Open and the Wimbledon women's singles crown.

1989 The biggest ever British banking computer error gave an extra £2 billion to customers in a period of just 30 minutes. A Citibank subsidiary stated that customers had returned 99.3 per cent of the money.

14 SEPTEMBER

BORN THIS DAY

HISTORY

1886 Jan (Garrigue) Masaryk, Czech statesman, son of the country's President, who was foreign minister from 1940 in exile in London, returning in 1945. (*See* DIED THIS DAY)

NATURAL HISTORY

1769 (Friedrich Heinrich Alexander) Baron von Humboldt, German scientist who explored Central and South America collecting data for 30 volumes which form the foundation of the study of earth science (ecology), which he initiated.

1909 Sir Peter (Markham) Scott, English artist and ornithologist, son of Sir Robert Falcon Scott. He has many books and television programmes to his credit popularizing ornithology and the ecology to support bird life.

ARTS

1760 Luigi Cherubini, Italian composer remembered mainly for his sacred music which includes a mass and two requiems. His opera *The Water Carrier* influenced Beethoven's *Fidelio*.

1867 Charles Dana Gibson, US artist, creator of the 'Gibson Girl', with which idealized view of American femininity at the turn of the century he set a new style. His wife was his model for these pen-and-ink drawings which appeared in *Collier's Weekly* earning him an unprecedented $50,000 a year.

ENTERTAINMENT

1910 Jack Hawkins, leading English actor in both British and US films even after cancer of the larynx in 1966 lost him his distinctive voice. Charles Gray was used to dub dialogue on his later films. His film career started in 1930 and lasted until his death in 1973, and included *The Cruel Sea* (1953), *The Bridge on the River Kwai* (1957) and *The League of Gentlemen* (1960).

DIED THIS DAY

AD258 St Cyprian, bishop of Carthage, the first bishop-martyr of Africa condemned to death and beheaded by the emperor Valerian in a new bout of persecution.

1321 Dante Alighieri, great Italian poet who wrote *The Divine Comedy*, buried with great pomp at Ravenna.

1851 James Fennimore Cooper, US novelist who wrote *The Last of the Mohicans* (1826).

1852 The Duke of Wellington, the English commander at the victory over Napoleon at Waterloo, and later British Prime Minister. He was given one of the biggest state funerals ever seen in London. Nothing would rival it until that of Winston Churchill (30.1.1965).

1901 William McKinley, 25th US President, after being shot by an anarchist while opening an exhibition in Buffalo, New York on 6 September.

LADY KILLERS Cars were the instrument of death for two famous US women who died this day over half a century apart, but not far from the same spot. In 1927, the unconventional and legendary dancer Isadora Duncan was setting off from Nice in the south of France, for a drive in a red Bugatti sports car when the fringe of her shawl was caught in the rear wheel. As the car pulled away, her neck was broken and she died instantly. She was 49. In 1982, on the mountain road between Monaco and Nice, the car driven by Princess Grace (formerly US actress Grace Kelly) with her daughter in the front passenger seat plunged off the road when the brakes apparently failed. Neither were wearing seat belts. While her daughter Stephanie escaped, Princess Grace died from head injuries. She was 52.

1937 Thomas Garrigue Masaryk. Czech revolutionary leader who was elected as the country's first president in 1918. He died on his son Jan's 51st birthday. (*see* BORN THIS DAY)

1984 Janet Gaynor (Laura Gainor), US actress who starred in the 1937 version of *A Star Is Born*.

ON THIS DAY

1752 The Gregorian Calendar, introduced into Britain on the (*q.v*) 3rd, 'lost' 11 days and became the 14th.

1759 The earliest dated English board game, *A Journey Through Europe, or the play of Geography* invented and sold from this day by John Jeffreys, at his house in Chapel Street, Westminster, priced 8s (40p).

1812 Napoleon entered Moscow which was abandoned by the Russians following their scorched earth policy. A fire broke out later this day, destroying a large part of the city. Winter was approaching, Napoleon would have to retreat.

1814 The US national anthem, 'The Star-spangled Banner' was written by Francis Scott Key, following the shelling by the British of Fort McHenry on the 13th. In the morning, Key saw the American flag still flying over the fortress and wrote his poem, which was printed anonymously under the title 'Defence of Fort McHenry' on 20 September. It was set to the tune of an English drinking song 'To Anacreon in Heaven'. It became the national anthem in 1931.

1868 The first recorded hole-in-one was scored by the legendary Scottish golfer Tom Morris on the 8th hole (166 yards) at Prestwick during the Open Championships.

1891 The first penalty kick in an English League football game was taken by Heath of Wolverhampton Wanderers against Accrington.

1901 Twelve hours after the death of President McKinley, Theodore Roosevelt became the 26th President of the US. Aged 42, he was the youngest.

1923 Miguel Primo de Riviera became dictator of Spain.

1959 The first spacecraft to reach and land on the moon was the Soviet *Lunik II*.

1975 Pope Paul VI canonized Elizabeth Ann Bayley Seton, the first US saint.

1987 Young German hackers known as the Data Travellers had successfully broken into the secret NASA network and other top secret world-wide computers, it was disclosed this day.

1988 A London taxi arrived in New Delhi with its meter running at London rates which showed a fare of £13,200. The six man expedition was *en route* to Sydney.

15 SEPTEMBER

The Battle of Britain day which marks the most active day of the battle when the RAF claimed to have shot down 185 German aircraft.

BORN THIS DAY

HISTORY

AD53 Trajan (Marcus Ulpius Trajanus), Roman emperor born in Spain who enlarged the empire geographically and also with a vast construction and social welfare programme.

1649 Titus Oates, English Anglican priest who invented a 'Popish Plot' in 1678 in an effort to create an anti-Catholic backlash. It worked. Fearful Londoners hailed him a saviour and his false testimony had 35 people executed before his fabrication was exposed. He was pilloried, flogged and imprisoned.

1857 William Howard Taft, 27th US President from 1908–12.

1909 Jean Batten, New Zealand aviator who became the first woman to fly solo from Australia to Britain and back, in 1935.

1984 Prince Henry of Wales (Henry Charles Albert David), second son of Prince Charles and Princess Diana.

ARTS

1789 James Fenimore Cooper, US novelist who wrote 50 novels, but is best remembered for *The Last of the Mohicans* (1826) and *The Deerslayer* (1841).

1887 (Jean) Hans Arp, French painter, sculptor and engraver who moved from Dadaism to Surrealism to the Abstract.

1890 Agatha (Mary Clarissa) Christie, English crime writer and one of the most successful novelists of all time. Her first novel, *The Mysterious Affair at Styles*, was published in 1920. She created Hercule Poirot, the Belgian detective, and Miss Jane Marple, spinster detective. Her play *The Mousetrap* is now the longest running play ever (25.11.1952), and *Witness for the Prosecution* (1953) was also a successful film as were many of her novels including *Murder on the Orient Express*. It is estimated that over one billion copies of her books have been sold world-wide.

1889 Robert (Charles) Benchley, US humorist who wrote *From Bed to Worse* (1930) and *Inside Benchley* (1942) as well as many short films and broadcasts.

1921 Richard Gordon (Dr Gordon Ostlere), English writer of humorous books, creator of the 'Doctor' books starting with *Doctor in the House* (1952) which led to a series of popular British comedies.

1945 Jessye Norman, US concert and opera singer, who is also a fine *lieder* singer with one of the most powerful soprano voices.

ENTERTAINMENT

1894 Jean Renoir, French film director, son of the famous painter, who made *La Règle du Jeu* (*The Rules of the Game*) (1939), considered his masterpiece and *The River* (1951) shot in India.

1904 Sheilah Graham (Lily Sheil), English journalist, former orphanage girl, housemaid and then Cochran young lady, who settled in Hollywood where she met Scott Fitzgerald and became his mistress; the character of Kathleen in *The Last Tycoon* is based on her. She wrote his biography, *Beloved Infidel*, recounting those sad last years of their life together.

1907 Fay Wray, US actress who will be remembered as the original screaming girl in *King Kong* (1933).

1916 Margaret Lockwood (Margaret Day), English actress, born in Karachi. As well as her stage career, she starred in many of the popular post-war British films including *The Man in Grey* (1943) and *The Wicked Lady* (1945).

DIED THIS DAY

1859 Isambard Kingdom Brunel, probably the greatest British engineer.

1864 John Hanning Speke, discoverer of Lake Victoria and the source of the Nile.

1898 William Seaward Burroughs, US adding machine pioneer.

1978 Wilhelm Messerschmitt, German aircraft designer and manufacturer.

1989 Robert Penn Warren, US author of novels including *All The King's Men* (1946) which won the Pulitzer prize.

ON THIS DAY

1830 The Liverpool and Manchester Railway was opened by the Prime Minister, the Duke of Wellington. William Huskinsson, head of the Board of Trade, became the first person killed by a train when he stepped out on to what appeared to be an empty line as Stephenson's *Rocket* came steaming down.

1871 The Army and Navy Co-operative began the first mail order business to meet the needs of its members in Britain and overseas. The first catalogue was available the following February.

1916 Tanks went into battle for the first time for the British Army, at Flers in the Somme. Designed by Sir Ernest Swinton, they revolutionized battle strategy.

1917 Kerensky proclaimed Russia a republic.

1928 A robot, the first made in Britain, was demonstrated at the Model Engineering Exhibition in London by its inventors, Captain Rickards and A. H. Renfell.

1956 The 'Ying Tong Song' entered the UK charts. This second hit from The Goons would reach No. 3, higher than their previous 'I'm Walking Backwards for Christmas'.

1964 The socialist *Daily Herald* closed, and in its place arose Rupert Murdoch's the *Sun* to become the biggest selling newspaper in Britain.

1966 The Queen Mother launched Britain's first nuclear submarine at Barrow, HMS *Resolution*.

1973 On the death of his father, King Gustavus VI, the Crown Prince, Carl Gustaf became King of Sweden.

1975 The civil war in Beirut began between Christians and Muslims.

1982 For the match between Aston Villa and Besktas of Turkey in the European Cup, there were no paying spectators due to a ban by UEFA as disciplinary action against Villa fans.

1985 Tony Jacklin's European team won the Ryder Cup from the US who had long dominated this competition.

1988 The Museum of the Moving Image, the world's largest museum devoted entirely to the cinema and television, opened on London's South Bank.

16 SEPTEMBER

National Day of Mexico marking the revolt against Spanish rule which began in 1810.

BORN THIS DAY

HISTORY

1387 Henry V, King of England, son of Henry IV, in Wales, who defeated the French at Agincourt on St Crispin's Day (24.10.1415).

1785 Thomas Barnes, editor of *The Times* from 1817, who enhanced its quality and viewpoint earning it the nickname the 'Thunderer'.

1858 Sir Edward Marshall Hall, English criminal lawyer who became famous for his dramatic defences of several major cases including the Seddon poisoning case in 1912.

1923 Lee Kuan Yew, Prime Minister of Singapore from 1959 who trained as a barrister in London.

1925 Charles Haughey, Irish Prime Minister first in 1979–81, again briefly in 1982 and once more in 1986.

ARTS

1685 John Gay, English poet and playwright who wrote the satiric *The Beggar's Opera* (29.1.1728) and enjoyed the longest known run at that time.

ENTERTAINMENT

1893 Sir Alexander Korda (Sandra Korda), British film producer born in Hungary who was the major figure in the British film industry in the 30s and 40s responsible for *The Private Life of Henry VIII* (1933) and *The Third Man* (1956), just two of the many films produced by his London Films.

1924 Lauren Bacall (Betty Joan Perske), US actress who made her debut opposite her future husband Humphrey Bogart in *To Have and Have Not* (1944). She was in three more films with him including *Key Largo* (1948).

1927 Peter Falk, US actor who graduated from University in public administration and eventually became the dishevelled Columbo in the television series of that name. He lost an an eye at three which gives him a perpetually quizzical expression.

1947 Russ Abbot, Scottish comedian, singer and actor, best known for his regular shows on television.

JAZZ

1925 Charlie Byrd, US jazz guitarist and composer who studied with Segovia, then returned to play clubs and record a hugely successful bossa nova album with Stan Getz (1962).

1925 (Riley) B.B. King, US blues guitarist who was the first black bluesman to tour Russia in 1979. He influenced a generation of rock guitarists including Eric Clapton.

SPORT

1951 Andy Irvine, Scottish rugby footballer who was considered one of the most exciting runners in the modern game. He played full back for Scotland from 1973 to 1984, and was the only Scotland player to win 51 caps.

DIED THIS DAY

1498 Tomas de Torquemada, Dominican monk who was the feared and hated Grand Inquisitor of the Spanish Inquisition.

1736 Gabriel Daniel Fahrenheit, German physicist who devised the thermometer scale that bears his name.
1824 Louis XVIII, King of France.
1945 Count John McCormack, Irish-born US tenor.
1977 Maria Callas (Cecilia Sophia Maria Calogeropoulos), US operatic soprano of Greek parents, of a heart attack, alone in her Paris flat.
1977 Marc Bolan, English lead singer and founder of T. Rex, when his car crashed on Barnes Bridge, London.

ON THIS DAY

1620 The *Mayflower* set sail from Plymouth with the Pilgrim Fathers led by Myles Standish.
1847 The United Shakespeare Company bought the house in which Shakespeare was born at Stratford-upon-Avon for £3,000, the first building in Britain to be bought for preservation.
1857 The song 'Jingle Bells' under the title 'One Horse Open Sleigh' was copyrighted by Jane Pierpont of Boston, written originally for a Sunday school entertainment.
1861 The Post Office Savings Banks opened in Britain.
1908 The US Buick and Oldsmobile car manufacturers merged to become General Motors.
1953 Cinemascope was demonstrated by 20th Century-Fox in New York with a screening of *The Robe*.
1963 Malaysia became independent and a mob of over 100,000 burned down the British Embassy.
1969 Biba opened in Kensington High Street, founded by Barbara Hulanicki, the trendiest store in 'swinging 60s' London.
1987 The first performance in South Africa of *Othello* played by a black actor. John Khani played the Moor, directed by Janet Suzman at the Market Theatre, Johannesburg.
1988 Thousands queued in the US to apply for a new credit card called the Elvis Presley credit card which featured Elvis. The card, promoted by a Memphis finance house and Graceland, the Presley enterprise company, allowed credit up to $3,500.

17 SEPTEMBER

BORN THIS DAY

HISTORY

1901 Sir Francis Chichester, English yachtsman and aviator who flew the first east to west crossing of the Tasman Sea in *Gipsy Moth*, the name he also used for his yachts. He was knighted for his solo round-the-world sailing voyage in *Gypsy Moth IV* (27.1.1967).
1906 Junius Jaywardene, President of Sri Lanka from 1977.
1918 Chaim Herzog, President of Israel from 1983.

ARTS

1883 William Carlos Williams, US poet and physician who wrote 'Journey to Love'.
1906 Sir Frederick (William Mallandaine) Ashton, British dancer, choreographer and director, born in Ecuador. He was a dancer and principal choreographer with the Ballet Rambert 1926–33 and with the Royal Ballet from 1933–70 and also its director from 1963. He created over 30 ballets including *Façade* with music by Walton and the

ballets for the film *The Tales of Hoffman* (1951).

1957 David Bintley, English principal choreographer with the Sadler's Wells Royal Ballet following in the steps of Ashton. Amongst his ballets, Bintley created the moving *'Still Life' at the Penguin Café* in 1989.

ENTERTAINMENT

1928 Roddy (Roderick Anthony Jude) McDowall, English-born US actor who went to the US as an evacuee during the Blitz, stayed on to become a Hollywood child star in *How Green Was My Valley* (1941) and survived to play adult roles in films including *Planet of the Apes* (1968).

1931 Anne Bancroft (Anna Maria Louise Italiano), US actress who made her name on Broadway in *The Miracle Worker* which she repeated in the film version (1962), collecting an Oscar for best actress. Other films include *The Graduate* (1967) and *The Turning Point* (1977).

POP

1947 Lol Creme, English rock guitarist and singer with Kevin Godley who formed 10cc in 1973. They later became successful pop video producers and directors.

SPORT

1929 Stirling Moss, English grand prix driver who was the first non-Italian driver to win the Mille Miglia (1955), but despite winning many grand prix races including the British and Monaco twice, he never won the world title. In 1962 at Goodwood he crashed at a 110 m.p.h. in his Lotus Climax and was severely injured (23.4.1962). He recovered and retired from the sport to devote himself to business interests.

1934 Maureen Connolly, US tennis player known as 'Little Mo' because of her height who became the first woman to win the Grand Slam: Wimbledon, the US, Australian and French singles in 1953. Her tennis career came to an end when she injured her leg in a horse-riding accident the following year.

1942 Desmond Lynam, laid-back British television sports presenter.

1946 Billy Bonds, British footballer who won an MBE in 1987 for services to the game.

BUSINESS

1897 Sir Isaac Wolfson, English retailer and honorary life president of Great Universal Stores (GUS), Britain's biggest mail order group as well as many high street stores. He also founded Wolfson College, Oxford.

DIED THIS DAY

1701 King James II of England, the last Stuart monarch.

1877 William Henry Fox Talbot, English photographic pioneer.

1948 Count Folke Bernadotte, Swedish diplomat and UN mediator in Palestine, shot dead in an ambush by the Jewish Stern Gang in Jersusalem.

1961 Adnan Menderes, former Turkish Prime Minister, publicly hanged by the new military rulers.

1985 Laura Ashley, Welsh designer and fabric retailer.

1986 Pat(ricia) Phoenix, English actress, best remembered as Elsie Tanner in television's *Coronation Street*, of cancer.

ON THIS DAY

1787 The US Constitution was approved by 39 of the 42 remaining delegates in the convention.

1894 *A Gaiety Girl* opened at Daly's Theatre, New York, the first British musical on Broadway.

1908 Lt Selfridge, on a test flight with Orville Wright to assess the value of the airplane for military purposes, was killed when the plane suddenly nose-dived and crashed. He was the first passenger to die in a air crash.

1931 Long-playing records (33⅓ r.p.m.) were demonstrated in New York by RCA-Victor, but the venture failed because of the high price of the players, and the first real microgroove records didn't appear until 1948 (21.6.1948).

1944 The British airborne invasion of Arnhem, Holland began as part of 'Operation Market Garden'. The objective was to secure a bridge over the Rhine to facilitate an Allied invasion of Germany, but after a battle which lasted until 27 September, the attempt failed.

1987 A Russian hunter fired at a flying duck, but instead a fish fell out of the sky. The fish (a pike) apparently tried to catch the duck to eat, but as the terrified bird took off and gained height, the fish had to let go and was bagged by the hunter; an odd twist to the one that got away.

18 SEPTEMBER

The National Day of Chile, marking the start, two days after Mexico, of the Chilean revolt against Spanish rule.

BORN THIS DAY

HISTORY

1709 'Dr' Samuel Johnson, English lexicographer and celebrated conversationalist. His *Dictionary*, published on 15.4.1755, remained the authorative reference book for over a century.

1895 John George Diefenbaker, Canadian Prime Minister from 1957–63. He took over after the Liberals had held power for 22 years, but lost the next election over his proposal for Canada to make its own nuclear weapons.

1909 Kwame Nkrumah, Prime Minister of Ghana from 1952, and President from independence in 1957. He declared Ghana a one-party state which ended with a military coup in 1966 and his exile in Guinea.

ENTERTAINMENT

1894 Fay Compton (Virginia Lilian Emmeline), English actress who had a long, distinguished career on both stage and screen including the films *Nicholas Nickleby* (1947) and *Uncle Vanya* (1963).

1905 Greta Garbo (Greta Louisa Gustafsson), the Swedish shopgirl who became one of the most legendary film stars of all time, yet who was only offered a Hollywood contract because they wanted her mentor, the director Mauritz Stiller, who insisted she be offered one as well. Her magnetic screen appearances in films such as *Queen Christina* (1933), *Camille* (1937) and her only comedy, *Ninotchka* (1939), still captivate audiences, and her star status seemed to increase despite not having made a single film since 1941.

1914 Jack Cardiff, English film director who first made his mark as a brilliant director of photography on films including *The African Queen* (1951). He began directing in 1958. His productions also include *Sons and Lovers* (1960) and *Death on the Nile* (1978).

SCIENCE

1819 Jean Bernard Leon Foucault, French physicist who invented the Foucault pendulum in 1851 which demonstrated the earth's rotation in the laboratory. The following year, he had developed the gyroscope to produce the same effect.

1907 Edwin M(attison) McMillan, US nuclear physicist and discoverer of plutonium with Glenn T. Seaborg with whom he shared the Nobel prize in 1951.

POP

1933 Bob Dylan (Robert Allen Zimmerman), US singer, songwriter, poet and cult figure who began in the folk idiom with songs such as 'The Times They Are A-Changin' (1964) which were linked with the protest movement of the 60s. His album *Highway 61 Revisted* caught the purists by surprise with the use of electronic instruments, and his conversion to Christianity in 1979 produced another ecletic change.

1939 Frankie Avalon (Francis Thomas Avallone), US singer and actor who started recording as a child, not as a singer but as a trumpeter. The recording company persuaded him to sing, but not until 'Venus' in 1959 did he get to No. 1 in the US and stay there five weeks. That same year, he had a hit with 'Why'.

SPORT

1935 John Spencer, English snooker player and former world champion in 1969, 1971 and 1977.

1949 Peter Shilton, England footballer who proved to be one of the best England goalkeepers of his time with a 113 caps.

DIED THIS DAY

1961 Dag Hammarskjold, Swedish Secretary-General of the United Nations who died when the DC6 airliner he and 130 others were travelling in crashed in the jungle on the approach to Ndola Airport, Northern Rhodesia.

1964 Sean O'Casey, Irish playwright of *Juno and the Paycock* (1924) among others.

1967 Sir John Cockcroft, English nuclear physicist who first split the atom.

1970 Jimi Hendrix, one of rock's leading guitarists during the 60s who first found success in Britain, died from a drug overdose in London, aged 27.

ON THIS DAY

1851 The *New York Times* was published for the first time.

1866 One of the first 'private eyes' appeared in the *New York Weekly*. Nick Carter was in a story entitled *The Odd Detective Pupil* by John Coryell. Over 1,000 Nick Carter stories appeared by various writers.

1879 The famous Blackpool illuminations were switched on for the first time.

1914 The Irish Home Rule Bill received Royal Assent.

1939 Irishman William Joyce, nicknamed Lord Haw-Haw, made his first Nazi propaganda broadcast to Britain.

1949 Sir Stafford Cripps, Chancellor of the Exchequer presided over the devaluation of the pound by 30%, from US$4.80 to US$2.80.

1981 France abolished the guillotine.

1988 Britain's youngest pupil passed A-level maths with top marks. Ganesh Sittampalam of London, aged nine years four months, passed four maths papers with grade A.

19 SEPTEMBER

BORN THIS DAY

HISTORY

1802 Lajos Kossuth, Hungarian patriot who proclaimed Hungarian independence of the Hapsburg rule in 1849.

TWO OF A KIND Two English manufacturers created mighty enterprises based on providing their workforce with good housing and welfare. Born 1839, George Cadbury, Quaker and chocolate manufacturer, expanded his father's business and established a model village for his workers at Bourneville. William Hesketh Lever, first Viscount Leverhulme, born 1851, began making soap from vegetable oils instead of tallow and created the new town of Port Sunlight, Merseyside to house the workers of Lever Bros.

ARTS

1911 Sir William (Gerald) Golding, major English author and winner of the Nobel prize in 1983 for Literature (1983), who wrote *The Lord of the Flies* (1954), *The Rites of Passage* (1980) and *The Paper Men* (1984).

1928 Penelope Mortimer, English novelist best known for *The Pumpkin Eater* (1962) which was later filmed.

ENTERTAINMENT

1932 Derek Nimmo, English comic actor, ideally cast as a curate on television in *All Gas and Gaiters* and as 'Bertie' in *The World of Wooster*.

1933 David McCallum, Scottish-born actor best known as the Russian Ilya Kuryakin in *The Man from UNCLE* both on television and film.

1948 Jeremy Irons, English actor who plays leads in major productions on stage and screen. He appeared in *Brideshead Revisited* on television, and in the film *The French Lieutenant's Woman* (1981).

1949 Twiggy (Lesley Hornby), English actress, singer and former model who proved she could make the transition to acting and singing in Ken Russell's film version of *The Boy Friend* (1971).

POP

1928 Pete(r) Murray, British radio DJ and television presenter (*6.5 Special*, one of the early pop shows) who has proved be one of the survivors.

1934 Brian Epstein, discoverer of the world's greatest rock group, the Beatles. It has been said that had it not been for him, the Beatles might have broken up before their first recordings.

1943 'Mama' Cass Elliot (Naomi Cohen), overweight US lead singer with the Mamas and the Papas before going solo. She had hits with 'Dream a Little Dream' (1968).

SPORT

1922 Emil Zatopek, Czech long distance runner who dominated the 10,000 metres and 5,000m from 1948, winning golds for both in the Helsinki Olympics in 1952 and another for the marathon, while his wife Dana set a new Olympic javelin record.

1948 Rosie (Rosemary) Casals, US tennis player and Wimbledon finalist.

FASHION

1940 Zandra Rhodes, English fashion designer.

DIED THIS DAY

1812 Meyer Amschel Rothschild, German founder of the banking dynasty.

1881 James Abram Garfield, 20th President of the US, who was shot on 2 July, four months after taking office.

1905 Dr Thomas (John) Barnardo, physician and philanthropist, founder of homes for children.

1963 Sir David (Alexander) Low, New Zealand-born British political cartoonist who created the immortal Colonel Blimp.

1968 Chester (Floyd) Carlson, US inventor of the Xerox photocopying system.

ON THIS DAY

1356 Led by Edward, the Black Prince, the English defeated the French at the Battle of Poitiers in the Hundred Years War.

1783 At Versailles, Marie Antoinette and Louis XVI watched the Montgolfier brothers achieve the first manned hot air balloon ascent. Passengers included a sheep, a duck and a rooster.

1876 Melville Bissell, US inventor, patented the carpet sweeper. (*See also* 25.9.1843)

1888 The world's first and probably the most discreet beauty contest, took place in Belgium. The winner was Bertha Soucaret, an 18-year-old Creole from Guadaloupe who collected the prize of 5,000 fr.

1893 New Zealand granted women citizens the vote and so became the first nation to confer this right.

1945 Lord Haw-Haw (William Joyce) was sentenced to hang for treason. (*See* 3.1.1946 *and* 18.9.1939).

1955 Juan Perón was overthrown in Argentina by a military junta and exiled to Paraguay.

1960 Chubby Checker's 'The Twist' entered the US Charts and began the dance craze, although it was only a cover of an original Hank Ballard song.

1960 The first parking tickets were issued in London, 344 by the new Traffic Wardens.

1975 The first episode of *Fawlty Towers* was broadcast by the BBC.

1977 Roman Polanski, director of the film *Rosemary's Baby*, was jailed for three months in the US for having sex with a 13-year-old girl.

1981 Simon and Garfunkel came together again for the first time in 11 years to play a concert in New York's Central Park to an audience of 400,000.

1987 The publishers of the *Oxford English Dictionary* announced that the word 'bonk' would appear in the 1989 edition.

1989 The New York Supreme Court reversed an earlier decision to award the America's Cup to New Zealand, and allowed the San Diego Yacht Club to retain the award. The New Zealand syndicate intended to appeal.

1989 A teddy bear was sold for a record-breaking £55,000 at an auction at Sotheby's, London.

20 SEPTEMBER

BORN THIS DAY

ARTS

1878 Upton (Beall) Sinclair, US author of 80 books including *The Jungle* (1906) and *Oil!* (1927).

ENTERTAINMENT

1869 Sir George Robey (George Edward Wade) English comedian and music hall star billed as 'the Prime Minister of Mirth'. He also trod the legitimate stage, playing Falstaff in *Henry IV*, Part 1.

1914 Kenneth More, English actor who specialized in likeable, somewhat chauvinistic male roles on stage and screen. He was in the award-winning *Genevieve* (1953), starred in *The Deep Blue Sea* on stage and in the screen version (1955), and was a memorable Douglas Bader in *Reach for the Sky* (1956). On television, he is best remembered for his role in *The Forsyte Saga*.

1927 Rachel Roberts, Welsh-born actress who divided her time between the theatre and films where she starred in *Saturday Night and Sunday Morning* (1960) and was nominated for an Oscar for *This Sporting Life* (1963).

1934 Sophia Loren (Sofia Scicolone), Italian actress who was discovered and groomed by Carlo Ponti whom she later married. Her Italian films are probably her best, although with Peter Sellers in *The Millionairess* (1960) she proved a skilled comedienne. Other films include her Oscar-winning *Two Women* (1960) and *Marriage Italian Style* (1964).

SCIENCE

1842 Sir James Dewar, Scottish physicist and chemist, who invented the vacuum flask to hold liquid oxygen which he succeeded in producing in quantity.

JAZZ

1885 Jelly Roll Morton (Ferdinand Joseph La Menthe Morton), US pianist, composer and singer and one of the very first jazz musicians, who first recorded in 1923.

1927 John (Philip William) Dankworth, English saxophonist, bandleader and composer who played clarinet and traditional jazz in the mid-40s before trying bebop. His wife, Cleo Laine sang in his band between 1953–64. Dankworth has also scored many films and television productions including *The Servant*.

DIED THIS DAY

1803 Robert Emmet, Irish patriot hanged for his part in trying to seize Dublin Castle.

1863 Jakob (Karl) Grimm, German philologist and collector of folk tales with his brother Wilhelm.

1947 Fiorello Henry La Guardia, extrovert mayor of New York, probably the only mayor to have a Broadway musical based on his life.

1957 Jean (Julius Christian) Sibelius, Finnish composer of *Finlandia*.

1988 Roy Kinnear, English comedy actor, the day after falling from a horse while filming *The Return of the Musketeers* in Spain. His wife Carmel said he was left in a Madrid hospital room for nine hours without receiving attention.

ON THIS DAY

1258 Salisbury Cathedral was consecrated.

1519 Ferdinand Magellan set sail from Seville with his fleet of five small ships in an attempt to circumnavigate the world. (*See* 6.9.1522)

1854 The Battle of Alma, fought by the British against the Russians in the Crimean War, produced six winners of the Victoria Cross.

1928 In Rome the Fascists took over the supreme legislative body, replacing the Chamber of Deputies.

1931 Britain came off the gold standard to stop foreign speculation against the pound. This devaluation brought strikes and even a near-mutiny on 15 navy ships berthed in Scotland.

1961 The first non-stop swim across the Channel and back was started by Argentinian Antonio Albertondo; he successfully completed the feat the following day after 43 hours five minutes.

1967 The *Queen Elizabeth 2* (QE2) was launched at Clydebank, Scotland by the Queen.

1984 The US Embassy in Beirut was attacked by a suicide bomber who drove into the compound with a lorry-load of explosive and set them off killing 40 people.

21 SEPTEMBER

National Day of Malta, marking its independence in 1964 from Britain after 164 years.

BORN THIS DAY

HISTORY

1452 Girolamo Savonarola, Italian preacher and church reformer who fought against a corrupt clergy and against the Medici rule, eventually setting up a democratic republic of Florence. But enemies ensured he was tried and he died a martyr.

1756 John Loudon McAdam, Scottish roadmaking engineer and inventor of the macadam road surface. He was later appointed surveyor of roads in Britain.

1902 Sir Allen Lane, English publisher and founder of Penguin Books who brought about the paperback revolution.

ARTS

1866 H(erbert) G(eorge) Wells, English author whose first work pioneered science fiction with *The Time Machine* (1896) and other stories. *Kipps* (1905) became one of his most successful novels, followed in 1910 by *The History of Mr Polly*. He will also be remembered for *The Invisible Man* (1897) and *War of the Worlds* (1898).

1874 Gustav (Theodore) Holst, composer, son of a Swedish father and English mother who gave English music a cosmopolitan style. His most popular works include the suite *The Planets* (1918) and an opera *The Perfect Fool* (1923).

1932 Shirley Conran, English author who established her career with her timely *Superwoman* (1975).

ENTERTAINMENT

1923 Jimmy Young, English singer and broadcaster who had a huge hit with 'Unchained Melody' in 1955. He turned DJ on radio. Later, on BBC Radio 2, he attracted interviewees such as the Prime Minister, Margaret Thatcher.

1931 Larry Hagman (Hageman), US actor and director, son of singer and actress Mary Martin of *South Pacific* fame. Her son will always be identified with 'JR' in *Dallas*, but he also appeared in films including *The Eagle Has Landed* (1976).

1934 Leonard Cohen, Canadian poet and singer who was one of the voices of the 60s, albeit bleak and depressing, who came back again in the late 70s. His songs include 'Suzanne', 'That's No Way to Say Goodbye' and 'Diamonds in the Mine'.

JAZZ

1921 Chico (Forestorn) Hamilton, US drummer who formed his own group, touring extensively. He also wrote scores for television and films.

SPORT

1902 Sir Learie (Nicholas) Constantine, West Indian cricketer who was born at Port of Spain in Trinidad. He was made a peer in 1960.

DIED THIS DAY

19BC Virgil, great epic Roman poet.

1832 Sir Walter Scott, Scottish historical novelist.

1936 Frank Hornby, English toy manufacturer who created some of the legendary British toys of this century including Meccano and Hornby model railways, as well as Dinky toys.

1957 King Haakon VII of Norway, who was acceeded by his son Olav V.

ON THIS DAY

1327 Edward II, deposed and imprisoned king of England was murdered with a red-hot poker in the dungeon of Berkeley Castle to ensure his son Edward III could succeed to the throne.

1745 Bonnie Prince Charlie and his Jacobite army defeated the English at the Battle of Prestonpans in Scotland.

1784 *The Pennsylvania Packet and General Advertiser* was published to become the first successful daily newspaper in the US.

1903 The film *Kit Carson* opened in the US. It ran 21 minutes and was probably the first western.

1915 Stonehenge and the surrounding 30 acres of land was sold by Sir Edmund Antrobus to Mr C.H. Chubb for £6,600 at auction. Three years later on 15 September 1918, Mr Chubb presented it to the nation.

1949 England suffered their first home defeat by a foreign football team when the Republic of Ireland beat them 2-0 at Goodison Park.

1987 Viscount Linley, son of Princess Margaret and Lord Snowdon, became the first royal to be banned from driving for six months after admitting travelling at 98 m.p.h. on the M4.

1989 Hurricane Hugo lashed the Atlantic coast states of South Carolina and Georgia causing widespread damage and loss of life.

1989 A Tennessee judge awarded temporary custody of seven frozen embryos to Mary Sue Davis, a divorced woman. The embryos had been fertilized by her former husband who had complained that he did not want to become a father against his will.

22 SEPTEMBER

BORN THIS DAY

HISTORY

1515 Anne of Cleves, Henry VIII's fourth wife; her features found no favour with the King and he had the marriage declared null and void.

1880 Dame Christabel Pankhurst, English suffragette who was the daughter of Emmeline, the leader of the movement.

ARTS

1931 Fay Weldon, English author brought up in New Zealand whose novels include *The Life and Loves of a She-Devil* (1984), which was also adapted for television and film.

ENTERTAINMENT

1885 Erich von Stroheim (Erich Oswald Stroheim) actor and film director who claimed to be a descendant of a Prussian military family and lived up to the image in Hollywood, earning himself the title 'The Man You Love to Hate'. He was actually the son of a Jewish hatter. A brilliant director, his drive for perfectionism led him to go over budget, as when he directed Gloria Swanson in *Queen Kelly* (1928) and was fired.

1902 John Houseman (Jacques Haussmann), producer, actor, writer and stage director who was born in Bucharest to an English mother and Alsatian father. After an English education, he went to the US, founded the famous Mercury Theatre with Orson Welles and co-wrote *Citizen Kane.* Years later (1973) he won an Oscar for his performance in *The Paper Chase* which he repeated in the television series.

1985 Paul Muni (Muni Weisenfreund), Austrian-born actor who was an established stage actor before moving to Hollywood to make films including *I Am a Fugitive From a Chain Gang*, which won his second Oscar nomination in 1932, and *The Story of Louis Pasteur* (1936), which won him the Oscar. His last film was *The Last Angry Man* (1959).

SCIENCE

1791 Michael Faraday, English physicist and chemist who worked as Humphrey Davy's assistant. He later carried out a variety of experiments to examine aspects of electricty and formulated many of the principles of electricity as well as inventing the dynamo.

SPORT

1948 Captain Mark Phillips, English equestrian and husband of Anne Princess Royal (they separated in 1989), who was in the British team at the Seoul Olympics, 1988.

DIED THIS DAY

1776 Nathan Hale, American revolutionary, hanged by the British for spying.

1828 Shaka, the Zulu chief, assassinated by his two half-brothers to end his psychotic behaviour. His 'voices' had led to the slaying of thousands of Zulus including pregnant women.

1985 Dickie Henderson, English comedian and dancer who was the star of the 50s television series, *The Dickie Henderson Show*.

1987 Jaco Pastorius, leading US bass

guitarist who died from injuries received from an assault. He played with Weather Report and Blood, Sweat and Tears. He also toured with Herbie Hancock and Joni Mitchell.

1987 Louis Kentner, Hungarian-born English virtuoso concert pianist.

1987 Dan Rowan, US comedian of the enormously successful television series *Rowan and Martin's Laugh-In*.

1989 Irving Berlin (Israel Baline), US songwriter of more 'greats' than any other in history. The man who gave us 'White Christmas', 'Alexander's Ragtime Band', 'Easter Parade' and 'There's No Business Like Showbusiness' died aged 101.

ON THIS DAY

1735 Sir Robert Walpole became the first prime minister to occupy 10 Downing Street, a five minute walk from the Houses of Parliament.

1827 Joseph Smith, son of an impoverished New England farmer, announced that he had received golden plates from an angel. From this he translated the *Book of the Mormon* which led to the founding of the Mormons.

1888 At the Electrical Conference in Paris, the terms 'ohm', 'volt' and 'ampere' were agreed.

1920 London's Metropolitan Police formed the motorized 'Flying Squad'.

1927 World heavyweight boxing champion Gene Tunney survived a seventh round knock-down when fellow US challenger Jack Dempsey failed to retire to a neutral corner delaying the count by five seconds. The extra time helped Tunney to revive and get up to continue and win the fight. (*See also* 11.2.1990)

1934 The worst pit disaster in Britain for 21 years killed 262 miners when a fire underground caused an explosion at the Gresford Mine near Wrexham, Wales. (*See* 14.10.1913)

1955 With the start of ITV, commercial television in Britain, the first commercial transmitted was for Gibbs SR toothpaste, and the lunchtime news had Britain's first woman newsreader, Barbara Mandell.

1972 Idi Amin gave the 8,000 Asians in Uganda 48 hours to leave the country.

1980 The Solidarity movement was born following Polish workers winning the right to organize free trade unions. Lech Walesa was elected leader.

1985 A severe earthquake in Mexico killed 2,000 people.

1986 A two and a half-month-old baby was given a heart and lung transplant, the youngest patient ever. The operation took place at the Harefield Hospital, Middlesex,

1988 In a village in South Sumatra two women believed to have died and been buried by robbers, crawled out of their grave to report the crime.

1989 An IRA bomb attack killed ten at the Royal Marines School of Music in Deal, Kent. 12 other bandsmen were injured.

23 SEPTEMBER

The National day of Saudi Arabia.

BORN THIS DAY

HISTORY

63BC Gaius Octavius Caesar, first Roman emperor and the autocratic genius who brought stability to the empire. He was the adopted son and heir of Julius Caesar, his great-uncle whose assassins he defeated at the battle of Philippi in 42BC.

ENTERTAINMENT

1920 Mickey Rooney (Joe Yule, Jr), US actor who was the most popular star in the US at the end of the 30s in a series of 'Andy Hardy' films which led to roles in *National Velvet* (1944), *Baby Face Nelson* (1957) and *It's A Mad, Mad World* (1963). On Broadway, in his mature years, he starred in *Sugar Babies* (1965) which he repeated in London in 1989.

SCIENCE

1819 Armand Hyppolyte Louis, French physicist who first measured the speed of light.

JAZZ

1926 John (William) Coltrane, US tenor saxophonist whose influential style was put to good use with Dizzy Gillespie.

1932 Ray Charles, US singer who was blind at the age of six. His recording of 'Georgia on My Mind' has become a classic together with 'Hit the Road, Jack' and 'I Can't Stop Loving You'.

POP

1943 Julio Inglesias, popular Spanish singer.

1949 Bruce Springsteen, US singer and songwriter who had a resounding hit with the album *Born to Run* in 1975, supported by a $200,000 publicity campaign. His other successful albums include *Darkness on the Edge of Town* (1978).

SPORT

1951 Jeff Squire, Wales and British Lions rugby footballer.

DIED THIS DAY

1870 Prosper Mérimée, French novelist who wrote *Carmen* (1852).

1889 (William) Wilkie Collins, English author of the first British detective story, *The Woman in White* (1860).

1939 Sigmund Freud, Austrian father of modern psychoanalysis, in London.

1987 (William) Bob Fosse, US director and choreographer of the autobiographical film *All That Jazz* (1979).

ON THIS DAY

1779 A naval battle between the American *Bonhomme Richard* commanded by the Scottish-born John Paul Jones, and the British *Serapis* and *Countess of Scarborough* in the North Sea off Flamborough Head, saw Jones score a dramatic victory. He uttered the now-immortal words, 'I have not yet begun to fight!'

1780 British agent John André was captured by the Americans during the War of Independence. He was carrying information that Benedict Arnold was about to betray the revolution by surrendering West Point. André was hanged, but his remains were later interred in Westminster Abbey.

1846 Astronomer Johann Galle discovered the planet Neptune.

1907 The Manchester Repertoire Theatre gave its first performance. Founded by Miss A. Horniman; it was the first repertory theatre.

1912 Mack Sennet's first Keystone Cops film was released, *Cohen Collects a Debt*.

1940 The George Cross was instituted for civilian acts of courage.

1964 The first performance of *Fiddler on the Roof* took place in New York, with Zero Mostel singing 'If I were a Rich Man'.

1973 Juan Perón was re-elected President of Argentina after being ousted almost 18 years previously (19.9.1955).

1974 The BBC Ceefax teletext service began, the world's first.

24 SEPTEMBER

BORN THIS DAY

ARTS

1717 Horace Walpole, 4th earl of Orford who wrote *The Castle of Otranto* (1765). The son of the Prime Minister, Sir Robert Walpole, he also entered Parliament, but is best remembered for his 3,000 letters published posthumously.

1896 F(rancis) Scott (Key) Fitzgerald, US novelist and short story writer who wrote the definitive 20s novel, *The Great Gatsby* (1925) as well as *Tender is the Night* (1934) and *The Last Tycoon* (never completed).

1918 Professor Richard Hoggart, English author of *The Uses of Literacy* (1957).

1932 Svetlana Beriosova, Russian prima ballerina with the Grands Ballets de Monte Carlo and the Sadler's Wells (now Royal) Ballet, creating the leads in *Le Baiser de la Fée* (1960) and *Persephone* (1961).

ENTERTAINMENT

1890 Sir A(lan) P(atrick) Herbert, English writer of light verse and independent member of Parliament who wrote musicals with Vivian Ellis including *Bless the Bride* (1947).

1931 Anthony Newley, English actor, co-author and lyricist who made his name as a child actor playing the Artful Dodger in the film *Oliver Twist* (1948). With Leslie Bricuse, he wrote musicals such as *Stop the World, I Want to Get Off* (20.7.1961) and *Roar of the Greasepaint – the Smell of the Crowd* (1965).

1936 Jim Henderson, US joint-creator of *The Muppets*.

SCIENCE

1898 Sir Howard Florey, Australian-born British pathologist who with Sir Ernest Chain developed techniques for producing penicillin in quantity.

POP

1941 Linda McCartney, US photographer married to Paul McCartney and singer with his group, Wings.

1942 Gerry Marsden, English pop musician who led Gerry and the Pacemakers during the 60s with hits 'How Do You Do It?', 'You'll Never Walk Alone' (both 1963) and 'Ferry Across the Mersey' (1955).

DIED THIS DAY

1842 Bramwell Brontë, brother of the Brontë sisters, who died of drugs and drink. He was the model for the drunkard Hindley Earnshaw in Emily Brontë's *Wuthering Heights* (1847).

1960 Melanie Klein, Austrian-born child psychoanalyst who settled in London in 1926, author of *The Psychoanalysis of Children* (1932).

1983 Dame Isobel Baillie, Scottish soprano who gave over 1,000 performances of Handel's *Messiah*.

ON THIS DAY

1776 The St Leger horserace was run for the first time at Doncaster.

1852 The first hydrogen-filled airship, powered by a 3 h.p. steam engine built by Henri Giffard, made its maiden flight at Versailles.

1930 The first performance of *Private Lives* by Noël Coward in London.

1960 The first nuclear-powered aircraft carrier, the USS *Enterprise*, was launched at Newport, Virginia.

1975 Douglas Heston and Douglas Scott made the first steep ascent of the south-west face of Everest to become the first all-British team to reach the summit.

1980 The Iran-Iraq conflict turned to full-scale war when the Iraqis blew up the Abadan oil refinery.

25 SEPTEMBER

BORN THIS DAY

HISTORY

1852 Field Marshal Sir John (Denton Pinkstone) French, first Earl of Ypres, who was the supreme commander of the British Expeditionary Force in France 1914–15, then of the Home Forces.

1921 Sir Robert (David) Muldoon, Prime Minister of New Zealand from 1975–84.

1933 Adolfo Suarez, Spanish Prime Minister from 1976 who speeded reforms. He was re-elected in 1977 and 1979.

ARTS

1683 Jeanne Philippe Rameau, French composer best known for his opera *Castor et Pollux* (1937).

1897 William (Harrison) Faulkner, US novelist and Nobel prize winner for Literature in 1949, who wrote *The Sound and the Fury* (1929) and *Sanctuary* (1931).

1903 Mark Rothko, Russian-born US painter who was a pioneer of Abstract Expressionism.

1906 Dmitri Shostakovich, one of the finest 20th-century Russian composers who began his first opera, *The Gypsies*, at the age of nine. His famous 7th Symphony, *The Leningrad* received an extraordinary première (9.8.1942).

1927 Sir Colin Davis, considered to be the most important British conductor since Beecham, who was musical director of Covent Garden 1971–86 as well as chief conductor with other orchestras including the BBC Symphony and the Bavarian Radio Symphony Orchestras.

ENTERTAINMENT

1872 Sir Charles (Blake) Cochran, English impresario who was called 'Britain's Greatest Showman'. From 1914 to 1949, he presented some of the best musicals and revues including five by Noël Coward, two by Rodgers and Hart, and two by Cole Porter. His chorus girls rejoiced under the title of 'Mr Cochran's Young Ladies'.

1929 Ronnie Barker, English comedian who spent over 20 years with Ronnie Corbett in television's *The Two Ronnies*, and who starred in the classic *Porridge* series and *Open All Hours*.

1932 Barbara Walters, million-dollar-a-year US television journalist and newsreader (and that was in 1977), and 1933 Andrew Gardner, not-a-million-dollar-a-year British television journalist and newsreader.

1944 Michael Douglas, US actor and

producer, son of Kirk, who starred in, produced and co-scripted *The China Syndrome* (1979), his sixth film, and has since established himself as a major star with *Wall Street* (1988).

1946 Felicity Kendal, English actress born in India where she appeared in *Shakespeare Wallah* (1965), but became a household name for her part in the classic television comedy series, *The Good Life*.

SKYMEN Two US actors born on the same day in 1952 are both identified with comic book heroes despite their other roles. Is it a bird? Is it a plane? No, it's Christopher Reeve as *Superman* (the first film in 1978), just as Mark Hamill will always be the gallant Luke Skywalker in the *Star Wars* films (the first in 1977).

INVENTION

1843 Melvyn Reuben Bissell, US inventor of the carpet sweeper (19.9.1876), inspired by his allergy to straw, which he had to use to pack china in his shop.

JAZZ

1937 Mike (Michael Clement Irving) Gibbs, Southern Rhodesian (now Zimbabwe) musician and composer who established himself as a trombonist in both Britain and the US, but made his real mark as a composer in the jazz-rock style, writing music for ballets and feature films.

SPORT

1946 Bishen (Singh) Bédi, former Indian Test captain.

DIED THIS DAY

1680 Samuel Butler, English poet, writer and satirist, in poverty.

1849 Johann Strauss the Elder, Austrian composer who wrote the *Radetzsky March*.

1960 Emily Post (Price), US columnist and writer on etiquette.

1970 Erich Maria Remarque, German author who wrote *All Quiet on the Western Front* (1929).

1974 Coco the Clown (Nikolai Poliakov), celebrated Russian circus performer.

1984 Walter Pidgeon, Canadian-born film actor who played opposite Greer Garson in films such as *Mrs Miniver* (1942).

1987 Mary Astor (Lucille Langhanke), US actress in *The Maltese Falcon* (1941).

1987 (George) Emlyn Williams, Welsh actor, playwright and director who will be remembered for his play *Night Must Fall* in which he played the lead.

ON THIS DAY

1690 The first newspaper in the US, *Publick Occurrences, Both Foreign and Domestic*, was published in Boston.

1818 The first blood transfusion using human blood, as opposed to earlier attempts with animal blood, took place at Guy's Hospital, London.

1897 Britain's first motor bus service started in Bradford.

1932 Catalonia in Spain became autonomous, with its own parliament, flag and language.

1954 'Papa' Doc (Dr François Duvalier) won the Haiti presidential elections.

1957 Over 1,000 National Guardsmen enforced de-segregation in Little Rock,

Arkansas and escorted nine black children into Central High.

NOT FOR THE SQUEAMISH On this day in 1986 a British police constable was jailed for biting off part of a colleague's ear during a rugby match in Wales, while in 1987 a Nigerian herdsman who chopped off the legs of his 12-year-old wife because she kept trying to run away was sent to prison for life.

26 SEPTEMBER

BORN THIS DAY

HISTORY

1897 Pope Paul VI (Giovanni Battista Montini).

ARTS

1791 (Jean Louis André) Theodore Géricault, French artist who painted *The Derby at Epsom* and other horse-racing pictures as well as the *Raft of the Medusa* (1816).

1888 T(erence) S(tearns) Eliot, US-born poet and critic who settled in Britain and worked as a schoolteacher and a bank clerk. In 1922 'The Waste Land', his major poem, established him as one of the most important 20th-century poets. *Old Possum's Book of Practical Cats* was published in 1939 and was later the basis of the Lloyd-Webber musical *Cats*, the longest-running British musical ever. His five plays include *Murder in the Cathedral* (1935).

ENTERTAINMENT

1895 George Raft, US actor who specialized in gangster and tough guy roles, and who in real life had close associations with the Mafia. His films include *Scarface* (1932) and *Some Like It Hot* (1959).

1898 George Gershwin (Jacob Gershvin), US composer who worked mostly with his lyricist brother Ira to produce memorable songs and musicals including *Funny Face* (1927), *Strike Up the Band* (1930) and *Porgy and Bess* (1935). He also wrote concert pieces including *Rhapsody in Blue* (1924) and *An American in Paris* (1928), as well as scores for Hollywood musicals including *Shall We Dance* (1937).

1909 Leonard Sachs, English actor best known as the chairman of the long-running television variety show, *The Good Old Days*.

INVENTION

1887 Sir Barnes Neville Wallis, English airship and aircraft designer whose ingenious invention, the 'bouncing bomb' dropped by the Dambusters Squadron, destroyed the Mohne and Eder dams during the Second World War.

POP

1945 Bryan Ferry, English singer, pianist and composer whose group, Roxy Music, attracted the talents of Brian Eno and others to produce hit albums. They split in 1976, but came back again in 1979 to record *Manifesto* and *Flesh and Blood*.

1948 Olivia Newton-John, English singer who spent most of her youth in Australia where her father was the dean of Ormond College, Melbourne. She returned to England and eventually began working with Cliff Richard. Her hits include 'You're the One I Want' from the film *Grease*, in which she starred with John Travolta in 1978.

SPORT

1943 Ian Chappell, Australian cricketer who was signed by Kerry Packer to lead one of the teams in a series of internationals planned in 1977 in Australia which was seen as a direct threat to the official international game.

DIED THIS DAY

1820 Daniel Boone, US frontiersman.

1909 Prince Ito of Japan, assassinated by a Korean revolutionary.

1915 James Keir Hardie, one of the founders of the British Labour Party.

1937 Bessie Smith, leading US blues singer, in a car accident. It was said that had she been white, she would not have bled to death waiting for an ambulance.

1945 Béla Bartók, Hungarian composer of *Bluebeard's Castle* (1918).

1947 Hugh Lofting, English author who wrote *The Story of Dr Dolittle* (1920).

1959 Solomon Bandaranaike, Sri Lankan Prime Minister, after being shot by a Buddhist monk on 25 September 1959.

ON THIS DAY

1580 The *Golden Hind* sailed into Plymouth under Sir Francis Drake, having sailed around the world in 33 months.

1687 The Parthenon was severely damaged when a mortar bomb, fired by the Venetian army besieging the Turks holding the Acropolis, set off the gunpowder supplies blowing off the roof and causing extensive damage to the walls, leaving one of the greatest monuments of classical times the ruin it is today.

1769 The body of Honoretta Pratt was burned in an open grave at St George's Burial Ground, Hanover Square, London; this was the first recorded cremation in Britain.

1861 Tom Morris won the first British Open at Prestwick (14.9.1868).

1887 Émile Berliner was granted a patent for his Gramophone.

1907 New Zealand became a Dominion.

1929 Alex Cheyne of Aberdeen scored the first goal direct from a corner in the Scotland-England international at Hampden Park.

1934 Cunard-White Star liner, the *Queen Mary*, the biggest and most powerful ship, was launched by Queen Mary at John Brown's Yard, Clydebank, Scotland.

1955 Birds Eye fish fingers went on sale in Britain.

1956 Manchester United beat Anderlecht 10–1 in a preliminary round of the European Cup, the highest score in a single match in this competition.

1957 The first performance in New York of *West Side Story*, the Bernstein-Sondheim musical.

1961 Bob Dylan made his debut at Gerde's Folk City in Greenwich Village, New York.

1968 Jaguar unveiled the XJ-6 luxury saloon.

1977 Freddie Laker's Skytrain took off from Gatwick for New York with tickets at only £59 – food extra – the first of the really cheap flights.

1983 Alan Bond's *Australia II* won the America's Cup, the first non-US winner for 132 years.

1984 China and Britain agreed that Hong Kong would revert to Chinese control in 1997.

SPEEDTRAPS In 1987, the fastest speeding motorist caught on the M3 in England was a doctor driving a sportscar at 149 m.p.h. with two faulty tyres. He was fined nearly £2,000 and banned from driving for two years. One of the world's fastest men on his feet, Ben Johnson, Canada's world-record holding sprinter, was stripped of his gold medal in the 100 metres at the 1988 Seoul Olympics after he failed a drugs test.

27 SEPTEMBER

BORN THIS DAY

HISTORY

1722 Samuel Adams, American revolutionary who helped plan the Boston Tea Party (the anti-taxation raid on British ships).

1862 Louis Botha, first Prime Minister of the Union of South Africa, who had promoted reconciliation between the British and the Boers.

ARTS

1792 George Cruikshank, English illustrator and caricaturist who was the leading political cartoonist of the day, and who illustrated over 850 books including *Oliver Twist*.

ENTERTAINMENT

1898 Vincent (Millie) Youmans, US composer, born one day after Gershwin to become the second most important composer in the popular music field of that era with shows such as *No, No, Nanette* (1925), which included songs 'I Want to Be Happy' and 'Tea for Two'.

1907 Bernard Miles (Lord Miles), actor and founder of the Mermaid Theatre, famous for his rustic characters. Besides his many stage appearances, he was also in films such as *In Which We Serve* (1942) and *The Smallest Show on Earth* (1957) to mention but two.

1948 Michele Dotrice, English actress who first came to the attention of huge audiences when she played the long-suffering Betty in the television comedy series *Some Mothers Do 'Ave 'Em* starring opposite Michael Crawford.

POP

1942 Alvin Stardust (Bernard Jewry), formerly Shane Fenton until 1974, English rock singer. He got to No. 1 with 'Jealous Friend' in 1974.

1948 Barbara Dickson, Scottish singer, songwriter and actress who had successes with her recording of 'Another Suitcase, Another Hall' from the original pre-show recording of *Evita*. In 1983 she starred in the London production of Willy Russell's hit musical play, *Blood Brothers*.

DIED THIS DAY

1917 (Hilaire Germaine) Edgar Degas, French painter.

1919 Adelina Patti, Spanish-born Italian opera singer who made her home in Wales where she died.

1921 Engelbert Humperdinck, German composer of the opera *Hansel and Gretel*.

1979 Dame Gracie Fields, singer and entertainer who gave the world 'The Biggest Aspidistra in the World' and her 'theme' song 'Sally'.

ON THIS DAY

1825 The Stockton and Darlington Railway, built by George Stephenson, ran its first train on the 27-mile track with 32 passenger wagons pulled by the steam locomotive *Active* at ten m.p.h., inaugurating the world's first public railway service.

1888 The Central News Agency in London received a letter which began 'Dear Boss, I keep on hearing the police have caught me, but they won't fix me just yet...' It was signed 'Jack the Ripper', the first time the name had been used.

1922 Constantine I, King of Greece abdicated following the Greek defeat in Turkey.

1930 Bobby Jones of the US won the US National Amateur Championships to complete the first golfing grand slam.

1938 Four years and one day after the launching of the *Queen Mary* (26.9.1934) the same yard saw the launching by the Queen Mother of an even bigger liner, the 80,000 ton *Queen Elizabeth*.

1960 Bank Underground Station in London opened the first travelator or 'moving pavement' in Europe.

1963 Cilla Black's first single was released, 'Love of the Loved' written by Lennon and McCartney and given to the former cloakroom attendant at The Cavern, Liverpool.

1968 The first theatrical presentation to take advantage of the end of British stage censorship was the musical *Hair* which had its first London performance with the cast in the nude for one scene, albeit in discreetly dim lighting.

1979 BBC's *Question Time* was broadcast for the first time with Robin Day in the chair. He stayed with the television programme for ten years.

1987 The Great Britain and European Ryder Cup Team defeated the US for the first time on US soil to retain the trophy. Tony Jacklin's 12-man team included Sevvy Ballesteros, Howard Clark, Eamonn Darcy, Sam Torrance and Bernhard Langer.

28 SEPTEMBER

The Feast day of Wenceslaus, Prince of Bohemia, patron saint of Czechoslovakia, the 'good King Wenceslaus' of the carol, who attempted to Christianize his nation and was murdered by his brother.

BORN THIS DAY

HISTORY

1789 Richard Bright, English physician, discoverer of the kidney disorder called 'Bright's Disease'.

1841 Georges Clemenceau, French Prime Minister from 1917–20.

ARTS

1573 Caravaggio (Michaelangelo Merisi), Italian Baroque painter who, after killing a man in a brawl in 1606, fled Rome and painted for a while in Naples, Malta and Sicily.

1803 Prosper Mérimée, French playwright and novelist who wrote *Carmen* (1846) which later became an opera by Bizet.

1888 'Sapper' (Herman Cyril McNeile), English novelist whose pen-name is the army word for an engineer, which he was from 1917-19. He created the character of 'Bulldog Drummond' in 1920, in a book subtitled *The Adventures of a Demobilized Officer who found Peace Dull*.

1909 Al Capp, US cartoonist who drew the 'Li'l Abner' strip which first appeared in 1934.

IN THE GARDEN Two people involved in the quality of work performed at Covent Garden share a birthday. Michael Soames, former English ballet dancer and *repetiteur* at the Royal Ballet, was born 1917, and Jeremy Isaacs, former head of Channel 4, now general director of the Royal Opera House, Covent Garden, was born 1932.

1916 Peter Finch (William Mitchell), Anglo-Australian actor who appeared on stage and in films in Australia. He was spotted by Olivier who brought him to London where he also established himself as a leading man in both the theatre and cinema. His films include *A Town Like Alice* (1956), *Sunday, Bloody Sunday* (1971), which won him an Oscar nomination, and *Network* (1976) for which he won a posthumous Oscar for best actor.

1923 Marcello Mastroianni, Italian actor who starred in films including *La Dolce Vita* (1960) and *Divorce Italian Style* (1961).

1934 Brigitte Bardot, French actress who starred in *And God Created Woman* (1956), directed by Roger Vadim, then her husband. The sensation she caused made her an international sex symbol.

1946 Peter Egan, English actor capable of both smooth comedy – see in television's *Ever Decreasing Circles* – and drama, in *A Perfect Spy*.

SPORT

1769 'Gentleman John' Jackson, English pugilist who managed to get boxing accepted as a legitimate sport, opening a school of self-defence in Bond Street following his retirement as English boxing champion. His pupils included Lord Byron.

1905 Max Schmeling, German heavyweight boxer who became world champion through a disqualification, the only time this has happened. (*See* 12.6.1930)

DIED THIS DAY

48BC Pompey the Great, the day before his 58th birthday; this great Roman statesman and general was treacherously murdered in Egypt where he had landed to seek asylum through the offices of Ptolemy.

1891 Herman Melville, US novelist who wrote *Moby Dick, or The Whale* (1851).

1895 Louis Pasteur, French chemist and bacteriologist.

1964 (Arthur) Harpo Marx, the mute harp-playing member of the Marx Brothers.

1970 Gamal Abdel Nasser, Eyptian President.

1973 W(ystan) H(ugh) Auden, English poet and playwright.

1986 Robert Helpmann, Australian choreographer, dancer and actor who was spotted at age 14 by Pavlova on a tour of Australia, and invited to join her company.

1989 Ferdinand Edralin Marcos, deposed president of the Philippines, in exile.

ON THIS DAY

1745 At a public performance at Drury Lane Theatre, London, a new patriotic song, 'God Save the King', was sung in response to the threat from the Young Pretender, Bonnie Prince Charles.

1894 Polish immigrant Simon Marks and Yorkshireman Tom Spencer opened their Penny Bazaar in Manchester. In 1887, Marks had started in business with a £5 loan. The new partnership required £300 from Spencer.

1923 The small band of British radio listeners were able to buy the *Radio Times* for the first time.

1978 Pope John Paul I, pope of only 33 days, was found dead.

1986 British welterweight boxer Lloyd Honeyghan became undisputed champion of the world when he forced US boxer Donald Curry to retire with a badly cut eye in the sixth round of their fight in Atlantic City.

1987 The first Lapp feature film entirely written, starring and directed by Lapps had its première in Oslo.

29 SEPTEMBER

BORN THIS DAY

HISTORY

106BC Pompey the Great, Roman statesman and general who captured Jerusalem on his birthday in 61BC, and made Syria a Roman province. Pompey first supported Julius Caesar, but became alarmed at his growing power and ambition. (*See also* 28.9.48BC)

1725 Robert Clive, Baron Clive of Plassey, who defeated the Indian forces in Bengal and became its administrator. It became a corrupt administration, but despite this he was honoured on his return to England.

1758 Horatio Nelson, Viscount, British naval commander who first distinguished himself at Cape St Vincent in 1797 and at the Battle of the Nile, the following year. His love affair with Emma, Lady Hamilton, scandalized London society, but he established himself as a national hero.

1899 Sir (William Edmund) Billy Butlin, South African-born British holiday camp pioneer who opened the very first at Skegness in 1936.

1943 Lech Walesa, Polish trade unionist and leader of the Solidarity movement.

ARTS

1518 Tintoretto (Jacopo Robusti), Italian painter and one of the most important of the Venetian school who painted the ceilings at the Prado, Madrid, as well as other works including *The Ascension*.

1547 Miguel de Cervantes (Saavedra), Spanish playwright and novelist of *Don Quixote* (1605). He lost his left hand as a soldier taking part in the sea battle of Lepanto (1571). He was later captured by the Turks, had further adventures before returning to Spain in 1580 and wrote his first book *La Galatea* five years later.

1810 Mrs Elizabeth (Cleghorn) Gaskell, English novelist who wrote *Wives and Daughters* (1866), but is best remembered for her biography *The Life of Charlotte Brontë* (1857).

THREE OF A KIND Born 1916 (Carl Ronald) Giles, English cartoonist for the *Daily* and *Sunday Express* from 1943. Gile's 'family', led by the formidable 'Grandma', satirized British life for over four decades. On his birthday, two great cartoonists died: in 1959 the British (Charles) Bruce Bairnsfather, who had created the famous 'Old Bill' cartoons of the Second World War, and in 1988, the US cartoonist of the ghoulish 'Addams Family', Charles (Samuel) Addams, which had featured in the *New Yorker*.

ENTERTAINMENT

1907 Gene Autry, US singing cowboy and actor who became one of the most popular Western stars during the late 30s and early 40s. He wrote and recorded over 200 songs and starred in 23 films including *South of the Border* (1939).

1908 Greer Garson, Northern Ireland-born actress who made her debut with the Birmingham Repertoire Theatre before appearing on the London stage. She was invited to Hollywood where she received an Oscar nomination for her first film, *Goodbye Mr Chips* (1939). Other films include *Mrs Miniver* and *Random Harvest* both in 1942 which made her a major international star.

1914 Stanley Kramer, US film producer and director whose successes include *On the Beach* (1959) and *Guess Who's Coming to Dinner* (1967).

1916 Trevor Howard, English actor who scored his major success in the now-classic *Brief Encounter* (1945) and won an Oscar nomination for *Sons and Lovers* (1960). He was a splendid Lord Cardigan in *The Charge of the Light Brigade* (1968).

SCIENCE

1901 Enrico Fermi, Italian-born US physicist and Nobel prize winner in 1938 for his work in the field of nuclear physics. The US Atomic Energy Commission instituted the Fermi awards for outstanding work in nuclear physics after awarding him the first in 1954.

POP

1935 Jerry Lee Lewis, US rock star who gave his first public performance at age 14. His big hit came in 1957 with 'Great Balls of Fire'. His British tour was cancelled after four days (27.5.1958) because he scandalized the British public with his young cousin-wife of 13 years of age.

SPORT

1934 Lance Gibbs, West Indian cricketer from Guyana.

1956 Sebastian Coe, English athlete and probably the best middle distance runner Britain has ever produced, with world records and Olympic golds in the mile, 800 metres and 1,500 metres between 1979 and 1981.

1956 Gareth Davies, Welsh international rugby footballer.

DIED THIS DAY

1902 Émile (Édouard Charles Antoine) Zola, French novelist, accidentally gassed by charcoal fumes.

1967 (Lula) Carson McCullers, US author of *The Heart is a Lonely Hunter* (1940).

1981 Bill (William) Shankly, manager of Liverpool Football Club who moulded the team into one of the world's finest and most exciting club sides.

ON THIS DAY

1399 The first British monarch to abdicate, Richard II, was replaced by Bolingbroke to whom he had surrendered without a fight. Bolingbroke ascended the throne as Henry IV.

1885 The first electric street trams in Britain ran in Blackpool.

1916 John D. Rockefeller became the world's first billionaire during the share boom in the US.

1930 George Bernard Shaw turned down a peerage.

1946 The BBC began broadcasting the Third Programme, now Radio 3.

1950 The US Bell Telephone Company tested the first automatic telephone answering machine.

1952 British and world water-speed record holder John Cobb was killed on Loch Ness when *Crusader* disintegrated after hitting waves at 240 m.p.h.

1983 Lady Donaldson was elected the first woman Lord Mayor of London.

1987 An Australian federal judge rejected the British government's plea for a further extension of the injunction banning the publication of Peter Wright's *Spycatcher* after almost two years.

30 SEPTEMBER

The National day of Botswana, formerly Bechuanaland, which became independent in 1966 with Sir Seretse Khama as its first President.

BORN THIS DAY

HISTORY

1788 Lord Raglan (Fitzroy James Henry Somerset, Baron Raglan), inexperienced British field marshal who gave the orders to the Earl of Cardigan at the Battle of Balaclava during the Crimean War which led to the disastrous 'Charge of the Light Brigade'.

ARTS

1906 Michael Innes/J(ohn) I(nnes) M(ackintosh) Stewart, Scottish author who, as Reader in English Literature at Oxford, has written both non-fiction and novels under both names, the first used for his crime novels featuring Inspector Appleby.

1908 David (Fyodorovich) Oistrakh, Russian virtuoso concert violinist.

1924 Truman Capote, US author of both novels and short stories including *Breakfast at Tiffany's* (1958) and the 'non-fiction novel' *In Cold Blood* (1966).

ENTERTAINMENT

1895 Lewis Milestone, Russian-born US film director who won his second Oscar for *All Quiet on the Western Front* (1930) and the 1962 version of *Mutiny on the Bounty*.

1905 Michael Powell, English film director, producer and screenwriter whose collaboration with Emeric Pressburger brought out his best work including *The Life and Death of Colonel Blimp* (1943) and the best ballet film ever made, *The Red Shoes* (1948).

1921 Deborah Kerr (Deborah J. Kerr-Trimmer), Scottish-born actress who was originally a dancer with the Sadler's Wells Ballet before turning to acting. Her films include *From Here to Eternity* (1953), *The King and I* (1956) and *The Sundowners* (1960), which won her three of her six Oscar nominations.

1931 Angie Dickinson (Angeline Brown), US actress who starred on television in the series *Police Woman*, and in films including *Rio Bravo* (1951) and *Sam Whiskey* (1969).

POP

1935 Johnny Mathis, US ballad singer who had his first hit in 1957 with 'Wonderful! Wonderful!' and 21 years later was back at No. 1 in the US charts with 'Too Much, Too Little, Too Late' with Deniece Williams. In between he recorded and performed other best-sellers including 'Chances Are' and 'The Twelfth of Never'.

DIED THIS DAY

1772 James Brindley, English engineer and canal builder.

1943 Richard Austin Freeman, English crime writer who created 'Dr John Thorndyke'.

1955 James (Byron) Dean, US actor who was the embodiment of the character he played in the film *Rebel Without a Cause* (1955) with a love of fast cars, killed when his Porsche crashed on the highway en route to a motor racing event in which he was due to take part. Aged 24, with only three major film parts to his credit, here was the true cult figure destined for immortality.

1989 Virgil Thomson, US composer.

ON THIS DAY

1791 The first performance of Mozart's *The Magic Flute* took place in Vienna.

1888 Jack the Ripper killed two women in London's East End in the early hours. The first, 'Long Liz' (Elizabeth Stride, 45), was found at 12.45 a.m. and it seemed the killer was disturbed as she was not mutilated. He moved on to Mitre Square, nearly a mile away and murdered Catherine Eddowes, also 45, at about 1.30 a.m. Undisturbed, he had time to perform his ritualistic mutilation.

1929 The first rocket-powered aircraft, invented by Franz von Opel, made its maiden flight.

1935 The first performance of *Porgy and Bess* opened in Boston four days after composer George Gershwin's 37th birthday.

1936 Pinewood Studios opened near Iver, Buckinghamshire to provide Britain with a film studio to compete with Hollywood.

1938 On his return from Germany, British Prime Minister Neville Chamberlain told a crowd at Heston Airport, London: 'I believe it is peace in our time,' and waved the agreement he had signed with Hitler.

1939 Poland cracked under the strain of the German 'blitzkrieg'.

1967 Tony Blackburn opened BBC's Radio 1 programmes by playing 'Flowers in the Rain'.

1987 British Member of Parliament Keith Best was sent to prison for four months and fined £3,000 for trying to obtain British Telecom shares by deception.

1988 The first US manned-space venture since the disastrous 1986 *Challenger* flight was successfully completed when five astronauts in the space shuttle returned to earth.

OCTOBER

The world continues to offer glittering prizes to those who have stout hearts and sharp swords
(Lord Birkenhead)

I OCTOBER

The Feast Day of Agnes of Lisieux, patron saint of florists.
The National Day of China marking the formation in 1949 of the People's Republic with Mao Tse-tung as chairman.
The National Day of Nigeria which became independent within the Commonwealth in 1960, and became a republic this day in 1963.

BORN THIS DAY

HISTORY

1207 Henry III, King of England, born at Winchester, son of King John. He reigned from 1216 to 1272 and, by all accounts, was totally incompetent.

1847 Annie Besant, English social reformer and theosophist who worked with Charles Bradlaugh, the radical atheist, to promote birth control for which they were both prosecuted.

1924 Jimmy (James Earl) Carter, 39th US President (1977–81) and peanut farmer who managed to get Egypt and Israel to sign the Camp David agreement ending hostilities between their countries.

ARTS

1644 Alessandro Stradella, Italian singer, composer and passionate lover who was murdered by one of his rivals.

1781 Sir Robert Smirke, English architect who built the British Museum.

1865 Paul Dukas, French composer best known for the *Sorcerer's Apprentice* (1897).

1904 Vladimir Horovitz, Russian concert pianist with a flawless technique and enormous repertoire. He once gave a series of 25 recitals with over 200 works, without once repeating a single piece.

ENTERTAINMENT

FOUR INTO TWO Three actors and one actress born this day, all have links with two musicals. Stanley (Augustus) Holloway, English actor and entertainer, born 1890, performed in the music hall, in the theatre and radio, and was nominated for an Oscar for his Alfred Doolittle in the film *My Fair Lady* (1964) which he created for the original stage production in New York. The leading role of Eliza Doolittle was played on stage by Julie Andrews (Julia Elizabeth Welles), English actress and singer born 1935, who went on to film successes with *Mary Poppins* (1964), and *The Sound of Music* (1965) and *Victor Victoria* (1983). Two actors who both played the same part, one on the stage in London, the other in the film of *Camelot* share this birthday. Laurence Harvey (Lauruska Mischa Skikne), Lithuanian-born South African actor, born 1928, who came to England to pursue a career which saw him play leads on both the British and US stage including *Camelot* (1964) at Drury Lane, and in films such as *Room on the Top* (1958) and *Darling* (1965), and Richard Harris who starred in the same role in the screen version of *Camelot* (1967) was born in 1933 in Ireland, where he made his name in the film *This Sporting Life* (1963) which won him an Oscar nomination. Other notable performances were in *A Man Called Horse* (1970) and *The Cassandra Crossing* (1977).

1920 Walter Matthau (Walter Matuschanskavasky), US actor who graduated from a supporting player – he won an Oscar for his part in *The Fortune Cookie* (1966) – to leading man in *The Odd Couple* on Broadway which he repeated in the film version (1968).

DIED THIS DAY

1684 Pierre Corneille, French playwright who wrote *Le Cid* (1637).

1873 Sir Edwin Landseer, English painter who is best remembered for his *Monarch of the Glen.*

1972 Louis Seymour Bazzett Leakey, English anthropologist who discovered giant animal fossils in Kenya.

ON THIS DAY

1792 Money orders were first issued in Britain.

1843 The *News of the World*, Britain's biggest circulation Sunday newspaper, began publication.

1868 St Pancras railway station in London was formally opened as a terminus of the Midland Railway.

1880 The Edison Lamp Works began operations in New Jersey to manufacture the first electric light bulbs.

1903 From this day it was possible to take a train from London to Dover, pick up the connection at Ostend and travel via Berlin as far as St Petersburg as European railways linked with Russian.

1906 The first hot-air balloon race was staged at Whitley, Yorkshire and was won by US Army Lieutenant Frank Lahm.

1908 Henry Ford introduced the Model T, the world's most popular low-priced car until the arrival of the Volkswagen Beetle. It was also the first left-hand drive vehicle.

1918 The Arab forces of Emir Faisal with British officer T.E. Lawrence captured Damascus from the Turks. An Australian Mounted division followed them in.

1936 The BBC began regular television broadcasts from Alexandra Palace, north London.

1936 General Franco took over as the head of the Nationalist Government in Spain.

1938 German forces entered Sudetenland, once part of Czechoslovakia which Hitler claimed he had liberated.

1938 The first edition of *Picture Post*, an 80-page photonews magazine ,went on sale for just 3d (less than 2p) and became a legend in British journalism.

1963 The Nuclear Test Ban Treaty signed by Britain, USSR and the US came into force.

1969 Olaf Palme became Prime Minister of Sweden.

1969 Concorde 001 broke the sound barrier for the first time during a test flight in France.

1971 Disney World opened in Florida.

1974 The Watergate Trial began. John Erlichman, H.R. Haldeman and John Mitchell, charged with obstructing the course of justice, were found guilty the following year (1.1.1975).

1974 The first McDonald's opened in London to speed up the fast food revolution.

1985 Liverpool youths went on the rampage in Toxteth, a decaying inner city area. The riots were some of the most serious experienced in Britain this century.

1987 Surrogate grandmother Mrs Pat Anthony, 48, gave birth to triplets for her daughter Karen Ferreira-Jorge, 25, in Johannesburg, South Africa.

2 OCTOBER

BORN THIS DAY

HISTORY

1452 Richard III, King of England from 1483 who proved a skilful ruler despite being suspected of the murder of Edward V and his brother.

1847 Paul (Ludwig Hans von Beneckendorff und) Hindenburg, German field marshal and president of the Republic from 1925 who was forced to invite Hitler to accept the Chancellorship in 1933.

1851 Ferdinand Foch, Marshal of France who was in command of the Allied armies in 1918 when the final advance to end the war was launched.

1869 Mohandas Karamchand Gandhi, Indian leader who campaigned for Indian independence using the techniques of civil disobedience.

1871 Cordell Hull, US statesman and diplomat, Roosevelt's secretary of state who has been called 'the father of the United Nations' and for which he was awarded the Nobel Peace prize in 1945.

1904 Shri Lal Banadur Shastri, Indian prime minister who campaigned with Gandhi, with whom he shares a birthday and with whom he was frequently imprisoned. Called the 'Sparrow' because he was such a small man, he took charge after Nehru's death in 1964, but died only two years later.

1921 Robert (Alexander Kennedy) Runcie, Archbishop of Canterbury who was the first to be appointed by the church and not by political consultation.

ARTS

1901 Roy Campbell (Ignatius Roy Dunnachie Campbell), South African poet who travelled abroad and was for a time a fisherman and a bullfighter in Provence.

1904 Graham Greene, English novelist, playwright, short-story writer and journalist with *The Times* who wrote novels such as *The End of the Affair* (1951) and *Our Man in Havana* (1958). His plays such as *The Living Room* (1953) and *The Potting Shed* were equally successful, and his films *The Third Man* (1950) and others based on his novels including *Brighton Rock* (1938) have become classics.

ENTERTAINMENT

1890 Julius Henry 'Groucho' Marx, the youngest of the three famous Marx Brothers comedy team after Gummo and later Zeppo bowed out. He was the one with the crazy slouched walk, odd moustache and large cigar. The Marx Brothers films include *Duck Soup* (1933) and *A Night at the Opera* (1935).

1895 (William) Budd Abbott, US comedian who partnered Lou Costello and made broad slapstick comedies including *Abbott and Costello Meet the Invisible Man* (1951).

SCIENCE

1832 Sir Edward Burnett Tylor, English anthropologist who is considered the founder of cultural anthropology.

1852 Sir William Ramsay, Scottish chemist, discoverer of the noble gases. Helped by Lord Rayleigh, he found argon in 1894 and helium in 1903, and went on to isolate neon, crypton and xenon.

1907 Alexander Robertus Todd, Baron of Trumpington, Scottish biochemist who won the Nobel prize in 1957 for his work which was related to the understanding of the workings of genes.

POP

1945 Don McLean, US singer and songwriter who had a huge hit with his *American Pie* (1972).

1951 Sting (Gordon Sumner), English singer, songwriter and bassist who got his name from the yellow and black sweater he liked wearing. Originally with the group the Police, he had hits with 'Message In a Bottle' (1979) followed by 'Walking On the Moon'. The Police had the top single in 1983, 'Every Breath You Take' written by Sting. Since going solo, he has also become involved with the fight to save the Amazon rain forests.

DIED THIS DAY

322BC Aristotle, the great Greek philospher died of a stomach illness.

1803 Samuel Adams, US statesman and one of the signatories of the declaration of Independence.

1931 Sir Thomas Lipton, English sportsman and merchant and America's Cup competitor.

1958 Marie Stopes, English birth control pioneer.

1973 Paavo Nurmi, Finnish distance runner and Olympic gold medallist.

1985 Rock Hudson, US actor, of AIDS.

1987 Catherine Bramwell-Booth, Commissioner of the Salvation Army and grandaughter of its founder, aged 104.

1987 Sir Peter Medawar, British biologist and Nobel prize winner for his work on skin grafting.

ON THIS DAY

1187 Saladin, the Muslim sultan, captured Jerusalem this day after an 88-year occupation by the Franks.

1608 Dutch lens maker Hans Lippershey demonstrated the first telescope.

1870 Rome was declared the capital of Italy.

1871 Brigham Young, Mormon leader, was arrested for bigamy.

1901 The first Royal Navy submarine was launched at Barrow, built by Vickers. There were five of these experimental six-man crew 'submarine boats' on order.

1907 Hampstead Garden Suburb, London's first garden suburb was officially opened by the Lord Mayor symbollicaly unlocking one of the houses.

1909 The first match was held at the famous Twickenham rugby ground between Harlequins and Richmond.

1925 London's first distinctive red double-decker buses, almost entirely enclosed, began service. The fully-enclosed vehicles entered service in 1935 by which time authorities were convinced it would not be unsafe.

1935 Italian forces invaded Abyssinia after Mussolini's bombers pounded border towns.

1940 *The Empress of Britain* en route to Canada with child evacuees, was sunk by a German submarine, but fortunately British warships rescued most of the 634 crew and passengers.

1942 The British cruiser *Curacao* sank off the coast of Donegal after colliding with the liner *Queen Mary* with the loss of 338 lives.

1950 Legal aid started in Britain.

1950 *Peanuts*, Charles M. Schulz's cartoon strip featuring Charlie Brown, first appeared. It was to have been called *Li'l Folks*, but the syndication agency United Features insisted it be changed to the name by which it is now known in 67 countries.

1953 The photograph of William Pettit wanted for murder was shown on BBC television by request from the police, the first time television was used in Britain to help find a wanted man.

3 OCTOBER

BORN THIS DAY

HISTORY

1928 Shridath Surendranath 'Sonny' Ramphal, Guyanese politician who became Secretary-General of the Commonwealth in 1975.

ARTS

1859 Eleanora Duse, Italian actress born while her theatrical parents were on tour in Lombardy and christened in a gilt theatrical property box. The play *La Gioconda* was written for her by her lover, D'Annunzio, in 1898.

1867 Pierre Bonnard, French painter mainly of Paris scenes and cleverly lit interiors with figures.

1900 Thomas Wolfe, US novelist who wrote *Look Homeward, Angel* (1929).

1916 James Herriott (James Alfred Wright), English author and vet who aged 50 began writing a series of novels based on the experiences of a Yorkshire vet; they became best-sellers and were made into a long-running television series and into films. They include *All Creatures Great and Small* (1972).

1925 Gore Vidal, US author and critic with a cool satirical bite who wrote *Myra Breckinridge* (1968) and the screenplay *Suddenly Last Summer* (1958).

ENTERTAINMENT

1911 Sir Michael Horden, distinguished English actor who has played many Shakespearian roles including King Lear, and made many television appearances including an angling series (his great passion) and in the films *Where Eagles Dare* (1969) and *The Medusa Touch* (1978) among others.

POP

1938 Eddie Cochran, US singer who had a hit with 'Summertime Blues' and 'C'mon Everybody' (1958). His early death (17.4.1960) has given him a certain cult status.

1941 Chubby Checker (Ernest Evans), US singer who introduced 'The Twist' in 1962 which became an international dance craze. After that he had hits with 'Let's Twist Again', 'Twistin USA' and 'Slow Twistin'' and 'Twist It Up'.

SPORT

1921 Ray Lindwall, Australian cricketer and one of the greatest fast bowlers ever. He demolished the England team in Bradman's last test for 52 all out.

DIED THIS DAY

1226 St Francis of Assisi, founder of the Fransciscan order who received the stigmata, the wounds of Christ, and suffered great pain for the two years leading up to his death.

1656 Myles Standish, one of the Pilgrim fathers who sailed in the *Mayflower*.

1867 Elias Howe, US inventor of the sewing machine in 1846.

1896 William Morris, English craftsman, poet and painter.
1967 Sir (Harold) Malcolm (Watts) Sargent, hugely popular leading British conductor.
1967 Woody Guthrie, US singer and songwriter of 'This Land is Your Land', from Huntington's chorea, a disease that destroys the nervous system.
1987 Jean Anouilh, French playwright of *Ring Round the Moon* (1947).

ON THIS DAY

1811 The first women's county cricket match between Hampshire and Surrey began.
1888 The first performance of Gilbert and Sullivan's *The Yeoman of the Guard* took place at the Savoy Theatre, London.
1899 A motor-driven vacuum cleaner was patented by J.S. Thurman of the US.
1900 At the Birmingham Festival, the first performance of Elgar's *Dream of Gerontius*, set to a poem by Cardinal Newman, was poorly received.
1906 SOS became the international distress signal replacing the call sign CDQ sometimes explained as 'Come Damn Quick!'
1922 Mrs Rebecca L. Fulton was elected the first US woman senator. She was sworn in on the 7th.
1922 The first facsimile picture was transmitted over the telephone between buildings in Washington DC by C.F. Jenkins.
1929 The Kingdom of Serbs, Croats and Slovenes was renamed Yugoslavia.
1932 *The Times* newspaper first used Stanley Morrison's Times New Roman print.
1941 The aerosol was patented by L.D. Goodhue and W.N. Sullivan.
1941 The première of *The Maltese Falcon*, starring Humphrey Bogart and directed by John Huston, took place in New York.
1952 The first British atomic device was detonated at the Monte Bello Islands off the north-west coast of western Australia.
1956 The Bolshoi Ballet appeared at Covent Garden for the first time.
1959 Post-codes were introduced into Britain.
1961 The Queen made Tony Armstrong-Jones, Princess Margaret's husband, an Earl, Lord Snowdon.

4 OCTOBER

BORN THIS DAY

HISTORY

1822 Rutherford Birchard Hayes, 18th US President from 1822–93, who reformed the US civil service.
1892 Engelbert Dollfuss, Austrian statesman appointed Chancellor in 1932 who was eventually murdered when the Nazis seized the Chancellery (25.7.1934).

ARTS

1720 Giovanni Battista Piranesi, Italian architect and engraver.
1814 Jean-François Millet, French painter who specialized in romanticized scenes of peasant life such as *The Reapers* (1854).
1884 Damon (Alfred) Runyon, US author and sports and crime writer whose short stories with distinctive

characters and vocabulary were collected as *Guys and Dolls* (1932).

1891 Henri Gaudier-Brzeska, French sculptor who was a member of the English Vorticist movement whose aims were to make art relate and reflect the modern industrial world.

1930 Sir Terence Conran, designer and chief executive of Habitat and Mothercare and a major influence on post-war British styles.

ENTERTAINMENT

1895 (Joseph Francis) Buster Keaton, US actor, director and screenwriter who began his career as The Human Mop in the family comedy act with father 'sweeping' the stage with the three-year-old. Learning classic comedy routines provided Keaton with the armoury to make some of the funniest, most masterful comedies in Hollywood avoiding the bathos of his rival Chaplin with *The Navigator* (1924) and *The General* (1927). Years later, he played a cameo in Chaplin's *Limelight* (1952).

1924 Charlton Heston (Charles Carter), US actor who came to films via stage and television where he specialized in classical roles. He won an Oscar for his role in *Ben Hur* (1959) and has played heavyweight leads in epics including *El Cid* (1961) and *Airport* (1975).

SPORT

1931 Basil d'Oliviera, South African-born England and Worcestershire cricketer who was the centre of a political controversy when he was dropped from a winter tour of South Africa. The Cape Coloured (mixed race) all-rounder had left South Africa in 1960 frustrated by his country's apartheid policies.

DIED THIS DAY

1582 St Teresa of Avila, Spanish nun, canonized in 1622 and created the first woman Doctor of the Church in 1970.

1669 Rembrandt (Harmenzoon van Rijn), the great Dutch painter.

1821 John Rennie, Scottish civil engineer and bridge designer.

1948 Sir Arthur Whitten Brown, English aviator who flew non-stop across the Atlantic with Alcock (14.6.1919).

1970 Janis Joplin, 27-year-old US singer, from an overdose of heroin in her room at the Landmark Motel, Hollywood.

ON THIS DAY

1535 Miles Coverdale's English translation of the Bible was published on or about this day.

1878 The first Chinese Embassy was opened in Washington.

1883 The Boys' Brigade was founded in Glasgow by Sir William Alexander Smith.

1887 The first European edition of the *New York Herald* (later retitled the Herald-Tribune) was published in Paris.

1895 The first US Open Golf tournament, played at Newport, Rhode Island, was won by Horace Rawlins (US).

1905 Orville Wright became the first to fly an aircraft for over 33 minutes.

1910 Portugal was proclaimed a republic when King Manuel II fled to Britain.

1911 Earls Court Underground station switched Britain's first escalator on this morning.

1922 As her husband lay dying this night in a street in Ilford, Edith Thompson called frantically for help, saying he had fallen down on their way home from the station. But the police said it was murder, arresting both Edith and her young lover, Frederick Bywaters. So began the celebrated Thompson-Bywaters case.

1952 The first external pacemaker, developed by Dr Paul Zoll of the Harvard Medical School, was fitted to David Schwartz to control his heartbeats. (The first internal pacemaker was not fitted until 1958).

1957 The first orbiting satellite, *Sputnik I* was launched by the USSR, beating the US into space.

1958 BOAC (now British Airways) began the world's first jet service operating two Comet IV jets, one departing from London, the other from New York.

1965 Pope Paul VI became the first pope to visit the US where he came to address the UN.

1976 British Rail's high speed train, the 125, which could reach 125 m.p.h. went into service between London and South Wales.

1988 Bavarian environment minister Alfred Dick asked people not to yodel in the Bavarian Alps as it was harmful to the environment. The noise scared the chamois and was driving off golden eagles and other rare birds.

5 OCTOBER

BORN THIS DAY

HISTORY

1728 Charles Geneviève Timothée d'Éon de Beaumont, known as Chevalier d'Éon who disguised himself as a woman to conduct spying missions for France. When his sex was questioned while working for the French ambassador in London, he was instructed to 'henceforth dress as a woman'. A brilliant fencer, he gave exhibitions in London where he was accidentally wounded and died on 21 May 1810. An autopsy pronounced him male.

1830 Chester (Alan) Arthur, 21st US President (1881–5) who took over after the assassination of President Garfield.

1936 Vaclav Havel, Czechoslovak playwright and President of his nation since 29.12.1989. As a spokesman for Charter 77 on human rights, he was jailed four times until just before the collapse of the Communist regime in December 1989. His works include *Garden Party* (1963), *Largo Desolato* (1985) and *Letters to Olga* (1989).

ENTERTAINMENT

1908 Joshua (Lockwood) Logan, US director and librettist of *Annie Get Your Gun* (1946), *South Pacific* (1949), and the films *Picnic* and *Bus Stop* in 1956.

1919 Donald Pleasance, leading English character actor best known for his menacing performances in films including *Halloween* (1978) as well as television films such as *Better Late Than Never*.

1923 Glynis Johns, husky-voiced South African-born British actress, daughter of Welsh actor Mervyn Johns, who performed in films including *Miranda* (1948) as the mermaid, and played the lead in the musical, *A Little Night Music* on Broadway introducing the song 'Send in the Clowns' (25 February 1973).

1924 Barbara Kelly, Canadian actress, who with her husband Bernard Braden, was a regular on British television during the 50s and 60s. She was a popular panellist on shows such as *What's My Line?*

POP

1954 Bob Geldof, Irish musician and lead singer with the 'Boomtown Rats' and international fund-raiser for famine relief who received an honorary knighthood and was nominated for the Nobel Peace prize in 1986.

SPORT

1953 Roy (James) Laidlaw, Scotland's most capped international rugby footballer (82) in the position of scrum half.

DIED THIS DAY

1880 Jacques Offenbach, German-born French composer of *The Tales of Hoffman*.

1985 Nelson (Smock) Riddle, US conductor and arranger whose orchestra played his distinctive arrangements for singers including Frank Sinatra.

ON THIS DAY

1880 Alonzo T. Cross patented his new stylographic pen, the earliest 'ball pen' which carried its own ink supply and had a retractable tip.

1908 Bulgaria declared its independence from Turkey.

1917 Sir Arthur Lee donated Chequers to the nation as a country retreat for British prime ministers. The first to use it was Lloyd-George.

1930 The British airship R101 crashed at the edge of a wood near Beauvais, France killing 48 of the 54 passengers and crew including Air Minister Lord Thompson who may well have contributed to the disaster. He brought luggage on board the flight to India equivalent to the weight of about 24 people, and the crash of the 777-foot craft was thought to be a result of overloading.

1936 The Jarrow march began in which unemployed shipyard workers delivering a petition with over 11,500 signatures to the Government in London.

1949 Having stabbed to death Stanley Setty, a crooked second-hand car dealer the night before, Brian Donald Hume dismembered the body in his north London maisonette and took the parcelled sections by car to Elstree private airport. He hired a plane and flew to the English Channel where he dumped the parcels, including the SS knife he had used to kill his victim when they had quarrelled. Hume was never found guilty of murder, but he later confessed to a newspaper. Only later, when he murdered again, did justice triumph.

1967 The first majority verdict by a British jury was taken in Brighton when 'The Terrible Turk' (Saleh Kassem) was found guilty of stealing a handbag.

1968 A civil rights march in Londonderry was broken up by police using water canon and batons and re-started more than two decades of undeclared civil war.

1969 The first *Monty Python's Flying Circus* was screened by the BBC with John Cleese, Eric Idle, Michael Palin, Terry Gilliam and Graham Chapman who died from cancer on the eve of the twentieth anniversary celebration (4.10.1989)

1970 Anwar Sadat succeeded Nasser as the Egyptian Premier.

1982 Sony began marketing two-inch flat television screen pocket sets.

1983 Cecil Parkinson admitted having an affair with his secretary, Sara Keays, and that she was expecting his baby. The Trade and Industry Secretary then offered his resignation and took a back seat to allow the scandal to die down before making a return to politics and high office.

1989 The Moulin Rouge celebrated its centenary.

6 OCTOBER

BORN THIS DAY

HISTORY

1552 Matteo Ricci, Italian Jesuit missionary who travelled out to China to establish a mission.

1773 Louis Philippe, the 'Citizen King' of France from 1830–48. He had spent much time abroad in the US and in England before his opportunity for the crown came with the abdication of Charles X.

1910 Barbara (Anne) Castle, English member of the European Parliament; formerly Chairman of the Labour Party, then Minister of Overseas Development in the Wilson government followed by other cabinet posts. She was once tipped as the first woman prime minister of Britain.

ARTS

1820 Jenny Lind (Johanna Maria Lind), the 'Swedish Nightingale', operatic soprano who made her debut in Stockholm in 1838. She had a loyal following wherever she sang. The great US showman Barnum arranged her successful US tour in 1850.

1887 Le Corbusier (Charles Édouard Jenneret), Swiss-born influential French architect who promoted the concept 'the house is a habitable machine'. He was commissioned to devise town-planning schemes for many cities including Buenos Aires and Marseilles.

1906 Janet Gaynor (Laura Gainer), US actress, the first to win an Oscar for best actress for her role in *Seventh Heaven* (1927) and an Oscar nomination for *A Star is Born* (1937).

1939 Melvyn Bragg, English author and television producer and presenter whose novels include *Autumn Manoeuvres* (1978).

SCIENCE

1732 Nevil Maskelyne, British Astronomer-Royal who improved optical instruments and methods of observation.

1846 George Westinghouse, US engineer and inventor of the railway air brake.

1903 Ernest (Thomas Stinton) Walton, Irish physicist who split the atom with Sir John Cockcroft and with whom he shared the Nobel Physics prize in 1951.

1914 Thor Heyerdahl, Norwegian explorer and anthropologist who led the Kon Tiki expedition in 1947. They sailed their balsa-log raft *Kon-Tiki* (named after of an Inca god) from the western coast of South America to the islands east of Tahiti to demonstrate that people from America could have colonized Polynesia. The 5,000 miles (8,000km) was covered in three and a half months.

SPORT

1905 Helen Wills-Moody, US tennis champion who won the Wimbledon women's single title eight times.

1919 Tommy Lawton, England international footballer.

1930 Richie Benaud, Australian cricket captain and one of the great all-rounders, he took a record 106 wickets in 18 matches when Australia toured South Africa in 1957–8, and also scored 817 runs in that same season. The following year he captained the team that won back the Ashes which England had held for five years.

1946 Tony (Anthony William) Greig, South African-born cricketer who came to England, played for Sussex and became England captain until he agreed to captain one of the teams in Kerry Packer's pirate cricket circus in Australia 1977.

DIED THIS DAY

1536 William Tyndale, English reformer and translator of the Bible, strangled and burned at the stake at Vivarde, near Brussels on the orders of Henry VIII.

1891 Charles Stewart Parnell, Irish politician described as the 'uncrowned king' of Ireland.

1891 W(illiam) H(enry) Smith, English newsagent, bookseller and politician.

1892 Alfred, Lord Tennyson, English Poet Laureate from 1850.

1896 George du Maurier, English author of the novel, *Trilby* (1894).

1951 Will Keith Kellogg, US breakfast food pioneer.

1969 Walter Hagen, US champion golfer.

ON THIS DAY

1829 Locomotive trials began at Rainhill near Liverpool to find an engine for use on the Liverpool and Manchester Railway. On trial were *Cycloped*, *Perseverance*, *Sans Pareil*, *Novelty* and the winner, Stephenson's *Rocket*.

1890 The Mormons in Utah renounced bigamy (2.10.1871).

1895 Sir Henry Wood's Promenade Concerts began at Queen's Hall, London.

1902 The 2,000-mile railway line from Cape Town to Beira, Mozambique was completed.

YOU AIN'T HEARD NOTHIN' YET

IN 1921, 'April Showers' was sung by Al Jolson during the first performance of *Bombo* on Broadway. The song drew 36 curtain calls. Six years to the day in 1927, Jolson starred in the first talkie, *The Jazz Singer* premièred in New York. Not a true full-length talkie, as sound was only used for Jolson's songs and some dialogue, the rest was standard silent movie, and not until (6.7.1928) did a film have sound throughout.

1928 Chang Kai-shek became President of China.

1941 Two men went to the electric chair in Florida. Their names were Willburn and Frizzel.

1968 British drivers took the first three places in the US Grand Prix; Jackie Stewart, Graham Hill and John Surtees.

1981 One day after the 11th anniversary of his election to office, Anwar Sadat was assassinated by Muslim extremists while watching a military parade .

1987 Fiji cut its ties with the UK when the island was proclaimed a republic by Colonel Sitveni Rabuka.

1988 A Italian lion tamer was badly

mauled in the circus ring when he tried to stop an amorous lion called Tarzan mating with a lioness named Susie during a performance. He was rescued and taken to hospital.

7 OCTOBER

BORN THIS DAY

HISTORY

1900 Heinrich Himmler, head of the Nazi SS from 1929 who was also in charge of the Gestapo, and became Hitler's second-in-command replacing Goering.

1931 The Most Reverend Desmond (Mpilio) Tutu, Archbishop of Cape Town, who is also the general secretary of the South African Council of Churches. In 1984 he was awarded the Nobel Peace prize.

ARTS

1912 Joseph Cooper, English pianist and broadcaster best known as the question master of *Face the Music* on BBC television.

1936 Thomas (Michael) Keneally, Australian author and Booker Prize winner with his novel *Schindler's Ark* (1982) based on a true story.

1939 Clive James, Australian-born writer and broadcaster on television of *The Late Clive James* and other witty programmes, and author of the autobiography, *Unreliable Memoirs* (1980), and verse including *Peregrine Prykke's Pilgrimage Through the London World* (1976).

1955 Yo Yo Ma, Chinese cellist who was born in Paris and trained in the US at the Juilliard School.

ENTERTAINMENT

1923 June Allyson (Ella Geisman), US actress who went from Broadway to Hollywood to play the same part in *Best Foot Forward* (1941) and went on to make a string of MGM musicals such as *Two Girls and a Sailor* (1944) and *The Glenn Miller Story* (1954).

1927 Al Martino, US singer who had hits with 'Here in My Heart' and 'Wanted' and also appeared in the film *The Godfather* (1973).

SCIENCE

1885 Niels Henrik David Bohr, Danish nuclear physicist who worked with Rutherford at Manchester and in the US on the atomic bomb.

SPORT

1957 Jayne Torvill, English ice skater of world champion Torvill and Dean duo who dominated the ice dancing scene in the mid-80s.

POP

1945 Kevin Godley, English pop musician and video maker, the other half of Godley and Creme both formerly with the group 10CC.

DIED THIS DAY

1849 Edgar Allan Poe, US writer, poet and author of stories such as *The Tell-Tale Heart* (1843).

1922 Marie Lloyd (Matilda Alice Victoria Wood), English music hall comedienne, 'One of the ruins Cromwell Knocked About a Bit', who collapsed on the stage of the Alhambra Theatre, London.

1956 Clarence Birdseye, US inventor of a process for deep-freezing food.

1959 Mario Lanza (Alfred Arnold Cocozza), US tenor and film actor in *The Great Caruso* (1951) who died from alcohol and drug abuse resulting in excessive obesity which brought on a heart attack, aged 38.

1988 Billy Daniels, US singer who made 'That Old Black Magic' such a great hit, selling over 12 million copies during the 40s.

1989 Bette Davis, US actress, in Paris.

ON THIS DAY

1571 The Battle of Lepanto between Christian allied naval forces and the Ottoman Turks attempting to capture Cyprus from Venetian rule, ended with the Turks losing 117 galleys and thousands of men in the four-hour battle.

1799 The bell was salvaged from the *Lutine* which sank off the coast of Holland. It was presented to Lloyds of London. Known as the Lutine bell, it has been rung ever since to mark a marine disaster.

1806 Carbon paper was patented by Ralph Wedgewood of London.

1908 Crete revolted against Turkish domination and united with Greece.

1913 Henry Ford unveiled his new 'moving assembly line' to speed up mass production of his cars at the Michigan plant.

1919 The oldest airline, KLM (Koninkklijke Luchtvaart Maatschappij of Holland was established, however the first scheduled flight was made only on 17 May the following year.

1922 The first royal broadcast was made by the Prince of Wales on 2LO eleven days before it changed its name to the British Broadcasting Company (18.10.1922).

1959 The far side of the moon was photographed for the first time and pictures relayed back to earth by Russia's *Lunik III*.

1985 The *Achille Lauro*, an Italian cruise liner with over 400 passengers on board, was seized by Palestinian terrorists. They surrendered two days later, but not before killing an elderly physically handicapped US passenger (on 11 October). Intercepted by military aircraft, the ship was diverted to Italy who, despite protests, allowed the terrorists to fly to Yugoslavia and to eventual freedom in the Middle East.

1986 The *Independent* was first published in Britain.

1988 An Alaskan hunter spotted trapped grey whales beating themselves against the ice trying to break it. They became the focus of an international rescue to save them from certain death. Ironically, many of those who helped in the rescue were normally their killers.

8 OCTOBER

BORN THIS DAY

HISTORY

1838 Montagu Lowry-Corry, first Baron Rowton, English politician and philanthropist who founded the Rowton houses for working men offering comfortable, low cost accommodation.

1895 Juan (Domingo) Perón, Argentinian general and president from 1946. Deposed in 1955, he was returned to power in 1973, and died in office in 1974.

1941 Reverend Jesse Jackson, US senator and black civil rights campaigner.

ARTS

1878 Sir Alfred Munnings, English artist who specialized in horses and sporting pictures. As President of the Royal Academy, he was an implacable critic of modern art.

1937 Dame Merle Park, Rhodesian-born ballet dancer and principal soloist at Covent Garden until she became director of the Royal Ballet School.

ENTERTAINMENT

1898 Rouben Mamoulian, US film and stage director of many major Broadway musicals including *Porgy and Bess* (1935) and *Oklahoma!* (1943).

1928 Bill Maynard, English comedian and actor who played the lead in television's *Oh No It's Selwyn Froggitt* and *The Gaffer*.

SCIENCE

1927 Cesar Milstein, British molecular biologist who shared the Nobel prize for Medicine in 1984 for his work on techniques to produce antibodies to immunize against specific diseases.

SPORT

1928 Neil Harvey, Australian cricketer.

1932 Ray Reardon, Welsh snooker champion and World Professional Champion in 1970, 1973–76, and the first snooker player to be featured on television's *This Is Your Life*.

DIED THIS DAY

1754 Henry Fielding, English author of *Tom Jones* (1749).

1869 Franklin Pierce, 14th US President (1853–7).

1953 Kathleen Ferrier, English contralto.

1967 Clement Attlee, British Prime Minister (1945–51).

ON THIS DAY

1085 St Mark's Cathedral was consecrated in Venice.

1806 The British used a form of rocket-propelled missiles for the first time in an attack on Boulogne.

1871 The Great Fire of Chicago started, according to popular belief, in Mrs O'Leary's barn in DeKoven Street when a cow upset a lantern. The fire burned until the 11th, killing over 250 people and making 95,000 homeless.

1891 Britain's first street collection was held in Manchester and Salford for Lifeboat Day.

1938 The British comic-book hero, Rockfist Rogan of the RAF appeared in the *Champion*, created by Frank S. Pepper who was also responsible for Colwyn Dane, the detective, and the sci-fi Captain Condor as well as his other famous character, Roy of the Rovers. Pepper used to write 5,000 words a day and used ten different pen names.

1952 The second worst rail crash in Britain took place in Harrow involving three trains, killing 112 and injuring over 200 people.

1965 Britain's tallest building, the Post Office Tower in London, was opened, with a revolving restaurant and viewing galleries which had to be closed to the public after IRA bomb threats.

1967 A motorist in Somerset became the first person to be breathalysed in Britain.

1973 The first commercial radio station in Britain opened when LBC (London Broadcasting) went on the air.

1980 British Leyland launched the Mini Metro.

9 OCTOBER

National Day of Uganda celebrating its independence in 1962 after 70 years of British rule. Milton Obote became first prime minister.

BORN THIS DAY

HISTORY

1890 Aimee Semple McPherson, US evangelist who was one of the first to use radio to reach a large audience. She built up a huge following and her theatrical style helped her amass a fortune. She married three times. On 27 September 1944, she died from an overdose of barbiturates, but by then her Temple had become a tourist attraction.

1907 Lord Hailsham (Quintin McGarel Hogg), British politician, later Lord Chancellor.

ARTS

1835 (Charles) Camille Saint-Saens, French composer and pianist who is best known for his symphonic poem, *Danse macabre* (1875), his opera, *Samson and Delilah* (1877) and the popular *Carnival of the Animals* (1886).

1933 Bill Tidy, English cartoonist who created *The Fosdyke Saga*.

1935 Donald McCullin, award-winning British war photographer.

ENTERTAINMENT

1900 Alaistair Sim, Scottish actor who brought a unique style of comedy to his roles on stage and screen including *Laughter in Paradise* (1951) and *The Belles of St Trinians* (1954), but could could also express an eerie menace as he did in *An Inspector Calls* (1954).

1908 Jacques Tati (Tatischeff), French actor, film director and screenwriter who made *Jour de Fête* in 1949, his first feature, but will be best known for *Monsieur Hulot's Holiday* (1953) and *Mon Oncle* (1958).

1923 Donald Sinden, English character actor on the British stage, screen and television including in the comedy series *Two's Company* and *Never the Twain*.

1937 Brian Blessed, leading English character actor who was in the influential television crime series *Z Cars*, and *I, Claudius* as well as films and stage productions, including the musical *Metropolis* in London (1989).

POP

1940 John Lennon, English singer, musician, songwriter and author of *In His Own Write* (1964). As the dominant personality of the Beatles with Paul McCartney, he helped change the entire popular music scene in the 60s, influencing a new youth culture. When the Beatles split, he went his way with wife Yoko Ono to perform with the Plastic Ono Band and to promote world peace through increasingly bizarre stunts until his assassination in 1980.

SPORT

1955 Steve Ovett, English middle distance runner and European champion (1974 and 1975) and gold medallist at the Moscow Olympics in 1980 in the 800m. In 1981, in a period of ten days he lost, regained and lost again his world mile record to his rival, Sebastian Coe.

DIED THIS DAY

1562 Gabriel Fallopius, Italian anatomist who researched the reproductive organs. The Fallopian tubes are named after him.

1958 Pope Pius XII (Eugenio Pascall).

1967 André Maurois, French author and biographer.

1987 Clare Boothe Luce, former US congresswoman, ambassador, novelist, editor and playwright who wrote *The Women* (1936).

1988 Jackie Millburn, English footballer and Geordie folk hero known as 'Wor Jackie' (Our Jackie), who was the uncle of the famous Charlton brothers. A golden goal scorer for Newcastle United, the club named a new grandstand after him.

ON THIS DAY

28BC The Temple of Apollo on the Palantine Hill, Rome, was dedicated.

1470 Henry VI was restored to the English throne after being deposed in 1461.

1701 Yale College received its charter.

1897 Henry Sturmey set off in his 4.5-h.p. Daimler from Land's End, Cornwall to be the first to drive to John O'Groats, Scotland, a journey of 929 miles which he completed on the 19th.

1947 The first call between a car telephone and one in a plane was made above Wilmington, Delaware, in the US.

1967 The legendary fighter who had supported Castro's struggle in Cuba, Ernesto 'Che' Guevara, Marxist revolutionary and guerrilla leader, was captured and shot in the village of La Higuera, near Vallegrande, Bolivia.

1973 Elvis Presley divorced Priscilla who received $1.5m and $4,200 a month as settlement, as well as half the sale of the house ($750,000) plus 5% interest in two of Elvis's publishing companies.

10 OCTOBER

BORN THIS DAY

HISTORY

1825 Paul Kruger (Stephanus Johannes Paulus Kruger), South African statesman and Boer leader who was born in the Cape Colony. He became President of the Transvaal, the gold rich area of South Africa, and his treatment of the Uitlanders, the British and non-Boer white residents, gave Britain the excuse to invade and so start the Boer War.

1877 William Richard Morris, first Viscount Nuffield, English car manufacturer and philanthropist who started the Morris Motor Company at Cowley, Oxfordshire in 1910 to build cars for those with modest incomes. He endowed Nuffield College, Oxford in 1937 and the Nuffield Foundation in 1943.

ARTS

1684 Antoine Watteau, French rococo painter who painted the famous in rural settings.

1738 Benjamin West, US-born painter who succeeded Sir Joshua Reynolds as President of the Royal Academy.

1813 Giuseppe (Fortunino Francesco) Verdi, Italian opera composer of *Rigoletto* (1851) and *Aida* (1871) who established himself as the master of romantic opera.

1924 James Clavell, English-born novelist, screenwriter, director and producer who settled in the US where he wrote the novels *King Rat* (1962) and *Tai Pan* (1966), which both ended up on the screen as did *To Sir With Love* (1967) which he also wrote and directed.

1930 Harold Pinter, leading English playwright who began as an actor before writing *The Birthday Party* (1958) which was a flop when first produced. His second play, *The Caretaker* (1960), which was also filmed, established him internationally as a major writer.

ENTERTAINMENT

1900 Helen Hayes (Brown), US actress who became known as 'The First Lady of the American Theater'. She won an Oscar for her first film, *The Sin of Madelon Claudet* (1931), and made others including *Airport* (1970) which won her another, but her greatest triumphs were on the stage in such plays as *Victoria Regina*.

1933 Daniel Massey, English actor, son of Raymond, who works mainly as a stage actor, but was nominated for an Oscar for his part as Noël Coward in *Star* (1968).

1936 Judith Chalmers, English television presenter, best known for her stint with the holiday programme, *Wish You Were Here*.

1946 Ben Vereen, black US dancer and actor who starred in television miniseries *Roots*.

1946 Charles Dance, English actor who starred in *The Jewel in the Crown* and *The Secret Servant* (1984).

SCIENCE

1731 Henry Cavendish, French-born English scientist and chemist who discovered hydrogen in 1766.

1861 Fridtjof Nansen, Norwegian scientist, polar explorer and statesman who led expeditions to Greenland and to the Arctic. After the First World War, he became League of Nations High Commissioner for refugees for which he won the Nobel Peace prize in 1923.

JAZZ

1920 Thelonius Monk, US jazz pianist and composer who pioneered bebop, best known for his 'Round Midnight'.

DIED THIS DAY

1964 Eddie Cantor (Edward Israel Iskowitz), US comedian, star of the Ziegfeld Follies and films.

1983 Sir Ralph Richardson, distinguished English actor who came to the theatre each day on his powerful motorbike.

LARGER THAN LIFE Two actors, both 70, both famed for playing large-scale characters died, 1985. Yul Brynner, despite roles in films such as *The Magnificent Seven* (1960), will always be associated with the musical, *The King and I* (1956) which he performed thousands of times. Orson Welles was the genius whose first film *Citizen Kane*, made in 1941, is rated one of the world's greatest. He will also be remembered as Harry Lime in *The Third Man* (1949).

1988 Frank Gollan, US scientist who isolated the polio virus and invented the first heart-lung machine, died with his wife in a double suicide.

ON THIS DAY

1903 Mrs Emmeline Pankhurst formed the Women's Social & Political Union to fight for female emancipation in Britain.

1913 US President Wilson detonated 40 tons of explosives by remote control from the White House to clear the last obstacles and open the Panama Canal.

1930 Three US airlines merged to form TWA (Transcontinental and Western Airlines).

1935 The first performance of *Porgy and Bess* by George Gershwin took place in New York. The 'first American opera' with the songs 'Summertime' and 'I've Got Plenty of Nothin'', was a financial failure though an artistic triumph.

1940 A German bomb destroyed the high altar of St Paul's, London.

1957 The Windscale nuclear accident which began on 7 October when an atomic pile was shut down for what should have been a routine operation at the Cumberland power station, ended up being a major radiation leak this day. The emergency was under control by the 12th, making it the worst nuclear accident prior to Chernobyl.

1958 *Any Questions?* was broadcast in the south-west region by the BBC before going national, with Freddy Grisewood as chairman.

1972 John Betjeman was appointed Poet Laureate.

1973 US Vice-President Spiro Agnew resigned because of charges of tax evasion.

1975 After a divorce in the early 70s followed by several reconciliations and separations, Richard Burton and Elizabeth Taylor re-married in a remote village in Botswana. They would divorce the following year.

1988 A 25-year-old haemophiliac became the first in Britain to be treated with a new genetically-engineered blood-clotting agent Synthetic Factor viii, at London's Royal Free Hospital.

1988 Igor Judge, a British QC, was sworn in as a High Court judge where he would be known as Mr Justice Judge.

11 OCTOBER

BORN THIS DAY

HISTORY

1738 Arthur Phillip, English admiral and first governor of New South Wales, who founded the first penal colony at Sydney.

1844 H(enry) J(ohn) Heinz, US food manufacturer who in 1905 formed H.J. Heinz Company Inc, and who adopted the slogan '57 Varieties' in 1896.

1884 (Anna) Eleanor Roosevelt, wife and cousin of the 32nd US President, Franklin D. Roosevelt. She was also a writer and civil rights campaigner.

1821 Sir George Williams, English social reformer and founder of the YMCA in 1844.

ARTS

1885 François Mauriac, French Nobel prize-winning novelist who wrote *The Desert of Love* (1925).

1918 Jerome Robbins (Rabinowitz), US dancer and choreographer of hit Broadway musicals such as *West Side Story* (1957) followed by *Gypsy* (1959) and *Fiddler on the Roof* (1967).

1928 Ennio Morricone, prolific Italian composer who became internationally known for his atmospheric scores for films including *A Fistful of Dollars* (1964) and *The Exorcist II* (1977).

SCIENCE

1884 Friedrich Bergius, German industrial chemist who invented a process to extract oil from coal. He shared the Nobel prize in 1931 with C. Bosch for research into high-pressure chemical techniques.

JAZZ

1919 Art(hur) Blakey, US drummer and leader of the influential Jazz Messengers, a 'hard-bop' co-operative which at times featured the likes of Freddie Hubbard and Chick Corea.

1927 (Cyril Anthony) Tony Kinsey, English percussionist, composer and arranger who was a founder member of the Johnny Dankworth Seven in the 50s. He played with other groups, accompanying many major jazz soloists including Oscar Peterson and Ella Fitzgerald. He has also written scores for films and orchestral suites.

SPORT

1910 Dr Danie Craven, South African rugby player and administrator considered the high priest of the once world champion Springboks and a leading figure in the sport.

1937 Bobby Charlton, former Manchester United and England international footballer who, with his brother Jackie, was in the World Cup winning team in 1966. Bobby had over 100 England caps and 49 goals to his credit.

1939 Maria (Ester Audion) Bueno, Brazilian tennis player who won Wimbledon aged 17 in 1959 and again in 1960, as well as 19 other major championships including the US crown four times.

1947 Alan Pascoe, English hurdler who won a gold in the European Championships in 1974 and was in the silver medal relay team at the Munich Olympics (1972).

DIED THIS DAY

1809 Meriwether Lewis, US explorer who with William Clark found the overland route to the Pacific.

1961 Leonard 'Chico' Marx, piano-playing member of the famous Marx Brothers comedy team.

1963 Jean Cocteau, French poet and writer.

ON THIS DAY

TIME WARP **In 1521 Pope Leo X conferred the title of 'Defender of the Faith' on Henry VIII for his book supporting Catholic principles. Twelve years later Henry broke with Rome to marry Anne Boleyn. On this same day over 400 years later in 1982, the *Mary Rose*, once the pride of Henry's fleet before it capsized and sank in 1545 in the Solent, was finally raised.**

1689 Peter the Great became Tsar of Russia.

1727 The coronation of George II took place in London.

1871 The Great Fire of Chicago was finally extinguished (started 8.10.1871).

1899 The Anglo-Boer War began.

1919 The first airline meals were served on a Handley-Page flight from London to Paris. They were pre-packed lunch boxes at 3s each (15p).

1951 Gordon Richards, champion British

jockey, rode his 200th winner for the sixth successive season.

1957 The Jodrell Bank radio telescope designed by Sir Bernard Lovell began operating.

1968 *Apollo 7* was launched with US astronauts Walter Schirra, Don Eiselle and Walter Cunningham.

1976 Chiang Ch'ing, Mao Tse-tung's widow and the 'Gang of Four' were arrested in Beijing.

1978 Nancy Spungeon, girl friend of English punk star Sid Vicious, was found murdered in her Greenwich Village bathroom. Sid was arrested the next day.

1980 Soviet cosmonauts in *Salyut 6* returned to earth after a record 185 days in space.

12 OCTOBER

Columbus Day in Spain commemorating this day in 1492 when Columbus sighted the New World.

BORN THIS DAY

HISTORY

1537 Edward VI, King of England, who was the son of Henry VIII and his third wife, Jane Seymour.

1860 Elmer Ambrose Sperry, US inventor of the gyroscopic compass and other gyroscopic devices as well as marine autopilots.

1866 (James) Ramsay MacDonald, Scottish statesman who was the first Labour British Prime Minister in 1924 with the support of the Liberals. He led a minority government again in 1929 which collapsed in 1931. He left the Labour Party to form a national government with backing from both Conservatives and Liberals.

1875 (Edward) Aleister Crowley, English occultist and author who promoted modern satanism. He settled in an abbey in Sicily with a group of disciples until rumours of orgies and magical ceremonies involving the sacrifice of babies had him expelled. He promoted himself as 'the wickedest man alive' and 'the great beast'.

ARTS

1872 Ralph Vaughan Williams, leading English composer best remembered for his *Sea Symphony* (1910), his *Sinfonia Antarctica* (1948), which was used in part as the film score for *Scott of the Antarctic*, and his popular setting of *Greensleeves* (1929).

1935 Luciano Pavarotti, leading Italian tenor, who excels in the classic Italian operas such as *Rigoletto*.

ENTERTAINMENT

1929 Magnus Magnusson, Icelandic-born writer and quiz master of the long-running *Mastermind* television series.

1944 Angela Rippon, English television presenter, former BBC newsreader.

SPORT

1921 Jaroslav Drobny, Czech tennis player who defected to the West. He was twice a finalist at Wimbledon, winning on his third attempt in 1953 and again in 1954 in what was the longest final ever, when despite a bad knee, he beat Ken Rosewall (2.7.1954).

DIED THIS DAY

1845 Elizabeth Fry, English social and prison reformer.

1859 Robert Stephenson, English rail and civil engineer.

1870 Robert E(dward) Lee, US Confederate general during the Civil War.

1915 Edith Cavell, English nurse, executed by a German firing squad for aiding the escape of British soldiers in Belgium.

1924 Anatole France, French author of *Penguin Island* (1908).

1940 Tom Mix, US film actor who starred in over 400 westerns.

1964 Ian Fleming, English creator of James Bond.

1965 Paul Muller, Swiss chemist and Nobel prize winner for his formulation of the insecticide DDT.

1987 Kenneth Uston, US card player who gave up his job as senior vice-president of the San Francisco Stock Exchange to concentrate on his technique of card-counting. It made him a fortune at Blackjack and he was eventually banned from many casino tables.

ON THIS DAY

1609 *Three Blind Mice* was published in London, believed to be the earliest printed secular song.

1822 Pedro the Great was proclaimed Emperor of Brazil.

1849 British inventor Charles Rowley patented the safety pin unaware of an earlier US patent this same year (10.4.1849).

1901 President Theodore Roosevelt renamed the Executive Mansion 'The White House'.

1923 The BBC appointed its first full time announcer, J.S. Dodson.

1924 The Z3 Zeppelin flew from Friedrichschafen to Lakenhurst, New Jersey.

1928 The first 'iron lung' was used at the Boston Children's Hospital, Massachusetts.

1948 The first Morris Minor, designed by Sir Alec Issigonis, came off the assembly line at Cowley, Oxfordshire.

1951 Florence Chadwick broke the English Channel swimming record. The US swimmer took just 13 hours 33 minutes.

1961 New Zealand voted to abolish the death penalty.

1971 *Jesus Christ Superstar* by Lloyd-Webber and Rice opened on Broadway, prior to its London production.

1984 During the Conservative Party Conference at the Brighton Grand Hotel, an IRA bomb badly damaged the hotel killing four and injuring 30 people including Norman Tebbitt, the Employment Secretary, and his wife. The Prime Minister Margaret Thatcher escaped unharmed on the eve of her 58th birthday.

13 OCTOBER

BORN THIS DAY

HISTORY

1925 Margaret (Hilda) Thatcher (née Roberts), British Prime Minister from 1979, daughter of a Grantham grocer. She entered parliament in 1959, became Minister of Education 1970–74, and defeated Edward Heath for leadership of the Conservative Party in 1975.

1946 Edwina Currie, British politician whose flair for self-publicity was her undoing when her remarks to the press on the amount of salmonella in British eggs set her against the powerful egg lobby. She was forced to resign her post as junior Minister of Health.

ARTS

1853 Lillie Langtry (Emilie Charlotte le Breton), daughter of the Dean of Jersey, who was known as the 'Jersey Lily', the title of Millais's portrait of her. An intimate of Edward VII when he was the Prince of Wales, she was an indifferent actress, but much admired in society for her beauty.

1915 Cornel(ius Louis) Wilde, who was a member of the US Olympic fencing team before he dropped out to concentrate on an acting career. He played the role of Chopin in *A Song to Remember* (1945) and his swordmanship was shown to effect in *Lancelot and Guinevere* (1963).

1921 Yves Montand (Ivo Livi), Italian-born French singer and actor whose anti-fascist parents fled to Marseilles. Edith Piaf guided his career both as a singer and actor. He proved his acting ability with *The Wages of Fear* (1953) and *On A Clear Day You Can See Forever* (1970).

1924 Lenny Bruce (Leonard Alfred Schneider), US social satirist whose use of obscenity offended some, yet opened the way for other comedians such as Richard Prior. He was arrested and charged with obscenity on several occasions, and was deported from Britain in 1963. The Australians banned him after one performance in Sydney.

POP

1941 Paul Simon, US singer, songwriter and musician, originally with Art Garfunkel who together established themselves as one of the major duos ever with a succession of hits including 'Bridge Over Troubled Water' (1970) and the film score for *The Graduate* (1967) with the song 'Mrs Robinson'. They split in 1975 and Paul's solo hits include '50 Ways to Leave Your Lover'.

DIED THIS DAY

AD54 Claudius I, Roman emperor who died after eating poisoned mushrooms as a result of a plot inspired by his wife, the Empress Agrippina.

1815 Joachim Murat, King of Two Sicilies, executed after attempting to repossess Naples.

1905 Sir Henry Irving, first actor to be knighted, of a heart attack outside his hotel in Bradford.

1966 Clifton Webb, US actor who starred in *Laura* (1944).

ON THIS DAY

1399 The first King of the House of Lancaster, Henry IV, was crowned.

1792 The foundation stone of the White House was laid by President George Washington. The building was designed by James Hoban.

1857 'Prioress' became the first US horse to win a major British race when it ran at Newmarket.

1884 Greenwich was adopted as the universal meridian (Greenwich Mean Time).

1894 Liverpool and Everton football clubs met in the first Merseyside 'derby' at Goodison Park with Everton winning 3–0.

1904 Sigmund Freud's *The Interpretation of Dreams* was published.

1924 Ramsay MacDonald made the first election broadcast on the BBC on behalf of the Labour Party.

1954 Chris Chataway broke the world 5,000m by a full 5 seconds beating the great Vladimir Kuts in 13 minutes 15.6 seconds in the London v Moscow championship at London's White City.

THE TRUTH WILL OUT This day in 1988, the British Government's 2½-year, £3m battle to suppress Peter Wright's book *Spycatcher* was given a further setback when the Law Lords lifted an injunction and allowed British newspapers to print extracts. In Italy, the Cardinal of Turin confirmed leaked press reports that scientific tests had proved the Shroud of Turin, believed to carry the imprint of the face of Christ, to be of medieval origin, around AD 1260 to 1390.

14 OCTOBER

BORN THIS DAY

HISTORY

1633 James II, King of Great Britain and Ireland, second son of Charles I. His pro-Catholic stand led to his overthrow by William of Orange.

1644 William Penn, English Quaker leader who was the founder of a Quaker colony in the US named Pennsylvania in his honour.

1882 Eamon de Valera, Irish Prime Minister and President, who was born in New York City. He was sent to Ireland for his schooling and later became a teacher. In 1917 he became president of Sinn Fein. In 1920 he was elected president but, wanted by the British, he went into hiding. When Ireland was divided, he refused to accept the treaty. He was elected again in 1932 and renegotiated with Britain, defeated in 1948, but back again in 1951–4 and 1957–9, and President 1959–73.

1890 Dwight D(avid) Eisenhower, US military commander in charge of the Allied invasion of Europe in the Second World War, and 34th US President from 1952–6 and again 1956–60 with Nixon as his Vice-President.

ARTS

1888 Katherine Mansfield (Beauchamp), New Zealand-born author who influenced the development of the modern short story. She settled in England in 1908 and married the following year, but left her husband the next morning. Her books include *The Garden Party and Other Stories* (1922).

1894 e e cummings (Edward Estlin Cummings), US poet and painter whose experimental style involved odd punctuation and an abstention from the use of capital letters. His poems include 'a clown's smirk in the head of a baboon'.

ENTERTAINMENT

1896 Bud Flanagan (Chaim Reeven Weintrop) who, with Chesney Allen, became one of the best-loved comedy duos in Britain. Their patter and songs such as 'Underneath the Arches' and 'Run Rabbit Run' became hits. They joined the Crazy Gang in 1932 for seven productions until the war interrupted, and then re-formed to occupy the Victoria Palace for decades.

1896 Lillian Gish, US actress who played the heroine in many D.W. Griffith silent film classics including *Birth of a Nation* (1915) and *Intolerance* (1916). She later appeared on television in *Arsenic and Old Lace* (1969).

1928 Roger Moore, English actor who established himself in television series such as *The Saint* before taking over as 007 from Sean Connery's James Bond with *Live and Let Die* in 1973.

1940 Christopher Timothy, English actor best known for his portrayal of James Herriott in the long-running television series, *All Creatures Great and Small.*

POP

1940 Cliff Richard (Harold Webb), English pop singer and film actor born in India, who had successes in the 50s with songs such as 'Living Doll' (1959), which he performed with his long-time backing group, the Shadows, and 'Bachelor Boy' (1963), and is still going strong 30 years later.

1946 Justin Hayward, English singer and multi-instrumentalist who joined the flagging Moody Blues to record 'Knights in White Satin' which became a smash hit on its re-release in 1972. He also formed the Blue Jays with John Lodge, and recorded 'Blue Guitar'.

SPORT

1960 Steve Cram, English middle distance runner and world record breaker in the mile in Oslo and the 2,000m in Hungary, both in August 1985.

DIED THIS DAY

1944 Rommel, the 'Desert Fox', took cyanide tablets and died within moments before he could be arrested for his part in the plot to kill Hitler.

1959 Errol Flynn, Tasmanian-born swashbuckling actor.

1976 Dame Edith Evans, leading English character actress.

1977 Bing Crosby, US crooner and actor, on a golf course in Madrid.

ON THIS DAY

1066 The Battle of Hastings was fought on Senlac Hill, seven miles from Hastings, where King Harold was slain as William the Conqueror's troops routed the English army.

1830 Belgium was proclaimed an independent kingdom.

1878 The first football match played under floodlights (four Siemens' arc lamps), took place at Bramhall Lane, Sheffield.

1884 George Eastman patented photographic film.

1893 The first performance of *The Gaiety Girl*, considered the first musical comedy, was presented in London by George Edwardes on his 38th birthday.

1912 President Theodore Roosevelt was shot at by a mentally unstable man named Schranke in an assassination attempt. He was saved by his thick coat and a bundle of manuscript paper in his breast pocket.

1913 Britain's worst mining disaster occurred as the result of an explosion at Universal Colliery in South Wales killing 439 miners. (*See* 22.9.1934)

1930 Ethel Merman made her Broadway debut in Gershwin's *Girl Crazy*. The cast included Ginger Rogers in only her second show and the orchestra featured Glenn Miller, Jimmy Dorsey, Gene Krupa and Jack Teagarden who all went on to become major jazz musicians. The music included 'I've Got Rhythm' and 'Embraceable You'.

1939 The Royal Navy battleship *Royal Oak* was torpedoed and sunk in Scapa Flow with the loss of 810 lives.

1947 Chuck Yeagar in his Bell XI rocket plane became the first man to break the sound barrier.

1964 Martin Luther King was awarded the Nobel Peace prize.

1968 The new Euston station was opened in London.

1969 The British ten shilling note was replaced with the seven-sided 50p coin.

1973 Egyptian and Syrian forces invaded Israel as the nation marked the holiest of holy days, Yom Kippur (the Day of Atonement). Despite an unprepared Israel by 26 October the Yom Kippur War was over when Israeli forces trapped the Egyptians in the Sinai and other Israeli troops were only 20 miles from Damascus. A cease fire was called.

1987 A man flushed 52 gold bars down an airliner toilet after failing to make contact with a fellow smuggler at Katmandu Airport, giving the Himalayan Kingdom of Nepal a windfall worth £100,000 when the bars were found by the cleaning crew at Hong Kong airport. The gold had to be legally returned to its place of origin, Nepal.

15 OCTOBER

BORN THIS DAY

HISTORY

1959 The Duchess of York, wife of Prince Andrew, formerly Sarah Ferguson.

ARTS

70BC Virgil (Publius Vergilius Maro), the greatest Roman poet, best known for his epic *Aeneid* which was unfinished when he died and included the legend of the founding of Rome.

1836 Friedrich Wilhelm Nietzche, German philospher who wrote *Thus Spake Zarathustra* (1835) in which he developed the idea of the *Ubermensch* (superman).

1881 P(elham) G(renville) Wodehouse, English novelist and librettist who settled in the US after the Second World War. He created the famous characters Bertie Wooster and 'the gentleman's gentleman' Jeeves, who first appeared in 1917, and wrote more than 90 books, collaborated on more than 30 plays and musical comedies and over 20 film scripts.

1905 C(harles) P(ercy) Snow (Lord Snow), English author who was a Parliamentary Secretary to the Ministry of Science and Technology. He wrote a sequence of novels under the general title *Strangers and Brothers* which includes *The Masters* (1951) and *The Corridors of Power* (1964)

1920 Mario Puzo, US novelist who wrote the best-selling *Godfather* (1969) which spawned the equally successful films.

ENTERTAINMENT

1900 Mervyn Leroy, US film director best remembered for *Random Harvest* (1942), *Quo Vadis* (1951) and *Gypsy* (1962).

SCIENCE

1608 Evangelista Torricelli, Italian mathematician who devised the barometer in 1643.

1908 Professor John K(enneth) Galbraith, Canadian economist whose books include *The Great Crash* (1955) and *The Affluent Society* (1958).

POP

1946 Richard Carpenter, US singer who formed the Carpenters with his sister Karen. Their hits included '(They Long to Be) Close to You' (1970), 'Top of the

World' (1973) and 'Please Mr Postman' (1975).

SPORT

1858 John L(awrence) Sullivan, US world heavyweight boxer who was known as the 'Boston Strong Boy'. He became champion by beating Paddy Ryan in 1882 and remained champion for ten years although he refused to fight the great Australian black heavyweight Peter Jackson.

DIED THIS DAY

1730 Antoine de la Mothe Cadillac, French soldier and founder of Detroit, and later Governor of Louisiana.

TRAITORS Two wartime collaborators were executed. In the First World War, Mata Hari (Magaretha Geertruida Zelle), legendary Dutch spy who danced in the nude, was executed in 1917 by firing squad in Paris. Pierre Laval, the French leader who led the Vichy government which collaborated with the Germans during the Second World War, was executed in 1945.

1946 Herman Goering, Nazi war criminal and founder of the Luftwaffe, took poison in Nuremberg Prison a few hours before he was due to face the hangman.

1964 Cole Porter, US composer and lyricist of Broadway shows including *Kiss Me Kate*.

ON THIS DAY

1581 The first major ballet was staged at the request of Catherine de' Medici in the palace at Paris. *Le Ballet comique de la reine* entertained an audience of 10,000 and was five hours of spectacle choreographed by Balthazar de Beaujoyeulx.

1666 The first waistcoat was worn by King Charles II, according to Pepys.

1815 Napoleon arrived in St Helena with a party of followers who were joining him in exile where he spent most of his time writing, and reading English newspapers.

1851 The Great Exhibition closed at Hyde Park, but its unique Crystal Palace was re-erected in south London.

1864 The *Church Times* published 'Onward Christian Soldiers', music by Arthur Sullivan, words by the Reverend Sabine Baring-Gould, written for a children's festival.

1887 Preston North End beat Hyde 26–0 in an FA Cup tie, the highest goal score ever by an English club in a major competition, with James Ross, the first player to score seven goals in a Division 1 match.

1928 The 'Graf Zeppelin' made its first transatlantic crossing from Friedrichshafen to Lakenhurst, New Jersey.

1951 The first British party political broadcast was televised by the BBC. Lord Samuel spoke on behalf of the Liberals.

1954 William Golding's *Lord of the Flies* was published in Britain.

1962 Amnesty International was formed in London.

1964 Nikita Kruschev was deposed while holidaying at the Black Sea and replaced by Leonid Brezhnev.

1964 Craig Breedlove of the US set a new landspeed record in his rocket propelled car reaching 526.28 m.p.h.

1978 Irene Miller and Vera Komakova became the first women to reach the summit of Annapurna One in the Himalayas.

1987 The worst hurricane to hit Britain since records began struck in the early hours of the morning, devastating southern England and causing at least 17 deaths.

16 OCTOBER

BORN THIS DAY

HISTORY

1758 Noah Webster, US lexicographer who originated the first US dictionary.

1863 Sir (Joseph) Austen Chamberlain, British statesman who won the Nobel Peace prize in 1925 for his work as Foreign Secretary, negotiating and signing the Locarno Pact.

1886 David Ben-Gurion, first Prime Minister of Israel in 1948 who was born in Poland as David Green; a visionary who was the leading force in the creation of the state.

ARTS

1854 Oscar Wilde (Fingal O'Flahertie Wills), Irish-born playwright who was one of the wittiest writers for the stage with plays such as *Lady Windermere's Fan* (1892) and *The Importance of Being Earnest* (1895). His novel, *The Picture of Dorian Gray* (1891) and poems including 'The Ballad of Reading Gaol' (1898) were his main works. He was accused of homosexual practices and imprisoned for three years. On release, he moved to Paris, where he died a broken man in 1900.

1888 Eugene (Gladstone) O'Neil, leading US playwright whose plays include *Mourning Becomes Electra* (1931) and *A Long Day's Journey Into Night* (written 1940, staged 1956) and he won the Nobel Literature prize in 1936.

1927 Gunter Grass, German author and sculptor who wrote *The Tin Drum* in 1963.

ENTERTAINMENT

1922 Max Bygraves, English entertainer. His records of 'sing-alongs', including 'Mr Sandman' (1955), have always been popular.

1925 Angela Lansbury, English actress who settled in New York at the beginning of the Second World War. On Broadway, she played in *Mame* (1966) and *Sweeney Todd* (1979) which won her Tony awards, and she was nominated for an Oscar for her first film *Gaslight* (1944). Besides her many supporting roles in films such as *Death on the Nile* (1978), she is best known for the television series, *Murder She Wrote*.

1936 Peter Bowles, English actor who is best known for his television appearances in comedy series such as *To the Manor Born*, *Lytton's Diary* and *Perfect Scoundrels*.

1940 Simon Ward, English actor who played the leading role in the television mini-series *Young Churchill*.

POP

1923 Bert Kaempfert, German conductor and composer who had a huge hit with 'Wonderland by Night' in 1961, and also wrote Sinatra's hit 'Strangers in the Night', amongst others.

SPORT

1947 Terry Griffiths, Welsh snooker player and world champion in 1979.

DIED THIS DAY

1555 Hugh Latimer and Nicholas Ridley, English Protestant reformers, found guilty of heresy and burnt at the stake opposite Balliol College, Oxford.
1793 Marie Antoinette was guillotined.
1951 Liaquat Ali Khan, Prime Minister of Pakistan, was assassinated.
1981 Moshe Dayan, colourful Israeli military leader and archaeologist with the black eye-patch.

ON THIS DAY

1822 The new Drury Lane Theatre was opened.
1834 Fire caused extensive damage to the Palace of Westminster, but firemen managed to save both Westminster Hall and St Stephen's Chapel.
1846 An anaesthetic was successfully used for the first time at the Massachussetts General Hospital where dentist William T.G. Morton used diethyl ether prior to removing a tumour from a young man's jaw. Soon after, John Snow, a physician in Britain, enthusiastically adopted the use of this anaesthetic.
1847 *Jane Eyre* by Charlotte Brontë was published under the pseudonym, Currer Bell.
1859 John Brown, US abolitionist whose anti-slavery activity led him to violence. He seized the US armoury at Harper's Ferry in Virginia, hoping to steal arms for his private militia. He and 21 followers were captured and later hanged.
1902 The first Borstal Institution to house young offenders was opened at the village of Borstal, Kent.
1906 British New Guinea became part of Australia.
1908 US aviator Samuel Cody demonstrated his aircraft at Farnborough and became the first man to fly in Britain.
1916 Margaret Sanger and Ethyl Byrne opened the world's first Birth Control Clinic in Brooklyn, New York.
1922 The longest railway tunnel in the world, the Simplon II under the Alps, was completed.
1923 John Harwood patented the self-winding watch in Switzerland, and in 1928 Marin Pipkin of the US patented the frosted lamp bulb.
1936 A meeting between press baron Lord Beaverbrook and King Edward VIII was held to arrange press silence on Edward's affair with Mrs Simpson (27.10.1936).
1946 Nazi war criminals were hanged at Nuremberg. They included von Ribbentrop, Rosenberg and Streicher.
1964 China exploded a nuclear device.
1964 Harold Wilson became Prime Minister of a Labour Government which won a General Election with a majority of four.
1978 Cardinal Karol Wojtyla of Poland became the first non-Italian pope since 1542 and also the youngest this century.

17 OCTOBER

BORN THIS DAY

HISTORY

1727 John Wilkes, English political agitator and advocate of press freedom who, despite being elected to Parliament four times, was not allowed to take his seat. Growing working- and middle-class support eventually secured him his rightful entry to Parliament where he fought for reforms and religious tolerance.

ARTS

1885 Baroness Karen Blixen (Karen Chnstence Dinesen), Danish author who settled in Kenya and wrote the novel *Out of Africa* (1938) under the pseudonym of Isak Dinesen.

1903 Nathaniel West (Nathaniel Weinstein), US author whose experiences as a Hollywood screenwriter are captured in *The Day of the Locust* (1939).

1915 Arthur Miller, leading US playwright who has continued the tradition and style of Eugene O'Neill (*b.* 16.10.1888) with universally acclaimed plays including *Death of a Salesman* (1949) and *A View From the Bridge* (1955). He also wrote the screenplay *The Misfits* (1961) for his wife, Marilyn Monroe, whom he divorced a week before its opening.

ENTERTAINMENT

1905 Jean Arthur (Gladys Georgianna Greene), US actress who specialized in comedies such as *Mr Deeds Goes to Town* (1936) and won acclaim as *Peter Pan* on Broadway in 1950.

1918 Rita Hayworth (Magarita Carmen Cansino), US actress and dancer who partnered Astaire in *You Were Never Lovelier* (1942). She also starred in *The Lady From Shanghai* (1948) directed by Orson Welles, her second husband. They were filing for divorce while the film was being made. Her affair and marriage to playboy Aly Khan lasted two years.

1920 (Edward) Montgomery Clift, US actor who gave sensitive performances in *The Heiress* (1949) and *Suddenly Last Summer* (1959). His early death from a heart attack, aged 45, ended a career still rich with promise.

1939 Evel Knievel, US stuntman who specialised in leaping rows of cars or buses on a motorcycle or in a car. On a British tour in 1975, he suffered spinal injuries when his car failed to jump 13 buses, but lived to leap another day.

1948 Margot Kidder, Canadian-born actress best known for her portrayal of Lois Lane in the Superman films.

SPORT

1925 Harry Carpenter, leading British sports commentator who is usually at the ringside at major events.

1938 Ann Jones (formerly Haydon), English tennis player who beat Billie Jean King in 1969 to win the women's singles at her 14th Wimbledon.

DIED THIS DAY

1849 Frédéric Chopin, Polish pianist and composer, from tuberculosis.

1910 Julia Ward Howe, US author of 'The Battle Hymn of the Republic'.

1912 Millie and Christine, US Siamese twins, died aged 60. They had been continually exhibited and even danced in a chorus line.

1979 S(ydney) J(oseph) Perelman, US humorist and Marx Brothers screenwriter.

ON THIS DAY

1651 Charles II, defeated by Cromwell at Worcester, fled to France, destitute and friendless.

1777 British commander General Burgoyne surrendered to General Horatio Gates at Saratoga, a victory for the American colonists.

1855 A steel-making process was patented by Sir Harry Bessemer.

1860 The first professional golf championship was held at Prestwick, Scotland, won by Willie Park.

1902 The first Cadillac was made in Detroit.

1945 Juan Perón was asked to take over the government of Argentina eight days after being ousted by the army.

1956 The Queen opened Calder Hall, Britain's first nuclear power station.

1965 Lesley Ann Downey's body was found in a shallow grave in the Pennines and was eventually to lead to the arrest of Ian Brady and Myra Hindley, the 'Moors Murderers'.

1985 Mrs Victoria Gillick lost the final round of her campaign to prevent doctors prescribing contraceptives to girls under 16 without parental consent when the House of Lords voted against such action.

1988 Beethoven's lost *Tenth Symphony* was performed for the first time in London as a result of researcher Barry Cooper piecing together fragments of Beethoven's manuscript and sketches discovered in Berlin. Critics said it should have been called 'Excerpts and Snippets'.

18 OCTOBER

The Feast Day of Luke, patron saint of doctors.

BORN THIS DAY

HISTORY

1674 Richard 'Beau' Nash, English gambler who made Bath a city of fashion, improving its streets and buildings.

1919 Pierre (Elliot) Trudeau, Prime Minister of Canada from 1968–79, then again in 1980 until his resignation in 1984.

1939 Lee Harvey Oswald, presumed US assassin of President John F. Kennedy in Dallas, Texas (22.11.1963).

ARTS

1697 Canaletto (Giovanni Antonio Canale), Italian painter of Venetian scenes, as well as views of London which he painted when he worked in England on commissions, 1746–55.

1741 Pierre (Ambroise François Choderlos) de Laclos, French author of *Les liaisons dangereuses*, his one masterpiece written in 1782 and two centuries later adapted by Christopher Hampton as a highly successful play and film.

ENTERTAINMENT

1900 Lotte Lenya (Karoline Blamauer), singer and actress closely identified with the work of Bertolt Brecht and Kurt Weill, her first husband. She played the role of Jenny in *Der Dreigroschenoper* (*The Threepenny Opera*). They left Nazi Germany to settle in the US where she appeared in *Cabaret* and later acted in films including the James Bond *From Russia With Love* in 1963.

1923 Melina Mercouri, Greek actress who is best known for her sparkling performance in *Never on Sunday* (1960) which won her an Oscar nomination. In 1977 she won a seat in the Greek Parliament and was promoted to Minister of Culture, Youth and Sports.

1927 George C(ampbell) Scott, US actor who won an Oscar for his performance playing the lead in *Patten* (1970) which he refused. His other films include *Movie Movie* (1978) and *The Changeling* (1979). On television, he played the lead in *Mussolini – the Untold Story* (1985).

POP

1926 Chuck Berry, US singer who was probably the most influential figure in rock and roll history influencing most of the English groups from the Beatles to the Rolling Stones and others. His 'Maybelline' was one of the first rock and roll hits and amongst others were 'Roll Over, Beethoven' and his enormously successful 'My Ding-a-Ling', suprisingly his only No. 1 in the US.

SPORT

1956 Martina Navratilova, Czech-born US tennis player who dominated the women's game from 1978 to 1987. She won the Wimbledon singles title nine times (six successive wins 1982–7) and 45 Grand Slam event titles.

DIED THIS DAY

1865 Lord Palmerston, twice British Prime Minister, who on his death bed said, 'Die, my dear doctor? That's the last thing I shall do!'

1871 Charles Babbage, English mathematician and inventor of a calculating machine, the forerunner of the computer.

1893 Charles Gounod, French composer of the opera *Faust* (1852–9).

1931 Thomas Alva Edison, prolific US inventor.

1966 Elizabeth Arden, US cosmetics magnate.

ON THIS DAY

1873 The rules of American football were formulated at a meeting in New York by delegates from Columbia, Princeton, Rutgers and Yale Universities.

1887 Russia transferred Alaska to the USA for $7,200,000. Negotiated by US Secretary of State William H. Seward, critics called the treaty, 'Seward's Folly' and claimed he 'was wasting money on a lot of ice'.

1898 The US took possession of Puerto Rico from Spain.

1910 The trial of Dr Hawley Harvey Crippen began at the Old Bailey (31.1.1910). Crippen and his mistress Ethel Le Neve (disguised as a boy) were arrested on board the SS *Montrose* bound for Canada (31.7.1910). The jury reached their verdict on 22.10.1910.

1922 The BBC (British Broadcasting Company) was officially formed.

1957 The Queen and Prince Philip visited the US and the White House to mark the 350th anniversary of the British settling in Virginia.

1963 Harold Macmillan resigned as Prime Minister and was succeeded by Lord Home.

1966 The Queen granted a royal pardon to Timothy Evans, convicted of the murder of his wife and child at 10 Rillington Place, west London. The real murderer was John Reginald Christie who had been hanged for mass murder in 1953. Unfortunately, Evans was hanged in 1950.

1970 The body of Pierre Laporte, Quebec's Minister of Labour, kidnapped by the separatist FLQ (Quebec Liberation Front), was found this day.

1977 Hilary Bradshaw, appropriately from Maidenhead, became the first woman to referee a rugby match when Bracknell played High Wycombe.

1977 Germany's anti-terrorist squad stormed a hijacked Lufthansa aircraft at Mogadishu Airport, Somalia killing three of the four Palestinian hijackers and freeing all the hostages.

1987 A small US company announced it was shipping 12 million pairs of chopsticks to Japan because of a shortage of timber there.

1988 British Home Secretary, Douglas Hurd banned all broadcasts involving terrorist spokesmen. IRA spokesmen could be seen, but not heard, but their statements could be reported by the media.

1989 Erich Honecker, the East German leader, was replaced by Egon Krenz in response to the failing economy and mass flight of young East Germans to the West.

1989 San Francisco was hit by an earthquake which measured 6.9 on the Richter scale killing at least 273 people and injuring 650.

19 OCTOBER

BORN THIS DAY

HISTORY

1859 Alfred Dreyfus, French army officer at the centre of the Dreyfus Affair, who was falsely accused of treason and sent to Devil's Island (*see* 22.12.1894).

1934 General Yakubu Gowon, Nigerian head of state who was educated at Sandhurst. He took control after a military coup in 1966 and tried to unite the country after the civil war (1967–70), but was himself overthrown by a military coup in 1975.

ARTS

1833 Adam Lindsay Gordon, Australian horsebreaker, steeplechase rider and first Australian poet to write in an Australian idiom. His work includes *Bush Ballads and Galloping Rhymes* (1870).

1931 John Le Carré (David John Moore Cornwell), English novelist who worked in the British Foreign Service in the 60s. His first success was in 1963 with *The Spy who Came in From the Cold*, followed by *The Looking Glass War* (1965). All his novels have been filmed or adapted for television or both.

ENTERTAINMENT

1909 Robert Beatty, Canadian actor who has played leads on both the London stage and in films including *2001: A Space Odyssey* (1968) and *Where Eagles Dare* (1969).

1925 Bernard Hepton, English actor in television serials including *Colditz*, *Secret Army* and Le Carre's *Tinker, Tailor, Soldier, Spy*.

1940 Michael Gambon, English actor who starred in *The Singing Detective* on television which won him a brace of awards. He is a leading stage actor as well as appearing in films including *Paris By Night* (1988).

INVENTION

1862 Auguste Lumière, French photographic pioneer who worked with his brother, Louis to develop and manufacture a motion-picture camera and projector called the 'Cinématographe' which is where the word 'cinema' came from. They made the first film, *Lunchbreak at the Lumière Factory* in 1895.

POP

1944 Peter Tosh, Jamaican reggae musician and an original member of Bob Marley's Wailers who went solo in 1975 until his murder in 1988. His hits include '(You Gotta Walk) Don't Look Back' (1978).

DIED THIS DAY

1216 King John of England, during the Civil War which was the result of his repudiating the Magna Carta signed the previous year.

1745 Jonathan Swift, Irish cleric and satirist, author of *Gulliver's Travels* (1726) who died insane.

1897 George Pullman, US designer and manufacturer of Pullman railway coaches.

1937 Ernest, first Baron Rutherford of Nelson, New Zealand-born physicist, founder of modern atomic theory and Nobel prizewinner.

1987 Jacqueline du Pré, one of Britain's finest cellists, from multiple scelrosis, aged 42.

ON THIS DAY

1741 David Garrick made his debut at Goodman's Fields Theatre in London's East End playing Richard III to tumultuous acclaim.

PEACE AND WAR The American War of Independence came to an end in 1781 when Lord Cornwallis surrendered to George Washington at Yorktown, Virginia. In 1864, during the American Civil War, the Battle of Cedar Creek ended with a victory to General Sheridan over the Confederates.

1860 The first company to manufacture internal combustion engines was formed in Florence. The engines were designed by Eugenio Barsanti and Felice Matteucci.

1901 An airship flew around the Eiffel Tower in an attempt to win the Deutsch Prize valued at around £1,000. Albert de Santos, a young Brazilian, made the round trip from a field near St Cloud in the permitted 30 minutes, but took 30 seconds too long to climb out of the gondola and was penalized; public consternation persuaded the judges to award him the prize.

1958 Driving for Ferrari, Mike Hawthorn became world motor racing champion despite coming second in the Moroccan Grand Prix to compatriot Stirling Moss, the winner.

1970 BP announced the first oil find in the North Sea.

1972 The first performance of *Crown Matrimonial* at the Haymarket Theatre, London, with Amanda Reiss portraying the Queen Mother in a drama about the abdication crisis of 1936. This was the first portrayal of a living member of the Royal family on the British stage.

1987 'Black Monday' on Wall Street wiped out millions on the stock markets around the world. Wall Street ended the day down 22%, lower than the 1929 crash.

1989 The 'Guildford Four' had their convictions quashed after serving 15 years for the IRA Guildford and Woolwich bombings.

20 OCTOBER

BORN THIS DAY

HISTORY

1784 Lord Palmerston (Henry John Temple, 3rd Viscount), English statesman, twice Prime Minister, in 1855–8 and 1859–65. Popular with the people, his imperious attitude did not amuse Queen Victoria.

1792 Colin Campbell, Baron Clyde, British commander-in-chief during the Indian Mutiny of 1857 who was nicknamed 'Old Careful' because of his sense of economy: this included winning battles by losing as few of his men as possible.

1926 Lord Montagu of Beaulieu, whose home houses the famous National Motor Museum with one of the world's finest collections of vintage cars.

ARTS

1632 Sir Christopher Wren, English mathematician and architect of St Paul's Cathedral, built between 1675–1710, and other London churches and major buildings including Marlborough House.

1822 Thomas Hughes, English author of *Tom Brown's Schooldays* published in 1857, the school being Rugby under its famous head, Thomas Arnold. Coincidentally Hughes was born on the 255th anniversary of Laurence Sheriff's death in 1567, the founder of Rugby School.

1854 Arthur Rimbaud (Jean Nicholas), French poet who wrote much of his best poetry before he reached the age of 20.

1874 Charles Ives, one of the first major US composers who influenced 20th-century music and set an 'American style', although his *Second Symphony* (1897–1902) was only performed in its entirety 50 years after its composition.

ENTERTAINMENT

1884 Bela Lugosi (Bela Blasko), Hungarian actor who emigrated to the US where he made his name playing the title role in *Dracula* in 1931, and from then became the master of the horror film appearing in *Son of Frankenstein* (1939) and *Bride of the Monster* (1956) among others.

1904 Dame Anna Neagle (Marjorie Robertson), English actress who started in the chorus of *Rose Marie* before starring in musicals including *Charlie Girl* in 1965 when she was 61. She also starred in many films for her husband, Herbert Wilcox, often playing famous women such as Queen Victoria in *Sixty Glorious Years* (1938) and the title role in *Nurse Edith Cavell* (1939), and in romantic films such as *Spring in Park Lane* (1948).

1934 Timothy West, English actor who, besides his many stage performances, played the lead on television in *Churchill and the Generals* and in the comedy series *Brass*.

SCIENCE

1891 Sir James Chadwick, English physicist who received the Nobel Physics prize in 1935 for the discovery of the neutron.

DIED THIS DAY

1524 Thomas Linacre, English physician to Henry VII and Henry VIII, founder of the Royal College of Physicians (1518).

1842 Grace Darling, English heroine of

the wreck of the *Forfarshire* (7.9.1838), from consumption.

1890 Sir Richard Burton, English explorer and translator of *The Arabian Nights*.

1964 Herbert Hoover, 31st US President (1929–33).

1968 Bud Flanagan (Chaim Reeven Weintrop), English comedian.

1987 Dr Phillip Levine, US scientist who discovered the rhesus factor in human blood.

1988 Sheila (Christine) Scott, English aviator, the first European woman to fly solo around the world (1966), from lung cancer.

1989 Sir Anthony Quayle, English actor who won an Oscar nomination for his portrayal of Wolsey in *Anne of the Thousand Days* (1969).

ON THIS DAY

1714 George I was crowned.

1818 The 49th Parallel was established by the US and Britain as a boundary between Canada and the US.

1822 The first edition of the *Sunday Times* was published in Britain.

1827 The Battle of Navarino, off the coast of Greece, ended with the combined British, French and Russian fleets completely destroying the Turkish and Egyptian fleets.

1935 One day short of a year, Mao Tse-tung's 'Long March' ended in Yenan, North China. He had led his threatened Communist army in a 6,000 mile semicircle to safety (21.10.1934).

1944 General MacArthur returned to the Philippines, now the liberator, fulfilling a promise he made when his forces retreated from the Japanese; while on the same day the Allies captured Aachen, the first German city in their drive to Berlin.

1960 D.H. Lawrence's novel, *Lady Chatterley's Lover* (1928) brought Penguin Books to the dock at the Old Bailey under the Obscene Publications Act. Mr Griffiths-Jones prosecuting asked 'Is it a book that you would even wish your wife or your servants to read?' Penguin and the late D.H. Lawrence were found not guilty.

1968 Jackie Kennedy, President Kennedy's widow, married Aristotle Onassis.

1973 The Sydney Opera House was opened by the Queen.

1987 Legal history was made at the Old Bailey again this day (*see* 1960), when a teenage girl gave evidence in a sex abuse case from behind a screen to save her the ordeal of facing her attackers.

21 OCTOBER

Trafalgar Day, commemorating Nelson's victory and his death.

BORN THIS DAY

HISTORY

1833 Alfred (Bernhard) Nobel, Swedish industrialist, chemist and inventor of dynamite. His factory once made nitroglycerine until it blew up in 1864 killing his younger brother. Three years later he found a safer explosive and patented dynamite in 1867. With the vast fortune he made from this and his oil field holdings, he founded the Nobel prize to honour the world's leading scientists, artists and peacemakers from 1901.

1868 Sir Ernest Dunlop Swinton, English tank inventor and the originator of the word 'tank' to describe the armoured vehicle.

ARTS

1760 Katsushka Hokusai, Japanese painter, wood engraver and master printmaker who became the greatest exponent of the Japanese colour prints, his most famous being *Thirty-Six Views of Mount Fuji.*

1772 Samuel Taylor Coleridge, English poet and author who wrote two of the most popular poems in the English language, 'The Ancient Mariner' (1798) and 'Kubla Khan' (1816).

1912 Sir George Solti, British conductor born in Budapest who was director of music at Covent Garden 1961–71 and the London Philharmonic (1979–83).

1921 Malcolm Arnold, English composer who played trumpet with London Philharmonic Orchestra. Besides composing symphonies and concertos, he also wrote ballets including *Homage to the Queen*.

1927 Nadia Nerina (Nadine Judd), South African-born prima ballerina with the Royal Ballet from 1951. Robert Helpmann created the ballet *Elektra* for her in 1963. She was also a guest dancer with the Kirov and Bolshoi ballets.

1933 Maureen (Patricia) Duffy, English novelist whose work includes *The Venus Touch* (1971) and *Gorsaga* (1981) which was adapted for television as *First Born*.

1936 Simon (James Haliday) Gray, English novelist and playwright whose first success, *Butley* (1971) established him as a leading writer. Other plays include *Otherwise Engaged* (1975) and *Close of Play* (1979).

ENTERTAINMENT

1956 Carrie Fisher, US actress, daughter of Eddie Fisher and Debbie Reynolds who made her debut in the film *Shampoo* (1975) and played Princess Leia in *Star Wars*, the first of the series in 1981. She also wrote the book *Postcards from the Edge* (1987).

JAZZ

1917 (John Birks) Dizzy Gillespie, US trumpet player, bandleader and composer of the jazz classic, 'Night in Tunisia'. He became a featured player in several major bands and recorded with Charlie Parker pioneering bebop. The US Government chose him as the first jazz musician to be sponsored on overseas goodwill tours with his band.

POP

1940 Manfred Mann (Michael Leibowitz), South African-born leader of the group of the same name who flourished in the 60s with hits like 'The Mighty Quinn' and 'Pretty Flamingo' with singer Paul Jones.

SPORT

1940 Geoffrey Boycott, Yorkshire and England cricketer, who was one of the best opening batsmen in the world. He played in over 100 tests, captaining four and scoring 139 centuries and passed 200 on ten occassions. He was the only English batsman to average over 100 for a season.

DIED THIS DAY

1931 Arthur Schnitzler, Austrian playwright best known for *La Ronde* (1896).

1969 Jack (Jean-Louis Lebris de)

Kerouac, US poet and novelist, inspirer of the 'Beat Generation' with his book, *On The Road* (1957).

ON THIS DAY

1805 At the Battle of Trafalgar, Nelson gave his famous signal, 'England expects...' which flew from the HMS *Victory* shortly after 1100hrs. The British won this important battle against Napoleon's combined French and Spanish fleets off Cape Trafalgar, south-west of Spain, but Nelson was one of the day's casualties. His body was sent home in a barrel of rum. One of the guards reported hearing gurgling coming from the barrel en route to Deptford where it was unloaded. After Nelson's corpse was removed, sailors found half a barrel of rum abandoned in the dockyard and apparently got 'pickled'. Neat rum is still known in the Royal Navy as 'Nelson's Blood'.

1824 Portland Cement was patented by Joseph Aspdin of Wakefield, Yorkshire.

1858 The first performance of Offenbach's *Orpheus in the Underworld* took place in Paris.

1923 The first planetarium opened in Munich.

1934 Mao Tse-tung's Long March with his 100,000-strong Communist army began after fighting their way out of the siege mounted by Chang Kai-shek's Nationalist armies in Funkien (20.10.1935).

1940 Ernest Hemingway's *For Whom the Bell Tolls* was published in New York.

1958 The first life peer and peeress, Lord Parker of Wassington and Baroness Swanborough, took their seats in the House of Lords.

1960 *Dreadnought*, the first British nuclear submarine, was launched.

1966 A coal slag slid and engulfed the Welsh village of Aberfan killing 116 children and 28 adults. Locals had warned coal board officials and others that the coal slag was unsafe and that there had been signs of a slide before, but these complaints and warnings had been ignored.

1967 Egyptian missiles sank the Israeli destroyer *Eilat* off the coast of Sinai with the loss of over 40 lives.

1969 Willy Brandt was elected Chancellor of West Germany.

1979 Grete Waitz of Norway became the first woman to break the 2hrs 30 minute marathon time, winning the New York marathon in 2 hours 27.6 minutes.

1984 Niki Lauda became world motor racing champion for the third time.

1988 A new service began in London promising to deliver a variety pack of condoms 'to your door, (or hotel room, cinema seat, office lift, car back seat, House of Commons, etc.).'

22 OCTOBER

BORN THIS DAY

HISTORY

1936 Colonel John Blashford-Snell, English adventurer and director of 'Operation Raleigh'.

ARTS

1811 Franz Liszt, Hungarian-born composer and piano virtuoso, a major composer of Romantic music who performed widely in Europe. He was the creator of the symphonic poem, whose most popular works are the lyrical *Liebestraum* and *Hungarian Rhapsodies*.

1870 Lord Alfred (Bruce) 'Bosie' Douglas, English poet and Oscar Wilde's lover. It was his father, the Marquis of Queensbury, who was prosecuted by Wilde for libelling him as a 'sodomite', but which led to Wilde being tried for performing homosexual acts.

1919 Doris Lessing, novelist and short-story writer, born in Persia, who lived in Rhodesia before settling in England where she wrote *The Golden Notebook* (1962) and the quintet of novels *Children of Violence* (1952–69) before moving on to what she calls 'inner space fiction'.

1925 Robert Rauschenberg, US artist who contributed to the Pop Art movement with his technique of blending photographic images into a painting. He had no interest in art until 1942, when, while serving in the US Navy, he happened to visit an art gallery and decided to study painting.

ENTERTAINMENT

1844 Sarah Bernhardt (Henriette Rosine Bernard), French actress called 'The Divine Sarah' by her admirers. She scored a huge success in the title role of Racine's *Phèdre* in 1893 and the theatre changed its name to Théâtre Sarah Bernhardt. She relaxed by lying in a coffin. On tour in South America, she injured her right knee jumping off a parapet in the last act of *Tosca*. Gangrene set in but, despite having her leg amputated in 1915, she was soon back performing in specially written parts.

1917 Joan Fontaine (Joan de Beauvoir de Havilland), US actress born in Tokyo to British parents, who settled in the US as a child with her sister, Olivia de Havilland. Her films include *Rebecca* (1940), which won her an Oscar nomination, and *The Constant Nymph* (1943) which won her an Oscar.

1938 Derek Jacobi, award-winning English actor on stage and screen, known also for his television roles including *I, Claudius*.

1943 Catherine Deneuve (Catherine Dolreac), French actress who played leads in both French and international films including *Repulsion* (1965) and *Belle de Jour* (1967). Her marriage to British photographer David Bailey ended in divorce.

DIED THIS DAY

1806 Thomas Sheraton, English furniture designer and maker.

1906 Paul Cézanne, French Impressionist painter.

1973 Pablo Cassals, Spanish cellist, composer and conductor.

ON THIS DAY

1797 The first parachute jump was made by André-Jacques Garnerin from a balloon 6,000 feet above the Parc Monceau, Paris.

1878 The first floodlit rugby match took place at Broughton, Lancashire.

1881 The first edition of the British magazine *Tit Bits* was published.

1883 The Metropolitan Opera House, New York opened.

1909 Élise Deroche who used the self-created title Baronne de la Roche, became the first woman to fly solo. She was the world's first qualified woman pilot (8.3.1910).

1910 Dr Hawley Crippen was found

guilty of murdering his wife. He was sentenced to be hanged on 23.11.1910 at Holloway Prison, a stone's throw away from the scene of the crime. His mistress, Ethel Le Neve, was tried separately and found not guilty.

1917 The Trans-Australian Railway was opened, running from Kalgoorlie to Port Augusta.

1930 The BBC Symphony Orchestra played their first concert, conducted by Sir Adrian Boult at the Queen's Hall, London.

1962 The Cuban Missile Crisis began when President Kennedy announced a naval blockade against Cuba in protest over the installation of Soviet missile bases on the island.

1962 Nelson Mandela's treason trial began in South Africa. He pleaded not guilty.

DIRTY TRICKS In 1962 William Vassall, an Admiralty clerk, was jailed for 18 years for spying. While in Russia he had been photographed during a homosexual party and blackmailed. This day in 1966, a leading Russian spy, George Blake, escaped from Wormwood Scrubs in west London, where he was serving a 40-year sentence.

1966 Britain's David Bryant won the first world bowls championship singles title in Sydney.

1972 Gordon Banks, England's star goalkeeper damaged his eyes in a car crash.

1986 The world's youngest heart transplant patient, a two-and-a-half-month-old baby from north-west London, was given the heart of a five-day-old Belgian boy by Professor Magdi Yacoub at Harefield Hospital, Middlesex.

1987 The first volume of the Gutenberg Bible (from Genesis to Psalms), was sold in New York for £3.26m ($5.39m) and became the most expensive printed book ever sold at auction.

1987 An aeroplane was found by a deer hunter in the branches of a tree in Star Lake, New York. It had taken off 65 miles away without its pilot who had cranked its propeller to start it. It fell tail first after it ran out of fuel.

23 OCTOBER

BORN THIS DAY

HISTORY

1844 Louis Riel, rebel leader of the Métis (people of Indian-white descent) in Canada. He and his followers captured Fort Garry (now Winnipeg) and established a provisional government (1869–70). The fort was soon recaptured, and Riel was outlawed. He led another rebellion in 1884 which ended in his execution.

ARTS

1844 Robert Bridges, English poet and Poet Laureate from 1913 who worked from 1869 to 1882 as a physician in London hospitals. His poems include 'London Snow' and 'On a Dead Child'.

1817 Pierre (Athanase) Larousse, French lexicographer and encyclopaedist who founded the Parisian publishing house in 1852.

ENTERTAINMENT

1925 Johnny Carson, US entertainer and leading chat show host of the *Tonight* show since 1962. He previously hosted *The Johnny Carson Show*.

1931 Diana Dors (Diana Fluck), English actress who was originally promoted as Britain's post-war sex symbol, and later proved a popular actress and personality in films including *A Kid for Two Farthings* (1955) and on television in the series *Queenie's Castle* (1970–2) as well as in various game shows.

SPORT

1900 Douglas (Robert) Jardine, England cricket captain, born Bombay, who was at the centre of the controversial 'bodyline' tour of Australia in 1932–3. (*See* 17.1.1933)

1940 Pelé (Edson Arantes do Nascimento), Brazilian footballer, one of the finest players the game has ever seen, who made his international debut at age 16 and ended up scoring over 1,000 goals. He is also the only player to have been in three World Cup-winning sides.

BUSINESS

1942 Anita Roddick, English entrepreneur who combined enviromental, health and fashion ideas to create one of the most successful 'niche' retail groups, The Body Shop.

DIED THIS DAY

42BC Marcus Junius Brutus who, five months after his involvement in the assassination of Julius Caesar, committed suicide when his army was crushed by Anthony and Octavian.

1915 W(illiam) G(ilbert) Grace, legendary English cricketer.

1921 John Boyd Dunlop, Scottish veterinary surgeon and the inventor of the pneumatic bicycle tyre.

1939 Zane Grey, US novelist who specialized in Westerns such as *Riders of the Purple Sage* (1912).

1950 Al Jolson (Asa Yoelson), US singer who billed himself as 'the world's greatest entertainer'.

ON THIS DAY

1642 The Cavaliers of Charles I clashed with Cromwell's Parliamentary Roundheads at the Battle of Edgehill in the Cotswolds, the first major but inconclusive encounter between these opposing forces. Sir Robert Welch and Captain John Smith won the first medals for gallantry (presented 1 June 1643)

1812 A rumour that Napoleon had died in Russia encouraged an anti-Napoleonic faction in Paris to try and mount a *coup d'état*. When news reached Napoleon, he hurried back from Moscow ahead of his retreating Grande Armée.

1922 The shortest term of office this century for a British Prime Minister began this day when Andrew Bonar Law took office. Due to ill health, he was replaced six months later (on 22 May 1923) by Stanley Baldwin.

1947 Twelve-year-old Julie Andrews made her debut in *Starlight Roof*.

1954 Britain, US, France and USSR agreed to end the occupation of Germany. On the same day, the Western nations agreed to allow West Germany to enter NATO.

1956 The Hungarian revolt against Soviet leadership began. Thousands of demonstrators called for the withdrawal of Russian forces in Hungary.

1970 The world land speed record of 631.367 m.p.h. was achieved by Gary Gavelich of the US in *Blue Flame*, a rocket-propelled car on Bonneville Salt Flats, Utah.

1972 Access credit cards were introduced in Britain.

GO TO JAIL In 1987 Lester Piggott, former British champion jockey, now a top trainer, was jailed for three years for tax evasion, while in San Antonio, Texas, a burglar sentenced to seven years complained that seven was his unlucky number. The judge raised it to eight years.

1987 Dolphins were first used by the US Navy in the Gulf War to help detect mines.

1988 A dog fell from the 13th floor of a Buenos Aires building and landed on a 75-year-old woman, killing her instantly. As a crowd gathered, a bus knocked down a woman, and a man who saw both incidents dropped dead from a heart attack.

24 OCTOBER

United Nations Day commemorating this day in 1945 when the UN Charter came into force.

The National day of Zambia. In 1964, Northern Rhodesia became independent and was renamed Zambia.

BORN THIS DAY

HISTORY

1769 Jacques Laffitte, French banker who made a vast fortune and became Governor of the Bank of France. During the Revolution, his house was its headquarters. In 1843 he was elected president of the Chamber of Deputies.

ARTS

1904 Moss Hart, US playwright, revue writer and lyricist who collaborated with George S. Kaufman to write the comedy hits, *You Can't Take It With You* (1936) and *The Man who Came to Dinner* (1939).

1915 Tito Gobbi, Italian baritone who excelled in the roles of Figaro in *The Barber of Seville* and Scarpia in *Tosca*.

ENTERTAIMENT

1882 Dame Sybil Thorndike, English actress who was the first to play George Bernard Shaw's Saint Joan and considered by many to have been the finest. She and her husband, Sir Lewis Casson appeared frequently at the Old Vic.

1893 Merian C. Cooper, US producer and director best remembered for the original *King Kong* (1933) and the first Cinerama production, *This is Cinerama* (1952).

1923 Sir Robin Day, influential, delightfully quirky English journalist, broadcaster and long-time chairman of television's *Question Time*.

1924 Jack Warner (Jack Waters), English actor who became famous as Dixon of Dock Green, first in the film *The Blue Lamp* (1950) and then on television.

SCIENCE

1632 Antonie van Leeuwenhoek, Dutch microscopist who was trained as a draper. His interest in microscopes led him to grind over 400 different lenses and he was the first man to see bacteria.

POP

1930 The Big Bopper (John P. Richardson), US singer and songwriter, best known for his hit, 'Chantilly Lace'. He died with Buddy Holly in a plane crash (3.2.1959).

1936 Bill Wyman (William Perks), English bass guitarist who joined the Rolling Stones in December 1962. On 2 June 1989, aged 52, he married his 19-year-old girlfriend, Mandy Smith.

SPORT

1948 Phil Bennett, Wales and British Lions rugby footballer.

BUSINESS

1906 Sir Fred Pontin, British holiday camp founder.

1906 Sir Robert Sainsbury, British grocery chain president.

DIED THIS DAY

1537 Lady Jane Seymour, third wife of Henry VIII, soon after giving birth to a son and heir (Edward VI).

1601 Tycho Brahe, Danish royal astronomer.

1945 Vidkun Quisling, former Norwegian Premier and Nazi collaborator, executed by firing squad in Oslo.

1948 Franz Lehàr, Hungarian composer of *The Merry Widow* (1905).

1957 Christian Dior, French fashion designer who created one of the major post-war styles, the 'New Look'.

1989 Mary McCarthy, US author of *The Group* (1963) among others.

ON THIS DAY

1857 The first football club was formed by a group of Cambridge University Old Boys meeting in Sheffield.

1861 The US transcontinental telegraph line was completed, and the Pony Express Mail Service which ran from St Joseph, Missouri to Sacramento, California, stopped running after just 18 months.

1901 To help pay the mortgage, Mrs Ann Edson Taylor of the US went over the Niagara Falls in a padded barrel.

1908 Emmeline Pankhurst and her daughter Christabel were sent to prison for 'inciting the public to rush the House of Commons'. Two Cabinet ministers were witnesses for the defence including Lloyd-George, then Chancellor of the Exchequer.

1924 A letter purporting to be from Grigori Zinoviev of the USSR calling for socialists in all countries to start a revolution was deliberately leaked to the British press on the eve of an election to help give the Tories a huge victory over Labour. The letter was later denounced as a forgery.

1931 Chicago gangster boss, Al Capone was given an 11-year jail sentence and fined $80,000 for tax evasion. He served eight years.

1937 New Zealand aviator Jean Batten landed in England after a record-breaking 5 day 18 hour and 18 minute flight from Australia.

1987 The most hyped boxing match in Britain took place at White Hart Lane helped along by Joe Bugner's second wife, Marlene, a fast-talking Australian. Frank Bruno, 25, knocked down Joe, 37, in the 8th putting an end to the heavyweight ballyhoo. Bruno took home £750,000, Bugner got £250,000.

1989 US television preacher Jim Bakker was given a 45-year jail sentence and fined $500,000 for swindling his followers of millions of dollars.

25 OCTOBER

The Feast Day of Crispin and his brother, Crispinian, patron saints of shoemakers, a craft they practised in Soissons, France after fleeing persecution in Rome. In 287, they were martyred when, according to one version, they were both thrown into molten lead, but more probably were beheaded. A Kentish claim was that their bodies were cast into the sea and floated ashore at Romney Marsh. St Crispin's Day is also the anniversary of the Battle of Agincourt in 1415.

BORN THIS DAY

HISTORY

1800 Lord Macaulay (Thomas Babington, Baron Macaulay), historian, essayist, poet and politician who advocated parliamentary reform and the abolition of slavery. He wrote the popular volume of verse, *Lays of Ancient Rome* (1842) and his four-volume masterpiece, *History of England* (1848–61).

1888 Richard E(velyn) Byrd, US naval officer, pioneer aviator and polar explorer who claimed for have flown over the North Pole on 9 May 1926. He made several visits to the Antarctic to explore the area from the air.

1936 Martin Gilbert, English historian and official biographer of Sir Winston Churchill.

ARTS

1825 Johann Strauss the Younger, Austrian composer known as 'the Waltz King' for his still-popular waltzes such as 'The Blue Danube' and operettas including *Die Fledermaus* (1874).

1838 Georges (Alexandre Cesare Leopold) Bizet, French composer; best remembered for his opera *Carmen* written just before his death in 1875 from a heart disease.

1881 Pablo Picasso, Spanish painter and sculptor, the most influential and versatile 20th-century artist, who held his first exhibition at age 16 before going on to paint *Les Demoiselles d'Avignon* (1907) a precursor of Cubism.

1889 Abel Gance, French film director of the rediscovered epic, the 17-reel *Napoleon*, one of the most extraordinary films of the late 20s which used advanced techniques, even a simultaneous three-screen effect.

POP

1941 Helen Reddy, Australian singer who went to the US. Her hit 'I Am Woman' (1972) went to No. 1.

DIED THIS DAY

1400 Geoffrey Chaucer, one of the greatest English poets, who died in his leased house in the garden of Westminster Abbey with his masterpiece, *The Canterbury Tales*, unfinished.

1647 Evangelista Torricelli, Italian mathematician and physicist who invented the barometer or as it was then called, 'Torricellian Tube'.

1760 George II, King of England, to be succeeded by his grandson, George III.

1987 Ivan Beshoff, Russian mutineer believed to be the last survivor of the crew of the battleship *Potemkin*. Bad food was the main cause of the famous mutiny in 1905. Beshoff came to Ireland where he owned a fish and chip shop, and was once jailed as a suspected IRA spy.

ON THIS DAY

1415 Just south of Calais in northern France, the Battle of Agincourt took place. One of the many battles of the Hundred Years War, Henry V's longbowmen routed the superior French knights on St Crispin's Day.

1839 Bradshaw's Railway Guide, the world's first railway timetable, was published in Manchester.

1854 Lord Cardigan led the Charge of the Light Brigade during the Battle of Balaclava in the Crimean War. An ambiguous order from the commander, Lord Raglan, led Cardigan's brave cavalry to charge the Russians while fire came from three different sides. As one of the generals was heard to remark as the courageous soldiers suffered heavy casualties, 'C'est magnifique, mais ce n'est pas la guerre'.

1881 The airbrush was patented by L.L. Curtis in the US.

1900 The British annexed the Transvaal, rich in minerals, especially gold.

1906 Professor Lee de Forest of the US patented the three-diode amplification valve, the Audion which made broadcasting possible.

1927 Bix Beiderbecke and his Gang recorded 'Goose Pimples' and 'Sorry'. They are still available today...on CD.

1936 The first radio request programme was broadcast. The station in Berlin introduced *You Ask – We Play*. The first British request programme was *From My Post Bag* on 19 May 1939.

1951 Margaret Roberts (Thatcher), at 26, was the youngest candidate to stand at a General Election. The Tories won by a narrow margin. She failed to win the seat.

1961 The first edition of *Private Eye*, the British satirical magazine was published.

1971 Taiwan was expelled from the UN to make way for the admission of the People's Republic of China.

1976 The National Theatre complex on the South Bank, designed by Denys Lasdun, was officially opened by the Queen. The first production had been staged in March, but not all three of the auditoriums had been completed.

26 OCTOBER

National Day of Austria.

BORN THIS DAY

HISTORY

1759 Georges Jacques Danton, French Revolutionary leader who exhorted the nation when the Revolution was threatened by invading allied armies, 'To conquer the enemies of the fatherland, we need daring, more daring, daring now and always, and France is saved!' While he tried to stabilize the Revolution and disapproved of the Reign of Terror, opposition grew and eventually he and his supporters were arrested and he was put on trial on 5 April 1794.

1803 Joseph Aloysius Hansom, English designer of the Hansom cab (the Patent Safety Hansom Cab) in 1834, with a front folding entrance door and room for two passengers. The driver communicated through a trap door on top. They proved the most popular of London's cabs and were later introduced into New York and Boston.

1879 Leon Trotsky (Lev Davidovich Bronstein), Communist leader who with Lenin, organized the October Revolution. After Lenin's death, Stalin ousted him from the Politburo and forced him into exile in 1929. After a Soviet court sentenced him to death in his absence, he found asylum in Mexico where he was eventually murdered. (20.8.1940).

1916 François Mitterand, founder of the French Socialist Party and President from 1981.

1919 Mohammed Reza Pahlavi, last Shah of Iran who became shah in 1941. He divorced Princess Soraya in 1958 and married Farah Dibah, a former shepherdess the following year. On his birthday in 1967, after 26 years, he crowned himself and his Queen, in Tehran and declared this to be the National Day of Iran. In 1979 Islamic fundamentalism asserted itself and he was eventually driven into exile.

ARTS

1685 Giuseppe Domenico Scarlatti, composer and harpsichordist, son of the equally prolific Alessandro (born 24 October 1659). He was a brilliant performer and composed over 600 sonatas, making a significant contribution to its development.

1930 John Arden, English playwright whose work, such as *Sergeant Musgrave's Dance* (1959) and *The Workhouse Donkey* (1963), featured political themes.

ENTERTAINMENT

1914 Jackie (Leslie) Coogan, US actor, best remembered for the part he played as the child in *The Kid* with Charlie Chaplin in 1921 which made him an international celebrity. His mother and stepfather deliberately withheld his earnings from him even when he came of age, and though he took them to court he found that the money had dwindled and he was only able to win back half. This led to the law protecting child stars in the US known as the Coogan Act.

1942 Bob Hoskins, English award-winning actor of *Mona Lisa* (1986) and *Who Framed Roger Rabbit?* (1988) who first made his mark on television in the highly-acclaimed *Pennies from Heaven*.

MUSIC

1911 Mahalia Jackson, US gospel singer. Her first recordings included 'Move on Up a Little Higher' and 'Silent Night' (1945) which won her international recognition, reinforced by her appearance in the film, *Jazz on a Summer's Day* (1959).

DIED THIS DAY

1440 Gilles de Rais who fought beside Joan of Arc (later St Joan) and was created a marshal of France, hanged after confessing to the murder of countless children (said to be around 150) sacrificed during sexual orgies in which black magic practices took place on his estates and then burnt at Nantes.

1764 William Hogarth, English artist and engraver of the famous *Rake's Progress*.

1972 Igor Sikorsky, Russian born US helicopter pioneer who developed the first successful helicopter in 1938.

1973 Sir Roger Hollis, head of MI5 (1956–65), who was suspected by some of being a Soviet agent.

ON THIS DAY

1825 The Erie Canal (the New York State Barge Canal) was opened linking the Niagara river with the Hudson.

1860 Garibaldi proclaimed Victor Emmanuel King of Italy.

1860 The Physical Society, Frankfurt was given the first demonstration of a telephone when its inventor, Johann Philipp Reis, transmitted verses of songs over a 300-foot line from the Society's meeting room to the neighbouring Civic Hospital, but it appeared the transmission was not sustained and only bursts of the song were ever heard.

1863 The English Football Association was formed in London.

1881 The Gunfight at the O.K. Corral took place outside Tombstone, Arizona Territory between the Ike Clanton gang and the Town Marshal Virgil Earp, his deputized brothers, Wyatt and Morgan, as well as the alcoholic Doc Holliday. In the gun battle, Ike Clanton's brother Billy was shot dead as well as two other members of the gang. Ike Clanton and Billy Claibourne escaped. Virgil and Wyatt Earp both died of old age.

1905 Sweden and Norway ended their union and Oscar II, the Norwegian king, abdicated.

1907 The Territorial Army (the British Volunteer Force) was founded by Secretary of State for War, Richard Haldane.

1912 The Woolwich Tunnel under the Thames was opened.

1927 Duke Ellington and his orchestra recorded 'Creole Love Song' with Adelaide Hall growling a wordless vocal to make this a jazz classic.

1955 *Village Voice*, the influential underground US newspaper, was first published. One of the backers was Norman Mailer.

1956 The International Atomic Energy Agency was formed.

1965 The Beatles received their MBEs at Buckingham Palace.

1984 Known to the outside world simply as Baby Fae, this Californian infant was given a baboon's heart to replace a defective one, but she died on 15 November 1984.

1986 Jeffrey Archer resigned as Deputy Chairman of the Conservative Party after allegations that he had made a payment to a prostitute to make her leave the country and avoid a scandal. He denied the allegations and fought a successful libel case.

27 OCTOBER

BORN THIS DAY

HISTORY

1728 Captain James Cook, English naval officer and one of the greatest navigators in history whose voyages in the *Endeavour* led to the European discovery of Australia, New Zealand and the Hawaiian Islands. Thanks to Cook's understanding of diet no member of his crew ever died of scurvy, the great killer on other voyages.

1811 Isaac Merit Singer, US inventor and manufacturer of domestic and industrial sewing machines despite Elias Howe's infringements case.

1854 Sir William Smith, founder of the Boys' Brigade movement in Glasgow.

1858 Theodore Roosevelt, 26th US President who, among his many accomplishments, won the Nobel Peace prize (1906) for his efforts in ending the Russo-Japanese war.

ARTS

1782 Niccolò Paganini, virtuoso Italian

violinist and composer who mastered such complicated techniques that he was said to be in league with the devil; he performed the *Devil's Dance*, a piece he wrote to show off his uncanny skill. There were other showy pieces in which he would deliberately cut off two of the violin strings and complete the performance without any noticeable effect. He composed violin concertos and other works but, despite being idolized, he ran up huge gambling debts, and at one time was forced to pawn his violin to pay them.

1889 Enid Bagnold (Lady Jones), English novelist best remembered for *National Velvet* (1935) and her successful play, *The Chalk Garden* (1954).

1914 Dylan (Marlais) Thomas, Welsh poet whose major work *Under Milk Wood* began as a radio play in 1954 and has been staged and filmed. Besides his poems, he also wrote a collection of autobiographical short stories, *Portrait of the Artist as a Young Dog* (1940).

1923 Roy Lichtenstein, US painter and pioneer of Pop art whose greatly enlarged comic strip pictures were an enormous success at his first one-man show in New York in 1962.

1932 Sylvia Plath, US poet and novelist of the autobiographical *The Bell Jar* (1967). She married the British poet, Ted Hughes in 1956, but they separated in 1962. The following year in London, she committed suicide.

ENTERTAINMENT

1915 Harry Saltzman, Canadian-born film producer brought up in the US, who set up business in Britain with his partner Albert R. Broccoli making an odd mixture of artistic and commercial films from *Look Back in Anger* (1959) to the highly lucrative James Bond films, the first, *Dr No* in 1962.

1918 (Muriel) Teresa Wright, US actress who had several Oscar nominations for her strong supporting roles in films such as *The Little Foxes* (1941), but finally collecting one for *Mrs Miniver* in 1942.

1939 John Cleese, English comedy actor and writer who established himself on television with the Monty Python series before playing the manic Basil Fawlty in the classic multi-award winning comedy series *Fawlty Towers*. His lead in the film *A Fish Called Wanda* (1988) was equally successful.

SPORTS

1931 David Bryant, English bowls player and world's bowls champion who popularized the game on television, introducing it to a new and large audience.

1957 Glen Hoddle, Tottenham and England international footballer.

DIED THIS DAY

1505 Ivan III, the first Tsar of Russia, known as Ivan the Great.

1969 Eric Maschwitz, English lyricist whose songs include 'These Foolish Things' and 'A Nightingale Sang in Berkeley Square'.

ON THIS DAY

1662 Charles II sold Dunkirk to Louis XIV for 2,500,000 livres.

1901 A 'get away car' was used for the first time when thieves robbed a shop in Paris and raced away.

1904 Mayor McLellan opened the New York Subway.

1936 Mrs Simpson was granted a divorce from her second husband.

1951 Winston Churchill, now aged 77, became Prime Minister once more after the fall of the Labour Government.

1971 The Republic of the Congo changed its name to the Republic of Zaire.

1978 The Nobel Prize Committee announced that the Peace prize would go to President Anwar Sadat of Egypt and Prime Minister Menachem Begin of Israel for their effort in establishing peace between their two countries. They received their awards on 10 December 1978.

1986 'Big Bang' Day in the City of London, brought about by the deregulation of the money market.

28 OCTOBER

BORN THIS DAY

HISTORY

1794 Robert Liston, Scottish physician who carried out the first operation with the aid of an anaesthetic in Britain (21.12.1846).

1846 George-Auguste Escoffier, 'King of Cooks', chef de cuisine of the Carlton and the Savoy in London who also wrote *A Guide to Modern Cookery* with some 5,000 recipes.

1912 Sir (William) Richard Doll, English physician and cancer researcher who first proved the link between cigarette smoking and lung cancer.

1914 Jonas (Edward) Salk, US microbiologist who developed an anti-polio vaccine which virtually eradicated polio in developed countries.

1938 David Dimbleby, English newspaper proprietor and broadcaster, son of the great Richard, who, like his father, commentates at major political and ceremonial occasions.

ARTS

1903 Evelyn (Arthur St John) Waugh, English novelist and journalist who wrote *Decline and Fall* in 1928, establishing him as a leading satirical novelist. Along with *Vile Bodies* (1930), *Scoop* (1934) and *Brideshead Revisted* (1945) he also wrote what some consider his most important novel, *The Ordeal of Gilbert Pinfold* in 1958.

1909 Francis Bacon, a major 20th-century British painter, born in Dublin, whose paintings of distorted and sometimes mutilated human figures are brilliantly disturbing.

1936 Carl Davis, prolific US-born composer and conductor, mainly of television and film scores, including silent classics such as *Napoleon*. Other credits include *The Naked Civil Servant*, and the history series, *The World at War*.

ENTERTAINMENT

1929 Joan Plowright (Lady Olivier), English actress mainly in Shakespearian and classical roles who appeared opposite her husband Laurence Olivier in *The Merchant of Venice* at the Old Vic in 1970.

JAZZ

1927 Cleo Laine (Clementina Dinah Campbell), English singer and actress who achieved international acclaim with many successful US tours. She began as a vocalist for the Johnny Dankworth Seven and his big band, later marrying John Dankworth. Her stage appearances include revivals of

The Seven Deadly Sins by Kurt Weill, *Showboat* and a musical co-written by Dankworth, *Colette*.

POP

1942 Hank Marvin, English guitarist and leader of the Shadows who not only backed Cliff Richard, but were also successful on their own with British No. 1s including 'Apache' (1960) and 'Wonderful Land' (1962).

SPORT

1948 Dennis Taylor, British snooker player and world champion in 1985.

DIED THIS DAY

1792 John Smeaton, English civil engineer who designed the Eddystone Lighthouse.

1899 Otto Morgenthaler, German inventor of the Linotype machine.

1975 Georges Carpentier, French boxer and world light heavyweight champion, 1920–22.

ON THIS DAY

1636 Harvard University was founded, the first in the US. It was named after John Harvard, the English-born Puritan minister who bequeathed £779 and a 300-volume library.

1746 An earthquake demolished Lima and Callao in Peru.

1831 Michael Faraday demonstrated the first dynamo.

1862 The Aereated Bread Company (ABC) began in London. It eventually developed into a major food and retail chain.

1886 The Statue of Liberty was presented by France to the US. It was dedicated by President Cleveland to mark the 100th anniversary of the Declaration of Independence. Designed by Auguste Bartholdi, it took nine years to complete.

1893 The first Royal Navy destroyer, HMS *Havock*, started trials.

1914 George Eastman announced the invention of a colour photographic process to be marketed by his Eastman Kodak Company.

1929 The first baby was born on a plane when Mrs T.W. Evans gave birth to a girl in a transport plane above Florida.

1949 The glove puppet character Sooty, with Harry Corbett, made his first appearance on BBC television.

1958 The state opening of the British Parliament was televised for the first time.

1962 The Cuban Missile Crisis came to an end when Kruschev announced that the USSR would withdraw its missiles from Cuba, and Kennedy said the US would lift the blockade.

1971 The House of Commons voted by a majority of 112 in favour of Britain joining the European Common Market.

1982 The Socialists won a landslide victory in Spain under the new Prime Minister, 40-year-old Félipe Gonzalez.

29 OCTOBER

National day of Turkey. Kemal Atatürk proclaimed Turkey a republic and became its first President.

BORN THIS DAY

HISTORY

1507 The Duke of Alba, Spanish soldier

and statesman who conquered Portugal and was the hated governor general of the Netherlands.

1879 Franz von Papen, German statesman and diplomat who played a leading role in overthrowing the Weimar government and helping Hitler come to power.

1897 (Paul) Joseph Goebbels, Nazi propaganda chief from 1929 and Minister of Propaganda from 1933, who turned from poisoning minds to poisoning himself as the Allies entered Berlin (1.5.1945).

ARTS

1740 James Boswell, Scottish diarist and biographer of Samuel Johnson whom he met in 1763. He accompanied Johnson on a tour retold in *Journal of the Tour to the Hebrides* (1785) before producing his *Life of Samuel Johnson* in 1791.

1882 Jean Giradoux, French author, diplomat and playwright whose work includes *Tiger at the Gates* (1935) and *The Madwoman of Chaillot* (1945).

ENTERTAINMENT

1891 Fanny Brice (Fanny Borach), US Broadway star who introduced the songs 'My Man' and 'Second Hand Rose' in the Ziegfeld Follies from 1910 to 1936. Her life story was immortalized in the musical *Funny Girl* both on stage and film (1968).

1925 Robert Hardy, versatile English actor in television's *All Creatures Great and Small*, *Winston Churchill – the Wilderness Years* and in the off-beat comedy series, *Hot Metal*.

1948 Richard Dreyfuss, leading US actor whose film appearances have included *Close Encounters of the Third Kind* (1977) and *The Goodbye Girl* that same year which won him an Oscar.

JAZZ

1922 Neil Hefti, jazz trumpeter and composer who has written scores for films and television.

SPORT

1877 Wilfred Rhodes, Yorkshire and England cricketer who played 58 tests scoring 2325 runs and taking 127 wickets. He played his last Test on 12 April 1930, aged 52 years, 165 days, the oldest ever to play in a Test.

DIED THIS DAY

1828 Luke Hansard, English publisher and printer to the House of Commons.

1924 Frances Hodgson Burnett, English-born US novelist best known for *Little Lord Fauntleroy* (1886).

1987 Woody Herman (Woodrow Charles Herman), US clarinettist and big band leader from 1936 known as 'the band that played the blues'.

ON THIS DAY

1618 Sir Walter Raleigh, English seafarer, courtier and writer, once a favourite of Queen Elizabeth I, (he named Virginia after her) was beheaded at Whitehall. He had been falsely accused of treason and sentenced to death commuted to imprisonment, but after 13 years had been released to try and find the legendary gold of El Dorado. He failed, and returned to an undeserved fate.

1787 The first performance of Mozart's opera *Don Giovanni* took place in Prague.

1863 The Red Cross was founded by Swiss philanthropist, Henri Dunant (*see* 24.6.1859). On the 46th anniversary of its formation in 1909, Dame Anne Bryans was born and would become the chairman of the Red Cross and Order of St John in Britain.

FINISHING POST Two champion English jockeys retired this day, separated by 99 years. In 1886 Fred Archer rode the last of his 2746 winners at Newmarket retiring after 16 years, and in 1985 Lester Piggott, champion jockey, ended his riding career with one winner out of five rides at Nottingham. He had won the Derby nine times.

1927 Russian archaeologist Peter Kozlov discovered the tomb of Genghis Khan.

1929 'Black Tuesday', so-called when Wall Street crashed leading to the Great Depression. Shares had begun to slide dramatically on 'Black Thursday' (24 October) and the fall only ended on 2 July 1932 when the Dow Jones Industrial Index average had fallen almost 90%.

1945 The Harwell Atomic Energy Research Establishment was set up in England.

1956 Israel invaded the Sinai Peninsula and troops were pushing on towards the Suez Canal, just 20 miles away.

1964 Tanganyika and Zanzibar became known as Tanzania when they united.

1967 Expo-67 opened in Montreal.

1975 The world's largest mining complex opened at Selby, Yorkshire.

1982 The Dingo Baby Murder Case ended in Australia with Lindy Chamberlain, the mother being convicted of the murder of her nine-week-old baby Azaria at Ayers Rock who, she claimed, had been carried off by a dingo. The Darwin Supreme Court sentenced her to life imprisonment, but she was later given a discharge.

1987 Thomas 'Hit Man' Hearns won the world middle heavyweight title, making him the first boxer to win a world title at four different weights.

1988 Two of Britain's greatest middle-distance runners, Sebastian Coe and Steve Cram re-ran the 'Chariots of Fire' race. In 1927 Lord Burghley and Harold Abrahams, later an Olympic gold medallist, decided to sprint around the Great Court, Trinity College, Cambridge, setting off as the clock began to strike twelve and completing the 367m circuit before the twelfth stroke. Seb Coe won in 45.52 seconds. In the original race (not in the film) Lord Burghley actually beat Abrahams crossing the line in 42.5 seconds.

30 OCTOBER

BORN THIS DAY

HISTORY

1735 John Adams, 2nd US President from 1797–1801, who signed the Declaration of Independence and went to France to negotiate the treaties that ended the War of American Independence.

ARTS

1751 Richard Brinsley Sheridan, Irish-born playwright and one-time owner of the Drury Lane Theatre, who wrote social comedies that are still considered the best in the language including *The Rivals* (1775) with the famous Mrs Malaprop, and *School for Scandal* (1777).

1840 Alfred Sisley, French-born painter

of English parents who had little or no recognition during his lifetime, but is now considered one of the most important Impressionists.

1885 Ezra Pound, US poet who lived mainly in Europe and whose poetry influenced Eliot, Joyce and Yeats. He was arrested by US troops in Italy in 1945 where he had spent the war broadcasting anti-semitic and pro-fascist propaganda. Found to be mentally unstable, he was sent to a mental home.

ENTERTAINMENT

1932 Louis Malle, French film director whose first film was with Jacques Cousteau, *The Silent World* (1956). His other films include *Zasie dans le Métro* (1960).

1935 Michael Winner, English film producer and director best known for *Hannibal Brooks* (1969) and the *Death Wish* series, with box offices coining it from 1974.

1945 Henry Winkler, US actor who played the now-cultish the Fonz in the television series *Happy Days* in the early 70s.

POP

1939 Grace Slick, US singer, originally with Jefferson Airplane until she went solo in 1974. She returned to record the album *Modern Times* with the Starship (as they were then called) in 1981.

SPORT

1960 Diego Maradona, outstanding Argentinian footballer who was sold to Barcelona in 1982 for a record £5m. In the 1986 World Cup, he was the player who fisted in an illegal goal against England which helped Argentina to win the quarter-final. He claimed it was 'the hand of God'.

DIED THIS DAY

1747 Admiral Edward Vernon ('Old Grog'), English naval commander who got his nickname when he ordered his captains to mix water with the official tots of rum to reduce the excessive drunkenness of the sailors. They still got a quarter of a pint of rum mixed with a quart of water each day.

1823 Edmund Cartwright, English inventor of the power loom.

1910 Henri Dunant, Swiss philanthropist who founded the International Red Cross.

1923 Andrew Bonar Law, Canadian-born British Prime Minister.

1959 (James Allan) Jim Mollison, Scottish aviator and holder of many flying records including the first solo flight from England to Cape Town. His marriage to his former rival, Amy Johnson, was dissolved in 1938.

1979 Sir Barnes Neville Wallis, British airship and aircraft designer who invented the famous 'bouncing bombs' which destroyed key German dams during the Second World War.

ON THIS DAY

1485 Henry VII established the Yeoman of the Guard.

1894 The Time Card recorder was patented by D.M. Cooper of New Jersey.

1905 The October Manifesto: The Tsar of Russia bowed to pressure and agreed to grant civil liberties and elections in the hope of preventing a revolution by striking workers and oppressed peasants.

1905 Aspirin went on sale in Britain. It was developed by the German pharmaceutical company Bayer. (*See* 6.3.1899)

1911 Pu Yi, the boy emperor of China, aged five, on the advice of the regent Prince Chun granted a new constitution to combat the growing support for the Republican army and officially ended three centuries of Manchu domination over China.

1914 The Battle of Ypres began. (It ended on 21 November.)

1918 Czechoslovakia was proclaimed a republic with leaders Tomăš Masaryk and Edvard Beneš.

1922 Benito Mussolini, who at 39 became Italy's youngest Prime Minister, formed a Fascist ministry in Rome.

1925 In his workshop in London John Logie Baird achieved the first television pictures using a dummy's head. He then persuaded a 15-year-old office boy, William Taynton to come and sit in front of the camera and to become the first live person captured on television.

1938 Orson Welles' radio production and adaptation of H.G. Wells story, *War of the Worlds* caused panic and at least one death through heart failure by convincing many that Martians had really landed in the US. It made 23-year-old Welles and many of his Mercury Theatre cast (including Joseph Cotton) household names.

1942 Montgomery's Eighth Army began its major offensive at El Alamein with thousands of guns lighting up the sky.

1959 Ronnie Scott's jazz club opened in London's Soho.

1967 Brian Jones of the Rolling Stones was jailed for nine months for drug offences, but released on bail pending an appeal.

1974 Muhammad Ali regained his world heavyweight boxing title when he knocked out George Foreman in the eighth round in Kinshasa.

1984 Father Jerzy Popieluszko aged 37, a friend of Solidarity who had been kidnapped 11 days earlier, was found beaten to death in a reservoir in central Poland murdered by government agents.

1988 The mass marriage of 6,516 couples who had only met the day before took place in a Seoul factory. The Reverend Sun Myung Moon, founder of the Moonies, conducted the service.

31 OCTOBER

Halloween (All Hallows Eve), the day the souls of the dead were supposed to revisit their homes.

BORN THIS DAY

HISTORY

1802 Benoit Fourneyron, French inventor who developed the water turbine based on a proposal by his former professor, Claude Burdin. It was only realized how important the turbine could be when it was installed on the US side of the Niagara Falls to turn generators to provide electricity.

1828 Sir Joseph Swan, English chemist and inventor. Both he and Edison are separately credited with the invention of the electric lamp. Edison was first, but his had a much shorter life and was therefore not practical.

1887 Chiang Kai-shek, Chinese general and leader of the Kuomintang (Nationalist People's Party) until ousted by the Communists. He remained as leader in exile on Taiwan.

ARTS

1632 Jan Vermeer, Dutch painter whose

life seems clouded in mystery.The rarity of his almost photographic paintings and their artistic value makes them much prized.

1795 John Keats, English Romantic poet best known for his 'Odes'; 'Ode on a Grecian Urn', 'Ode to a Nightingale' (both 1819) and 'Hyperion' (1818).

1920 Dick Francis, popular English crime novelist who sets his stories in the horse racing world where he orginally worked as a jockey.

1926 H(enry) R(eymond) F(itzwalter) Keating, English author who created Inspector Ghote of the Bombay Police, featured in many novels. He has also written extensively about crime and crime fiction.

ENTERTAINMENT

1922 Barbara Bel Geddes, US actress who plays the mother in the television soap *Dallas*, for which she won an Emmy in 1980.

1926 Jimmy Savile, OBE, former English wrestler turned television and radio presenter with his successful *Jim'll Fix It* programme. He has devoted much of his time to fund raising, and was honoured for his efforts. He also spends some time each week working as a hospital porter in Leeds.

POP

1961 Larry Mullen, Irish pop musician with the group U2.

SPORT

1929 Eddie Charlton, Australian snooker champion 1964–7, 1969–78, 1984 and three times runner-up in the World Professional Championships. 'Steady Eddie' became the World Matchplay champion in 1976.

DIED THIS DAY

1926 Harry Houdini, the US magician and escapologist, as a result of a burst appendix. He was lecturing to a group of students in Montreal about how his stomach muscles could withstand punches when a student punched him twice without warning. He died from peritonitis.

1961 Augustus John, Welsh portrait painter.

ON THIS DAY

1828 A beggar woman named Docherty was invited back to a house in Edinburgh by William Burke. William Hare turned up soon after and strangled her. She was the last victim of the infamous body snatchers, for her death was to be discovered and the police called.

1864 Nevada became the 36th state of the Union.

1888 Pneumatic bicycle tyres were patented by Scottish inventor John Boyd Dunlop.

1915 The first steel helmets were issued to British troops on the Western Front.

1940 The Battle of Britain ended. The Royal Air Force had lost 915 aircraft, the Luftwaffe 1,733.

1951 The first zebra crossings were introduced in Britain.

1952 The first hydrogen bomb was detonated by the US at Eniwetak Atoll, Marshall Islands in the mid-Pacific.

1955 Princess Margaret announced that she would not marry Captain Peter Townsend, a divorcee.

1958 In Stockholm, Dr Ake Senning implanted the first internal heart pacemaker.

1964 The Windmill Theatre off London's

Piccadilly Circus finally closed after 32 years excluding 12 compulsory days in 1939 at the start of the war. The slogan 'We Never Closed' was a tribute to the tiny theatre that stayed open to troops during the war and later saw new comedians get their first blooding in between the Windmill Girls and the posing nudes. Hancock, Sellers, Milligan and Bentine were just some who played in the Windmill's *Revuedeville* shows starting in the late morning and running non-stop till late evening.

1971 An IRA bomb exploded at the top of the London Post Office Tower near the revolving restaurant. The building has been closed to the public ever since.

1984 Mrs Indira Gandhi, Prime Minister of India was shot dead by a Sikh member of her bodyguard in New Delhi while walking to a meeting with Peter Ustinov to discuss making a documentary about her.

1987 A London bank allowed a trainee accountant, 23-year-old Anil Gupta to run up debts of more than £1m to deal in traded options. When shares dropped dramatically, he lost all and admitted not 'having a bean'.

1987 Two young people beheaded themselves in a bizarre double suicide near Canberra, Australia. They were found strapped in the front seat of their car with their heads in the back, but Australian police refused to say how this was done.

THE PAN BOOK OF DATES

NOVEMBER

We are tomorrow's past
(Mary Webb)

I NOVEMBER

BORN THIS DAY

HISTORY

1762 Spencer Perceval, British Prime Minister from 1809 who was assassinated in the House of Commons (11.5.1812).

ARTS

1500 Benvenuto Cellini, Italian sculptor and goldsmith who made celebrated pieces including a remarkable salt-cellar now in Vienna and much sculpture such as his famous *Perseus*. He was one of the most picturesque characters of the Renaissance, a brawler who killed a rival goldsmith and was absolved by Pope Paul III. He was imprisoned for embezzlement, but escaped.

1757 Antonio Canova, leading Italian Neo-classical sculptor who did several tombs for the Popes including the well-known *The Tomb of Clement XIII* (1783–7).

1871 Stephen Crane, US author of *The Red Badge of Courage* (1895), a masterpiece on the American Civil War, remarkable for its realism, especially as the author had not seen battle when he wrote it.

1887 L(awrence) S(tephen) Lowry, English painter of cult status whose his distinctive 'matchstick' characters inhabit his north England industrial landscape.

1897 Naomi Mitchison, Scottish author noted for her historical novels including *The Conquered* (1923) and *The Far Harbour* (1957).

1923 Victoria de los Angeles (Victoria Gomez Cima), Spanish soprano who established her operatic and recording career with strong performances as Mimi, Butterfly, Carmen and other dramatic roles.

ENTERTAINMENT

1915 Michael Denison, English actor who played leads both on the British stage and screen, including the film *The Importance of Being Earnest* (1952) and in various television thrillers.

SPORT

1935 Gary Player, South African golfer who won the South African Open 11 times, and who has a long list of victories including the US Masters, US Open, the Australian Open (seven times), and is one of only a handful to have won all four of the world's major championships.

1962 Sharon Davies, English swimmer and Olympic silver medallist in Moscow (1980) in the 400m medley.

DIED THIS DAY

1793 Lord George Gordon, British anti-Catholic who stirred up the infamous 'Gordon Riots' in 1790, but who died in Newgate Prison convicted of libelling Marie Antoinette.

1972 Ezra Pound, major US poet.

1985 Phil Silvers (Philip Silver), US comedian best remembered as the immortal Sergeant Bilko.

1988 Louis (Albert) Johnson, leading New Zealand poet.

ON THIS DAY

1695 The Bank of Scotland was founded.

1755 An earthquake reduced two thirds of Lisbon to rubble. It is said 60,000 died in the catastrophe.

1848 W.H. Smith opened their first railway bookstall at Euston station, London, the start of Britain's first multiple retailer.

1895 The first motoring organization, the American Motor league was founded, a month before the Self-Propelled Traffic Association was formed in Britain (10.12.1895).

1922 The first radio licences went on sale this day in Britain at a cost of ten shillings (50p).

1927 Betting tax was first levied in Britain. Two days later, the bookies went on strike at Windsor in protest.

1940 A prehistoric painting was discovered in a cave at Lascaux in the Dordogne.

1946 The première of *A Matter of Life and Death* with David Niven, which was also the first Royal Command Film Performance, was held at the Empire, Leicester Square.

1947 *Sports Report*, the BBC radio's Saturday afternoon programme, first went on the air. It celebrated its 40th birthday in 1987, making it the world's longest running radio programme.

1950 Two Puerto Ricans attempted to assassinate President Truman; he escaped uninjured but his guard was shot dead and two others were wounded.

1956 Premium Bonds went on sale in Britain. (First winner, 1.6.1957.)

1959 The first stretch of Britain's first motorway, the M1, was opened.

1961 The body of the now-disgraced Stalin was removed from Lenin's Mausoleum in the Red Square.

1981 The world Mastermind championships (the board game) was played in the Temple of Luxor and won by John Seargent from Leicester, a 19-year-old mathematics student, champion since 1976.

1984 Rajiv Gandhi was sworn in as Prime Minister of India.

1988 After 48 years as Batman's sidekick, Robin the Boy Wonder was dynamited by the Joker in this month's edition of DC Comics' *Batman* (Number 428). This was in response to a reader poll which voted he should go. (Batgirl was killed off in the late 60s.)

2 NOVEMBER

BORN THIS DAY

HISTORY

1734 Daniel Boone, legendary American frontiersman and hunter who led a party to find a trail through the Cumberland Gap in the Apalachian Mountains and eventually settled in Kentucky. Although he was captured by the Indians, he was adopted as a son of the Shawnee chief, Blackfish, before returning to the settlement.

1755 Marie Antoinette, Austrian princess and Queen Consort of Louis XVI of France, whose arrogant and extravagant behaviour helped fuel the unrest that led to the Revolution. Of the poor she said, 'If they have no bread, let them eat cake.'

TWO OF A KIND Two US Presidents were born and two US states joined the Union. James (Knox) Polk, 11th US President was born 1795 and took office in 1844. He was an expansionist president, adding California and New Mexico to US territory. Warren (Gamaliel) Harding, 29th US President, born 1865, who took office in 1921 but his administration was blighted with corruption. He died before the end of his term. In 1889, North and South Dakota became the 39th and 40th states of the Union.

ENTERTAINMENT

1906 Luchino Visconti (Count Don Luchino Visconti di Mondrone), Italian film director who made *The Leopard* (1963) and *Death in Venice* (1971).

1913 Burt(on Stephen) Lancaster, US actor, a former circus acrobat who has made some of the more interesting films to come out of Tinseltown over the past 40 years: *The Sweet Smell of Success* (1957), *Elmer Gantry* (1960), which won him an Oscar, and *The Birdman of Alcatraz* (1962).

SPORT

1954 Ken Rosewall, Australian tennis player who reached the Wimbledon final four times between 1954 and 1974. He first made history playing in the longest singles match (2.7.1954). The next two finals he lost to fellow Australians. Aged 39, he fought his final battle with the crowd willing him on, but was beaten by Jimmy Connors.

POP

1948 Keith Emerson, English keyboard player and singer, first with the Nice and later with Emerson, Lake and Palmer. They had no individual hits, but their albums, including *Brain Salad Surgery* (1973), sold well. Their stage appearances were frenetic, but Emerson injured his hands when his keyboard blew up in a stunt that went wrong.

DIED THIS DAY

1887 Jenny (Johanna Maria) Lind, known as the 'Swedish Nightingale' for the purity of her voice, died in Malvern Wells, Worcestershire.

1950 George Bernard Shaw, British playwright, critic, pamphleteer and Nobel prize winner.

1961 James (Grover) Thurber, US humorist and cartoonist who created 'Walter Mitty'.

ON THIS DAY

1871 In Britain, photographs of prisoners were taken for the first time, originating the world's first Rogues Gallery.

1896 The first motor insurance policies were issued in Britain but they excluded damage caused by frightened horses.

1899 The Siege of Ladysmith in Natal began, with the Boers encircling the town.

1903 The *Daily Mirror* was first published in Britain, devised as a daily paper for women.

1917 The Balfour Declaration, in reality a letter from Lord Balfour, British foreign secretary to Lord Rothschild, stated the government's sympathies for Jewish Zionist aspirations for a Jewish homeland in Palestine and promised British aid to Zionist efforts to support this aspiration.

1920 KDKA in Pittsburg became the world's first regular broadcasting station.

1924 The first crossword appeared in a British newspaper, the *Sunday Express*, 11 years after first appearing in the US (21.12.1913).

1930 Ras Tafari was crowned Haile Selassie, Emperor of Ethiopia.

1936 The first daily high definition television transmission in Britain was broadcast by the BBC from Alexander Palace, north London.

1954 The classic comedy series, *Hancock's Half Hour* began on BBC radio.

1963 Archaeologists in the US found evidence of the Vikings dated 500 years before Columbus.

1964 Prince Faisal ascended the throne succeeding his brother, the deposed King Saud of Saudi Arabia.

1976 Jimmy Carter was elected 38th US President.

1982 Channel 4 was launched on British television.

3 NOVEMBER

BORN THIS DAY

HISTORY

1801 Karl Baedeker, German publisher, famous for his guide books.

1901 Leopold III, who became King of the Belgians from 1934.

ARTS

1801 Vincenzo Bellini, Italian opera composer best known for *Norma* (1831) and *La Sonnambula* (1831).

1919 Ludovic Kennedy, Scottish broadcaster and author whose books and television programmes on Timothy Evans, Stephen Ward and others he felt were victims of injustice were highly effective. In the case of Evans, it brought about his pardon, even if it was after he had been hanged.

ENTERTAINMENT

1921 Charles Bronson (Charles Buchinsky), US actor who first appeared in the films *House of Wax* (1953), and *Vera Cruz* (1954)) under his real name. As the craggy-faced Bronson he appeared in many films such as *The Magnificent Seven* (1960) and *Death Wish* (1974).

1933 John Barry, English composer and conductor of many film and television scores including *A Lion in Winter* (1968), which won him an Oscar, and several Bond films.

1935 Jeremy Brett (Peter Jeremy Huggins), English actor who established himself on television as the most mannered, yet totally convincing, Sherlock Holmes.

POP

1948 Lulu (Marie McDonald McLaughlin), pint-sized Scottish singer who had an international hit back in 1967 with the theme song of the film *To Sir With Love* in which she played a small part. But she is associated with her earlier hit 'Shout', which suprisingly never got to No. 1. In 1960, she married Bee Gee Maurice Gibb, and later hairdresser John Frieda.

1954 Adam Ant (Stuart Goddard), English singer with the Ants who had hits including two No. 1s in 1981, 'Prince Charming' and 'Stand And Deliver'.

DIED THIS DAY

1926 Annie Oakley (Phoebe Anne Oakley Moses), the legendary US sharpshooter with 'Buffalo Bill's Wild West Show'.

1954 Henri Matisse, French painter and sculptor.

ON THIS DAY

1706 The town of Abruzzi in Italy was destroyed by an earthquake which killed around 15,000 people.

1843 Nelson's statue was hauled to the top of the column in Trafalgar Square. The operation which began this day was completed on the 4th when the statue's two sections were assembled.

1903 Panama proclaimed its independence from Columbia.

1942 Montgomery's Eighth Army broke through Rommel's front line in Africa taking 9,000 prisoners and destroying 300 tanks in the next days.

1949 The BBC bought the Shepherd's Bush Studios in west London from the Rank Organisation.

1957 The Russian dog, Laika became the first in space inside *Sputnik II*.

1975 The Queen opened the North Sea pipeline, the first to be built underwater, which brings 400,000 barrels of North Sea oil ashore each day at Grangemouth Refinery on the Firth of Forth.

1976 The first £100,000 Premium Bond was won by someone in Hillingdon.

1978 The 'Muldergate Scandal' broke in South Africa when it was discovered that Information Minister, Connie Mulder had misused a £37 million propaganda fund.

VICTIMS OF VIOLENCE In 1984 Mrs Indira Gandhi, Prime Minister of India, was cremated after being assassinated by a Sihk bodyguard, and in Poland Father Jerzy Popieluszko was buried after being murdered by Polish Secret Police. Over 200,000 attended his funeral.

1985 Two French agents in New Zealand pleaded guilty to sinking the Green Peace ship, *Rainbow Warrior* and to the manslaughter of a photographer on board. They were sentenced to ten years imprisonment.

1988 Koo Stark was awarded £300,000 libel damages over articles in the *Sunday People* which implied she had an adulterous affair with Prince Andrew after her marriage.

4 NOVEMBER

BORN THIS DAY

HISTORY

1650 William III, King of England, Scotland and Ireland, born in Holland, posthumous son of William II, Prince of Orange. On the day after his 38th birthday he landed at Torbay with an army of English and Dutch troops, and when Parliament declared the throne empty, he was proclaimed king (13.2.1689).

1740 Augustus Montague Toplady, controversial English vicar of Hembury, Devon who was a staunch defender of Calvinism and the writer of the ever-popular hymn 'Rock of Ages'.

ENTERTAINMENT

1879 Will Rogers (William Penn Adair Rogers), US humorist and actor famous for his homespun wit who began his career with a rope-twirling and lassoing act. His humorous political commentary while appearing in Ziegfeld's *Midnight Follies* in 1915 led to a syndicated newspaper column. His films include *Connecticut Yankee* (1931) and *State Fair* (1933). He died in a plane crash with Wiley Post (15.8.1935).

1916 Walter Cronkite, award-winning US journalist, television newsreader and commentator with CBS.

1918 Art Carney (Arthur William Matthew Carney), US actor who played leads on Broadway including *The Odd Couple* in 1960, and in films such as *Harry and Tonto* (1974), which won him an Oscar.

1944 Loretta Swit, US actress who was Hotlips Houlihan in the long-running, acclaimed television series *M*A*S*H*.

1963 Lena Zavaroni, Scottish child star who won *Opportunity Knocks* aged ten, but later suffered from anorexia nervosa which she conquered to appear (as an adult) in her own television specials.

DIED THIS DAY

1847 (Jakob Ludwig) Felix Mendelssohn-Bartholdy, German composer and pianist.

1918 Wilfred Owen, English poet, killed in action on the Western Front.

1921 Takashi Hara Kei, Japanese Prime Minister who was assassinated by a Korean the day before Prince Hirohito ascended the throne.

ON THIS DAY

BLESS THIS HOUSE The Houses of Parliament celebrate four anniversaries this day. In 1605 Guy Fawkes was arrested when around 30 barrels of gunpowder camouflaged with coals and faggots were discovered in the cellar under Parliament. Robert Catesby's small band of Catholic zealots who planned to blow up James I and Parliament were only arrested after Fawkes revealed their names when tortured on the rack. This same day in 1852 the House of Commons Press Gallery was opened, and 100 years later in 1952 Queen Elizabeth II opened her first Parliament. In 1958 Baroness Elliott of Harwood became the first woman to address the House of Lords.

1879 The first cash register was patented by James Ritty who owned a saloon in Dayton, Ohio.

1890 The Prince of Wales travelled by Underground electric railway from King William Street to the Oval to mark the opening of what is now the City Branch of the Northern Line. This was the first electrified underground railway system and the carriages were illuminated by electric lights.

1914 The first fashion show was organized by Edna Woodman Chase of *Vogue* magazine and held at the Ritz-Carlton Hotel, New York.

1946 UNESCO (United Nations Educational, Scientific and Cultural Organization) was established.

1952 Dwight David Eisenhower was elected 34th US President.

1979 Iranian students stormed the US Embassy in Tehran and held over 60 staff and US Marines hostage.

1980 Ronald Reagan was elected 40th US President.

1987 Millionaire Peter de Savary bought Land's End.

5 NOVEMBER

Guy Fawkes Night in Britain since 1607, marking the discovery in 1605 of the Gunpowder Plot to blow up the Houses of Parliament (4.11.1605), when Guy Fawkes was arrested. The setting off of fireworks is still preceded by children asking for 'a penny for the Guy', a grotesque effigy of Guy Fawkes which is burnt on a bonfire this night.

BORN THIS DAY

ARTS

1884 James Elroy Flecker, English poet and playwright best known for his poem 'The Journey to Samarkand' (1913) and the play *Hassan*, performed with music by Delius in 1923.

ENTERTAINMENT

1905 Joel McCrea, US actor and a leading man in films such as Hitchcock's *Foreign Correspondent* (1940) and *Ride the High Country* (1962).

1912 Roy Rogers (Leonard Sly), US actor who inherited the title, 'King of the Cowboys' from Gene Autry, as a singing cowboy in films and television. His horse, Trigger, 'the smartest horse in the business', was also probably the better actor, not that Rogers need care. A shrewd businessman, he was reckoned to be worth over $100m.

1913 Vivien Leigh (Vivien Mary Hartley), English actress born in India who starred opposite her husband-to-be, Laurence Olivier, in *Fire Over England* (1937). They married soon after her worldwide success as Scarlett O'Hara in *Gone with the Wind* (1939), which won her an Oscar, and in 1951 she won her second for Blanche in *A Streetcar Named Desire*.

1940 Elke Sommer (Elke Schletz), German actress who speaks seven languages fluently. Films include *A Shot in the Dark* (1964).

1963 Tatum O'Neal, US actress who began as a child star opposite her father Ryan in *Paper Moon* (1973). It made her the youngest recipient of the Oscar and she also became the highest paid child star ever.

SCIENCE

1892 John (Burdon Sanderson) Haldane, English physiologist and geneticist who was a popularizer of biology and pioneered research in population genetics and evolution.

POP

1931 Ike Turner, US singer, songwriter and multi-instrumentalist who with his wife, Tina, and the miniskirted Ikettes had a hit with 'River Deep – Mountain High' before they split.

1942 Art Garfunkel, US singer and other half of the talented and successful duo with Paul Simon whose first hit was, 'The Sound of Silence' in 1966.

SPORT

1935 Lester Piggott, English champion jockey who had nine Derby wins and became a trainer in 1985 when he retired. In 1987, he was sent to prison for a year for tax evasion.

DIED THIS DAY

1960 Mack Sennett (Michael Sinnott), Canadian-born 'King of Comedy' who created Hollywood's immortal 'Keystone Cops'.

1979 Al Capp (Alfred Gerald Caplin), US cartoonist who created 'Li'l Abner' in 1934.

1987 Eamonn Andrews, Irish-born broadcaster who presented *This Is Your Life* on British television 1952–87.

1989 Vladimir Horowitz, Russian-born pianist, in New York.

ON THIS DAY

1854 The combined British and French armies defeated the Russians at the Battle of Inkerman during the Crimean War.

1909 Woolworth's first store in Britain opened in Liverpool.

1912 The British Board of Film Censors was appointed. They decided on only two classifications: Universal and Not Suitable for Children.

1914 Cyprus was annexed to Britain.

1919 The world's greatest screen lover, Rudolph Valentino, married actress Jean Acker, and found he was locked out on his wedding night. The marriage lasted less than six hours.

1922 Howard Carter discovered Tutankhamun's tomb in the Valley of the Kings near Luxor, Egypt, undisturbed since 1337BC.

1927 Britain's first automatic traffic lights were installed at Princess Square road junction in Wolverhampton.

1932 Gillespie Road London Underground station, which also served Arsenal Football Club's Highbury ground, had its name changed to Arsenal after representations by the club.

1940 Roosevelt won a record third term as US President. He won his fourth term four years later on 7 November 1944, while in 1968 Richard Nixon was elected 37th US President.

1971 Princess Anne was voted 'Sportswoman of the Year' by the British Sportswriters Association.

6 NOVEMBER

BORN THIS DAY

HISTORY

1638 James Gregory, Scottish mathematician and astronomer who described the first practical reflecting telescope and contributed towards the discovery of calculus.

1814 (Antoine-Joseph) Adolphe Sax, Belgian musical instrument maker who invented the saxophone in 1840, patenting it in 1846.

1861 James A. Naismith, US inventor of basketball while he was physical education director of the International Young Men's Christian Association Training School, Springfield, Massachusetts. He also invented the 'A' as a second name.

1892 Sir John Alcock, English aviator who flew the first non-stop flight across the Atlantic in 1919 with Sir Arthur Whitten-Brown.

ARTS

1854 John Philip Sousa, US conductor and composer of around 140 marches, which earned him the title the 'March King'. His compositions include 'The Stars and Stripes Forever' (1897).

1941 James Bowman, English counter tenor who has sung many of the castrato roles in Handel operas, fortunately without the need of an operation.

ENTERTAINMENT

1923 Donald Houston, Welsh actor who had major roles in films including *Where Eagles Dare* (1969) and *The Sea Wolves* (1980).

1930 Donald Churchill, English actor and

playwright best known for his television comedy in which he also appeared, *A Bit of a Lift* and his role in the sitcom *Spooner's Patch*.

1931 Mike Nichols (Michael Igor Peschkovsky), German-born US director who came to the US with his parents in 1938. He formed a successful partnership with Elaine May, performing satire until they parted in 1961 when he made his debut as a Broadway director. In Hollywood, he directed *Who's Afraid of Virginia Woolf?* (1966), and won an Oscar with *The Graduate* (1967).

1949 Nigel Havers, English actor, son of the Attorney General, best known for his role as the young Dr Latimer in television's *Don't Wait Up*.

JAZZ

1916 Ray Coniff, US trombonist, arranger and composer who also made successful albums with Bob Crosby and others, including *Just Kiddin' Around*.

1923 Don Lusher, English trombonist and bandleader known as the master technician of his instrument. He performed with Henry Mancini and many leading bands before forming his own.

POP

1938 P.J. Proby, US pop singer who split his jeans as a gimmick at concerts until he was banned on his British tour. (*See* 1.2.1965)

1948 Glenn Frey, US musician, singer and songwriter with the Eagles who had a succession of No. 1s in the US starting with 'Best of My Love' in 1975 and 'Hotel California' in 1977.

SPORT

1954 Gareth Williams, Welsh international rugby footballer.

DIED THIS DAY

1893 Peter Ilyich Tchaikovsky, Russian composer who died during a cholera epidemic in St Petersburg.

1901 Kate Greenaway, English illustrator of children's books.

ON THIS DAY

1429 Henry VI was crowned King of England. Two years later he was also crowned King of France in Paris.

1860 Abraham Lincoln was elected the 16th US President, and Herbert Hoover was elected 31st US President in 1928.

1924 Tory leader Stanley Baldwin was elected Prime Minister and he appointed Winston Churchill, former Liberal, as the Chancellor of the Exchequer.

1956 The construction of the Kariba High Dam began on the Zambezi River between Zambia and Zimbabwe.

1987 The busy Patna railway station in the Indian state of Bihar was thrown into a state of chaos as passengers rushed to watch a pornographic film which had appeared on the television screens meant for the train times. A railway official was sacked.

1988 A virus which crippled 6,000 US Defence Department computers was spread by a 23-year-old graduate whose father headed the country's computer security agency.

7 NOVEMBER

The National Day of Russia, when in 1917, Lenin's Bolsheviks led the overthrow of the moderate Kerensky socialist government.

BORN THIS DAY

HISTORY

1917 Helen Suzman, South African anti-apartheid and civil rights campaigner, a leading member of the South African Progressive Federal Party and former Member of Parliament.

1918 (William Franklin) Billy Graham, US evangelist who campaigned for Christ using all the techniques of modern communication to address huge audiences in the US and world-wide.

1942 Jean Shrimpton, leading English model whose face and figure, enhanced with a miniskirt, set the fashion for the 60s.

ARTS

1913 Albert Camus, Algerian-born French author and Nobel prize winner for Literature in 1957 who wrote *The Stranger* (1942) and *The Rebel* (1952).

1924 Wolf Mankowitz, English author and playwright best known for his novel and screenplay of *Make Me An Offer* (1954) and *A Kid for Two Farthings*, also from his novel, in 1955. His musical play *Expresso Bongo* (1959) was also a hit as a film.

1926 Dame Joan Sutherland, Australian operatic soprano who scored an enormous success as Lucia in Donizetti's opera at Covent Garden in 1959. She has excelled in other roles, and the role of Jenifer in Tippett's *Midsummer Marriage* was created for her.

1936 Dame Gwyneth Jones, Welsh operatic soprano who makes frequent guest appearances at leading opera houses in London, Vienna, Rome, Milan, Munich and San Francisco, and sang in the centenary Bayreuth Festival in 1976.

ENTERTAINMENT

1897 Herman J. Mankiewicz, US screenwriter who was largely responsible for the screenplay of the Oscar-winning *Citizen Kane* (1941) in collaboration with Orson Welles.

1949 Su Pollard, English comedy actress best known for her role as the chalet maid in the television series *Hi Di Hi*.

SCIENCE

1867 Marie Curie (Marya Sklodowska), Polish-born physicist who married her professor, Pierre, with whom she worked in isolating the radioactive element in pitchblende. They shared the 1903 Nobel Physics prize with Becquerel, who was also investigating radioactivity. When Pierre died, she became the first woman professor at the Sorbonne, and was awarded a second Nobel prize in 1911 for her discovery of radium. Their daughter, Irene, was also to receive the Nobel prize for Chemistry related to her research into radioactivity in 1935.

1878 Lise Meitner, Austrian physicist and a discoverer of nuclear fission with Otto Hahn and Fritz Strassmann.

1888 Sir Chandrasekhara Venkata Raman, Indian physicist who won the 1931 Nobel prize for Physics for his discovery of the changing wavelengths of light when diffused through transparent material.

POP

1943 Joni Mitchell (Roberta Joan Anderson), Canadian-born singer and songwriter who sang in Canadian coffee houses before she made her first album *Song to a Seagull* (1968). Her songs include 'Help Me' and 'Big Yellow Taxi'.

SPORT

1953 Lucinda Green, English horsewoman.

1961 Mark Hateley, England footballer who has also played for Coventry and AC Milan.

1963 John Barnes, Liverpool and England footballer who was born in Jamaica.

DIED THIS DAY

1962 (Anna) Eleanor Roosevelt, US writer, lecturer and wife of the 32nd US President, who threw herself into active causes to compensate for marriage to a president who was in love with her social secretary for most of their time at the White House.

1978 (James Joseph) Gene Tunney, US heavyweight boxing champion.

1980 (Terence Steven) Steve McQueen, US actor in *The Great Escape* (1963).

ON THIS DAY

1783 The last public hanging in Britain took place at Tyburn, near where Marble Arch now stands.

1865 The Erie Pocket Lighter, the first ever, was manufactured by the Repeating Light Company of Springfield, Massachusetts.

1872 The *Marie Celeste*, the ill-fated brigantine, sailed from New York to be found mysteriously abandoned some time later.

1885 After four and half years' work, the last spike was driven in to complete the Canadian Pacific Railway.

1916 Jeanette Rankin of Montana became the first woman member of the US Congress.

1961 Konrad Adenauer was elected German Chancellor for the fourth time.

1972 Richard Nixon was re-elected US President, a term that would end in his resignation.

1974 At 9.45 p.m., the Countess of Lucan burst through the door of the Plumber's Arms pub in Belgravia, London wearing only a nightdress. Bloodstained from head wounds and hysterical, she screamed 'Help me! Help me! I've just escaped from a murderer... He's murdered the nanny.' The accused, her husband Lord Lucan, disappeared on the night his children's nanny was beaten to death and his wife seriously assaulted. He has never been seen since.

8 NOVEMBER

The Feast of the Four Crowned Ones still marked by some English freemasons, commemorating four masons martyred by Emperor Diocletian for refusing to sculpt a a pagan god.

BORN THIS DAY

HISTORY

1656 Edmond Halley, English astronomer and mathematician best known for the comet named after him and for his work predicting its orbit. He also produced the first meteorological chart ever published and commanded a war sloop on the first sea voyage undertaken exclusively for scientific purposes.

1802 Sir Benjamin Hall, commissioner of works at the time of Big Ben's installation in the tower at the Houses of Parliament and from whom the famous clock with its 13-ton bell gets its name.

1866 Herbert Austin, later Baron Austin, English motor car manufacturer who first went to Australia where he managed several engineering works. He returned to England and produced his first car in 1895. He joined the Wolsey Company and then opened his own works in 1905.

1922 Professor Christiaan (Neethling) Barnard, South African heart transplant pioneer who carried out the world's first at Groote Schuur Hospital in Cape Town (3.12.1967).

ARTS

1847 (Abraham) Bram Stoker, Irish author of *Dracula* (1897) and who was also Sir Henry Irving's partner in running London's Lyceum Theatre.

1883 Sir Arnold (Edward Trevor) Bax, English composer and Master of the King's Music whose romantic, evocative music contributed much to the revival of interest in British composers. His work includes the symphonic poem *Tintagel* (1916–17) and seven symphonies dedicated to his favourite composers.

1900 Margaret Mitchell, US author of one of the biggest bestsellers of all time *Gone With the Wind*, published in June 1936. It took her ten years to write and was her only book.

1951 Nigel West (Rupert Allason), English author of revealing and seemingly authoritative non-fiction spy books who was also Britain's youngest Member of Parliament.

ENTERTAINMENT

1916 June Havoc (Ellen Evangeline Hovick), US actress, younger sister of Gypsy Rose Lee. Their ambitious mother made sure she was a vaudeville star aged five, and she married her first husband when she was 13. In Hollywood, she made films such as *My Sister Eileen* (1942).

1927 Ken Dodd, Liverpudlian comedian, creator of the imaginary Diddymen who inhabit the real Knotty Ash (near Liverpool).

1935 Alain Delon, French actor involved in a drugs and sex scandal that shocked France in 1968. It enhanced his image as a tough guy in films such as *Once A Thief* (1965) and *Airport '79* (1979).

SPORT

1940 Martin Peters, England and West Ham footballer who scored the goal that put England ahead in the World Cup final against West Germany in 1966, before the dramatic equalizer in the last minute which forced extra time.

DIED THIS DAY

1674 John Milton, blind English poet who wrote *Paradise Lost* (1667).

1865 Tom Sayers, English pugilist who took part in the first international heavyweight championship despite standing only five feet eight and a half inches.

1886 (Frederick James) Fred Archer, English champion jockey who won the Derby five times, shot himself, aged only 27.

ON THIS DAY

1793 The Louvre was opened to the public by the revolutionary government, although only part of the great collection could be viewed.

1889 Montana became the 41st state of the Union.

1895 William Rontgen discovered X-rays during an experiment at the University of Wurzburg with the flow of electricity through a partially evacuated glass tube.

1920 Rupert Bear made his first appearance in the *Daily Express*.

1923 The first Welsh language broadcast was made from 5WA, Cardiff.

1932 Franklin Delano Roosevelt won a massive victory against Herbert Hoover on his 'New Deal' ticket.

1939 A bomb exploded in the Buergerbraukeller in Munich on the 16th anniversary of the 1923 Beer Hall *putsch* where Hitler was delivering his traditional anniversary speech. The bomb went off just after Hitler left.

1974 Covent Garden ceased to be the location of London's famous flower and vegetable market as it moved across the Thames, leaving the old warehouses and Floral Hall to be rejuvenated.

1980 *Heaven's Gate* was premièred in New York. It proved to be the most expensive flop of all time ($30 million), and put its production company United Artists out of business.

1987 An IRA bomb exploded shortly before a Remembrance Day service at the Cenotaph in Enniskillen, Northern Ireland killing 11 people.

1987 A man serving 17 years for murder in a Californian prison decided to sue a juror for $24 million for sleeping through most of the trial and contributing to what he claimed was a wrongful conviction.

1989 The first black state governor in US history and the black mayor of New York were elected this day. Virginia chose Douglas Wilder, a grandson of freed slaves, as their Governor, while New Yorkers, by a slim majority, voted in David Dinkins.

9 NOVEMBER

BORN THIS DAY

HISTORY

1841 King Edward VII, eldest son of Queen Victoria and Prince Albert, who was the first British prince to tour Canada and the US. He was 61 when he was crowned and gave his name to the Edwardian age in English manners, fashion and literature.

ARTS

1818 Ivan Sergeyevich Turgenev, Russian playwright and novelist whose work includes the play *A Month in the Country* (1855) and his great novel *Fathers and Sons* (1862).

1928 Hugh Leonard, Irish playwright who also has written for television including *The Little World of Don Camillo* (1981).

1934 Ronald Harwood (Horwitz), South African-born playwright and novelist best known for his award-winning play, *The Dresser* (1980) and adapted for the screen in 1983. His work includes writing and presenting the television series (and book) *All the World's a Stage* (1984) and the play *Another Time* (1989).

ENTERTAINMENT

1881 Dr Herbert Thomas Kalmus, US inventor of Technicolor in 1912 making the first Technicolor one-reeler, *The Gulf Between*, in 1917. The first full-length Technicolor film was *The Black Pirate* in 1926.

1902 Anthony Asquith, English film director and producer, son of the British Prime Minister whose films include *Pygmalion* (1938) which he co-directed with its star, Leslie Howard, and *The Millionairess* (1960).

1909 Katherine Hepburn, US actress who established herself on stage and screen, but will be best remembered for her many film roles which won her a record eight Oscar nominations and four Oscars for *Morning Glory* (1933), *Guess Who's Coming to Dinner* (1967), *The Lion in Winter* (1968) and *On Golden Pond* (1981), while her performance in *The African Queen* (1951) was equally deserving.

1913 Hedy Lamarr (Hedwig Eva Maria Kiesler), US actress born in Vienna who was billed as the most beautiful woman in the world. Her most successful film was *Samson and Delilah* (1949).

JAZZ

1906 (Francis Joseph) Muggsy Spanier, US cornet player who was one of the central figures in the development of Chicago Dixieland throughout the 20s and 30s, playing with various bands from Ted Lewis to his own Muggsy Spanier's Ragtime Band.

SPORT

1942 Tom Weiskopf, US golfer who won the British and Canadian Opens and three other major tournaments in an eight-week period in 1973, and was runner-up in the US Masters four times.

DIED THIS DAY

1932 Nadya Aliluieva, Stalin's wife, aged 30, whose death is believed to have been suicide.

FOUR EVER No less that four major statesmen died this day including two British Prime Ministers, Ramsay MacDonald in 1937, while on a cruise for health reasons, and Neville Chamberlain, at last finding peace in his time in 1940. The first President of Israel, Chaim Weizmann, died in 1952 and President of France, Charles de Gaulle, in 1970.

1953 Dylan (Marlais) Thomas, hard-drinking Welsh poet, playwright and short-story writer, best remembered for *Under Milk Wood* (published 1954).

ON THIS DAY

1847 In Edinburgh, Dr James Young Simpson delivered Wilhemina Carstairs while chloroform was administered to the mother, the first child to be born with the aid of anaesthesia.

1859 From this day, flogging was no longer permitted in the British Army.

1888 At 3.30 a.m. near 13 Millers Court in London's Whitechapel, 25-year-old Mary Kelly became Jack the Ripper's last known victim.

1922 The SS (Schutzstaffel or 'Protection Squad') was formed in Germany.

1960 John F. Kennedy was elected the youngest ever president of the US, aged 43. Nixon conceded defeat shortly after midnight.

1961 Brian Epstein went to a lunchtime session at The Cavern in Liverpool to see for himself why his record shop was receiving so many requests for records by a group that had apparently made none. When he saw and heard the Beatles, he decided he wanted to be their manager.

1965 The biggest power cut in US history blacked out sections of New York and nine other states. There was a significant increase in births nine months later.

1985 In Moscow, Gary Kasparov became world chess champion beating Anatoly Karpov who had held the crown for ten years.

1989 Following demands for political reform from its citizens, the East German government decided to lift the 'iron curtain' and allow free travel through the Berlin Wall. Soon after the announcement, many thousands of jubilant East Berliners swarmed through the crossing points into West Berlin. The following day bulldozers moved in and began demolishing the 28-year-old barrier.

10 NOVEMBER

BORN THIS DAY

HISTORY

1483 Martin Luther, German religious reformer who attacked church abuses and began the Reformation.

1683 George II, King of England from 1727 to 1760 who leaned heavily on his prime minister, Sir Robert Walpole. He had a passion for opera and was Handel's patron.

ARTS

1668 François Couperin, French composer and harpsichordist known as 'Le Grand' because he was considered the most gifted of this musical family. He composed over 240 works for the keyboard.

1697 William Hogarth, English painter and engraver, best known for his 'strip cartoons' such as the eight-picture series, *The Rake's Progress* (1733–5), and his 'morality picture', *Marriage à la Mode* painted between 1743–50.

1728 Oliver Goldsmith, Irish poet and novelist who wrote *The Vicar of Wakefield* (1766) and the comedy *She Stoops to Conquer* (1773), and died in serious debt.

1759 Johann Christoph Friedrich von Schiller, German poet and playwright who wrote 'Hymn to Joy' which Beethoven used for his ninth symphony.

1880 Sir Jacob Epstein, British sculptor born in the US, whose work such as his symbolic *Adam* (1938), was often the subject of controversy and charges of indecency. They are now, however, recognized as masterpieces including the aluminium *St Michael and the Devil* (1958) for the new Coventry Cathedral.

1893 J(ohn) P(hillips) Marquand, US novelist who created the Japanese detective in *Thank You, Mr Moto* (1936) and the novel on Boston society, *H.M. Pulham, Esquire* (1941).

ENTERTAINMENT

1889 Claude Rains, English actor who moved to Hollywood after a distinguished stage career and began making films in 1933 when he played the title role in *The Invisible Man*. He will probably be remembered for his role as the French police chief in *Casablanca* (1942) although he never won an Oscar for any of his fine performances.

1911 Harry Andrews, British actor who combined a busy stage career often playing major Shakespearian roles, with films, including *Ice Cold in Alex* (1958), *Entertaining Mr Sloane* (1970) and *Death on the Nile* (1977).

1925 Richard Burton (Richard Walter Jenkins), Welsh-born actor who was with the Old Vic before devoting his career to films, some memorable like *The Spy Who Came in from the Cold* (1965) and *Who's Afraid of Virginia Woolf?* (1966) in which he starred opposite his wife, Elizabeth Taylor, others less interesting than his much publicized private life.

1944 Tim Rice, English lyricist and writer who worked with Andrew Lloyd Webber on most of his successes including *Jesus Christ Superstar* (1970) and *Evita* (1978), then worked on the musical *Chess*. He has also written books on cricket and on pop music history.

DIED THIS DAY

1938 Kemal Atatürk, the founder of modern Turkey.

1979 Dennis (Yately) Wheatley, English novelist who specialized in crime and the occult.

1982 Leonid Brezhnev, President of the USSR from 1977.

ON THIS DAY

1871 Henry Morton Stanley, sent out to Africa by his newspaper to find Scottish missionary David Livingstone, finally made contact with him at Ujiji on Lake Tanganyika with the immortal words, 'Dr Livingstone, I presume'.

1913 Battersea elected the first coloured mayor in Britain, John Archer, born in Liverpool of Jamaican parents.

1928 Hirohito was crowned Emperor of Japan. The Crown Prince, aged 27, had been regent for seven years before taking over from his sick father.

1938 'Kristallnacht' in Germany, when in the early hours Nazis burned 267 synagogues and destroyed thousands of Jewish homes and businesses, smashing shop windows which gave the night its name.

1987 The wreck of the US brig *Somers*, the infamous ship on which Herman Melville based his story *Billy Budd* (1924), was reported found off the coast of Veracruz, Mexico. In 1842, three of its crew were hanged for mutiny, and the Captain who ordered the hangings was himself charged with murder, but was acquitted. It is said that the ghosts of the hanged men haunted the ship and many tried to avoid sailing on her. During the US-Mexican war, she capsized and sank (12 December 1846) while pursuing a Mexican ship.

11 NOVEMBER

Feast Day of St Menas (or Mannas), who was believed by the Greeks to have the power to locate lost objects, especially sheep.

BORN THIS DAY

HISTORY

1885 George Smith Patton, US general who led the first US troops to fight in North Africa in the Second World War. In 1944, he headed the Third Army which swept across France.

ARTS

1821 Fyodor Mikhailovich Dostoyevsky,

Russian author who joined the revolutionary circles, and was arrested and sentenced to death. Reprieved, he was sent to face hard labour in Siberia. He called on his experiences for his novel *The House of the Dead*. His masterpiece, *Crime and Punishment* was published in 1866.

1922 Kurt Vonnegut, US novelist whose mixture of fantasy, science fiction and black comedy have made him a cult writer of novels including *Cat's Cradle* (1963) and *Slaughterhouse 5* (1969).

ENTERTAINMENT

1898 René Clair (Chomette), French film director who also made films in the US and Britain including *Under the Roofs of Paris* (1930) and *I Married a Witch* (1942).

1918 Stubby Kaye, US actor and singer, best known for creating the role of Nicely-Nicely Johnson in *Guys and Dolls* on Broadway and in London as well as in the 1955 film. He was also in *Cat Ballou* (1965) and *Sweet Charity* (1969).

1925 June Whitfield, English comedy actress who will be remembered for her part in the radio comedy series *Take It From Here*, and then in her own television series with Terry Scott, *Happy Ever After*.

1935 (Birgitta) Bibi Andersson, Swedish actress in many of Bergman's films including *Smiles of a Summer Night* (1955) and *Scenes from a Marriage* (1973).

SPORT

1947 Rodney (William) Marsh, Australian Test cricketer who dismissed a record 355 while he kept wicket, including 343 catches and 12 stumpings all in 96 matches.

DIED THIS DAY

1936 Sir Edward German (Edward German Jones), English composer of *Merrie England* (1902).

1945 Jerome (David) Kern, US composer and creator of stage musicals including *Show Boat* (1927).

ON THIS DAY

1880 (Edward) Ned Kelly, Australian bank robber whose daring raids with his gang in 1878–80, made him a legend. The last of the bushrangers, he was finally wounded in a shoot out. He was hanged at Melbourne jail, aged 25.

1889 Washington became the 42nd state of the Union.

IN MEMORIAM In 1918 the armistice was signed between the Allies and Germany in a guarded railway carriage in the forest of Compiègne. To mark the occasion three years later, the British Legion held their first Poppy Day. Irving Berlin's patriotic song, 'God Bless America' was sung for the first time in 1918 by Kate Smith. In 1920, the body of the unknown soldier was buried under the Arc de Triomphe, while the body of an unknown British soldier returned from France was interred in Westminster Abbey. This ceremony was recorded using a microphone by Lionel Guest and H.O. Merriman, the first electrical recording made.

1925 The BBC broadcast their first radio play, *The White Château* by Reginald Berkley.

1940 Willys launched the Jeep (called so

from the initials 'GP', for general purpose car).

1944 The Home Guard was disbanded in Britain.

1946 Stevenage was designated the first new town in Britain.

1952 The first video recorder was demonstrated at Bing Crosby Enterprises in Beverley Hills, California by inventors John Mullin and Wayne Johnson.

1953 The BBC television programme *Panorama* was first broadcast.

1965 Ian Smith's all-white Rhodesia government unilaterally declared independence from Britain.

1975 Australian Prime Minister Gough Whitlam was dismissed by the Governor-General Sir John Kerr because, unable to get his budget plans through Parliament he refused to call a general election.

1975 Angola became independent from Portugal.

1987 British customs seized the biggest haul of cocaine ever known in Europe, 208 kilos worth an estimated street value of £51 million.

1987 An amateur pilot, dubbed the Black Baron for his illegal night-time flights over Paris when he buzzed the Champs-Élysées, was grounded by a French court after a massive manhunt. He was fined £5,000 and banned from flying for three years.

1988 Soviet cosmonauts Vladimir Totov and Musa Manarov spent their 326th record breaking day in space.

12 NOVEMBER

BORN THIS DAY

HISTORY

1684 Edward Vernon ('Old Grog'), English admiral. (*See* 30.10.1747)

1866 Sun Yat-sen, first president of the Republic of China (1911–12), the father of modern China who worked for the overthrow of the Manchu dynasty.

1911 Reverend Chad Varah, founder of the Samaritans, the voluntary group who counsel those in distress. Originally established at St Stephen's Church, London, it provides a service day and night, every day of the year.

ARTS

1834 Alexander Porfiryevich Borodin, Russian composer best known for his uncompleted opera *Prince Igor* and his tone poem *In the Steppes of Central Asia* (1880).

1840 (François) Auguste Rodin, French sculptor who was granted a studio in Paris by the state and whose first exhibition in 1900 gained him an international reputation with works including *The Thinker* (1880) and *The Kiss* (1886).

1939 Lucia Popp, Czech-born Austrian soprano who appears as a guest artist at many leading opera houses.

ENTERTAINMENT

1929 Grace Kelly (Princess Grace of Monaco), US actress who won an Oscar for best supporting actress in *Mogambo* (1953) and an Oscar for *The Country Girl* (1954), but who will probably be best remembered for *Rear Window* (1954) and *High Society* (1956). In 1956 she married Prince Rainier III, the ruler of Monaco, and did much to revive the country's fortunes.

SCIENCE

1842 Lord Rayleigh (John William Strutt), English physicist and Nobel prize winner in 1904 for successfully isolating the inert gas argon.

POP

1918 Jo Stafford, US singer, popular during the late 40s and 50s and who was No. 2 in Britain's first chart (14.11.1952) with 'You Belong to My Heart'.

1945 Neil Young, Canadian-born rock singer and guitarist with the Buffalo Springfield who had a big hit with 'For What It's Worth'. When the group split, he worked for a while with Crosby, Stills, Nash and Young before going solo.

SPORT

1961 Nadia Comaneci, Romanian gymnast who as a 14-year-old stole the show at the 1976 Olympics at Montreal when she won the first-ever maximum score in an Olympic event in the asymetric bars in a team competition and won a total of three gold medals. She defected to the West on 28 November 1989.

DIED THIS DAY

1035 Canute II (the Great), King of England and Denmark from 1016, who put Viking chiefs in charge of Northumbria and East Anglia.

1865 Mrs Elizabeth (Cleghorn) Gaskell, English author who wrote *Cranford* (1853) and a biography of the Brontës.

ON THIS DAY

1859 Leotard made his debut in Paris. The daring young man on the flying trapeze, which he devised, was a sensation at the Cirque d'Été for which he was paid 500 francs a day, a large sum of money at this time. He also performed without a safety net.

1919 The first flight from England to Australia began from Hounslow with Ross and Smith in a Vickers Vimy. They landed safely on 13 December 1919.

1923 Hitler was arrested after his failed Beer Hall *putsch* in Munich on the 8th.

1928 The New Oxford Theatre, the first cinema outside the US to show 'talking pictures', opened in Manchester.

1942 Pharmaceutical giant Bayer patented polyurethane.

1974 A salmon was caught in the Thames, the first since around 1840.

1987 Van Gogh's *Irises* was sold for a then world record £30.2 million. He painted it while a patient at the St Rémy lunatic asylum. (*See* 16.5.1990)

13 NOVEMBER

BORN THIS DAY

HISTORY

1312 Edward III, King of England from 1327 whose incompetence reached a climax when he invaded Scotland and was soundly beaten at Bannockburn by Bruce. He was the father of Edward 'the Black Prince' and John of Gaunt.

ARTS

1850 Robert Louis (Balfour) Stevenson, Scottish author and traveller who wrote the classics *Treasure Island* (1883), *Kidnapped* (1886) and *The Strange Case of Dr Jekyll and Mr Hyde* (1889).

1912 Eugene Ionesco, Romanian-born French playwright who was a pioneer of the Theatre of the Absurd with *The Bald Prima Donna* (1950) and *Rhinoceros* (1958).

ENTERTAINMENT

1930 Adrienne Corri, Scottish-born actress who has appeared in many films including *A Clockwork Orange* (1971).

FASHION

PUTTING ON THE STYLE This day celebrates the birth of one great fashion designer and the death of two others. Born 1825, Anglo-French costumier Charles Frederick Worth went to Paris in 1846. He established himself as a leading fashion designer and attracted the patronage of the Empress Eugénie. The first to use girls as models, he also pioneered the replication of designer dresses in Parisian workrooms for international distribution. In 1954 designer Jacques Faith died and in 1973 Elsa Schiaperelli died. Born in Rome, she was at the centre of world fashion for 40 years with her collections, often featuring exotic colours such as shocking pink.

DIED THIS DAY

1854 John Peel, English farmer and huntsman who is recalled in the hunting song 'D'ye ken John Peel' (by John Graves) and is buried in Caldbeck in the Lake District.

1974 Vittorio de Sica, Italian film director of *The Bicycle Thieves* (1948).

1982 Chesney Allen who, with partner Bud Flanagan, was part of the famous Crazy Gang. Ironically, Allen stopped performing in the early 50s because of health problems, and then outlived the Gang.

1987 Pieter Nicolaas Menten, Dutch Nazi war criminal accused of killing dozens of Jews in Poland where he served as a translator for the SS and where he also allegedly stole art treasures.

ON THIS DAY

1851 The telegraphic service between London and Paris began operating.

1907 The first helicopter rose 6½ feet above ground in a field in Normandy powered by two motor-driven propellors above the pilot.

1936 King Edward VIII told Prime Minister Baldwin he intended to marry twice-divorced Mrs Simpson.

1940 Walt Disney's *Fantasia* opened in New York.

1945 General Charles de Gaulle was elected President of the provisional French government.

1947 Hugh Dalton, British Chancellor of the Exchequer resigned after admitting he had disclosed tax proposals to a reporter from the *Star* minutes before he presented the Budget (on the 12th).

1950 The first World Bridge Championship, held in Bermuda, was won by the US.

1987 The first criminal conviction based on genetic 'finger printing' led to a rapist being sentenced to eight years imprisonment at the Bristol Crown Court.

1987 The first condom commercial was screened by the BBC with the brand name removed.

14 NOVEMBER

BORN THIS DAY

HISTORY

1765 Robert Fulton, US engineer who developed the first commercially viable steamboat. He also built the first US submarine in 1800.

1863 Leo (Hendrik) Baekeland, Belgian-born US chemist who invented the first commercial plastic, which he named Bakelite.

1889 Jawaharial Nehru, the first prime minister of an independent India from August 1947, who was eventually followed by his daughter Indira and her son, Rajiv.

1908 Joseph (Raymond) McCarthy, US senator who led the notorious Senate enquiry into alleged communists in the 50s which blacklisted thousands of people from politicians to film stars. He was finally shown to be falsifying evidence which put a belated end to his witchhunt. He left his name to posterity: 'McCarthyism' – to accuse without evidence.

1935 King Hussein of Jordan (Hussein ibn Talal).

1948 Prince Charles (Charles Philip Arthur George), Prince of Wales and enthusiastic and concerned environmentalist.

ARTS

1840 Claude (Oscar) Monet, French Impressionist painter who gave the movement its name with his painting *Impression, Sunrise* (1872).

1900 Aaron Copland, US composer of the popular *Appalachian Spring* (1944), the ballet music for *Billy the Kid* (1939) and *Rodeo* (1942) which established a distinctive American style for both the music and the dance.

1930 Dame Elizabeth Frink, English sculptor whose works include *Horseman* opposite London's Ritz Hotel.

SCIENCE

1891 Sir Frederick Grant Banting, Canadian physician who with Charles H. Best discovered insulin in 1921. They were the first to produce it in a form in which it could be used to treat diabetes successfully. He was a co-recipient in 1923 of the Nobel prize with Professor Macleod, in whose laboratories at the Univerisity of Toronto the research was carried out. Best was not honoured, but Banting shared his portion of the award with his colleague.

SPORT

1904 Harold Larwood, Nottinghamshire and England fast bowler who was at the centre of the infamous 'body-line' Test series for delivering head high breaks that did both physical and mental damage to Australian batsmen (17.1.1933).

1934 Bernard Hinault, French cyclist and Tour de France champion.

DIED THIS DAY

CHARLIE'S ANGELS Two mistresses of King Charles II died this day separated by 57 years. In 1687 Nell (Eleanor) Gwynn, English actress, daughter of a Covent Garden brothel madam, died. She had two children by Charles. She was stricken by apoplexy and partially paralysed when she died aged 37, and was buried in the Church of St Martin-in-the-Fields with a sermon preached by the future Archbishop of Canterbury. In 1734 Louise de Kerouallle, Duchess of Portsmouth died. She was first introduced to Charles to influence him in favour of a French alliance. Unlike Nell, she was universally disliked by the court and public.

1905 Robert Whitehead, English inventor of the self-propelled torpedo in 1866.

1946 Manuel de Falla, Spanish composer best known for his ballet music *El Amor Brujo* (1915) and *The Three-Cornered Hat* (1919).

1988 Jaromir Vejvoda, Czech song composer who wrote the 'Beer Barrel Polka' ('Roll out the barrel...').

ON THIS DAY

1770 Scottish explorer James Bruce discovered the source of the Blue Nile in north-east Ethiopia, which was then considered the main stream of the Nile.

1889 *New York World* star female reporter Nellie Bly set sail from New York to beat Phileas Fogg's 80 days to go around the world as described in Jules Verne's classic. She filed stories during her travels and ran a competition for readers to guess what her time would be, attracting nearly one million entries. She actually did it in 72 days, 6 hours, 11 minutes and 14 seconds having travelled by sea, on sampans, on horseback, by rail and road.

1896 The speed limit for horseless carriages in Britain was raised from 4 m.p.h. (2 m.p.h. in towns) to 14 m.p.h. It was marked by the first London to Brighton Car Run, which only became a regular and official event from 1927, sponsored by the *Daily Sketch*. Curiously, the two most famous cars associated with the event in the classic film comedy *Genevieve* would not qualify for the event as they were both built in 1905, and only cars built by 1904 are allowed to enter.

1910 At 3.16 p.m., Eugene Ely made the first take off in an aircraft from the deck of a US light cruiser.

1922 The first programme was broadcast at 6 p.m. from 2LO London (later the BBC). A news bulletin, repeated again at 9 p.m., and a weather report were the entire programme.

1940 Coventry's centre was bombed, killing over 1,000 civilians and destroying the medieval cathedral.

1952 Britain's first music chart was published in the *New Musical Express* with Al Martino's 'Here in my Heart' at No. 1 and Vera Lynn in at 7, 8 and 10. (The first US chart, 4.1.1936.)

1963 A volcanic eruption under the sea off Iceland created the new island of Surtsey.

1969 The BBC began colour television programmes.

1973 Bobby Moore made his final and 108th appearance for England against Italy at Wembley.

1973 Princess Anne married Captain Mark Phillips at Westminster Abbey.

15 NOVEMBER

The Feast Day of Albert the Great, patron saint of medical technicians. Albert was a pioneer of books for students of natural sciences.

BORN THIS DAY

HISTORY

1638 Catherine of Braganza, Queen to Charles II. Her dowry to the King of England included Tangiers and Bombay.

1708 William Pitt the Elder, 1st Earl of Chatham, British Prime Minister and noted orator.

LIFE AND DEATH Born 1891 Erwin Rommel, legendary German field marshal, commander of the Afrika Corps of the North African campaign during the Second World War. He shares his birthday with Count Claus von Stauffenberg, a fellow German officer born 1907 who was involved in the attempt to assassinate Hitler (20.7.1944). A hunt for the plotters led not only to von Stauffenberg, who was executed, but also to Rommel who Hitler pressurized into committing suicide to avoid the scandal of trying a national hero for treason.

1897 Aneurin Bevan, British Labour politician, son of a miner, who was the architect of the National Health Service.

1977 Peter Phillips, son of Princess Anne and Captain Mark Phillips.

ARTS

1862 Gerhart Hauptmann, German playwright and novelist, winner of the Nobel prize in 1912, who wrote the verse epic, *Till Eulenspiegel* (1928).

1930 J(ames) G(raham) Ballard, British author of *Empire of the Sun* (1984) and science-fiction novels.

1942 Daniel Barenboim, Argentinian-born Israeli pianist and conductor with many international orchestras as well as musical director of the Orchestre de Paris since 1975. He was awarded the Légion d'honneur in 1987 and was married to the late Jacqueline du Pré.

ENTERTAINMENT

1905 Mantovani (Anuzio Paulo), Italian conductor and arranger of light music featuring 'the singing strings'. He was musical director of many of Noël Coward's musicals before forming a popular broadcasting orchestra in Britain in 1927.

1932 Petula Clark, English singer and actress who began her career as a child star in *Here Come the Huggetts* (1948). As a singer she is best known for her hits in the 60s including 'Downtown' (1965) and 'This is My Song' (1967). Her films include *Finian's Rainbow* (1968) and *Goodbye Mr Chips* (1969).

SCIENCE

1738 Sir William Herschel, German-born British astronomer and organist. In 1781, he discovered the planet Uranus.

DIED THIS DAY

1802 George Romney. English portait painter. An infatuation with Emma Hart, later Lady Hamilton, led him to paint numerous portraits of the lady.

1908 Tz'u-hsi, dowager empress of China, the day after her nephew, the Emperor Kuang-hsü had died, presumed poisoned. On 2 December, two-year-old Pu-Yi, who was enthroned under the regency of his father, the second Prince Chun. Pu-Yi was to be the last Manchu emperor, eventually deposed by the revolution led by Sun Yat-sen.

1916 Henryk Sienkiwicz, Polish-born author of the best-seller *Quo Vadis* (1896).

1954 Lionel Barrymore, US actor and Oscar winner, and the original Dr Gillespie in television's *Dr Kildare*.

1958 Tyrone Power, US actor.

1971 Rudolf Ivanovich Abel, Soviet master spy who ran a spy ring from a

Brooklyn photographic shop. He was caught and imprisoned, but swapped in 1962 for Gary Powers, the pilot of the U-2 spy plane which was shot down over Russian territory on 1.5.1960. (*See also* 19.8.1960)

ON THIS DAY

1777 Following the American War of Independence, the Articles of Confederation for the union of the United States of America were finally adopted by the Congress of Philadelphia.

1837 Isaac Pitman published details of his short-hand system, 'Stenographic Sound-Hand'.

1864 General Sherman began his march from Atlanta to Savannah with 60,000 men. His scorched earth policy destroyed towns and farms on the 300 mile march to the sea, an atrocity that would haunt him the rest of his life.

1889 Brazil became a republic on Pedro II's abdication following a revolution.

1899 The SS *St Paul* became the first ship to receive radio messages, transmitted from the Needles wireless station off the Isle of Wight.

1899 Winston Churchill was captured by the Boers while covering the war as a reporter for the *Morning Post*. He escaped a few weeks later.

1901 An electrical hearing aid was patented by Miller Reese of New York, however the device was certainly not portable. It was not until 1935 that A. Edwin Stevens of London, devised one that could be worn.

1918 Victory Day in Britain following the end of the First World War.

1923 Rampant inflation in Germany reached a peak this day when the mark, (4.2 to $1 in 1914) had risen to 4,200,000,000 to $1.

1926 NBC (National Broadcasting Corporation) was inaugurated in the US.

1956 *Love Me Tender*, Elvis Presley's first film, was premiered in New York. It recouped its production costs after three days.

1965 Craig Breedlove, US, set a world speed record of over 613 m.p.h. using a jet-engined car, *Spirit of America* on Bonneville Salt Flats, Utah.

1968 The liner *Queen Elizabeth* completed her final passenger voyage before being sold to a US group who planned to moor her in Florida as a tourist attraction.

1969 ATV (Midland) screened the first colour television commercial in Britain for Birds-Eye Peas at just £23 for the off-peak 30-second spot.

1983 The Greenham Common women's group mounted their first protest as Cruise missiles arrived at the US airbase in Berkshire.

16 NOVEMBER

BORN THIS DAY

HISTORY

42BC Tiberius Claudius Nero, second emperor of Rome, succeeding Augustus in AD14, who improved and strengthened the principate, but was depicted as cruel and perverted by historians.

1717 Jean le Rond d'Alembert, French author and mathematician who was found abandoned the day after his birth on the steps of the Church of St Jean le Rond from which his name was taken. He added 'Alembert' later.

1896 Oswald Mosley, English politician who was successively a Conservative and Labour Member of Parliament before forming the British Union of Fascists. Provocative marches through the Jewish east end of London prior to the Second World War led to major confrontations. He was interned during the war and later lived in exile in France.

ARTS

1895 Paul Hindemith, German composer and viola player who was one of the most important musical figures of the 20th century. Hitler banned his music in 1933 and he eventually went to the US in 1939 where he taught pupils including Leonard Bernstein. He left behind a vast amount of music including theatre pieces, symphonies, chamber music and communal and educational music.

ENTERTAINMENT

1889 George S(imon) Kaufman, US playwright and director of his plays and musicals written in collaboration with Moss Hart, Marc Connelly and others including the musical *Of Thee I Sing* (1931) and the play with Hart, *The Man Who Came to Dinner* (1932).

1908 Burgess Meredith, US actor who appeared in many films including *Of Mice and Men* (1940), *Rocky* and *Rocky II* (1976/79), but is probably best known for his role as the Penguin in television's *Batman* series.

1953 Griff Rhys Jones, British actor and writer who first became known in the television satirical comedy series *Not the Nine O' Clock News* followed soon by *Alas Smith and Jones* with his plump partner, Mel Smith.

JAZZ

1905 (Albert Edwin) Eddie Condon, US guitarist, bandleader and a major figure in the development of Chicago jazz who on 10 December 1927 co-led the first Chicago-style jazz recordings. He later opened a club which attracted the stars of show business, music and sport.

SPORT

1942 Willie Carson, Scottish-born jockey who was five times English champion.

1961 Frank Bruno, English boxer who was the former European and then British heavyweight boxing champion and world contender.

DIED THIS DAY

1724 Jack Sheppard, Stepney-born highwayman whose first robbery took place in 1720. He inspired ballads and plays as well as a tract by Defoe, and escaped the noose four times before he was finally hanged in front of 200,000 people at Tyburn.

1885 Louis Riel, leader of the Métis rebellion in Canada. He was captured and hanged after having established a rebel government which was put down by the British.

1960 Clark Gable, US film actor and Oscar winner who died soon after shooting the final scenes of *The Misfits* opposite Marilyn Monroe for whom this was also the last film.

1960 Gilbert Harding, one of the first British television and radio personalities renowned for his bluff, unconventionally frank manner in chat and game shows.

1981 William Holden (William Franklin Beedle), US actor who won an Oscar for *Love is a Many Splendored Thing* (1955).

1983 Arthur (Bowden) Askey, English comedian mainly on stage and radio, known as 'Big Hearted Arthur'.

ON THIS DAY

1824 Australian explorer Hamilton Hume discovered the Murray River, the longest in Australia, 1,609 miles (2,589 km).

1848 Frédéric Chopin gave his last public performance at London's Guildhall. He was one performer in a charity concert, where he played despite illness and a disinterested audience who spent most of the evening in the refreshment areas.

1869 The formal opening of the Suez Canal took place. It had taken ten years to make the 100-mile canal devised by Ferdinand de Lesseps. He celebrated his 64th birthday three days later. In 1974, the Suez Canal was re-opened following its closure in the 1967 Suez conflict.

1907 Oklahoma became the 46th state of the Union.

1913 The first volume of Marcel Proust's classic *Remembrance of Things Past* was published in Paris.

1917 Georges Clemenceau became Prime Minister of France.

1928 Bow Street Magistrates Court, London was the scene of an obscenity charge against the novel by Radclyffe Hall, *The Well of Loneliness*, a crusading lesbian novel which had the *Sunday Express* claiming it was 'A Book That Must Be Supressed'. It was not reprinted until 21 years later in 1948 when it hardly raised an eyebrow.

1938 Willie Hall of Spurs scored five goals for England against Ireland with his three goals in 3½ minutes, setting a record for the fastest ever in an international.

1959 *The Sound of Music* was performed for the first time on Broadway starring Mary Martin. The show ran 1,443 performances.

1965 The USSR launched *Venus III*, an unmanned spacecraft that successfully landed on Venus.

17 NOVEMBER

The Feast Day of Hilda, patron saint of business and professional women.

BORN THIS DAY

HISTORY

1755 Louis XVIII, first King of France after the fall of Napoleon.

1887 Field Marshal Viscount Montgomery of Alamein (Bernard Law Montgomery), English soldier who was a painstaking planner which contributed to his most successful battle in North Africa when he broke through Rommel's lines during the Second World War. 'Monty' was also a superb communicator, which assured his popularity with his men.

1931 Michael Freeman, English orthopaedic surgeon who pioneered new surgical procedures for replacement of hip, knee and ankle joints.

ARTS

1925 Sir (Alan) Charles Mackerras, Australian-born conductor with an international reputation who was the conductor of the English National Opera 1970–78.

1939 Auberon (Alexander) Waugh,

English writer, son of Evelyn, who wrote a regular column for the satirical magazine *Private Eye*. His novels include *The Foxglove Saga* (1960).

ENTERTAINMENT

1925 Rock Hudson (Roy Scherer), US film and television star remembered for his romantic roles with Doris Day in *Pillow Talk* (1962) and other films, but he also made *Giant* (1956) and the popular television series, *Macmillan and Wife*.

1937 Peter Cook, English writer and entertainer, one of the original *Beyond the Fringe* team who revolutionized British comedy, a process begun by the Goons. He and his partner, Dudley Moore, with television series *Not Only, But Also*, created one of the best double acts in Britain.

1942 Martin Scorsese, US film director whose films include *Taxi Driver* (1976) and *Raging Bull* (1979).

POP

1938 Gordon Lightfoot, Canadian singer and songwriter who had hits with 'If You Could Read My Mind' (1971) and 'Sundown' in 1974. Other songs include 'Early Morning Rain'.

DIED THIS DAY

1558 Mary I, Mary Tudor also known as 'Bloody Mary', the Catholic queen in Protestant Britain who was succeeded by Elizabeth I.

1917 Auguste Rodin, French sculptor of the sensuous *The Kiss*.

1971 Dame Gladys Cooper, English actress, and former Gaiety Girl.

1988 Sheilah Graham (Lily Shiel), London orphan born about 1908, who worked as a cleaning maid, won a beauty contest, and married a much older and well-off major who let her go off to the US in 1933, where she began her *Hollywood Today* gossip column and later became F. Scott Fitzgerald's lover. She was the model for the heroine in his unfinished final novel, *The Last Tycoon* (1941).

ON THIS DAY

1603 The trial of Sir Walter Raleigh began. Falsely accused of treason, he had been offered a large sum of money by Lord Cobham, a critic of England's King James I, to make peace with the Spanish and put Arabella Stuart, James's cousin, on the throne. Raleigh claimed he turned down the offer, but Lord Cobham told his accusers that Raleigh was involved in the plot.

1800 The US Congress met for the first time and John Adams became the first President to move into the Executive Mansion (later renamed the White House).

1869 The first cycle road race, 83 miles from Paris to Rouen, was won by England's James Moore.

1880 The first three women to graduate in Britain received their Bachelor of Arts degrees at London University.

1922 The last Sultan of Turkey was deposed by Kemal Atatürk.

1922 Siberia voted for union with the USSR on the same day that Britain elected its first Communist member of parliament, J.T. Walton-Newbold standing for Motherwell, Scotland. He eventually joined the Labour Party.

1954 King Farouk of Egypt was sent into exile, and General Nasser became head of state.

1955 Anglesey became the first authority in Britain to introduce fluoride into the water supply.

1959 Two Scottish airports, Prestwick and Renfrew, became the first to offer duty free goods in Britain. London Heathrow followed soon after.

1970 The unmanned Soviet *Luna 17* landed on the moon.

1970 The *Sun* newspaper pictured its first Page Three girl, Stephanie Rahn.

1988 Franz Kafka's manuscript of his classic novel, *The Trial* (1925) was sold at Sotheby's in London for £1 million, a world record for a modern literary text. Kafka died in poverty in 1924.

18 NOVEMBER

BORN THIS DAY

HISTORY

AD9 Vespasian (Titus Flavius Vespasianus), Roman emperor who consolidated the empire, directed the pacification of Wales and northern Britain and established extensive sales and excise taxes, including one on public urinals.

1789 Louis Daguerre, French photography pioneer who developed the daguerrotype, a one-off picture without a negative, said to have been discovered when he accidentally spilt iodine on some silvered plates.

1860 Ignace Jan Paderewski, famous international Polish pianist, composer who became Poland's first Prime Minister after it achieved independence in 1919. Although he resigned a year later, he continued to raise money for war victims with his concerts. He made a guest appearance in the 1936 film *Moonlight Sonata*.

1906 Sir Alec (Alexander Arnold Constantine) Issigonis, born in Turkey of a Bavarian mother and a Greek father. He came to Britain in 1922 and made his way slowly in the motor industry designing the Morris Minor in 1948, the first British car to sell more than a million. In 1959 he had his greatest triumph when he unveiled the Mini Minor which ten years later became the first British car to sell over two million.

1901 George (Horace) Gallup, US organizer of public opinion surveys who devised the Gallup Poll. He conducted his first poll in 1932 for an advertising company.

ARTS

1786 Carl (Maria) von Weber, German composer who managed to break away from the strong Italian influence. His work includes the operas *Der Freischutz* (1817–21) and *Oberon* (1825–6).

1889 Amelita Galli-Curci, self-taught Italian soprano who won much acclaim for her roles, especially as Gilda in *Rigoletto*.

ENTERTAINMENT

1836 Sir W(illiam) S(chwenck) Gilbert, English humorist and librettist who collaborated with Sir Arthur Sullivan to produce their series of light operas including *HMS Pinafore* (1878), *The Pirates of Penzance* (1880) and *The Gondoliers* (1989).

1909 Johnny Mercer, US composer and lyricist who wrote lyrics for Broadway musicals and Hollywood including the songs 'That Old Black Magic', 'Come Rain, Come Shine', 'Autumn Leaves' and 'Moon River' as well as *Seven Brides for Seven Brothers* (1954).

1928 Mickey Mouse, US cartoon character who was created by Walt Disney and the brilliant chief animator, Ub Iwerks who received the screen credit for Mickey's realization. The voice was Disney's. Mickey made his first and last silent appearance under the name of Mortimer Mouse in a short film called *Plane Crazy* before being renamed for his first sound film. (*See* ON THIS DAY)

1941 David Hemmings, English actor, director and producer, who began as a painter before making films including *Blow-Up*, (1966) in which made his name, and *Juggernaut* (1974).

1944 Linda Evans, US actress in the television soap *Dynasty*.

POP

1960 Kim Wilde, English singer, daughter of former pop singer Marty who acts as her producer with brother Ricky. Her first big hit was in 1981 with 'Kids in America'.

DIED THIS DAY

1922 Marcel Proust, French novelist of *Remembrance of Things Past* (13 volumes, 1913–27).

1962 Niels Henrik Bohr, Danish physicist and Nobel prize winner for his work on the quantum theory and atomic structures.

ON THIS DAY

1477 Caxton's first dated book, the *Dictes or Sayengis of the Philosophres*, was published.

1626 St Peter's in Rome was consecrated.

1852 The state funeral of the Duke of Wellington took place, one of the biggest ever held in London with the procession making its way to St Paul's Cathedral.

1905 Prince Carl of Denmark became King Haakon VII of Norway when that country voted itself independent of Denmark.

OF MOUSE AND FUNNYMAN Two of the most internationally popular US entertainers after Chaplin made their debut this day. In 1928 the first Mickey Mouse cartoon, *Steamboat Willie* was screened in the US. It was the first experimental sound cartoon and, although not strictly the first Mickey cartoon (see 'Born This Day'), it was the first with his amended name. 1933 saw Bob Hope make his first major appearance on Broadway in Jerome Kern's *Roberta* as Huckleberry Haines. The show introduced the song 'Smoke Gets In Your Eyes'.

1963 Bell Telephone introduced push button telephones.

1977 President Sadat became the first Egyptian leader to visit Israel and address the Knesset.

1978 In Guyana, a US sect led by the 'Reverend' Jim Lloyd murdered three visiting newsmen and a US congressman who had come to investigate the movement. Lloyd then ordered his 900 men, women and children to commit mass suicide by drinking a soft drink, Kool Aid, laced with cyanide. Probably the largest mass suicide in modern times was discovered on the 29th.

1983 Mrs Janet Walton of Liverpool gave birth to sextuplets after taking a fertility drug.

1987 The worst fire in the history of the London Underground killed 30 people. The blaze began in the machinery below a wooden escalator in King's Cross Underground station and soon filled the tunnels with dense, choking smoke and intense heat.

19 NOVEMBER

BORN THIS DAY

HISTORY

1600 Charles I, King of England and Scotland who believed the king ruled by Divine Right, until his action in dissolving Parliament led to the civil war with Cromwell and his eventual execution.

1805 Viscomte Ferdinand de Lesseps, French diplomat and engineer who supervised the construction of the Suez Canal 1859–69. He was to be responsible for the construction of the Panama Canal but was prosecuted for embezzling funds.

1831 James (Abram) Garfield, 20th US President from 1881, who was assassinated three months later.

1875 Hiram Bingham, archaeologist and US senator who in 1911 discovered the route in the Peruvian Andes to the lost Inca capital of Vilcabamba at Machu Picchu.

1888 José Raùl Capablanca, Cuban chess champion who won the world title from 1921–7 and was instrumental in the development of the modern game.

1917 Indira Gandhi, Prime Minister of India, daughter of Nehru, who served as Prime Minister from 1966–77 and again in 1980–84. She was a controversial leader and in 1975 her election to parliament was declared void and a state of emergency was declared.

ENTERTAINMENT

1891 Clifton Webb (Webb Parmallee Hollenbeck), US actor who also trained as a dancer. He began in musical comedies such as *As Thousands Cheer* (1933) in which he sang 'Easter Parade'. His film career included *Laura* in 1944 and *The Razor's Edge* (1946) and he won Oscar nominations for both as best supporting actor.

1900 Anton Walbrook (Adolf Anton Wilhelm Wohlbruck), Austrian actor who, after a short career in German and Austrian films, went first to Hollywood, then settled in London. He was in *The Life and Death of Colonel Blimp* (1943) and *The Red Shoes* (1948) as well as the French classic *La Ronde* (1950).

1905 Tommy (Thomas) Dorsey, US trombonist and bandleader who split with his equally famous elder brother, Jimmy, over disagreements on the running of their Dorsey Brothers Band. Each started his own band and Tommy's attracted singers such as Sinatra, Dick Haymes and Jo Stafford. His theme song, 'I'm Getting Sentimental Over You', was heard on radio and in ballrooms. The brothers got together in 1947 for the film *The Fabulous Dorseys*.

1963 Jodie Foster, US actress who made her first film when she was only three, and later played leads in *Taxi Driver* (1976) and *Bugsy Malone* (1976). She was also in the television series *Paper Moon*. She played the rape victim in *The Accused* (1988) which won her an Oscar nomination.

SPORT

1918 Auriol Sinclair, first official woman National Hunt trainer.

1949 Dennis Taylor, Irish snooker

champion who won the world title in 1985 wearing his distinctive and specially designed glasses which helped him improve his game.

DIED THIS DAY

1703 *The Man in the Iron Mask*, the subject of a novel by Alexandre Dumas, was based on the mysterious prisoner in the Bastille whose identity was never revealed but was believed to have been Count Anthony Matthioli. He is recorded as having died this day. The infamous mask was in reality made of velvet and strengthened by bands of whalebone.

1828 Franz Schubert, prolific Austrian composer, of typhus.

1988 Christina Onassis, US-born daughter of the Greek shipping magnate, Aristotle who was the embodiment of 'the poor little rich girl'. Four times married, she struggled constantly with weight problems and died from a heart attack aged only 37, in Argentina.

ON THIS DAY

1850 Lord Tennyson became Poet Laureate.

1863 President Lincoln delivered his famous Gettysburg address after the American Civil War with the immortal phrase '...that government by the people, for the people, shall not perish from the earth'.

1893 The first colour supplement was published in the Sunday *New York World*.

1951 The white football became official.

1960 The first VTOL (vertical take-off aircraft) made by the British Hawker Siddeley Company was flown for the first time.

1960 Pele scored his 1,000th goal with a penalty while playing for Santos in his 909th first class match.

1987 A 1931 Bugatti Royale was sold for £5.5 million at an auction at the Royal Albert Hall, a record for a car.

20 NOVEMBER

BORN THIS DAY

HISTORY

1787 Sir Samuel Cunard, shipowner born in Nova Scotia who came to Britain in 1838 and, together with two partners, established what became the Cunard Line in 1839. Their first ship, the *Britannia*, set sail the following year taking 14 days and 8 hours to cross the Atlantic.

1908 (Alfred) Alistair Cooke, British-born US-based broadcaster and journalist who began his famous commentaries, *Letters from America*, in 1938. He also presented the television series *Alistair Cooke's America* (1973) which was followed up with a best-selling book.

1925 Robert Kennedy, younger brother of the 35th President, John F. Kennedy. He became the Attorney-General (1961–4), then as Senator for New York, announced his intention to stand for president in 1968, but was assassinated that year (5.6.1968).

ARTS

1906 Alexandra Danilova, Russian prima ballerina with the Ballets Russes, choreographer and teacher. She went to the US in 1933 where she introduced Russian techniques. She continued as a guest artist with many international ballet companies including the Sadler's Wells.

ENTERTAINMENT

1920 Dulcie Gray (Dulcie Bailey), English actress born in West Malaysia who, with husband Michael Denison, played leads in British theatre and films such as *The Glass Mountain* (1948). She also played a major role in the television series, *Howard's Way*.

1920 Gene Tierney, US actress who starred in the title role of *Laura* (1944) and in *Leave Her to Heaven* (1945) which won her an Oscar nomination.

SPORT

1912 Wilfred Wooler, former Cambridge University and Glamorgan cricketer and Welsh rugby international.

1917 Bobby (D'Arcy) Locke, South African golfer who won four British Open championships between 1949 and 1957. He won the Open in South Africa, New Zealand, Canada and other countries and was three times winner of the Vardon Trophy.

DIED THIS DAY

1847 Henry Francis Lyte, Scottish composer of 'Abide with Me'.

1910 Count Leo Tolstoy, Russian author of *War and Peace* (1864–9).

1967 Casimir Funk, Polish-born US biochemist who gave the world the word 'vitamin'.

1975 General Franco, Spanish dictator.

ON THIS DAY

1805 The first performance of Beethoven's *Fidelio* took place in Vienna.

1818 Simón Bolívar declared Venezuela independent from Spain.

1906 Charles Stewart Rolls and Frederick Henry Royce formed Rolls-Royce. This day in 1931, the company bought up Bentley Motors.

1929 Salvador Dali's first one-man show was held in Paris.

1944 The lights of Piccadilly Circus and the Strand were switched back on after five years of blackout.

1945 The Nuremberg War Crimes trial of Nazis including Goering, Hess, Ribbentrop and Streicher began. It lasted 218 days.

1947 Princess Elizabeth married Lt Philip Mountbatten RN in Westminster Abbey. The BBC made the first telerecording of the event, which was broadcast in the US 32 hours later.

1951 Snowdonia in Wales was designated a National Park.

1959 Top US DJ Alan Freed refused to deny being involved in a big payola scandal and was sacked from both television and radio programmes.

1970 The ten-shilling note (50p) was officially withdrawn by the Bank of England.

1979 Anthony Blunt, the Surveyor of the Queen's Pictures, was stripped of his knighthood after admitting to being a spy for Russia, thereby exposed as the Fourth Man in the Burgess, Maclean and Philby spy scandal.

1984 British Telecom shares went on sale and were over-subscribed several times over.

21 NOVEMBER

BORN THIS DAY

ARTS

1694 Voltaire, French philospher and satirist who was a crusader against tyranny and bigotry and who wrote *Candide* (1759).

1898 René (François-Ghislain) Magritte, Belgian painter who was dubbed 'one of the most ambiguous painters of our time' for his surrealistic paintings.

1934 Beryl Bainbridge, English author, originally an actress, whose novels include *The Bottle Factory Outing* (1974).

ENTERTAINMENT

1888 Harpo Marx (Adolph, known as Arthur Marx), US comedian who was the second eldest of the four-man Marx Brothers. (The fifth, Gummo, left the team before it reached Broadway.) He taught himself to play the harp, developed his skills as a mime artist and never spoke a word. With his red wig, old-fashioned taxi horn and clownish expression, he became an international favourite overcoming language barriers.

1922 Telly (Aristotle) Savalas, US actor who was a senior director for ABC News until he went into films, winning an Oscar nomination for his supporting role in *The Birdman of Alcatraz* (1962). But it was as television's 'Kojak', the detective with a penchant for lollipops, that he is most closely identified.

1941 Juliet Mills, English actress, Hayley's older sister, who made films and appeared on stage in Britain, but now works mainly in the US on television. Her films include *In Which We Serve* (1942), made when she was 11 months old.

1945 Goldie Hawn, US actress who made her name as the dizzy blonde in the television comedy show, *Rowan and Martin's Laugh In* before going on to Hollywood to make films including *Cactus Flower* (1969) and *Private Benjamin* (1980), receiving Oscar nominations for both.

JAZZ

1904 Coleman (Randolph) Hawkins, US virtuoso tenor saxophonist with Fletcher Henderson's Orchestra, who was the main influence in raising the saxophone to its current position of prominence.

DIED THIS DAY

1695 Henry Purcell, English composer of 'Nymphs and Shepherds'.

1913 Prince Keiki Tokugawa, the last of the Shoguns whose family re-established the shogunate in the 16th century.

1916 Franz Josef, Emperor of Austria.

ON THIS DAY

1783 Man's first free-flight was made by Jean de Rosier and the Marquis d'Arlandes in the Montgolfier brothers' hot-air balloon. They rose 500 feet above Paris and after 25 minutes, landed a few miles south.

1789 North Carolina became the 12th state of the Union.

1831 Michael Faraday read his first series of papers at the Royal Society in London on 'Experimental Research into Electricity'.

1843 Thomas Hancock patented vulcanized rubber. In 1825 he had produced the first toy balloons in Britain, consisting of a bottle of rubber solution and a condensing syringe.

1934 The first performance in New York of Cole Porter's *Anything Goes* with words by Guy Bolton and P.G. Wodehouse which included the song 'I Get A Kick Out of You'. It made Ethel Merman a star.

1953 The discovery of 'The Piltdown Man' skull by Charles Dawson in Sussex in 1912 was finally revealed as a hoax.

1958 Work began on the Forth Road Bridge in Scotland, and in 1964, the world's longest single span bridge, the Verrazano-Narrows Bridge across New York City Harbor, was opened.

22 NOVEMBER

The feast day of Cecilia, the patron saint of music, singers and poets.

BORN THIS DAY

HISTORY

1808 Thomas Cook, English travel agent who began his pioneering tour business, Thomas Cook & Son, when he organized the first publicly advertised railway excursion to a temperance meeting on 5 July 1841. In the early 1860s he stopped running his own personal tours and became an agent for domestic and overseas travel tickets.

1890 General Charles (André Marie Joseph) de Gaulle, French soldier and leader of the Free French in England during the Second World War. He returned to France in triumph at the end of the war and headed the provisional government, but later resigned. In 1958, with France in a critical state of unrest and with a fragile economy, he was invited to return. The following year he took office as President.

1899 Wiley Post, US aviator who was the first to fly solo around the world on 15.7.1931.

ARTS

1819 George Eliot (Mary Ann Evans), English author who assumed a male pen-name and who wrote *The Mill on the Floss* (1860) and *Silas Marner* (1861) among others.

1859 Cecil James Sharp, founder of the English Folk Dancing Society, who collected and published many of the old English folk songs and dances.

1913 (Edward) Benjamin Britten, English composer who established a festival in the coastal village Aldeburgh where he lived, and composed such operas as *Peter Grimes* (1945) to be sung by his friend, the tenor Peter Pears who lived with him. His other work includes his moving *War Requiem* performed at the dedication of Coventry Cathedral in 1962. He was made a Life Peer in 1976.

ENTERTAINMENT

1930 Sir Peter (Reginald Frederick) Hall, director of the National Theatre until 1988. His career as a director has included *Waiting for Godot* (1955) and *Amadeus* (1979).

1932 Robert Vaughn, US actor best known for his role on television and films as *The Man from UNCLE*.

1940 Terry Gilliam, US film animator based in England, actor and director who made his name in the classic television series *Monty Python's Flying Circus* before going on to act and direct in films including *Life of Brian* (1979), and *The Adventures of Baron Munchausen* (1989).

1941 Tom Conti, Scottish-born actor on the British stage and screen known for his film role in *Shirley Valentine* (1989) and on television with *The Glittering Prizes* and *The Norman Conquests*. In 1990, he took over from Peter O'Toole in the London stage success, *Jeffrey Bernard is Unwell*.

SCIENCE

1918 Sir Andrew Huxley, English physiologist and Nobel prize winner for his research into nerve impulse conduction and muscle contraction.

JAZZ

1899 Hoagy Carmichael (Howard Hoagland Carmichael), US songwriter remembered for his songs 'Stardust' (1927), 'Lazy River' (1931) and 'In the Cool, Cool, Cool of the Evening', written in 1951 and which won an Oscar when sung in the film *Here Comes the Groom*.

SPORT

BILLY AND BORIS Two Wimbledon champions share a birthday. One became champion in 1961, winning her 20th title in 1977 when she and Martina Navratilova won the doubles: Billy Jean King (née Moffit) was born in 1943 and proved one of the greatest women tennis stars of this century. Boris Becker, West Germany's Wimbledon champion when only aged 17 (1985), was born in 1967. He repeated the performance the following year and again in 1989.

DIED THIS DAY

1718 Edward Teach, English pirate who sailed under the name of Blackbeard, killed off the coast of North Carolina.

1774 Robert Clive, English soldier and administrator in India who avenged the 'Black Hole of Calcutta' deaths, from an overdose of opium.

1900 Sir Arthur (Seymour) Sullivan, English composer best remembered for his partnership with Sir W.S.Gilbert to produce light operas.

1916 (John Griffith) Jack London, US novelist who wrote *Call of the Wild* (1903).

1943 Lorenz (Milton) Hart, US lyricist who collaborated with Richard Rodgers on such shows as *On Your Toes* and *Pal Joey* and wrote songs including 'With a Song in My Heart'.

1980 Mae West, US actress and show business legend.

1982 Jean Batten, New Zealand aviator who broke the Australia-to-England record in 1937, aged 72, of a heart attack on the terrace of a cheap lodging house near Palma airport, Mallorca, where she had ended up, seeking seclusion. Her death was only made public in 1987 when her New Zealand biographers found she had been buried in a pauper's grave in a black bag with five Spaniards.

ON THIS DAY

1497 Portuguese navigator Vasco da Gama rounded the Cape of Good Hope in his search for a route to India.

1830 Container transport was introduced by Pickford's by agreement with the Liverpool & Manchester Railway Company.

1927 The first performance of George Gershwin's *Funny Face* starring Fred and Adele Astaire in New York with the song ''S Wonderful'.

1930 The first Irish Sweep Stake was held, on the Manchester November Handicap. The grand prize was £204,764 won by a Belfast civil servant.

1946 The first Biro ballpoint pen went on

sale, invented by Hungarian Laslo Biro and manufactured by a British company.

1963 John F. Kennedy was assassinated as he was driven in an open car on his official visit to Dallas, Texas. Lee Harvey Oswald was charged with the killing, a charge still overflowing with controversy.

1975 King Juan Carlos was sworn in as King of Spain following the death of Franco two days before.

1986 Mike Tyson at age 20, became the youngest ever world heavyweight boxing champion when he beat Trevor Berbick in Las Vegas in just two rounds.

23 NOVEMBER

BORN THIS DAY

HISTORY

1804 Franklin Pierce, 14th US President from 1852 who was nominated as a compromise candidate. He retired from active politics in 1857 when his unpopular actions lit a long fuse which would set off the Civil War.

1859 Billy the Kid (William H. Bonney), US outlaw who was the legendary gang leader in the Lincoln County cattle war in New Mexico. He murdered a sherrif, was sentenced to death, escaped, killing two guards and was eventually shot by Sherrif Pat Garrett, but not before the 22-year-old psychopath had murdered 21 people, the first when he was only 12 years old.

1869 Valdemar Poulsen, Danish engineer who invented the tape recorder which he patented on 1 December 1898. He was unable to find backers in Europe and finally took his invention to the US, but the device, which recorded on piano wire, had limited application.

ARTS

1876 Manuel (Maria) de Falla (y Matheu), Spanish composer of *Nights in the Gardens of Spain*, which he began in 1909; but it was the ballets *El Amor brujo*, with the popular 'Ritual Fire Dance' (1915), and *The Three-Cornered Hat* (1919) which really confirmed his success.

ENTERTAINMENT

1887 Boris Karloff (William Henry Pratt), English actor who went to the US via Canada. He appeared in the first of his 140 films in 1916 and his classic roles include the monster in *Frankenstein* (1939), which he played with great subtlety. He appeared in many horror films and was a huge success on Broadway in the black comedy *Arsenic and Old Lace* (1950).

1911 Sir Peter Saunders, British impresario who must have taken seriously the saying: 'If you build a better mousetrap, the world will beat a path to your door.' He staged Agatha Christie's *The Mousetrap*, and they did.

1917 Michael Gough, English actor born in Malaya who has established himself as a leading character actor on stage and screen including *The Go-Between* (1971) and *The Boys From Brazil* (1978).

SPORT

1934 Lew Hoad, Australian tennis player; twice Wimbledon champion in 1956–7 and a finalist in 1959.

1956 Shane Gould, Australian swimmer who collected four gold medals (200m,

400m, 800m freestyle and 200m medley) and a silver in the 100m freestyle at the Munich Olympics in 1972.

DIED THIS DAY

HANGING TALES In 1499, Perkin Warbeck, the Flemish imposter claiming to be Richard, Duke of York who had been murdered in the Tower, was hanged at the Tower of London after twice attempting to escape. In 1910, Dr Hawley Harvey Crippen, who poisoned his wife to seek a new life with his lover, Ethel Le Neve, was hanged at Holloway Prison, London, a short walk from his home in Hilldrop Crescent where he had killed and buried the body of his wife, and a few blocks from where he had purchased the poison.

1979 Merle Oberon (Estelle Merle O'Brien Thompson), Tasmanian-born actress who starred in *Wuthering Heights* (1939).

1985 Leslie Mitchell, British radio personality and the BBC's first television announcer.

ON THIS DAY

1670 The first performance in Paris of Molière's *Le Bourgeois Gentilhomme*.

1852 The first pillar boxes were erected in St Helier, in the Channel Islands where, according to a Post Office surveyor sent over to inspect postal facilities, 'there were no receiving offices for people in distant parts of the town'. The surveyor later became famous as the novelist, Anthony Trollope.

1889 The first juke box was installed in Palais Royal Saloon in San Francisco.

1915 'Pack Up Your Troubles in Your Old Kit Bag', the famous First World War song, was published, music by Felix Powell and words by George Asaf, who were really two brothers from Wales.

1963 The first episode of the BBCTV serial *Dr Who* was screened in Britain. The first Dr Who was played by William Hartnell, and Ann Ford was his first female companion. The producer, Sydney Newman, thought the Daleks, designed by Ray Cusick, were 'bug-eyed monsters' and totally wrong for the series.

1988 The grand sumo champion Chionofuji became only the fifth sumo wrestler in recorded history to win 50 matches in a row. Known as the Wolf, his name will be carved into a cenotaph.

24 NOVEMBER

BORN THIS DAY

HISTORY

1784 Zachary Taylor, 12th US President who was a popular military figure with heroic victories against Santa Ana and his Mexican army before taking office in 1848. He died in office two years later.

1815 Grace Darling, English lighthouse-keeper's daughter who rowed out to rescue survivors of the *Forfarshire* (7.9.1838) and became a national heroine fêted by royalty, befriended by the aristocracy, written about by Wordsworth and Swinburne. She died of consumption, aged 27.

ARTS

1713 Laurence Sterne, Irish clergyman and author of *The Life and Opinions of Tristram Shandy* (1760).

1849 Frances (Eliza) Hodgson Burnett, English-born novelist who emigrated with her parents to Tennessee. She is remembered for two novels, *Little Lord Fauntleroy* (1886) and *The Secret Garden* (1909).

1864 Henri (Marie Raymond) de Toulouse-Lautrec, French painter and lithographer, born into a wealthy, aristocratic family. At 14, he had a horse riding accident and broke both legs which then failed to grow. He set up as a painter in Montmartre. His paintings together with posters for the Moulin Rouge captured the spirit of the age with studies of cabaret artistes and prostitutes.

1912 Garson Kanin, US writer and director who had a hit on Broadway with his play, (later filmed) *Born Yesterday* (1946). Other films include *Adam's Rib* (1949).

1925 Alun Owen, British playwright for both the stage and television with plays such as *No Trams to Lime Street* (1959) and *Kisch, Kisch* (1983).

ENTERTAINMENT

1914 Geraldine Fitzgerald, Irish-born US actress who had a successful stage career playing leads in productions including *Long Day's Journey into Night* (1971) and in the films *Wuthering Heights* (1939), which won her an Oscar nomination for best supporting actress, and *Rachel, Rachel* (1968).

1919 David Kossof, English actor, author and illustrator who was in *A Kid for Two Farthings* (1955). He scored a personal success with his broadcast of an earthy version of popular bible stories which were also published as *Bible Stories Retold by David Kossoff* (1968).

1942 Billy Connolly, Scottish comedian.

SCIENCE

1903 Hans Popper, Austrian-born hepatologist who founded the modern science of hepatology, the study of liver disorders, together with Dame Sheila Sherlock.

JAZZ

1868 Scott Joplin, pianist and composer who played his ragtime in the brothels of Chicago and St Louis. He composed the first ragtime opera *A Guest of Honor* (1911), but it was mainly due to Joshua Rifkin in the mid 70s that his work was revived and revalued.

1925 Al(vin Gilbert) Cohn, US tenor saxophonist and arranger who was featured in Buddy Rich's band in 1947 and then with Stan Getz and Zoot Sims.

SPORT

1894 Herbert (William) Sutcliffe, Yorkshire and England cricketer who was a high-scoring batsman. In 54 tests, he totalled 4,555 runs.

1955 Ian (Terence) Botham, former England cricket captain, who made his debut for Somerset in 1974. Certainly one of the most exciting, unpredictable and controversial cricketers in the game and one of the best all-rounders, he has been a record wicket-taker and a hard hitting batsman capable of high scores.

DIED THIS DAY

1572 John Knox, founder of Scottish Presbytarianism.

1848 Lord Melbourne, twice British Prime Minister.

1916 Sir Hiram Maxim, English-born US machine gun inventor and manufacturer.

1929 Georges Clemenceau, twice French Prime Minister.

ON THIS DAY

1434 The River Thames froze over, and exactly 281 years later, it froze again hard enough for a Frost Fair to be held on the ice.

1642 Dutch navigator Abel Tasman discovered Van Diemen's Land which he named after his captain, but it was later renamed Tasmania.

1859 Darwin's controversial *Origin of Species* was published.

1939 Imperial Airways and British Airways merged to become BOAC (British Overseas Airways Corporation, which later merged with British European Airways and returned to one of the previous names, British Airways).

1951 Austin and Morris Motors agreed to merge.

1962 The satirical television programme *That Was the Week That Was* went out live from the BBC, introduced by a new presenter, David Frost, and with some material written by an equally unknown John Cleese. Produced by Ned Sherrin, the programme broke new ground.

1963 Lee Harvey Oswald was shot dead by Jack Ruby in the underground car park of the Dallas Police Headquarters. Harvey, charged with the assassination of President Kennedy, was being transferred to the County Jail when the strip club owner (real name, Jack Rubinstein) suddenly appeared and fired a gun at point blank range before being overpowered and arrested, adding one more curious and disturbing element to the mystery.

1989 The Czechoslovak party leadership resigned following huge and violent protests in Prague and elsewhere in the country. The Communist Party's domination finally ended on 28 November.

25 NOVEMBER

Some biblical scholars claim this was the day in 2348BC when the Flood began.

BORN THIS DAY

HISTORY

1835 Andrew Carnegie, Scottish-born US industrialist and philanthropist who rose from telegraph boy to iron and steel multimillionaire. He devoted his vast wealth to libraries and universities including the Carnegie Hall in New York which opened in 1891.

1844 Karl Friedrich Benz, German engineer and motor car pioneer who built the world's first practical internal-combustion vehicle in 1885, patented the following year (26.1.1886). In 1926, his company merged with Daimler.

1915 General Augusto Pinochet, president of Chile who ousted Dr Salvador Allende in a CIA-backed military coup instituting a repressive regime.

POP

1946 Bev Bevan, English drummer with the Electric Light Orchestra which combined strings, and at one time, a 30-voice male choir for their album, *Discovery* (1979) and who recorded the sound-track for the film *Xanadu* (1980).

SPORT

1931 Dickie Jeeps, former England rugby football international and chairman of the Sports Council.

1952 Imran Khan Niaz, Pakistan cricket

captain who also played for Lahore, Worcestershire, Oxford University and Sussex. His bowling made him his country's highest wicket-taker.

DIED THIS DAY

1937 Dame Lilian (Mary) Baylis, founder of the Old Vic.

1949 Bojangles (Bill Robinson), US tap dancer and entertainer who also appeared in films with Shirley Temple.

1970 Yukio Mishima (Kimitake Hiraoka), Japanese novelist who was involved in a political cult to restore traditionalist values to modern Japanese society. Disillusioned, he commited ritual suicide after first seizing control of military headquarters near Tokyo and addressing a crowd from the balcony, attacking the weakness of Japan for accepting a constitution that forbade it to re-arm.

1974 U. Thant, Burmese diplomat and UN Secretary-General, 1962–71.

ON THIS DAY

1884 Evaporated milk was patented by John Mayenberg of St Louis, Missouri.

1896 William Marshall became the first person in Britain to receive a parking summons after leaving his car in Tokenhouse Yard in the City of London, but the case was dismissed.

1932 British Equity, the actors' union, voted for a closed shop to begin operating in 1933.

1952 Agatha Christie's *The Mousetrap* opened at the Ambassadors Theatre, London starring Richard Attenborough and Sheila Sim.

1953 Hungary, led by their talented footballer Ferenc Pushkas, beat England 6–3 at Wembley to become the first foreign team to achieve an away win at Wembley.

1969 John Lennon returned his MBE in protest against British involvement in Biafra and British support of US involvement in Vietnam.

1988 Lorraine Miles made legal history when her civil action, the first unsupported by a criminal conviction for rape, was upheld at an Essex court. She was awarded £25,108 in damages.

26 NOVEMBER

BORN THIS DAY

HISTORY

1810 William George Armstrong (Baron Armstrong), English inventor of hydraulic equipment, originally for military use, but which led to the development of the first hydraulic crane.

1908 Lord Forte (Charles Forte), British business magnate, chairman of Trusthouse Forte, one of the largest hotel and restaurant groups in the world.

ARTS

1731 William Cowper, English poet who suffered a mental breakdown. Released from the asylum, he was taken under the wing of a succession of women. Besides poetry and a collection of letters, he wrote hymns including 'God Moves in a Mysterious Way'.

1922 Charles Schulz, US cartoonist who created 'Peanuts', one of the best and most successful cartoon strips ever. Shulz studied cartooning through a correspondence course. Originally titled *Li'l Folks*, the strip featured Charlie

Brown, Snoopy, Linus, Lucy and others (*see* 2.10.1950). It inspired the musical *You're a Good Man, Charlie Brown* in 1967.

ENTERTAINMENT

1905 (George) Emlyn Williams, Welsh playwright and actor who appeared in his own plays including *Night Must Fall* (1935) and *The Corn is Green* (1938), both later filmed. He was also in many British and Hollywood films including *Jamaica Inn* (1939) and *David Copperfield* (1970).

1910 Cyril Cussack, South African-born actor who was brought up in Ireland where he made his first stage appearance. Much in demand, both on stage and screen, his film appearances include *Odd Man Out* (1947) and *The Day of the Jackal* (1973).

JAZZ

1939 Art(hur Edward George) Themen, English saxophonist and consultant orthopaedic surgeon, who performed with the early British blues players including Alexis Korner, before moving on to play with the likes of Stan Tracey.

1945 Jim Mullen, Scottish guitarist who played with the Average White Band and others in the US before collaborating with Morrisey to form Morrisey-Mullen.

POP

1939 Tina Turner (Annie Mae Bullock), US singer who began as half of a duo with husband Ike whose hits included 'River Deep, Mountain High' (1967). When their marriage and partnership broke up, she established herself as a raunchy solo performer with hits including 'What's Love Got to Do With It' (1984).

DIED THIS DAY

1836 John Loudon McAdam, Scottish road surface inventor.

1956 Tommy Dorsey, US bandleader in the era of big band 'swing', choked to death in his sleep, age 51.

ON THIS DAY

1832 John Mason introduced the first trams in New York running the Prince Street-14th Street route.

1867 Mrs Lily Maxwell of Manchester cast her vote in a parliamentary election. She had been placed on the electoral register in error and had to be escorted by a bodyguard to protect her from loutish opponents to women's suffrage.

1922 Howard Carter and the Earl of Carnarvon, Carter's sponsor, became the first men to see inside the tomb of the Pharaoh Tutankhamun near Luxor since it was sealed 3,000 years before. Having escaped detection by tomb robbers, it was complete with golden statues and golden throne inlaid with gems.

1928 The first twins delivered by Caesarean section in Britain were born in a Manchester hospital to a mother who was hunchbacked.

1942 The Soviet forces counterattacked at Stalingrad, ending the siege and forcing General von Paulus's Sixth Army to retreat.

1966 President de Gaulle opened the world's first tidal power station in Brittany.

1983 The Brinks Mat security warehouse

at London's Heathrow Airport was robbed of £25 million worth of gold bars weighing three tons.

1987 Drawings of English bank notes by US artist James Boggs were declared works of art and not illegal replicas of UK currency by an Old Bailey jury.

1988 Mrs Rita Lockett of Torquay, Devon spent £10,000 to repeat her daughter's wedding two months after the event because she did not like the video. The couple went through the reception with all 200 wedding guests wearing the same outfits and having to listen to the same speeches, this time with a professional video crew on hand.

27 NOVEMBER

BORN THIS DAY

HISTORY

1874 Chaim (Azriel) Weizmann, first president of Israel, born in Russia who was a chemistry professor in Geneva where he became active in the World Zionist Movement. After settling in Britain in 1904 he assisted the British munitions industry during the First World War when he devised a way of extracting acetone (needed for cordite) from maize. In return, the British government promised to help his cause and establish a Jewish state in Palestine.

1894 Konosuke Matsushita, Japanese industrialist who founded the Matsushita Electric Industrial Company in 1918 which later made products under the Panasonic name.

1921 Alexander Dubček, former first secretary of the Czechoslovakian Communist Party who introduced short-lived reforms during the Prague Spring of 1968, before the Russians invaded. When democracy was eventually re-introduced, he became Chairman of the Czechoslovak parliament on 28 December 1989.

ENTERTAINMENT

1809 Fanny (Frances Ann) Kemble, popular English actress who saved her father, actor-manager Charles Kemble, manager of Drury Lane, from bankruptcy by her success. She later toured the US where she married a Southern planter.

1925 Ernie Wise (Wiseman), English comedian, one half of Morecambe and Wise who were one of the best double acts in the history of British comedy. (*See* 14.5.1926)

1929 Alan Simpson, English scriptwriter who, with partner Ray Galton, was responsible for some of the classic comedy series on British television including *Hancock's Half Hour* and *Steptoe and Son*.

1938 Rodney Bewes, English comedy actor who first attracted attention in the comedy television series *The Likely Lads*.

1940 John Alderton, English actor who was in the television series *Please Sir*, *Upstairs, Downstairs* and later *Forever Green* opposite his wife Pauline Collins.

SCIENCE

1701 Anders Celsius, Swedish astronomer who devised the Celsius thermometer, also known as the centigrade thermometer, in 1742.

POP

1942 Jimi Hendrix, US guitarist and singer who formed the Jimi Hendrix

Experience in Britain in 1966 which had success with 'Purple Haze' and 'The Wind Cries Mary', both in 1967.

DIED THIS DAY

1811 Andrew Meikle, Scottish agricultural engineer who invented the threshing machine in 1786.

1895 Alexandre Dumas (fils), French playwright and author of *La Dame aux Camélias* (1848).

1953 Eugene O'Neill, leading US playwright and Nobel prize winner, who wrote *The Iceman Cometh* (1939.

1975 Ross McWhirter, twin brother of Norris, compilers of the *Guinness Book of Records*, shot on his doorstep by an Irish gunman.

ON THIS DAY

1582 On or about this day William Shakespeare, aged 18, married Anne Hathaway. They had a daughter in 1583 and a twin boy and girl in 1585. The boy died aged 11.

1914 The first two trained policewomen to be granted official status in Britain, Miss Mary Allen and Miss E.F. Harburn reported for duty at Grantham, Lincolnshire.

1942 As German troops arrived in Toulon the French fleet was scuttled in Toulon harbour to prevent the warships falling into enemy hands.

1944 Between 3,500 and 4,000 tons of high explosives went off in a cavern beneath Staffordshire killing 68 people and wiping out an entire farm. The explosion was heard over 100 miles away in London, and recorded as an earthquake in Geneva.

1967 President de Gaulle said 'Non' to British entry into the Common Market.

1987 A young man in Somerset tried seven times to kill himself following a row with his girlfriend. He threw himself in front of four cars, and jumped under the wheels of a lorry. He tried to strangle himself and jumped from a window. The real victims were a driver of one car who suffered a heart attack, a policeman who injured his back trying to restrain the man, and a doctor who was kicked in the face when the struggling man reached hospital.

28 NOVEMBER

BORN THIS DAY

HISTORY

1765 Captain George Manby, English inventor of life saving equipment which he developed while barrack-master at Yarmouth.

1820 Friedrich Engels, German political thinker who settled in England where he worked with Marx on the *Communist Manifesto* (1848). He had previously written *Condition of the Working Classes in England* (1844).

1837 John Wesley Hyatt, US inventor who discovered a process for making celluloid while trying to find a substitute for ivory billiard balls.

1908 Claude Lévi-Strauss, French anthropologist who examined the reason for myths in society and decided they were created to overcome 'contradictions' in life.

ARTS

1632 Jean Baptiste Lully (Giovanni Battista Lulli), Italian composer who became a French citizen and music master to the Royal Family. He collaborated with Molière in a series of comedy-ballets, was the first to introduce women dancers into ballets and make opera popular in France.

1757 William Blake, mystic and visionary English poet and painter who studied under Reynolds. He both engraved the text and illustrations to his *Songs of Innocence* (1789) as well as illustrating Milton's *Paradise Lost* and other works.

1895 Jose Iturbi, Spanish-born pianist and conductor who also appeared in films including *Anchors Aweigh* (1945). He helped to popularize classical music in the US.

1904 Nancy (Freeman) Mitford, English novelist and biographer who is best known for her novel *Love in a Cold Climate* (1949) and her biography *The Sun King* (1966).

1907 Alberto Moravia (Alberto Pincherle), Italian author whose novels include *Conjugal Love* (1951) and *Two Women* (1958).

ENTERTAINMENT

1931 Hope Lange, US actress nominated for an Oscar for her role in *Peyton Place* (1957).

POP

1943 Randy Newman, US singer and songwriter who attracted a cult following for his songs 'I Think It's Gonna Rain Today' (1966) and 'Living Without You' (1967) and who composed the score for the film *Ragtime* (1981) which won him an Oscar nomination.

SPORT

1919 Keith (Ross) Miller, Australian Test cricketer who played 55 Tests taking 170 wickets and scoring 2958 runs.

1959 Stephen Roche, Irish cycling champion who won the Tour de France (26.7.1987).

DIED THIS DAY

1859 Washington Irving, US author who wrote *Rip van Winkle* (1819).

1911 'Lord' George Sanger, English circus impresario, found murdered.

1945 Dwight Filley Davis, sponsor of the Davis Cup tournament.

1962 Wilhelmina, Queen of the Netherlands.

1968 Enid (Mary) Blyton, English children's book author and creator of 'Noddy'.

ON THIS DAY

1660 The Royal Society was founded in London.

WOMEN IN LABOUR This day celebrates the first time any nation granted the vote to its women, the first time a Labour government was elected and the first time a woman was elected to the British parliament. In 1893 women went to the polls in New Zealand as a result of a bill passed by a majority of two votes. In 1899 the world's first Labour Prime Minister took office. Anderson Dawson formed the first ever constitutionally appointed socialist government to sit in the Queensland Parliament, but it only lasted a day. Australia also elected the first Labour Prime Minister in 1904, but John Christian Watson lasted only four months. It was only in 1919 that Nancy Astor won the election as the Member of Parliament for Plymouth and became Britain's first woman MP.

1905 The Irish political party Sinn Fein was founded by Arthur Griffith in Dublin.

1924 The skull of a fossil child from Taung, near Kimberley in the northern Cape Province, was identified by Professor Raymond Dart, Australian anthropologist, as a 'southern African ape with a brain size capable of human intelligence', thereby establishing the missing evolutionary link between ape and man which Darwin had predicted.

1935 The Miles quadruplets (three boys and a girl) were born in England and were the first British quads to survive infancy.

1948 Dr Edwin Land's first Polaroid cameras went on sale in Boston.

29 NOVEMBER

National Day of Yugoslavia celebrating its proclamation as a Federal People's Republic in 1945.

BORN THIS DAY

HISTORY

1834 Tz'u-hsi, dowager empress of China who became the most powerful woman in Chinese history, retaining power by suppressing much needed reforms. (*See* 15.11.1908)

1932 Jacques Chirac, French politician who became Prime Minister first in 1974 to President Giscard d'Estaing and again in 1986 under François Mitterand.

ARTS

1797 Gaetano Donizetti, Italian composer whose operas include *Lucia di Lammermoor* (1835) and *Don Pasquale* (1843).

1832 Louisa M(ay) Alcott, US author of the autobiographical novel, *Little Women* (1868), one of the most popular books for girls.

1898 C(live) S(taples) Lewis, born in Belfast, educated at Oxford, this scholar and author wrote *The Screwtape Letters* (1942), and although it became a best seller, he has become better known through his *The Narnia Chronicles* stories for children, the first written in 1950.

ENTERTAINMENT

1895 Busby Berkeley (William Berkeley Enos), choreographer and director who devised a new style of choreography and photography which revolutionized Hollywood musicals. His kaleidoscopic ballets, with overhead shots to show the changing patterns his dancers could create, were his trademark in films including *42nd Street*, *The Gold Diggers of 1933* (both 1933) and *Babes in Arms* (1939).

1928 Derek Jameson, the cockney lad who grew up to be a Fleet Street editor and now a radio and television broadcaster on BBC Radio 2 and Sky satellite television.

SCIENCE

1803 Christian Johann Doppler, Austrian physicist who described the Doppler effect in simple terms as the change in pitch of a siren as it comes towards one and then recedes, and which has more significant applications when examining the red shift of light from distant stars.

1849 Sir John Ambrose Fleming, English electrical engineer who invented the diode or Fleming valve in 1904 which, together with the amplifier grid invented by Lee De Forest, is the basic requirement for most electronic apparatus.

POP

1929 Berry Gordy, Jr, US songwriter and record producer who founded the first all-black record company, Motown Records, in 1959. His recording artists included The Jackson Five, Diana Ross and the Supremes, Lionel Ritchie, Stevie Wonder and other chart toppers. The name Motown came from Detroit, the motor town where the studio was based.

1933 John Mayall, pioneer British rhythm and blues musician who led his group the Bluebreakers in the early 60s, and encouraged an interest in blues music in Britain. He later went to the US.

JAZZ

1915 (William) Billy Strayhorn, US composer of the great classic, 'Take the A-Train' which Duke Ellington made his theme tune in 1941.

1934 (Anthony George) Tony Coe, English saxophonist and clarinettist, considered one of the finest in Britain, who has played with many leading groups and bands as well as for films. His is the distinctive sax on the title music of 'The Pink Panther' films.

SPORT

1952 Dusty Hare, England rugby footballer.

DIED THIS DAY

1530 Thomas Wolsey, English Cardinal and Lord Chancellor, *en route* from York to London.

1780 Maria Theresa, Empress of Austria and Queen of Hungary and Bohemia, who renewed Austria's power and authority.

1872 Horace Greeley, US editor and founder of the *New York Tribune*.

1924 Giacomo (Antonio Domenico Michele Secondo Maria) Puccini, Italian opera composer whose works include *Madame Butterfly* (1904).

1952 Rosa Lewis, English working-class cook who rose to become the owner of the fashionable Cavendish Hotel in London,

1954 Sir George Edward Robey, English comedian and actor, known as 'The Prime Minister of Mirth' who introduced the song, 'If You Were the Only Girl in the World'.

1975 Graham Hill, champion English racing driver killed when a private aircraft in which he was travelling crashed in Hertfordshire.

ON THIS DAY

1864 A black day in US history. Several hundred Cheyenne and some Arapaho Indians who had surrendered to the US, had been given permission to camp at Sand Creek, Colorado Territory while negotiating a peace formula. Their chief Black Kettle, had agreed to the disarming of their troops. Colonel John M. Chivington with 1,200 troops mounted a surprise attack on the camp, and despite Black Kettle hoisting aloft the US flag and a white flag, the troops shot dead 400 men, women and children and set off the Arapaho-Cheyenne war.

1929 US admiral Richard Byrd became the first man to fly over the South Pole with his pilot Bernt Balchen.

DANCING TIMES The first performance in 1932 of Cole Porter's *The Gay Divorce* in New York starring Fred Astaire and featuring the song 'Night and Day'. In 1936, Rogers and Hart's *On Your Toes* opened in New York, the first Broadway musical to integrate balletic dance (choregraphed by George Balanchine) for the 'Slaughter on Tenth Avenue' sequence.

30 NOVEMBER

St Andrew's Day, patron saint of Scotland and also of golfers and fishermen.

BORN THIS DAY

HISTORY

1869 Nils Gustaf Dalen, Swedish physicist and inventor, winner of the Nobel prize for his development of the automatic sun valve used on buoys and unmanned lighthouses. He also invented the Aga cooker and continued to work though blinded by an experiment with gases in 1913.

1874 Sir Winston Leonard Churchill, British statesman, journalist, historian and Nobel prize winner for literature, a descendant of the great Duke of Marlborough, born in Blenheim Palace. The great wartime Prime Minister, with his highly quotable speeches, was considered by many as 'the greatest living Englishman'. From Boer War newspaper correspondent to first Lord of the Admiralty to Prime Minister, Churchill dominated British history for much of the 20th century.

ARTS

1508 Andrea Palladio, Italian architect who built the Villa Rotonda and other mansions for wealthy Venetians and influenced Western architecture with his neo-classical style.

TWO OF A KIND Born in 1628 John Bunyan, English minister and preacher, and author of one of the most popular books in the English language, *The Pilgrim's Progress* (1678) was baptized on this day. He spent 12 years in prison for holding beliefs which did not conform to those of the established church. Another cleric who found the pen more potent than the sermon was born in 1667 in Dublin. Jonathan Swift, who became Dean of St Patrick's, Dublin after political services in England, wrote his first satirical novel *A Tale of a Tub* in 1696–99, and his masterpiece *Gulliver's Travels* was published in 1726.

1835 Mark Twain (Samuel Langhorne Clemens), US humorist who was a Mississippi riverboat pilot ('mark twain' is a call to the pilot to let him know the depth of water), a journalist and odd job man before he produced *The Adventures of Tom Sawyer* (1876) and *The Adventures of Huckleberry Finn* (1885).

1900 Geoffrey (Edward West) Household, English author best known for his gripping *Rogue Male* (1938) also made into a film and television film, and *A Rough Shoot* (1951).

ENTERTAINMENT

1920 Virginia Mayo (Virginia Jones), US actress who graduated from showgirl to a showgirl-type leading lady in films such as *The Princess and the Pirate* (1944) and *The Kid from Brooklyn* (1946).

1926 Richard Crenna, US actor in both cinema and television films including *Breakhart Pass* (1976).

SPORT

1960 Gary Lineker, English footballer who was the top goal scorer at the 1986 World Cup for England. The talented Lineker played for Barcelona before returning to England in 1989 to join Spurs.

DIED THIS DAY

1900 Oscar (Fingal O'Flahertie) Wilde, Irish-born playwright, in a Paris hotel, poverty stricken and all but forgotten by his admirers since his release from jail and self-imposed exile in France.

1957 Benjamino Gigli, celebrated Italian tenor.

1977 Sir Terence (Mervyn) Rattigan, English playwright of *The Deep Blue Sea* (1952).

1979 Zeppo (Herbert) Marx, member of the Marx Brothers for a brief spell before becoming their agent.

1979 Joyce (Irene) Grenfell, English entertainer and writer famous for her humorous monologues which she presented in her one-woman show.

ON THIS DAY

1840 Napoleon I's remains were returned from St Helena to Paris.

1872 The first football match between England and Scotland took place in Glasgow. It ended in a 0–0 draw.

1913 Charlie Chaplin made his film debut without the moustache and cane in *Making a Living*, a Mack Sennett one-reeler.

1922 The first purpose-built aircraft carrier, the Japanese navy's *Hosho* began its first sea trials.

1931 HMV (His Master's Voice) and Columbia Records merged to form EMI (Electrical and Musical Industries).

1936 Crystal Palace was destroyed by fire. The spectacular blaze was seen miles away. Designed by Sir Joseph Paxton, it was originally erected in Hyde Park for the Great Exhibition in 1851.

1944 HMS *Vanguard*, Britain's largest ever battleship, was launched at Clydebank. It was to be the last.

1956 Floyd Patterson became the youngest boxer to win the world heavyweight title, at age 21, when he knocked out Archie Moore in Round Five in Chicago.

1983 Dutch brewing millionaire, Alfred Heineken was kidnapped in Amsterdam, but was tracked down and freed by the police in a raid on the 30th.

THE PAN BOOK OF DATES

DECEMBER

Does God know the earth has reached its 'sell-by' date?
(Anon)

1 DECEMBER

BORN THIS DAY

HISTORY

1761 Madame Marie Tussaud (Grosholz), Swiss-born French waxworks modeller. During the French Revolution she made death masks from the severed heads of the famous. In 1800, separated from her husband, she toured Britain with her waxworks, eventually setting up a permanent exhibition in London.

1844 Queen Alexandra, wife of Edward VII, who was the eldest daughter of King Christian of Denmark.

ARTS

1895 Henry Williamson, English author of *Tarka the Otter* (1927) and *Salar the Salmon* (1935).

1910 Alicia Markova (Lilian Alicia Marks), English prima ballerina who made her debut at age 14 with Diaghilev's Ballets Russes. In 1933 she became the first prima ballerina of the Vic-Wells Ballet. With Anton Dolin, she established the Markova-Dolin Ballet and later London's Festival Ballet.

1952 Stephen Poliakoff, English playwright who wrote *Bloody Kids*, made into a film in 1979, and the television plays, *Caught on a Train* (1980) and *Strawberry Fields* (1986).

ENTERTAINMENT

1913 Mary Martin, US actress and singer who starred on Broadway in *South Pacific* (1949) and in the original production of *The Sound of Music* (1959). She is the mother of Larry Hagman of *Dallas* fame.

1935 Woody Allen (Allen Stewart Konigsberg), US comedian, writer and director who both scripted and performed in his first film *What's New, Pussycat?* (1965). The Oscar-winning *Annie Hall* (1977) was written by, directed by and starred Allen.

1940 Richard Pryor, US comedian and actor who won an Oscar for best supporting actor in *The Lady Sings the Blues* (1972) and went on to make *California Suite* (1978) and *Richard Pryor Alive in Concert* (1979).

1945 Bette Midler, US singer and comedienne who has made several television specials as well as the film *The Rose* (1979). A Los Angeles concert was also filmed as *Divine Madness* (1980).

POP

1946 (Raymond Edward) Gilbert O'Sullivan, Irish-born singer best known for his hits 'Alone Again (Naturally)' which got to No. 1 in the US in 1972, and the song 'Clare' about his producer Gordon Mill's daughter which reached No. 1 in the UK chart the same year.

JAZZ

1951 (John Francis) Jaco Pastorius, US bassist with the jazz-rock group Weather Report and later with his own group, Word of Mouth. He died after being beaten up trying to enter a club in Fort Lauderdale, Florida in 1987.

SPORT

1939 Lee Trevino, US golfer known as 'Supermex', who won the US Open in 1968 and 1971, and the British Open in 1971 and 1972. He was the first to win the US, British and Canadian Opens in a single year (1971).

DIED THIS DAY

1581 Edward Campion, (later St Edward) and three other Jesuits were martyred. He was tried on a charge of treason for promoting Catholicism and hanged in London.

1973 David Ben-Gurion, Israel's first Prime Minister.

1987 James Baldwin, US author and playwright, who wrote *The Amen Corner* (1955).

ON THIS DAY

1640 The Spanish were driven out of Portugal and the country regained its independence.

1768 The Royal Academy of Arts was founded in London.

1887 Beeton's Christmas Annual went on sale on or about this day with *A Study in Scarlet* by A. Conan Doyle which first introduced the detective, Sherlock Holmes.

1906 The Cinema Omnia Pathé, the world's first purpose-built picture palace, opened in Paris.

1919 Lady Astor became the first woman to take her seat in the House of Commons as a Member of Parliament.

1939 The world première in New York of *Gone with the Wind* starring Clark Gable, Vivien Leigh and Olivia de Havilland.

1942 The Beveridge Report written by Sir William Beveridge proposed a welfare state for Britain.

1951 The first performance at Covent Garden of Benjamin Britten's opera *Billy Budd* with Peter Pears.

1953 Marilyn Monroe was featured as the centre-spread nude in the first edition of Hugh Heffner's *Playboy* magazine which he started with just $10,000.

1987 The Department of Trade inspectors were ordered into the giant Guinness company to investigate allegations of misconduct which ended up with four arrests being made, including the chairman Ernest Saunders.

1989 In Rome, Pope John Paul II and Mikhail Gorbachev ended seventy years of hostility between the Roman Catholic Church and the Soviet Union.

2 DECEMBER

BORN THIS DAY

ARTS

1859 Georges Seurat, French painter who was a founder of the Neo-Impressionist school popularly known as Pointillism. His paintings made a major contribution towards the development of modern art.

1899 Sir John (Giovanni Battista) Barbirolli, English conductor with many major orchestras including Covent Garden, the Hallé and international orchestras such as the Berlin Philharmonic and the Chicago Symphony Orchestra.

ENTERTAINMENT

1915 Adolf Green, US lyricist and librettist who collaborated with Betty Comden to create some of Broadway's greatest shows and songs including *Wonderful Town* (1953) and *The Bells Are Ringing* (1956).

INVENTION

1906 Peter Carl Goldmark, Hungarian-born US inventor of long-playing records. The LP record utilizing micro-grooves was introduced in 1948, and in 1950 he came up with the scanning system which allowed the US Lunar Orbiter spacecraft to relay pictures back to earth.

DIED THIS DAY

1547 Hernán Cortés, Spanish conqueror of Mexico.
1594 Gerhardus Mercator (Gerhard Kaufmann), Belgian-born map maker.
1814 Marquis de Sade, French novelist after whom sadism is named, in the asylum at Charenton.
1859 John Brown, militant US anti-slavery campaigner who was hanged for his attack on the Federal arsenal at Harper's Ferry (16.10.1859).
1918 Edmond (Eugène Alexis) Rostand, French playwright of *Cyrano de Bergerac* (1897).
1951 Stephen Potter, English author on 'gamesmanship'.
1985 Philip (Arthur) Larkin, English poet and critic.

ON THIS DAY

1697 The rebuilt St Paul's Cathedral, the work of Sir Christopher Wren, was opened.
1804 Napoleon was crowned Emperor in Paris by Pope Pius VII. On this day, one year later in 1805, Napoleon defeated the Austro-Russian force at the Battle of Austerlitz.
1823 US President James Monroe's Monroe Doctrine was proclaimed, opposing foreign, especially European interference and involvement in US policies.
1901 In the US King Camp Gillette marketed a safety razor he patented in 1897. It had a double edged disposable blade.
1907 English footballers formed the Professional Footballer's Association.
1942 At the University of Chicago, the world's first nuclear chain reaction took place as the first atomic pile began operating under the direction of physicists Enrio Fermi and Arthur Compton.
1982 The first artificial heart was fitted, to dentist Dr Barney B. Clark, at the Univeristy of Utah Medical Center, Salt Lake City. He died the following March.
1981 Colonel 'Mad Mike' Hoare and his 44 mercenaries posing as the Froth Blowers Club found their frothy cover blown soon after landing in the Seychelles and had to shoot their way out of the airport lounge, hijack an Air India plane and make the pilot fly them to South Africa where they had originally been sponsored to fly over and topple the Seychelles government. The Froth Blowers were arrested by South African officials.

3 DECEMBER

BORN THIS DAY

ARTS

1857 Joseph Conrad (Teodor Jozef Konrad Korzeniowski), Polish-born English author who turned to writing after 20 years at sea. He wrote *Lord Jim* (1900), *Heart of Darkness* (1902), *The Secret Agent* (1907) and *Under Western Eyes* (1911) amongst others.
1883 (Friedrich Wilhelm) Anton von Webern, German composer who wrote most of his works in memory of his mother. He was accidentally shot by a US sentry in 1945.
1923 (Cecilia Sophia Anna) Maria Callas (Calogeropoulos), US-born operatic

diva who studied in Greece where she made her debut in 1940. She enlarged the normal operatic repertoire and earned herself the title 'La divina' for her performances of Norma, Violetta and Tosca. Her private life was anything but private, and added to the Callas phenomenon.

ENTERTAINMENT

1930 Jean-Luc Godard, French film director who introduced new cinematic techniques in his low-budget first film, *Breathless* (1959). His other films include *A Woman is a Woman* (1961) and *Alphaville* (1965).

1946 Paul Nicholas, English actor and singer in the musical revival *Me and My Girl* in London, but is best known for his television sitcom *Just Good Friends*.

1952 Mel Smith, English comedy actor and writer who was in television's *Not the Nine O'Clock News* and *Alas Smith and Jones* with his colleague, Griff Rhys Jones.

INVENTION

1753 Samuel Crompton, English inventor of the spinning-mule, the first major mechanisation of the cotton industry. He could not afford to patent his device and revealed its secrets to mill owners in return for a promise to pay him a royalty. All he ever received was £60.

1795 Sir Rowland Hill, English postal pioneer who invented the idea of the Penny Post (10.1.1840) while postmaster-general. He was also an educationalist and founder of the Society for the Diffusion of Useful Knowledge.

POP

1930 Andy Williams, US ballad singer who made several television specials. He had his only No. 1 in the UK with 'Butterfly' in 1957.

SPORT

FAST AND SLOW Born 1905, Lesley (Ethelbert George) Ames, Kent and England cricketer who scored a record 123 before lunch against South Africa at the Oval in 1935; while Trevor (Edward) Bailey, Essex and England cricketer born in 1923 has the distinction of scoring the slowest half century (357 minutes) against Australia at Brisbane in 1958.

DIED THIS DAY

1552 Francis Xavier, Jesuit missionary who was canonized in 1622.

1894 Robert Louis Stevenson, Scottish author who wrote *Treasure Island* (1883).

1910 Mary Eddy Baker, US founder of the Christian Science movement.

1919 Pierre Auguste Renoir, French Impressionist painter.

1980 Sir Oswald (Ernald) Moseley, leader of the British Union of Fascists, in exile in Paris.

ON THIS DAY

1660 Margaret Hughes received a rousing reception for her performance at the Vere Street Theatre as Desdomona in *The Moor of Venice*, Thomas Killigrew's version of *Othello*. It was the first time a professional actress had ever appeared on the British stage.

1818 Illinois became the 21st state of the Union.

1836 Three people were killed at Great Corby, near Carlisle in Cumbria in the first fatal railway derailment.

1910 Neon lighting, developed by French physicist George Claude, was displayed for the first time at the Paris Motor Show.

1926 In an episode as puzzling and intriguing as any in her many novels, Agatha Christie disappeared from her Surrey home and was discovered on the 14th staying under an assumed name at the Old Swan Hotel, Harrogate. She said she had no recollection of how she came to be in Yorkshire.

1967 At Groote Schuur Hospital, Cape Town, Dr Christiaan Barnard carried out the world's first heart transplant. The heart of the first donor came from Denise Darvall, a 25-year-old bank clerk who was found dying after a road accident and agreed to give her heart to a 53-year-old grocer, Louis Washansky. He died 18 days later as a result of tissue rejection.

4 DECEMBER

One-time Feast Day of Barbara, patron saint of artillery men and miners. Her heathen father is said to have beheaded her for her faith and was immediately struck by lightning and died.

BORN THIS DAY

HISTORY

1865 Edith (Louisa) Cavell, English nurse in Brussels 1914–15, who was accused of helping Allied soldiers escape occupied Belgium over the Dutch border and was executed by the Germans (12.10.1915).

1892 General Francisco Franco (Bahamonde), Spanish dictator who was formerly the Chief of Staff of the Spanish Army before being demoted to Governor of the Canary Islands and then dismissed by the Republican government. With German and Italian assistance, he initiated the Civil War and in 1939 became the head of a Fascist government.

ARTS

1795 Thomas Carlyle, Scottish historian and writer, best known for his *French Revolution* in 1839 which established his reputation as a literary genius.

1835 Samuel Butler, English satirical novelist who was for a time a sheep farmer in New Zealand. He wrote his classic *Erewhon* (1872) which is (almost) 'Nowhere' backwards and which is a world where much is inverted; crime is an illness, illness a crime.

1875 (Richard Horatio) Edgar Wallace, English thriller writer who was adopted by a Billingsgate fish porter. After odd jobs and a spell in the army serving in South Africa, he became one of the most prolific writers with some 175 books and 15 plays including *Saunders of the River* (1911) and *The Terror* (1930). He also collaborated on the film script of the original *King Kong* shortly before his death in 1932.

1943 Yvonne Minton, Australian mezzo-soprano with an international reputation who created the role of Thea in Tippett's *The Knot Garden* (1970).

ENTERTAINMENT

1861 Lillian Russell (Helen Louise Leonard), leading US singer and actress, the most photographed woman of her age. She starred in light operas and comedies in both the US and on the London stage. The film *Lillian Russell* stars Alice Faye as the actress.

1912 Jimmy Jewel, English comedian who appared with Ben Warriss before going on to an acting career which included appearances in television series including *Nearest and Dearest*.

1922 (Edna May) Deanna Durbin, Canadian singer and actress whose career began at age 14. She lost out on a contract with MGM to Judy Garland, but began making films at Universal such as *That Certain Age* (1938) and *Up in Central Park* (1948).

1930 Ronnie Corbett, diminutive Scottish-born comedian often associated with Ronnie Barker in such television series as the award-winning *The Two Ronnies* which ran for well over 20 years, and in his own series, *Sorry!*

1942 Gemma Jones, British actress best known for her television role as *The Duchess of Duke Street*.

1949 Jeff Bridges, US actor, son of Lloyd, who won an Oscar nomination for his performance in *The Last Picture Show* (1971), and starred with brother Bill in *The Fabulous Baker Boys* (1989).

1950 Pamela Stephenson, Australian comedienne who settled in England and shone in television's *Not the Nine O'Clock News* and other shows. She is married to comedian Billy Connolly.

SPORT

1938 Richard Meade, British Olympic horseman who won a gold medal at the Munich Olympics in the individual three-day event in 1972.

DIED THIS DAY

1642 Cardinal Richelieu, French statesman and chief minister to King Louis XIII.

1732 John Gay, English playwright who wrote *The Beggar's Opera* (1728).

1798 Luigi Galvani, Italian physiologist who discovered galvanic electricity or animal electricity.

1850 William Sturgeon, English physicist who built the first electromagnet.

1976 Benjamin Britten, English composer of *Peter Grimes* and other major 20th-century operas.

ON THIS DAY

1154 The only Englishman to become a pope, Nicholas Breakspear became Adrian IV.

1791 The *Observer*, Britain's oldest Sunday newspaper, was first published.

1921 'Fatty' Arbuckle, US silent film comedian was found not guilty by 10–2 of rape and manslaughter. He was retried twice, found not guilty both times, but his career was ruined.

1937 *The Dandy* comic was first published by D. C. Thomson featuring Desperate Dan, the brainchild of Dudley Watkins. With a fan club of over 350,000, Dan proved a durable character. A copy of this first edition is worth between £850 – £1,000.

1947 The first performance on Broadway of Tennessee Williams' *A Streetcar Named Desire* starring Marlon Brando and Jessica Tandy.

1948 George Orwell completed the final draft of *Nineteen Eighty-Four* which was published on 8 June 1949.

1961 The birth control pill became available on the National Health Service in Britain.

1965 The US launched *Gemini VII* into space for a link-up with the orbiting *Gemini VI*.

1988 Lorin Maazel conducted Beethoven's nine symphonies in one day at the Royal Festival Hall, London using three orchestras.

5 DECEMBER

BORN THIS DAY

HISTORY

1782 Martin van Buren, 8th US President, from 1835–40.

1839 George Armstrong Custer, US cavalry commander famous for his 'last stand'. He attacked Sitting Bull's Sioux and Cheyenne Indian encampment on the Little Bighorn River in Montana and all 250 of his men were killed, because he failed to wait for reinforcements to arrive. He had previously been court martialled for leaving his fort without a commander to go off and visit his wife.

ARTS

1830 Christina (Georgina) Rossetti, English poet, sister of Dante, whose religious beliefs are reflected in her poetry.

1946 José Carreras, Spanish operatic tenor who performed in many leading opera houses, and many successful recordings, but in the late 80s his career was temporarily halted for three years by leukaemia.

ENTERTAINMENT

GOODNIGHT, VIENNA Two Viennese film directors who both ended up in Hollywood after fleeing the spectre of Nazism were born this day. In 1890 Fritz Lang who made the classics *Metropolis* (1927) and *M* (1931) was born. He was offered the chance to direct major Nazi productions but left Vienna before it was discovered he was Jewish. In Hollywood he directed many films including *Ministry of Fear* (1944) and *The Big Heat* (1953). Born 1906, Otto Preminger first worked in the theatre as an assistant of the great Max Reinhardt. Ironically, in Hollywood, this Jewish refugee played a bald-headed Nazi in the film *The Pied Piper* (1942) and stayed to direct *Carmen Jones* (1954), *The Man with the Golden Arm* (1955) and *Anatomy of a Murder* (1959).

1901 Walt Disney, US cartoon film producer whose first production company, Laugh-O-Gram went bankrupt. He fared better when he started a new company in partnership with his brother Roy and the animator and creative genius, Ub Iwerks. He produced some of the greatest animated films in history, featuring such characters as Mickey Mouse, Donald Duck and Snow White; and films including *101 Dalmations* (1961) to *Mary Poppins* (1964) and *The Jungle Book* (1967). In 1955, he opened Disneyland.

1902 Emeric Pressburger (Imre Pressburger) Hungarian-born British film maker (director, producer, screenwriter) of such films as *Behold a Pale Horse* (1964), before his partnership with Michael Powell (30.9.1905) with films including *The Red Shoes* (1948).

POP

1935 Little Richard (Richard Penniman), US rock 'n roll innovator, and probably the first to gain international popularity with 'Tutti Frutti' (1956) and 'Long Tall Sally' the same year. His last major hit was 'Good Golly, Miss Molly' (1958) before the self-styled King of Rock 'n'

Roll was born again and went on the gospel circuit.

DIED THIS DAY

1791 Wolfgang Amadeus Mozart, Austrian composer who died from typhus and was buried in an unmarked grave with several other paupers. His unfinished *Requiem* was completed by his former pupil, Süssmayr.

1870 Alexandre Dumas *père* (Davy de la Pailleterie), French author of *The Count of Monte Cristo* and *The Three Musketeers* (both 1844).

1926 Claude-Oscar Monet, French painter and a founder of the Impressionist movement.

1983 Robert Aldrich, US film director of *The Dirty Dozen* (1967).

ON THIS DAY

1766 The founder of the famous auctioneers, James Christie held his first sale in London.

1839 The postage rate in Britain was changed to a standard charge of 4d a half ounce instead of being charged by distance.

1904 The Russian fleet was almost totally destroyed by the Japanese at Port Arthur.

1928 England beat Australia by a record 675 runs in the Test at Brisbane.

1933 Prohibition ended after 14 years in the US.

1956 Miss Rose Heilbron QC was appointed Recorder of Burnley to become Britain's first woman judge.

1958 The Queen dialled Edinburgh from Bristol to inaugurate the first direct dialled trunk call (STD).

1958 Prime Minister Harold Macmillan opened the Preston bypass in Lancashire, the first stretch of motorway in Britain.

DOUBLE MYSTERY In 1872, the *Marie Celeste* was found abandoned, drifting in the Atlantic with a cargo of alcohol. The captain, Benjamin Briggs and his crew were never heard of again. This day 1945, five US Navy bombers took off from Fort Lauderdale, Florida on a training flight. Contact was lost and an aircraft was sent to look for them. It too lost contact and no trace of any of the aircraft or their 27 crew members was ever found in the area which became known as the Bermuda Triangle.

6 DECEMBER

The Feast day of Nicholas, patron saint of youth, popularly known as Santa Claus. He is also the patron of merchants, thieves, sailors and travellers.

The National Day of Finland marking the day in 1917 when it proclaimed its independence from Russia.

BORN THIS DAY

HISTORY

1732 Warren Hastings, first Governor General of Bengal who established the foundations of British administration in India. He was impeached for corruption on his return to England in 1785, but later acquitted.

ENTERTAINMENT

1896 Ira Gershwin (Israel Gershvin), US lyricist who, with brother George, wrote the songs that made their many musicals successful, 'Fascinating

Rhythm', 'Lady Be Good', Someone to Watch Over Me' and 'I've Got Rhythm'.

1888 Will Hay, English music hall comedian who later made films including *The Goose Steps Out* (1942).

SCIENCE

1778 Joseph Louis Gay-Lussac, French physicist and chemist who made ballooon ascents to study the weather. In his investigations of gases he found the way to produce sulphuric and other acids.

1863 Charles Martin Hall, US chemist who pioneered the manufacture of aluminium around 1885.

JAZZ

1920 Dave (David Warren) Brubeck, US pianist, composer who studied under Darius Milhaud. His classical training enabled him to become of one jazz's finest innovators as demonstrated by his quartet, formed 1951 and with his compositions including his popular 'Take Five' (with Paul Desmond).

SPORT

1914 Cyril Washbrook, Lancashire and England cricketer whose career spanned 1933 to 1964 in which he accumulated over 3,400 runs averaging 42.67.

DIED THIS DAY

1793 Madame du Barry, mistress of Louis XV of France, by the guillotine after being found guilty by the Revolutionary Tribune of 'having wasted the treasures of the state'.

1882 Anthony Trollope, English novelist of the *Barsetshire Chronicles*.

1889 Jefferson Davies, former President of the Confederate States of America.

1988 Roy Orbison, US rock and roll singer with hits like 'Only the Lonely' and 'Oh Pretty Woman', of a heart attack, aged 52.

ON THIS DAY

1492 Christopher Columbus discovered Hispaniola (now Haiti and the Dominican Republic).

1774 Austria became the first nation to introduce a state education system.

1877 Thomas Alva Edison recited 'Mary had a Little Lamb' into his Phonograph and made the world's first recording of the human voice.

1921 Irish independence was granted for the 26 southern states which became known as the Irish Free State. Six counties which formed Ulster (Northern Ireland) remained as part of the UK.

1975 The Balcombe Street siege, watched by millions on television, ended when the four IRA gunmen who had taken a couple hostage following a gun battle and chase finally gave themselves up without a shot being fired.

1989 The worst mass killing in Canadian history took place when a gunman burst into an engineering class at the University of Montreal and shot dead 14 women students and wounded nine others and four men before turning the gun on himself.

7 DECEMBER

BORN THIS DAY

HISTORY

1924 Dr Mario Soares, President of Portugal, who lived in exile during the period of dictatorship, but returned in 1974. He was elected Prime Minister in 1976, and President in 1986.

1928 Professor Noam (Avrom) Chomsky, US linguist who revolutionized the study of linguistics. He also became well known for his opposition to US involvement in Vietnam.

ARTS

1598 Gian Lorenzo Bernini, Italian sculptor, architect and painter who did much of his work for St Peter's Basilica in Rome, including the colonade enclosing the piazza.

1863 Pietro Mascagni, Italian composer whose one-act opera, *Cavalleria Rusticana* won the first prize in competition sponsored by a music publisher in 1889. He later became a devoted follower of Fascist dictator Mussolini.

1888 (Arthur) Joyce (Lunel) Cary, Irish author who created vivid characters in novels such as the painter Gully Jimson in *The Horse's Mouth* (1944).

ENTERTAINMENT

1915 Eli Wallach, US actor who came from Broadway to play 'heavies' in films including *Baby Doll* (1956), *The Misfits* (1961) and *Firepower* (1979).

1932 Ellen Burstyn (Edna Rae Gillooly), US actress who was nominated for Oscars for her performances in *The Last Picture Show* (1971) and *The Exorcist* (1973) and finally won an Oscar for her role in *Alice Doesn't Live Here Anymore* (1975). She picked up her third Oscar nomination for *The Same Time Next Year* (1978).

DIED THIS DAY

43BC Cicero (Marcus Tullius), the great Roman orator who was a strong opponent of Mark Antony, and delivered 14 brilliant orations (or phillipics) against him. When Mark Antony came to power, he had Cicero executed.

1815 Marshal Ney, French soldier and Napoleon's most famous general, who was shot in Paris for high treason after supporting Napoleon at Waterloo when he was originally instructed to arrest him.

1817 William Bligh, rear-Admiral who was the captain of HMS *Bounty* at the time of the famous mutiny (28.4.1789), died in London.

1894 Ferdinand de Lesseps, French diplomat and the man behind the building of the Suez Canal.

1985 Robert Graves, English poet and author of *I, Claudius* (1934).

1988 Peter Langan, Irish restaurateur, co-owner with Michael Caine of the famous London brasserie, Langans. The colourful Langan, who is said to have consumed 12 bottles of Bollinger champagne a night, died in a fire at his ten-bedroom home which had been started deliberately.

ON THIS DAY

1732 The first Covent Garden Opera House, then called the Theatre Royal, opened in London.

1783 William Pitt, the Younger, aged 24, became the youngest British Prime Minister.

1787 Delaware became the first US state.

1889 The first performance at the Savoy of Gilbert and Sullivan's *The Gondoliers*, their last real success.

1907 Eugene Corri became the first referee to officiate *inside* a boxing ring at the Tommy Burns – Gunner Moir fight at the National Sporting Club, London.

1916 David Lloyd George became Prime Minister of a British coalition government.

1941 The Japanese attacked the US fleet in Pearl Harbor. Without any official declaration of war, they sank or damaged five battleships, 14 smaller warships, 200 aircraft and killed 2,400 people.

1972 The US launched *Apollo 17* on its way to make the sixth landing on the moon.

1982 Charles Brooks Jr, a prisoner on death row at Fort Worth Prison, Texas, was executed by being given a lethal injection, the first to die by this method in the US.

1988 A severe earthquake hit Soviet Armenia killing thousands and causing wide-spread destruction.

8 DECEMBER

BORN THIS DAY

HISTORY

1542 Mary, Queen of Scots, who reigned as Scotland's Queen from 1542 and married her cousin the Earl of Darnley. After Darnley was assassinated, she married the Earl of Bothwell. A rebellion led to her abdication and later Elizabeth I imprisoned her for the plot to restore the Roman Catholic religion and to take the throne from Elizabeth.

ARTS

1865 Jean (Julius Christian) Sibelius, Finnish composer, many of whose works have strong Finnish associations, including his popular *Finlandia* (1900).

1894 James (Grover) Thurber, US humorist, writer and cartoonist, whose work appeared in the *New Yorker* which he joined in 1933. His classic short stories include *The Secret Life of Walter Mitty* (1932).

1922 Lucian Freud, English painter, grandson of Sigmund Freud, whose disturbingly realistic nudes and portraits have maintained his position as a major artist.

1939 James Galway, Northern Irish flautist who became principal flautist with major London orchestras before joining the Berlin Philharmonic. He went solo in 1975, appearing regularly on both concert stage and television. Despite a serious accident, he continued his career and has proved a successful recording artist.

ENTERTAINMENT

1916 Richard Fleischer, US film director, son of the cartoonist who created Betty Boop. His films include *20,000 Leagues Under the Sea* (1954), *Dr Dolittle* (1967) and *Soylent Green* (1973).

1925 Sammy Davis Jr, US actor, singer and dancer, the son of vaudeville artists, he went on the stage when he was three and never looked back. A top US entertainer, he appeared in Broadway musicals including *Mr Wonderful* (1956) in which he sang 'Too Close for Comfort'. His film appearances include

Porgy and Bess (1959), *Ocean's 11* (1960) and *Sweet Charity* (1969).

1930 Maximillian Schell, Austrian actor, writer and director whose family fled the Nazis in 1938 and settled in Switzerland. In the US, he played German officers in stage and film productions, and won an Oscar for his role in *Judgement at Nuremberg* (1961) and Oscar nominations for *The Man in the Glass Booth* (1975) and *Julia* (1977).

1940 David Carradine, US actor best known for his role in the quirky television series *Kung Fu*.

INVENTION

1765 Eli Whitney, US inventor who patented the cotton gin (1793) which separated seeds from cotton fibre and totally revolutionized the cotton growing business.

POP

1943 Jim Morrison, US lead singer with hard rock group the Doors, formed in 1965 and renowned for the poetic quality of Morrison's lyrics. Their first big hit was 'Light My Fire' (1967).

SPORT

1941 Geoff Hurst, West Ham and England footballer who was the only player to score six goals in a Division 1 Football League match against Sunderland.

DIED THIS DAY

1859 Thomas de Quincey, English author best remembered for his autobiographical *Confessions of an English Opium-Eater* (1822). He lived to age 74 despite having taken opium since he was 19 years old, originally to relieve the pain of facial neuralgia.

1978 Golda Meir (Goldie Mabovich), Israeli Prime Minister from 1969 to 1974.

ON THIS DAY

1841 Prince Albert Edward, later King Edward VII, became the Prince of Wales.

1854 Pope Pius IX declared the dogma of the Immaculate Conception of the Blessed Virgin Mary to be an article of faith.

1863 The world's first heavyweight boxing championship took place at Woodhurst, Kent between Tom King (England) and John C. Heenan (US). King became the first world champion.

1864 The Clifton Suspension Bridge over the River Avon at Bistol, designed by Brunel, was opened.

1941 The US, Britain and Australia declared war on Japan following the Pearl Harbor attack the previous day.

1980 A mentally unstable 'fan', Mark David Chapman shot John Lennon dead outside his New York apartment as he and his wife Yoko Ono were returning from a recording session.

1987 Presidents Gorbachev and Reagan signed the first-ever treaty to reduce USSR and US ground-based intermediate-range missiles.

1988 Scientists at Liverpool University reported they had etched an image of Marilyn Monroe on to an area smaller than a pinhead using a revolutionary new instrument, an ultra-powerful 'field emission electron microscope', devised by Professor Colin Humphreys who said the device was capable of etching the entire contents of the 29 volumes of the *Encyclopaedia Britannica*. The machine can store 1,000 times more information in a given space than any other medium.

9 DECEMBER

The National Day of Tanzania, celebrating its independence in 1961. Originally Tanganyika, it became a republic on the first anniversary of independence, remaining within the Commonwealth and with Julius Nyerere as the first President.

BORN THIS DAY

HISTORY

1886 Clarence Birdseye, US inventor of a process to deep-freeze foodstuffs in small packages for retailing, who got the idea from his days as a fur trader in Alaska where he had seen the Eskimoes do exactly that (6.3.1930).

1895 Dolores Gomez Ibarruri, Spanish politician, known as 'La Pasionaria' who won a seat in the Cortes (parliament) in 1936. She was a great orator; her passionate speeches against the Fascists, and her cry of 'They will not pass' became the battle cry for the Republican soldiers during the Civil War. She eventually fled to Russia only returning to Spain in 1977 and where she died on 12 December 1989.

1902 Richard Austen ('Rab') Butler, progressive British Conservative politician born in India who was Minister of Education, Chancellor of the Exchequer, Home Secretary, Foreign Secretary but never the role he was most tipped for, that of Prime Minister. Instead he served no less than four Prime Ministers.

1929 Bob (Robert) Hawke, Prime Minister of Australia from 1983.

ARTS

1608 John Milton, English poet of *Paradise Lost* (1667), *Paradise Regained* (1677) and the drama *Samson Agonistes* (1677). By 1652 his sight had failed totally and his greatest work had to be produced with the aid of amanuenses including his three daughters.

1848 Joel Chandler Harris, US author of the classic Uncle Remus tales published in 1879, which were based on negro folk tales and featured Brer Rabbit.

1915 Elizabeth Swarzkopf, German opera and concert singer and one of the greatest sopranos of her age. She settled in England and became a member of the Covent Garden Opera from 1948-51. In 1951 she played the role of Anne Trulove, created for her by Stravinsky in his opera *The Rake's Progress*.

ENTERTAINMENT

1909 Douglas Fairbanks, Jr, US actor and the son of Douglas, Snr. He gave creditable performances in *Catherine the Great* (1934), *The Prisoner of Zenda* (1937) and *Sinbad the Sailor* (1947). An Anglophile, he was awarded an honorary knighthood in 1949 for his special services to the Allied effort during the Second World War.

1918 Kirk Douglas (Issur Danielovitch, changed to Demsky), US actor who excelled in intensely dramatic roles, seen to best effect in *Champion* (1949), *Lust for Life* (1956) as Van Gogh, and *Spartacus* (1960).

1929 John Cassavetes, US actor, screenwriter and director who made his very distinctive *Shadows* (1961) and *Husbands* (1970), just two of the low-budget films using actors often on deferred fees. Many of his productions were improvised, but clever editing resulted in interesting films. He has also appeared in many films including *The Killers* (1964) and *The Killing of a Chinese Bookie* (1976) which he also scripted.

1934 Dame Judi Dench, English actress and director who plays both Shakespearian leads and bubbly contemporary television sitcom roles with equal success including *A Fine Romance* opposite her husband Michael Williams.

1941 Beau Bridges (Lloyd Vernet Bridges III) US actor, son of Lloyd, seen in *Two Minute Warning* (1976) and in many television productions including *The Four Feathers* (1978).

POP

1952 Joan Armatrading, English singer and songwriter who had a hit with 'Love and Affection' in the late 70s.

1957 Donny Osmond (Donald Clark Osmond), US singer who was one of the successful Osmond Brothers. He went solo in 1971 when he had a No. 1 in the US chart with 'Go Away Little Girl'. He also recorded duets with sister Marie including 'Deep Purple'.

SPORT

1942 Billy Bremner, former Leeds footballer and captain of Scotland who was banned from playing for Scotland in 1975 over an alleged brawl in Copenhagen.

DIED THIS DAY

1641 Sir Anthony van Dyke, Flemish painter at the court of Charles I, died in his London studio.

1814 Joseph Brahmah, English inventor of the beer pump and a handy machine printing bank notes.

1936 Juan de la Cierva, Spanish inventor of the autogiro who was killed in an aircrash in Britain with 14 others.

1964 Dame Edith Sitwell, English poet and author of *The English Eccentrics* (1933).

ON THIS DAY

1783 The first executions took place at Newgate Prison.

1868 Gladstone became Prime Minister for the first time. He would win office for three more terms.

1905 Richard Strauss's opera *Salome*, based on Oscar Wilde's play, was first performed at Dresden.

1955 Sugar Ray Robinson knocked out Carl Olson to regain his middleweight boxing title.

1960 The first episode of *Coronation Street* was screened on ITV.

1987 The first martyrs of the 'intifada' in the Gaza Strip were created when an Israeli patrol attacked in the Jabaliya refugee camp.

10 DECEMBER

BORN THIS DAY

HISTORY

1819 Count Felice Orsini, Italian political activist who was a member of a secret political group trying to assassinate Napoleon III in an effort to spread revolution from France to Italy.

1851 Melvil Dewey, US librarian who devised the library cataloguing system which bears his name.

1924 Michael Manley, Prime Minister of Jamaica from 1972–80 and again in 1989. His father Norman, had been Prime Minister ten years before.

ARTS

1822 César Auguste Franck, Belgian composer known for his Romantic and religious music including his *Symphonic Variations* (1885).

1830 Emily (Elizabeth) Dickinson, US poet who had only seven poems published during her lifetime. When she died, she had left around 800 poems.

1903 William Plomer, South African-born much-travelled poet and author who wrote *Dado* (1931) and the libretti for several Benjamin Britten operas including *Gloriana* (1953).

1908 Olivier Messiaen, influential French composer and organist who used birdsong in many of his works as well as a distinctive use of rhythm.

ENTERTAINMENT

1914 Dorothy Lamour (Mary Leta Dorothy Kaumeyer), US actress best remembered for her exotic roles in the 'Road' films with Bob Hope and Bing Crosby.

1960 Kenneth Branagh, Belfast-born British actor, writer and producer who played leading roles by age 23 with the Royal Shakespeare Company. He went on to star in films *A Month in the Country* (1987) and his acclaimed *Henry V* (1989) which he also adapted for the screen and directed. He is the founder of the Renaissance Theatre Company.

SPORT

1963 Jahangir Khan, six times world champion squash champion (from 1981–8) who was born in Karachi.

DIED THIS DAY

1896 Alfred Bernhard Nobel, Swedish chemist and industrialist who made much of his fortune from his invention of dynamite (1867) and used it to found the Nobel prizes.

1946 Alfred Damon Runyon, US writer, author of *Guys and Dolls* (1932).

1967 Otis Redding, who sang '(Sitting On) The Dock of the Bay', was killed in a plane crash in Wisconsin.

1987 Jascha Heifetz, Lithuanian-born US virtuoso violinist.

1988 Dr Roger Altounyan, English inventor of the anti-asthma drug Intal and the inhaler now commonly used by asthmatics.

ON THIS DAY

1817 Mississippi became the 20th state of the Union.

1845 Civil engineer Robert Thompson patented pneumatic tyres in London. Later manufacture had to be by hand and were too expensive to catch on. That was left to Dunlop in 1888.

1868 *Whitaker's Almanac* was published for the first time.

1896 The first performance of *Ubu Roi*, the first Theatre of the Absurd play by Alfred Jarry, conceived when he was 15, presented when he was 23. The second performance was called off after rioting, but the play influenced much 20th-century literature and theatre.

1898 Cuba became independent of Spain following the Spanish-American War.

PRIZE DAY In 1901 the first Nobel prizes

were awarded on the anniversary of the death of Nobel. In 1903, Madame Marie Curie became the first woman to win the award which she shared with husband Pierre and Henri Becquerel for their work on radio activity. In 1974, Russian writer Alexandr Solzhenitsyn collected his award for Literature...four years late, after originally being blocked by the USSR.

1917 The first postmark slogan was stamped on envelopes in Britain: 'Buy British War Bonds Now.'

1919 The Smith brothers became the first aviators to fly from Britain to Australia.

1928 Piccadilly Circus Underground station opened.

1931 Alasara Zamaora became Spain's first constitutionally elected President.

1983 Raul Alfonsin became the first civilian president of Argentina for eight years following the rule of the military junta.

11 DECEMBER

BORN THIS DAY

HISTORY

1882 Fiorello Henry La Guardia, three-times mayor of New York, who fought corruption and did much to improve the city. Known as Little Flower, he was a colourful, legendary character whose actions ranged from providing a Jewish police escort for a visiting Nazi delegation and reading the comic strips on radio during a newspaper strike. He was later the subject of the hit musical, *Fiorello*.

ARTS

1803 (Louis) Hector Berlioz, French composer often seen as a romantic. His most successful work includes *Symphonie fantastique* (1832), *Romeo et Juliette* (1838) and *The Damnation of Faust*, a cantata (1828–46).

1918 Alexandr Solzhenitsyn, Russsian novelist and Nobel Prize winner who suffered under Stalin's regime and was sent to a labour camp which he writes of in his novel *One Day in the Life of Ivan Denisovich* (1962) and again in *Cancer Ward* (1968) and *The Gulag Archipelago* (1973). He became a US citizen in 1974. (*See 10.12.1974*)

1929 Sir Kenneth MacMillan, Scottish choreographer who directed the Royal Ballet from 1970–77 and created some its most exciting new ballets including *Anastasia* (1967–71) for Canadian dancer Lynn Seymour, *Elite Syncopations* (1974) and *Mayerling* (1978).

ENTERTAINMENT

1905 Gilbert Roland (Luis Antonio Damaso de Alonso), Mexican-born US actor in many films spanning 50 years from *Camille* (1927) to *Cabo Blanco* (1979).

1913 Carlo Ponti, Italian film producer mainly in partnership with Dino de Laurentiis to make films including *La Strada* (1954) and *The Cassandra Crossing* (1977). He married Sophia Loren in 1957, but ran into difficulties over his previous marriage, and then for currency smuggling.

1942 Anna Carteret, English actress who is best known for her role in the television series *Juliet Bravo*, although originally the female police officer was played by Stephanie Turner.

SCIENCE

1781 Sir David Brewster, Scottish

physicist who did much work with optics and polarized light. In 1816 he invented the kaleidoscope.

1843 Robert Koch, German physicist who was one of the founders of the science of bacteriology. In 1882 he identified the tubercle bacillus (which causes tuberculosis) and the following year, the cholera bacillus.

POP

1944 Brenda Lee (Brenda Mae Tarpley), US singer who had hits with 'I'm Sorry' and 'I Want to Be Wanted' both 1960.

DIED THIS DAY

1282 Llywelyn ap Gruffudd, prince of Gwynnedd in northern Wales. The only native to be recognized by the English as Prince of Wales; a year after his death, Wales fell completely under the English rule.

1965 Ed Roscoe Murrow, US journalist and broadcaster.

ON THIS DAY

1769 Venetian blinds were patented by Edward Beran of London.

1894 In Paris, the first motor show opened. There were nine exhibitors.

1903 The first wildlife preservation society was formed in Britain to protect fauna, called the Society for the Preservation of Wild Fauna of the Empire.

1914 The Royal Flying Corps which later became the RAF, adopted the red, white and blue roundel to identify its aircraft.

1936 Edward VIII abdicated and slipped away in the early hours to an exile in France. He was succeeded by his brother, George who became George VI. Edward planned to marry Mrs Wallis Simpson and, before he left the country, made a final farewell broadcast.

1952 Derek Bentley, aged 19, and 16-year-old Christopher Craig, were found guilty of the murder of a policeman in south London. Because of his age, Craig was sentenced to be detained at Her Majesty's pleasure, while Bentley, who did not fire the gun, was sentenced to hang. Despite a public outcry, the sentence was carried out on 27 January 1953.

1987 Charlie Chaplin's famous cane and bowler were sold at Christies in London for £82,500 and his boots for £38,500.

12 DECEMBER

The National Day of Kenya marking its independence, with Jomo Kenyatta as the first Prime Minister, in 1963. He became President when Kenya became a republic in 1964.

BORN THIS DAY

HISTORY

1724 Admiral Samuel Hood, first Viscount, British naval commander and one of the most skilful tacticians who had notable victories including those in the West Indies in 1782.

ARTS

1786 Carl Maria (Friedrich Ernst) von Weber, German composer best known his opera *Der Freischutz* (1821).

1821 Gustave Flaubert, French novelist who was a pioneer of realism and who was prosecuted for an allegedly immoral novel, his masterpiece *Madame Bovary* (1857).

1863 Edvard Munch, Norwegian painter much influenced by Van Gogh and Gauguin, who painted *The Scream* in 1893. Like Van Gogh he went insane, in 1908.

1929 John (James) Osborne, English playwright who changed the mould of British drama with his first play, *Look Back In Anger* (1956), depicting 'the angry young men' of the post-war generation. His next play, *The Entertainer* (1957), brought Laurence Olivier to the West End as the seedy variety comedian, Archie Rice.

ENTERTAINMENT

1893 Edward G. Robinson (Emanuel Goldenburg), US actor, born in Bucharest, who began playing powerful gangster roles in films such as *Little Caesar* (1931) and *Key Largo* (1948). He had one of the finest private collections of modern paintings, and it is said he made so many films, some not worthy of his talents, to pay for paintings. Sadly, he had to sell the collection in a divorce settlement.

1915 Frank Sinatra, US singer and actor who began as a vocalist with the Harry James and Tommy Dorsey bands before his successful singing career led to the creation of the first 'bobbysoxers' or screaming teenage fans. In films, he won an Oscar for his supporting role in *From Here to Eternity* (1953) and other films include *Guys and Dolls* and *The Tender Trap* and *The Man with the Golden Arm*, all in 1955. His hit songs include 'Three Coins in the Fountain', 'Chicago' and 'You Make Me Feel So Young'.

POP

1938 Connie Francis (Concetta Rosa Maria Franconero), US singer who had hits in the 60s with 'Who's Sorry Now' which was originally written in 1923, 'Everybody's Somebody's Fool' and 'Where the Boys Are'.

1941 Dionne Warwick (Marie Dionne Warrick), US singer, one-time backing singer as part of the Sweet Inspirations before going solo with 'Don't Make Me Over' in 1963. Her big hits include 'Do You Know the Way to San José' (1968) and 'There's Always Something There to Remind Me' (1968).

SPORT

1946 Emmerson Fittipaldi, Brazillian motor racing champion.

1962 Tracy Austin, US tennis player who caused a sensation at Wimbledon in 1979 when, aged only 16, she beat the then queen of tennis, Billie-Jean King in the singles quarter-finals, but didn't reach the final which was between Navratilova and Evert.

DIED THIS DAY

1889 Robert Browning, English poet of 'The Ring and the Book'.

1939 Douglas Fairbanks, Snr (Douglas Elton Ulman), US actor best remembered as a swashbuckling hero in silent films.

1968 Tallulah (Brockman) Bankhead, legendary US actress.

1977 Clementine, Baroness Spencer-Churchill, Sir Winston's widow.

1985 Anne Baxter, US actress in *All About Eve* (1950).

ON THIS DAY

1787 Pennsylvania became the second state of the Union.

1896 Marconi gave the first public demonstration of radio at Toynbee Hall, London. The same day in 1901, Marconi carried out the first transatlantic radio transmission from Poldhu, Cornwall to St John's, Newfoundland.

1913 The Mona Lisa which had been stolen from the Louvre (*see* 21.8.1911) was recovered from its hiding place in a bedroom of a small hotel in Florence. Vincenzo Perugia and three others were arrested.

1915 The first all-metal plane, made by German aircraft builder Hugo Junkers, was flown for the first time.

1955 Christopher Cockerell patented his prototype of the hovercraft.

1955 Bill Haley and the Comets recorded 'See You Later Alligator' at Decca Recording Studios, New York.

1957 Five months before he divorced his second wife, singer Jerry Lee Lewis married 13-year-old Myra Lewis, daughter of his cousin. The scandal nearly ruined his career, and his child-bride's appearance in Britain caused his tour to be cancelled.

1988 Britain's worst rail crash for 20 years killed 35 and injured 113 people when a packed express from Bournemouth ran into the back of a stationary commuter train near Clapham Junction.

1988 The first satellite pictures were beamed to 2,200 London betting shops to allow them to watch the races live from many race courses.

1989 Billionaire Leona Helmsley who said, 'Only the little people pay taxes,' was fined $7 million and sentenced to four years imprisonment for tax evasion. Dubbed the 'Queen of Greed', she and her husband Harry owned a chain of luxury hotels worth $5 billion.

13 DECEMBER

BORN THIS DAY

HISTORY

1915 Balthazar Johannes Vorster, South African Prime Minister from 1966–78 and President from 1978–9, resigning the office following the 'Muldergate' propaganda slush fund affair (*see* 3.11.1978).

ARTS

1797 Heinrich Heine, German Romantic poet and writer who moved to Paris in 1831 and lived there until his death. His poems include his 'Book of Songs' (1826–7) some of which were set to music by Schumann and Schubert.

1903 John Piper, English painter best known for his Second World War paintings of air raids and his theatre designs.

1906 Laurens van der Post, South African-born writer of *The Lost World of the Kalahari* (1959) and *Heart of the Hunter* (1961).

1942 Howard Brenton, English playwright best known for his controversial *The Romans in Britain* (1980) which contained a simulated homosexual sex scene which was the subject of legal action to have it banned.

ENTERTAINMENT

1925 Dick van Dyke, US actor who starred in television's *The Dick Van Dyke Show* opposite Mary Tyler Moore and made films including *Chitty Chitty Bang Bang* (1968).

1929 (Arthur) Christopher (Orme) Plummer, Canadian actor who played Baron von Trapp in the film version of *The Sound of Music* (1965).

1949 Paula Wilcox, English actress in television sitcoms such as *Man About the House*.

1954 Jim Davidson, English comedian who won a New Faces competition and went on to host television's Jim Davidson Show.

INVENTION

1816 Ernst Werner von Siemens, German inventor and founder with his brothers of the electrical firm of Siemens.

SPORT

1952 John Francome, English jockey who became only the second National Hunt jockey to ride over 1,000 winners – the other was Stan Mellor.

DIED THIS DAY

1784 Dr Samuel Johnson, English writer and dictionary compiler.

1983 Mary Renault (Mary Challans), English author of *The Last of the Wine* (1956) and other historical novels set in ancient Greece, died in Cape Town, South Africa where she had settled.

ON THIS DAY

1577 Francis Drake set sail from Plymouth in the *Golden Hind* on his circumnavigation of the world (26.9.1580).

1642 Abel Tasman, the Dutch navigator sighted New Zealand, but several of his men were killed when he attempted to land.

1779 The first Smithfield Show organized by the Smithfield Cattle and Sheep Society was held at Wooton's Dolphin Yard in London.

1847 On or about this day, *Wuthering Heights* by Ellis Bell (Emily Brontë) was published, as was *Agnes Grey* by Acton Bell (Anne Brontë).

1878 The Holborn Viaduct in London was illuminated by electricity, the first street lighting in Britain, installed by a French contractor who had lit a street in Lyon in 1857, the first in the world.

1884 A coin-operated weighing machine was patented by Percy Everitt.

1903 Ice cream cones (or moulds) were patented by Italo Marcione of New York.

1904 The Metropolitan Underground railway in London went electric.

1937 Sellotape was first marketed in Britain.

1939 The Battle of the River Plate with action by British cruisers *Exeter*, *Ajax* and *Achilles*, who drove the great German battleship *Admiral Graf Spee* to seek shelter off Montevideo, Uruguay (17.12.1939).

1967 King Constantine of Greece fled the country after his attempt to overthrow the Greek Military junta had failed.

1989 A deaf choir from South Wales gave what was claimed to be the first concert using sign language. Performed in unison with a leading male voice choir, it enabled deaf members of the audience to enjoy the concert at the Gwyn Town Hall in West Glamorgan.

14 DECEMBER

BORN THIS DAY

HISTORY

1503 Nostradamus (Michel de Nostradame), French astrologer and physician who published his celebrated book of prophecies, *Centuries*, in 1555. It seemed many of his prophecies were fulfilled; his fame spread and he was invited to cast horoscopes for Catherine de Medici, the queen consort.

1546 Tycho Brahe, Danish astronomer and mathematician who, with Kepler, proved that the planets orbit the sun in ellipses. The Danish King Frederick II provided an island for an observatory where Brahe was able to carry out some of the most advanced astronomy in Europe.

1895 King George VI, the second son of George V and Mary who succeeded Edward VIII when he abdicated, and led the British through the war years.

ENTERTAINMENT

1935 Lee Remick, US actress whose film credits include *The Long Hot Summer* (1958), *Anatomy of a Murder* (1959) and *The Days of Wine and Roses* (1962). Since coming to England in the 70s she has made both stage and television appearances collecting a BAFTA award for *Jennie* (1974).

1938 Jeanette Scott, English actress, Thora Hird's daughter, who appeared in films from a child. As an adult, she was in *The Good Companions* (1957) and *The Day of the Triffids* (1963).

JAZZ

1920 Clark Terry, US trumpeter and flugelhorn player who featured in many leading bands including those of Count Basie, Duke Ellington and Oscar Peterson.

1932 Charlie Rich, US country singer.

SPORT

1946 Stan Smith, US tennis player who was twice a Wimbledon finalist in the men's singles. He lost to Ile Nastase in 1971, but beat John Newcombe in 1972 to take the title.

1957 Alain Loreieux, French rugby football international.

DIED THIS DAY

1799 George Washington, first president of the US.

1861 Prince Albert, consort to Queen Victoria, of typhoid fever.

1947 Stanley Baldwin, three-times British Prime Minister.

1959 Sir Stanley Spencer, English painter who immortalized Cookham church.

1989 Andrei Sakharov, Soviet scientist, human rights activist and Nobel Peace prize winner in 1975, who was exiled to Gorky in 1980 until 1986 when invited to Moscow by Mikhail Gorbachev.

ON THIS DAY

1819 Alabama became the 22nd state of the Union.

1900 Professor Max Planck of Berlin University revealed his revolutionary Quantum Theory.

1911 Norwegian explorer Raold Amundsen and his three companions reached the South Pole 35 days ahead of Scott's expedition and planted the Norwegian flag on top of an ice mound.

1918 The first woman elected to Parliament was Constance, the Countess

Markievicz who won for Sinn Fein contesting a Dublin seat. She was unable to take her seat as she was in Holloway Prison, London, which is why Lady Astor is officially recognized as the first woman member (1919). The 1918 General Election was also the first time women in Britain had the vote.

1920 The first scheduled airliner disaster in aviation history occurred when an airliner with six passengers and two crew took off from Cricklewood Airport, London, for a flight to Paris. Barely airborne, the plane crashed into a house in neighbouring Golders Green killing the crew and two passengers. The others escaped from the wreckage.

1922 The man who would play a significant part in the history of British broadcasting, John Reith was appointed General Manager of the fledgling BBC.

1932 The first floodlit rugby league match was held at London's White City Stadium between Leeds and Wigan.

1959 The shortest murder trial in British legal history took place. In 30 seconds at Winchester Assizes, Brian Cawley pleaded guilty to murder of Rupert Steed and was later sentenced to life imprisonment.

1962 US *Mariner II* sent the first close up pictures of the planet Venus back to earth.

1973 John Paul Getty II, teenage grandson of the oil tycoon, was set free by his Italian kidnappers after part of his ear had been cut off and sent by post, together with a ransom note demanding $750,000 which was paid by his grandfather.

15 DECEMBER

BORN THIS DAY

HISTORY

AD37 Nero, the fifth Roman emperor, who put to death his mother in AD59, his wife Octavia in 62, and saw Rome destroyed by fire in 64. His behaviour inspired a revolt which eventually led to his suicide.

1832 Alexandre Gustave Eiffel, French engineer who built the great landmark that bears his name for the Paris Exhibition of 1899. The Eiffel Tower stands 300m (984 feet) high and, when originally proposed, aroused a good deal of hostility and fear that the structure would be an ugly, tall edifice.

1852 Antoine Henri Becquerel, French physicist who shared the Nobel prize in 1903 with the Curies for his discovery of radiation coming from uranium salts.

1859 Dr Lazarus Ludovic Zamenof, Polish oculist and linguist who invented the artifical language of Esperanto in 1887.

1892 Jean Paul Getty, US multimillionaire who was president of the Getty Oil Company from 1947. He later founded the world's richest art gallery in California which bears his name.

1918 Ahmed Ben Bella, Algerian Prime Minister who led the War of Independence against the French.

ARTS

1734 George Romney, fashionable English portrait painter who kept his fees low, his paintings flattering and made himself a successful society painter.

1888 Maxwell Anderson, US playwright who wrote *What Price Glory* (1924) with Laurence Stallings, and the poetic drama *Winterset* (1935) based on the Sacco and Vanzetti case.

1930 Edna O'Brien, Irish novelist who wrote *The Country Girls* (1960). She adapted her novel *The Lonely Girl* (1962) as the successful film, *The Girl with the Green Eyes* (1965).

POP

1922 Alan Freed, US DJ who is said to have coined the term 'rock 'n' roll' in the 50s. He fell from the heights in 1960 in the first major payola scandal.

1942 Dave Clark, English drummer and founder of the Dave Clark Five, who later staged the costly musical *Time* which opened in London on 11 April 1986.

SPORT

1951 Joe Jordan, former Scottish international footballer.

DIED THIS DAY

1675 Jan Vermeer (Jan van der Meer van Delft), Dutch painter.

1683 Izaak Walton, English author of *The Compleat Angler* (1653).

1890 Chief Sitting Bull, Sioux Indian of great dignity who later gained fame in Buffalo Bill's Wild West Show. He retired to his reservation, but his influence remained and there were fears that he would lead a rebellion. He was falsely arrested and in the scuffles that followed, he was shot dead by the arresting Indian police.

1943 (Thomas Wright) 'Fats' Waller, jazz pianist and composer of 'Aint Misbehavin'' and 'Honeysuckle Rose'.

1962 Charles Laughton, English actor who played Captain Bligh in *The Mutiny on the Bounty* (1935).

1966 Walt(er Elias) Disney, US cartoon film producer and creator who also gave the world Disneyland and Disney World.

ON THIS DAY

1654 A meteorological office established in Tuscany began recording daily temperature readings.

1840 The remains of Napoleon returned from St Helena were interred at Les Invalides, Paris.

1916 The Battle of Verdun ended with 364,000 Allied soldiers and 338,000 Germans dead.

1927 The British Parliament rejected the New Book of Common Prayer because it 'leaned too far towards Rome' and it was returned for further revision.

1939 Billie Holliday recorded 'The Man I Love' in New York.

1939 Nylon yarn was first produced commercially in Delaware.

1964 The Canadian Parliament adopted the maple leaf as the official symbol for the national flag.

1965 Two US spacecraft achieved the first space rendezvous when *Gemini 7*, with Frank Borman and James A. Lovell, Jr, and *Gemini 6* with Walter M. Schirra, Jr and Thomas Stafford travelled side by side for four hours.

1978 Laser videodiscs were launched in Atlanta, Georgia by Magnavision, part of Philips/MCA.

1979 Two 30-year-old Canadians, Chris Haney, picture editor on the Montreal *Gazette* and sports writer, Scott Abbott came up with the idea for a game called Trivial Pursuit. It was eventually manufactured in 1982 and sold 45 million copies world-wide in its first five years.

1987 A company in Bedford became the

first to be fined (£500) for failing to register personal computer records under the Data Protection Act.

16 DECEMBER

BORN THIS DAY

HISTORY

1485 Catherine of Aragon, first of Henry VIII's wives. She bore him six children but only one survived (Mary I), and Henry divorced her against the Pope's wishes, in his pursuit for a male heir.

1742 Gebhard Berecht von Blucher, Prussian general nicknamed 'Marshal Forward'. In the Battle of Waterloo, his forces supported Wellington and tipped the balance against Napoleon.

1790 Leopold I, King of Belgium, the first of an independent nation. He was Queen Victoria's uncle.

ARTS

1775 Jane Austen, English novelist whose work appeared anonymously during her lifetime. Her first novel *Sense and Sensibility* (1811) was followed by *Pride and Prejudice* (1813). Completed in 1803 but not published, *Northanger Abbey* had to be bought back from the original publishing house and finally appeared in 1818.

1882 Zoltan Kodaly, Hungarian composer who collected folk songs to form the foundation of some of his music including *Variations on an Hungarian Folksong* (1939).

1928 Arthur C(harles) Clarke, best-selling English science fiction writer, twice chairman of the British Interplanetary Society, and awarded the Kalinga Prize by UNESCO for popularising science. His books include *2001: A Space Odyssey* (1968) which was made into a now-cult film by Stanley Kubrick.

ENTERTAINMENT

1889 Sir Noël (Pierce) Coward, English playwright, composer, lyricist, actor, producer and director who brought a distinctive style and sophistication to theatre and films with plays such as *Hay Fever* (1925), *Private Lives* (1930) and *Blithe Spirit* (1941), and films including *In Which We Serve* (1942) which he wrote, directed, starred in and even composed the score. Most of his plays and several short stories were adapted for the screen. He wrote some of the classic songs of the 20s, 30s and 40s including 'Mad Dogs and Englishmen', 'Poor Little Rich Girl' and 'A Room with a View'. He was rightly nicknamed the Master.

1939 Liv Ullman, Norwegian actress born in Tokyo who made her name in Bergman films such as *Cries and Whispers* (1972) and *Scenes from a Marriage* (1973).

SCIENCE

1857 Edward Emerson Barnard, US astronomer who discovered Barnard's Star in 1916, the second closest star to the sun.

1901 Dr Margaret Mead, US anthropologist who popularized anthropology with *Coming of Age in Samoa* (1928) and other works.

SPORT

1882 Sir (John) Jack Hobbs, one of the finest batsmen England has produced and who also played for Surrey. In his

41 Tests against Australia, he averaged 54.26 with a total 3,636 runs.

1953 Joel Garner, Barbados, Somerset and West Indies bowler who took 6 wickets for 56 in one competition match.

DIED THIS DAY

1859 Wilhelm Grimm, German folklorist who, with his brother Jacob, collected and published classic fairy tales.

1897 William Terris (William Charles James Lewin) English actor who was stabbed by embittered small-part actor Richard Arthur Prince as he left the stage door of the Adelphi Theatre, London. It is said that his ghost haunts the theatre.

1921 Charles Camille Saint-Saëns, French composer of the *Carnival of Animals* (1886) who died in Algiers.

1944 Glenn Miller, US band leader and arranger who went missing on a flight from England to France. No wreckage or bodies were ever discovered.

1965 William Somerset Maugham, English novelist and playwright.

ON THIS DAY

1653 Following the execution of Charles I, Oliver Cromwell failed to get the Parliament he wanted and became Lord Protector, turning himself into an uncrowned king for the next four years.

1773 Taxes by Britain on tea and other commodities led Samuel Adams and 150 'Sons of Liberty' disguised as Mohawk Indians to hold the Boston Tea Party in which 342 tea chests worth £18,000 were tossed off Griffin's Wharf into Boston Harbor. The War of Independence had begun.

1809 Napoleon divorced his wife Joséphine by Act of the Senate to marry Marie Louise, daughter of the Hapsburg Emperor.

INTO THE LAAGER In 1838 the Boers on their Great Trek away from British rule in the Cape Colony, clashed with the mighty Zulu nation. At the Battle of the Blood River, their superior weaponry and clever tactics of forming a laager – a circular fortress using their ox wagons – defeated the Zulus. In 1856, Marthinus Pretorius who founded Pretoria the previous year, now established a Boer Republic in the Transvaal. In 1949, the Voortrekker Monument was unveiled in Pretoria, commemorating the Great Trek north and the consolidation of the Afrikaaner nation.

1850 The first immigrant ship, the *Charlotte Jane* arrived at Lyttleton, New Zealand.

1853 Santa Anna became dictator of Mexico.

1914 German warships bombarded the seaside resort of Scarborough believing it to be a major British port. Several other east coast resorts were hit.

1925 Construction work began on the Mersey Tunnel which would take nine years to complete.

1929 Barnes Wallis saw his R100 airship carry out its first test flight.

1937 The first performance in London of Noel Gay's *Me and My Girl* which introduced 'The Lambeth Walk'.

1944 The Battle of the Bulge began in the Ardennes when German forces under Field Marshal von Runstedt caught the invading Allied forces at their weakest.

1949 Ahmed Sukarno was elected the first President of Indonesia.

1951 Freddie Steele was transferred from

Mansfield to Port Vale, the first footballer to be involved in a transfer deal.

1954 Professor H.T. Hall at GEC Laboratories in the US produced the first synthetic diamonds.

1955 London Heathrow opened its new terminal buildings and established itself as the world's busiest international airport.

1987 Italy's biggest Mafia trial convicted 13 Mafia bosses to life sentences this day, 22 months after the trial opened. 1,314 people testified and of the 474 defendants, two were shot while out on bail.

1987 Himalayan herdsmen were reported to have offered a £44 reward for help in catching thieves who cut off yaks' tails for use as dusters or decorations and in certain religious ceremonies.

17 DECEMBER

BORN THIS DAY

HISTORY

1874 William Lyon Mackenzie King, three-times Prime Minister of Canada during a period from 1921 to 1948.

ARTS

1770 Ludwig von Beethoven, German composer and pianist (baptized this day), who was the dominant influence in 19th-century music and probably the most performed composer over the past 200 years. His father was a drunken Court Singer, and young Ludwig, aged 11, became the deputy organist at the Court of the Elector of Cologne. His first published music was three pianoforte trios in 1795, and his enormous output diminished little when he began to go deaf in 1788. He was made a freeman of the city of Vienna.

1903 Erskine Caldwell, US author of realistic novels set in the southern states, who wrote *Tobacco Road* and *God's Little Acre*, both 1933.

ENTERTAINMENT

1891 Robertson Hare, English actor who excelled in the Aldwych farces including *Rookery Nook* and *Cuckoo in the Nest* with his cry, 'Oh, calamity!'

1936 Tommy Steele (Thomas Hicks), English pop star turned actor who first made his name in the 50s with the hits 'Singing the Blues' (1957) and 'The Little White Bull' (1959). He made the film *The Tommy Steele Story* in 1957 and then scored a huge success in the musical *Half a Sixpence* in London (1963) as well as on Broadway and in the film version which led to further musicals and TV specials.

1944 Bernard Hill, English actor acclaimed for his role in *The Boys from the Blackstuff* on television.

SCIENCE

1778 Sir Humphrey Davy, English chemist and inventor of the miner's safety lamp, and discoverer of the metals sodium, potassium and strontium.

1908 Willard Frank Libby, US chemist who developed the method of radiocarbon dating later used for proving the Turin Shroud a fake.

SPORT

1937 Kerry Packer, Australian media magnate who promoted World Series cricket which caused a major split in the international cricket world.

1938 Peter Snell, New Zealand athlete who first came to world attention when he won the 800m at the 1960 Olympics in Rome, beating the world-record holder. In 1962, in New Zealand he set a new world record running on grass of 3 minutes 54.5. He triumphed again at the Tokyo Olympics in 1964 when he became only the second man ever to win both the 800m and the 1500m.

DIED THIS DAY

1830 Simón Bolívar, South American revolutionary leader who was known as the Liberator. Bolivia is named in his honour.

1917 Elizabeth Garrett Anderson, first English woman physician and later, the first woman mayor in England.

1957 Dorothy L(eigh) Sayers, English author who created the upper-class detective, Lord Peter Wimsey.

1967 Harold (Edward) Holt, Australian Prime Minister who was drowned in a swimming accident at Portsea, Victoria.

1988 (Melvin James) 'Sy' Oliver, US composer, arranger and trumpeter who had hit records in the 30s including 'It Aint Whatcha Do'.

ON THIS DAY

1843 *A Christmas Carol* by Charles Dickens was published.

1892 The first performance of *The Nutcracker* at St Petersburg (now Leningrad), with music by Tchaikovsky, choreography by Ivanov and danced by the Russian Imperial Ballet.

1849 Thomas and William Bowler, felt hatmakers sold their first bowler to William Coke which he purchased at Lock's of St James.

1903 The Wright brothers aircraft made the first flight of a heavier-than-air machine. It made four flights from Kitty Hawke, North Carolina, the longest lasting just under a minute, and all piloted by younger brother Orville.

1939 The German battleship, *Admiral Graf Spee* was scuttled in the River Plate off Montevideo, Uruguay (13.12.1939).

1971 Zulfikar Ali Bhutto became the first Prime Minister of Pakistan.

1986 Mrs Davina Thompson became the world's first heart, lungs and liver transplant patient in a Cambridge Hospital.

1989 Brazilians had their first opportunity for 29 years to elect a president. They chose Fernando Collor de Mello.

18 DECEMBER

BORN THIS DAY

HISTORY

1707 Charles Wesley, English hymn writer who was an evangelist like his brother John, the founder of Methodism. Amongst his 5,500 hymns is 'Jesu, Lover of my soul'.

1913 Willy Brandt (Karl Herbert Frahm), the illegitimate son of a shop assistant and anti-Nazi who became one of the most charismatic post-war German politicians and West Germany's chancellor in 1969. He changed his original name after fleeing Germany in 1933 to Norway where he temporarily became a citizen until he could return to Germany after the war.

ARTS

1879 Paul Klee, Swiss painter who was in the forefront of the avant-garde movement with his fantastic and abstract pictures.

1907 Christopher (Harris) Fry, English poet and playwright who won acclaim for his verse play *The Lady's Not For Burning* (1948) and *The Dark is Light Enough* (1954). He also collaborated on the screenplays of *Ben Hur* (1959) and *Barabbas* (1962).

ENTERTAINMENT

1779 Joseph Grimaldi, English pantomimist who created the white-faced clown known ever since as a 'Joey' in his honour. His career began as a baby clown with his Italian immigrant family of clowns and dancers.

1861 Lionel Monckton, English composer of musical comedies including *Our Miss Gibbs* (1909) and *The Quaker Girl* (1910).

1911 Jules (Julius) Dassin, US film director who became associated with European film making when the Communist witch-hunts in Hollywood drove him out. He made *Rififi*, one of the best crime films ever, in France in 1955, and *Never on a Sunday* (1960) in Greece.

1916 (Elizabeth Ruth) Betty Grable, US singer, actress and dancer whose legs were insured for $1 million and made her the No. 1 Second World War pin-up with the US forces. Her films include *Pin-Up Girl* (1944) and *Mother Wore Tights* (1947).

1928 Galt MacDermot, Canadian composer who is best known for the musical *Hair* (1967).

1947 Steven Spielberg, US film director who won international success with *Jaws* (1975) and the cult film *Close Encounters of the Third Kind* (1977) for which he also wrote the story.

SCIENCE

1856 Sir Joseph John Thomson, English physicist who discovered the electron and who made the Cavendish Research Laboratory at Cambridge the centre of atomic research. He won the Nobel prize in 1906.

1890 Edward Howard Armstrong, US engineer whose work on frequency circuitry led to his invention of FM radio. He was involved in a lengthy battle over patents with Lee De Forest.

POP

1943 Keith Richards, English guitarist and Rolling Stone who was a student at the London School of Economics where he met Mick Jagger.

DIED THIS DAY

1737 Antonio Stradivari, great Italian violin maker who perfected the instrument; the secret is said to be in the varnish.

1919 Sir John William Alcock, English pioneer aviator who flew the Atlantic non-stop with Brown (14.6.1919). While delivering an amphibian aircraft to Paris, he ran into bad weather and was killed in a crash.

1971 (Robert Tyre) Bobby Jones, champion US amateur golfer who was the only man to achieve the Grand Slam in a single year.

1980 Ben Travers, English playwright who wrote the popular Aldwych farces (because they were presented at the Aldwych Theatre, London) including *A Cuckoo in the Nest*.

ON THIS DAY

1787 New Jersey became the third US state.

1865 The US officially abolished slavery

with the ratification of the 13th Amendment.

1912 The Piltdown Man was discovered in Sussex by Charles Dawson, claimed to be the fossilized skull and remains of the earliest known European. In 1953 it was proved to be a hoax. The skull was that of an orangutan.

1971 Stan Mellor, champion English National Hunt jockey rode his 1,000th winner.

1987 Ivan Boesky, the former US 'King of Arbitrage' was sentenced to three years imprisonment for insider stock exchange dealings. Some of Boesky's revelations led to the investigation by the Department of Trade and Industry in Britain into Guinness's takeover of Distillers.

19 DECEMBER

BORN THIS DAY

HISTORY

1906 Leonid Ilyich Brezhnev, Soviet politician and President from 1960–63. The following year he became General Secretary and combined this with the position of President.

ARTS

1910 Jean Genet, French novelist and playwright, an unwanted child who became a tramp, pickpocket and male prostitute. He began to write while in prison. His novels include *Funeral Rites* (1968), and plays *The Maids* (1954) and *The Screens* (1962).

ENTERTAINMENT

1902 Sir Ralph Richardson, leading English stage and screen actor who was with the Old Vic during the 30s and 40s, and proved equally successful in contemporary roles. He earned an Oscar for his role in the film *The Heiress* (1949). Other films include *The Fallen Idol* (1948) and *David Copperfield* (1970) as Micawber.

1915 Edith Piaf (Edith Giovanna Gassion), legendary French singer, the 'little sparrow' who began singing in the streets of Paris when she was 15 and lived a life of lovers, alcohol and drugs. Her song *'Je ne regrette rien'* summed up her outlook on life.

1922 Eamonn Andrews, Irish-born British broadcaster who was famous for chairing the popular television game, *What's My Line* and then presented the top-rated *This Is Your Life* for ten years on the BBC from 1959 before going over to Thames to present it up to his death in 1987, a non-stop run of 28 seasons.

1923 Gordon Jackson, Scottish actor who became recognized by an international audience when he appeared in the television series *Upstairs, Downstairs* and has since appeared regularly on both stage and screen. His films include *Whisky Galore* (1949) and *The Prime of Miss Jean Brodie* (1969).

DIED THIS DAY

1741 Vitus Jonassen Bering, Danish-born explorer, from scurvy when his ship was wrecked on the shore of Bering Island during an ill-prepared expedition to the Gulf of Alaska.

1848 Emily (Jane) Brontë, English novelist who wrote *Wuthering Heights*, aged 30, from tuberculosis.

1851 Joseph Mallord William Turner, most successful and wealthy English land and seascape painter who anticipated the French Impressionists, died in his Chelsea house under the assumed name of Booth, where his demand for privacy had been strictly enforced by his old housekeeper. His fortune never went to help 'decayed artists' as he requested. Litigation managed to divert it to his relations.

1980 Alexei Nikolayevich Kosygin, Russian leader from 1964–80.

1989 Stella Gibbons, English author of *Cold Comfort Farm* (1932).

ON THIS DAY

1154 Henry II became King of England. It was during his reign that the conquest of Ireland began.

1863 Linoleum was patented by Frederick Walton of London.

1955 Carl Perkins recorded his 'Blue Suede Shoes' at the Sun Studios, Memphis, Tennessee.

1984 Britain and China signed an agreement for the return of Hong Kong to China in 1997.

1987 Gary Kasparov defeated Anatoly Karpov in Seville to retain his title as world chess champion for a further three years.

20 DECEMBER

BORN THIS DAY

HISTORY

1894 Sir Robert (Gordon) Menzies, Australian Prime Minister from 1939. He returned as leader of the Opposition in 1943. The following year he formed the Australian Liberal Party and in 1949 became Prime Minister of a coalition government which was re-elected six times from 1951 to 1963, retiring as Prime Minister in 1966. He was both knighted and made Lord Warden of the Cinque Ports in 1965, formerly held by Churchill.

1906 Sir Dick White, one-time head of Britain's secret services, MI5 and MI6.

ARTS

1923 (Thomas) James Leasor, English author of *Follow the Drum* (1976), *Ship of Gold* (1984) and *Tank of Serpents* (1986).

1924 Errol John, West Indian actor, playwright and author, born in Trinidad, who wrote the classic Caribbean play, *Moon on a Rainbow Shawl* (1956). He played Othello at the Old Vic and appeared in films such as *The African Queen* (1952).

ENTERTAINMENT

1904 Irene (Marie) Dunne, US actress who won an Oscar nomination for *I Remember Mama* (1948). Other films include *Anna and the King of Siam* (1942) and Queen Victoria in *The Mudlark* (1950) before becoming President Eisenhower's delegate to the UN.

1946 Uri Geller, Israeli psychic (or illusionist?) whose demonstrations of the paranormal, from metal bending to telepathy, have amazed and baffled scientists and public alike, but which, for the most part can be repeated by several professional magicians including his fiercest critic, James Randi.

1952 Jenny Agutter, English actress in the film *The Railway Children* (1970) and *The Riddle of the Sands* (1979).

SCIENCE

1805 Thomas Graham, Scottish chemist

who did much to establish the science of physical chemistry and also discovered the principle of dialysis.

POP

1958 Billy Bragg, English songwriter and singer of 'A New England'.

DIED THIS DAY

1954 James Hilton, English novelist who wrote *Goodbye Mr Chips* (1934).

1968 John Steinbeck, US Nobel prize winning author of *The Grapes of Wrath* (1939).

1973 Bobby Darin (Robert Waldon Cassotto), US singer who had a hit with 'Mack the Knife', died during open heart surgery.

1982 Artur Rubinstein, Polish-born US virtuoso pianist.

ON THIS DAY

1804 A new game, 'Emulation' was published 'designed for the Amusement of Youth of both Sexes and calculated to inspire their Minds with an Abhorrence of Vice and a Love of Virtue'. The game was over when a player moving his or her token along the board and passing through various virtues and vices eventually reached the centre where 'Virtue is its Own reward'. It never caught on.

1915 The ANZACS, Australian and New Zealand forces with British troops were evacuated from Gallipoli. Over 90,000 men, their weapons and animals were rescued after their expedition, which started in February against the Turks, went seriously wrong. (*See* 25.4.1915)

1928 Harry Ramsden started his fish and chip restaurant in a hut near Bradford, West Yorkshire, which soon became the most famous fish and chip restaurant in the world.

1933 Fred Astaire's first film with partner Ginger Rogers, *Flying Down to Rio*, was premièred in New York.

1957 At the height of his career Elvis Presley received his call-up papers.

1973 The Spanish Prime Minister, Admiral Luis Carrero Blanco was killed when a bomb hidden in a tunnel exploded as his car passed over.

1987 A Philippine ferry with more than 1,500 passengers sank in shark-infested waters south of Manila after colliding with an oil tanker. More lives were lost than when the Titanic went down.

1989 General Manuel Noriega, Panama's former military leader, dictator and alleged drugs baron, was overthrown by a US invasion force invited by the head of the new civilian government, Guillermo Endara.

21 DECEMBER

The Feast Day of St Thomas the Apostle, patron saint of Portugal, and of architects.

BORN THIS DAY

HISTORY

1804 Benjamin Disraeli, first Earl of Beaconsfield, British Prime Minister and novelist, author of *Endymion* (1881). He became the first Conservative Prime Minister in 1868, but was defeated at the next election. He was Prime Minister again in 1874 with a substantial majority which allowed him to carry out reforms.

1879 Joseph Stalin (Josef Vissarionovich Dzhugashvili), Russian revolutionary who Lenin had wanted to remove, but died before he could leaving Stalin to impose his harsh ideology, carrying out purges to eliminate critics.

1918 Dr Kurt Waldheim, Austrian chancellor, former secretary-general of the United Nations (appointed this day in 1971), who lied about his war record and was later alleged to have links with Nazi atrocities.

ARTS

1917 Heinrich Böll, German author of *Acquainted with the Night* (1954) and *The Clown* (1963) who won the Nobel prize for Literature in 1972.

1944 Michael Tilson Thomas, US conductor who made his debut in 1970 with the London Symphony Orchestra.

ENTERTAINMENT

1937 Jane Fonda, US actress, daughter of Henry, who was an active anti-Vietnam war and civil rights campaigner as well as the recipient of Oscars for *Klute* (1971) and *Coming Home* (1978). She was also acclaimed for her role in *The China Syndrome* (1979) and, opposite her father in his last film, *On Golden Pond* (1981).

SPORT

1892 Walter (Charles) Hagen, US golf champion, nicknamed 'The Haig' who raised the social standing of the game. Winner of the US Open in both 1914 and 1919, the British Open four times, and six times playing captain of the US Ryder Cup team, he was one of the sport's most colourful characters.

1938 Greville (Michael Wilson) Starkey, English jockey whose wins include Ascot and Prix de l'Arc de Triomphe. He rode 107 winners in his 1978 season.

1943 Walter Spanghero, French rugby footballer who was capped 72 times. His younger brother Claude played with him in seven France internationals.

1954 Chris Evert, US tennis champion who has been in five Wimbledon women's singles finals from 1980 when she lost to Evonne Goolagong. She won the crown the following year, but was beaten in 1982, 1984 and 1985 by her rival and friend, Martina Navratilova.

POP

1940 (Francis Vincent) Frank Zappa, US rock singer and composer with the Mothers of Invention, one of the most innovative groups combining rock and jazz. Often outrageous, (his Albert Hall concert was banned by the management), he had success with his controversial 'Jewish Princess' and 'Dancin' Fool', less with 'Why Does It Hurt When I Pee?'. He was seriously injured when pushed from the stage of London's Rainbow Theatre in 1971, but returned to the recording studio the following year.

1946 Carl Wilson, US singer with his brothers, the Beach Boys, who scored enormous successes in the 60s with 'I Get Around', 'Surfin'', and 'Good Vibrations'.

DIED THIS DAY

1375 Giovanni Boccaccio, Italian author of the *Decameron* (1348–53).

1940 F(rancis) Scott (Key) Fitzgerald, US author of *The Great Gatsby* (1925).

1945 General George Smith Patton, US general nicknamed 'Old Blood and Guts'.

1963 Sir (John Berry) Jack Hobbs, the first cricketer to be knighted.

1970 Cicero (Elyesa Bazna) probably Albanian, who was one of the most famous Second World War spies. He worked as a valet in the British Embassy in Istanbul and photographed secret documents which he sold to the Germans. He was paid vast sums, all in counterfeit British money. The Germans never trusted his information despite accurate details of the proposed D-Day landings. He spent his last years as a nightwatchman in Munich.

ON THIS DAY

1620 The Pilgrim Fathers in the *Mayflower* landed at Plymouth Rock in Massachusetts.

1719 The first edition of the Boston *Gazette* was published.

1846 Robert Liston used anaesthetic (ether) for the first time in a British operation at University College Hospital, London to perform an amputation of a leg.

1879 The first performance of Ibsen's *A Doll's House* at the Royal Theatre, Copenhagen, with a specially revised happy ending to oblige the leading lady. The more realistic ending soon replaced it.

1880 An act passed by the House of Keys on the Isle of Man granted women the vote, provided they were widows or spinsters with a property rated annually at £4 or over. The first opportunity to vote was in April, the following year. In 1901, Norwegian women were allowed to vote, but in local elections only.

1911 The Jules Bonnot gang escaped from a bank hold-up in Paris in what is believed to be the first getaway car.

1913 The *New York World* printed the first crossword puzzle.

FILM HISTORY Two films were premiered this day, both milestones in film history. In 1925 Eisenstein's *Battleship Potemkin* was first screened in Moscow, and in 1935, Walt Disney's *Snow White and the Seven Dwarfs*, the first full-length colour and sound animated cartoon was shown in the US.

1958 Charles de Gaulle became President of France.

1963 Undersoil heating was used for the first time at the Leeds Rugby League ground for their match against Dewsbury.

1968 *Apollo 8* was launched from Cape Kennedy to orbit the Moon on 27 December.

1988 A US jumbo jet carrying more than 270 people blew up and crashed on to the Scottish town of Lockerbie. The aircraft, en route to New York, had taken off from London after completing its first leg from Germany. The bomb had been hidden in a transistor radio.

1988 Two Russian cosmonauts and a French astronaut returned to earth after a record 366 days in space.

22 DECEMBER

BORN THIS DAY

ARTS

1639 Jean Racine, French playwright, was baptized. His dramas offered leading ladies of the day such as Rachel a chance to shine in plays including *Phèdre* (1677).

1858 Giacomo (Antonio Domenico Michele Secondo Maria) Puccini,

Italian composer of popular operas including *La Bohème* (1896), *Madame Butterfly* (1904) and the great masterpiece *Turandot*, which he never completed.

ENTERTAINMENT

1839 John Nevil Maskelyne, English magician who advanced modern presentation of magic. A trained watchmaker, he used his skills to create his box trick and automata. In 1865 he exposed fraudulent spiritualists which made him a national celebrity. He toured with his magic show and later took on a partner, David Devant, who collaborated with him on the first authorative book on magic.

1907 Dame Peggy Ashcroft, one of the major English actresses of this century who played Desdemona to Paul Robeson's Othello and Juliet to John Gielgud's Romeo in 1935. In the 80s she won awards for performances in the television series *The Jewel in the Crown* (1984) and the David Lean film, *A Passage to India* (1985).

1909 Patricia Hayes, English character actress who won a BAFTA award in 1981 for her role in Jeremy Sandford's television play *Edna the Inebriate Woman*.

1936 James Burke, British writer and television presenter of science programmes such as *Connections* (1978) and *The Day the Universe Changed* (1985).

1948 Noel Edmonds, English DJ and television game show host.

POP

1949 Maurice and Robin Gibb, born on the Isle of Man. Their parents moved to Australia where they and elder brother Barry (1.9.1946) were brought up, and where they formed the internationally successful group, the Bee Gees with hits including 'Massachusetts' and 'I've Gotta Get a Message to You'.

DIED THIS DAY

1880 George Eliot (Mary Ann Evans), English author of *The Mill on the Floss* (1860).

1940 Nathanael West (Nathan Weinstein), US author of *The Day of the Locust* (1939) killed with his wife in a motor accident in California.

1943 Beatrix Potter, English author and artist.

1944 Harry Langdon, US silent film comedian with the famous 'babyface' who died of a cerebral haemorrhage while trying to make a comeback.

1989 Samuel (Barclay) Beckett, Nobel prize winning Irish author and playwright, in Paris.

ON THIS DAY

1715 James Stuart, the Old Pretender landed at Peterhead to lead a Jacobite rebellion which failed.

1864 Savannah, Georgia fell to General Sherman's Union troops in the American Civil War.

1877 Liquid oxygen was formulated by Raoul Pictet, Geneva.

1894 Alfred Dreyfus, the French officer who was found guilty of selling military secrets, was sent to Devil's Island. Innocent of the crime, his conviction sparked off the Dreyfus Affair and he was eventually exonerated.

1895 Rontgen made the first radiograph or x-ray of his wife's hand.

1965 The 70 m.p.h. speed limit was introduced in Britain.

1975 Pro-Palestinian terrorists led by Carlos seized 70 hostages at OPEC's Vienna headquarters. Austria decided to let the terrorists escape in return for freeing most of the hostages. The remainder were freed once the terrorists landed at Algiers.

1987 Chinese thieves caused chaos in the streets of Xianyang in north China when they stole 2,249 manhole covers to sell back to government departments.

23 DECEMBER

BORN THIS DAY

HISTORY

1777 Alexander I, Tsar of Russia whose armies fought Napoleon when he made his disastrous march into Russia.

1805 Joseph Smith, US leader of the Church of Jesus Christ of Latter Day Saints, better known as the Mormons, who claimed he had been directed by an angel to buried golden plates written by Indians who were descendants of the Biblical Hebrews.

1812 Samuel Smiles, English author of *Self Help* (1859) which sold over 250,000 copies, followed by other self-improvement books such as *Thrift* (1875) which were meant as the tools of Victorian virtues.

1918 Helmut Schmidt, West German Chancellor following Willy Brandt's resignation in 1974, and who supported the deployment of US missiles on German soil.

INVENTION

1732 Sir Richard Arkwright, English inventor of the 'spinning frame' which infuriated his Preston spinners in 1768 who felt their jobs were at stake. He also introduced steampower into his Nottingham factory.

DECIPHERING THE PAST Two leading Egyptologists were born this day, separated by twenty years, but both pursuing the same goals. Born 1790, French Egyptologist Jean-François Champollion deciphered the Rosetta Stone by recognizing that the Egyptian symbols were not just alaphabetic or syllabic, but could express an entire idea. His work was both complemented and advanced by Karl Richard Lepsius, German Egyptologist born 1810 who was the founder of modern archaeology by introducing a more scientific approach. He measured the Valley of the Tombs of the Kings near Luxor, was the first to estimate the date of the pyramids and made thousands of casts of inscriptions and temple reliefs.

ARTS

1908 Yousuf Karsh, Turkish-Armenian photographer who emigrated to Canada to escape persecution. He studied art and became an apprentice photographer. His wartime portrait of Churchill brought him international fame, and he became recognized as one of the finest portrait photographers in the history of photography. As a way of thanking Canada for its hospitality, he always signed himself, Karsh of Ottawa.

ENTERTAINMENT

1827 'Lord' George Sanger, English circus proprietor with his brother John from 1853. Their circus also performed at Astley's Amphitheatre, London (1871). In the late 1870s, the partnership ended and the brothers continued with separate shows.

1888 J(oseph) Arthur Rank, 1st Baron, English film magnate who began producing films for religious and instructional aids while chairman of his family business of Rank Hovis McDougall. In 1935 he moved into features and purchased the cinemas in which to screen them.

1909 Maurice Denham, English character actor who was in *Sunday, Bloody Sunday* (1971) and *Julia* (1977).

DIED THIS DAY

1944 Charles Dana Gibson, US illustrator who created the 'Gibson Girl'.

1948 Hideki Tojo, the Japanese Prime Minister was hanged for war crimes. He had tried unsuccessfully to commit ritual suicide and together with several other Japanese generals met his fate in Sugamo Prison, Tokyo.

1987 (Thomas) Henry Cotton, who raised the level and status of professional golf in Britain and won his first British Open in 1934 by five strokes despite severe stomach cramps.

ON THIS DAY

1834 English architect Jospeh Hansom patented his 'safety cab', better known as the Hansom cab.

1848 The *London Illustrated News* published the first Christmas supplement with advice on 'making the Christmas Pudding'.

1888 Vincent Van Gogh, suffering severe depression which was increased by his companion Gauguin's decision to leave their lodgings at Arles to escape winter, cut off his ear.

1922 The BBC began daily news broadcasts.

1970 *The Mousetrap* reached its 7511th consecutive performance to break the world record for the longest running play.

1973 The Shah of Iran announced that his country would increase oil prices 100 per cent.

CHRISTMAS SPIRIT In 1987 the first 'Scrooge' award by the Low Pay Unit was made to a Wiltshire stable-owner who paid a qualified groom only £28 a week. The runner-up was a doctor employing a telephonist for 30p an hour. The prize was an illustrated edition of *A Christmas Carol*. This same day, Santa Claus, by arrangement with the Finnish Tourist Board, had an audience with the Pope to prove that 'the Finnish Santa is the genuine article'.

24 DECEMBER

Christmas Eve

BORN THIS DAY

HISTORY

1167 King John, youngest son of Henry II, King of England who was forced by the barons to sign the Magna Carta. When he tried to revoke his authorisation, civil war broke out.

1491 Ignatius Loyola, Spanish solder who became a religious convert when injured in battle and who formed the Jesuits.

1809 (Christopher) Kit Carson, US frontiersman, trapper, scout, Indian agent and national folk hero who played an important part in the westward expansion of the US. He served the Union cause during the Civil War and was made a colonel. Carson City, Nevada was named after him.

1905 Howard (Robard) Hughes, US tycoon who inherited the Hughes Tool Company on his father's death and invested some of the money in Hollywood productions including *Hell's Angels* (1931) and later Jane Russell's films including *The Outlaw* (1943) in which he insisted on designing her bra. He was considered a lady's man during this period, dating many stars including Ava Gardner. He worked under an assumed name for American Airways, then left after less than a year with enough knowledge not just to start his own aircraft company, but also to design an aircraft to take the airspeed record (12.9.1935). In 1950, he became a recluse living by all accounts, a bizarre lifestyle.

ARTS

1822 Matthew Arnold, English poet and critic remembered for his poems, 'The Gypsy Scholar' and 'Dover Beach'.

ENTERTAINMENT

1888 Michael Curtiz (Mihaly Kertesz), Hungarian-born US film director remembered for his classic *Casablanca* (1942) which won him an Oscar, and *White Christmas* (1954).

1922 Ava Gardner (Lucy Johnson), US actress first considered a Hollywood sex symbol until she managed to prove herself a serious actress in films like *The Barefoot Contessa* (1954) and *The Cassandra Crossing* (1977).

1931 Jill Bennett, British actress born in Malaya who established herself at Stratford-upon-Avon and later in films including *Inadmissable Evidence* (1968) written by her husband, John Osborne.

SCIENCE

1818 James Prescott Joule, English physicist whose research into various forms of energy led to the basic laws of the conservation of energy. Work he did with William Thomson (later Lord Kelvin) on the effects of gas as a coolant led to the development of the modern refrigeration industry.

SPORT

1932 (Michael) Colin Cowdrey, England and Kent cricket captain born in Bangalore, India who was a high scoring batsman, making over 7,600 runs in 114 Test matches, an average of 44.06.

DIED THIS DAY

1524 Vasco da Gama, Portuguese navigator who found the sea route from Europe to the East and helped make Portugal a major power and trading nation, died on his second voyage shortly after landing in Cochin, India.

1863 W(illiam) M(akepeace) Thackeray, English author of *Vanity Fair* (1847–8).

ON THIS DAY

1582 Water piped to private houses by the London Bridge Waterworks began flowing.

1814 The war of 1812 between the US and Britain was brought to an end with the signing of the Treaty of Ghent.

1818 The first performance of the song 'Silent Night' ('*Heilige Nacht*'), music by Franz Gruber with words by his friend Jospeh Mohr, a priest, at the church in Obertsdorf, Bavaria.

1828 The trial of William Burke began in Edinburgh. The other body-snatcher, William Hare had turned King's evidence and was not therefore brought to trial. Burke had published his full confession in the Edinburgh *Courant*. Dr Knox, who bought the bodies was not even called to give evidence. Burke charged sixpence to artists wishing to draw him while in court. Sentenced to death, he was hanged on 28 January, 1829, when the rhyme appeared: 'Burke's the murderer, Hare's the thief/And Knox the boy who buys the beef'.

1851 Part of the Capitol building in Washington and the entire Library of Congress was destroyed by fire.

1871 The first performance of Verdi's opera *Aida* was presented in Cairo.

1904 The London Coliseum opened with the first revolving stage in Britain.

1906 The first radio telephone broadcast was demonstrated by Canadian-born Professor Reginald Fessenden from a radio station at Brant Rock, Massachusetts to ships' radios within a five-mile range.

DEATH FROM THE SKIES In 1914 a German monoplane dropped a single bomb on Dover, the first ever to be dropped on British soil. It landed on a rectory garden lawn and blew out the house windows. Exactly 28 years later in 1942, at Peenemunde, the Germans launched the world's first surface-to-surface guided missile, the V1. This day in 1944, the Germans flew the first jet aircraft for wartime use.

1922 The BBC broadcast *The Truth About Father Christmas* by Phyllis M. Twigg, the first play written for radio in Britain.

1943 General Dwight D. Eisenhower was appointed by Roosevelt to be Commander-in-Chief of the invasion of Europe. The desk-bound general had never fought a single campaign.

1965 A meteorite weighing about 100lbs landed on Leicestershire, possibly the largest to fall on Britain in modern times.

1974 The Beatles partnership was legally dissolved.

1979 Soviet troops invaded Afghanistan as the Kabul government fell.

25 DECEMBER

Christmas Day.

BORN THIS DAY

HISTORY

1876 Mohammed Ali Jinnah, Indian politician who, as a Muslim, opposed Gandhi's policies for a united India, demanding a separate Muslim state. He was made the first Governor-General of Pakistan in 1947.

1887 Conrad (Nicholson) Hilton, US hotelier who founded one of the largest groups in the world. He began by helping his father turn their large New Mexican house into an inn for travelling salesmen.

1918 Anwar Sadat, President of Egypt from 1970 who initiated peace talks with Israel's hard-line Prime Minister Begin. They both shared the Nobel Peace prize for accomplishing a reconciliation.

ARTS

1771 Dorothy Wordsworth, sister of the English Romantic poet, William, whose journals, published posthumously give a detailed and intimate description of their lives.

1883 Maurice Utrillo, French painter whose surname was that of a Spanish art critic as his mother was not sure who the father was. An alcoholic in his youth, he took up painting to try to overcome this obsession, with haunting, atmospheric pictures of Montmartre.

1892 Dame Rebecca West (Cicely Isabel Fairfield), British writer born in Ireland, educated in Edinburgh who reported on the Nuremberg trials after the Second World War establishing herself as a leading writer. She also wrote *The Meaning of Treason* (1949) and novels including *The Birds Fall Down* (1966).

ENTERTAINMENT

1899 Humphrey (DeForest) Bogart, legendary US actor who owed his film career to English actor, Leslie Howard who insisted Bogart be included in the film version of *The Petrified Forest* (1936) as the gangster, the role he had played in the stage version with Howard. Bogart's film career includes some of Hollywood's finest films and he always contributed a polished, memorable performance yet only collected one Oscar, for *The African Queen* (1952). His other films include *The Maltese Falcon* (1941), *Casablanca* (1942) and *To Have and Have Not* (1945).

1907 Andrew Cruikshank, Scottish actor who is best known for his television role as Dr Finlay in *Dr Finlay's Casebook*, but was a leading stage actor whose credits included *The Master Builder* and *Dial M For Murder*. His last play before his death in 1988, was Jeffrey Archer's *Beyond Reasonable Doubt*.

1907 Lord Grade (Lew Winogradsky), Russian-born British impressario, film and television chief executive who was a world champion Charleston dancer, then an agent before running his own television station and making films which he promoted to the US. *The Saint*, *Dangerman* and *The Muppets* are part of his success story.

1912 Tony Martin, US actor and singer who was a popular vocalist as well as leading man in light romantic films such as *Till the Clouds Rolls By* (1946) and *Deep in my Heart* (1954).

1944 Kenny Everett, zany English DJ who became a wild, whacky performer in the television series *The Kenny Everett Video Show*.

1949 Sissy Spacek, US actress who scored a success with her role in *Carrie* (1976) and went on to other challenging roles such as *Coalminer's Daughter* (1979) which won her an Oscar.

SCIENCE

1642 Sir Isaac Newton, English mathematician, founder of modern physics who began research into gravity in 1666, publishing his theory of gravitation in 1685. His major work is his *Philosophiae Naturalis Principia Mathematica*, the three volumes published between 1686–7.

1906 Ernst Ruska, German scientist who was the main force behind the invention of the electron microscope. In 1938, the giant Siemens company made the first prototype.

JAZZ

1907 Cab (Cabell) Calloway, US jazz vocalist and bandleader who, with the Missourians, recorded their theme song, *Minnie the Moocher*, a big hit in the early 30s which they performed at the Cotton Club. He starred in the Broadway production of *Bubbling Brown Sugar* in the 70s.

POP

1954 Annie Lennox, Scottish singer, with the Eurythmics with partner Dave Stewart whose hits include 'Sweet Dreams (Are Made of This)', a US No. 1 in 1983, and 'There Must Be An Angel Playing with My Heart' (1985).

DIED THIS DAY

1938 Karel (Matelj) Capek, Czech playwright of *R.U.R* in which he coined the word 'robot'.

1946 W(illiam) C(laude Dunkenfield) Fields, US actor and screenwriter who said, 'Any man who hates small dogs and children can't be all bad.'

1977 Sir Charles Chaplin who at his peak was probably the best known man in the world.

ON THIS DAY

1066 William the Conqueror was crowned at Westminster Abbey.

1176 The first eisteddfod took place at Cardigan Castle.

1741 The Centigrade temperature scale was devised by Anders Celsius and incorporated into a Delisle thermometer at Uppsala in Sweden.

1800 The first Christmas tree in Britain was erected at Queen's Lodge, Windsor by the German-born Queen Charlotte, wife of George III who brought the idea over from Germany where the first reports of Christmas trees go back to 1521.

1864 The traditional swim in the ice-cold Serpentine in London's Hyde Park was initiated.

1866 The US yacht *Henrietta* sailed in to Cowes harbour, Isle of Wight, the winner of the first transatlantic yacht race.

1914 The famous Christmas truce between British and German troops bogged down in the trenches on the western front during the First World War led to fraternizing and swapping presents in no-mans land. At midnight, they began to shoot each other again.

1926 Hirohito acceded to the throne of Japan on the death of his father Yoshihito.

1932 King George V made the first Royal Christmas broadcast to the Empire. Queen Elizabeth II made her first Christmas broadcast in 1952, and her first television Christmas message was broadcast in 1957.

1941 Hong Kong fell to the Japanese after a seven-day battle.

1950 The Stone of Scone, the Scottish coronation stone which had been in Westminster Abbey for 650 years was stolen by Scottish nationalists. The Stone, weighing 458lbs, was said to have been taken from Scotland by Edward I.

1959 Sony launched their transistor television set, the Sony TV 8 -301 in Japan.

1972 The Nicaraguan capital Managua was devasted by an earthquake which killed over 10,000 people.

1989 The former dictator of Romania, Nicolae Ceaucescu and his wife Elena, who had been in hiding since 22 December when the hated regime was toppled, were arrested, tried and found guilty of 'genocide' by a military court. They were executed this Christmas day.

26 DECEMBER

Boxing Day, also the traditional starting day for English pantomimes, the first in 1717, Harlequin Executed *presented by*

John Rich at Lincoln's Inn Fields Theatre, London. The BBC presented the first televised panto, Dick Whittington, *in 1932.*

BORN THIS DAY

HISTORY

1893 Mao Tse-tung, Chinese Communist leader who was a founder of the party in 1921 and organized the Long March. He led his nation after the war of liberation, from 1947 to his death. Chairman Mao's famous *Little Red Book* with his thoughts, was issued to all the population.

ARTS

1716 Thomas Gray, English poet who wrote 'Elegy Written in a Country Churchyard' at Stoke Poges in 1750.

1891 Henry Miller, controversial US novelist whose novels originally were banned as pornographic including *Tropic of Cancer* (1934) and *Tropic of Capricorn* (1938).

ENTERTAINMENT

1822 Dion Boucicault, Irish actor and playwright of *London Assurance* (1841). He went to the US where he settled and wrote and acted in *The Poor of New York* (1857) and other successful plays.

1914 Richard Widmark, US actor whose films have included *The Alamo* (as Jim Bowie) in 1960 and *Madigan* (1968).

1944 Jane Lapotaire, English actress best known for her remarkable portrayal of Edith Piaf both on stage and television.

INVENTION

1792 Charles Babbage, English inventor of a calculating machine. In 1823, a government grant allowed him to design a machine capable of doing more complex computations, the forerunner of the electronic computer.

POP

1940 Phil Spector, US songwriter and record producer who developed the 'Wall of Sound' recording technique popular in the 60s.

SPORT

1935 Rohan (Babulal) Kanhai, Guyana-born cricketer who also played for Trinidad, the West Indies, Warwickshire, Western Australia and Tasmania. He made a world record second wicket batting partnership (with John Jameson) of 465 (he scored 213) for Warwickshire against Gloucestershire at Birmingham in 1974.

DIED THIS DAY

1890 Heinrich Schliemann, German archaeologist who discovered Troy.

1957 Charles Pathé, French film pioneer.

1961 Frank Richards (Charles Harold St John Hamilton), creator of Billy Bunter.

1970 Lillian Board, 22-year-old English athlete and gold medallist in the European Games in Athens in the 800m and winner of the silver medal in the 1968 Mexican Olympics in the 400m, died of cancer in a Bavarian Clinic where she had gone for treatment.

1972 Harry S. Truman, 33rd US President.

1974 Jack Benny (Benjamin Kubelsky), US comedian.

ON THIS DAY

1898 Marie and Pierre Curie discovered radium while experimenting with pitchblende.

1906 The world's first feature film, *The Story of the Kelly Gang* made in Australia, was screened in Melbourne.

1908 'Galveston Jack' Johnson, became the first black boxer to win a world-heavyweight title when he beat Tommy Burns in Sydney, Australia. It shocked white boxing fans and so began the quest for the Great White Hope to put this 'uppity nigger in his place'.

1943 The last major German battleship, the *Scharnhorst* was sunk by the Royal Navy.

1948 Bertrand Russell delivered the first Reith Lecture on the BBC, entitled *Authority and the Individual.*

27 DECEMBER

BORN THIS DAY

HISTORY

1571 Johannes Kepler, German astronomer who discovered and confirmed Copernicus's theory that the earth and planets circle the sun in elliptical orbits.

1773 Sir George Cayley, English pioneer of the study of aerodynamics who built the first successful glider to be flown by a man – his reluctant coachman – in 1853. One of his later inventions was the caterpillar tractor.

1822 Louis Pasteur, French chemist and bacteriologist who discovered that micro-organisms cause fermentation and infection and later developed a vaccine for rabies. His pupil Lister developed this research into the field of antiseptic surgery.

ENTERTAINMENT

1879 Sydney Greenstreet, English actor who was an established stage actor both in Britain and the US when he finally landed his first film part in *The Maltese Falcon* (1941). He was then much in demand to play sophisticated sinister roles in *Casablanca* (1942) and other films.

1904 Marlene Dietrich (Maria Magdalena von Losch), German actress whose performance in *The Blue Angel* (1930) led to a Hollywood contract where she starred in a succession of films of varied quality from *Destry Rides Again* (1939) to *Rancho Notorious* (1952). In later life, billed as 'the world's most glamorous grandmother', she toured in her one-woman show singing her famous song 'Falling In Love Again'.

SPORT

1931 John Charles, Welsh footballer who became Italian Footballer of the Year (1958).

DIED THIS DAY

1972 Lester Pearson, Prime Minister of Canada and Nobel prize winner.

ON THIS DAY

1831 Charles Darwin set sail in the *Beagle* from Plymouth on his voyage of scientific discovery.

OPENING NIGHTS In 1904 the first performance in London of James Barrie's *Peter Pan* with Nina Boucicault as the first Peter and Gerald du Maurier as Captain Hook. On the same night, the world's first state subsidised theatre, the Abbey in Dublin, opened with two short plays, one by Yeats, the other by Lady Gregory. In 1927 Broadway saw the first performance of Jerome Kern's musical *Show Boat*, presented by Florenz Ziegfeld. It introduced songs including 'Ol' Man River' and 'Bill' (with words by P.G. Wodehouse).

1945 The International Monetary Fund (IMF) was established in Washington.

1975 The Sex Discrimination and Equal Pay Acts came into effect in Britain.

1984 The four police officers accused of killing the pro-Solidarity priest, Father Jerzy Popieluszko went on trial in Poland.

28 DECEMBER

BORN THIS DAY

HISTORY

1856 (Thomas) Woodrow Wilson, 28th US President, elected 1912 and 1916, who was one of the founders of the League of Nations.

ARTS

1927 Simon (Arthur Noel) Raven, English author and playwright whose novels include *Alms for Oblivion*, *Friends in Low Places* (1965) and *The Judas Boy* (1968). He adapted Huxley's *Point Counter Point* and Trollope's *The Way We Live Now* for television (1968–9).

1956 Nigel Kennedy, English violinist who studied at the Menuhin School, England and Julliard in New York where he made his debut in 1972 aged 16, and his London debut in 1977. In 1981 he toured Australia with the Hallé Orchestra and became internationally recognized as a leading performer in both the classical and jazz fields.

ENTERTAINMENT

1908 Lew Ayres, US actor best remembered for his performance as a young patriotic German soldier who discovers the realities of war in *All Quiet on the Western Front* (1930), and was the original Dr Kildare in the film (not television) series which began with *Young Doctor Kildare* (1938).

1934 Maggie Smith, award-winning English stage and screen actress who collected an Oscar for best actress in *The Prime of Miss Jean Brodie* (1969), and for best supporting actress in *California Suite* (1978), as well as nominations for her performances in *Othello* (1965) and *Travels with My Aunt* (1972). She also starred in *A Room with a View* (1986) and on stage, in *Lettice and Lovage* (1987).

JAZZ

1905 Earl 'Fatha' Hines, US pianist and songwriter, and later bandleader. He was later recognized as one of the great jazz pianists of all time.

DIED THIS DAY

1694 Queen Mary II from small pox leaving William III to reign alone.

1734 Rob Roy (Robert Macgregor), legendary Scottish Robin Hood immortalized by Sir Walter Scott in his novel, *Rob Roy* (1818), but who appears to have been an opportunistic cattle stealer and even a blackmailer, ending up in Newgate Prison before eventually being pardoned.

1923 (Alexandre) Gustave Eiffel, French

designer and builder of the famous tower.

1937 Maurice (Joseph) Ravel, French composer, best remembered for his *Bolero*.

1984 Sam Peckinpah, US film director of *Straw Dogs* (1971).

ON THIS DAY

1846 Iowa became the 29th state of the Union.

1879 The Tay railway bridge collapsed when the Edinburgh to Dundee train was crossing. The engine and carriages plummeted into the icy river below killing 90 people.

1904 The first weather reports relayed by wireless telegraphy were published in London.

1908 An earthquake killed over 75,000 at Messina in Sicily.

1926 At Melbourne, the highest score in a single innings in first-class cricket was 1,107 hit by Victoria. New South Wales bowler, Arthur Mailey ended with a world record 362 runs for four wickets.

1950 The first British national park was designated: the Peak District.

1963 The last *That Was The Week That Was*, television's first satirical show, was broadcast by the BBC. It was pulled off while still commanding huge audiences because 1964 was to be election year; it was felt the show could influence voters.

29 DECEMBER

BORN THIS DAY

HISTORY

1721 Jeanne Antoinette, Marquise de Pompadour, mistress of Louis XV, a woman of fashion who attracted the eye of the King. She became involved in matters of state and also diverted its wealth to meet her own lavish lifestyle.

1808 Andrew Johnson, 17th US President, the former military governor of Tennessee who became Vice-President in 1865 and took over the presidency on Lincoln's assassination. His unpopular policies led to impeachment proceedings being brought against him but he was acquitted.

1809 William (Ewart) Gladstone, four-times British Prime Minister in 1868–74 which allowed him to carry out major reforms. He was elected in 1880–85, and again in 1866. When his Home Rule Bill was defeated, he resigned. He became Prime Minister again in 1892 and resigned two years later, this time when his Home Rule Bill was rejected by the Lords.

1911 Emil Julius Klaus Fuchs, German physicist and spy who settled in Britain in 1933 and studied at Edinburgh and Bristol Universities. During the war he was involved in the Manhattan Project – the development of the atomic bomb – but he was meeting Soviet agents and passing them secrets. He was later charged with spying, confessed and served nine years in prison.

ARTS

1876 Pablo Casals, Spanish virtuoso cellist who went into exile during Franco's rule. Considered the finest cellist of this century, he also composed and conducted including his 'Hymn to the United Nations' (1971).

1893 Vera (Mary) Brittain, English author, pacifist and feminist who wrote the autobiographical *Testament of Youth* (1933).

1915 Robert (Chester) Ruark, US author who wrote mainly of Africa in the novels *Horn of the Hunter* (1953) and *Uhuru* (1962).

ENTERTAINMENT

1928 Bernard Cribbens, English character actor on stage and screen, in a multitude of productions including the railwayman in the film classic, *The Railway Children* (1971).

1937 Mary Tyler Moore, US actress who co-starred in the successful *Dick Van Dyke Show* television series before landing her own *Mary Tyler Moore Show*.

1938 Jon Voight, US actor who has landed roles in some of Hollywood's best films including *Midnight Cowboy* (an Oscar nomination), *Deliverance* (1972), and *Coming Home* (1978) which won him an Oscar.

INVENTION

RUBBER GOODS Three men who experimented and developed products with rubber were born this day. In 1766, Charles Macintosh, Scottish chemist and inventor of waterproofed clothing was born. In 1800, Charles Goodyear, US inventor of vulcanized rubber, whose patents were infringed in both the US and Europe and landed him in prison for bankruptcy. In 1813, Alexander Parkes, English chemist and inventor of another way to vulcanize rubber, who is better known as the inventor of an electroplating method, and especially xylonite (celluloid) which he patented in 1855.

SCIENCE

1908 Dr Magnus Pyke, British scientist who helped popularize science in his 70s television programmes.

POP

1946 Marianne Faithfull, English singer and actress who had a hit in the 60s with 'As Tears Go By' and lived in the glare of publicity as Mick Jagger's girlfriend, suffering a miscarriage, an attempted suicide and an arrest for drugs. In 1990 she made a successful comeback.

SPORT

1881 Jess Willard, US heavyweight boxer, 'the great White Hope' who knocked out Jack Johnson (the first black champion) on 5 April 1915. His reign ended in 1919 when he was beaten by great Jack Dempsey.

1938 Harvey Smith, English show-jumper and British champion who caused a rumpus in 1971 when he gave a two-finger gesture at the British Championships in Derby.

DIED THIS DAY

1170 St Thomas à Becket, Archbishop of Canterbury, murdered in his cathedral by four knights acting on the orders of Henry II with whom he was in conflict. His martyrdom led to Henry being forced to offer concessions which Becket had always wanted.

1952 James Fletcher Henderson, US jazz pianist, composer and bandleader, from a stroke, aged 55.

ON THIS DAY

1720 The Theatre Royal, Haymarket opened.

1845 Texas became the 28th state of the Union.

1860 The first iron-clad screw-driven British warship, HMS *Warrior* was launched.

1890 The last major battle between US forces and the Indians took place at Wounded Knee, South Dakota when 200 Sioux Indians under Chief Big Foot were massacred by Colonel Forsyth's 7th Cavalry.

1895 The Jameson Raid into the Transvaal to aid the Uitlanders (mainly British settlers) in the Boer Colony, began.

1911 Sun Yat-sen became the first president of a republican China following the revolution.

1930 Radio Luxembourg began broadcasting.

1937 The Irish Republic changed its name to Eire as the new constitution was implemented.

1940 German bombers dropped 10,000 bombs on London on one of the worst night's ever during 'The Battle of Britain'.

1951 The first transistor hearing aid went on sale in the US.

1952 The Coelacanth, a prehistoric fish believed to be extinct, was caught off the coast of South Africa.

1972 The 16 survivors from the crashed Uruguayan Fairchild F227 which had been chartered by an amateur rugby team en route to Montevideo, were rescued on the Andes. The crash had taken place on 13 October, and it was only later that the 16 revealed their survival had been possible because they ate the flesh of their dead companions.

1989 Vaclav Havel was sworn in as President of Czechoslovakia.

30 DECEMBER

BORN THIS DAY

ARTS

1865 (Joseph) Rudyard Kipling, English author born in India where some of his best novels and short stories are set: *Plain Tales from the Hills* and the two *Jungle Books* (both in the 1880s). He also wrote poetry that now seems jingoistic, but was exceptionally popular such as 'Mandalay', 'If' and 'Gunga Din'. Other successes were *Captains Courageous* (1897) and *Puck of Pook's Hill* (1906).

1869 Stephen (Butler) Leacock, British-born Canadian humorist who became internationally popular with more than 30 books beginning with *Literary Lapses* (1910), followed by *Nonsense Novels* (1911).

ENTERTAINMENT

1906 Sir Carol Reed, English film director and stage actor who became one of Britain's leading film-makers with *Odd Man Out* (1947), *The Fallen Idol* (1948) and *The Third Man* (1949), yet it was the film of the musical *Oliver!* that won him his only Oscar in 1968.

1959 Tracy Ullman, English comedienne who was in *Three's Company* on television in 1980 and *Kick Up the Eighties* 1981–2. She became one of the few British comedy stars to make it on US television with her own *Tracy Ullman Show*.

JAZZ

1927 Stan(ley William) Tracey, English pianist and composer now internationally recognized. His compositions include *Under Milk Wood* (1965).

1928 Bo Didley (Elias McDaniel McCombe) US singer, songwriter and guitarist who was a major influence on groups such as the Rolling Stones and the Who.

SPORT

1934 Barry Briggs, New Zealand international speedway racing champion who was world champion in 1957, 1958, 1964, and 1966.

1937 Gordon Banks, England and Leicester goalkeeper who was considered one of the safest in Europe. His career ended soon after a car accident in 1972 which damaged his eyes.

DIED THIS DAY

1691 Robert Boyle, Irish-born chemist and natural philosopher who formulated Boyle's Law on gases.

1894 Amelia Jenks Bloomer, US social reformer who gave the world the garment 'bloomers'.

1916 Gregory Yefimovich Rasputin, influential Russian monk and illiterate mystic who was a favourite of Nicholas II and Alexandra, but feared and detested by others. Nicknamed 'The Debauched One' and the 'Mad Monk', Rasputin was alleged to work magic, but his scandalous behaviour forced the Tsar to expel him. Alexandra allowed him to return to help her haemophiliac son. A group of extreme conservatives led by Prince Feliks Yusupov decided to save the monarch from further embarassment and gave Rasputin cakes laced with poison, but he seemed to withstand the effects of the cyanide. Yusupov then shot the monk while in the basement of the Moika Palace. He appeared to be dead, but recovered and then attacked Yusupov. The other conspirators then battered the monk into a state of unconciousness and dumped his body in the icy river Neva where he was found drowned and frozen.

1979 Richard (Charles) Rodgers, US composer of *The Sound of Music*.

ON THIS DAY

1672 The first public concert was held in London. The musicians performed behind a curtain while patrons ate cakes and drank ale.

1879 The first performance of Gilbert and Sullivan's *The Pirates of Penzance* at Paignton, Devon.

1880 Transvaal became a republic with Paul Kruger as the first president.

1887 A petition addressed to Queen Victoria with over one million names of women appealing for public houses to be closed on Sundays was handed to the Home Secretary.

1922 Russia officially became the USSR – the Union of Soviet Socialist Republics.

1948 The first performance of Cole Porter's *Kiss Me Kate* in New York with songs 'Wunderbar' and 'Always True to You In My Fashion'.

1973 The head of Marks and Spencer's, Lord Sieff was wounded by an Arab gunman at his home in St John's Wood.

31 DECEMBER

New Year's Eve, and Hogmany in Scotland.

BORN THIS DAY

HISTORY

1491 Jacques Cartier, French navigator who explored the St Lawrence river and named the site of Montreal during his Canadian explorations.

1720 Bonnie Prince Charlie (Charles Edward Stuart), also known as the 'Young Pretender', was born in Rome. With his followers he landed in Scotland in 1745, capturing Edinburgh and setting up court at the Palace of Holyrood. He scored a further victory at Prestonpans (21.9.1745), but his decision to march on London brought him head on with the British army and defeat at Culloden (16.4.1746).

1880 George Marshall, US general and statesman who directed the Marshall Aid plan to help the post-war recovery of Europe.

ARTS

1869 Henri Matisse, French painter and member of the group known as les Fauves inspired by the work of Van Gogh. His work influenced many 20th-century artists.

ENTERTAINMENT

1905 Jule Styne (Julius Kerwin Styne), US composer who was born in London. He gave up his career as a concert pianist to write musicals including *Gypsy* (1959) and *Funny Girl* (1964), with songs 'Everything's Coming Up Roses', 'People' and 'Diamonds Are a Girl's Best Friend'.

1937 Anthony Hopkins, Welsh-born actor with an impressive theatre and film career including *The Lion in Winter* (1968) and *A Bridge Too Far* (1977), with a BAFTA award-winning performance in television's *War and Peace* (1972).

1943 Ben Kingsley, English actor who won an Oscar in 1982 for his portrayal of the Indian statesman in *Gandhi*. He was also in *Pascali's Island* (1989).

1941 Sarah Miles, English actress who played opposite Olivier in her first film *Term of Trial* (1962). Her other appearances include *Ryan's Daughter* (1970), *Lady Caroline Lamb* (1972) and *The Big Sleep* (1978).

POP

1943 John Denver (Henry John Deutschendorf, Jr.), US singer associated with the cheerful 'Take Me Home, Country Roads', who had a No. 1 with 'Annie's Song', 'Sunshine on My Shoulders' (both 1974), and 'I'm Sorry' and 'Thank God I'm a Country Boy' (both 1975).

1948 Donna Summer (LaDonna Andrea Gaines), US singer with a long list of hits including 'MacArthur Park' (1978) and 'No More Tears (Enough Is Enough')(1979) with Barbra Streisand.

SPORT

1929 Peter (Barker Howard) May, England and Surrey cricket captain and later Chairman of the England cricket selectors. He and Colin Cowdrey scored the highest England partnership in 1957, (285 and 154 respectively) against the West Indies.

1952 Jean-Pierre Rives, French rugby football captain.

DIED THIS DAY

1948 Sir Malcolm Campbell, English land and water speed record holder and first man to clock 300 m.p.h. in his car, *Bluebird*.

1985 Rick Nelson, US pop singer, together with his fiancée and five members of the Stone Canyon Band, killed when their aircraft crashed in Texas.

ON THIS DAY

1687 The first Huguenots set sail from France for the Cape of Good Hope where they would escape religious persecution and create the South African wine industry with the vines they took with them on the voyage.

1695 The window tax was imposed in Britain which resulted in many being bricked up, evidence which remains to this day.

1890 Ellis Island in New York was opened as the immigration depot to handle the 'huddled masses'.

1911 Marie Curie received her second Nobel prize, unprecedented in the history of the award.

1917 Sugar was rationed in Britain as a result of shortages during the First World War, the first time food rationing had ever been imposed in Britain on a national scale.

1923 The chimes of Big Ben were broadcast by the BBC for the first time.

1935 Charles Darrow patented his board game 'Monopoly', which he had first invented in 1933. (*See also* 28.8.1967)

1938 In Indianapolis, Dr R.N. Harger's 'Drunkometer' was officially used to breathalyse drivers by the Indianapolis Police Department.

1960 The farthing ceased to be legal tender in Britain at midnight.

1968 The Russian supersonic airliner TU-144 made its inaugural flight from Moscow to Alma Ata, several months ahead of the Anglo-French Concorde.

1973 The three-day week began in Britain as a result of power strikes; it would lead to the downfall of Prime Minister Edward Heath and his government.

1988 At midnight, when the Queen's New Year honours list was revealed, world champion Eric Bristow – 'the Crafty Cockney' – became the first ever darts player to receive an MBE.

INDEX

DISTRIBUTORS
for the Wordsworth Reference Series

AUSTRALIA

Reed Editions
22 Salmon Street
Port Melbourne
Vic 3207
Australia
Tel: (03) 646 6716
Fax: (03) 646 6925

GERMANY, AUSTRIA
& SWITZERLAND

Swan Buch-Marketing GmbH
Goldscheuerstraße 16
D-7640 Kehl am Rhein
Germany

GREAT BRITAIN & IRELAND

Wordsworth Editions Ltd
Cumberland House
Crib Street
Ware
Hertfordshire SG12 9ET

ITALY

Magis Books SRL
Via Raffaello 31/C
Zona Ind Mancasale
42100 Reggio Emilia
Tel: 0522-920999
Fax: 0522-920666

SINGAPORE, MALAYSIA
& BRUNEI

Paul & Elizabeth Book Services
Pte Ltd
163 Tanglin Road No 03-15/16
Tanglin Mall
Singapore 1024
Tel: (65) 735-7308
Fax: (65) 735-9747

SPAIN

Ribera Libros S.L.
Poligono Martiartu, Calle 1-no 6
48480 Arrigorriaga, Vizcaya
Tel: 34-4-6713607 (Almacen)
34-4-4418787 (Libreria)
Fax: 34-4-6713608 (Almacen)
34-4-4418029 (Libreria)

PORTUGAL

International Publishing Services Ltd
Rua da Cruz da Carreira, 4B
1100 Lisboa
Tel: 01-570051
Fax: 01-3522066

SOUTHERN AFRICA

Struik Book Distributors (Pty) Ltd
Graph Avenue
Montague Gardens
7441
P O Box 193
Maitland
7405
South Africa
Tel: (021) 551-5900
Fax: (021) 551-1124

USA, CANADA & MEXICO

Universal Sales & Marketing
230 Fifth Avenue
Suite 1212
New York, NY 10001 USA
Tel: 212-481-3500
Fax: 212-481-3534